Literary Criticism and Theory

This incredibly useful volume offers an introduction to the history of literary criticism and theory from ancient Greece to the present. Grounded in the close reading of landmark theoretical texts, while seeking to encourage the reader's critical response, Pelagia Goulimari examines:

- major thinkers and critics from Plato and Aristotle to Foucault, Derrida, Kristeva, Said and Butler;
- key concepts, themes and schools in the history of literary theory: mimesis, inspiration, reason and emotion, the self, the relation of literature to history, society, culture and ethics; feminism, poststructuralism, postcolonialism, queer theory;
- genres and movements in literary history: epic, tragedy, comedy, the novel; Romanticism, realism, modernism and postmodernism.

Historical connections between theorists and theories are traced and the book is generously cross-referenced. With useful features such as key-point conclusions, further reading sections, descriptive text boxes, detailed headings, and a comprehensive index, this book is the ideal introduction to anyone approaching literary theory for the first time or unfamiliar with the scope of its history.

Pelagia Goulimari is a member of the English Faculty of the University of Oxford, where she lectures on literary theory, and a former convenor of Oxford's graduate programme in Women's Studies. She is general editor of *Angelaki: Journal of the Theoretical Humanities*. Her publications include *Postmodernism: What Moment?* (2007) and *Toni Morrison* (2009).

"Pelagia Goulimari sets a new standard for reading theory in context, introducing and summarizing theories and theorists without being reductive, contextualizing the broad intellectual and aesthetic movements from which theory emerges, while constantly keeping the focus on deep literary critical understanding. The critical readings are wonderfully fresh and insightful, with constant illumination of the theory through reference to literary authors such as Beckett, Woolf, and Morrison. This truly is a fresh and lively reading of the theoretical scene, offering inspirational insight for beginners and more experienced critics alike."

Richard Lane, Vancouver Island University, Canada

"Incredibly useful, and a miracle of concision. A one volume account of over 2,500 years of literary criticism that manages to be both informative and readable. I will recommend it to all my students."

John McGowan, *University of North Carolina, USA, co-editor of the* Norton Anthology of Theory and Criticism

"Amongst the many texts seeking to introduce readers to literary theory, Pelagia Goulimari's *Literary Criticism and Theory* stands out for its careful and patient reading of critical texts, admirably weaving together older and more recent traditions in a way that helps make coherent sense of the lines of filiation that run through Western and postcolonial understandings of the literary."

John Frow, *University of Sydney, Australia*

Literary Criticism and Theory

From Plato to postcolonialism

Pelagia Goulimari

LONDON AND NEW YORK

First published 2015
by Routledge
2 Park Square, Milton Park, Abingdon, Oxon OX14 4RN

Simultaneously published in the USA and Canada
by Routledge
711 Third Avenue, New York, NY 10017

Routledge is an imprint of the Taylor & Francis Group, an informa business

British Library Cataloguing in Publication Data
A catalogue record for this book is available from the British Library

Library of Congress Cataloging in Publication Data
Goulimari, Pelagia.
Literary criticism and theory / Pelagia Goulimari.
pages cm
Includes bibliographical references and index.
1. Criticism–History. 2. Literature–History and criticism–Theory, etc.
3. Literature–Philosophy–History. I. Title.
PN86.G684 2014
801'.9509–dc23
2014002914

ISBN: 978-0-415-54431-3 (hbk)
ISBN: 978-0-415-54432-0 (pbk)
ISBN: 978-0-203-48719-8 (ebk)

Typeset in Times New Roman
by Taylor & Francis Books

Contents

Acknowledgements

I have been very fortunate to receive an exceptional amount of help and encouragement in writing this book. Gerard Greenway made a huge contribution to the book in every respect. I am very grateful to colleagues for their criticisms and suggestions on chapters in the area of their specialism. They are Pamela Sue Anderson, Louise Braddock, Philip Bullock, Stephanie Clare, Robert Douglas-Fairhurst, Stephen Gill, Roger Griffin, Louise Gyler, Jane Hiddlestone, Ken Hirschkop, Susan Jones, Karen Leeder, Sabina Lovibond, Ben Morgan, Bernard O'Donoghue, Georgina Paul, Andrew Sillett, Helen Small, Ida Toth and Robert J. C. Young. The book evolved out of lectures given at the English Faculty of the University of Oxford since 2006 as well as classes and tutorials at Oxford colleges – Pembroke, Lincoln and Wadham – and my students have provided me over the years with invaluable feedback. My thanks to Routledge's anonymous and eponymous reviewers – Pat Waugh, John Frow, Robert Eaglestone – for their comments on an early version of the manuscript. My thanks to Routledge's editorial team, Polly Dodson, Elizabeth J. Levine, Ruth Moody, Emma Hudson, Megan Hiatt, Laura Emsden – Polly's enthusiasm has been vital. I am grateful to the librarians of Faculty and College libraries at the University of Oxford.

My love to Max, Roula, Fotis, Maria and of course Gerard – thank you for your love and support!

Introduction

"Literary theory" has a contemporary or recent ring about it, evoking developments in literary studies in the English-speaking world that gathered momentum in higher education in the 1970s. But of course literary theory and criticism are as old as their object of study, literature, and a vital, multidisciplinary and international current in intellectual history, open to the world and to the broad course of culture and society. To move outside the contemporary critical canon and explore this field, in its historical depth and geographical breadth, is a salutary counter to the orthodoxies of the present, revitalizing our enjoyment of literature and our critical language. One of the discoveries I have made is how literary and critical innovation has been inextricable from revisiting and reanimating the past, and this book is intended as an introduction to resources for future innovation.

As I approached the writing of the book, the initial daunting challenge was how 2,500 years of thinking and writing could be adequately represented in the available space. Textbooks are introductory outlines of their subject, but there is a danger, especially in this case with so much to cover, that discussion will summarize in too headlong and cursory a way, and the reader learn little. I therefore decided to ground the book in close readings of selected texts, readings that are good to think with, that stimulate discussion and entice readers to visit the texts themselves. In this way, the book is itself a literary-theoretical exercise, and I have endeavoured to remain alert and to include some critical discussion. In selecting texts I have striven to pay attention to marginalized voices (e.g. Plotinus, Wole Soyinka, Zora Neale Hurston).

The order of the chapters is broadly chronological, but each chapter focuses on specific themes and moves backwards and forwards historically. So each chapter is, to a degree, a free-standing history of an area of literary theory, complementing close readings with historical and biographical contextualization. Particular weight is accorded to the twentieth century's extraordinary and often neglected variety and geographical spread of movements. Chapters include biographical boxes, a key-point conclusion, long chapter titles, subtitles and section titles listing main critics, movements, themes and concepts covered, and cross-references to other chapters. Cross-references have been generously created to highlight connections and correspondences.

1 *Mimēsis*

Plato and the poet

Plato and modern Platonic variations: Rousseau, Wordsworth, Arnold, Nietzsche, Pater, Huxley, Brecht, Benjamin, Marcuse, Derrida, Deleuze, Baudrillard, Plath, Kristeva

Plato is one of the great fountainheads of the Western intellectual tradition and is considered by many to be its greatest philosopher. His *Republic* is the most famous book of philosophy and the founding text of Western political thought. With his teacher Socrates, Plato is the great champion of philosophy as the way to wisdom and as a way of life. Nobody wishing to develop a broad understanding, or a broad critique, of the history of Western thought can avoid serious attention to Plato. Three thinkers of recent times who have sought to develop such a critique and who have also been major influences on literary studies and theory are Friedrich Nietzsche, Martin Heidegger and Jacques Derrida. All of them engaged intensively with Plato in their work, seeing the Western intellectual tradition as significantly Plato's legacy. But Plato was also a founder of literary theory in his own right; his views on literature and the arts intimately related to the rest of his philosophy, with the *Republic*, once again, being the most famous source of his ideas. In addition, Plato as visionary thinker and as literary artist has had a greater influence on literary writers than any other philosopher. To mention just a few names, from among those that feature in this book, he was a source of inspiration to writers as diverse as Sir Philip Sidney, Percy Bysshe Shelley, Matthew Arnold and Oscar Wilde. In order to examine Plato's ideas about literature we will be concentrating on his dialogues *Ion*, *Republic* and *Phaedrus*.

Plato (*c.* 427–347 BC) was born to a prominent Athenian family and lived in the city-state of Athens. He composed dialogues, a new genre he invented as the instrument of his dialogical or *dialectical* method (*dialektikē*). The dialogues feature the character of Socrates interrogating interlocutors who hold unexamined beliefs (*doxa*) on subjects such as the nature of poetic inspiration, wisdom, knowledge, truth, virtue, reason, the emotions or pleasure, and then attempting to advance a better definition or encouraging *them* to do so. Plato's Socrates is fictive and bears a tenuous relation to the historical Socrates, certainly as Plato begins to develop his own ideas. The prose of the dialogues is exquisite and, to many, Plato is not only the first major theorist of literature, he is also a supreme stylist of the ancient Greek language. Creator of the dialogue as a genre, superb stylist and poet in his youth, Plato is both a great philosopher and a great literary artist. Perhaps he was the original "Critic as Artist", to use Oscar Wilde's memorable phrase.

Longinus, in the first century AD, analyses Plato's texts as literature, for example in terms of the metaphors Plato uses. In his *On the Sublime*, which became a crucial document for the late-eighteenth-century and early-nineteenth-century movement of Romanticism and its own notion of the sublime, Longinus views Plato as a sublime (i.e. "high", "lofty") writer and a literary genius. Longinus is writing in a tradition within which Plato was being read as literature rather than philosophy, and being criticized for his literary qualities. Longinus defends Plato against previous critics who "pull Plato to pieces, on the ground that he is often carried away by a sort of Bacchic possession in his writing into harsh and intemperate metaphor and allegorical bombast" (Longinus 1995, 265); for his critics, Plato's is "the language of a poet who is far from sober" (267). Ironically, these harsh critics' figurative language of possession and intoxication is borrowed from Plato, who uses it himself against poets, as will become clear shortly. Against such critics, Longinus claims that Plato uses metaphors and other literary tropes "still more divinely" than other magnificent writers (263). Giving many examples of Plato's use of figurative language, he praises his style for its "natural grandeur" and "sublimity" (265). (See *On the Sublime* [32.5–8].) Longinus concludes that Plato is one of a few "writers of genius", "greatness" and "true excellence" (277–8).

Plato himself saw things differently. He uses his dialogues to establish a new opposition between poetry ("poetry" is the closest equivalent to "literature" in the classical world) and the way of life and path to knowledge of which he is the spokesman: *philosophia*, literally the love of wisdom, or the pursuit of wisdom through reason or the intellect. Poetry preoccupied Plato. He didn't compose an *ars poetica*, but he returns to the question of poetry in several dialogues. For the Athenians of Plato's time, the pre-eminent literary figure was Homer, and the pre-eminent works were his epic poems, the *Iliad* and the *Odyssey*. They were composed without the aid of writing and were performed orally by rhapsodes, who were professional storytellers. Poetry, especially Homer, was central to Athenian life and education. Homer was admired by everyone, including Plato, and was viewed as a great authority on all manner of subjects. Second in importance, after Homer and epic poetry, was tragic poetry (drama): the tragedies of Aeschylus, Sophocles, Euripides. The performance of tragedy was very popular, attracting large audiences. So what constituted literature in Plato's time was epic and tragic poetry; and poetry's role, its function, was that of a great authority, a source of wisdom for life, playing a central role in the education of children.

The argument between poetry and philosophy is most famously staged in the *Republic*, where Plato is shockingly negative in his assessment of poets and poetry. Why would he want to attack such an important cultural institution?

In Plato's time, not all was well with Athenian democracy, the great invention of which Aeschylus was so proud a few decades earlier. (See, for example, Aeschylus's tragedy, *Persians*, juxtaposing Persian despotism and Athenian democracy.) Plato was born and spent his formative years during the Peloponnesian War (431–404 BC), a savage war between the Greek city-states of Athens and Sparta, and the other Greek city-states under their respective influence. Probably brought on by the circumstances of war, certainly worsened by them, a devastating plague in Athens claimed the great statesman Pericles's life in 429 BC. Plato witnessed the defeat of Athens, the crisis of Athenian democracy and its oscillation between ochlocracy and populist leaders on the one hand, oligarchic coups on the other. The political persecution and execution, by a democratic government, of Socrates, Plato's teacher, in 399 BC – depicted by Plato in the *Apology*, *Crito* and *Phaedo* – was a sign of the times. So was Plato's turn away from politics, his expected path given his family background, towards philosophy. To understand the strength of Plato's criticism of poetry, it is important to bear in mind that Plato was writing after the ancient Greek equivalent of World War I or World War II.

Plato lived in traumatic times and his response to them was to question everything and to search for new foundations. He saw the authority of poetry in Athenian culture as resting on shaky grounds. Poetry was an important old rival to be confronted: a survivor from the golden age of Athenian democracy, the Pentecontaetia (50 years) between the defeat of the second Persian invasion by a broad alliance of Greek city-states in 479 BC and the beginning of the Peloponnesian War. But in the light of the traumatic history he had lived through, Plato had serious doubts as to the role that poetry should play in a well-ordered and secure city-state.

Plato's literary theory: *Ion*, *Republic*, *Phaedrus*

We will begin our reading of Plato's dialogues with *Ion*, an early dialogue written in approximately 390 BC. *Ion* outlines the theory of poetry as *inspiration* – it is a dialogue especially important to Sidney as well as to Shelley and the Romantics. Plato brings onto the stage Ion, a rhapsode specializing in the performance of Homer. Ion has just won first prize in an important Pan-Hellenic competition of rhapsodes. Socrates questions him to discover his thoughts on Homer and on the art of poetry. Ion's initial answers suggest an unthinking man, obsessed with Homer to the exclusion of other poetry: "when someone converses about any another poet I … can't make any worthwhile contribution at all, but just doze off – whereas when anyone mentions Homer, I am awake in a flash" [532b–c] (Plato 2005). But Ion soon presents Socrates with a puzzle and becomes a puzzle himself: "on Homer I am the finest speaker of mankind … and everybody else agrees what a good speaker I am – but not on the other poets. Now then, see what that amounts to!" [533c].

To solve this enigma Socrates outlines for Ion a theory of poetry as divine possession, which recasts Ion as unreflecting but inspired, possessed by Homer rather than mastering him. To build his hypothesis Plato uses literary tropes, beginning with the simile of the poetic Muse as divine magnet. Socrates tells Ion: "What moves you is a divine power", like a magnetic stone that moves iron rings; this stone "not only attracts" those rings, it also "confers on them a power", so that they in turn can "attract other rings" – and there is "sometimes quite a long chain". In the same way, "the Muse herself makes" the poets "inspired", and then through those who are inspired a chain of other enthusiasts is "strung out". Good epic poets are not masters of their subject, "but in a state of inspiration and possession" [533d–e throughout]. This passage allows for a multiplicity of interpretations. A contemporary of Plato might think that Plato is a conventionally pious man who reaffirms the moral authority of Homer. Are not the poets inspired by the gods themselves? Yet to many philosophers and critics it has seemed very clear that the purpose of this dialogue is to contrast the poet's possession with true mastery and true knowledge as pursued by the philosophical intellect.

Plato then shifts his frame of reference. Socrates now puts it to Ion that poets are "out of their senses" and "possessed" by "Bacchic frenzy" – possessed by the god of wine, Dionysus, also called Bacchus [534a]. Dionysus, though a son of Zeus, is not one of the ruling twelve Olympian gods, but his power and the visionary intensity and potential destructiveness of Bacchic possession were definitively depicted in Euripides's *Bacchae* (or *Bacchanals*), first perfomed posthumously in 405 BC. In the *Bacchae*, Pentheus, king of Thebes, receives reports of the "wondrous deeds" of the bacchante women, the female devotees of the god, led by Pentheus's mother, Agave: they made water, milk and wine gush "forth unstinted" out of the earth while (fairly flagrant in its erotic connotation) "dripped the while/Sweet streams of honey from their ivy-staves" (Euripides 1988a, 59, 61). But Pentheus opposes Dionysus. To show his power Dionysus uses the bacchante women against Pentheus: in deep possession the bacchante women dismember him, and Agave tears off her own son's head. Out of the honey-making of the terrifying bacchante women, Plato develops a gentler simile of the poet as bee in a pastoral idyll. Socrates tells Ion of poets in "gardens and glades of the Muses", "gathering" their songs "from honey-springs" and "flying through the air like bees", bearing songs to us as bees carry pollen; a poet is an airy thing, "a light thing … winged and holy, and cannot compose before he gets inspiration and loses control of his senses and his reason has deserted him" [534b] (Plato 2005).

Perhaps it is tempting to read this passage as a lyrical defence of artistic inspiration enthralling the reader with its beauty. However, its links to the

Bacchae cannot be ignored. The gentle bee-poet is one whose productions depend on the flight from reason and the ordinary senses into inspiration, in a way that is in continuity with the delirium of the Bacchic women; and if the bee is a symbol of gentle, social and industrious nature, in the context of Bacchic excess we might recall that bees can show another nature, swarming and suicidally stinging. Sylvia Plath's bee poems in *Ariel* evoke this other nature of the bee as a metaphor for a (female) desire to escape social conventionality, in poems with more than a hint of a primitive nature cult. Plath's bees are not the sedulous workers of pastoral idyll or of the perfectly ordered society that Plato envisions in the *Republic*, but "a box of maniacs" ("The Arrival of the Bee Box", Plath 2010b, 63) who will swarm and attack a male "scapegoat" ("Stings", Plath 2010a, 66). Or if the hive is imagined as a well-ordered society, a honey engine full of "unmiraculous women,/honey drudges" – just as the poet feels herself to have become in her proper social role as wife and mother – she searches the hive for a transfigured identity, her true identity as poetess: "I/Have a self to recover, a queen" ("Stings", 65–66). The poem ends with the Bacchic flight of the queen beyond the social "wax house", the hive, "More terrible than she ever was, red/Scar in the sky, red comet/from the engine that killed her–/The mausoleum, the wax house" (67). This little flight of my own at least serves to introduce Plato's fundamental political anxiety in regard to poetry: that it is dangerous to social order. No doubt Plato would have felt that Sylvia Plath's powerful poetry was a case in point.

We might see *Ion* as a first attempt to master poetry and stand outside its chain of possession. *Ion* can be viewed as the birthplace of the literary critic and of literary theory, in that it offers the outline of a first poetics, poetry mastered as a whole by the intellect, a pursuit of which Plato sees his contemporary poets, performers and audience as incapable. Let us make Plato's anxieties about poetry and art a bit more concrete. Ion, the featherbrained rhapsode, seems incapable of rational reflection on those subjects closest to him, the poetry of Homer and his profession as rhapsode. Very well, he is a creature of inspiration. But why is this such a cause for concern? Ion himself seems inoffensive enough. But inspiration is very closely allied to something that is a major concern for philosophy and which poetry (art more generally) holds as one of its highest values: emotion and passion. Inspiration is a state of heightened emotion, producing poetry of heightened emotion. The rhapsode, entranced channeller of the muse, brings to life the words of the poet with the fullest emotional power he or she can achieve. The more pathetic, the more terrible, the more thrilling, the more appalling, the better we like it. The more vivid and transporting the evocations of battle, lust, cruelty, pride, humiliation, the more spine tingling, the more heart stopping, the more hair raising, the more we like it, the more our eyes widen, our cheeks flush, our throats parch. Excitement, passion is what we desire. To feel, to be aroused, to be moved is what we constantly *desire*. And we know as well as Plato that the value of emotion and passion exists independently of rationality and ethics and that they are very often enemies. We know well from our experience of literature and the arts, and other modern-day entertainments or infotainments, that we are often not too concerned about the ethical aspect of what we are being presented with. Or we are aware that we are indulging something rather objectionable in ourselves and that we really shouldn't be watching or reading or clicking, but we watch and read on, we click on. Indeed even when the moral, rational and emotional are properly connected (see Aristotle on tragedy, Chapter 2), the emotions have a value, a pleasure, independent of the ethical.

Ion himself, well qualified for his job, is a creature of strong emotion, as he intimates to Socrates: "I'll tell you in all frankness. When I say something piteous, my eyes fill with tears. When it's something frightening or terrible, my hair stands on end with fear" [535c]. He likes Homer the best of all the poets, yet so unreflective is he that he cannot say why. It seems pretty clear to us: Homer is the most exciting to him. Glancing through Homer's epics we can see what Ion saw in them: tales of passion to the point of madness, insane pride, blood feud, nations plunged into years of war because of personal jealousy or slight, the thrill of battle, the glory of slaughter, trickery and cunning, unbounded passions for bodies, riches, honour, fame. Do we start to see Plato's point? Emotion, passion is of the body, of the body's desire for suffusion, tension, pleasure, connecting with the most primitive and fearsome part of our nature, independent of and often dramatically opposed to reason and sound ethics. Poetry and art are the unashamed champions of emotion, passion, feeling, seeking to provoke it at every turn, and valued and sought out to the degree that they do so. They seem a legitimate concern for a thinker about to develop his vision of the rational *polis* and individual.

Ion has characterized poetry as the product of irrational inspiration and not of practical or rational knowledge. We must remember the central importance of poetry in the Greece of Plato's time as an authority on all aspects of life and behaviour, and its place at the heart of Greek education. The dialogue can be seen as an initial move by Plato to undermine the authority of Homer (and poetry generally). Plato had serious doubts about the appropriateness of Bronze Age heroes, of warriors and adventurers like Odysseus and Achilles, and the activities of Zeus and the other gods in Homer's epics and elsewhere in popular poetry, being held up as examples of virtue in classical urban Athens. Of course, that something is the result of divine inspiration does not undermine its authority, quite the opposite: the divine is a *source* of authority. But what we see Plato attempting to effect is exactly a change of the source of authority, from tradition, the divine, the prophetic and inspired to knowledge grounded in rational and critical thought about matters as they present themselves here and now to reasonable people. Philosophy is to be the new source of authority on values and how to live one's life. Indeed philosophy, before it starts philosophizing, is already an ethics, already an alternative value system to what Socrates and Plato saw prevailing in Athens. For the virtues required for rational philosophical dialogue in search of the truth – calm, control of emotion, non-assertiveness (not seeking to dominate for egotistical or dogmatic reasons), tolerance of others and their views, impartiality, honesty, etc. – are not merely intellectual virtues, they are general moral and political virtues, at least for a society like Athens. And the opposites of these intellectual virtues – egotism, dogmatism, lack of respect for others, partiality, uncontrolled passion, emotion, bodily pleasure and materialism, rhetorical and logical trickery, etc. – are the stuff of our complaints about our societies' moral, political and economic life just as they were for Socrates and Plato nearly 2,500 years ago. Socrates and Plato add the argument that only the pursuit of intellectual virtues leads to a truly fulfilling life, aligning the pursuits of knowledge, virtue and happiness. Socrates and Plato are thus able to put forward an extremely powerful claim for the authority of philosophy as the rational pursuit of truth that is also the practice of personal and political virtue and, in itself, the way of life that brings true human happiness.

In the *Republic* (*c.* 375 BC), written during Plato's middle period, Plato imagines an ideal *polis*, city-state. However, the dialogue is a striking mixture of the utopian and the dystopian, at least for those of us who think of literature and the arts as an integral part of the good life. On the one hand, Plato is exhilaratingly visionary. For example, he dares to think that women might have the intellectual and moral potential to be among the rulers of the ideal city, that there would be philosopher-queens as well as philosopher-kings, even though Plato's own society refused women even citizenship. (On the equality of women see Plato 1992b [449a–471e].) On the other hand, the *Republic*, one of the most famous and influential books ever written, contains perhaps the most famous attack on literature and the arts, with Plato's pronouncements aimed squarely at the great artists of the age: Homer, Hesiod and the tragedians.

Socrates, Plato's mouthpiece in the *Republic*, claims that poetry does not have knowledge, that it is full of bad example, that poetry and the other arts, with their power to provoke emotion and passion, to whip up feeling, and their tendency to innovation and novelty, are forces that are highly dangerous to the just city and the well-ordered and truly happy individual. Finally the claim is made that poetry and visual art are (metaphysically) lost in the realm of illusion and becoming that is this world, in contrast to the spiritual realm of the Forms. All those who have argued down the centuries for the danger of literature and art, their tendency to irrationality and immorality, to licentiousness, their tendency to turn heads and disorder personalities, their threat to public order, have Plato as their great forebear. Yet in Plato's ideal city poetry and art will continue to play a central role, as they had done. But they must be unfailingly controlled in order to support and inculcate the virtues of calm, order, stability. It is notable just how much importance Plato attaches to literature and the arts, as Socrates says:

> those in charge must cling to education and see that it isn't corrupted without their noticing it, guarding it against everything. Above all, they must

> guard as carefully as they can against any innovation in music and poetry … [I]t is in music and poetry that our guardians [the philosopher-kings] must build their bulwark.
>
> [424b–d]

Socrates also proposes censoring the existing literary canon, particularly the following kinds of passages: gods or heroes being violent towards members of their families; gods "warring, fighting, or plotting against one other" [378c]; gods being anything but good and responsible for good things; gods represented as shape-shifting; gods misleading humans; death presented in a negative light; heroes weeping, wailing and mourning the death of loved ones; gods or heroes who are "lovers of laughter" [388e]; gods and heroes being disobedient or lacking self-discipline; heroes being mercenary "money-lovers" [390d]; immoral people being happy and moral people unhappy; passages stimulating pain or even pleasure in the audience. Socrates gets his interlocutor to admit that excessive pleasure "drives one mad just as much as pain does" [402e]. According to Socrates, such passages are both untrue and morally corrupting.

Censorship along these lines is in fact a demolition of Homer and the tragedians – not a single work remains standing. Here are four famous and much-loved passages from the *Iliad* and the *Odyssey* featuring Achilles, which need to be cut according to Plato's proposals:

- Achilles's address to the leader of the Greek army, Agamemnon: "Wine-bibber, with the eyes of a dog and the heart of a deer" [389e].
- When Hector kills Achilles's friend Patroclus, Achilles, unhinged by grief, pours ashes over his head.
- Achilles kills Hector and then drags his body around, mutilating it. Old King Priam, Hector's father, is "[r]olling around in dung" in grief [388b].
- In the *Iliad*, Achilles chooses to fight and die young over a long life, marriage and children; but in the *Odyssey* – and this is the passage that offends Plato – Achilles, now a ghost in the underworld, famously declares: "I would rather labor on earth in service to another … Than be a king over all the dead" [386c]. In other words, he would rather be a living slave than a dead hero.

Given the extent of censorship that Socrates proposes, it is unsurprising that, later on in the *Republic*, Socrates calls for a ban on Homer and Greek tragedy in the ideal *polis*. A new art of true and morally improving stories is announced, where the *intellect* of the poet would develop moral goodness in the form of "a fine and good character" [400e]. To understand Plato's language, it is important to sketch his theory of *mimesis* (*mimēsis*) and its relation to the ideal world of Forms. Framing Plato's assessment of literature in the *Republic* are his highly influential theories as to the nature of the self and the nature of reality. According to Plato, the self – or the "soul" – has three parts:

the rational, which is the superior part; the desiring or appetitive, which is the inferior part; and the spirited, which allies itself with the rational part when it is not corrupted by dangerous literature and bad education (see Plato 1992b [434d–442d]). These parts of the soul correspond to the three social classes of his city: the philosopher-kings (rationality), the workers or commercial class (lower desires and appetites) and the warrior class (the spirited and honour-loving part of the soul).

It can be argued that Plato fears this world, distrusts the evidence of the senses and perceives people's desires as dangerous and destructive; at least this is Nietzsche's view in *Twilight of the Idols.* As a result, Plato postulates an ideal world of Forms, which he considers more real than this world – the true reality – and which can only be properly accessed by our rational part. Our world is an inferior copy of the ideal world of Forms – an appearance – while literature is an inferior copy of our world, and therefore an inferior copy of an inferior copy, twice removed from the truth. Literature, according to Plato, is *mimesis* (representation, imitation), but it represents or imitates appearance, not reality.

To make this hypothesis more vivid – and the path from appearance to reality more desirable – Plato devises his famous allegory of the cave (see Plato 1992b [514a–522b]). Imagine, says Socrates, prisoners in a cave, chained, forced to watch a perpetual shadow-theatre performed by puppeteers. The prisoners would take this shadow-theatre as the only reality and, if an escaped prisoner came back to tell them of the world outside the cave and of the sun, they would doubt him and try to kill him (as the Athenians killed Socrates). One possible interpretation of this allegory is that we are these prisoners, literature is our shadow-theatre, poets are puppeteers, while the escaped prisoner is the philosopher (though sophists, popular educators, demagogues, etc. are also viewed as puppeteers).

Whereas in *Ion* the poet was divinely inspired, in the *Republic* he is a conjuror, a trickster, a sorcerer who deceives and harms. This view is built on the *opposition* of the rational part and the desiring part of the soul. As Socrates says, the poet "arouses, nourishes, and strengthens" the desiring part, "and so destroys the rational part", just as one "destroys the better sort of citizen when he strengthens the vicious ones and surrenders the city to them" [605b]. Not only does *mimesis* "produce work that is far from the truth", but it also "consorts with a part of us that is far from reason" and nothing "sound nor true" can emerge from this relationship; instead *mimesis* is "an inferior thing that consorts with another inferior thing to produce an inferior offspring" [603a–b]. As Jessica Moss points out, virtue in the *Republic* is "a harmonious ordering of the soul, in which there are no conflicts or tensions"; for Plato "such a state is stable and uniform" (Moss 2007, 434). If this is the true reality or the ideal Form of virtue, the gods and heroes of Homer and the tragedians, by contrast, are models of "vice" (Moss 2007, 443). These "varied" and "contradictory" characters *appear* excellent but are "in reality … vicious" since "true human excellence lies in stability and uniformity of soul" (Moss

2007, 430). But apart from their changeableness – Zeus is always changing shape – they have very questionable values: cunning, lust for honour, pride, stubbornness, furious passion. Homer and the tragedians copy "appearances of human affairs, and of human excellence", but these appearances "differ drastically from the reality" (Moss 2007, 443), i.e. the true reality of the ideal world of Forms.

In the *Republic* the supreme entity in the world of Forms is the Good, the coincidence of truth and goodness that is the divine principle of Reason, origin and sustainer of all things in their essential goodness and order. The band of elite intellectuals whose life-long labours in learning and dialectic will finally afford them this mystic and inspired vision are of course the guardians, the philosopher-kings. Philosophy, having cleared away the old gods, knowledge and values, and the poetry embedding them, is now invested with divine sanction. Plato then argues for something which seems rationally unassailable to him: philosophy must reluctantly return from the spiritual heights to fulfil its duty to bring the good life to all the people so far as their natures allow. Indeed it is the only hope for the good life for the city. The philosopher-kings must come down from the acropolis to assume the political power that Socrates and Plato had turned their backs on.

In the meantime, while Socrates pursues the relation of literature to the desiring part, he makes the following paradoxical observation about the pleasure of *mimesis*: when Homer or the tragedians represent the hero "sorrowing", "lamenting" and "beating his breast, … we enjoy it" – "even the best of us"; we "give ourselves up" and "sympathize", and "enjoy and praise" exactly what we would consider "unworthy and shameful" in real life [605c–e]. In other words, we can experience with pleasure in art what we would recoil from in life. This intuition will later become a cornerstone of Aristotle's *Poetics.* But if he touches on the idea of what would later be called aesthetic distance, Socrates's anxiety is still the lack of distance between life and art, and the likelihood of heightened emotions on stage spilling out into the audience and beyond the theatre. Once "the pitying part" is "nourished and strengthened" by poetry, it "won't be easily checked when we ourselves suffer"; and poetry has "the very same effect" on "sex, anger, and all the desires, pleasures, and pains": it "nurtures and waters" what "ought to wither and be ruled" [606b–d]. Yet if Socrates remains steadfast in his criticism of poetry he is not going to foreclose dialogue: "we'll allow" those who are "lovers of poetry" to defend it and try to "show that it not only gives pleasure but is beneficial" [607d–e]. Plato's student, Aristotle, adopts Plato's insight, but draws an antithetical conclusion from it, as we will discuss in Chapter 2.

That Plato's work inspired Aristotle, but to very different conclusions, is exemplary of Plato's legacy and points to Plato's fruitfulness and *polyvocity.* His dialogues are part of an ongoing and never-completed investigation. The very genre of "dialogue" that Plato invented is open-ended, dynamic and full of tensions. As Barthes would say, Plato's dialogues are texts, not works. While the character of Socrates is generally considered Plato's voice, Socrates is changing from dialogue to dialogue, displays contradictions within dialogues and voices ideas undermined by the plot. Nor are Plato's dialogues necessarily practising what Socrates sometimes seems to be preaching. For example, and this is just one of Plato's many "paradoxes", the *Republic* advocates the cool use of reason, only to close with a visually stunning and emotionally uplifting literary representation of life after death, the myth of Er [x. 614b ff.] (Plato 1992b). This is one of many myths, or allegorical stories, in Plato; and at the heart of the *Republic*, the allegory of the cave is an inspiring poetic vision, not a piece of philosophical analysis.

Plato's attitude towards literature and passion expressed in *Republic* is the one he is most famous for, but in the *Symposium* he can be seen to develop a more positive attitude to literature, inspiration and passion, particularly the erotic. Interestingly, these two dialogues were written in roughly the same period. At the drinking party of *Symposium*, Socrates and company amuse themselves by attempting to define love. Love is described as the child of Lack and Invention, lack providing the spur to invention. Love, the erotic, is the origin of all creativity. The word for creativity is "poetry" (*poiēsis*), meaning originally "making" [205e] (Plato 1951). All making – craft, law-making, philosophy or literature – is driven by lack that draws us ever onward. Regarding sexual love, Socrates describes the lover's progress from love of another person towards the spirit of love itself: the Form of the beautiful, which is the spirit of all that is good and desirable. In addition, this spiritual love, because the most valued, purifies us of the lower expressions of eros, gross passions such as pride, greed, lust, etc. This connection of refined love with visionary inspiration, and the control of lower passion, has been of extraordinary importance, and the ideas are to be found in many writers, for example Shakespeare, Dante, T. S. Eliot. Similar views about love, passion and inspiration are developed in the *Phaedrus* in relation to rhetoric.

Elizabeth Asmis insists on "the tensions and variations" in Plato's literary theory: "Trying out various approaches in different dialogues, Plato enters into a dialogue with himself" (Asmis 1992, 339). Plato's dialogues seem to us surprisingly polyvocal and open to a variety of interpretations. However, Plato himself may wish to assert that there is a limit to this polyvocity, that interpretations cannot go beyond the meaning that he intends and that he is the repository of his meaning, if we judge by Socrates's myth about writing in Plato's middle dialogue *Phaedrus* (*c.* 370 BC). This myth was famously read by Derrida in "Plato's Pharmacy". Derrida uses Plato to critique Plato – as Nietzsche used Plato to critique Plato before him – thereby demonstrating the polyvocity of Plato. What Derrida finds in the *Phaedrus* is the emergence, for the first time, of the figure of the author as the father and source of meaning of his work. The *Phaedrus*, Derrida argues, establishes a

> schema that assigns the origin and power of speech … to the paternal position … [T]he "speaking subject" is the *father* of his speech … *Logos* [in Greek, word, speech, account, reason] is a son, then, a son that would

be destroyed in his very *presence* without the present *attendance* of his father.

(Derrida 1981b, 76–7)

The birth of the author as father of his work goes hand in hand with an attack on the written word. In the *Phaedrus* Plato invents a myth by reassembling Greek and Egyptian mythological elements; Socrates tells the story of Ammon, Egyptian father of the gods, and Theuth, inventor of writing. Theuth goes to Ammon, saying: "O King, … I have discovered a potion [a *pharmakon* in the original] for memory and for wisdom" [274e] (Plato 1995). This *pharmakon* is writing. The term *pharmakon*, as Derrida points out, signifies both medicine and poison; it is ambiguous, and Plato attempts to exorcise the ambiguity of writing, as *pharmakon*, by offering an account of it which is clear and unambiguous – an account which is, paradoxically, itself written. (We will return to Derrida's "Plato's Pharmacy" to discuss it in detail in the final section of this chapter.) Ammon contradicts Theuth on the value of his gift, stating about writing: "Your invention will enable [your students] to hear many things without being properly taught, and they will imagine that they have come to know much while for the most part they will know nothing" [275a–b]. Socrates spells out the meaning of his myth: "those who think they can leave written instructions for an art, as well as those who accept them, thinking that writing can yield results that are clear and certain, must be quite naive" [275c]. This is because writing, unlike speech and dialogue and Socrates's dialectical method, is separated from the body of its father and is, as a consequence, barren and dead [277a]. With writing, says Socrates, "if you question anything that has been said because you want to learn more, [writing] continues to signify just that very same thing forever. … And when it is faulted and attacked unfairly, it always needs its father's support" [275d–e].

In other words, the meaning of a text is independent of the signs used by the author, and pre-exists the text in the interiority of the author's mind: only what is "written in the soul concerning what is just, noble, and good can be clear, perfect, and worth serious attention" [278a]. Speech has a living relationship with its father, but writing doesn't. According to Plato, then, his thought cannot be adequately understood when read. The history of literary theory shows that, on the contrary, once Plato's thought was separated from its father, it started an intense and fruitful life. The second section of this chapter will sketch important moments in Plato's modern afterlife since Romanticism. However, we will be returning to Plato throughout this book, to discuss his transformations in the work of Aristotle in Chapter 2, Plotinus and Sir Philip Sidney in Chapter 3, etc.

Modern Platonic variations

Jean-Jacques Rousseau, announcing Romanticism, reads Plato as his precursor. Peter Gay argues that, "[l]ike his favorite philosopher, Plato, Rousseau sought to discover and produce the moral man who would make the moral society, and a moral society that would foster the moral man" (Gay 1996b, 535). The founding assumption of Rousseau's philosophy is that man is born good, but is corrupted by society. The purpose of education ought to be to prevent or undo this corruption and return man to his natural state. In the opening pages of *Émile*, Rousseau concedes that "[i]n popular estimation" Plato "stands for all that is fanciful and unreal", but defends Plato as a reformer who "sought to purge man's heart"; he praises the *Republic* as "the finest treatise on education ever written" (Rousseau 1993, 8–9).

William Wordsworth, in his 1800 Preface to *Lyrical Ballads*, famously states that "good poetry is the spontaneous overflow of powerful feelings" (Wordsworth 2012, 508). While Wordsworth doesn't name Plato, he follows Plato's *Ion* in describing the poet as an inspired creature and in stressing the role of feeling rather than reasoning for the poet as well as for his audience; as with Plato, for Wordsworth the poet imparts pleasure. Wordsworth here resonates with Coleridge (who contributed ideas to the Preface) and Shelley. Though Wordsworth probably didn't read Plato at Cambridge, he certainly would have done so after meeting Coleridge in 1795. Wordsworth, however, breaks with Plato, at least with those views that Plato expresses about poets in the *Republic*, in order to address the situation of the poet in his own time and place. Caught between the emotionally hollow and formulaic elevated speech that counted as good poetry in England at the beginning of the nineteenth century, on the one hand, and the cheap thrills that urban men seek to counter the monotony of their working life, on the other, the poet uses the power of his imagination to generate the kinds of insight that reveal "the primary laws of our nature" (Wordsworth 2012, 507). What exists in nature and in the "common" "rustic" man, the poet re-creates and synthesizes in the poetic imagination for the benefit of modern urban man (507). We can imagine Wordsworth saying to Plato: Yes, Plato, the poet is inspired; yes, he feels deeply and has vivid sensations; yes, his greatest faculty is his imagination. But let me tell you, Plato, that inspiration, imagination and emotion can bring enlightenment and can have moral purpose. There is also a telling contrast between their visions of ideal reality. For Plato we feel the Forms transcend this world, for Wordsworth the "motion and … spirit … [that] rolls through all things" is of this world, immanent (Wordsworth 1998, 59). This sense of things aligns him with the following figure.

Friedrich Nietzsche, whose influence on contemporary literary theory cannot be overestimated, returns to Plato compulsively in most of his works. He had begun his career as a brilliant young classics professor, and understands almost all European philosophy as belonging to an idealist and rationalist tradition inaugurated by Plato. However, where others saw the dawn of Western civilization, Nietzsche saw the beginning of European *decadence*. For Nietzsche Plato's work is an epochal break with the life-affirming Homeric world and pre-Socratic thought, and is the inauguration and symptom of a new era of decline lasting over two millennia. Nietzsche gives himself the impossible task of extricating Western thought from Platonism and the "Platonism for 'the people'" of Christianity (Nietzsche 1973, 14).

Nietzsche's revolution of Western thought and culture, his transvaluation of all values, involves wholesale demolition of all things Platonic. (Earlier anti-Platonists would include William of Ockham, Niccolò Machiavelli, Thomas Hobbes, David Hume and others.) There is no immutable and eternal world of Forms. The apparent world – *this* world – is all there is. Life is flux and becoming and suffering. Plato is a coward running away from life itself, his idealism devaluing life itself. Nietzsche turns to the earlier, Homeric and pre-classical world for alternative values. (See especially Nietzsche [1887] 1989, 28–31 and editor's note 2 on 29.) Yet Nietzsche also finds in Plato himself inspiration to critique Plato, as well as to critique the Western civilization that Plato has been so important to. For example, he finds and appropriates "a new kind of *agon*": the critical, agonistic and iconoclastic spirit that makes Socrates and Plato such enemies of *doxa* (unexamined belief) and dogmatism (Nietzsche [1889] 1968, see especially "The Problem of Socrates" on 29–34). Whatever their differences, Nietzsche shares with Socrates and Plato the spirit of his radical opposition to his time. Matthew Arnold had also recently advocated the critical spirit of Plato's Socrates – or at least his own version of it – in *Culture and Anarchy* (1869). Arnold argued that his contemporary Victorians suffered from a dangerous excess of moral feeling. To counter-balance this, he turned to Plato to find the ideal of a reflective and examined life (see Chapter 5).

Walter Pater's last book, *Plato and Platonism* (1893), reads Plato's *Republic* in the context of nineteenth-century "aestheticism". Pater, trained as a classicist, had been a seminal figure for the late-Victorian Aesthetic Movement since the publication of his first book, *The Renaissance* (1873). In the last chapter of *Plato and Platonism*, "Plato's Aesthetic", Pater presents Plato as a certain kind of aesthete. Plato's attention to aesthetic form – his love and appreciation of the beauty of form – "anticipates the modern notion that art as such has no end but its own perfection, – 'art for art's sake'" (Pater 1909, 268). For Pater Plato's attention to music in the *Republic* resonates with aestheticism's idea that literature, indeed all the arts, should aspire to the state of music, in that music is the most formal (the least representative) art form. Pater boldly argues that formal-aesthetic qualities such as "harmony … symmetry, aesthetic fitness, tone" form the basis for Plato's conception of virtue; and that Plato understands philosophy itself as "the sympathetic appreciation of a kind of music in the very nature of things" (268). At this point Plato's transformation into an aesthetic critic – into Pater – is complete.

Pater's Plato, like Pater himself, believes that literature affects its readers morally, not through its content (*logoi*) but through its form (*lexis*): "its qualities, concision, simplicity, rhythm, or, contrariwise, abundance, variety, discord" (Pater 1909, 271). However, unlike Pater, Plato endorses the former qualities and rejects the latter. Plato's aesthetic was "austere" (271), "dry" (283), "manly" (280), ascetic, "self-denying" (274) – cutting, simplifying, correcting, controlling Plato's own "fluent and luxuriant" (283) nature, and to be imposed (in *Republic*) on the flower of Athenian youth for the sake of social order and discipline. This is then Pater's oxymoron of Plato's ascetic aestheticism, a "fervently aesthetic community" of "very fervent … ascetics" (271): "We are to become – like little pieces in a machine! you may complain. – No, like performers rather … in a perfect musical exercise" (273). Pater argues that what is valuable in ascetic-aesthetic literature is its allusiveness: it "solicits a certain effort from the reader or spectator", requires "great attentiveness" and addresses the reader "as a scholar, formed, mature and manly" (280). Pindar would be exemplary here: "With those fine, sharp-cut gems or chasings of his, so sparely set, how much he leaves for a well-drilled intelligence to supply in the way of connecting thought" (283).

Pater might call the art Plato endorses a *centripetal classicism*, the art he rejects a *centrifugal romanticism* – a distinction Pater first outlined in his 1876 essay "Romanticism", later included in his *Appreciations* (1889). Pater resurrects the perspective of the founders of the ideal *polis* vividly, if ironically: "We are here to escape from, to resist, a certain vicious centrifugal tendency in life" (Pater 1909, 273). But Pater argues that, if we were to ban the centrifugal, we would ban writers such as Homer and Shakespeare, whose "genius" is "'like a mirror turning all about'" (274). We would be effectively banning "fluidity" and multiplicity: the transfigurative power of the imagination; the "myriad-minded" poet "able by his genius … to become all things … in turn, and able to transform us too into all things" (276). Fluidity and multiplicity are the very values Pater is implicitly advocating here and explicitly in his earlier work (see also Chapter 5).

Aldous Huxley, in *Brave New World* (1932), revisits the *Republic* to describe a possible future world, the World State, where literature and the emotions are chillingly abolished and where everyone is vacuously contented. Huxley's hero is John the Savage, who was brought up on Shakespeare in the Savage Reservation and who has an intense emotional life. When John leaves the Reservation and is brought to live in mainstream society, his interactions with these new people are unsuccessful, his intense emotional life descends into violence, and he hangs himself to escape – a bleak view of literature as having no place in the totally engineered society. In "'Everybody is happy now'" Margaret Atwood discusses *Brave New World* within the context of the genre of "utopia/dystopia" and its ancestry in Plato's *Republic.* Atwood herself made a notable contribution to the genre with her science-fiction novel on a totalitarian society, *The Handmaid's Tale* (1985).

Plato, but particularly Plato's Socrates, as the champion of undogmatic thinking and the enemy of *doxa* – the power of arbitrary authority – inspired many, both on the right and on the left, who see themselves opposed to the existing order of things, from the anti-democratic Nietzsche to the German Marxists of the early twentieth century (Brecht, Benjamin, Marcuse). Bertolt Brecht – playwright, theatre director and theoretician – outlines his theory of the theatre in "A Short Organum for the Theatre" (1949). Brecht follows

Plato in distrusting emotion in literature and rejecting the audience's emotional identification with the hero in theatre. Brecht instead theorizes – and attempts to create in his own theatre – what he calls the "alienation effect" or estrangement (Brecht 1964, 180). In other words, Brecht aims to break the audience's passive emotional identification with the hero in order to enable an active critical and thinking attitude. Pericles Lewis argues that Brecht's theatre followed Plato in that it "appealed to reason rather than feeling", in spite of the two thinkers' obvious political differences: while "Plato's critique of theater had a conservative element to it", Brecht's theatre was politically radical (Lewis 2007, 193) (See also Chapter 7).

Benjamin had already developed a comparable perspective in an essay written in 1936, "The Work of Art in the Age of Mechanical Reproduction". Benjamin, a major influence on contemporary literary theory, argues that the work of art has been traditionally endowed with an almost sacred "aura" that invited in the audience an attitude of "contemplative immersion" (Benjamin 1992c, 231): passive contemplation, emotional identification and loss of the spectator's self in the artistic object. Benjamin, in his commitment to a critically detached and politically active audience, opposes "aura" and aims for what he calls "distraction" (231) and "heightened presence of mind" (232). The emancipation of the audience from art's aura or "cult value" (218) "permits the audience to take the position of a critic" (222) and fuse "visual and emotional enjoyment with the orientation of the expert" (227). Benjamin insists that this is an emancipation of art itself, and argues for the revolutionary potential inherent, especially, in the new medium of film. For Benjamin, a German Jew, what is at stake in Germany in 1936 is nothing less than to imagine an art and an audience capable of resisting the rise of Nazism. He is aware that film, in spite of its revolutionary potential, can be used to resurrect aura and "cult value". Alluding to the use of film in Nazi propaganda deifying Hitler, he writes of the "violation of the masses, whom Fascism, with its *Führer* cult, forces to their knees" (234). Benjamin would commit suicide in 1940 to escape capture by the Nazis (see Chapter 7).

Herbert Marcuse left Germany in 1933, emigrated to the United States in 1934 and taught in American universities; his students at Brandeis included Angela Davis, activist in the civil rights movement and one of the pioneers of black feminism. Marcuse's *One-Dimensional Man* (1964), though deeply pessimistic about the future, coincided with the civil rights movement that ended racial segregation in the United States, and became the bible of the 1960s student movements in the US and Europe. In *One-Dimensional Man* Marcuse argues that Plato inaugurates critical and dialectical thinking. He values the "transcendent, negative, oppositional elements" of Plato's concept of reason (Marcuse 1991, 97). Postulating an ideal world allows us to step outside our society and look at it critically. Plato allows us to distinguish between what is and what *ought to be* – "between the 'is' and the 'ought', between essence and appearance" – an indispensable distinction if we want to change the world (97).

Marcuse develops his reading of Plato in Chapter 5, "Negative Thinking: The Defeated Language of Protest", basing it on Plato's Socrates as the enemy of *doxa*. Marcuse writes:

> the Socratic discourse is political discourse inasmuch as it contradicts the established political institutions. The search for the correct definition, for the "concept" of virtue, justice, piety, and knowledge becomes a subversive undertaking, for the concept intends a new *polis*.
>
> (134)

Marcuse here outlines Plato's potential – what Plato ought to be. He argues that Plato's dialectical thinking is rooted in his historical experience; it "reflects the experience of a world antagonistic in itself – a world afflicted with want and negativity" (125). However, Plato does not acknowledge this. On the contrary, his thought "leaves history behind, unmastered, and elevates truth safely above the historical reality" (129) and, importantly, dissociates itself from "material practice", i.e. political action for change (134). Marcuse sees his own work of historicizing and politicizing Plato as the completion and fulfilment of Plato's thinking: his work is the moment when "the ontological tension between essence and appearance, between 'is' and 'ought' becomes historical tension" (141) and political activism. (Marcuse owes much to G. W. F. Hegel's appropriation of Plato's dialectical method [see Chapter 4] and, of course, to Karl Marx's historicization and politicization of Hegel's dialectic [see Chapter 5].)

Since the late 1960s the poststructuralists (Chapter 11), following Nietzsche and Heidegger and with the same grand scope of critiquing all of Western history and culture, returned to Plato's work as the founding moment of Western metaphysics. Thinking in a post-Saussurean context, the post-stucturalists' central concept was "difference" (as opposed to identity). For Saussure there are no positive terms in language; there are only differences (Chapter 7). The meaning (or signified) of any term is arrived at negatively, through this term's relations to other terms in chains of signifiers. The post-structuralists mobilized "difference" to critique Plato's tradition-defining emphasis on identity. They simultaneously mobilized Plato to critique the limitations of Saussure's static or synchronic concept of "difference". For example, Derrida's concept of *pharmakon* or Gilles Deleuze's "simulacrum" – both derived from Plato – (re-)inject movement and Nietzschean "becoming" into difference. (Plato also has a lot to say about difference in the *Sophist* [Plato 1993].)

In "Plato's Pharmacy" (1968; 1972), concentrating on *Phaedrus*, Derrida argues that Plato's work "sets up the whole of Western metaphysics in its conceptuality" (Derrida 1981b, 76). Derrida defines Western metaphysics as a system of binary oppositions: presence/absence; essence/appearance; true/false; good/evil; inside/outside. Within each opposition, the former term is valued, the latter devalued and desired to be excluded. Each one of these terms "must be simply *external* to the other" term in each opposition (103); the valued term is understood as an "inside" completely insulated from an "outside" inhabited by its opposite. Derrida therefore argues that the opposition inside/outside is "the matrix of all possible opposition" (103).

However, while Plato is working to establish these oppositions, in *Phaedrus* his own concept of *pharmakon* is working to undo them, to cross the "border" (108) between opposing terms and in this sense to "deconstruct", to undermine from within, his system, against his own intentions. The *pharmakon* – philtre, recipe, drug, medicine, remedy, poison – "introduces itself into the body of the discourse with all its ambivalence" (70) and generates a "passage among opposing values" (98). The passage from remedy to poison crosses the frontier between good and evil. One might describe the *pharmakon* (and writing as *pharmakon*) as "non-presence", "non-truth" (68), "nonessence" (70). However, this doesn't mean at all that they belong to the latter terms of the oppositions described above. Rather, the irreducible polysemy and ambiguity of the *pharmakon* and of writing, difference, "precedes" these oppositions: it is the very spectre that these oppositions attempt to exorcise yet is also their very condition of possibility – the "original medium" within which they are produced (99). (Derrida is here coming very close to Plato's *Timaeus* and its concept of the *chora* [*chōra* or *khōra*] as he briefly acknowledges [159–60]. We will return to this concept in the discussion of Kristeva in this chapter.)

Derrida discerns two simultaneous movements in Plato: a movement to establish the "exteriority of writing" in relation to the author's intentions; and a movement displaying writing's "ability to affect or infect what lies deepest inside" (110), so that "[t]he outside is already *within*" (109). However, what does Derrida mean by "writing" and what kind of literature would qualify as writing in the spirit of "writing"? This would be an art of *mimesis* as "play": "writing or play … hav[e] no essence" but "introduc[e] difference as the condition for the presence of essence" (157). If literature has a reality effect, this sense of reality is generated by the play of "differences", relations and "intervals" (163). It is against and out of this background that the real emerges. Against those who see literature as the "full intuition of truth", Derrida advocates the principle of *sumplokē* (in ancient Greek, intertwining, combination, interimplication) (166). Literature and philosophy generate their reality and truth out of polysemy, polyphony and intertextual play. Derrida announces the "necessity of the multiplicity of genres and ideas, of relation and difference" (167). Against a literature (and a practice of reading) faithful to the father-author's intention, this literature (and this reading) would be "parricidal" (164), in that it would have no kernel of hidden meaning which, once grasped by the reader, would put an end to the movement of *différance* (Derrida's neologism condensing *difference* and *deferral* – see Chapter 11). Derrida's own reading of Plato avoids such an interpretation of Plato to capture the movements of Plato's text and the way in which it exceeds the intended meaning of the father-author. But reading Derrida's text alongside *Phaedrus* also captures Derrida's unacknowledged debt to it, given the themes (touched above) of *Phaedrus*: philosophy's relation to rhetoric, inspiration and stories. The idea of "play" is one that is developed during the course of the dialogue in relation to philosophy, with Socrates remarking towards the end, "Well, then: our playful amusement regarding discourse is complete" [278b] (Plato 1995).

The poststructuralist philosopher Gilles Deleuze confronts Plato in "Plato and the Simulacrum" (1969; first version "Reversing Platonism" 1967). Deleuze, whose *Nietzsche and Philosophy* was published in 1962, here returns to Nietzsche's engagement with Plato and asks: what does Nietzsche mean when he defines the aim of his philosophy as "to reverse Platonism" (Deleuze 1990b, 253)? Deleuze focuses on Plato's distinction between the *icon* and the *simulacrum* in the *Sophist* [236b, 264c] (Plato 1993) and other texts. To continue our earlier discussion of the *Republic*, the *icon* would be the true representation of the immutable and eternal world of Forms to which philosophy aspires, while the *simulacrum* would be the false and morally corrupting representation of the ever-changing world of appearance (this world) that is the literature of Homer for Plato.

Deleuze argues that the "motivation" or the "project" of Platonism (Deleuze 1990b, 253) is this: the "construction of a model" – the ideal world of Forms – according to which the philosopher's claims to knowledge and truth can be judged in relation to the pretensions of rival claimants: the poet, the sophist, etc. (255). So Deleuze reverses Platonism in arguing that, rather than being a primary ontological reality, the ideal world of Forms is a Nietzschean idol, a myth, constructed to legitimize Plato's ambition for philosophy as the path to truth, to the "well-founded" *icons* "guaranteed by resemblance" (256) to True Reality, and to delegitimize the claims of poets as unfounded *simulacra* resembling nothing. However, as with Nietzsche and Derrida, Deleuze finds in Plato the means for the reversal of Platonism: Deleuze claims that in the *Sophist* Plato "discovers … that the simulacrum is not simply a false copy, but that it places in question the very notations of copy and model … Was it not Plato himself who pointed out the direction for the reversal of Platonism?" (256).

Deleuze's task is to imagine and redefine the *simulacrum* once it has been freed from the logic of resemblance – and it is a highly significant reversal that he turns to literature for help. Modern literature, in its radical multi-perspectivism, is a *simulacrum*: "It is not at all a question of different points of view on one story supposedly the same" and functioning as the common centre of concentric circles; rather it is "a question of different and divergent stories, as if an absolutely distinct landscape corresponded to each point of view" (Deleuze 1990b, 260). This doesn't mean at all, according to Deleuze, that perspectives, in this de-centred system, are isolated and non-communicating: "Between these basic series, a sort of *internal resonance* is produced; and this resonance induces a *forced movement*, which goes beyond the series themselves" (261). (The movement is "forced" in the sense that it has no author or father but is co-authored by differential relations between the series.) This is, in effect, a quick sketch of Deleuze's radical-democratic philosophical project of valorizing de-centralized multiplicities of selves and social groups in perpetual motion without beginning or end – Deleuze's version of a philosophy of "difference" (262). Highly Nietzschean in spirit, Deleuze like Nietzsche valorizes "becoming" rather than immutable and eternal Being – Deleuze calls the *simulacrum* "Proteus" (shape-shifting god as well as reference to James Joyce's *Ulysses*). "Becoming" follows no model, has no end and fulfils no end (such as Ulysses's return to Ithaca in the *Odyssey*): Deleuze describes the movement of the *simulacrum* as wandering: "chaodyssey (*chao-errance*)" (264). If copying a model is the definition of morality according to Plato (interpreted by Nietzsche), Deleuze (interpreting Nietzsche) describes the *simulacrum*'s practice of tracing paths without a model as "aesthetic existence" (257).

Plato describes the philosopher's Odyssey or *nostos* (journey home) through the allegory of the cave in the *Republic*: the philosopher will reject the aesthetic existence of the puppet theatre inside the cave, will leave the cave and ascend towards the sun. Against Plato, Deleuze affirms a *different* role for the philosopher, consisting of aesthetic wandering, quoting Nietzsche: "behind each cave another that opens still more deeply" (263), each cave a mask behind a mask behind a mask. Quoting from the first version of Derrida's "Plato's Pharmacy" Deleuze describes the *simulacrum*'s rejection of the Sun as "against the father" (257). (Luce Irigaray, in *Speculum of the Other Woman* [1974], will read Plato's cave as a world of proximity to the maternal body, see Chapter 12).

In Deleuze's Odyssey, the philosopher's aesthetic wandering is only one among many divergent wanderings, involving those who, for Plato, were the "others" of the philosopher, such as the poet. An Odyssey rewritten along these lines would tell the story not only of the wandering of Odysseus but would include the wanderings and crossing paths of Penelope, Circe, Cyclops Polyphemus, the Sirens, the suitors, the maids: "At least two divergent series are internalized in the simulacrum … There is no longer any privileged point of view … The non-hierarchized work is a condensation of coexistences and a simultaneity of events" (262). Joyce's *Ulysses*, Derek Walcott's *Omeros* and Margaret Atwood's *Penelopiad* are Deleuzean *simulacra*. Deleuze's concept of the *simulacrum* captures the "critical edge" of "modernity" and "modern" philosophy and literature (including Kafka and Beckett, both authors discussed by Deleuze and his collaborator, Félix Guattari) (265) – see Chapter 11. He announces hopefully that "Modernity is defined by the power of the simulacrum" (265). This power or force (*puissance*), simply stated, is "belief in the future" (265).

Deleuze's radical redefinition or creative misundertanding of Plato's *simulacrum* is in turn radically redefined by the poststructuralist sociologist Jean Baudrillard. In *Symbolic Exchange and Death* (1976) and especially in *Simulacra and Simulation* (1981) and subsequent work, Baudrillard develops his theory – or perhaps science fiction – of the end of modernity and the coming of a new age: the "*precession of simulacra*" (Baudrillard 1994, 1), simulation and hyper-reality. This theory became a constant reference point in the gigantic interdisciplinary debate on postmodernism and postmodernity of the 1980s and 1990s (see Chapter 9).

Baudrillard follows Deleuze's definition of the *simulacrum* as a copy without an original, a representation that does not correspond to an external reality. Simulation "has no relation to any reality whatsoever: it is its own pure simulacrum" (Baudrillard 1994, 6); "truth, reference, objective cause have ceased to exist" (3). However, whereas Deleuze embraced simulation as the critical edge of modernity, embodied in modern art and its valorization of multiplicity and becoming, Baudrillard claims that modernity is over and that the "system" (16) or "power" (*pouvoir*) now works through simulation, which is becoming an instrument of social control and "deterrence" (22). Baudrillard focuses on the explosion of mass media and of new information, communication and virtual-reality technologies, and the ensuing saturation – overtaking, precession – of "real life" by excessive flows of representations or *simulacra*. He claims that *simulacra*, rather than mirroring reality, prepackage reality into formulaic and restrictive simulation models that attempt to control our lives, as part of a generalized "strategy of deterrence" (7). This is a spreading form of "imperialism" where "present-day simulators try to make the real" – each and every one of us – "coincide with their simulation models" (2). Furthermore, simulacra hide their own status – they "dissimulate that there is nothing" (6) – and masquerade as true mirrors of reality. In Baudrillard's terms, simulacra, having liquidated reality, have to resurrect it artificially by pursuing a "strategy of the real, of the neoreal and the hyperreal" (7) as the necessary complement of their strategy of deterrence. In Plato's and Deleuze's terms Baudrillard's *simulacra* are *icons* as regards their purpose, in that they pretend to correspond with a pre-existing reality to mask their exercise of power.

What ought to be the role of theory and literature today, according to Baudrillard, and what is the status of his own work? While Baudrillard condemns contemporary representations as simulacra (copies without an original) masquerading as icons (true copies), he simultaneously suggests the possibility of a more pure form of simulation: a simulation that presents itself, avowedly and self-consciously, as simulation. Baudrillard's excessive style – the crass generalizations, the paranoid scenarios, the science-fiction imagery, the comically hyperbolic pessimism, the contradictions, the sense of clowning or buffoonery, the use of irony – undercuts the scientificity, objectivity and reliability of his analysis in order to lay claim to this purer form of simulation. In this sense, Baudrillard's theorization of contemporary culture presents itself as fiction rather than truth.

To turn now to Baudrillard's theorization of literature, on the one hand he suggests the liquidation of literature and art more generally. The contemporary explosion of representations, the ubiquity of images of (previously challenging and experimental) art has caused a loss of its modern autonomy, critical edge, outsider status and avant-garde role. This argument is made by Baudrillard at length in *The Transparency of Evil* (1990). At the same time, Baudrillard's textual and rhetorical strategies as they perform a more pure simulation – or *hypersimulation* – are borrowed from the literary avant-gardes. Baudrillard seems to position himself as the inheritor of an avant-garde line of modern literature, creating absurdist worlds parallel to our own and mining this line's critical potential. The line includes Alfred Jarry – famous for his play, *Ubu Roi* (1896) and his pseudo-science of "pataphysics" – followed by surrealists and post-surrealists and the Theatre of the Absurd: Jorge Luis Borges, Raymond Queneau, Eugène Ionesco, Jean Genet, Boris Vian. Baudrillard pointed to his debt to Jarry many times, and it is significant that he opens *Simulacra and Simulations* with a discussion of a Borges story; the story is not named but seems to be Borges's 1946 short story "On Exactitude in Science".

We will conclude this chapter with Julia Kristeva's use of Plato's *chora*, a cornerstone of her literary theory in *Revolution in Poetic Language* (1974) and particularly of her influential concept of *the semiotic*. Plato developed his aporetic or catachrestic concept of *chora* (*chōra* or *khōra*) in his late cosmological dialogue *Timaeus*. Heidegger discusses the *chora* in his 1953 *Introduction to Metaphysics* (Heidegger 2000, 69–70). Irigaray engages with it in "Plato's *Hystera*" in *Speculum of the Other Woman*. Derrida returns to it in his 1993 essay "Khōra". Judith Butler turns to *chora*, Irigaray and Kristeva in *Bodies that Matter* (1993, 35–55).

Plato outlines the idea of *chora* in the *Timaeus* [48–52] (Plato 1977). In earlier dialogues Plato distinguished between an "intelligible and unchanging model" and a "visible and changing copy of it" [48]. Here Socrates's interlocutor, Timaeus, posits a third term that is "difficult and obscure" and calls it *chora*: it is the "receptacle and … nurse of all becoming" and "provides a position for everything that comes to be" [49]. Timaeus compares the *chora* to "a kind of neutral plastic material" and suggests that we "compare the receptacle to the mother" [50]. The model is intelligible and the copy accessible to the senses; the *chora*, on the other hand, is neither accessible to the senses nor intelligible properly speaking: it is "puzzling" and "very hard to grasp" [51] and is "apprehended … by a sort of spurious reasoning … we look at it indeed in a kind of dream" [52]. "Chora" is itself a spurious – aporetic or catachrestic – sort of concept.

Kristeva brings Plato's *chora* into dialogue with the work of psychoanalyst Melanie Klein on the pre-Oedipal, in order to theorize the avant-garde literary practices of Stéphane Mallarmé, Virginia Woolf, Joyce and others. Kristeva transposes Plato's *chora* and the dreamlike reasoning associated with it onto the unconscious signifying processes mediated by the intensely ambivalent pre-Oedipal relation to the mother theorized by Klein. These signifying processes – Kristeva calls them *the semiotic* – summon and orchestrate the material properties of language in rhythm and rhyme, alliteration and assonance, playing out and signifying the fluctuation of affects (from love to hate and back again) towards the "bad mother" and the "good mother" of unconscious psychic reality. Kristeva argues that "only certain literary texts of the avant-garde … manage to cover the infinity of the process, that is, reach the semiotic *chora*" (Kristeva 1984, 88) (see also Chapter 6).

Conclusion

- Plato did not write a single poetics but developed his thinking on poetry and authorship dialectically throughout his dialogues. Our discussion of *Ion*, *Republic* and *Phaedrus* shows the tensions and contradictions in Plato's literary theorizing.
- Plato is a major founder of literary theory, but despite expressing at points in his writing, most famously in the *Republic*, firm (and very critical) ideas about literature, he is in fact a highly polyvocal thinker. His dialogues have invited an astounding variety of interpretations, appropriations and creative misunderstandings – conservative and radical, idealist, materialist, rationalist, etc. Thinkers and writers – whether they critiqued violently or embraced enthusiastically – have returned to Plato to privilege different Platonic dialogues or ideas, and have refashioned Plato to fit their own original purposes and what they perceived as the needs of their time.
- Plato's literary theory introduces terms and debates of crucial and ongoing importance: *mimēsis*, inspiration, the emotions and reason, truth and virtue, *doxa* and the critical spirit, dialogue and the dialectical method.
- As discussed in this chapter, Longinus, Rousseau, Wordsworth, Arnold, Nietzsche, Pater, Huxley, Brecht, Benjamin, Marcuse, Derrida, Deleuze, Baudrillard and Kristeva read Plato very differently. Most of these thinkers are discussed in more detail in subsequent chapters.

Further reading

Any of the texts discussed in this chapter would be useful further reading. You might begin with Plato's *Ion*, *Republic*, *Symposium* and *Phaedrus*; Asmis 1992 and Moss 2007 provide useful interpretations; Nietzsche 1968, Derrida 1981b and Kristeva 1984 are especially important for contemporary literary studies.

2 Aristotle and tragedy

From *Poetics* to postcolonial tragedy

Aristotle, Horace, Sidney, Richardson, Johnson, Hegel, Shelley, George Eliot, Nietzsche, Bakhtin, Steiner, Williams, Soyinka, White, Nussbaum, Cixous, Eagleton, Quayson, Reiss

In this chapter we will outline Aristotle's literary theory, focusing on his *Poetics* and his understanding of tragedy. We will then trace Aristotle's influence and sketch out the development of tragic theory and practice up to the present.

Aristotle (384–322 BC) studied with Plato for many years. Unlike Plato, he was not an Athenian, though he lived, studied and taught in Athens for a large part of his life. Aristotle came from the kingdom of Macedonia, a region of the ancient Greek world that, in his lifetime, rose to succeed Athens and Sparta as the leader of that world, first with Philip II and then with Alexander the Great. Aristotle's father was the royal physician to Alexander's grandfather, while Aristotle himself was Alexander's tutor. He benefited from this association until Alexander's early death, though Alexander's great favourite was the *Iliad* and its hero Achilles, rather than the works of his tutor.

Aristotle's early works, like Plato's, were dialogues; unfortunately none of them have survived. His mature works are systematic expositions of their subject area aiming at comprehensiveness, that is, they are more like philosophical works as we tend to think of them than are Plato's dialogues. Unlike Plato's works, no one could mistake Aristotle's works for literature or read them for aesthetic pleasure. At first glance, the difference between Plato and Aristotle is deceptively huge. One could say that Plato insists on the difference between philosophy and literature but writes philosophical works in a literary form; Aristotle argues for a rapprochement of philosophy and literature but doesn't practice it. Unlike Plato, who is a visionary often starting from the ideal world of Forms as the realm of being and truth, Aristotle is more of an empiricist and a scientist tending to start from careful observation of the particular and the already existing and then moving up, classifying the particular into general categories, as part of a system. However, these are oversimplifications, as Plato's method has both an "upward" and a "downward" path, and Aristotle follows him in this.

Aristotle was a polymath, the original Renaissance man. He worked and wrote on a great variety of subjects, from biology to metaphysics and poetics, indeed he is the founder of a number of subjects. His two works most relevant to literary criticism are *Rhetoric* (*c.* 340 BC) and *Poetics* (*c.* 330 BC). His *Poetics*, in particular, is the first sustained exposition of *ars poetica* in Western thought and remains a canonical text in literary theory. It has been the starting point for many boldly innovative revisions of tragic theory and practice over the centuries, alternatively invoked as admired authority or attacked as wrongheaded obstacle to understanding.

Reading Aristotle's *Poetics*

Aristotle's *Poetics* only survives in part. In the existing large fragment Aristotle analyses poetry – especially tragedy but also epic – systematically. Comedy is thought to have been treated in the missing fragment. His systematic approach proves de facto that, unlike Plato, he considers poetry to be a complicated affair. Again unlike Plato, Aristotle considers that poetry at its best requires great skill, and also differentiates between good and bad poetry on clear and systematic aesthetic grounds. He accepts Plato's insight that the emotions are important to poetry, but rejects Plato's distrust of the emotions. According to Aristotle, tragedy in particular is a genre that sets out to create *pity and terror* (*eleos kai phobos*) in the audience, but this has a positive end (*telos*), which he calls catharsis (*katharsis*; purification, purgation, clarification). Good tragedy brings catharsis and catharsis is good for us.

Aristotle classifies tragedy, epic and comedy as subspecies of poetry, while classifying poetry as a species of the genus of *mimēsis* (representation, imitation). Mimesis, as we saw in Chapter 1, is a term used by Plato to define literature: our world, according to Plato, is a mimesis of the ideal world of Forms, whereas literature is a mimesis of our world, and therefore twice removed from the ideal world of Forms which only philosophy can approach. Aristotle's understanding of mimesis is subtly different. Plato attempts to separate completely philosophy and literary theory on the one hand and poetry on the other, and refuses to see his own works as mimetic. For Aristotle, on the other hand, the category of mimesis would include Plato's dialogues, as well as dance, music and painting. This rapprochement of philosophy and poetry in Aristotle goes hand in hand with a positive reappraisal of Plato's insights on mimesis:

> (i) Representation is natural to human beings from childhood. They differ from other animals in this: man tends most towards representation and learns his first lessons through representation. Also (ii) everyone delights in representations ... [W]e delight in looking at the most detailed images of things which in themselves we see with pain ... The cause of this is that learning is most pleasant, not only for philosophers but for others likewise.
> [4.1448b] (Aristotle 1987 throughout unless otherwise indicated)

As we discussed in Chapter 1, Plato intuits that the spectators of tragedies watch a spectacle of suffering and feel pleasure. He interprets this as evidence of poetry's dangerous effects. In his view, poetry indulges that part of us – the emotions – that should be left to wither. Aristotle actually follows Plato's insights quite closely but draws antithetical conclusions and drastically changes the tone of his account.

As to Aristotle's "poetry" as a species of the genus of mimesis, what Aristotle means by poetry is much broader than our own understanding: it is mimesis using the different media of "rhythm, speech and melody" [1.1447a] either combined or separately. It can be classified and divided into subspecies: first, from the point of view of its use of these three media of "rhythm, speech and melody". Second, poetry can be classified according to whether it represents people as better, worse or as good as they are in reality. Comedy represents people as worse than they are; tragedy represents them as better than they are. Third, poetry can be classified according to whether it represents by means of narration (as do Homer and epic poetry) or whether it represents by means of dramatic enactment (as do tragedy and comedy). Aristotle then turns to his famous analysis of tragedy. He starts from the following working definition and then analyses its constituent parts:

> Tragedy is a representation of a serious, complete action which has magnitude, in embellished speech [with rhythm and melody] ... ; accomplishing by means of pity and terror the catharsis of such emotions.
> [5.1449b]

Aristotle argues that this is also the essence of epic poetry, so our discussion of tragedy is also applicable to the epic. Indeed Aristotle himself draws Homer and epic poetry explicitly into the discussion of tragedy, so connecting his theory of tragedy to a more general theory of poetry.

Tragedy is the mimesis of a single and complete action with a beginning, a middle and an end, where the middle flows out of the beginning rather than simply following it, and the end flows out of the middle. Tragedy's "parts ... ought to be so constructed that, when some part is transposed or removed, the whole is disrupted and disturbed. Something which ... explains nothing [else], is no part of the whole" [8.1451a]. Unity of action is vital. However, plots cannot be unified by focusing on a single person because "[a]n infinitely large number of things happens to one person" [8.1451a]. Homer is "marvellous compared to the others" because whereas "other [poets] compose about a single man, [or] a single time", Homer built both the *Iliad* and the *Odyssey* around a single action [23.1459a]. Aristotle argues that the good poet, unlike the historian and the bad poet, creates unity of action:

> [J]ust as in tragedies, [the epic poet] should construct plots ... about a single whole action ... The constructions [of the incidents] should not be like histories; in [histories] it is necessary to produce a description not of a single action, but of a single time, with all that happened during it ... ; each [event] relates to the others at random ... [O]ne thing sometimes comes about after another, but from these there comes about no single end. But this is what the majority, almost, of epic poets do ... Homer appears marvellous compared to the others, in that he did not undertake to put into his composition even the [Trojan] war as a whole, although it has a beginning and an end.
>
> [23.1459a]

What is involved in poetic mimesis is much more than copying reality. Aristotle assumes that poetry is difficult and good poetry is rare. Unlike the historian, he claims, the poet goes to past events and myths in order to extract out of the mass of details a single and complete action, selecting, synthesizing and inventing all at once. Whereas the historian relates what actually happened, the poet presents the significant and essential core of events. If Aristotle seems unappreciative of the artistry and selectivity of Thucydides, for example, we can see Aristotle's point clearly enough as the first drawing of a distinction between art and life. He concludes, in direct contrast with Plato, by raising poetry alongside philosophy on the plane of the universal, of general truths and essences: "poetry is a more philosophical and more serious thing than history; poetry tends to speak of universals, history of particulars" [9.1451b].

Because of the centrality of the single and complete action, out of the six parts of tragedy – "plot, characters, diction, reasoning, spectacle and song" – the most important part is plot or "the structure of the incidents" [6.1450a]. Plot is "the origin and as it were the soul of tragedy, and the characters are secondary" [6.1450a]. As to the parts of the plot, they are three: first, *peripeteia* or reversal (change of the intended effect of an action to its opposite and subsequent reversal of fortune); second, *anagnōrisis* or recognition ("change from ignorance to knowledge" [11.1452a]); third, suffering ("a destructive or painful action" [11.1452b]). The tragic "single" action is "simple" when it involves suffering but doesn't involve recognition or reversal; and "complex" when it does involve recognition and reversal as well as suffering [10.1452a]. For example, in *Oedipus the King* Oedipus's killing of his father is complex, in that it involves both Oedipus's *peripeteia* and *anagnōrisis.* According to Aristotle, "the finest tragedy should be not simple but complex, and moreover it should represent terrifying and pitiable events" [13.1452b]; "Necessarily, then, a plot that is fine is single … and involves a change not from misfortune to good fortune, but conversely, from good fortune to misfortune, not because of wickedness but because of a great error [*hamartia*]" [13.1453a]. For tragedy to achieve its end of arousing pity and terror, "[f]irst and foremost, the characters should be good" [15.1454a]. To give a modern example from Thomas Hardy, who engaged with the genre of tragedy in many of his novels, Tess, in *Tess of the D'Urbervilles*, has to be good for the novel to work as a tragedy. The subtitle called her "A Pure Woman" and provoked a wave of hostile comments from its readers in 1891. Presumably they didn't consider a sexually unchaste peasant woman good enough to be a tragic heroine. Aristotle would also have been critical of the accidents that play an important role in Hardy's plots, and would have felt that they were arbitrary and unmotivated.

For Aristotle tragedy – and poetry in general – is at its most effective in arousing the emotions when the poet is able to experience them himself:

> Those [poets] who experience the emotions [to be represented] are the most believable, i.e. he who is agitated or furious [can represent] agitation and anger most truthfully. For this reason, the art of poetry belongs to the genius or the madman; of these, the first are adaptable, the second can step outside themselves.
>
> [17.1455a]

Once again Aristotle follows Plato in thinking of poetry as a form of madness or divine possession and in depicting the poet as living the emotions he represents. But Aristotle reverses Plato's judgement (at least in the *Republic*). In line with his own view of tragedy as operating on the universal level of truth, Aristotle sees the ability of the writer to sympathetically identify with his characters' emotions, and therefore express them more "truthfully", as increasing art's power to express universal truth.

***

Aristotle's *Poetics* gives rise to a number of questions, particularly from a contemporary perspective, which I will now try to outline. Concerning the relation of poetry and history, in 1978 the historian Hayden White famously returned to Aristotle in a canonical essay entitled "The Historical Text as Literary Artifact". White argues that "the distinction, as old as Aristotle, between history and poetry obscures as much as it illuminates about both" and asks us to consider "the *mimetic* aspect of historical narratives" (White 2001, 1727). White argues that historical narratives are just that, "narratives", and therefore they are not purely objective. Out of an infinite mass of events, historians select, order, prioritize, synthesize, just as much as literature does – historians *emplot* or practice "emplotment" (1714). White gives the example of the historians of the French Revolution, who emplotted it very differently: Michelet as a "drama of Romantic transcendence", Tocqueville as an "ironic

Tragedy" (1715). We might conclude that, if histories are not fact pure and simple, literary critics cannot unproblematically turn to historians in order to illuminate literary texts.

Aristotle defends tragedy (and poetry more generally) by positing its philosophical universality against the particularity of history. He claims that the tragic hero is a type (that is, a universal) rather than a particular individual; and that tragedy is primarily mimesis of an action (*praxis*), not of a character with personal qualities or a person [1450a] (Aristotle 1995; see Halliwell's note b on 51). This can be understood as part of Aristotle's intensive dialogue with Plato, mobilizing Plato's terms to defend tragedy against Plato's accusations. At the same time, contemporary readers might well retrospectively interpret this in the light of Raymond Williams's passionate plea in *Modern Tragedy* (1966) not to cut off tragedy, as a literary genre, from real-life tragedy and historical catastrophe. Terry Eagleton reiterated Williams's plea in *Sweet Violence: The Idea of the Tragic* (2003). Does the universalism that Aristotle claims for tragedy run the risk of devaluing and bracketing off history, as Nietzsche in the new spirit of nineteenth-century historicism accused Plato of doing? Aristotle certainly doesn't put tragedy (or indeed the epic and comedy) in the context of Greek history. Nor does he ask whether the catharsis of pity and terror might be beneficial – and for whom – within the turbulent context of Greek history. Arthur Miller's *Death of a Salesman* springs to mind as an example of the sort of play that Williams and Eagleton would welcome, but I argue in this chapter that postcolonial tragedy is the major twentieth-century example of tragedy that is both historically grounded and universalizing.

As regards the question of Aristotle's "formalism", Aristotle's dehistoricized and depoliticized account of tragic and poetic form, in the sense discussed above, has lent itself to an oft-rehearsed assumption that his is a formalist poetics. (For example, see Peter Wilson 2005, 184.) In twentieth-century and contemporary literary theory there is a divide between, on the one hand, the "intrinsic" criticism of formalists such as the Russian Formalists (see Chapter 7) and the Anglo-American New Critics (see Chapter 9) and, on the other hand, the "extrinsic" criticism of "reader-response theory" (e.g. Stanley Fish, see Chapter 9). However, Aristotle is both a formalist and a reader-response critic, the latter in the sense that his starting point is a definition of tragedy in terms of its effect on the audience: the *catharsis* of pity and terror. Eagleton calls the *Poetics* an early example of "reception theory", studying the effects of tragedy on the audience (2003, 3), while George Steiner calls it a formal theory (2004, 4); I suggest we put the two together.

In relation to catharsis, the meaning of the *katharsis* of pity and terror is obscure, contested and open to ever-new interpretations. Aristotle does not say what he thinks the larger purpose of *katharsis* might be. And yet it is the starting point of Aristotle's *Poetics*, in that many other elements of his tragic theory – whether descriptive or prescriptive – are deducible from or necessitated by it, at least in his view. Pity and terror require undeserved "suffering", the hero's vulnerability to luck (*tuchē*), his or her reversal (*peripeteia*) of fortune from good fortune to misfortune, their fall. Further, Aristotle claims that the fall – the "action" – cannot be of someone who is completely good or bad. The fall of someone who is completely good would be simply repugnant (*miaron*) [13.1452b] (Aristotle 1995), while the fall of someone who is completely bad would also fail to generate pity and terror. He argues that we feel pity for the victim and terror at the prospect of such misfortune befalling someone who, neither superhumanly good nor bad, might be us. Martha Nussbaum argues that the very fragility of the tragic hero's goodness, in Aristotle's *Poetics* and in Greek tragedy, is a crucial ethical insight conducive to our "richness and fullness of life" (1986, 421). Why is goodness fragile? See Nussbaum's indispensable discussion of *hamartia*, pity and terror in relation to the "gap" between goodness and "good activity" (380), and *katharsis* as "cognitive clarification" or "illumination" (390–91) involving the emotions (378–91).

Concerning tragic characters, to fulfil the *telos* of tragedy Aristotle prescribes a character or rather an action (*praxis*) that is elevated (*spoudaios* and *kalos*) while also displaying fallibility (susceptibility to *hamartia*). In an effort to clarify this point further he embarks on the well-known comparison of the genres of tragedy and comedy: comic heroes are not wholly bad but "worse" than existing humans [2.1448a] and "rather inferior – not, however, with respect to every [kind of] vice" [5.1449a] – while tragic heroes are "better than we are" [14.1454b]. Social or moral pre-eminence is not a requirement for tragedy, as Aristotle is well aware: "Sophocles said that he himself portrayed people as they should be, but Euripides portrayed them as they are" [25.1460b]. The emphasis on socially elevated tragic characters owes more to sixteenth- and seventeenth-century neoclassical dogma than to Aristotle himself. In modern tragedy, in the genre of the novel itself, in postcolonial tragedy, the common man and downtrodden humanity ask to be taken seriously, so "fall" cannot be understood as fall from social eminence. It would be wrong to declare this attention to common people the death of tragedy, as George Steiner famously does in *The Death of Tragedy* (1961). Ancient Greek tragedy itself doesn't quite fit into the dogma of social pre-eminence. This is especially true of the marginal characters in Euripides, but it is also true of Sophocles's Philoctetes, for example, who is not only a minor and marginal figure on the Greek side during the Trojan War, but who suffers as a surrogate victim for the crimes of the leaders of the Greek army.

Concerning endings, Aristotle contrasts tragic fall and misfortune with the improbable happy endings of comedy where the worst enemies – say Orestes and Aegisthus – are reconciled. Aristotle concludes that, as a result, tragedy is a demanding art. He strongly rejects a moralistic and didactic form of tragedy where the good end well and the bad badly, as in the *Odyssey* and in comedy, because it panders to the "weakness" of the audience [13.1453a]. However, Aristotle is not programmatically against happy endings. On the contrary, and against current stereotypes, what he considers most appropriate to the *telos* of tragedy (the *catharsis* of pity and terror) is recognition (*anagnōrisis*) just before the reversal of fortune, which averts that reversal; "the best" plot [14.1445a] is "to be about to do something deadly in ignorance, but to recognise it before doing so" [14.1453c]. For example, in Euripides's *Iphigenia in Tauris*, Iphigenia, a priestess about to sacrifice a captive stranger, recognizes her long-lost brother Orestes and averts his ritual sacrifice. A bad ending is not a requirement in Aristotle's tragic theory; and it is certainly not a *sine qua non* of extant Greek tragedies, as several tragedies end well for at least some characters (for example, Euripides's *Helen* and *Alcestis* end well). Greek tragedies were written and performed as trilogies, to be followed by a closing satyr play whose comic elements and comic effect on the audience have to be taken into account. In Aeschylus's *Oresteia*, the only surviving trilogy, the concluding tragedy, *Eumenides*, ends well for Orestes. That the *Eumenides* ends well for all had seemed uncontroversial, until the recent strong feminist disagreement of Hélène Cixous, who argues that the *Eumenides* does not end well for the (female) Furies themselves (Cixous 1997, 431, 447–8).

Beckett's *Waiting for Godot*, originally written in French in 1948–53 and premiering in French in 1953, is given the subtitle "a tragicomedy in two acts" in Beckett's own English-language translation. This led to a strong critical interest in this mixed genre and to the claim that Beckett and the playwrights of *the absurd* more generally, from Eugène Ionesco to Harold Pinter and Tom Stoppard – as far back as the now tragicomic Anton Chekhov (e.g. *The Cherry Orchard*) – signalled a historic transition from tragedy to tragicomedy. Martin Esslin argued that "the Theatre of the Absurd transcends the categories of comedy and tragedy and combines laughter and horror" (Esslin 1961, 401), but "tragicomedy" was still a very minor theme in his 1961 book, gaining in critical currency in subsequent decades. In this context it is important to point out that tragedy has been mixing with comedy since its very inception. Aristotle's surviving comments on comedy (discussed above) contrasting tragedy and comedy so sharply are unfortunate and misleading, as there is nothing in his theory of poetic genres that requires him to conceive of them as mutually exclusive.

In *The Death of Tragedy* and more recently in his 2004 article "'Tragedy', Reconsidered" Steiner makes the case for the death of tragedy after World War II. He argues that one of the conditions of possibility of Greek tragedy was a shared worldview, and that this is now impossible. For example, the plots of Greek tragedy, far from being original, were based on a mythology shared by everyone. This is of course one of the truisms about Greek tragedy. However, Aristotle contradicts this – it is "ridiculous" to seek to keep to the traditional stories, "since even the well-known [incidents] are known only to a few people" – and calls on tragedians to innovate [9.1451b]. Shelley, in his Preface to his *Prometheus Unbound*, is reiterating Aristotle's point and seems to be heeding his advice: "The Greek tragic writers … by no means conceived themselves bound to adhere to the common interpretation or to imitate in story their rivals and predecessors … I have presumed to employ a similar licence" (Shelley 2003e, 229). Steiner arguably projects onto the ancient world a conflict-free unity that was never there. There is a danger of classicizing the classics (Greek tragedy and Aristotle) to fit the mould of current dogma.

Another claim made by Steiner to support his "death of tragedy" thesis is that the chorus, a vital part of Greek tragedy, is now dead. Aristotle confirms the importance of the chorus and calls for its greater integration: the chorus should be "one of the actors. It should be a part of the whole, and contribute to the performance" [18.1456a]. So is the chorus dead today? If it is dead among the white male European writers discussed by Steiner, the chorus is alive, active and participating in the action, in the spirit of Aristotle, in Wole Soyinka's *Death and the King's Horseman* (1975), to be discussed shortly, or in Hélène Cixous's *La ville parjure ou le réveil des Erinyes* (The perjured city, or the awakening of the Furies) (1994). Toni Morrison, in "Rootedness: The Ancestor as Foundation" (1984), a theoretical text defining what she calls her Black art, describes the presence of the chorus as one of its core elements. Indeed *Beloved*, particularly the long-delayed and long-awaited community of thirty women gathering outside Sethe's house and preventing her killing of Bodwin, can be read as the coming together of tragic hero and chorus.

Reading Aristotle's *Poetics* one is surprised by what Aristotle doesn't say, and which we expected him to say because it is part of our most basic understanding of tragedy. There is nothing about freedom and the individual battling against Fate or Necessity – *hybris* as the individual's willful confrontation with the social order, cosmic order or (perhaps dating from Milton and Shelley) arbitrary and tyrannical power – as in modern readings of Aeschylus's *Prometheus Bound*. This is a modern and particularly a Romantic view. There is nothing about conflict between two initially incompatible goods and its resolution (Hegel), as in Sophocles's *Antigone*. Nothing about dissonance (Nietzsche); nothing about Steiner's existentialist reading of tragedy as "ontological homelessness ... This is what tragedy is about" (Steiner 2004, 2).

Aristotle's *Poetics* became canonical in Europe in the sixteenth century, but its rediscovery and canonization was accompanied by a narrow neoclassicist reading of the *Poetics*. Western dramatic theory on the whole isolated Aristotle's thoughts on unity of action (and the resulting unities of time and place) and his thoughts on noble characters, turning them into a dominant but increasingly ossified and repressive neoclassicist dogma, while other aspects of his work, such as his emphasis on the emotions, were ignored. Philip Sidney, in his treatise, *The Defence of Poesy* (1580–81), is formulaically neoclassical in his comments on tragedy and his reading of Aristotle, anxious to downplay his own boldly innovative understanding of poetry. Shakespeare's tragedies, as is well known, never did fit this neoclassical mould. An overview of (post-) Renaissance English, Spanish, French and German tragic drama is beyond the scope of this chapter, but see Bushnell 2005.

In the seventeenth century, the neoclassical reading of Aristotle inspired the great drama of Corneille and Racine, but in the eighteenth century Aristotle's *Poetics* was increasingly used to discredit innovation. Reacting to this situation,

Samuel Johnson, in the preface to his eight-volume edition of Shakespeare (1765), defends Shakespeare for breaking the neoclassical rules of unity of action, time and place, but also astutely dissociates thc unities of time and place from Aristotle (Samuel Johnson 2001, 476–79). In defending Shakespeare, Johnson opens the way for the rule-breaking of Romanticism. This is repeated in other European literary cultures. For example, between the 1740s, when Shakespeare was translated into German, and the 1820s, when Shakespeare's current reputation as a genius was finally firmly established, a debate raged in Germany among critics, with Aristotle often being used against Shakespeare.

Modern tragedy

Hegel's post-Romantic theory, in his *Lectures on Aesthetics* and other texts, defines tragedy as the "collision" or "contradiction" of two equally "*justified*" perspectives – the major example being the collision between Antigone and Creon and their respective moral claims in Sophocles's *Antigone* – and the "resolution" of the conflict from a "further" or higher perspective which is a synthesis of those perspectives (Hegel 1998, 26). Hegel privileges "the feeling of reconciliation" (29). In Hegel's dialectic, thesis and antithesis are followed by synthesis, which in turn becomes a new thesis encountering a new antithesis and leading to a new and higher synthesis. Roche stresses Hegel's "conciliatory focus", his insistence on the possibility of "unity" and "harmony" and assumption that "all conflict is in principle solvable" (Roche 2005, 52, 55, 62–3). Antigone dies and Creon loses his wife and son. However, the conciliatory unification of their conflicting moral imperatives takes place within the "consciousness of the audience"; for Hegel catharsis is the audience's recognition of the untenable "one-sidedness" of each one of the conflicting positions, leading to their higher synthesis (57).

Against Hegel, Nietzsche's first book, *The Birth of Tragedy* (1872), focuses on conflict without resolution or synthesis, in a stunningly original rewriting of Aristotle's *Poetics.* Nietzsche starts his career as a brilliant classicist with a thorough knowledge of Plato and Aristotle. His emphasis on conflict (*agōn*) makes him modern in an exemplary way – in spite of the Platonic and ancient Greek roots of *agōn* in his thinking – as does his abrasive and antagonistic relation to modernity. Together with Freud, Marx and Saussure, Nietzsche is one of the cornerstones of contemporary literary theory. He has influenced twentieth-century thinkers and movements as diverse, if not antagonistic, as Heidegger, the Frankfurt School, the existentialists and the poststructuralists.

Nietzsche does not even bother to engage with the neoclassicist appropriation of Aristotle. Neoclassicism is no longer the enemy, Romanticism has already happened, and Nietzsche is engaged, as his later itinerary will make clear, in a critique of the limitations of Romanticism, while at the same time remaining strongly influenced by the Romantic tradition. Nietzsche goes to Aristotle's *Poetics* in search of what is vital in his thought. What is valuable to Nietzsche is Aristotle's understanding of tragedy as suffering transmuted into a pleasurable spectacle, an aesthetic phenomenon that delights – or, in Nietzsche's case, that is conducive to and an expression of a heightened sense of vitality.

Art is very important to Nietzsche. Writing *The Birth of Tragedy* after the Franco-Prussian War of 1870–71, Nietzsche is unexcited by the Prussian victory and military superiority. His view is that the Prussian military victory over France doesn't amount to much because France is superior in the arts – a reversal of fortune since the time of Goethe, when Germany was militarily weak but superior artistically. Before we discuss *The Birth of Tragedy*, a note about the difficulties of reading this book. As Walter Kaufmann argues and as Nietzsche himself requests in his "Attempt at a Self-Criticism" (included in the 1886 edition and in Nietzsche 1967), it is important to read this book in the context of Nietzsche's later work in order to avoid misunderstandings. Some of the passages of *The Birth of Tragedy* show Nietzsche emerging as an original thinker out of a radical rewriting of Aristotle, while other passages show Nietzsche repeating Schopenhauer and Wagner and rehearsing views which he later found utterly objectionable. I will focus on the former passages.

Life is suffering, states Nietzsche in *The Birth of Tragedy*. What Nietzsche comes to understand by "suffering" already takes him away from Aristotle. If, abandoning the shallow optimism and beautiful fictions of mainstream culture, philosophy and religion, we have the courage to look down below, into the depths, into the abyss, into the terrible substratum of existence, we will see life as suffering, as *becoming*, as the "ceaseless flux" that Plato shrank from (104), life as conflict, bringing about terrible destructions and rebirths. We will see "the hard, gruesome, evil, problematic aspect of existence" (17) – "the terrible destructiveness of so-called world history as well as the cruelty of nature" (59). Unlike the shallow optimism of Victorian science, whose perspective was that life is comprehensible and manageable and history an upward curve of progress and enlightenment, art allows us to gaze into the abyss and yet live – it is "the quintessence of all prophylactic powers of healing" (125). His words clearly announcing the twentieth-century existentialism of Jean-Paul Sartre and Albert Camus, Nietzsche writes:

> Conscious of the truth he has once seen, man now sees everywhere only the horror or absurdity of existence … he is nauseated. Here, when the danger to his will is greatest, *art* approaches as a saving sorceress, expert at healing. She alone knows how to turn these nauseous thoughts … into notions with which one can live.
>
> (60)

Art is a "supplement", a supplement to life – art can "transfigure" life (140; see also Derrida's "… That Dangerous Supplement …" on Rousseau in *Of Grammatology*).

For Nietzsche there are two kinds of art – Dionysian and Apollinian – and he finds in Greek tragedy a meeting of the two. Dionysian art is an expression of life as terrible creations and destructions, an expression coming from a *pre-individual*, unconscious part of us; Dionysian art does not express the suffering, the desires and affects of an *individual*, as Nietzsche accuses Romanticism of doing, fairly or unfairly. It converts metaphysical pessimism, even abjection, into a sense of power and joy. Dionysus has this double aspect. He is both the abyss and the unconquerable power – the nausea, the absurdity and the meaninglessness of human life converted into an ecstatic vision of eternal becoming and the expenditure of energy without end or reason out of sheer over-abundance of vitality (the excess that Georges Bataille will later take up). Apollinian art, on the other hand, is an art of restraint, measure and harmony, in response to "gruesome night" (67). It harnesses destructive forces by creating boundaries. It is a *plastic* art ("plastic" in the earlier sense of creating forms, not in the current sense of artificial) that turns chaos into images of "brightest clarity" and turns suffering into "calm delight" (139). The Apollinian is, as Nietzsche concludes, a "power of transfiguration" (143). In a strong sense, the two sorts of art are opposed, but the union of Apollo and Dionysus in Greek tragedy allows us to say yes to life, to celebrate it as ultimately "indestructibly powerful and pleasurable" (59), without idealizing it, argues Nietzsche. The cryptic aphorism that sums up Nietzsche's view in *The Birth of Tragedy* is that "it is only as an *aesthetic phenomenon* that existence and the world are eternally *justified*" (52).

In his later thought Nietzsche keeps returning to the Dionysian, while the Apollonian fades out. Nietzsche scholars have argued that this is because the Dionysian, as later used by Nietzsche, combines both the Dionysian and the Apollinian, as defined in *The Birth of Tragedy.* For example, Kaufmann argues that, in Nietzsche's later thought, "the Dionysian stands for the creative employment of the passions and the affirmation of life in spite of suffering – as it were, for the synthesis of the Dionysian, as originally conceived, with the Apollinian" (Kaufmann 1967, 20).

Twice in *The Birth of Tragedy* Nietzsche expresses his hope for an art of the future that would attempt what at the time looked impossible: a coupling of the Dionysian and the Apollinian with a third force, a Socratic-critical force. This is a co-existence of the aesthetic (as the Dionysian and Apollinian) and the critical/theoretical. Nietzsche invokes as a figure of this coupling the "artistic Socrates" (92, 106) – not the disenchanting rationalizer that Nietzsche attacks the historical Socrates for being, but a Dionysian poet equipped with the power of dialectic and radically opposed, as Socrates was, to the values of his age. Perhaps the artistic Socrates was Nietzsche's formula for his future role.

As to Nietzsche's originality, it seems to me that the one element of Nietzsche's rewriting of Aristotle that simply cannot be derived from Aristotle is life as conflict or contradiction. After Hegel's all-reconciling dialectic, Nietzsche sees in Greek tragedy conflict between different systems of law, different worldviews, etc. Towards the end of *The Birth of Tragedy* Nietzsche keeps thinking of "dissonance" and disharmony (140–41, 143). This emphasis on conflict and dissonance leads away from Hegelian synthesis and reconciliation, towards the irreducible multiperspectivism of Nietzsche's later thought, which can be summarized as follows: there is no one Truth, only a multiplicity of perspectives reflecting each other, combining with each other or struggling with each other. In this Nietzsche resonates with Marx's emphasis on conflict and struggle, and anticipates Bakhtin, Sartre and Foucault. Yet already, in his emphasis on life as aesthetic phenomenon, Nietzsche has in this early work devalorized Truth in favour of artistic vision.

Mikhail Bakhtin, though not engaging with Nietzsche, uses Nietzsche's metaphor of dissonance as well as the related metaphors of resonance and orchestration to describe the relations between the different voices in modern society and in the genre of the novel. Bakhtin, one of the most influential twentieth-century literary critics, describes reality as pluralistic, multiperspectival, centrifugal, *polyglossic* and *heteroglossic* (of many different languages) (see Chapter 7). In "Discourse in the Novel" (1930–36) Bakhtin praises the novel, still considered secondary to poetry at the time. The novel, he argues, intensifies and orchestrates the heteroglossia or polyvocity of language and society, and fights the centralizing, centripetal, *monological* (of one language) forces in language and society. Bakhtin reads Aristotle very differently from Nietzsche. He views Aristotle's poetics, with its emphasis on unity of action, as an ally of those monological, "centripetal" forces (Bakhtin 1981b, 271).

If in the eyes of critics and even novelists themselves the novel, as a new genre, lacked the *kudos* of poetry, the birth and rise of the novel is one of the great events in the history of literature. However, Samuel Richardson in his 1748 postscript to his epistolary novel, *Clarissa*, connects *Clarissa* to Aristotle and classical tragedy and seems to downplay the novelty of its form. If *Clarissa* is "a Story designed to represent real Life" (Richardson 1964, 368), Richardson argues against those who "looked upon it as a mere *Novel*" (367). He presents *Clarissa* as a tragedy in the Greek mould, and defends its unhappy ending from those readers who were "against Tragedies" and favoured "reforming Lovelace, and marrying him to Clarissa" (348–9). He argues that his plot is "justified … by the greatest master of reason, and the best judge of composition, that ever lived. The learned Reader knows we must mean ARISTOTLE" (351). Acknowledging that some Greek tragedies end happily, he claims that the Athenians "had fortitude enough to trust themselves with their own generous grief, because they found their hearts mended by it" (356).

It can be argued that the novel, in its nascent state, makes use of tragic elements and Aristotle's tragic theory in order to strengthen its claim to artistic legitimacy and seriousness. However, against neoclassical dogma (that tragedy concerns itself with the fate of the socially prominent), the novel as a genre is committed, in particular, to the *serious* treatment of common people, as Erich Auerbach famously claims in *Mimesis* (1968, e.g. 554, 556). Extending this view, it can be argued that the novel democratizes and in this sense truly universalizes the tragic hero: the urban middle classes, as well as the "low" and the disenfranchised – the urban working classes, rural labourers, "fallen women" – are all worthy of the dignity of the tragic hero. As with the modern play, critics and novelists have asked whether the novel is compatible with the universalism of tragedy, as understood by Aristotle. To the extent that the novel is, as a genre, wedded to realism, the observation and detailed description of a particular social context and of particular individuals within it, can it rise to the resonance of the universal? Can concretely particular individuals also be tragic heroes? Are "lowly" characters capable of *anagnōrisis* (that moment of the clear-sighted recognition of their actions and situation) and the articulacy required to put recognition into words, or does the omniscient narrator have to step in? For example, to what extent is Hetty able to recognize her infanticide in George Eliot's *Adam Bede*? Are the middle classes, who comprise the majority of the reading public for novels, capable of extending their "sympathy" – the key to George Eliot's aesthetic – to socially "lowly" tragic heroes, and does tragedy work if this sympathy is withheld, as for example was the case with Thomas Hardy's *Tess* at the time of publication? These questions are rehearsed in Jeanette King's *Tragedy in the Victorian Novel* (1978).

Terry Eagleton argues that the European novel turns increasingly to tragedy as the nineteenth century unfolds because the bourgeoisie loses its character as a revolutionary class promising the liberation of the whole of society – or at least optimistically and energetically planning its reform – and enters into a period of "epochal decline in the later nineteenth century" (2003, 179). However, Isobel Armstrong in *Victorian Poetry: Poetry, Poetics and Politics* develops an equally materialist but very different and in my view more persuasive argument. Starting from the 1830s and Carlyle's reading of modernity as alienated and alienating, she explores the alienated and fractured modern consciousness in what she calls "the text as struggle" and "the double poem" as simultaneously symptomatic of modernity and enabling its critique (Armstrong 1993, 13–14).

Armstrong's focus on struggle and fragmentation resonates with George Eliot's definition of tragedy. Eliot is familiar with Greek tragedy and Aristotle's tragic theory. Her description of Maggie (*The Mill on the Floss*) as a "character essentially noble but liable to great error – error that is anguish to its own nobleness" (quoted in King 1978, 80) clearly indicates her familiarity with tragic theory, but she goes on to highlight her modern preoccupation with the psychological interiority of the individual. Eliot's description of Sophocles's *Antigone* as "an antagonism between valid claims" (quoted on 78) indicates her reading of Hegel. Her view that "[a] good tragic subject … to be really tragic … must represent irreparable collision between the individual and the general" (quoted on 84) signals the importance of the modern conflict between individual and society in her work, a conflict often played out within the individual; but Eliot diverges from Hegel in her emphasis on conflict without resolution or reconciliation – conflict between "two irreconcilable 'oughts'" (quoted on 86). "Irreconcilable" conflict not only suggests a valid reading of some of her own texts, such as *The Mill on the Floss*, but anticipates Nietzsche's understanding of the tragic as "dissonance" without Hegelian reconciliation (Eliot's comments above were made in the 1850s and 1860s). Other texts by Eliot are arguably closer to Hegelian reconciliation or un-tragic, in the sense that tragedy is either averted or embedded within a larger un-tragic or optimistically progressive narrative (e.g. Hetty's tragedy in *Adam Bede*).

Critics have long considered Thomas Hardy a tragic – perhaps the most tragic – novelist (Kramer 1975; King 1978). More recent criticism confirms this, but also suggests irreconcilable conflict as the key concept in Hardy's version of tragedy. Linda M. Shires, in "The Radical Aesthetic of *Tess of the D'Urbervilles*" (1999), focuses on Hardy's "aesthetic of incongruity" (149), conflict of perspectives and absence of a common standard. Tess is a fractured rather than unified character; her fate is overdetermined by multiple and incompatible causes and laws; the perspectives of Alec, Angel and the narrator on Tess all undercut each other so that each one of them appears reductive and limited; the novel mixes several genres and discourses that undercut each other's reality and truthfulness in favour of a Nietzschean "hall of mirrors" (156). Hardy's so-called awkwardness is therefore due to his exploration of jarring non-coherence, as in the description of Zeus as "President of the Immortals", staging a clash of the lexical registers of modern politics and mythology, in the closing lines of this novel. Shires concludes that there is in *Tess* "no … satisfying resolution" (162). However, she traces a *single* origin of Hardy's aesthetic: the struggle and doubleness of Victorian poetry theorized by Isobel Armstrong. I suggest that "irreducible conflict" is a modern European paradigm emerging in *several* sites, largely independently. For example, Hardy was not influenced by Nietzsche and even disliked him.

For Bakhtin both tragedy and carnivalesque laughter are opposed to "any kind of premature and 'abbreviated' harmony in what exists (when the very thing that would accomplish the harmonizing is not present … Tragedy and laughter equally fearlessly look being in the eye)" (quoted in Eagleton 2003, 185). The twentieth-century practice of mixing tragedy and comedy is already discussed in Plato. In the concluding lines of the *Symposium*, at daybreak and after an entire night's talking and drinking, Socrates is found in conversation with the comic poet Aristophanes and the tragic poet Agathon: "Socrates was compelling them to admit that the man who knew how to write a comedy could also write a tragedy, and that a skilful tragic writer was capable of being also a comic writer" (Plato 1951, 113). To some degree this is a self-reflexive statement, for in *Symposium* itself love is presented in many guises, including Aristophanes's tragic myth of human *hybris* and our separation into two parts that long to find each other; Socrates's sublime account of love as an ascent to a vision of the Forms; and the comedy of a drunken Alcibiades breaking in on the party and paying tribute to the object of his jealous love, Socrates. In his *Ars Poetica* Horace writes: "comedy does sometimes raise her voice, and angry Chremes [in Aristophanes] perorates with swelling eloquence. Often too Telephus and Peleus in tragedy lament in prosaic language"

[93–96] (Horace 1989). Ionesco certainly makes the case more strongly; he refers to "our tragicomic human condition" and claims: "I have never been able to understand the difference that is made between the tragic and the comic" (quoted in Esslin 1961, 187).

In *Tragicomedy* David L. Hirst claims that tragicomedy is the "dominant dramatic form" of the twentieth century (1984, xi). In an account centred on the Theatre of the Absurd, Hirst reconstructs a long tragicomic line including Henrik Ibsen, George Bernard Shaw, Chekhov, Luigi Pirandello, Antonin Artaud, Brecht, Beckett and Ionesco. He is particularly interested in tragicomedy not as a "synthesis" of tragedy and comedy but as a "volatile mix" of the two "so that different effects", comic and tragic, are "contrasted" (xi). The model here is Ionesco: "I tried … to confront comedy and tragedy … these two elements do not coalesce … they show each other up, criticize and deny one another" (Ionesco quoted in Hirst 1984, 113–14). Hirst argues that, in a "post-Freudian, post-Einsteinian" (128), faithless world without "clearly defined ideals and absolutes" (102), pure tragedy, pure comedy and catharsis are all impossible. John Orr, in *Tragicomedy and Contemporary Culture* (1991), understands "tragicomedy" narrowly as a neomodernist or second-wave modernist genre that emerged in the mid 1950s but whose moment has now passed (Orr 1991, 43–5). He focuses on Beckett, Pinter and Sam Shepard and all too briefly mentions Soyinka and Athol Fugard; he treats Pirandello as a precursor, but excludes Artaud and Brecht. Richard Dutton, in the even more narrowly focused *Modern Tragicomedy and the British Tradition: Beckett, Pinter, Stoppard, Albee and Storey* (1986), argues that the form exhausted itself in the mid 1970s, when the work of the authors discussed "passed into new phases" (Dutton 1986, 4). To return to Orr, he defines neomodernist tragicomedy as a ludic genre asserting "disrecognition" ("failures" or "refusals" of recognition) and "play" (Orr 1991, 17). It emerges out of liberal modern tragedy – as exemplified by Ibsen's *Hedda Gabler* or *A Doll's House* – and is both an intensification and a critique of it. The multiperspectivism of liberal modern tragedy is intensified into epistemological uncertainty and breakdown of (self-)perception (disrecognition), while the multiplicity of the self is intensified into roles, performances of self, in the absence of the unifying rational core self assumed by liberalism (play). Instead of the liberal modern conflict between society and individual, the self is now in a moral vacuum and lacks depth and interiority, so that it is no longer possible to distinguish between resistance and compromise. Liberal optimism is punctured, while empathy, (self-)recognition and catharsis are short-circuited. Orr situates neomodernist tragicomedy in the postwar Western context of "commodification" (as theorized by Horkheimer and Adorno), the "one-dimensional" administered society (Marcuse) and consumer capitalism (Baudrillard) (Orr 1991, 4–5). Tragicomedy's exploration of disrecognition and play ludicly exposes this new society and its structures of feeling. Examples of neomodernist tragicomedy would include Beckett's *Endgame* (1957), Pinter's *The Birthday Party* (1958), Stoppard's *Rosencrantz and Guildenstern*

Are Dead (1967), Shepard's *Fool for Love* (1984). More recently, Sarah Kane's *Phaedra's Love* (1996) can be read as a feminist tragicomedy revising ancient tragedy and neomodernist tragicomedy.

The "grand" contemporary debate on tragedy was conducted between George Steiner and Raymond Williams in the 1960s; Terry Eagleton renewed it in 2003, prompting Steiner's response. While Steiner's *The Death of Tragedy* (1961) is now deservedly a classic, particularly in its close readings of European verse drama, it is a flawed classic, in that it high-handedly asserts as self-evident a series of very debatable propositions, three of which I will outline below. First, Steiner asserts that Greek tragedy and the entire Western tradition primarily re-enact "private" suffering (3). However, Aristotle's tragic theory asserts that the soul of tragedy is not the interiority of character but the externality of action, and that the best tragedies move beyond suffering towards *peripeteia* and *anagnōrisis.*

Second, Steiner posits that, necessarily, "Tragedies end badly" (8) – that is, with the hero's ruination. As we discussed above, some Greek tragedies do not end badly; and Aristotle's sense of "the best" kind of tragic plot (timely recognition that averts disaster) counters this axiom. Problematically, Steiner uses his axiom to assert that Christianity, Marxism, Romanticism and Goethe are anti-tragic. Steiner views Romanticism as incompatible with tragedy because of its optimism (128). He sees Goethe's "ideal of growth and education" in *Faust*, *Wilhelm Meister* and elsewhere as anti-tragic (169; see 166–9). However, it can be argued that it has some affinity with ancient Greek tragic recognition. For example, in Aeschylus's *Agamemnon* (ll. 177–8) there is learning in suffering (πάθει μάθος) (Aeschylus 2002). Christianity, Steiner claims, is anti-tragic in that it seeks spiritual redemption and salvation, while Marxism is anti-tragic in its focus on "temporal remedies" (291; see also 323–4 and 342). These are very narrow definitions of Christianity and Marxism, unfitted to account for Walter Benjamin's Jewish-mystical Marxism, for instance. Steiner adds that atheism is as anti-tragic as Christianity: tragedy "requires the intolerable burden of God's presence" (353). Is the "intolerable burden of God's presence" to be found in such tragedies as *Macbeth*, *Antony and Cleopatra*, *Hamlet*, *King Lear*, Camus's *Caligula*, Miller's *Death of a Salesman*? The answer is clearly "no".

Third, Steiner argues that tragedy is incompatible with democracy: "There is nothing democratic in the vision of tragedy" (241). Steiner contentiously reads Athenian democracy as a "stable" (194) and conflict-free organic society led by an aristocracy whose worldview is shared by everyone; he is arguably projecting onto classical Athens a unity that was never there. By contrast Steiner views the modern process of democratization as spelling the death of community and the death of tragedy (292, 318, 320). Steiner further claims that tragedy is compatible with verse (as aristocratic) and incompatible with prose, because prose "must correspond to our sensual perceptions" (241). It is difficult to know how to respond to such a statement, except to say that it has the same validity as "poetry must not correspond to our sensual perceptions".

Steiner's "death of tragedy" thesis variously refers to any one of several factors: a growing preference for happy endings; modern optimism in relation to the perfectibility of society and man; modern rationalism; Romantic egotism; decline of verse drama and rise of the novel; rise of prose and democracy; lowly characters; lowly audiences unfit for verse drama. His views are entirely imbued with a cultural-pessimist view of history as spiritual decline. He is in highly distinguished company. Nietzsche, Heidegger and very many other modern thinkers and critics take the same totalizing view. Steiner does not focus on the Theatre of the Absurd and does not view tragicomedy as contributing to the "death of tragedy". He shares the view that the Elizabethans "mixed tragedy and comedy", though he resists the idea of Greek tragicomedy (192).

While Raymond Williams does not name Steiner, *Modern Tragedy* (1966) is an implicit but very sustained critique of Steiner. First, Williams argues that the role of the chorus in Greek tragedy suggests that tragedy is rooted not in "individual" but in "collective" experience (18). According to Williams, emphasis on the individual and the "personal" points narrowly only to modern "liberal tragedy" (34, 58). Tragedy's roots in collective life support the idea of the continuity of tragedy as literary form and real-life tragedy. The view that tragedy does not concern itself with social and political life, ordinary people and everyday life is an "alienated" view (48–9).

Second, Williams points out that "not many … tragedies … end with the destruction of the hero" (55). He argues for a political reading of tragedy geared not towards happy endings but towards hope, the possibility of action, *emergent* forces; he argues against quietism, against the "complacent" understanding of tragedy as the representation of inevitable or "transcendent evil" and against the ideologically motivated suppression of historical human struggle against historical "evils" (58–9). Finally, Williams points out the proximity between Hegel's tragic theory and Hegelian Marxism (including Marx's early Hegelianism) in order to counter the argument that Marxism is incompatible with modern tragedy.

Third, Williams posits that ages of stable belief, and correspondence between belief and experience, "do not seem to produce tragedy of any intensity" (54). On the contrary, tragedy's condition is the "tension between the old and the new" (54), and "revolutionary societies have been tragic societies" (74). Turning his attention to the decolonization struggles of his time, he comments that "other peoples have been violently opposed in the very act of their own liberation" (79): "Korea, Suez, the Congo, Cuba, Vietnam, are names of our own crisis" (70). He diagnoses a "gap" between contemporary tragic theory announcing the death of tragedy and contemporary "tragic experience" (84).

Williams only discusses European and American tragedy, but his attention to decolonization struggles and his definition of the literary form of tragedy as rooted in historical struggle resonate with an emergent wave of anticolonial and postcolonial tragedy. For example, Aimé Césaire's tragic drama, *A Season in the Congo*, also published in 1966 in its first version, explores the history of Congolese independence and its tragic hero, Patrice Lumumba (see Gayatri Chakravorty Spivak's 2010 translation).

Eagleton's tragic theory in *Sweet Violence* (2003) is an idiosyncratic synthesis of Steiner and Williams. He recasts Steiner's apolitical theory of tragedy as ruination into the terms of the Lacanian Marxist critic Slavoj Žižek (see Chapter 6). In a bold politicization of Steiner, Eagleton defines "authentic politics" as anchored in the recognition of human frailty and vulnerability (xv) or of tragic "suffering" (Aristotle's term). Similarly, Eagleton reads Christianity and Jesus in the light of Kierkegaard's existentialist *Fear and Trembling.* In Žižek's Lacanian terms, Eagleton posits the traumatic encounter with the Real (repressed desires and hidden or disavowed aspects of reality that erupt, tearing the web of normality and the status quo) as the price to pay for "genuine emancipation" (58), without any guarantee that "the bargain will prove worth it" (60). Tragedy is redefined as paying the highest price for one's fidelity to the Real of one's desire for truth and justice (57, 234). This desire is not based on smug certainty; on the contrary, Eagleton speaks of "fissure", aporia and the unknowable (281–2). The only "objectivity" available is that of mutual "selfless attention to another's needs" and solidarity and identification with the disenfranchised (284, 289).

Eagleton explicitly endorses, develops and updates Raymond Williams's tragic theory. He develops Williams's insight that the dominant twentieth-century ideologies – Marxism, Freudianism and existentialism – are tragic, against Steiner's "death of tragedy" thesis. He also develops Williams's view of tragedy as compatible with "hope" and "the possibility of social progress" (40). Suffering is not ennobling, but one might choose it reluctantly in the hope of a more just society. Eagleton, finally, shares Williams's anticolonial and anti-Eurocentric perspective. He endorses "the anti-colonial struggle" (65) and scathingly rejects Eurocentric definitions of tragedy as exclusionary: "Only Western cultures need apply" (71). And yet, among the large, expansive, inclusive group of tragedies Eagleton reads in his book, how surprising that he does not so much as mention a single tragedy written by a postcolonial writer! In relation to tragedies by women writers, only *Wuthering Heights* and *Beloved* are mentioned, while *The Mill on the Floss* is on Eagleton's list of "near-misses" (178). Eagleton shares with Steiner an *attention* to European and American male writers and a lack of attention to everyone else, which narrows and undercuts his self-proclaimed "self-less attention" to the needs of others. While he tries to establish a distinction between conservative/traditionalist (Steiner) and radical/political (Williams, Eagleton) theories of tragedy, his narrow canon undermines the usefulness of this distinction.

Steiner's "'Tragedy', Reconsidered" (2004) can be read as a response to Eagleton. While Eagleton aimed to politicize tragedy and Christianity, Steiner aims to redefine "the abyss" as the necessarily "theological" core of tragedy (5). Steiner's theology posits the "divine malignity" and "sadism" of "daemonic and godly forces", unalleviated by the possibility of "redemption or repair" (12). Steiner also posits that this divine malevolence and envy is directed necessarily towards men of "[s]ocial status" (10). The decline of tragedy "was concomitant with the democratization of western ideals" because tragedy requires social "eminence"; Steiner rejects the idea that this is an elitist view, as "pseudo-Marxist chatter would have it" (9). The core of tragedy for Steiner is the *oxymoron* that the king of the city becomes *apolis*, an unwelcome guest in the world, as he is exposed to his "ontological homelessness" (2). He views Euripides's *Bacchae* (or *Bacchanals*) as exemplary of his tragic theory: Pentheus, king of Thebes, is felled by Dionysus.

Steiner states that this very narrow view of tragedy is very much the basis of his 1961 book: he had "inferred this categorical imperative" when writing *The Death of Tragedy* but "had not underlined it adequately" (4). However, he has difficulty fitting his favourite texts into this mould. For example, unwilling to give up on Shelley's *The Cenci* as a tragedy, he is forced to argue that *The Cenci* expresses a protest "against the arbitrary tyranny of the gods" (7), surely a misreading. He concludes that there are still "no persuasive grounds on which to retract" his 1961 "death of tragedy" thesis. Steiner's tragic reading of tragedy as a fallen genre is supported by the un-tragic fate of his own book, "now … in its seventeenth language" (15).

Steiner has reformulated his idea of tragedy as the human condition, not a literary genre. This condition is one of staring at the "abyss" and "ontological homelessness". He thus alludes to an important tradition – Nietzsche (Chapter 5), Heidegger, Sartre (Chapter 10), Beckett – primarily addressing the intolerable *absence* of God (the opposite of Steiner's "intolerable burden of God's presence" thesis). Instead of engaging with it, he translates the rich theme of "ontological homelessness" into a very reductive religious myth of divine malignity, which is clearly irrelevant to most tragedies, so that the death of tragedy is little more than the dearth of tragedies in this narrow mould. Even as a reading of the *Bacchae* – arguably Euripides's most political play – his thesis is reductive. Steiner seems happy to rest in the nebulosity of high- or deep-sounding generality: "man is made an unwelcome guest of life or, at best, a threatened stranger on this hostile or indifferent earth" (2). We remain here entirely in the realm of mythic metaphor with, in addition, an odd but telling sense of solitariness, the use of the collective "man" making all of us lonely wanderers in an elemental nature. Here is a large part of the trouble with Steiner. For Oedipus, K, Tess, Willy Loman, Macbeth and Lady Macbeth are not solitary wanderers in the eternal wilderness. Nobody is, not even King Lear. The world may be a hostile place for Willy Loman, in *Death of a Salesman*, but it is a tough socioeconomic mid-twentieth-century American reality, not an elemental wilderness. Willy's ontological homelessness has involved him spending many years paying off the mortgage on his home. If he feels unfulfilled, lacking, and is finally driven to death by this, it may be due to incurable ontological lack, but first and foremost it is due to his desire to be a success in terms of the masculine values of the time and the ideals of the American Dream.

The strife of the decolonizing process and its postcolonial aftermath were the context for a return of tragedy, to which Steiner and Eagleton are strangely blind. Wole Soyinka's work is exemplary here, but we might go further back: to Aimé Césaire's *La tragédie du roi Christophe* (1963) and Walcott's *Henri Christophe* (1949), both on Haiti; or to Chinua Achebe's tragic novel on the Igbo people, *Things Fall Apart* (1958), intertextually referring to W. B. Yeats's poem "The Second Coming"; to Yeats's tragic drama and the theme of tragic joy in his poetry; as well as to the tragic drama of J. M. Synge.

In Euripides's *Bacchae* (see Chapter 1), Pentheus, king of Thebes, scorns Dionysus's divine regenerative powers; the god then possesses Pentheus's mother, Agave, who leads a group of Theban Bacchantes, dismembering Pentheus in their trance. The play ends in mourning and Agave's banishment. Soyinka's *The Bacchae of Euripides* (1973) substantially rewrites Euripides's play. Soyinka's play was written for the British National Theatre and its first production was by all accounts a failure (see Soyinka's account in Soyinka 1988c). In Soyinka's version, the leader of a chorus of slaves (one of Soyinka's innovations) acknowledges Dionysus's transformative and regenerative potential: "his mesh of elements/Reconciles a warring universe" (251). After Pentheus's dismemberment by Agave and the Bacchantes, unlike the Greek play, "red jets" of wine spring from Pentheus's impaled head. Everyone, including Agave, moves towards the "fountain", and they collectively drink from Pentheus's head in a ritual bringing the community together after the violent conflict (307). The play is appropriately subtitled "a communion rite". Soyinka, while acknowledging the destructiveness of Dionysus, affirms his ultimately regenerative powers and prioritizes community-building.

In his theoretical piece on Yoruba tragedy, "The Fourth Stage" (1973), the Yoruba-Nigerian Soyinka posits the proximity of the destructive/regenerative Dionysus (as theorized by Nietzsche) and the Yoruba god Ogun, god of "creativity" and "war" (34). Soyinka describes Ogun as Dionysus's "twin" (33). Yoruba cosmology is based on the "contemporaneous existence" (23) of our world, the world of the ancestors and the world of the unborn, but these worlds are separated by a "transitional abyss" (32), and Ogun-like powers are required to cross it. Soyinka defines Yoruba mythology as affirming "the final resolution of things and the constant evidence of harmony" (28). However, to avoid "complacency" (31), he stresses his awareness that "harmonious resolution" is "antithetical to the tragic challenge of Ogun" on which it depends (29).

In Soyinka's Yoruba tragedy written in English, *Death and the King's Horseman* (1975) – written while Soyinka was a visiting academic at Cambridge and given a first reading there – the traditional official role of the King of Oyo's "Horseman", Elesin, is to commit ritual suicide after the king's death in order to forge a path for the king across the transitional gulf to the world of the ancestors. When Elesin's ritual suicide is interrupted by a combination of failure of the will and intervention by the colonial authorities, his Western-educated son paradoxically steps in and takes his place in an attempt to salvage the interrupted communication with the world of the ancestors.

In "Using Tragedy against its Makers: Some African and Caribbean Instances" (2005) Timothy J. Reiss argues that postcolonial tragedy deviates both from metaphysical/universalist and from historical/political accounts of tragedy. Though Steiner, Williams and Eagleton are not mentioned, Reiss effectively posits the need for an account of postcolonial tragedy that is substantially different from theirs, and then outlines just such an account. Reiss claims that while tragic theory has either stressed the social/political or the metaphysical, postcolonial African practitioners of tragedy "annul such a distinction" (511). Postcolonial tragedy, more generally, "turns" (adapts) tragedy against its makers by "joining realms of being and experience, not marking the division" (520). Reiss acknowledges that crossing the boundary between the political and the metaphysical is of course not exclusive to postcolonial tragedy but is already present in Greek tragedy. The example he gives is *Oedipus at Colonus*. (Arguably Williams and Eagleton also cross this boundary.)

What Reiss particularly objects to in relation to modern tragic theory and practice is an "insuperable divide" between individual and an impersonal cosmic or social order: "a modern Western sense of 'self' as individually facing a greater divine, social, or political whole … facing-*off* with it in … anguished conflict" (506). He argues that, in a colonial context, this narrative or mythic template has historically allowed Westerners to perceive "the 'tragic Indian,' 'tragic mulatto,' or anthropological indigene [as] irrevocably doomed" by the impersonal logic of "civilization's march" rather than by their own actions or inaction, and to abdicate their "responsibility" towards them (506). By contrast, postcolonial tragedies "turn tragedy on its head" by affirming and celebrating human agency, solidarity, "community", reconstruction and "remaking" (532).

Reiss traces the emergence of African and Caribbean postcolonial tragedy between Derek Walcott's 1949 *Henri Christophe* and Aimé Césaire's 1963 *La tragédie du roi Christophe*. The former, Reiss argues, followed the above modern Western tragic pattern, and was written when Haiti was an isolated instance of (hardly successful) decolonization. The latter "differs wholly" (532) and inaugurates postcolonial tragedy emerging in response to unfolding decolonization struggles.

Soyinka is central to Reiss's account of postcolonial tragedy. His *The Bacchae of Euripides* "joyfully affirms a culture that unites death and life, divine and secular, social and natural worlds", and the "disaster and exile" that end Euripides's *Bacchae* are "upturned" (510). This 1973 play displays an "optimism" that sub-Saharan tragedy "would not show for much longer", as political conditions worsened (510). However, *Death and the King's Horseman*, though less optimistic, continues to assume the continuity of the world of the ancestors and the historical world, "establishes the source of disjunction" and "offers more than a hope of rejoining produced from the play of social and political forces" (514). In spite of the variety of postcolonial tragic narratives – from precolonial conflicts to the horrors of colonization to postcolonial conflicts of values to neocolonialism and corrupt elites – and in spite of changing conditions, many postcolonial tragedies affirm "reparation for disjunction within the individual psyche", "harmony in the universe" and "cosmic adjustment" (Soyinka quoted Reiss 2005, 518), in texts where "[s]ociopolitical critique joins with what Soyinka calls the 'sacred'" (532).

Reiss posits the collectivism of postcolonial tragedy and its critique of individualist values. Often "the main tragic 'hero' is the community" (Reiss 2005, 529, quoting Lokangasa Losambe) or, even if the individual "agent of renewal suffers", "the community is healed" (519) or there is "communal participation" (529, quoting Ola Rotimi). Reiss endorses Ato Quayson's argument (to be discussed shortly) that viewing real-life events such as the murder of the writer Ken Saro-Wiwa through this postcolonial tragic prism "arouse[s] a silent people into an engagement with their history" (533, quoting Quayson). Reiss concludes that postcolonial tragedy is both politically proactive and engaged in "turning" modern tragedy towards the redefined metaphysics and ethics of the African diaspora.

Ato Quayson in "African Postcolonial Relations through the Prism of Tragedy" (2003) argues that Saro-Wiwa took a leading role in the struggle of the Ogonis against the Nigerian state and Shell exactly because he interpreted the history of Ogoniland as a tragedy. Quayson interprets Saro-Wiwa himself as a tragic hero, combining elements of the tragic theories of Aristotle, Raymond Williams and Wole Soyinka. However, Quayson cautions against Soyinka's emphasis on the tragic hero: as in Christian conceptions of tragedy, Soyinka hints at the "redemptive quality of the hero's death", but this idea "can breed quiescence and apathy ... since the hero is taken as carrying the responsibility for salvation" (74). Quayson suggests that, on the contrary, political hope resides in a "continual reappraisal of the life and death of the hero as a means of renewing the resolve to struggle on in the process of challenging the dominant structural and discursive relations begun by the hero" (74).

I regret that I can only note here the substantial contribution of feminist thinkers, from a variety of traditions, to contemporary tragic theory, and I regret that I cannot discuss them here. Important texts include María Zambrano's *La tumba de Antígona* (Antigone's tomb) (1967), Martha Nussbaum's *The Fragility of Goodness* (1986), Adriana Cavarero's "On the Body of Antigone" (1995), and Judith Butler's *Antigone's Claim* (2002).

Conclusion

- Aristotle's *Poetics* outlines his literary thinking on: *mimēsis* and poetry (the name for literature at the time); the role of the emotions; and, famously but sketchily, the *katharsis* of pity and terror, unity of action, plot, endings, *peripeteia* and *anagnōrisis*, the tragic hero and *hamartia*, the relation of tragedy and comedy. Aristotle's literary theory involves both a critique and a refashioning of Plato.

- Canonized since the sixteenth century, the *Poetics* was appropriated by an increasingly rigid neoclassicism, from which Samuel Johnson tried to detach it. For Shelley, Aristotle is an ally. Hegel and Nietzsche, in their original response to Aristotle, are major voices of modern tragic theory. Since Samuel Richardson tragedy finds a place within the new genre of the novel, with Eliot and especially Hardy being examples. Since the 1960s Steiner and Williams have proposed antagonistic theories of tragedy, with Eagleton joining the debate more recently. Since the mid-twentieth century, postcolonial tragedy, as practised and theorized by Soyinka and others, returned to Aristotle and Greek tragedy with revisionist intent. Since the 1980s feminist philosophers have also been revisiting classical tragic theory and practice.

Further reading

In addition to reading Aristotle's *Poetics*, see especially the following: Hegel 1998 and 1975; Nietzsche 1967; Steiner 1961 and 2004; Williams 1992; Soyinka 1988b; Nussbaum 1986, particularly "Interlude 2"; Eagleton 2003; Reiss 2005.

3 Medieval and Renaissance criticism

From mimesis to creation

Plotinus, Augustine, Aquinas, Dante, Boccaccio, Pico, Sidney. With an appendix on Byzantine literary criticism.

This chapter posits an epochal shift from literature understood as mimesis of ideal or divine reality to literature as human self-creation, within a wider shift of emphasis from a God-centred view to a human-centred view, from theology to humanism, from man's submission to God and the authority of the church to an emphasis on human dignity and creativity. Particularly, it explores the shift from Plotinus's late-antique idea of literature as contemplation of and ascent to the ideal world to medieval scriptural interpretation of the Word of God to the Renaissance idea of literature as human creation and fiction. It focuses on medieval literary theory and considers the highly contested transitions from the late-antique into the medieval period and from late medieval into the Renaissance.

Neoplatonism is arguably the philosophical movement exerting the strongest and most uninterrupted influence throughout the late-antique, medieval and Renaissance periods. Plotinus, its founder, sees Plato as his philosophical master and is generally considered to be "the last great philosopher of late antiquity" (Henry 1991, xlii). The chapter will trace two divergent readings of Plotinus and Neoplatonism: Augustine's reading leading to medieval scriptural interpretation intended to overcome the ambiguity of figurative language in order to reach the Word of God through authoritative and definitive textual interpretation; and late-medieval and Renaissance readings leading to a humanist understanding of literature as fiction and man's creation.

Plotinus (*c.* 204/5–270 AD) studied Greek philosophy in Alexandria and was also well-versed in Homer and Greek mythology. He moved to Rome at the age of 39, where he taught and wrote until his final illness. His *magnum opus, The Enneads*, written in Greek, was published posthumously, edited by his pupil and biographer Porphyry. Gregory argues that Plotinus's mysticism and asceticism have to be understood in the context of the third century AD as a "calamitous" period of "unprecedented disaster" for the Roman empire (1991, 15). The crucial issue, in my view, is the extraordinary longevity and depth of his multiform influence over the centuries. The pagan Plotinus was translated into Christianity by St Augustine and others. At the same time, it is vital to see that Plotinus himself already offers the first important hybrid of classicism and Christianity. Though he is not a Christian thinker, we can see the influence of Christianity in his rewriting of Plato and the influence of Plato in his rewriting of Christian doctrine.

In Plotinus Plato's thought undergoes a transformation or shift of emphasis that is very important for Western thought. In Plato's *Republic* our world is the inferior copy of the ideal world of Forms, while poetry is an inferior copy of our world, and therefore an inferior copy of an inferior copy. Although this sense can be discerned in Plato, for Plotinus the ideal world of Forms is much more emphatically a *creative force* out of which things emanate, like the Christian God. Plotinus mixes the properties of the Christian God, as the spirit and creator of the world, with the worldview of the *Republic*. (This can be seen to emerge in Plato's late *Timaeus*, outlining the figure of a creator of the world or "Demiurge", a myth highly influential to Plotinus's great rivals, the Gnostics, who were also a powerful current in early Christianity.)

Porphyry acknowledges the difficulty of Plotinus's style: Plotinus is "concise, dense with thought, terse, more lavish of ideas than of words" (1991, cxii). Sketching out Plotinus's sublime and complex view of reality and the artist, and simplifying Plotinus's terminology, the ideal world of Forms has three parts: the One, the Intellect and the Soul. The One creates the Intellect, which in turn creates the Soul, which in turn creates the world. This descent, the creation of the lower by the higher, is complemented by an ascent, where the lower returns to the higher: the individual contemplating the ideal world of Forms can return to communion with the higher world. This contemplation, and this is the important point for us, is not so much a matter of painstaking reasoning, as it is in Plato (with the enormously demanding education in dialectic that the philosopher must go through in the *Republic*). Contemplation is much more a matter of intuition and the artist is the perfect figure of intuitive contemplation. Art is not an imitation of external reality but an *intuitive contemplation of ideal reality*. Plotinus writes:

> the arts are not to be slighted on the ground that they create by imitation of natural objects … [T]hey give no bare reproduction of the thing seen but go back to the Reason-Principles [the One, the Intellect and the Soul] from which Nature itself derives, and, furthermore, that much of their work is all their own; they are holders of beauty and add where nature is lacking. Thus Pheidias wrought the [statue of] Zeus upon no model among things of sense but by apprehending what form Zeus must take if he chose to become manifest to sight.
> (1991, 411)

Plotinus attempts to clarify intuitive contemplation:

> If we have failed to understand, it is that we have thought of knowledge as a mass of theorems and an accumulation of propositions, though that

> is false even for our sciences of the sense-realm … [T]he artist himself goes back, after all, to that wisdom in Nature which is embodied in himself; and this is not a wisdom built up of theorems but one *totality*.
>
> (415–16, my italics)

In other words, the intuitive understanding of the artist grasps true reality *at once and synthetically*, not gradually and analytically.

The medieval sign: Christian allegory

> For now we see through a glass [mirror], darkly [*en ainigmati*, in an enigma].
>
> (St Paul, 1 Corinthians 13.12)

This section will introduce medieval thought on the nature of signs and the problems of interpretation of figurative language, especially the problems of Scriptural interpretation. We will focus on Augustine (354–430 AD) and Aquinas (1225–74 AD). How does the medieval sign, as defined by them, compare to the modern sign, as defined by Ferdinand de Saussure, the structuralists and the poststructuralists? I will discuss Saussure's simultaneous critique and reiteration of aspects of the medieval sign, as Jacques Derrida argues (Derrida 1997c).

Augustine's semiology (theory of signs) and hermeneutics (theory of interpretation) dominated Western criticism throughout the middle ages. The semiology opposed by Saussure in his path-breaking *Course in General Linguistics* is essentially established by Augustine. The work of Augustine, written in Latin, can be situated intellectually in relation to his Christian rewriting of Plotinus and in relation to the work of the Grammarians (Hellenistic philologists) on tropes. As Kirwan points out "no one disputes" that Plotinus had "the greatest importance for his formation" (Kirwan 2001, 195). According to Augustine's reading of Plotinus, literature – as figurative language or allegory – though ambiguous or enigmatic, gives us access to true reality: it illuminates the ideal world of Forms – or, in Augustine's Christian terms, the Word of God and the Divine Realm. Augustine's aim is to ascend, through interpretation, from the figurative language of Scripture to its true meaning, the Word of God.

In *On Christian Doctrine*, Augustine provides a definition of signs and distinguishes between: signs and things; natural and conventional signs; literal and figurative signs. A sign is "a thing which causes us to think of something beyond the impression the thing itself makes upon our senses" (Augustine 1958, 34). Whereas natural signs – for example, the tracks of an animal – signify "without any desire or intention of signifying", conventional signs are intentional signs that "living creatures show to one another" in order to communicate "the motion of their spirits or something which they have sensed or understood" (34–5). Finally, signs are literal when they are "used to designate those things on account of which they were instituted"; signs are figurative when "that thing which we designate by a literal sign is used to signify something else" – for example, when St Paul uses "ox" to signify the apostles (43).

In common with literature, Scripture uses figurative signs. Augustine recognizes that figurative language poses acutely the problem of "ambiguous signs" (43), but his aim is to overcome the ambiguity of figurative signs in order to open the path to a stable and authoritative Scriptural interpretation. Of course knowledge of the variety of literary tropes, as discussed by the Grammarians, is "necessary to a solution of the ambiguities of Scriptures" (104). Tropes include: *allegoria* (saying one thing but meaning another), *aenigma* (allusive or obscure speech; see "*en ainigmati* [in an enigma]" in this section's epigraph), *parabola* (teaching moral lessons by means of extended metaphors), *catachresis* (improper use of words), *irony or antiphrasis* (saying one thing but meaning the opposite) (102–4).

Augustine also addresses the problem that the text of Scripture is not stable: in the absence of standard authoritative editions and translations at the time, the text of Scripture was in versions in three languages (Hebrew, Greek, Latin) and an "infinite variety" of "innumerable" Latin translations (43–4). For Augustine the multiplicity of sign systems and different versions emerges as a nightmarish enemy: it is a cacophonous Tower of Babel erected by "the sin of human dissension" and the "dissonant" voices of "impious men" (36). Augustine also begins to address the relation between the Word of God and the word of man – the Scriptural problem of "signs given by God" but "presented to us by the men who wrote them" (35). He continues to address this problem in *On the Trinity.*

Augustine's *On the Trinity* is especially useful for a comparison between the medieval sign and the modern sign. Augustine posits the precession and ontological primacy of the signified over the signifier, in particular the primacy of a "transcendental signified" (Derrida's term), the Word of God, which "precedes all the signs by which it is signified" (Augustine 2002, 188). Augustine further posits a *necessary*, mimetic relation between signified and signifier. There is a necessary, mimetic relation of "likeness" (188–9) or mirroring between the Word of God (signified) and human thought as "the word which we speak in our heart" incorporeally (186) (signifier); and a necessary, mimetic relation of "likeness" between human thought (signified) and human language passing "through the body" (188) (signifier). Augustine posits these mimetic relations while acknowledging that the mimesis at stake is not direct reflection but allegorical figuration, where "one thing is understood from another"; particularly, out of the "very many species" of allegory, "obscure allegory" or enigma (183). Through the "word of man … the Word of God may in some manner be seen as in an enigma" (183). Augustine often quotes St Paul's *en ainigmati* (see Colish 1983, 26, 35, 49, 53). Colish argues that Augustine understands this Pauline phrase in the context of his own Neoplatonic "intuitionism" (110): "metaphorical signification" is deemed better suited to the expression of realities that are "obscure and difficult to understand", and the difficulties of an *aenigma* "enhance rather than reduce its expressive power" (53).

Saussure, in *Course in General Linguistics*, posits the primacy of the signifier over the signified and the "arbitrary", non-mimetic relation between signifier and signified (Saussure 1960, 67). For Saussure a signifier acquires a signified as an effect emerging at the intersection of syntagmatic and paradigmatic chains of signifiers. The (arbitrary) linking of a signifier to a signified is arrived at retroactively (see Chapter 7). In Augustine's terms, Saussure argues that language, as the socially mediated word of man, precedes and constructs the Word of God, as well as preceding the private thought of man, rather than mirroring and imitating it obscurely. However, Saussure, like Augustine, is committed to the possibility and the desirability of determining the signified (the meaning) and explicitly aims to offer a "*semiology*", a science of signs, to achieve this (16). By contrast, poststructuralist thinkers – Lacan (see Chapter 6), Derrida, Barthes (see Chapter 11), etc. – posit that the signified is infinitely deferred. Derrida calls this *différance* (Derrida 1982b) while Lacan calls it the "sliding of the signified under the signifier" (Lacan 1977a, 154). In other words, they posit that texts do not have a determinate and definitive meaning that can be reached through a canonical and authoritative interpretation. So they plunge texts back into the openness and plurality of interpretation and the "dissension" feared by Augustine. While Saussure critiques the medieval sign and its "metaphysics of presence" (Derrida's term), Derrida argues that Saussure's understanding of writing as a signifier mimetic of the signified of speech goes against Saussure's own understanding of the relation between signifier and signified as arbitrary, and shows the extent to which Saussure is still inside the metaphysics of presence (Derrida 1997c).

Augustine scholar Thomas Williams argues that Augustine's *On Christian Doctrine* does not aim to police interpretations or to arrive at a single authoritative interpretation at the expense of all others. Though for Augustine God speaks "in my inward ear", Augustine acknowledges that the truth is the "common property of all right-thinking people" (Augustine quoted in Williams 2001, 63, 67). The only limit Augustine imposes on interpretation is the principle of charity. For example, charity requires a figurative reading of the anointment of Jesus's feet:

> no one would seriously believe that the Lord's feet were anointed with precious ointment by a woman, as is the custom among extravagant and worthless men whose entertainments we abhor … the good odor is the good fame that anyone leading a good life will have through his deeds, when he follows in the footsteps of Christ.
>
> (Augustine quoted in Williams 2001, 70)

Charity, understood by Augustine as the "motion of the soul toward enjoying God for his own sake and oneself and one's neighbor for God's sake", is the aim of interpretation (Augustine quoted on 67). What is to be avoided is cupidity, "enjoying oneself, one's neighbor, or any bodily thing for the sake of something other than God" (Augustine quoted on 67). Further, Williams insists that Augustine, as a teacher of rhetoric, was interested in the human author's text and how its language works rhetorically (the literal sense, in Augustine's terms). Augustine's exegesis of Genesis in his *Confessions* might have "squeezed some 9,000 words of commentary" from a text of 17 words, but he paid attention to both literal and allegorical senses (Williams 2001, 59–60).

Christopher Kirwan warns against too simplistic an understanding of Augustine's view of language. According to Kirwan, Augustine "repudiated" the view that "the individual words in language name objects" (2001, 189). This would have been a philosophy of language limited to nouns or names, but Augustine "knew better, because he knew his grammar" (188). Kirwan claims that Augustine's originality lies in the concept of "inner words" (195), which was introduced in Plato's *Theaetetus* and the *Sophist.* In particular, Augustine assumed a one-to-one "correspondence between the elements of a sentence, which are words, and the elements of the thought signified by that sentence" (202). According to Kirwan this view (a "speech-thought isomorphism") is "demonstrably false", but Augustine's very description of it allows us to see that he was wrong (203).

I will now turn to Thomas Aquinas (1225–74). I will situate his *Summa theologiae* (written in Latin) intellectually in relation to Neoplatonism and Augustine, on the one hand, and Aristotle, on the other hand. Aquinas's milieu was the University of Paris, "electric with theological controversy" at the time (Colish 1983, 133). The new intellectual force was Aristotle's logic, the arrival of his "*logica nova*" in Western Europe *c.* 1130 leading to the emergence of a new science of theology, with progressive theologians using logic rather than quoting Scripture in support of their arguments (Colish 1983, 139).

Aquinas had no direct knowledge of Plotinus but was familiar with the later Neoplatonist, Proclus (Gregory 1991, 179). In keeping with Neoplatonism and Augustine, Aquinas argues that Scripture uses the figurative language of literature – "metaphors taken from corporeal things" – to give access to "intellectual truths" (Aquinas 1991, 239–40). Aquinas acknowledges that, while Scripture aims towards "the elucidation of the truth", it uses metaphors and that arguably "the truth is actually obscured by likenesses of this sort" (239), in contrast with Augustine. Aquinas also recognizes that, in Scripture as in literature, words have several senses, but aims to establish that this polysemy is compatible with determinate meaning and access to truth. He defines four senses very precisely: 1. historical or literal; 2. allegorical (interpreting the Old Testament as allegorically signifying the New Testament); 3. tropological or moral (texts signifying "what we ought to be doing"); 4. anagogical or escatological (texts signifying "eternal glory", the Christian metaphysical reality) (242). The last three are all species of the "spiritual sense". He posits that these senses are not in conflict but build on each other. In particular, the spiritual sense (and its three species) is "based upon the literal sense and presupposes it" (241). As a result, Aquinas is able to conclude: "the fact that there is more than one meaning does not create ambiguity or any kind of mixture of meanings" (242). In other words "no confusion results … since all the senses are based on one, namely the literal sense" (242). As Aristotle begins with an observation of the existing and the particular in a "scientific" manner and then moves upwards to the ideal and the general, Aquinas starts from the text's "literal" sense and moves upwards to its "spiritual" senses. This is Aquinas's "Aristotelian empiricism" (Colish 1983, 110).

Eleonore Stump is keen to highlight Aquinas's reliance on the literal sense. Following on the influential work of Beryl Smalley, Stump argues that Aquinas clarified the relation between literal and spiritual sense and helped "bring under some control" interpretations of the spiritual sense by placing "a strong and sensible emphasis on the literal sense" (Stump 1993, 257). At the same time, Stump points out that Aquinas's medieval understanding of the literal sense was very different from ours. For example, he is unconcerned by the fact that he is reading Hebrew and Greek biblical texts in a variety of Latin translations and makes no effort to "recover the text in its original form" (256).

Today many critics question the distinction between literal and figurative meaning on which Aquinas's science of interpretation is based. Roland Barthes in *S/Z* critiques his earlier distinction between "denotation" and "connotation". In *Mythologies* he distinguished between a first, "literal" meaning – for example, a black soldier saluting the French flag on the front cover of *Paris Match* in 1955 (denotation); and a second, metaphorical/mythological meaning (connotation) – for example, the greatness of the French Empire, our colonies love us, etc. (1973, 121–2). In *S/Z* he rejects this distinction: there is only connotation (1975, 9) (see Chapter 11).

To return to Aquinas, Umberto Eco's *The Aesthetics of Thomas Aquinas* argues that Aquinas's aesthetics is exemplary of the medieval worldview. According to Eco the medieval period is an "era of dissolution and ruin" (1988, 138), a period of sustained change and turbulence, whose aesthetics prioritized hierarchy and "harmony" (19). With Aquinas medieval aesthetic theory "perfected its aesthetic image of political and theological order just when this order was threatened on all sides" (212). The medieval aesthetic aspires to an ideal of "coherence" (xi), "organic wholeness" (87) and "consonance" (*consonantia*) of a "multitude of orders" (90–91). Its criteria of beauty are: "due proportion or consonance", "integrity or perfection", and "clarity" (Aquinas quoted on 65). "Proportion" and "integrity" include the "suitability of matter" to a form and the "compatibility" of a form or a thing with its ideal form (196); clarity points to the medieval view that things are "intelligible and knowable" (120). The medieval mind is looking to ascend towards God: it has a "theophanic" or "anagogical" orientation (14). St Paul's "For now we see through a glass, darkly" is central to the medieval sense of the world (139). However, within this view, Aquinas represents a late-medieval scientific turn.

The world as a "storehouse of symbols" vanishes in Aquinas under the impact of "Aristotelian physics"; Providence is now not a "marshalling of signs" but a "reifying of forms" – a "symbolic vision" is turned into a "naturalistic vision" (140–41). Unlike Plotinus, for whom contemplation emphasizes the intuitive act of the mystic and poet, contemplation for Aquinas is the gradual and painstaking work of the scientist (in agreement with Plato). While Aquinas is himself a "trained and skilful" poet (154), he considers poetry an "*infima doctrina*" (inferior teaching or knowledge) (148). Eco argues that Aquinas's own superior aim, in his distinction of four senses, was "the correct decoding" of Scripture and the taming of the polysemy of texts and of the world (145, 147).

Eco, as both a medievalist and a structuralist semiologist, is ideally placed to comment on the relation between Aquinas and Saussurean structuralist linguistics. Both Aquinas and Saussure theorize a synchronic structure whose parts are understood in their relations to each other. For Aquinas this is the real "synchrony of being" itself, inherent in the "logic of things themselves" (217); "'cultural' structure" is "made up of relations among 'full' elements – namely, [Aristotelian] substantial forms" (219). For Saussure, by contrast, language is a synchronic structure "made up of the relations among 'empty' values – values that are defined only by their difference from other values" (219).

Eco views Dante, to whom our discussion will now turn, as a medieval figure whose project is very much within the medieval worldview: for Dante poets "continue the work of the scriptures", and his monumental *Divine Comedy* is a "new instance of prophetic writing … endowed with spiritual senses just as the scriptures are" (162). (Later in this chapter we will return to Eco and his theorization of the break between medieval and Renaissance aesthetics.)

Dante Alighieri (1265–1321) posited the "hidden truth" of poetry. He outlined his hermeneutics and poetics in *Il Convivio* (The banquet) (1306–9) and in "Epistle to Can Grande della Scala" (1319), of questionable authorship but believed by most critics to be at least partially written by him. Dante sets out to transpose Aquinas's principles of scholarly allegorical biblical exegesis in Latin to the interpretation of poetry in the European vernacular languages spoken by everyone. In writing *The Divine Comedy* in Italian Dante was a pioneer in the literary use of European vernacular languages. In *The Banquet* Dante collects and interprets *canzoni* (short vernacular poems). Setting out his method of allegorical interpretation, he outlines a *depth* model of hermeneutics adapted from medieval scriptural commentary. The interpreter needs to go *below* the surface of the text to reach its *hidden* true meaning. While the literal sense "does not go beyond the *surface* of the letter", the allegorical sense is "*that which hides beneath* the mantle … a truth *hidden beneath* a beautiful falsehood" (Dante 1991a, 396; my emphasis). Out of Aquinas's quadripartite system, Dante singles out as central the distinction between literal sense and allegorical sense ("allegorical" now understood more broadly): "I shall first discuss the literal meaning of each *canzone* and, after that, will discuss its allegory, that is, its hidden truth. And occasionally ... I shall touch upon the other senses" (398). This model relies on the distinction between a valuable inside and an expendable or instrumental outside, as Dante makes clear: the literal is the sense "which contains in its meaning (*sentenza*) all other meanings ... [F]or each thing that has *an inside and an outside* it is impossible to come to the inside without first coming to the outside" (397, my emphasis). (See Derrida's "Plato's Pharmacy" on the reliance of Western thought since Plato on binary oppositions between a privileged term and a devalued term; see also Chapter 1).

D. W. Robertson looks closely at inter-related medieval metaphors of grain and chaff, nucleus and shell, as commonplaces of medieval exegesis sharing a model of inside/outside: "typical of the general attitude of medieval exegetes" was to penetrate the enigma or the "puzzle" to reach the "*nucleus*" under "the 'shell' of poetic fiction" (Robertson 1962, 32). Robertson discusses a multitude of examples. For Augustine what matters is "the pleasure arising from the discovery of truth, not the incidental pleasure of the 'shell'" (54); the truth "beneath a puzzling figurative surface" (55). For St Gregory the Great "the letter covers the spirit as the chaff covers the grain" (quoted on 58). For Rabanus when "the bark [*cortex*] of the letter is taken away, the interior whiteness is shown allegorically" (quoted on 317). For Berchorius "just as honey is contained in a honeycomb and is clarified and pressed forth, in the same way the letter contains an inner sense" (quoted on 302). Medieval exegetes use the Latin verb "*enucleare* [to extract the nucleus]" to describe "the process by which the *nucleus* of the spirit is derived from the *cortex* of the letter" (309). In Chaucer's *Canterbury Tales* the Parson declares that he "will mingle no chaff with his wheat" (quoted on 335) – in other words, "Taketh the fruyt, and lat the chaf be stille" (Chaucer, quoted on 367). This view survives into the Renaissance: for Erasmus "the surface and, as it were, the *siliqua*" (pod) is "hard" and "bitter" but "[d]ig out the spiritual sense, for there is nothing more sweet" and "succulent" (quoted on 314). Dante is far from unique in emphasizing poetry's function as purveyor of higher truths concealed under false covering (see 345–5).

Robertson argues that, in the medieval distinction between a more valuable inside (or spirit as grain, honey, nucleus) and a less valuable outside (or letter as chaff, honeycomb, shell, cortex), the relation between the two terms is one of ordered hierarchy between a superior and an inferior term: spirit and letter are not "modern 'opposites' which are mutually exclusive" (304). In this view, it is the "abuse of the letter rather than the letter itself" that needs to be "cast aside" (303). What is required of the reader and the exegete is to ascend from the lower and outer term towards the higher and inner one. This is exemplary of all medieval ordered hierarchies. For example, marriage "in medieval terms" is a "well-ordered hierarchy" between a morally superior term (man, spirit) and a morally inferior term (woman, body) (375). Medieval misogyny consists in equating women (and male effeminacy) with "lack of virtue" (361).

This becomes a problem when women do not accept their place. For example, in Chaucer's *Canterbury Tales* the Wife of Bath is disrespectful of the hierarchy of "spirit over the flesh", "do[ing] her best to subvert the traditional hierarchy of husband and wife" and representing "rampant 'femininity' or carnality" (317, 321, 330). This is arguably Chaucer's contestation of medieval hierarchy; see also Christine de Pizan's contestation of medieval misogyny in *The Book of the City of Ladies* (1405).

To return to Dante, "Epistle to Can Grande della Scala", written in Latin, reaffirms Dante's distinction between the literal and the allegorical. He returns to Aquinas's schema and argues that what Aquinas distinguishes as the allegorical, moral and anagogical senses should all come under the same category of "allegorical" and be distinguished from the literal: "although these mystical meanings are called by various names, they may one and all in a general sense be termed allegorical, inasmuch as they are all different (*diversi*) from the literal or historical" (Dante 1991b, 460).

In *Mimesis* Auerbach offers an influential and controversial reading of Dante as the early originator of the humanist notion of the individual. Dante reveals the individual "man's inner life": in Dante the indestructibility of the individual man, "rooted in the divine order … turns *against* that order … The image of man eclipses the image of God" and "the figure becomes independent" (Auerbach 1968, 202). Let us see briefly how Auerbach comes to this conclusion. He argues that Dante's *Comedy* is not allegorical: while in allegory the literal, historical or individual points (and invites an ascent) towards a higher eternal divine reality, the *Comedy* is primarily committed to individual, living human beings: "The beyond becomes a stage for human beings and human passions … [Dante] brings to life … every single human being who crosses his path!" (201). Auerbach highlights the "earthly" realism of Dante's dead sinners: his "undisguised incursions into the realm of real life" (185); the "almost painfully immediate impression of the earthly reality" of human beings (199) – such as Farinata and Cavalcante – whose "individual character is manifest in all its force" (192). In this sense, Auerbach argues, Dante joins the literal/historical/individual with the spiritual, "integrating what is characteristically individual and at times horrible, ugly, grotesque, and vulgar with the dignity of God's judgment" (194). In other words, Dante's afterlife possesses historical phenomenality and an "overwhelming realism", so that it is both "eternal" and "phenomenal", "changeless" and "full of history" (197). Auerbach's claim is that what he views as Dante's new individualism is "Christian in spirit and … in origin" (198), in the sense that it emerges out of "the Christian idea of the indestructibility of the entire human individual" (199).

To turn now to Colish's reading of Dante in *The Mirror of Knowledge*, she argues that Dante inherits from Augustine and Aquinas a theory of signs according to which signs represent reality "truly but partially" (1983, 150, 167). However, though Aquinas pays serious attention to the allegorical language of Scripture, he avoids allegorical language himself and considers poetic allegory false because of the inherent falseness of poetry (160, 266). Dante, on the other hand, puts forward with increasing confidence vernacular poetry as the proper didactic medium of religious and moral instruction. Colish argues that in the "Epistle to Can Grande" Dante finally "assimilat[es] to poetry ... the mission of theology" and "arrogates to himself as a poet the tasks, methods, and powers of theology" (189). So Aquinas and Dante share a theological orientation but pursue it differently: the former through Aristotelian logic and the latter through vernacular poetry. At the same time, in Colish's view, Dante is only half theologian. In keeping with Auerbach's reading of Dante, she argues that in the *Comedy* poetic form and content as well as literal and allegorical sense "do not stand over against each other"; "the literal meaning may never be discarded as irrelevant or merely ancillary to the allegorical meaning" (191). Instead there is a "twofold thrust": in Plotinian terms descent is as valuable as ascent, for example, the literal/historical meaning of Beatrice is as important as her allegorical meaning (191–3). While the literal or historical is ancillary to the ascent towards the spiritual in Aquinas, Colish joins Auerbach in discerning in Dante a humanist turn from God to man.

In "Allegory and Autobiography" the Dante scholar John Freccero revisits influential readings of Dante – by Luigi Pirandello, Auerbach, Leo Spitzer, Charles Singleton, Bruno Nardi – before outlining his own *intertextual* view (to be explained shortly). Freccero's response to Auerbach is that "[p]raise for Dante's realism ... masked Auerbach's impatience" with the *Comedy*'s "theological import" (2007, 175). Freccero argues, against Auerbach, that while "modern biographies ... seek to establish above all the uniqueness of their subject", Dante's autobiography in the *Comedy* is "allegorical and conforms to biblical and classical patterns" (162). Dante's journey on the classical winged monster Geryon is not only a "mythic representation of biography" (165), but also a Christianized allegory of conversion from pride to humility. While Dante's journey on Geryon is a "descent into himself" and "distinctly confessional" (164), it is important to understand that "[t]he confession itself is completely generic" (167). Just as Catholic confession "requires the translation of individual experience into general terms", Dante's journey is allegorical, in the sense that it "generalize[s] experience" (166): it is "neither a poetic fiction nor a historical account", but "exemplary" – "both autobiographical and emblematic" (168). In understanding the allegorization of biography and autobiography in the *Comedy*, Freccero focuses critical attention away from its historicity and "mimetic power" and towards its intertextuality and its "narrative structure" as a "conversion" (177). As in Dante's treatment of Beatrice and Virgil "intertextuality counterfeits a history" (167); it is undecidable whether Dante's conversion in the *Comedy* "corresponds to an experience or is an illusion created by the narrative" (178). In this new and redefined sense, Freccero argues that the *Comedy* "conform[s] to the definition of the 'allegory of poets' given in the *Convivio*: 'truth hidden under a beautiful lie'" (169).

Giovanni Boccaccio (1313–75) is an important transitional figure in the history of literary theory; some critics view him as essentially late medieval, others as an exemplary Renaissance figure. He outlined his literary theory in *The Genealogy of the Gentile Gods*, written in Latin (1350–62). Following Aristotle and Horace, Boccaccio views poetry as requiring great skill and as worthy of serious attention. Poetry is a "practical art (*facultas*)" (Boccaccio 1991, 422) dependent on the poet's and the reader's skill. Its "difficult involutions" (431) make serious interpretative demands: "you must persevere … and exert the utmost power of your mind … until … you will find that clear which at first looked dark" (431). At the same time, Boccaccio gives voice to a new, Renaissance humanist view of poetry. Poetry is not *mimesis*, as Aristotle and Horace thought, but human *invention* and *expression*. Poetry is "a sort of fervid and exquisite invention, with fervid expression … of that which the mind has invented" (420).

Auerbach in *Mimesis* views Boccaccio as a secular humanist who broke with Dante's theological worldview. While Dante's world was "pervaded" by a "Christian conception", Boccaccio's characters "live on earth and only on earth" (Auerbach 1968, 224). Minnis and Scott, on the other hand, argue for the late-medieval continuity between Aquinas's medieval scholasticism, Dante and Boccaccio in their influential *Medieval Literary Theory and Criticism c. 1100–c. 1375* (1991). They maintain that Aquinas (and other Aristotelian schoolmen), Dante and Boccaccio represent a major late-medieval break with the immediate past that is more important than the shift between late-medieval and Renaissance thought emphasized by so many. This is a break in favour of the literal sense, i.e. the "letter" and intention (*intentio*) of human authors (*auctores*). In other words, Minnis and Scott dispute the "alleged gulf between late-medieval scholasticism and early Renaissance humanism" and affirm the modern debt to "Parisian schoolmen" (Minnis and Scott 1991, 9). Aquinas is a part of the thirteenth-century shift of emphasis "from the divine author to the human author of Scripture" (3) and of the increasing interest in the literal sense, i.e. the intention and historical context of human writers of sacred and profane literature, and the human author's "letter" (style, etc.) (66–71, 197). In Minnis and Scott's bold view, Aquinas and the schoolmen "privilege" the literal sense (203), which "was identified as the expression of the intention of the human author" (205); this encourages a "literary sensibility" (206) and gives authors "responsibility for what they said and the ways they said it" (207), while focusing the critic "(in humanist fashion) upon the letter of the text rather than upon extra-literary sources of inspiration" (451).

Furthermore, Minnis and Scott argue, the Neoplatonist influence on Aquinas and the schoolmen led them to the view that "[t]he truest poetry is the most obviously feigning" or the most inventive (Minnis and Scott 1991, 126) – a Renaissance view in the eyes of some critics. For the Neoplatonist Christian theologian Pseudo-Dionysius (fifth and sixth centuries, exact dates not known), an influence on Aquinas and Paris schoolmen, jarringly inappropriate, ugly and base figures are most successful in lifting the mind towards God in a negative fashion, because paradoxically they have a more powerful effect on our attempts to grasp more fully the nature of God than conventional and positive terms (167–73). Hence the late-medieval view that "figures, fiction, and other poetic devices ... are particularly valuable by reason of their very non-referentiality"; "the more fictional and inappropriate they are the better" (126).

Minnis and Scott highlight Dante's debt to scholasticism (372) and simultaneously position Dante and Boccaccio among "the most innovative literary theorists of the later Middle Ages" (212). Their novelty lies, first, in their redeployment of the Latin commentary (or hermeneutic) tradition, including its methods and vocabulary of exegesis, to interpret and authorize new vernacular literature (vi–vii). Dante's "Epistle" (whether authentic or not) was indisputably influential and "momentous" in that the methodologies of scriptural exegesis and commentary on venerated ancient authors are now "applied" to Dante's *Comedy*, the work of a "living" poet using "his own vernacular" (444). This is not only an "aggrandizement of the vernacular" (386), but also a democratization including the "common masses" (440). The use of the vernacular in the *Comedy* meant that "everyone could ... participate" to the great consternation of some scholars; and Boccaccio with his 1373 public lectures on the *Comedy* repeats, with some unease, Dante's gesture by giving these lectures on a vernacular text in the vernacular (458) – while others write Latin commentaries on the *Comedy* in an attempt to classicize it (439). Second, there is a coming together, under the broad category of poetry, of sacred and secular, pagan and Christian, traditional canonical *auctores* (meaning "authors" but having the double sense of "authorities") and new authors writing in the vernacular literature (387, 393). Boccaccio's novelty in particular lies in reversing the traditional relation of theology and poetry: rather than poetry being theology by other means, theology is "a poetry of God" (455). As a result, he focuses on Dante's "literary (rather than visionary, political, or religious) achievement" (456). Opposing the view that poetry is "composed under heavenly guidance" (390), Boccaccio argues that the poet is not divinely inspired, but rather divinely gifted with "a god-given and unusual natural talent" (392).

In contrast to Minnis and Scott, Eco discerns a radical break between medieval and early Renaissance literary theory, but posits the beginning of the Renaissance earlier, in the work of "proto-humanists such as Albertino Mussato" (1261–1329) (Eco 1988, 166). For Eco, Aquinas as well as Dante, Mussato's contemporary, are part of a medieval view of art as an allegorical and cognitive craft, while the Renaissance views art as "inventive or 'creative'" (162) – as "a method of creation" (166). Within the medieval worldview, artistic autonomy is an "absurd" idea (184) because art is "ontologically dependent" (173) on the superior spiritual reality it attempts to represent. For medieval thought, it is "unthinkable ... that the human spirit would engage in creation" (169). One of the conditions of possibility of the emerging Renaissance (and more broadly modern) conception of the artist as an "inventor and creator" was the historical experience of the new merchant class as "citizens of the new self-governing communities" (214).

Robertson attempts a comparison between medieval and (broadly) modern aesthetic theory. He contrasts the medieval use of *allegoria* or *aenigma* that alludes to spiritual "invisible truth" (1962, 15) and looks "inward ... to find God" (16) and modern "self expression" (12). While for the medievals the spiritual meaning is by no means created by the author but points to "a common language of faith" (350), the modern artist emerges increasingly as an individual in "dynamic opposition" to his society (10) – Robertson's model is Romanticism.

Renaissance humanism

Renaissance humanism was driven by the positive re-evaluation of classical antiquity as a source of moral value and a human-centred worldview, the revival of classical learning and the renewed philological study of previously neglected or inaccessible Greek and Latin texts in the original. Renaissance humanists – Petrach, Marsilio Ficino, Erasmus, Thomas More – criticized scholasticism and church orthodoxy, but were often devoutly pious. They searched for and collected manuscripts, studied, translated and disseminated classical texts (e.g. previously neglected Platonic dialogues, Aristotle's *Poetics*, etc.).

In "The Death of the Author" Barthes famously proclaims the death of the idea of the writer as an Author-God creating the text *ex nihilo*. In "What Is an Author?" Foucault historicizes this idea: he sees it as a *modern* idea related to the rise of capitalism and private property. Derrida, on the other hand, traces the idea of the author as father of his text as far back as Plato's *Phaedrus* in "Plato's Pharmacy". In this chapter we are witnessing the historical emergence of the modern idea of literature as man's creation. *On the Dignity of Man* by Giovanni Pico della Mirandola (1463–94) is a "principal" philosophical work of Renaissance humanism (Gregory 1991, 179) and presents a striking assertion of human freedom. As Gregory and Paul J. W. Miller (1998) make clear, Pico's text and Renaissance humanism are not absolutely novel, but rather offer a novel interpretation of Plotinus and Neoplatonism, marked by a rediscovery of Plato, Plotinus and the Neoplatonic tradition. Gregory points out, in particular, that Pico's representation of Man as "a microcosm of all creation, free to determine his destiny" is Neoplatonist (179), while Miller pays tribute to Pico's teacher, Ficino, and Ficino's reading of Plotinus and Plato (and we will add that Ficino translates all of Plato into Latin).

Pico's *On the Dignity of Man* can be selectively quoted to suggest man's absolute freedom as (self-)creator or (self-)inventor – for example, "man fashions, fabricates, transforms himself" (Pico della Mirandola 1998, 6). This, however, would be a distortion. Pico presents man as a "chameleon" (5), a creature of "indeterminate form" (4) who is morally free to choose which of his gifts to develop. God placed in man "every sort of seed and sprouts of every kind of life. The seeds that each man cultivates will grow and bear their fruit in him" (5). Pico insists, for obvious reasons, that his view is not heretical but "confirm[s] the holy and Catholic faith" (29). In existentialist terms, man has no fixed nature: you may claim "the seat, the form, the gifts which thou thyself shalt desire" (4); "thou art confined by no bounds; and thou wilt fix limits of nature for thyself"; you are "the molder and maker of thyself" (5). Man is free to soar (in Plotinian terms to ascend) – to "grow upward from thy soul's reason into the higher natures which are divine"– or to plummet, descend, "grow downward", thereby "abusing the very liberality of the Father" who gave him freedom and harming himself (5). Pico, as Miller points out, does not posit man as a God-like creator *ex nihilo*: "the making activity of man operates upon potencies which are already given" (Miller 1998, xv). Nevertheless, the emphasis on potencies in itself marks Pico off from the Catholic theological emphasis on man's wretchedness and impotence without God's grace.

François Rabelais was probably born in 1494, the year of Pico's death, and died in 1553, a year before Philip Sidney's birth. Mikhail Bakhtin's reading of Rabelais's *Gargantua and Pantagruel* in *Rabelais and His World* has been an important influence on contemporary literary theory – particularly Bakhtin's concepts of "the carnivalesque" (Bakhtin 1984, 218) and "grotesque realism" (18). Bakhtin discerns a schism between two cultures in the medieval world. "The men of the Middle Ages participated in two lives, the official and the carnival life" (96): an official, rigidly hierarchical and serious high culture inculcating fear and consecrating "inequality" (10); and a popular, democratic, "nonofficial" (6) and carnivalesque low culture of the marketplace, cultivating laughter, "fearlessness" (39), community, "inventive freedom" (34), the "parody" (84) and "suspension" (15) of the powerful official world and grotesque realism. Grotesque realism turns to the body as an "ambivalent" (151) and "contradictory" (62) source of both degradation and regeneration. If classicism perceives the body as self-contained and closed off, grotesque realism pays attention to the ways in which bodies transgress and exceed their boundaries, their points of contact with the outside, their collective and even cosmic aspects; indeed the "style" of grotesque realism is one of "exaggeration, hyperbolism, excessiveness" (e.g. excessive eating, drinking, sexuality) (303). Bakhtin argues that the medieval carnivalesque low culture is an important origin of the Renaissance and of Rabelais's "democratic", "radical popular" and "nonofficial" work (2–3). In this sense Bakhtin claims a "struggle" between medieval low and high culture (437), and a deep continuity between the fearless claim to freedom in medieval low culture and the humanist emphasis on man's freedom in Renaissance high culture.

We will now turn to Sir Philip Sidney's treatise, *The Defence of Poesy*. It is Sidney's dialogue with his historical and intellectual contexts: Plato, Aristotle, Horace, Plotinus, Christianity, European Renaissance humanism, the contemporary arts and sciences (especially English literature), the Elizabethan monarchy. While ostensibly following ancient authorities, Sidney introduces Renaissance humanist innovations, though he is not keen to advertise the fact.

Against Plato's *Republic*, he argues that the poet does not lie because he does not affirm anything as true: poetry is "a good invention". Sidney's treatise is not original, but it is arguably exemplary of Renaissance humanism: it is "epoch-marking," not "epoch-making" (Shepherd 1973, 16).

Sir Philip Sidney (1554–86) was a high-ranking member of Elizabethan high society, whose father had "at various points in time, run both Ireland and Wales for the Queen" (Alexander 2004, liii). At the age of 22, Sidney was appointed ambassador to the Holy Roman Emperor Rudolph II. His mission was brilliantly successful and he looked set for a glittering political career. And yet this career never materialized. As with Plato, whose privileged background destined him for a prominent role in politics but who chose philosophy against the grain, Sidney had nothing to gain by wasting his time on literary pursuits. And yet, as inexpediently as in the case of Plato, Sidney wrote poetry and plays in the English vernacular, at a time when English literature was still in its nascent state, and attempted to translate several classical works into English, including Aristotle's *Rhetoric* (highly relevant to Sidney's view of poetry's "forcibleness"), with varying degrees of success. He also wrote *The Defence of Poesy*, alternatively titled *An Apology for Poetry* (c. 1580–81), considered the outstanding Elizabethan treatise on poetry and arguably the first major piece of literary theory in English. Unlike Plato, Sidney didn't publicly choose literature or abandon his political aspirations. He did not intend his literary works for publication, perhaps because publication was considered indecorous for a courtier. None of his many literary works were published in his lifetime, though he circulated manuscripts privately within a narrow circle of friends. Katherine Duncan-Jones has argued that as the queen approached the end of her child-bearing years, and especially after the collapse of plans to marry Alençon in 1582, Sidney was "in the eyes of some almost a crown prince" (2002, ix). However, by 1585 Sidney was personally poor and politically undervalued and underused. Then his fortunes appeared to be changing for the better when Elizabeth appointed him governor of Flushing in the Netherlands, where the queen had sent troops against Spain. In Flushing Sidney was wounded by a bullet during a raid, the wound became infected and he died a "soldier's death" (Duncan-Jones 2002, vii) in 1586 at the tender age of 32. His work was published after his death to European acclaim.

Sidney wrote *The Defence of Poesy* before Shakespeare, Marlowe, Donne and Ben Jonson had reached maturity. He doesn't strive for originality; indeed originality is not an established literary ideal at the time. On the contrary, he devotes a lot of space to engaging with the classical tradition. Sidney pronounces his respect for and shows detailed knowledge of various works of Plato and Aristotle. He refers to many passages in Plato and Aristotle, including those we have discussed in previous chapters.

Beginning with his engagement with Plato, Sidney turns to those sections of the *Republic* where Plato accuses poets of being liars, sorcerers, conjurors feeding that part of us – the emotions – that should be deprived of nourishment. Sidney vividly summarizes the point of view of the *Republic* and its many followers (and poetry's detractors): poetry is "the mother of lies ... infecting us with many pestilent desires" (Sidney 2002c, 234). Sidney then uses Plato against Plato. He uses those passages in Plato's *Ion* where the poet is described as an airy and divinely possessed creature against the Plato of the *Republic* (see 240). Indeed, echoing Longinus, Sidney adds that Plato is "most worthy of reverence" because "of all philosophers he is the most poetical" (238). But Sidney also responds to the *Republic* with an altogether different and new argument – a Renaissance humanist argument. While the poet's peers in the secular arts and sciences affirm many things and inevitably sometimes stray from the truth, the poet never lies because he does not affirm anything as true. Sidney writes:

> Now for the poet, he nothing affirms, and therefore never lieth ... The poet never maketh any circles [as in sorcery] about your imagination, to conjure you to believe for true what he writes. He citeth not authorities of other histories, but even for his entry calleth the sweet Muses to inspire into him *a good invention.*
>
> (235, my italics)

When Sidney formally defines poetry, he seems absolutely determined to paraphrase as many classical authorities as possible:

> Poetry therefore is an art of imitation, for so Aristotle termeth it in the word *mimesis* – that is to say, a representing, counterfeiting, or figuring forth – to speak metaphorically, a speaking picture – with this end, to teach and delight.
>
> (217)

In addition to naming and following Aristotle here, Sidney also pays tribute to Horace, to whom we will briefly turn. Horace (65–08 BC) was the first important poet to write an *ars poetica.* He follows Aristotle in viewing poetry primarily as a craft and as a matter of skill, not as a matter of inspiration. As an excellent and mature practitioner, he offers valuable technical advice to fledgling poets. Perhaps the most famous passage in his *Ars Poetica* is the following:

> Poets aim either to do good or to give pleasure – or, thirdly, to say things which are both pleasing and serviceable for life [*dulce et utile*] ... The

> man who combines pleasure with usefulness wins every suffrage, delighting the reader and also giving him advice.
>
> (Horace 1989, 106–7)

Here Horace cuts the Gordian knot of the convoluted debate between Plato and Aristotle as to poetry and pleasure, the emotions, knowledge and moral goodness, by saying quite sensibly that good poetry both delights and instructs. The Roman orator and philosopher Cicero modelled the aim of the orator on the ideal poet: *docere, delectare, movere* (to instruct, to give pleasure, to move). In *Ars Poetica* Horace, Cicero's junior by 40 years, returns Cicero's formula back to poetry (Alexander 2004, xxxv–xxxvi). In Sidney's time rhetoric and poetry are of renewed importance in the curriculum and Sidney was very familiar with Horace's text. Horace also famously writes: "Poetry is like painting [*ut pictura poesis*]" (Horace 1989, 107). This refers back to the description of poetry as a "speaking picture" (*pictura loquens*) attributed by Plutarch to Simonides of Ceos (Shepherd and Maslen 2002, 143). Sidney, in his definition of poetry, combines both of Horace's famous sayings, describing poetry as "a speaking picture – with this end, to teach and delight."

While Sidney is ostensibly following ancient authorities, he is also quietly innovating, away from Plato's theory of poetry as a *mimesis* of appearance and Aristotle's theory of poetry as a *mimesis* of universal ideal reality towards a new view of poetry as "a good invention" which does not lie because it does not affirm anything. This shift towards invention is visible in Renaissance humanism and already discernible in Boccaccio, Pico and others, as discussed above. The shift was enabled by a certain reading of the work of Plotinus, who is perhaps the greatest (if unnamed) influence on Sidney in *The Defence of Poesy.*

If Plotinus, the last pagan philosopher, offers the first hybrid of classicism and Christianity, Sidney also offers a hybrid of Christianity and classicism in *The Defence of Poesy.* Indeed on occasion Sidney sounds just like a Christian Plotinus. For example, Sidney claims that the best poets "to imitate borrow nothing of what is, hath been, or shall be; but range, only reined with learned discretion, into the divine consideration of what may be or should be" (Sidney 2002c, 218). Is not Sidney following Plotinus here, to argue that the poet contemplates not external reality but ideal reality, in this instance God's cosmological plan?

However, there is an important shift of emphasis and an important new ingredient discernible in Sidney. In brief, Sidney adopts Plotinus's theory of creation or generation – where the ideal world of Forms is a creative force out of which things emanate – but extends this creativity to humanity. On the one hand, Sidney refers explicitly to the Christian God and believes in God, while Plotinus doesn't. On the other hand, Plotinus's theory of art is still largely a theory of imitation, where art imitates the divine realm; Sidney's is a theory of invention, shifting the emphasis from God to man. (Plotinus arguably anticipates his Renaissance readings when he comments on the arts that "much of their work is all their own; they … add where nature is lacking" [Plotinus 1991, 411, quoted above].) Sidney's originality, when compared with classical authors, lies in his Renaissance humanist emphasis on the poet as creative, fashioning and self-fashioning. Poetry is not a revelation of the Truth. *Poetry is fiction.*

Sidney stages a contest between the poet and his secular competitors, such as the astronomer, the geometer, the philosopher, the lawyer, the historian, the physician. Each one of the poet's competitors takes "the works of nature for his principal object, without which they could not consist, and on which they so depend" (Sidney 2002c, 215–16). Sidney continues:

> Only the poet, disdaining to be tied to any such subjection, lifted up with the vigour of his own invention, doth grow in effect an other nature, in making things either better than nature bringeth forth, or quite anew, forms such as never were in nature, as the Heroes, Demigods, Cyclops, Chimeras, Furies, and such like: so as he goes hand in hand with nature, not enclosed within the narrow warrant of her gifts, but freely ranging only within the zodiac of his own wit [mind, intellect, understanding].
> (216)

Sidney is here turning Lucretius's language and examples against him. At the beginning of *On the Nature of Things* the Roman poet Lucretius greeted the father of his atomic physics, the Greek philosopher Epicurus, as a liberator who lifted us above religious "superstition" (and its attendant fears and anxieties) with "his mind's might and vigor" [1.62–79] (Lucretius 2001). For Lucretius, science is about "fixed law", according to which monsters such as the mythological Chimaeras are impossible in nature [2.700–711]; similarly, the Furies "do not exist and cannot exist anywhere at all" [3.1011–13]. Sidney, in a new twist, elevates the poet to an Epicurus-like mighty figure who frees himself, ironically enough, from the narrow confines of science. (The Scientific Revolution will later force a reformulation of the relation between literature and science.)

Sidney's poet, "freely ranging only within the zodiac of his own wit", reappears in many guises and variations in *The Defence of Poesy*, with each new variation pronouncing the poet's creative freedom. The poet is an "artificer" who has within himself the "*idea* [Plato's word for Form] or fore-conceit of the work" (Sidney 2002c, 216); "fore-conceit" is Sidney's neologism for a mental conception before it finds artistic expression. The best poet is the one who takes the "course of his own invention" (218). What makes the poet is not writing in verse but their imagination: not "rhyming" but "feigning" or fiction-making (218–19). As Sidney finally concludes:

> where all other arts retain themselves within their subject and receive, as it were, their being from it, the poet only bringeth his own stuff, and doth

> not learn a conceit [mental conception] out of matter, but maketh matter for a conceit.
>
> (232)

While reconfiguring the poet as a mini-God, Sidney's Renaissance humanism is compatible with Christianity and conventional piety, and he praises God who "gave us so good minds" – "the immortal goodness of that God who giveth us … wits to conceive" (246).

Geoffrey Shepherd makes a point familiar to us from the discussion of Boccaccio and Pico. Sidney is claiming, not man's creation *ex nihilo,* but his exercise of God-given reason. Poetry is not divine possession, but human power of conception. In this Sidney rehearses a European view rooted in Renaissance Neoplatonism (Shepherd 1973, 66). Katherine Duncan-Jones and J. A. van Dorsten highlight the "Christian-Platonist" provenance of Sidney's emphasis on the "powers of the mind" and his view of poetry as "invention" of "another nature" (Duncan-Jones and van Dorsten 1973, 189, 193). Confronting the "fallen state of man", poetry is the "effort of an individual mind to bridge the gap between the sinful state and the lost paradise" (190, 193).

R. W. Maslen argues that a line of influence connects Boccaccio, Chaucer and Sidney (Maslen 2002, 18). He highlights Sidney's rationalism: the role of the intellect – Sidney's "erected wit" – in poetry's mission against the fall (43). Poetry, as envisaged by Sidney, affirms not objective facts but the poet's "I think" (*cogito*) (Maslen 2002, 60) – a capacity for reason later captured in René Descartes's *cogito ergo sum* (I think, therefore I am). Shepherd and Maslen point towards the multiple origins of Sidney's text: Boccaccio, the Florentine Neoplatonists Ficino and Pico and Protestantism. Boccaccio in the *Genealogy* already "shows that as poetry does not claim to convey literal truth it cannot reasonably be charged with not providing it" (Shepherd and Maslen 2002, 203). Ficino and Pico have already emphasized conception and the *idea.* For Ficino and Pico "beauty was … infused into the mind of man from the mind of God, and existed there independent of any sense-impressions"; man can create a *second nature* because he has a God-given creative power, though on a much smaller scale than God (Shepherd and Maslen 2002, 140–42). At the same time, Sidney's text can be read in the context of Protestantism: the "efficacy" of Sidney's God-given "inward light" of reason is "characteristic of Protestant thought" (176), which places "heavy emphasis on the personal mental act" (140–41).

In *The Defence of Poesy* the thread of poetry as invention or creation is interwoven with a second important new thread. This is the thread of poetry's *force* and *authority,* and it emerges out of conventional material. Initially we find Sidney following a Plotinian line. Most of the poet's competitors try to illuminate "the works of nature" (Sidney 2002c, 215–16, quoted above) but wander into error. Even when the philosopher succeeds in giving us "infallible grounds of wisdom", these infallible grounds "lie dark before the imaginative and judging power, if they be not illuminated or figured forth by the speaking picture of poetry" (222). Sidney's Plotinian argument at this point is that poetry alone illuminates the incorporeal. Sidney continues on this line, giving vivid and convincing examples. The Stoic philosophers define anger as a short madness, but what *illuminates* anger for us is Sophocles's *Ajax*. Ajax, furious that the Greeks chose to give Achilles's weapons to Odysseus rather than to him after Achilles's death, slaughters sheep thinking they are his Greek rivals, then wakes up from his madness and kills himself in shame. Cicero states that love of one's country is a powerful emotion, but the *Odyssey* gives us insight into this emotion, when we see Odysseus, "in the fullness of all Calypso's delights[,] bewail his absence from barren and beggarly Ithaca" (Sidney 2002c, 222).

Then a process of semantic slippage or "sliding" (Lacan 1977a, 154, quoted above) happens, and Sidney moves imperceptibly from illumination and insight to force. Let's look at this process in slow motion. The philosopher defines virtues, vices, passions, states of mind, but he "teacheth *obscurely*" and as a result "teacheth them that are already taught" (Sidney 2002c, 223, my emphasis; "obscurely" as the opposite of "clearly"). On the other hand, the "feigned image of poetry … hath the more *force* in teaching" (223, my emphasis). Suddenly, the opposite of obscurity is not clarity or illumination but force, as power to evoke emotion but also power to inspire action. From this point on in the text, Sidney develops the thread of poetry as force. He goes back to the classical sources. Aristotle was right to say that poetry delights. "[P]oetical invention" (227) delights, and in delighting it moves, and in moving it is effective. When poetry moves us, it gets us to do something: for example, Alexander the Great was inspired to greatness by Achilles's deeds in the *Iliad*, not by his teacher Aristotle's definition of greatness (237–8).

An idea developed in Plato's work is that we never knowingly do wrong, which allows Plato to conclude that knowledge is goodness. For Plato, knowledge (*gnosis*) is action (*praxis*), for not to do what one knows to be right would be to knowingly do wrong. Aristotle, more realistically, recognizes a gap between the two (though Plato's use of emotionally captivating myths throughout his work and endorsement of good rhetoric in *Phaedrus* suggest his awareness of this gap). Sidney, in an ingenious reading of Aristotle, views poetry and its ability to move and motivate as closing the gap between *gnosis* and *praxis*. Sidney writes in a scintillating passage:

> who will be taught, if he be not moved by desire to be taught? And what so much good doth that teaching bring forth (I speak still of moral doctrine) as that it moveth one to do that which it doth teach? For, as Aristotle saith, it is not *gnosis* but *praxis* must be the fruit. And how *praxis* can be, without being moved to *praxis*, it is no hard matter to consider … [T]o be moved to do that which we know, or to be moved with desire to know: *hoc opus, hic labor est* [from Virgil's *Aeneid*, "this is the work, this is the toil", i.e. this is the difficult part].
>
> (226)

So as poetry moves, it can get the reader to do something, and thus poetry is obeyed. Unlike its competitors it has this power and authority. For example, when Sidney discusses the claims of the historian, he begins by rehearsing the argument in favour of poetry against history in Aristotle's *Poetics*, but he quickly returns to his own argument for the poet's unique "authority":

> the best of the historian is subject to the poet; for whatsoever action, or faction, whatsoever counsel, policy, or war stratagem the historian is bound to recite, that may the poet … with his imitation make his own, beautifying it both for further teaching, and more delighting, as it please him: having all, from Dante's heaven to his hell, under the *authority* of his pen.
>
> (225, my emphasis)

In their contest with poetry, all the secular arts and sciences show themselves to be "serving sciences" directed towards the higher end of a "mistress-knowledge, by the Greeks called *architektonike*": namely, "the knowledge of a man's self, in the ethic and politic consideration, with the end of well-*doing* and not of well-*knowing* only" (219; my emphases). Poetry is this mistress-knowledge. Finally, Sidney describes the poet as monarch: "of all [secular] sciences … is our poet *the monarch*. For he doth not only show the way, but giveth so sweet a prospect into the way, as will entice any man to follow it" (226, my emphasis).

Katherine Duncan-Jones and J. A. van Dorsten suggest that this thread of poetry's effectiveness in its ability to move is a Protestant "belief in the power of the *inward light*" (Duncan-Jones and van Dorsten 1973, 198). Shepherd, Maslen and Alexander, on the other hand, offer a variety of political interpretations. Geoffrey Shepherd argues for the centrality of politics in Sidney's ambitious vision for the new vernacular literature. Sidney is a political animal, whose orientation is practical, proactive and secular. His "astonishingly frank" 1580 letter to Queen Elizabeth, arguing against her proposed marriage to the French Catholic Duke of Alençon, the French king's brother, is characteristic of him (Shepherd 1973, 7). He is a "firm nationalist" and a "royalist, an absolutist within limits", whose militant Protestantism is inseparable from his sense of patriotism (Shepherd 1973, 25); accordingly, his prose has a "strong, masculine … style" (Shepherd 1973, 90). Gavin Alexander argues that Sidney's text is calling for a public role for vernacular English literature in its "fledgling state", in the context of a "nascent British Empire" (Alexander 2004, xxii). Sidney attempts to establish the sovereignty and ambitions of England *and* its poetry, inextricably, during a period of "nation building" and "colonization" (Alexander 2004, xviii–xix). R. W. Maslen argues that Sidney's text "implies" a critique of the Elizabethan government's early "quietist attitude to Catholic Europe" (Maslen 2002, 12) and "more or less covertly criticizes … its foreign and domestic policies", with "considerable risks" to Sidney (Maslen 2002, 1). Maslen presents Sidney, simultaneously, as a hawk calling for a more aggressive foreign policy and as an advocate of the poet's "political liberty" (47). On the one hand, Sidney views poetry's force as "quasi-martial" and as a "stimulus to military action" (Maslen 2002, 65); against the comparative peace of Elizabeth's early reign, Sidney envisages an aggressively ambitious international role for English poetry and for England (Maslen 2002, 36–7, 41, 67, 72). On the other hand, Maslen views Sidney's text as implying a proto-Enlightenment "resistance to tyranny" and "hostility to despotism" (51), in Sidney's "passion for 'libertie and freedome'" (56). In this respect, poetry's force and authority in Sidney's text is anti-authoritarian: "invariably oppositional, either explicitly or implicitly critical of the ruling authorities" (15).

In *The Defence of Poesy* Sidney celebrates the creativity and the "forcibleness or *energia* (as the Greeks call it) of the writer" (246). However, the poet's sovereign creativity cannot be unambiguously and unproblematically celebrated, as the melancholy of Sidney's literary work attests. Critics describe his literary work as characterized by "deep melancholy" (Edward Dyer), "deadlock" (John Carey), "emotional impasse", "stagnation", "inward torment" (Duncan-Jones 2002, xii–xiii). Critics seem to agree that there is, in Sidney, a "deep misery … welling up beneath the bright, witty … surface" (Duncan-Jones 2002, xii). Perhaps Sidney's voice testifies to a painful disjunction between the writer's imagination and desire, on the one hand, and the realities of Elizabethan England, on the other hand, even for someone as privileged as Sidney – a painful disjunction that poetry cannot remedy. Sidney describes the poet as a monarch in a passage that idealizes monarchy as giving "so sweet a prospect into the way, as will entice any man to follow it." But while Sidney describes the poet as a monarch, Sidney was very palpably the subject of Queen Elizabeth, his fortune as a high-born courtier entirely dependant on her, preferment or otherwise. Duncan-Jones asks why Sidney's very successful ambassadorial mission to the Holy Roman Emperor Rudolph II didn't lead to other commissions, leaving Sidney lacking in income and underemployed. She suggests that "Sidney may have been rather *too* successful" for Queen Elizabeth's "liking, as he could not be trusted not to take independent initiative" (xv).

Whatever the answer to this particular riddle, it seems that, already in Sidney and Renaissance humanism, the modern shift of emphasis – from the ideal world of Forms and from God to man himself, and from literature as mimesis to literature as creation and forceful action in the world – is painful as well as joyful. In other words, this modern shift of emphasis is an aspiration rather than a reality of Elizabethan society. Yet in this aspiration Sidney anticipates the forces of the future. Shepherd argues that Sidney's privileging of reason is a "groping forwards" towards René Descartes's anthropocentric rationalism and, more broadly, the seventeenth-century Scientific Revolution; Sidney is therefore a Renaissance man "on the eve of Cartesianism" (Shepherd 1973, 60). R. W. Maslen goes further, reading Sidney as a harbinger of the Enlightenment (Maslen 2002).

Perhaps it seems difficult to reconcile the Neoplatonists to whom Sidney is indebted and Descartes's rationalism (and his desire to found knowledge on something indubitably true), which he arguably anticipates. Nevertheless, Descartes's *cogito ergo sum* is also an act of human freedom, independent of the senses and of God. Descartes also spoke of a light of reason that allowed him to arrive at certain truths independent of experience, which he believed had been placed in the human mind by God. In this sense, there is a line connecting the Renaissance humanist affirmation of human freedom, Descartes's rationalism and the Enlightenment.

Appendix: Byzantine literary criticism

The Byzantine Empire (*c.* 330–1453 AD) was originally the eastern, mostly Greek-speaking part of the Roman Empire. Constantine moved the imperial capital from Rome to Constantinople in 330 and, following the collapse of the western Roman Empire in the fifth century, the Byzantine Empire thrived as an independent entity until the Fall of Constantinople to the Ottoman Empire in 1453. Its official language was Greek, its official religion Christianity, and its official culture largely modelled on ancient Greek texts. Literary and critical production was often linked to the imperial court and to state functions. This appendix provides a brief survey of the little-known field of Byzantine criticism, drawing heavily on some good sources.

Throughout the history of Byzantium *mimesis* and *authority* were fundamental to Byzantine literary criticism. The Byzantines mostly wrote "under the 'authority' of a patron … and in 'imitation'" of older, often classical, models (Agapitos 2008, 77). However, these constraints, far from disabling innovation, forced writers towards oblique, indirect and "creative approaches" (78). They challenged canons, genres and their own society "by pretending not to do so" (78). Michael Psellos's (or Psellus) eleventh-century *Chronographia* can be read as "social and political criticism couched as praise" (81). Byzantine funerary literature is cast in genres whose terms are inherited from antiquity, but their "meaning and structure have been substantially altered to the point of completely cancelling the traditional rhetorical patterns" (80). More generally, Byzantine practice and criticism shows a "steady trend in juxtaposing convention and innovation or in experimenting with mixture and deviation" (79). One might quote examples of more explicit innovation. In the tenth and eleventh centuries, John Sikeliotes was "not afraid to depart from received wisdom" in his commentary on the Greek rhetorician Hermogenes (second century AD) and John Doxapatres was not "afraid to be critical of 'the ancients'" (Conley 2005, 677–8). In the twelfth century Nikephoros Basilakes, in his prologue to an edition of his works, defends his "use of an extremely experimental … style" (Agapitos 2008, 79). The Byzantines developed the genre of autobiography without precedent in an ancient genre (often with a strong metafictional element). For example, historiographers created an authorial persona within their works. Or, as in the twelfth-century epic,

Alexiad, by Anna Komnene (or Comnena), one might claim originality for images of "authorial *maternity*" (82, my italics). Nevertheless, poststructuralist notions of *intertextuality* and *resignification* (see Chapters 11 and 12) are more appropriate to Byzantine literature than the valorization of originality.

A third Byzantine principle, *usefulness* (*to chrēsimon*), needs to be added to *mimesis* and *authority*. Byzantine critics – from Photios (ninth century) to Psellos (eleventh century) and Theodoros Metochites (fourteenth century) – lived under a monarchy and were often public servants in the imperial court and church officials, composing texts "appropriate" to the local needs of their particular "setting" (Conley 2005, 669). Photios, as government official and patriarch, was involved in "political and ecclesiastical relations with the West, the evangelisation of the Slavs, and, in the East, diplomatic relations with Baghdad" (675). In his *Bibliotheca* (reviewing 279 books), though Hermogenes is a "conspicuous 'authority'", Photios uses him very selectively and deploys a wide range of "authoritative critical materials" for "his own" purposes (674). Photios's overriding principle of critical evaluation is not aesthetic but practical, *to chrēsimon*, to be understood in a number of senses. Literary texts are useful when they "lead the reader" to "moral and spiritual improvement", but Photios is also very aware that stylistic and rhetorical skill is "required of anyone holding public office" (673–5). It is pragmatically useful when "denouncing heresy" or towards "professional success and the maintenance of orthodox morality" (675). Psellos's careerism and "self-promotion" dictate, ironically, his evaluation of authors for their "moral character" (680), in keeping with orthodox morality. He thus promotes his career by arguing that the "pagan greats" only aimed at "short-term benefit" while Christian eloquence "aims at the refinement of virtue and spiritual salvation" (680).

In the Komnenian era (1081–1204) especially, literary criticism is a "staggeringly complex affair" involving both increased state interference – an "administrative aesthetic" that is "dictated 'from the top'" – and censorship as well as increased innovation, with writers and critics "striking out in new directions even as they bear witness to traditional literary values" (Conley 2005, 681). While literature is often written "on commission for high-ranking personages" (681), twelfth-century readers display a new and "lively interest" in "erotic romance and satire" and in "literary compositions in 'demotic' Greek" (685). (Byzantine texts were written in three linguistic registers: a classicizing high register, a middle register [*koinē*] and a vernacular or demotic low register.) So the overall picture is a "remarkable mix of conservatism and innovation" (681). On the side of innovation, literary taste shifted significantly away from classical Attic orators (e.g. Demosthenes) towards Homer and postclassical authors, the Old Testament, the Psalms and David, patristic and more recent authors. Criteria of literary evaluation shifted away from the imitation of authorities towards usefulness in the sense of *kairos* (contingent circumstances), "appropriateness to the rhetorical situation" (684). Innovation becomes more pronounced, in the form of "creative forays beyond the limits" of stylistic and even "moralising conventions", and there develops a "much wider range of acceptance" for non-canonical and demotic literature (686), such as the anonymous demotic epic *Digenis Akritis*.

Late Byzantine literary criticism is exemplified by Theodoros Metochites's *Epistasia kai Krisis*, comparing two orators in the Greek tradition, Aristides and Demosthenes. Though Demosthenes is synonymous with "traditional literary premises", in a context of political instability Demosthenes's association with democracy summons the "spectres of *ataxia*" (social disorder) and "political disaster", so Metochites pronounces against him (690). For Metochites literature cannot be "set apart from other 'modes' of discourse" and his comments "confound literary principles and political aims", showing an "overlap" of aesthetic, rhetorical, moral and political issues (669). He uses past authorities as "weapons" and the "decisive" role of "frank political considerations" in his evaluation of authors is unprecedented in Byzantine criticism (689). However, late Byzantine literature and criticism arguably also display an increasing democratization. There is a "new trend" towards writing in a Greek "closer" to the demotic spoken by the common people, and the circulation of simplified versions of texts – for example, Komnene's *Alexiad* or major historiographic works initially written in a high register – suggests a democratization of the reading public (691). The demotic erotic romance written by Emperor Michael VIII Palaiologos's nephew, Andronikos Palaiologos (thirteenth and fourteenth centuries), *Kallimachos and Chrysorrhoē*, seems to belong to a new generation of texts "composed for the entertainment of the literate members of the lower classes, outside court circles" (691). At the same time, late-Byzantine writers and scholars played an important part in the transfer of classical manuscripts and the transmission of classical scholarship to the West, leading to the revival of Platonism and the emergence of Renaissance humanism.

Conclusion

- Plotinus understands poetry (and art more generally) as part of the attempt to ascend to the vision of spiritual reality.
- Augustine devises a theory and practice of Scriptural interpretation aiming to overcome the ambiguity of figurative language and to reach its stable and authoritative true meaning, the Word of God.
- Aquinas's solution to the ambiguity of figurative language is to distinguish clearly between the "literal" sense and three "spiritual" senses: "allegorical", "moral" and "escatological". There is no conflict of meanings because the spiritual senses are all based on the literal sense.
- Dante views poetry in the vernacular as the proper medium of religious and moral instruction and transposes Aquinas's principles of biblical exegesis to the interpretation of poetry, criticism aiming to reveal poetry's "hidden truth". His model of literary interpretation, adapted from medieval Scriptural interpretation, is based on metaphors of inside/outside, grain/chaff, nucleus/shell.

- For Boccaccio poetry is not mimesis (of the Word of God) but human "invention" and "expression". Pico claims that man is a "chameleon" without fixed nature, free to choose which of his God-given potentials to cultivate and whether to ascend toward the spiritual or descend toward the material and bestial.
- Sidney theorizes poetry as creation, "a good invention" that does not affirm anything as true, a fiction emanating from human reason and its powers of conception, but he also posits poetry's practical and political forcibleness, effectiveness and authority.
- Byzantine literature and criticism were dominated by (sometimes conflicting) principles of mimesis, authority and moral and political usefulness. The Byzantines often tacitly deviated from the classical authorities they claimed to imitate, in response to moral concerns and especially political considerations. Indirection, hidden polemic and rhetorical appropriateness to local and topical political circumstances often prevailed. Literature and criticism of the Komnenian era, especially the twelfth century, is a particularly complex mix of conservatism and innovation. In late Byzantine literature and literary criticism there is a shift away from the mimesis of canonical literary models towards explicit considerations of political order and authority. Meanwhile there is also an increasing democratization of literary language towards vernacular Greek and of literary address and audiences, which increasingly include the lower classes. Byzantine critics were involved in the dissemination of classical scholarship to Italy.

Further reading

In addition to the primary texts by Plotinus, Augustine, Aquinas, Dante, Boccaccio, Pico and Sidney discussed in this chapter, the following have been influential: Auerbach 1968, Bakhtin 1984, Colish 1983, Eco 1988, Minnis and Scott 1991, Robertson 1962. In relation to Byzantine criticism see Agapitos 2008 and Conley 2005.

4 The Enlightenment and Romanticism

Reason and imagination

Hume, Burke, Wollstonecraft, Kant, Coleridge, Shelley, Hegel. With an appendix on the rise of the mass media.

In this chapter we will be focusing on the Enlightenment and Romanticism, and thinking about literature in its relation to "reason" and the "imagination" as conceived by the Enlightenment and Romanticism.

"Reason" is a key term in Enlightenment critical and literary texts: the criticism and fiction of Mary Wollstonecraft and William Godwin; the exchanges on the French Revolution between Edmund Burke and Thomas Paine; the Jacobin novel; the writings on aesthetics of Edmund Burke, David Hume and Joshua Reynolds, to give some examples in English. Enlightenment "reason" refers far back to classical figures such as Plato's Socrates, the implacable enemy of *doxa* (unexamined belief), but by now it is also strongly associated with the seventeenth-century Scientific Revolution and pioneers of this revolution, such as Isaac Newton. Enlightenment reason boldly connects ancient thought and modern science to a promise of universal emancipation. In 1784, in a short text entitled "An Answer to the Question: 'What Is Enlightenment?'", Immanuel Kant (1724–1804) called upon everyone to think for themselves, echoing Socrates 2,000 years previously as Kant would be echoed by Foucault in the twentieth century. Kant famously exclaimed the "motto of enlightenment", quoting Horace: "*Sapere aude!* Have courage to use your *own* understanding!" (Kant 1991b, 54). He added that his age, the eighteenth century, was an "age of *enlightenment*", but was not yet an "*enlightened* age" (58).

Enlightenment involved the following in the eyes of its eighteenth-century advocates: a call to cultivate critical reason rather than unthinkingly following orders and obeying authorities; a critique of religious intolerance and superstition and, in some instances, a rejection of Christianity; a turn towards classical antiquity as the cradle of critical and self-critical thinking (embodied in Socrates); endorsement of the Scientific Revolution of the seventeenth century (embodied in Newton) and of the empiricist philosophy of John Locke; a political admiration for contemporary England, considered less despotic in its government than European Continental countries; at least initially, endorsements of the American and French Revolutions; a belief in the power of human beings to shape their lives; an attitude towards history, society and the natural world that was active, optimistic, confident, practical, experimental, democratizing, meritocratic, cosmopolitan, universalizing. This summary, needless to say, downplays the variety of Enlightenment thought, the heated disagreements and the important role of different national contexts (though "nation" is at this time an emerging rather than established idea), with different levels of religious and political tolerance, censorship, literacy and independence from patrons for men of letters.

In the twentieth century, after World War II, there were important critiques of the Enlightenment and its emphasis on reason. Faced with a technologically advanced war and a "rationally administered" genocide, the Holocaust, postwar thinkers felt that the exercise of reason led to enslavement and unprecedented crimes against humanity rather than the liberation and utopian civilization the Enlightenment had promised. Since the 1980s, we have witnessed a widespread rejection of the Enlightenment. The Enlightenment seemed to have become synonymous with many questionable values: naïve optimism, blindness to the destructive potential of science, the arrogance and sterility of reason, selective or despotic universalism. Enlightenment universalism was seen as the attempt to impose Western values and prejudices on everybody else; or the famous rights of man advocated by Enlightenment thinkers (see Thomas Paine's *Rights of Man*) in practice only applied to the Western male middle class, not to the poor, to women, to slaves and the colonized.

Increasingly formulaic rejections of the Enlightenment have referred their legitimacy to the more complex earlier critiques by such thinkers as Horkheimer and Adorno (see Chapter 10), Foucault and Derrida (Chapter 11). (See Horkheimer and Adorno 1998; Derrida 1978, 1982c; Foucault 1986b, 2002.) Since the late 1990s there has been some correction of this attitude. A comparison between Zygmunt Bauman's 1987 *Legislators and Interpreters* and his 2000 *Liquid Modernity* would illustrate this widespread change. Derrida, in one of his last pieces before his death in 2004, "Enlightenment Past and to Come", looks to Europe "as a proud descendant of the Enlightenment past and a harbinger of the new Enlightenment to come" (Derrida 2004). In this new climate, it is becoming possible again to study the Enlightenment seriously without having to be either simply for or simply against it. As Michel Foucault urged, "we must free ourselves from the intellectual blackmail of 'being for or against the Enlightenment'" and "proceed with the analysis of ourselves as beings who are historically determined, to a certain extent, by the Enlightenment" (1986b, 45, 43). For example, in the free exercise of their reason, Enlightenment thinkers did write texts marked by appalling gender and race stereotyping. At the same time we owe to the Enlightenment one of the first classics of feminist literary criticism, Mary Wollstonecraft's *Vindication of the Rights of Woman*, as well as critical and literary texts advocating the abolition of slavery. (See the "Gender and Race" section in Kramnick 1995; and Robert Bage's Jacobin novel, *Hermsprong*.)

Peter Gay, in his important work, *The Enlightenment*, argues in relation to the strong association with reason that most Enlightenment thinkers actually valorized the body, sensuality, passion, the senses, the subjective. Gay also sees the aesthetic of the sublime – which explores the relation between presentation and the unpresentable and which is commonly identified with the Romantics – as an Enlightenment aesthetic (see "The Revolt against Rationalism" in Gay 1996b, 187–207). It can be strongly argued that most Enlightenment calls to reason are rooted in empiricism and question belief in universal objective a prioris, in contrast with the "rationalism" of previous philosophy, which held that certain universal truths could be discovered by reason alone. This is why Enlightenment literary criticism focuses on taste – which inevitably varies – not on objective laws of great literature, and why Enlightenment literary criticism only recognizes a rough empirical universality, for example that of widespread agreement that Homer is great. The empiricist David Hume would be, it seems to me, exemplary in this sense; while a comparison between Hume and Shelley would illuminate the complex relation between the Enlightenment and Romanticism.

David Hume and Edmund Burke

David Hume, a major Enlightenment thinker, was born in Edinburgh in 1711. It is often claimed that the Enlightenment deified reason, but this cannot be claimed of Hume. He is an empiricist, not a rationalist. As an empiricist he trusts only in experience and appropriates the "observational" and "experimental" method of the natural sciences first developed by Francis Bacon (Norton 1993b, 3, 5). At the heart of his empiricism is an iconoclastic scepticism that leaves no faith (either religious faith or the faith of common sense) untouched, in a way that can still disturb and inspire. He targets his scepticism equally at the belief in God, but also at the confidence that reason and science will guide us in a Godless world. His *Dialogues on Natural Religion* is a brilliant and witty classic of scepticism which speaks finally for tolerance and an end to fanaticism, whether theist or atheist. Hume died in 1776, 13 years before the beginning of the French Revolution, an atheist until the end.

Hume's major philosophical work is *A Treatise of Human Nature*, written when he was only in his mid twenties and published in 1739–40. Seen by his opponents as a work of alarming atheism and scepticism, it prevented him from gaining a Chair at the University of Edinburgh in 1745 and the University of Glasgow a few years later. *An Enquiry Concerning Human Understanding*, published in 1748, is a condensed and popularized version of part of the *Treatise.* During our discussion of Shelley, we will return to these two works – particularly to Hume's notions of the "imagination" and "sympathy" – as an important influence on Shelley.

We will now turn to Hume's major literary essay, "Of the Standard of Taste" (1757). While it is not a systematic work of academic philosophy, it is a masterly combination of rigorous philosophical thinking and delightful literary style appreciable by a wide audience and so very much in keeping with Hume's ideals. It is exemplary of Hume's essays, which his friend John Home described as "at once popular and philosophical … a rare and happy union of profound Science and fine writing" (quoted in Eugene F. Miller 1987, xvii), and whose popularity along with his historical writing made Hume a wealthy man and one of the best-known writers of his time, a happy state enjoyed by few philosophers!

Earlier chapters featured commentary by Plato, Aristotle, Horace, Plotinus, Sidney and others on a shared literary canon including, for example, Homer and the three ancient Greek tragedians, Aeschylus, Sophocles and Euripides. The first sentences of Hume's "Of the Standard of Taste" burst open this small world of shared literary values: "The great variety of taste, as well as of opinion, which prevails in the world, is too obvious not to have fallen under every one's observation" (Hume 1987b, 226). "[G]reat inconsistence and contrariety" of taste are observable both within a "narrow" group sharing the same education and "prejudices" and when contemplating "distant nations and remote ages" (227). Hume concludes: "We are apt to call *barbarous* whatever departs widely from our own taste and apprehension: But soon find the epithet of reproach retorted on us" (227). The proper response to such a "contest of sentiment" is scepticism: our arrogance is checked and "scruples … to pronounce positively in its own favour" (227). We come to see that – due to "diversity in the internal frame or external situation", etc. – "a certain degree of diversity in judgment is unavoidable, and we seek in vain for a standard, by which we can reconcile the contrary sentiments" (244). For example:

> A young man, whose passions are warm, will be more sensibly touched with amorous and tender images, than a man more advanced in years … One person is more pleased with the sublime; another with the tender; a third with raillery. One has a strong sensibility to blemishes, and is extremely studious of correctness: Another has a more lively feeling of beauties, and pardons twenty absurdities and defects for one elevated or pathetic stroke. The ear of this man is entirely turned towards conciseness and energy; that man is delighted with a copious, rich, and harmonious expression. Simplicity is affected by one; ornament by another … Such preferences are innocent and unavoidable, and can never reasonably be the object of dispute, because there is no standard, by which they can be decided.
>
> (244)

Hume's scepticism must have felt to many of his contemporary readers like a demolition machine levelling everything in his denial of any grounds for objective discrimination. While Hume talks of facts, such as the great variety of taste, which ought to have "fallen under every one's observation", what *falls* under Hume's sceptical eye is neoclassical dogma (see Chapter 2), belief in the givenness of a standard of literary greatness and belief in the givenness of the literary canon.

On the level ground he has cleared, Hume will then attempt to rebuild a literary canon. He will develop two different arguments, which I will call the "popular" argument and the "expert" argument.

- Hume's "popular" argument is that, in spite of the great diversity of taste, the fact is that authors such as Homer have been considered great and enjoyed widely by different peoples throughout the ages. This is empirical evidence of a universality of sorts in matters of taste.
- Hume's "expert" argument is that taste can be cultivated. A long and serious engagement with literature, involving arduous practice, tireless comparisons and a shedding of prejudices, could lift the individual reader to a truer and more universal taste (and Matthew Arnold could not agree more with Hume, see Chapter 5) (241).

After the fascinating movement of iconoclastic scepticism, Hume's reconstructive movement opens many questions. In relation to Hume's "popular" argument, for example, Hume claims that, when it comes to literature (unlike philosophy and science), the popular affection does not err for long (242–3). But why is that? If, as Hume argues, refined taste is very rare, why does not the unrefined taste of the many, throughout the ages, err? By what amazing good luck or Providence does the taste of the nonexpert many come to coincide with the taste of the expert few? Or by what process of ideological persuasion and subtle indoctrination, as Terry Eagleton asks in *The Ideology of the Aesthetic*? Hume would answer by returning to those few figures that combine great popularity and great critical acclaim by the most refined few. Today Shakespeare would be perhaps the ultimate example. Is not Shakespeare's combined popularity all over the world and recognition by professional critics an indication of a sort of universality in judgements of literary value? And yet in *The History of England* Hume found Shakespeare "too often tasteless" (quoted in Jones 1993, 260). A second set of questions, in relation to Hume's "expert" argument, would be as follows. Why should a long apprenticeship in reading literature, why should refinement, lead to agreement rather than disagreement among the refined few? Why should it lead to universal taste rather than irrevocably irreconcilable differences of taste? Is Hume observing a fact or rehearsing an Enlightenment ideal or, worse, an unexamined prejudice?

A comparison of Hume's "On the Standard of Taste" to Edmund Burke's contemporaneous *A Philosophical Enquiry into the Origin of our Ideas of the Sublime and Beautiful* (1757, second edition 1759) will show the radicalism of Hume's scepticism and version of empiricism. Like Hume, Burke turns to experimental science as his model for aesthetic investigation but, unlike Hume, what he thinks he can find there is grounds for agreement.

Burke's method is an inward-looking empiricism – the "diligent examination" of his "own mind" (Burke 1990, 152) – on the assumption that it will reveal a commonly shared, universal human nature. He is particularly interested in the "passions" affecting the human "imagination" – emotive responses to the world and to aesthetic objects (especially poetry) – and their effects on the human body. He distinguishes between a variety of "passions", categorizing them, attempting to describe their "exact boundaries" (48) and to provide "distinct knowledge" of them (117). His focus is on the difference between feelings of the beautiful and the sublime, as they arise in response to beautiful and sublime aesthetic objects. Beautiful aesthetic objects are small, polished, clear, light and delicate. They give rise to commonly shared feelings of pleasure as well as bodily effects of relaxation, thus furthering society, according to Burke. Sublime aesthetic objects are vast, rugged, dark and gloomy, massive, obscure. They excite feelings of "*pain*" and "*danger*" – tensing the body and furthering self-preservation – but mixed with "delight" that, due to our aesthetic distance, pain and danger do not "press too nearly" (36). (See Aristotle's theory of tragedy, Chapter 2.) Burke believes his enquiry reveals the providential mechanisms of human nature, as a "powerful machine" (98) created by God. He thus claims to provide aesthetic criticism with secure "principles" grounded in "laws" of human nature (149, 160–61).

On the one hand, Burke defines aesthetic criticism as an autonomous field with a distinct object, "Taste", understood as judgement of "the works of imagination and the elegant arts" (Burke 1990, 13). On the other hand, Burke claims that the method of aesthetic enquiry should be modelled on the experimental method of the natural sciences; this method of "investigation" is preferable because it "tends to set the reader himself in the track of invention, and to direct him in those paths in which the author has made his own discoveries" (12–13). However, Burke presupposes that what will be discovered will be universal laws. While the purpose of his enquiry is to find "*whether* there are any principles, on which the imagination is affected, so common to all, so grounded and certain, as to supply the means of reasoning satisfactorily about them" (13; my emphasis), he has already concluded that "it is probable that the standard … of … Taste is the same in all human creatures" (11); the alternative would be as "highly absurd" as to suppose that "the same cause … will produce different effects" (13–14). Even if this principled aesthetic universality does not exist yet (except as unrealized potential), Burke is optimistically confident that the development of aesthetic criticism into a science will bring it about. Taste can be improved "by extending our knowledge, by a steady attention to our object, and by frequent exercise" (25). As artists and critics extend their "ideas to take in all that nature comprehends" (12), the arts as well as the "science of criticism" progress towards a perfection indissociable from their universality (25).

However, the irony of Burke's enquiry is that it seems to reveal the pivotal role of "passions", the imagination and art (especially poetry) in the workings of human nature and society, and the limited and negative role of aesthetic enquiry itself. In looking for differences and clear boundaries Burke's aesthetic enquiry is not well suited to its object, especially the aesthetic of the sublime in its boundlessness and obscurity. The very "clearness" and "perspicuity" of critical enquiry undercut its emotional impact and power (Burke 1990, 160). Critics have rightly commented on Burke's ambivalence and his liminal position between Enlightenment and Romanticism.

Burke claims that "weakness", "imperfection" and a "fair" (not "dusky") skin colour are properties of female beauty universally and by "nature" (Burke 1990, 100, 106). To many contemporary readers the universalism of Hume, Burke and other Enlightenment figures feels like an attempt to impose modern Western values and prejudices on everybody else. Hume is a kindred spirit when he writes: "We are apt to call *barbarous* whatever departs widely from our own taste and apprehension. But soon find the epithet of reproach retorted on us" (Hume 1987b, 227, quoted above). However, in spite of his iconoclastic zeal, we find evidence of his fake or suspect universalism, his own unexamined prejudices and his own "barbarism" when he calls the Koran a "wild and absurd performance" (229) and when he claims that the "coarsest daubing … would affect the mind of a peasant or Indian with the highest admiration" (238). It seems that it is not always possible to distinguish between observable fact and prejudice. However, Enlightenment universalism is not necessarily politically suspect. For example, universalism is in the service of the liberation of women in Mary Wollstonecraft's *Vindication of the Rights of Woman*.

Mary Wollstonecraft

Mary Wollstonecraft (1759–97) is considered the first major feminist thinker. She was born into middle-class poverty in 1759 and was self-taught. Having initially explored the narrow field of female professional work in order to make a living, she then supported herself by writing. In 1790 she published *Vindication of the Rights of Men* in heated response to the French Revolution. In 1792 she published *Vindication of the Rights of Woman*, shortly after Thomas Paine's *Rights of Man*. Wollstonecraft led an experimental life. A radical intellectual, after the publication of *Vindication of the Rights of Woman* she went to France in 1792, and returned from France in 1795 a single, unmarried mother, deserted by her lover Gilbert Imlay. She wrote theoretical, literary and historical works (2007, 2008a). In 1797 Wollstonecraft was engaged in writing a new novel when she contracted a fatal post-natal infection, just a few days after giving birth to her second child, Mary. Mary was brought up by her father, the radical intellectual William Godwin, in a stimulating and bohemian environment. She became Shelley's mistress, bore him illegitimate children, married him, and lost him to an early death. Of her own writings she is most famous for *Frankenstein*. Mary Shelley came to know her mother through her writings alone.

In *Vindication of the Rights of Woman* Wollstonecraft puts universalism in the service of liberating women from what she calls the "tyranny of man" (Wollstonecraft 1985, 100). In thinking about the relation between literature and patriarchy, she turns to Milton's *Paradise Lost*:

> Women are told from their infancy, and taught by the example of their mothers, that a little knowledge of human weakness, justly termed cunning, softness of temper, *outward* obedience, and a scrupulous attention to a puerile kind of propriety, will obtain for them the protection of man; and should they be beautiful, everything else is needless, for at least twenty years of their lives. Thus Milton describes our first frail mother [Eve]; though when he tells us that women are formed for softness and sweet attractive grace, I cannot comprehend his meaning, unless … he meant to deprive us of souls, and insinuate that we were beings only designed by sweet attractive grace, and docile blind obedience, to gratify the senses of man when he can no longer soar on the wing of contemplation.
>
> (100–101)

According to Wollstonecraft, much of what is considered great literature participates in the oppression of women. Her reading of Milton is implicitly accusing the literary canon of oppression. She claims, more explicitly: "man, from the remotest antiquity, found it convenient, to exert his strength to subjugate his companion, *and his invention to show that she ought to have her neck bent under the yoke*" (109, my emphases). His literary invention has also played its part.

Quoted by Wollstonecraft, Milton describes Eve addressing Adam as follows: "To whom thus Eve with *perfect beauty* adorn'd./ My author and disposer, what thou bid'st/*Unargued* I obey; so God ordains;/God is *thy law, thou mine*: to know no more/is woman's *happiest* knowledge and her *praise*." (101, emphases added by Wollstonecraft). However, and this is an important point, Wollstonecraft also finds in Milton's *Paradise Lost* a longing for companionship between man and woman, but a longing that cannot be satisfied, given the existing ideal of femininity (exemplified by Milton's Eve) and the system of educating and constraining women to match this ideal. Wollstonecraft quotes Milton's Adam saying to God: "Hast thou not made me here thy substitute,/ And these inferior far beneath me set?/Among *unequals* what society/Can sort, what harmony or true delight?/ … of *fellowship* I speak/ Such as I seek, fit to participate/All rational delight … " (102, emphases added by Wollstonecraft). According to Wollstonecraft, in these lines man blames God for a loneliness that is of his own making. In systematically bringing up woman to become an obedient and decorative creature, man has deprived himself of an intellectual and moral equal and a friend. Milton's poem gives voice to a desire for shared rational delight and fellowship but also seeks to justify an order of things that prohibits it. "[J]ustify[ing] the ways of God to men", as Milton famously described the purpose of his epic poem, meant also to justify the contemporary ways of men to women!

How does Wollstonecraft put universalism in the service of the liberation of women in *Vindication of the Rights of Woman*? She argues that female education, geared as it is towards trivial "feminine" accomplishments, bars women from serious intellectual pursuits. As a result the seed of reason is not cultivated in women. This makes it impossible for women to be truly virtuous, in that true virtue requires a rigorous exercise of reason, not blind obedience: "It is a farce to call any being virtuous whose virtues do not result from the exercise of its own reason" (103). This is an argument very indebted to Plato and Aristotle's *Nicomachean Ethics.* However, Wollstonecraft would have criticized them too for, on the one hand, describing reason as a defining feature of the human being and, on the other hand, depriving all manner of humans (women, slaves, etc.) of full reason and therefore full humanity. The upbringing of women produces a creature for the narrow benefit of man, in that this creature is pleasing and obedient to man. This is why an altogether different standard is forced upon women. However, the seed of reason *is* universal, *is* present in women as well as men. Wollstonecraft argues that if men want better wives and mothers, they should *universalize* their own standard of intellectual and moral excellence to include women, and they should *universalize* the education that develops that excellence to include women.

In common with other Enlightenment thinkers, Wollstonecraft celebrates a free-thinking being leading an examined life, advocates the universal cultivation of the universal capacity for reason and rejects ways of life where people are "prey to prejudices", "taking all their opinions on credit" and "blindly submit[ting] to authority" (106). Impatiently she calls for enlightenment, for men to examine their prejudices regarding women, their own lack of reason: "What nonsense! When will a great man arise with sufficient strength of mind to puff away the fumes which pride and sensuality have thus spread over the subject?" (108). And she calls on women to "unfold their own faculties and acquire the dignity of conscious virtue" (109).

Immanuel Kant

In "What Is Enlightenment?" Foucault defines the Enlightenment as critique of the present, exemplified by Kant's "An Answer to the Question: 'What Is Enlightenment?'". Kant originates the "attitude of modernity", understood as an "ethos" of "permanent critique of our historical era" (Foucault 1986b,

38, 42). Foucault thus traces modernity and its thinkers, such as Baudelaire and Nietzsche, back to Kant and the Enlightenment. While Kant shared in the Enlightenment call on everyone to think critically for themselves, what is distinctive about his ground-breaking and monumental project is "critique" as the philosophical enterprise of defining the nature and limits of reason, morality and aesthetic judgement.

Kant's Third Critique, *Critique of Judgment* (1790), published one year into the French Revolution, defines aesthetic judgement as judgement without rules. The search for universal laws of aesthetic judgement misunderstands the nature of aesthetic judgement in Kant's eyes. Judging an object beautiful is not an act of cognition, but a refined pleasure taken in the *disinterested* contemplation of the form of the beautiful object. By contrast, our relation to the agreeable or the good is one of "interest" and "desire" (Kant 1987, 51). When we declare an object agreeable we express an "interest" in and "desire" for that object and its sensuous "enjoyment"; similarly, when we declare an object good (as in moral judgements) we express a rational interest in that object because we desire the good (48). While the agreeable pertains to our experience of the material world and the pleasure of the senses, and the good to our interaction with the ideal world of reason and morality, aesthetic pleasure has the crucial role of bridging the gap between the two, according to Kant. Put differently, while the Scientific Revolution (and empiricism) is turned towards the material world and the laws of nature, and the idealism dominating Western thought since Plato is turned towards the ideal world as the realm of freedom from the strict determination of the material, the aesthetic – for example, the production and consumption of literature – has the crucial role of overcoming this split within the human self, providing an aspect of our experience where the oppositions can mingle to a degree. Taste is thus an important bridge: it "enables us … to make the transition from sensible charm to a habitual moral interest without making too violent a leap" (230).

Kant's aesthetics is strictly formalist. Even colour is rejected in favour of pure form, "*design*", "*composition*" (72) and "shape" (77). We call an object or presentation beautiful when our "pleasure is connected with mere apprehension" of its "form", without reference to what that object is meant to be or cognition of it; "taste" is "our ability to judge by such a pleasure" (29–30). Aesthetic delight in form, in its disinterestedness, promises to be a path to universality and freedom. When we find an object beautiful we believe it to be universally beautiful because we "cannot discover" any underlying "private conditions" or "inclination" or "interest" (54). By "abstracting from the limitations" of our particular judgement, by "leaving out as much as possible whatever is matter, i.e. sensation" and by "paying attention solely to the formal features", we hope to reach a *sensus communis* or "*common human understanding*" potentially shared by all (160). Even if this "common sense" doesn't already exist, we want to bring it about – and we are declaring that "there is a possibility of reaching such agreement" (89–90). Another name for this process is enlightenment. It involves a combination of thinking "for oneself", in the sense of thinking in an "*unprejudiced*" manner free from "*superstition*", and thinking beyond petty interests and "private subjective conditions", in a "*broadened*" manner encompassing "the standpoint of everyone else" (160–61). So Kant optimistically assumes that "transferring" oneself "to the standpoint of others" is possible, and considers that taste and aesthetic judgement involve the exercise of our *sensus communis* in exemplary fashion (161).

In its disinterestedness, aesthetic pleasure is inherently "*free*" (52, 54). Freedom, a double freedom from the subjective as well as the objective, is at the heart of Kant's aesthetics: literature (and art more generally) frees us both from private interests and inclinations and from artistic or otherwise obedience to rules. It is creation and aesthetic pleasure without objective rules and without subjective compulsions: "[t]here can be no objective rule of taste … that determines … what is beautiful" (79). If there were, the judgement of what is beautiful would not be free, but determined by the rule. On the contrary, due to the absence of objective rules, aesthetic judgements are "singular", though they lay claim to universal validity through their disinterestedness (97). Kant says they are "subjective universal" judgements, for when we judge something beautiful we feel that everybody *should* think so too, though we know that this is not likely to be the case in reality. Similarly, true aesthetic creation is the work of genius, understood as "originality" and "freedom from the constraint of rules" (186–7). The very exercise of creative genius can give rise to new rules for art, in the sense that it "gives rise to a school" whose rules are extracted retrospectively from the free exercise of genius (187). However, in the relation of genius to genius, the only rule to be taught or learned is rule-breaking: one genius arouses in another genius only the "feeling of his own originality" and the exercise of his "freedom from the constraint of rules" (187). At the same time, in his dual critique of both empiricism and idealism, Kant warns against an unbridled idealism by pointing out that there is in art an element of "constraint" or "*mechanism*" without which "the *spirit* … would have no body", so "free art" is not "mere play" (171).

Following Kant's thinking very closely, Jean-François Lyotard calls this rule-breaking "postmodern" in his influential essay "Answering the Question: What Is Postmodernism?" His argument is that there are two ever-recurring moments following each other within modern art and literature: a "postmodern" rule-breaking moment "working without rules in order to formulate the rules of what *will have been done*" (Lyotard 1984b, 81) and a "realist" moment codifying these new rules into a dogma whose very repetition and naturalization carries with it strong if delusive "effects of reality" (74), falsely appearing to "seize reality" (82) (see Chapter 9).

To return to *Critique of Judgment* Kant adopts Burke's distinction between the beautiful and the sublime, but greatly refines it. As with Burke, while the form of the beautiful is "bounded", the form of the sublime is "*unboundedness*" in its "totality" (Kant 1987, 98). Kant distinguishes between three faculties within the human mind: the understanding, turned towards nature and working on sensuous experience; the imagination, associated with aesthetic production and consumption; and reason, turned towards suprasensible ideas. Kant defines the distinction between the beautiful and the sublime within this schema, in the following manner. When we judge an aesthetic object to be beautiful, there is a "free play" (62), "free harmony" (186) or "attunement" between imagination and understanding (113). We experience aesthetic pleasure in response to the "*accordance*" of imagination and understanding (115). While beautiful objects or presentations are sensuous ones, hence the role of the understanding, sublime objects are ideal and suprasensible ones and involve a harmonization or attunement of the imagination with reason. (Kant thinks that no sensuous object is properly speaking sublime. The sublime is to be found not in "nature" but "within ourselves" [100].) However, in relation to the sublime, the imagination's attunement with reason is a "*conflict*" rather than an "*accordance*" (115–16) – and is experienced as a mixture of pleasure and pain or attraction and repulsion (98). With the sublime, the mind "finds all the might of the imagination still inadequate to reason's ideas". This makes "intuitable for us the superiority of the rational vocation" over sensibility. We experience "displeasure" because of the imagination's inadequacy in relation to reason and "pleasure" because "this very judgement" is "in harmony with rational ideas" (113–15 throughout). For example, we know the estimated age and size of the universe but we cannot imagine it adequately.

In "Answering the Question: What Is Postmodernism?" Lyotard's updating of Kant lingers especially on the sublime (77ff.). The aesthetic of postmodernism should be an aesthetic of the sublime, he argues, setting out to present the unpresentable in its very unpresentability. Instead of claiming to be an adequate and truthful presentation of reality, literature and art have to bear witness to the unpresentable, i.e. what can be conceived by reason but defies the powers of the imagination. Lyotard is writing in defence of the twentieth-century avant-gardes and conceptual art, while simultaneously secularizing and historicizing Kant's sublime. While for Kant an example of the sublime would be the idea of "the infinite *as a whole*" (Kant 1987, 111), for Lyotard such an example would be the Holocaust and other traumatic historical events brought about by modern totalitarian "terror" (Lyotard 1984b, 82). The word inevitably recalls "the Terror" beginning in 1793 in France, four years after the French Revolution, in which the revolutionary government conducted violent repression against the populace. Published in 1790, Kant's *Critique of Judgment* established the idea of disinterestedness, an idea that has had a rich history in aesthetics and literary theory. The *Critique* appears detached from the French Revolution but its ideas of the beautiful and the *sensus communis* as a force for the overcoming of the oppositions dividing the modern individual and modern society, and the utopian promise of a community founded on a common ground of shared values beyond class and other "interests", were a potent message in troubled times.

Samuel Taylor Coleridge

Samuel Taylor Coleridge (1772–1834) is perhaps the most important intellectual in English history. A major poet, his diverse prose writings made highly influential contributions to literary theory and criticism and social and political theory. He spent time in Germany and was also responsible for introducing Britain to the philosophy of Kant and his successors, the German idealists.

Kant (and those who followed him, such as Fichte and Schelling) was a major influence on Coleridge's *Biographia Literaria* (1817), as the text itself often and readily acknowledges. However, Coleridge displays different priorities, in response to different historical and personal concerns. In relation to reason and the imagination, Kant ultimately privileged the former, Coleridge the latter. While for Kant the imagination makes "intuitable for us the superiority of the rational vocation" (Kant 1987, 113, quoted above), for Coleridge the imagination is a supreme "esemplastic" (a neologism whose meaning in Greek is "transforming into one or unifying") power promising to cure the traumatic disharmony witnessed during the French Terror brought about by the excesses of Jacobinism.

Coleridge's use and modification of Kant can perhaps best be approached through Coleridge's complex version of artistic and critical disinterestedness. Disinterestedness, in its many forms, is emphatically asserted throughout *Biographia Literaria.* To begin with, Coleridge influentially posits the poet's impersonality – an attitude to which T. S. Eliot returns in his famous essay, "Tradition and the Individual Talent" (see Chapter 8). Coleridge boldly asserts the poet's "alienation" or the "utter *aloofness* of the poet's own feelings"; he avoids "private interests and circumstances" and is "unparticipating in the passions" (1975, 176–7). Against "doleful egotism" (14), the man of genius has no strong "sensation of self", as he "lives most in the ideal world" (25). Coleridge presents himself as the opposite of a man of the world: as an outsider who has "lived either abroad or in retirement" (31) and who wishes to detach literature from the marketplace, "*never pursue literature as a trade*" (127). He claims that the French Revolution soon bred in him "thorough disgust and despondency, both with regard to disputes and the parties disputant"; in search for a cure "I retired to a cottage … and devoted my thoughts and studies to the foundations of religion and morals" (110–11).

In his search for secure foundations, Coleridge turns to earlier critical projects: Descartes's methodological doubt establishing the certainty of the thinking subject (*cogito ergo sum*) (144) and, most importantly, Kant's critical project establishing the limits and conditions of knowledge (pure reason), morality (practical reason) and aesthetic criticism (judgement). Condemning "quacks in criticism" (40), critics who "write from humour or interest" (33) in the new fashionable reviews whose circulation vastly exceeded the sales of books of poetry, Coleridge (who felt he had personally suffered badly at the hands of malicious critics) is obsessively looking for secure and "permanent principles" (122) of literary criticism, as the basis of his literary theory and practice. He is searching for "fixed canons of criticism" (36); a "poetic creed" deduced "from established premises" (53); a "disclosure and establishment of principles" against "superstition and despotism" (104); an impartial "enlightened adherence to a code of intelligible principles" (117); a critics' "constitution and code of laws" (239) that stand above the "interference of national party" (240); "general grounds or rules" (241).

Coleridge views his struggle as a project of enlightenment, in the "best interests of humanity" (40), and sums it up in Kantian style: "I labored at a solid foundation on which permanently to ground my opinions in the component faculties of the human mind itself" (11). Coleridge is very aware that his labours, unlike Kant's, didn't take the form of systematic philosophy, and describes *Biographia Literaria* as "so immethodical a miscellany" (52) that his deductions of principles of literary creation and criticism are "like the fragments of the winding steps of an old ruined tower" (166). So what are the principles Coleridge elaborates? And does he manage to avoid the pseudo-scientific criticism beloved of Burke and rejected by Kant?

First, following Descartes and Kant, Coleridge affirms the postulate – the groundless ground – of self-consciousness as the ultimate condition of human knowledge. Self-consciousness, as a "primary act of self-duplicating" (153), is the condition of "all our possible knowledge" (154). Coleridge's distinctive contribution, derived from German idealism, understands self-consciousness as an active "will" and "freedom" (153), whose exemplary manifestation is the imagination. Distinguishing between "fancy" and "imagination", Coleridge defines fancy as "the aggregative and associative power" and imagination as the higher "shaping or modifying power" (160) – a transfigurative *esemplastic* power "shap[ing] into one" (91). While fancy works piecemeal and calculatively, piecing together existing impressions, imagination is true creation (252) and the "formation of a second nature" (264) – Coleridge (not by chance) here echoes Sir Philip Sidney's Plotinian phrase discussed in Chapter 3. The imagination "re-create[s]" and "struggles to idealize and to unify" (167); it is "synthetic" and imparts "unity" and "the balance or reconciliation of opposite or discordant qualities" (174).

Coleridge's second postulate is the need for unification and integration: the "end and purpose of all reason" is "unity and system" (155). Coleridge acknowledges his particular debt to Plato, Plotinus and the Neoplatonic tradition's emphasis on the ultimate principle of "the One" (Plotinus's term): Plato's "sublime truths of the divine unity" (129). His claim that Plato and the Neoplatonists – Plotinus, Proclus and Ficino – prepared him for Descartes (80) suggests that Idealism and modern critical philosophy are compatible in his eyes. However, his idealist turn towards oneness also serves an urgent political purpose. Having diagnosed sectarianism as "the cause of our failures" (142), Coleridge sets up the *esemplastic* imagination as the medium of "genuine reformation" (117). He effectively replaces political freedom and emancipatory politics with the spiritual freedom of the *esemplastic* imagination (140), whose "love of peace" he trusts will lead to the "progressive amelioration of mankind" (130). This is literature's difficult civilizing mission; Coleridge now discerns a tendency towards "disjunction and separation" of the "component parts" (201) in the language of common uneducated men, in which Wordsworth and his own younger and more democratic self had put so much faith in the Preface to *Lyrical Ballads*.

On these postulates Coleridge founds what he calls "practical criticism" (175): applied criticism of literary texts, particularly poems, involving close reading. Twentieth-century Anglo-American Practical Criticism as well as several influential critical ideas descend from *Biographia Literaria*. Coleridge's practical criticism posits four literary ideals: unity of form, defamiliarization, universality and originality.

Unity of form or "harmony and integrity" (243) is the main, and most distinctive, principle of practical criticism. Coleridge inherits Kant's formalism but redefines it as a search for harmonious and unified form – an ideal fully adopted by twentieth-century Anglo-American Practical Criticism and American formalism and shared by some structuralists. The poem must be a "harmonious whole" (173) whose "parts … mutually support and explain each other" (172). Poetic power consists in "reducing multitude into unity of effect" and "one predominant thought or feeling" (176). To bring about unity and harmony, the multitude of parts need to be assimilated to "the more important and essential parts" (211) – Coleridge here anticipates Roman Jakobson's classic structuralist essay, "The Dominant" (1935) (see Chapter 7). The formal unity of the great poem is like an impregnable and everlasting edifice: it is easier to "push a stone out from the pyramids with the bare hand than to alter a word, or the position of a word, in Milton or Shakespeare … without making the author say something else, or something worse, than he does say" (12). Indeed great poetry contributes to peace in this way: for example, in Shakespeare the creative and the intellectual "in a war embrace" but they reconcile "with one voice" (179–80). On the other hand, "disharmony in style" or "incongruity" is a poetic defect (249). For example, Wordsworth's "undue predilection for the dramatic form" leads to "incongruity of style", due to the incongruity between the diction and thoughts of character(s) and poet (257). It is a defect in Wordsworth that he "sinks too often and too abruptly" to a low prosaic style, unpleasantly forcing the reader to "alternate states of feeling" that are too dissimilar (248). (Coleridge discusses "organic form" already in his 1812–13 series of lectures on Shakespeare [Coleridge 1989, 53].)

Coleridge's poetic ideal of defamiliarization – deduced from the transfigurative power of the imagination – is explicitly adopted by Shelley and anticipates the Russian Formalist Viktor Shklovsky's theory of "defamiliarization" outlined in his classic essay, "Art as Technique" (1917) (see Chapter 7). For Coleridge poetic defamiliarization is a superior, heightened form of observation, an intensified and novel perception: it represents "familiar objects as to awaken … that freshness of sensation"; poetic "genius produces the strongest impressions of novelty" (49). The novelty of the poetic imagination "awaken[s] the mind's attention from the lethargy of custom" and peels off "the film of familiarity and selfish solicitude" (169). (Shelley borrows "film of familiarity" in his own account of defamiliarization; see Shelley 2003b, 698.) Defamiliarization brings together external reality and the ideal, observation and imagination, the essence of things and the unique singularity of genius: "spreading … the ideal world, around forms, incidents and situations of which … custom had bedimmed all the lustre" (49), poetic genius (and Wordsworth in particular) does not distort objects but "brings out a vein and many a tint which escape the eye of common observation … on the dusty highroad of custom" (265).

In poetry Coleridge is looking for two seemingly contradictory qualities, universality (or generality or commonality) and originality (or singularity or uniqueness), which defamiliarization promises to bring together. "Universality" refers back to Kant's "disinterestedness" (discussed above) as well as to Aristotle's discussion of poetry as superior to historiography, in that poetry attempts to capture the essential and unchanging universal human nature while historiography deals with historical particularity (see Chapter 2) (Coleridge 1975, 192–4). Arguing against Wordsworth's Preface to *Lyrical Ballads* (discussed in Chapter 1) (Coleridge does not acknowledge that he contributed ideas to the Preface and urged Wordsworth to write it) and attacking caricatures of Wordsworth as writing poems in low language, Coleridge tries to show that Wordsworth's language is not exclusively the language of low and rustic life, but an ordinary language shared by all classes and simultaneously uniquely his own. Poems must be "representative" (256) and an element of Wordsworth's greatness is his ability to discern "the sameness of the nature" irrespective of rank (270). Anxious to repudiate the democratic identification with the lowly in the Preface to *Lyrical Ballads*, Coleridge argues that a "low profession" (254) is not a guarantee of virtue or poetic freshness, as there is "but one Burns among the shepherds of Scotland" (255). He is equally anxious to repudiate the literary engagement with specific historical contexts so vigorously pursued by so many novels and by realist literature more generally. "[S]pecific and individual" characters and descriptions in modern poetry (181) are considered a defect. "[L]aborious minuteness and fidelity in the representation of objects" and "the insertion of accidental circumstances" in Wordsworth are also a defect, incompatible with the "liberty" of the poet and "fetter[ing] his feet in the shackles" of historians, who "have entered into bond to truth" (251). Instances in Wordsworth of "minute adherence to matter-of-fact in character and incidents" (253) are rejected. Coleridge similarly rejects novels "meant to pass for histories" such as Defoe's *Moll Flanders*, though Sterne is more acceptable

(256). Simplifying somewhat, George Eliot's version of realism is a complete reversal of Coleridge, in its programmatic attention to historical context (see Chapter 5).

While advocating poetry's search for an existing if hidden universality – and the moral and emotional heights to be "found in all ranks" (253) – Coleridge also posits the poet's unique and singular originality as a power of spiritual reform to come (rather than political reform). Having rejected "egotism", he praises the "peculiarity" (263) of Shakespeare, Milton and Wordsworth: how "singular" that Wordsworth, the defender of *lingua communis*, has a diction which like Shakespeare's and Milton's is "the most individualized and characteristic" (229)! Anticipating modernist heroes, Wordsworth's diction is "peculiarly his own" (232); even his "grammatical construction" is "peculiar" (235). In Wordsworth's *Excursion* the pedlar's diction is not really characteristic of the profession, but Wordsworth's own (257). Coleridge thus redefines Wordsworth's greatness as residing in the originality of his imagination: his imagination is comparable to Shakespeare's and Milton's but "perfectly unborrowed and his own" (271) so that the real tendency of his mind is its elevated imagination, "his own majestic movements" (247). The poet's imagination allows escape from the everyday world and the poet's – and reader's – everyday "egotism" into the spiritual freedom of a higher self.

Coleridge builds a pyramid of principles of practical criticism, whose base is shared by universality and the poet's unique originality, combined in the poetic practice of defamiliarization, and whose peak is harmony and unity. Are his principles the permanent foundations he believes them to be, or are they temporary postulates suited to his historical situation as he sees it? While Sir Philip Sidney's version of Platonism leads him to advocate a role for literature in national politics (as Shepherd, Maslen and Alexander argued, see Chapter 3), Coleridge's version of Platonism configures the true poet as an exceptional individual standing above national politics and offering what national politics cannot deliver for the benefit of all humanity. This goes hand in hand with a classist and racist devaluation of common humanity: the uneducated are prone to disunity; the "degraded" and "half human savages of New Holland" are only capable of mimicry and lack the transfigurative power of the imagination (45); the inner sense is "not yet born" in the "Esquimaux or New Zealander" (144); missionaries are familiar with the "obstacle" of the limited language of "uncivilized tribes", which lacks the "internal acts" of the imagination (197). Coleridge's poet thus emerges as the vanguard in the civilizing mission of the British Empire, serving the "love of liberty" (117).

Recalling Pico (Chapter 3), Coleridge claims that there is some truth in most "philosophical sects" (141). However, he is hostile to natural or mechanical philosophy, empiricism and Hume, while he endorses Plato and Neoplatonism, Descartes (Chapters 1 and 3), Kant and especially Schelling, with whom he recognizes a "genial coincidence" (86), asking the reader not to confuse it with plagiarism. In turn, Coleridge is politicized and radicalized by Shelley, who read *Biographia Literaria* "as soon as it appeared" (Watson

1975, xix). Coleridge's emphases on disinterestedness, sweetness, temperance, harmony, oneness and his vision of a "secular clerisy" as priests of culture greatly influenced Matthew Arnold (see Chapter 5); while his emphases on formal unity (or organic form) and the words on the page (neither a word nor its position in Shakespeare and Milton can be changed without altering and spoiling the text) became tenets of twentieth-century Anglo-American criticism (see Chapters 8 and 9).

Percy Bysshe Shelley

Percy Bysshe Shelley was born in 1792, the year *Vindication of the Rights of Woman* was published, into a wealthy aristocratic family. He was a declared atheist, in the spirit of Locke's and Hume's empiricism, already in his teens. He read Thomas Paine and William Godwin and corresponded with Godwin. In 1811 Shelley got himself expelled from Oxford for co-authoring a pamphlet, *The Necessity of Atheism*, and sending it to the heads of Oxford colleges. As a result of his refusal to renounce this work, together with his scandalously bohemian love life – eloping with Harriet Westbrook, then marrying her, then deserting her for Mary Godwin – he was disinherited by his family. He found an intellectual equal in Mary Godwin and together they led a rootless, creatively productive, bohemian life, until his early death in a boating accident in Italy in 1822. Shelley wrote "A Defence of Poetry" in 1821, but it remained unpublished until 1840, when Mary Shelley was finally able to overcome the objections of his family in order to edit it and publish it. It is one of the most widely read theoretical statements on literature to this day and has attracted enormous admiration as well as criticism.

In "A Defence of Poetry", the focus of our discussion, Shelley pursues the democratic ideals of the Enlightenment and the French Revolution – "*liberté, egalité, fraternité*" – by new means in response to the times. By 1821 the French Revolution had neither spread across the channel nor fulfilled its democratic promise. Wollstonecraft's bright hope that the exercise of reason would bring about true human fellowship had not materialized. In France the Terror was criticized by many (e.g. Burke) as reason gone mad. In England, the cultivation of the seed of reason was instrumentalized and put in the service of self-interest and profit. In the pursuit of narrow self-interest, the gap between rich and poor had increased. Shelley is grateful to Locke, Hume, Gibbon, Voltaire and Rousseau for their past exertions on behalf of "oppressed and deluded humanity" (2003b, 695) – and salutes the "emancipation of women" (690) – but argues that reason is now in the hands of (what we would today call) technocrats in England. The speculations of technocrats tend to increase the "extremes of luxury and want" (694). This is because technocrats serve the twin masters of anarchic middle-class economic self-interest and political despotism: "The rich have become richer, and the poor have become poorer; and the vessel of the state is driven between the Scylla and Charybdis of anarchy and despotism" (694) – a complaint still very current as I write in 2013! Shelley claims:

> The cultivation of those sciences which have enlarged the limits of the empire of man over the external world, has, for want of the poetical faculty, proportionally circumscribed those of the internal world, and man, having enslaved the elements, remains himself a slave. To what but a cultivation of the mechanical arts in a degree disproportioned to the presence of the creative faculty which is the basis of all knowledge is to be attributed the abuse of all invention for abridging and combining labour, to the exasperation of the inequality of mankind.
>
> (695–6)

In 1821 and while travelling in Europe, Shelley had somehow grasped early an English problem that would later preoccupy the Victorian novel. While the middle classes are flourishing, the urban poor, the new industrial working classes, are starving in England – and novels by Charlotte Brontë, Dickens, Disraeli, George Eliot, Elizabeth Gaskell, Charles Kingsley and George Gissing would give us chilling depictions of hunger in England later in the century. Indeed Shelley expresses in this passage an analysis that not only Marx (Chapter 5) but Heidegger (without the class concern) (Chapter 10) will fundamentally share.

In response to this new situation, Shelley reiterates the Enlightenment condemnation of despotism and superstition, condemns "the dissonance of arms" witnessed during the French Revolution and the Napoleonic Wars (1803–15), but also identifies the new urgency of another target: "the dull vapours of the little world of self" (690–91). Kant's "disinterested" imagination, endorsed by Coleridge, anticipates this problem to a degree. But Shelley also argues that we need new means for Enlightenment ends. What is required in order to bring about *fraternité* – or Hume's moral "sympathy" or Wollstonecraft's "fellowship" – is neither Hume's radical scepticism nor Wollstonecraft's exercise of reason, but the poet's imagination. So Shelley reconnects Coleridge's "imagination" (and the self) to everyday social reality, through Hume's moral "sympathy" (Shelley returns to poetry the identification with the lowly that Coleridge abstracted from Wordsworth). While Coleridge is the major influence on Shelley, Coleridge's "imagination" is primarily about the self and Shelley's "imagination" is about social others: a synthetic force that will build the "social sympathies" (675) – sympathies among parts of society separated by an ever-increasing chasm – and fight selfishness. Shelley argues:

> The great secret of morals is Love, or a going out of our own nature, and an identification of ourselves with the beautiful which exists in thought, action or person, not our own. A man to be greatly good, must imagine intensely and comprehensively; he must put himself in the place of another and of many others … The great instrument of moral good is the imagination … Poetry enlarges the circumference of the imagination.
> (682)

In this sense, without poetry there is "utter anarchy and darkness" (688).

For Shelley "Reason respects the differences, and Imagination the similitudes of things" (675) – the former is analytical and the latter synthetic. Imagination is a power of association. The new poet "create[s] afresh the associations which have been … disorganized" (676). Shelley here radically rewrites Hume on the imagination and on sympathy. According to Hume, we perceive the external world as images. Imagination is fancy, the practice of associating or connecting images. However, the associations we make with our imagination are not inherent in things but are of our own making. The lynchpin of Hume's moral theory is "sympathy" or "benevolence", which is a matter of imagination: of making a connection where there isn't one already. Hume optimistically declares that this sympathy or benevolence is a commonly shared "feeling for humanity" that is "obvious" even to "the most careless observer", while selfishness is "contrary" both "to common feeling and our most unprejudiced notions" (Hume 1975b, 298).

While Hume stresses that imagination is just fancy and argues the need to dispel the fumes of superstition, Shelley celebrates the power of the imagination in passages that radicalize Coleridge and anticipate the early-twentieth-century Russian Formalist idea of "defamiliarization". In 1917 Viktor Shklovsky defines it as follows: "art exists that one may recover the sensation of life … Art removes objects from the automatism of perception" (Shklovsky 1998, 18). Shelley writes that poetry "creates anew the universe after it has been annihilated in our minds by the recurrence of impressions blunted by reiteration" (698). For Shelley the language of poets is "vitally metaphorical; that is, it marks the before unapprehended relations of things" (676). Poetry "contains within itself the seeds at once of its own and of social renovation" (687). In the nineteenth and twentieth centuries, artists and critics posed the question whether literature is the power to understand what is foreign and alien to us and to bring together those kept apart; or, on the contrary, whether literature is just the imaginary resolution of real and continuing conflicts. The debate still goes on.

Shelley doesn't only advocate new and unprecedented associations and does not only claim with bravado that poetry "subdues to union under its light yoke all irreconcilable things" (698). He also attempts himself an unprecedented association or combination in "A Defence of Poetry". He combines what to many are indeed "irreconcilable things": Hume's Enlightenment radicalism and Plotinus's Neoplatonist idealism. Shelley's rewriting of Hume (discussed above) is already a Plotinian one, as I hope will become clear. In Plotinus's theory of art (see Chapter 3), the ideal world of Forms has three levels: the One, the Intellect and the Soul. The One creates the Intellect, which creates the Soul, which creates the world. While the higher creates the lower, the lower contemplates the higher – man contemplates the spiritual realm that culminates in the One. Contemplation is not a rational process grasping the One gradually and analytically. Contemplation is, at least finally, poetic intuition, grasping the One instantaneously as a whole. "A Poet participates in the eternal, the infinite and the one" (677), states Shelley in impeccable Plotinian language (which would have gained Coleridge's wholehearted assent). The poet participates in the eternal through intuition that, like Prometheus, brings "light and fire from those eternal regions" (696). Intuition, as in Plotinus, is instantaneous conception: "Milton conceived the *Paradise Lost* as a whole before he executed it in portions" (697). Shelley contrasts the instantaneousness of intuitive conception with the time of actual composition: "[Conception] is as a mirror which reflects, [expression] as a cloud which enfeebles, the light of which both are mediums of communication" (678). In other words, "the most glorious poetry that has ever been communicated to the world is probably a feeble shadow of the original conceptions of the poet" (697). Coleridge, in his own Neoplatonism, took a similar view in *Biographia Literaria*: words are the "shadows of notions" (Coleridge 1975, 140); the "language of words" is only the "vehicle" of the "language of spirits" (158). A contemporary audience, brought up on Roland Barthes's "writing is the destruction of every voice, of every point of origin" (Barthes 1977b, 142) (see Chapter 11) – anticipated by Oscar Wilde's "language … is the parent, and not the child, of thought" (Wilde 1961, 60) (see Chapter 5) – is likely to find such instances of Shelley's (and Coleridge's) idealism suspicious.

"A Defence of Poetry" keeps reiterating that intuition is unconscious rather than willed, short-lived and humbling rather than self-aggrandizing. Shelley writes of "evanescent visitations" and "an inconstant wind" during which the "self appears as what it is, an atom to an Universe" (697–8). Yet Shelley also reiterates his Platonic/Neoplatonic belief that poetry reveals the Truth: the One, eternal World of Being underlying the apparent world of becoming, multiplicity and conflict. The thinkers of modernity (discussed in the next chapter) will tell us that the apparent world is all there is; and Shelley occasionally and fleetingly intuits a multiperspectivism to come, when for example he defines poetry as "*a prismatic and many-sided mirror*, which collects the brightest rays of human nature" (685, my italics).

G. W. F. Hegel

German philosophical developments after Kant culminated in Georg Wilhelm Friedrich Hegel (1770–1831). Central to Hegel's philosophy is the dialectic – thesis, antithesis, synthesis – which is the mechanism by which the mind and historical reality itself progress towards their final form and truth, the reconciliation of man and the world, the spiritual and the real. Hegel's knowledge of the visual arts is vast, but along with the egomaniacal nature of his philosophy goes a full-fledged Eurocentrism.

Hegel's *Lectures on Fine Art* (1835), first published posthumously, is a severe rebuke to the Romantics and their aspirations. It shockingly announces the modern irrelevance of aesthetic production as "a thing of the past" that "no longer fills our highest need" (Hegel 1975, 10–11). In world history, art had a central role as the self-conscious expression of the spirit of entire epochs, but in the modern world the artist is alienated and expresses only himself, while the cognitive vocation of art is now best served by philosophy, that is to say by Hegel's philosophy.

Hegel positions his aesthetics as the dialectical synthesis and overcoming of two opposed but equally inferior and defective earlier aesthetics. First, following Kant and Romanticism, he rejects neoclassical "rule-providing theories" of art (Chapter 2): their "prescriptions" are not conducive to great art; on the contrary, "what can be carried out on such directions" is purely "mechanical" and has no artistic value in itself (26). Rather than obeying external rules, "artistic production" is an inner individual freedom: a "spiritual activity" that works "from its own resources" and summons "richer content and more comprehensive individual creations" (26). Second, he also rejects Kant and Romanticism and effectively brings the imagination under the control of reason. Hegel claims that Romanticism – initiated by Goethe's and Schiller's first works – views "genius" as purely free, spontaneous and unconscious, to the exclusion of thinking, effort and historical constraints. This defective view understands genius as a "*specially gifted* spirit" giving "free play … *only* to its own particular gift", without "attention to universally valid laws" and without "conscious reflection interfering with its own instinctive-like productive activity" (26). In other words, this is a view of inspiration whose defects are: that it is blind to aspects of artistic production such as "external workmanship" and "[s]kill in technique"; and blind to "study whereby the artist brings" the spirit and the heart "into his consciousness" – "consciousness" in the actual process of artistic production is considered "superfluous" and "even deleterious" (27–8).

Hegel makes an important distinction about the object of aesthetics, giving a prominent place to human consciousness and self-consciousness, at the expense of nature. Because of the artist's consciousness, the work of art is superior to nature. While nature is "unconscious" and "far below consciousness in worth", man is "conscious and actively self-productive spirit" (30). This is another critique of Kant, who greatly favoured nature, particularly flowers, as examples of beauty. In other words, man "*duplicates* himself" in two senses. In a theoretical sense, man brings both himself and the world before him in consciousness; in a practical sense, he "deliberately alters" himself and the world, impresses on the world "the seal of his inner being" and transforms the world into an "external realization of himself" (31). Art is, in exemplary fashion, man's "self-production in external things"; it satisfies man's universal rational need to make "what is within him explicit to himself" and others and to give "outward reality" to himself (31–2). Having imbued the world with his spirit, he is no longer alienated from the world (though art achieved this to perfection in a previous age, as we'll see). Hegel's account of man's productive externalization of his essence will be radically reworked by Marx, in his *Economic and Philosophic Manuscripts*, into a distinction between *unalienated labour* and *alienated labour* under capitalism (see Chapter 5).

A further notable difference with Kant is Hegel's historical approach. For Hegel art is "bound up with the most universal views of life and the religious interests of whole epochs and peoples" (30). He gives an account of three world-historical epochs of art: the early *symbolic* art of the East; the *classical* art of ancient Greece, which Hegel considers the most perfect art; and what he calls the *romantic* art of the entire Christian era, encompassing the middle ages and the Renaissance, up to his time (not to be confused with Romanticism). Untypically for the Hegelian dialectic, the dialectical development of art shows no "progression" but is "parabolic: marked by the gradual ascent, climax and eventual descent of the representative powers of art" (Beiser 2005, 302). There is progress to ancient Greece, then decline.

In the early "*symbolic*" art of the East (ancient Egypt, India and China), claims Hegel, there is a "*mere search* for portrayal" rather than "true representation" because "the Idea" presented by art is "still in its indeterminacy and obscurity" (76). Hegel is clear that the early "symbolic" art of the East lacks the developed spirituality/rationality of modern Europeans. ("Idea" here refers to the content of Eastern art: the religions and spirit of the cultures of the ancient East.) As a result of flawed content, the expression of Eastern art is also inadequate. The very inadequacy of early art leads to progress, in that it allows consciousness to perceive, for example, "the foreignness of the Idea to natural phenomena" (76). However, the objections that power the dialectic as it evolves to the next stage will take us away from the East. After its early and unsatisfactory appearance, the East disappears from world history, as History and Spirit move Westwards, according to Hegel.

In *classical* art, by which Hegel means primarily statuary, shape – the human form – and Idea are in "free and complete harmony" (77); here the human body is spiritualized and "purified" from "the purely sensuous" and "contingent finitude"; at the same time – and this is the defect in Christian eyes – "the spirit is … determined as particular and human, not as purely absolute and eternal" (77–9). In classical art, in the "blending" of spirit and human form, spirit is not "represented in its *true nature*" – so classical art still lacks in rationality; *romantic* art turns towards this "*true* element", which is "the *inwardness of self-consciousness*" and the Christian God as absolute spirit (79–80). Hegel's understanding is explicitly Protestant, Hegel's religion. In Romantic art the Idea is conceived properly as "*inner* world" and spirit, though, due to this "higher perfection", the Idea "is not susceptible of an adequate union with the external" – art *in its sensuousness* can only point negatively to the sublimity of the inner world (80–81), the superiority of Hegel's philosophy and its own irrelevance.

Hegel's philosophical activity aims to show that history and spirit have reached a rational perfection in his time and his philosophy and is obviously incompatible with Shelley's commitment to the amelioration of social conditions. However, Hegel's philosophy was a major influence on Marx and shaped the materialist thinker's vision of history, modernity and revolution. The thinkers of modernity, responding to Hegel's emphasis on the inner world and accusation that the modern artist expresses nothing but himself, will take the exploration of interiority in new and surprising directions.

Appendix on the rise of the mass media

The role of print in early modern Europe was limited for a variety of political, legal and financial reasons. Philip Sidney (late sixteenth century) was part of an exclusive court culture and circulated his poems in manuscript within a narrow circle (see Chapter 3). The writings of Kant and Hegel were produced in the context of a university culture that had access to a limited printing industry and claimed a degree of independence from the state and state censorship (the German states that preceded the unification of Germany as a nation-state). The range of their writings appealed to a variety of audiences but were primarily addressed to the academic world. However, Britain in the eighteenth century witnessed an explosion of print culture, particularly the prominence of high-circulation commercial periodicals addressing primarily an educated middle-class audience. Broadly defined literary journalism (anonymous and eponymous reviewing of new publications, literary criticism and essays) became an increasingly prosperous if highly precarious modern profession, whose finest examples include the radical William Hazlitt (a very modern figure) and the conservative Thomas De Quincey. Publishers, editors and reviewers sought to shape their large readership into a literary audience and a literary culture, and were in turn shaped by it, fighting "cultural wars" to arbitrate and define artistic taste (Schoenfield 2009, 2). The *Gentleman's Magazine* (founded 1731) and the *Monthly Review* (1749) led the market until the end of the nineteenth century. The beginning of war with revolutionary France in 1793 led to a backlash against political radicals in the second half of the 1790s, and Coleridge (among others) was ridiculed in the periodicals. The *Edinburgh Review* (1802), dominant at the beginning of the nineteenth century, aimed at "high" (expert and disinterested) journalism and took a distance from the war, but still attacked Coleridge as a heterodox populist. The *Quarterly* (1809), also aspiring to "high" journalism, took a more patriotic stance (see Butler 2010). The war ending in 1815, the *Quarterly* led "public opinion" through a continuing period of conservative reaction, attacking the younger Romantic generation, especially Byron. Its "savage" anonymous review of Keats's *Endymion* in 1821, followed by Keats's death from tuberculosis, led Shelley to accuse the critic of murder in *Adonais*, his elegy for Keats (Shelley 2003c, 529). Keats was "pierced by the shaft which flies/In darkness" (531). Byron agrees with a few lines after "Who Killed Cock Robin": "Who kill'd John Keats?/I, says the Quarterly,/So savage and Tartarly …" (quoted Schoenfield 2009, 172). Coleridge, in *The Statesman's Manual* (1816), had already "associated the dominance of the periodical press with a disease of the body politic" (Schoenfield 2009, 239), in spite of his own significant forays in periodical publication and writing.

The Romantics might have professed indifference or hostility to the periodical industry, attempting to distance themselves from it, even, in part, leaving the country because of it. Romantic texts, nevertheless, had to negotiate their relation to modern audiences through periodicals. In the last fifteen years Andrew Bennett, Lucy Newlyn and, more recently, Andrew Franta have been addressing this relation (Franta 2007, 188–9), questioning the assumption that Romantic literary theory and practice is solely expressivist (focused on poetic self-expression) and exploring the Romantics' reception anxiety. For example, Franta argues that Shelley's "A Defence of Poetry" hesitates between two conceptions of authorship: authorship as ownership of texts, involving conscious or unconscious authorial intentionality, whose model is copyright law; and authorship as triggering unintended effects on audiences/readers, whose model is libel law. On the one hand, Shelley reads Dante and Milton as glorious "closet heretics" who intended their heresy (Franta 2007, 133). On the other hand, Shelley suggests, approvingly, that their "masking and indirect expression of their views", which remain inaccessible, enable the reader's freedom, in that they allow for diametrically opposed interpretations, which they "could not have foreseen" and "would not have endorsed" (133–4). Thus Franta suggests that Shelley is anticipating reader-response criticism, in the context of Shelley's engagement with a new culture industry. To put this recent work in context, Raymond Williams's *Culture and Society* (1958) is still the classic account of the Romantics' relation to the first mass media, arguing that Coleridge initiated a British tradition of thinking critically about culture (see Chapter 8).

Conclusion

- The empiricist Hume doubts the existence of a standard of literary greatness. The literary canon is the empirical consensus of popular opinion and expert opinion that certain authors are great.
- Burke, by contrast, believes in an autonomous rational science of criticism, superior to the aesthetic productions of the imagination and based on universal principles.
- Wollstonecraft calls for the cultivation of the seed of reason to become truly universal and include women. She questions the literary canon, showing that great literature participates in (but also resists) the oppression of women.

- Kant defines criticism as judgement without rules, based on disinterested aesthetic pleasure that is free from objective rules, conceptual content and subjective desires and interests. Aesthetic production itself is freedom from rules, at least in the creation of original aesthetic forms by the genius, and a force to heal the oppositions of the modern mind and modern society. He distinguishes between an aesthetic of the beautiful and of the sublime.
- Coleridge privileges the imagination and advocates the writer's disinterested impersonality. The unifying (*esemplastic*) power of the imagination is the healing power that art (poetry) can offer society. His "practical criticism" espouses four literary ideals, all thoroughly consistent with the imagination: unity of form, defamiliarization, universality and originality.
- Shelley views poetry (and the synthetic power of the imagination) as the exemplary medium for the radical political aims of the Enlightenment. Literature is both intuition of the eternal Truth and defamiliarization of the historical and political world, whose aim is social justice and renewal.
- Hegel's anti-Romantic aesthetics claims the irrelevance of art (including literature) in the modern world. The early art of the East, Greek classical art and the art of the Christian era expressed the spirit of their eras. However, philosophy expresses the modern world; Romantic artists express only themselves.

Further reading

In addition to the primary texts by Hume, Burke, Wollstonecraft, Kant, Coleridge, Shelley and Hegel discussed in this chapter, see the following: Horkheimer and Adorno 1998; Derrida 1978, 1982c; Eagleton 1990; Foucault 1986b, 2002; Gay 1996a, 1996b; Lyotard 1984a.

5 Modernity, multiplicity and becoming

Marx, George Eliot, Baudelaire, Arnold, Pater, Nietzsche, Wilde, Mallarmé

In the last chapter we discerned in Shelley's work a coming change of orientation, in literature and criticism, from the ideal world (a suprahistorical world of unity, harmony, immutable essences and "being") to a new world of history. In what ways was this new current of understanding articulated? How did writers and thinkers contribute to the creation of this new sense of the world, how did they respond to it? In addressing these questions we will examine Karl Marx, George Eliot, Charles Baudelaire, Matthew Arnold, Walter Pater, Friedrich Nietzsche, Oscar Wilde and Stéphane Mallarmé, and discuss in relation to them these key themes and ideas: modernity; multiplicity and becoming; conflict; the city and the streets; realism and Aestheticism.

A new critical question is being posed, that of the relation between literary text and historical context. This question arose in the nineteenth century with such urgency because of the new volatility of modernity: the nineteenth century is the century of history as rapid change, releasing a multiplicity of displaced and unstable groups and subjectivities in flux. Understanding and responding to this jolt to thought, in a time of unprecedented upheaval, became a major ask – arguably *the* task – for the literature and criticism of the period, for nineteenth-century realism as well as for Aestheticism and modernism.

Karl Marx and George Eliot: revolution and reform

For Karl Marx (1818–83) modernity emerges out of a new economic system: capitalism. In *The Communist Manifesto*, co-written with Friedrich Engels in 1848 – a year of revolution throughout Europe – Marx both celebrates and condemns capitalism. Capitalism is the best and the worst that could happen to us. What Marx and Engels embrace and find revolutionary in capitalism is that it is a force of rapid and unceasing change, sweeping away old powers and authorities. "All that is solid melts into air," they famously announce, echoing Shakespeare (Marx and Engels 1985, 83). They liken capitalism to Prometheus, who disobeyed the father of the gods, Zeus, to bring fire to men.

What they condemn in capitalism in 1848 is what we saw Shelley condemning in 1821: the gap between rich and poor. Marx and Engels, born into the affluent bourgeoisie (in 1818 and 1820, respectively), noting the appalling rates of infant mortality among the working class, comment that the bourgeoisie might have been a revolutionary class before the French Revolution but it is now so callous and stupid as to fail to look after the perpetuation of the workforce on which it relies for its profits.

The Industrial Revolution progressed most rapidly in England, producing new industrial centres such as Manchester, where Engels was sent as a young man by his industrialist father. But rather than observing the newest methods of industrial production, as his father had intended, from 1842 to 1844 Engels conducted a sociological study of the Manchester working class, detailing their shocking and life-threatening working and living conditions in *The Condition of the Working Class in England* (first published in German in 1845).

In *A New View of Society* (1813–16) the industrialist Robert Owen gave an account of his experiment with a more humane form of industrial production in New Lanark Mills in Scotland: he writes, to discover a remedy to current industrial conditions and "try its efficacy in practice, have been the employments of my life ... I am now anxious you should all partake of its benefits". Owen calls for legislative reform of industrial conditions as a high priority for the British public: "your primary and most essential interests are deeply involved". A pioneering Christian socialist, Owen argues that looking after workers is in everyone's interest, and just as rational and profitable as looking after the industrial machinery. In relation to "living mechanism" (workers), "it would ... prove true economy to keep it neat and clean; to treat it with kindness" in order to avoid "irritating friction"; and "supply it regularly with a sufficient quantity of wholesome food and other necessaries of life, that the body might be preserved in good working condition, and prevented from being out of repair, or falling prematurely to decay" (Owen 1813–16 throughout).

While Owen was proposing reform from above, an array of independent working-class protest movements, under the umbrella term "Chartism", emerged in England in the 1830s and the "hungry" 1840s (a period of economic depression affecting especially textile workers). Thomas Carlyle, one of the great Victorian "sages", addressed what he called the "ominous matter" of "the condition and disposition of the Working Classes" in his pamphlet, *Chartism* (Carlyle 1840, 1). In Chapter VI, "Laissez-Faire", Carlyle argues that the dire conditions and growing anger of the working classes require reform and guidance, and rejects *laissez-faire* principles (of non-interference with the laws of the market). In *Past and Present* (1843), Carlyle outlines a paternalistic and neofeudal model of reform from above. Another eminent Victorian and critic of industrial capitalism was the art critic and thinker John Ruskin, who developed his highly critical view of capitalism and its degradation of people, built environment and landscape in *Unto This Last* (1862), arguing a moral case for a living wage. Very contentious when it was first published, *Unto This Last* exercised a long-lasting influence, not least on Mahatma Gandhi. Responding to Ruskin, William Morris founded the Arts and Crafts movement in the 1860s, an anti-industrial applied-arts and design movement valorizing traditional materials and craftsmanship, as part of a larger focus on social and economic reform. In the 1880s, influenced by Marx, William Morris developed his own version of *fin-de-siècle* socialism, as seen in his numerous political speeches and literary writings such as the novel *News from Nowhere* (1890).

George Eliot's (1819–80) theoretical elaboration of nineteenth-century literary "realism" – or "classic realism", as critics now call it – has to be understood in this context. Viewed as the exemplary nineteenth-century moral realist, Eliot outlines her developing understanding of realism in the essay "The Natural History of German Life" (1856) and in Chapter 17 of *Adam Bede* (1859). In this chapter, entitled "In Which the Story Pauses a Little", George Eliot posits "truthfulness" and "sympathy" as the twin aims of her art: both truthfulness and sympathy are required, and they have to come together. (In the novel, Adam Bede's gaze is at first "keen" [Eliot 1996, 6], intelligently observant, but lacks sympathy.) Truthfulness, as she makes clear here, has a complex meaning for her. We can disentangle at least five different threads.

- First, it involves close observation of external reality and detailed description of it. Eliot likens her art to life-drawing. (Coleridge would have disapproved, see Chapter 4.)
- Second, truthfulness aspires to democratic inclusiveness. Eliot's field of vision was wide enough to take in people with "work-worn hands" (178) – lowly and previously neglected and misunderstood social groups. The main protagonists of *Adam Bede* are a carpenter, Adam; a cotton-mill hand, Dinah; and the poor dependant of a tenant farmer, Hetty.
- Third, it involves observation and description of the *complexity* of internal reality, the *complexity* of character. Real people are "inconsistent" (176). The good and the bad are "entangled" within them (176).
- Fourth, truthfulness involves a sense of moral seriousness and responsibility: "I feel as much bound to tell you, as precisely as I can, what that reflection [of men and things in my mind] is, as if I were in the witness-box narrating my experience on oath" (175).
- Fifth, it involves an anxious recognition of difficulties. Literature as life-drawing is risky: instead of drawing an imaginary "griffin", Eliot has the challenging task of drawing a living "lion" (177). One of the difficulties in

this is that the author is a mirror, but "the mirror is doubtless defective" (175) (just like the mirror in Hetty's room). Why is the mirror defective? Eliot explains in "The Natural History of German Life": in a divided society such as Eliot's own, one has to summon formidable powers of observation and social sympathy in order to avoid unwittingly projecting the perspective of one's own social group onto others. Another difficulty has to do with the nature of the novelist's medium, language: "one word stands for many things, and many words for one thing; the subtle shades of meaning, and still subtler echoes of association, make language an instrument which scarcely anything short of genius can yield with definiteness and certainty" (Eliot 1990, 128). Eliot, however, embraces the "fitful shimmer of many-hued significance" and rejects "a patent deodorized and nonresonant language" (128). This is confirmed in the figurative language of Chapter 17, where Eliot is a trial witness in a courtroom one moment and drawing lions the next.

- While affirming *truthfulness* in all the above senses in this chapter, Eliot self-consciously examines its limits elsewhere in *Adam Bede*. For example, she explores the limits of observation. In spite of Adam's intelligence and keen eye, he repeatedly misreads Hetty's and Dinah's signs.

Eliot's ideals of truthfulness and social sympathy highlight the complex net of continuities and discontinuities connecting her to the eighteenth-century realist novel, Romanticism and Charles Dickens. While the eighteenth-century realist novel, for example Fielding's *Tom Jones* (1749), already displays observation, attention to the present and recent past, common people, complex individualized characters (as Ian Watt argues), it treats the lives of common people comically or as light entertainment, following an age-old tradition in literature (as Auerbach argues in *Mimesis*). Eliot inherits from Wordsworth the *serious* treatment of – and sympathy for – "low and rustic life", as announced in his 1800 Preface to *Lyrical Ballads* (Wordsworth 2012, 507), while she inherits social "sympathy" from Shelley (as discussed in the last chapter). However, Eliot's anxious sense of obstacles to sympathy – and her self-conscious exploration of the limits of truthfulness and sympathy – are arguably new. Finally, despite striking differences in style from Dickens, her great contemporary, Eliot shares with him a reforming spirit. For example, in his postscript to *Our Mutual Friend* Dickens positions his novel in relation to his severe criticisms of the Poor Law – fed by the ideology of the undeserving poor – and the "shameful cases of disease and death from destitution" to which it has led (Dickens 1997, 799), highlighted in the novel through the destitute but very deserving Betty Higden. Both novelists attempt to avoid idealizations and demonizations: the moral and psychological simplification of characters into stereotypes of goodness and badness. In his preface to *Oliver Twist* Dickens rejects "Romance" – idealizations and flights from reality – for the "stern truth" (Dickens 1949, ix): "I had read of thieves by scores … But I had never met (except in Hogarth) with the miserable reality ... It appeared to me that ... to show them as they really were ... would be to attempt a something which was needed, and which would be a service to society. And I did it as I best could" (vii). (Dickens's style, unlike Eliot's, shares with Hogarth truthfulness through exaggerated description.) The novels of Dickens and Eliot also share an elastic form. Their realism includes "the romantic side of familiar things", as Dickens writes in his preface to *Bleak House* (Dickens 1894, vii). It includes the imagination. It thrives on metaphor and metonymy, as J. Hillis Miller argues. It recognizes conflicts of perspective among and within characters – or shifting perspectives, as George Levine argues, or "heteroglossia" and "dialogism", as Bakhtin argues (Bakhtin 1981b; see Chapter 7). But they work to avoid falsity and the dogmatic imposition of empty formulae on life, as Eliot makes clear in Chapter 17 and as Dickens insists in *Hard Times.* However, from Dickens to Eliot there is an increased attention to psychological realism, as Eliot herself argues in her critique of Dickens in "The Natural History of German Life" (111); in her view Dickens had not, up to that point (1856), avoided idealizations and demonizations.

Looking ahead, the study of literary characters' subjectivity, passions and impressions, initiated by Romanticism, will be further intensified in Thomas Hardy and Henry James (as they argue themselves), partly in response to the Aestheticism of Walter Pater and others. Leo Bersani has argued that there is an assumption of the unity of the self underlying the complexity of characters in nineteenth-century realism. My argument is that, in the transition from Romanticism to Aestheticism, the Romantic unity of the self (discussed in the previous chapter) gives way to multiplicity. At the same time, from Eliot to Hardy and Henry James, an important shift in narrative voice is discernible. In Chapter 17 of *Adam Bede* Eliot uses an authorial persona addressing the reader directly. (That the author addressing us here is a fictive George Eliot is made clear when she meets Adam Bede in his old age.) This authorial persona makes its presence felt throughout the novel: it tells us the story and is passionately engaged in the telling. As an omniscient third-person narrator, it conveys the perspectives of many characters, but also stands above them and guides our interpretations. This narrator is Eliot's *attempt* at an ideal synthesis of the characters' conflicting perspectives and the perfect combination of truthfulness and sympathy. For example, the narrator's view of Hetty attempts to mediate Mrs Poyser's keen but unsympathetic view of her and Dinah's overly sympathetic one. Later in the century, in Gustave Flaubert and partly in response to Flaubert, this Shelley-inspired synthetic labour is abandoned as impossible or undesirable. The narrator becomes impartial and ironizing. We are shown a fictional reality and invited to draw our own conclusions. (See also Jean-Paul Sartre on Flaubert, Chapter 10.)

While Eliot attempts to write from a perspective ideally synthesizing a variety of individual and group perspectives, this synthesis is grounded in serious study of social context in its historical development. This new emphasis is fed by her interest in the new science of sociology, pioneered in France by Auguste Comte (1798–1857); it then receives a new impetus with the epoch-making publication of Charles Darwin's *The Origin of Species* in 1859. Environment is crucially important in Darwin's theory of evolution, and receives heightened attention in literature following publication of his revolutionary book.

Eliot's humble provincial origins and off-centre commitments – for example, her sympathetic account of low, marginal, disenfranchised and endangered cultures, such as Dinah's Methodism and Mrs Poyser's local oral linguistic creativity – make her an important precursor for a long line of regional novelists, including Thomas Hardy and D. H. Lawrence. Their texts broach the fraught interaction (both external and within the self) between a dominant national culture or perspective and a socially marginalized one. Today the conflict between colonizer and colonized cultures continues to be a vital theme in postcolonial writing, for example in Tsitsi Damgarembga's *Nervous Conditions* (1988). In her 1919 article, "George Eliot", Virginia Woolf defends Eliot vigorously against the late-Victorian devaluation that she suffered. Sketching Eliot's "very humble foundation" as "the granddaughter of a carpenter" (Woolf 2003, 164), she reminds us of Eliot's own sense that "by becoming a blue-stocking she was forfeiting her brother's respect" (165). Woolf concludes the essay with an affirmation of Eliot's bi-cultural orientation, combing high and low cultural perspectives:

> she must reach … and pluck for herself the strange bright fruits of art and knowledge. Clasping them as few women have ever clasped them, she would not renounce her own inheritance – the difference of view, the difference of standard.
>
> (171)

In assessing the merits of Eliot's literary form, Woolf's enthusiasm for Eliot is a reminder to us to avoid too sharp a contrast between nineteenth-century realism and twentieth-century avant-garde literature. Lyotard's distinction between realism and postmodernism, discussed in the previous chapter, is an example of the overly quick dismissal of realism. Lyotard defines realism as the docile following of existing aesthetic rules; postmodernism as the creation of new rules (Lyotard 1984b). (Lyotard himself is probably following the polemically anti-representational and anti-realist ethos of the French *nouveau roman* and of modernist experimentation more broadly.) Eliot attempts a new novel and explicitly sets out to replace the familiar conventional idealizations or demonizations of lowly groups in literature with realist sympathy. However, in assessing Eliot's reforming vision, some (Marxist, feminist, etc.) critics argue that it lacks political boldness.

The most influential of the more radical writers contemporary with Eliot was, of course, Marx. His materialist vision of revolution and *unalienated labour* emerges out of his early philosophical work in *Economic and Philosophical Manuscripts* of 1844, heavily critical but simultaneously heavily indebted to the idealist philosophy of Hegel (see Chapter 4). For Hegel thought is driven by conflict – the antagonism of the dialectic – from its initial experience of raw sense data towards the ultimate end of Absolute Knowledge. Every thesis, every hypothesis about the nature of the truth, is countered by another idea: the antithesis. But the antithesis is not just a contradiction of the thesis, rather it supplies a part of the truth that the thesis lacked. The initial conflict of thesis and antithesis therefore turns into their combination: the synthesis. In this way thought develops ever onwards towards the ultimate completeness of Absolute Knowledge. Hegel claims that his dialectic is necessary and inevitable, every lacking thesis inevitably causing the antithesis to arise in order to complete it. It is enormously significant that Hegel sees history itself as embodying this unfolding of thought towards completeness, with different stages of history, different cultures and ideologies, as stages in the development of the truth towards final completeness. What we therefore have in Hegel is a thoroughgoing vision of history as a necessary rational development towards an ultimate goal: the realization of Absolute Knowledge, which will also be the realization of the perfect society.

Marx felt that Hegel had discovered the truth or rather the *image* of the truth. Hegel believed in the priority of the mind and of the mysterious rational force of Spirit. This was where he had gone wrong. Hegel's "greatness" lies in understanding man "as the result of his own labour" (Marx 1977c, 101), but it is not the labour of Spirit and thought that drives history, but material economic life. Just as Spirit's necessary unfolding determined history for Hegel, so for Marx the inevitable development of the economic base of society explained history and was also the explanation of every aspect of human life, including higher culture, literature and the arts. For Marx too history would inevitably culminate in the realization of the perfect society. Capitalism's degradation of the workers would finally cause them to rise up. The Revolution would seep away capitalism, private property, all the institutions, every aspect of that rotten and corrupt world. In its place there would arise the new and perfect society, the final synthesis: communism.

In *Economic and Philosophical Manuscripts* Marx distinguishes between *alienated labour* under capitalism, where the worker is separated from the fruits (products and profits) of his labour, which belong to the capitalist, and "degraded to the most miserable sort of commodity" (Marx 1977c, 77) and *unalienated labour*, the returning of the workers' human productive or transformative potential, to be brought about by the revolutionary overthrow of capitalism. In *Capital* Marx describes capitalism as an inverted and alienated world. While Hegel and Marx have revealed that the "products of labour" are nothing but "material expressions of the human labour spent in their production" (Marx 1977b, 438), capitalism enslaves human productivity in the service of capital and commodities. Capitalist methods of production "mutilate the labourer into a fragment of a man, degrade him to the level of an appendage to a machine" and "drag his wife and child beneath the wheels of the Juggernaut of capital" (Marx 1977b, 482–3). While objectifying and commodifying humans, capitalism fetishizes commodities (Marx 1977b, 435ff.) and glorifies or idealizes capital, which "becomes a quite mysterious being" and "appears … as productive" (Marx 1977b, 516).

Unalienated labour, for Marx, is what labour should be, with the worker once again feeling that he or she vitally expresses themselves in their work, and through it materially and spiritually making the world a place in which they feel that they belong. One can see that it is very difficult to reconcile industrial work with such a vision, which seems to see labour strongly in artisanal and crafts-like terms. Many other Victorian critics of capitalism, such as Ruskin and Morris, share a similar vision of material labour as applied art. Marx, however, felt that he had a great advantage over other critics of nineteenth-century capitalism and industrialism. Carlyle, Ruskin and others had no theory of history; or if they did they did not have the true and fully worked-out theory of history. All they could do was to attempt to convince people that society must change. For Marx such critics were "idealist", in the philosophical sense that they did not accept the truth of materialist economic history. They were mere utopians, dreamers, whereas Marx believed he had discovered in class conflict the key to history. Marxism thus had a clear practical task, to aid the workers in the coming of the Revolution. (We will be discussing versions of Marxist literary criticism in all subsequent chapters.)

This quick sketch of Marx's Hegel-inspired theory of history highlights the limits of Eliot's radicalism. Eliot's early realism works mostly at the level of individual sympathies, rather than abstract historical thought. Her later work aims to meld realist fiction with the attempt to understand large-scale historical processes. (See, for example, her historical novel *Romola* [1862–3] on Renaissance Florence.) Politically, Eliot is a liberal progressivist, while Marx espouses revolution, but both desire to immerse themselves in the concrete and the historical. Marx, Eliot and other nineteenth-century figures fix their attention on historical humanity. Marx pays attention to the emergent, metropolitan, industrial working class, calling for revolution; Eliot to the residual, provincial, rural poor of the recent past, calling for reform. But what about the slaves and the colonized? The Indian Mutiny of 1857 forced the world's attention. In the US the abolitionist movement gathered momentum and slavery was abolished after the Civil War in 1863. In Jamaica in 1865 the Morant Bay Rebellion – a black rebellion triggered by worsening economic conditions and continuing disenfranchisement for the great majority of former slaves – was brutally suppressed by the British Governor, Edward Eyre. The atrocities divided British metropolitan men of letters: John Stuart Mill, Charles Darwin, Thomas Huxley, Herbert Spencer and others sought Eyre's prosecution; Thomas Carlyle, Charles Dickens, Charles Kingsley, John Ruskin, Alfred Lord Tennyson defended him. Patrick Brantlinger, in *Rule of Darkness: British Literature and Imperialism, 1830–1914*, offers an influential account of the engagement of British literary texts with British colonialism and imperialism.

Baudelaire's *modernité*, Arnold's "culture", Nietzsche's multiperspectivism

The Parisian poet Charles Baudelaire (1821–67), contemporary of Marx and George Eliot, coins the term *modernité* (modernity) in "The Painter of Modern Life". In this essay, written between November 1859 and February 1860 and published in 1863, Baudelaire looks at modern life as a life of speed, a life where the fleeting and the ephemeral rule. In this ever-changing context, the figure of the artist is very close to the *flâneur* – the man about town strolling aimlessly along the new giant boulevards of Paris, which were being built by Haussmann from *c.* 1853 as part of his modernization plan for the capital – as the *flâneur* is able to capture the fleeting, which is the proper subject of modern art. Back in his attic room, the speed of the fleeting impression "imposes upon the artist an equal speed of execution" (Baudelaire 1992, 394), and the sketches fly from his pen as he works at his table. Baudelaire continues, in a section entitled "Modernity": the artist, "this solitary mortal endowed with an active imagination, always roaming the great desert of men, has a nobler aim than the pure idler [the *flâneur*] … He is looking for that indefinable something we may be allowed to call 'modernity', for want of a better term to express the idea in question. The aim for him is … to distil the eternal from the transitory" (402). What is important to note here is that Baudelaire is not proposing an escape from the fleeting: the eternal is to be sought in the transitory, not away from it.

Baudelaire's view of the modern artist implies a critique of Romanticism and Romantic idealism, and more generally a critique of the (Neo)Platonism that dominated the history of literary criticism (see Chapters 1–4). Baudelaire returns to this theme in his 1865 post-Romantic prose poem on the poet's fall into his new life, "Loss of a Halo" ("Perte d'Auréole"), in *Paris Spleen* (*Le Spleen de Paris*), a collection published posthumously in 1869. The poet, traditionally the Parnassian "ambrosia eater" and "drinker of quintessences", finds himself in the streets. The poet recounts: "as I was crossing the boulevard in a great hurry … my halo slipped off my head and fell into the mire". The poet declares this fall from the Ideal to the real world to be a fortunate one, from innocence into experience: "I am bored with dignity"; "I can now … be as low as I please and indulge in debauch like ordinary mortals. So here I am … exactly like yourself" (Baudelaire 1970, 94). Walter Benjamin turns to this hitherto neglected prose poem in the last section of his essay, "On Some Motifs in Baudelaire", quoting it in its entirety. Benjamin's comment – "Of all the experiences which made his life what it was, Baudelaire singled out his having been jostled by the crowd as the decisive, unique experience" (Benjamin 1992b, 189) – is a reminder of Baudelaire's participation in the Revolution of 1848 (one of a number in Europe in that year).

While Baudelaire valorizes the poet's descent into the historical world, Matthew Arnold (1822–88), Baudelaire's British contemporary, on the contrary, outlines in his *Culture and Anarchy* (1869) a literature and criticism once again "above" social conflict and strife, as the solution to social conflict. Arnold was born a member of the affluent and highly educated stratum of the Victorian middle classes and retained this privileged position and insider status throughout his life. He was, at the same time, one of Victorian England's sharpest critics. In *Culture and Anarchy* Arnold fails to be remotely impressed by the condition of English culture. In response to the Victorians' optimism, single-minded pursuit of practical goals and moral zeal for a variety of issues, he diagnoses "the diseased spirit of our time" (Arnold 1993b, 152). The "disease" Arnold identifies is the social multiperspectivism of Victorian England. For Arnold, Victorian society has become deeply divided into three social classes that have developed antagonistic social perspectives. The social classes Arnold calls: the Barbarians (the aristocracy); the Philistines (the middle classes); the Populace (the working classes, in whom Arnold seems to have a limited interest). As each class has its own virtues and defects and, most importantly, as each class now sees things from the point of view of its own prejudices and interests, society is ailing, due to the absence of common ground, shared values and a shared sense of identity.

Arnold's antidote to this "disease" is "culture". In order to understand what he means by culture, we will begin by trying to clarify the main conceptual distinction on which his analysis rests. Arnold identifies two great tendencies in the life of humanity: Hellenism and Hebraism. Hebraism is his name for the attitude supporting the perceived sectarianism of Victorian society; Hellenism, his name for the path to culture. He defines them as follows: "The governing idea of Hellenism is *spontaneity of consciousness*; that of Hebraism, *strictness of conscience*" (128). The latter is "the staunch adherence to some fixed law of doing" (138); the former "tends continually to enlarge our whole law of doing" (149). In Arnold's view, in Victorian England there is too much Hebraism, "strictness of conscience", in the sense of there being an excess of moral feeling invested in the blind overactive pursuit of unexamined aims that tend to coincide with one's class interests.

Arnold places himself and his reader in the position of a new Socrates: "in his own breast does not every man carry about with him a possible Socrates" (186)? Like Socrates, the implacable interrogator of *doxa* (unexamined belief), Arnold attacks repeatedly the "blind following of certain stock notions as infallible" (177), reliance on one's "habits and interests" (162) and the "staunch mechanical pursuit of a fixed object" (172) – all of which he summarizes as the triumph of "machinery" over real thought. Two of the examples Arnold gives of *doxa* or excessive Hebraism are the Victorian middle-class obsessions with free trade and with very large families, both of which they pursue relentlessly and with great moral fervour. It might be fair to say that Arnold does not object to multiperspectivism per se; he objects to perspectives that become rigid, dogmatic and incapable of admixture and dialogue. I will return to this issue in my closing remarks on Arnold.

Hellenism, on the other hand, finds a place for the critical spirit of Socrates as one of its elements. It also involves harmonious development and temperance, or as Arnold calls it "*sweetness and light*" (66). Hellenism cultivates "a human nature complete on all its sides" (69): Hellenism is multifaceted and promises harmonious relations between the different parts. As to its "spontaneity of consciousness", this is a "free inward play of thought" (191), a "[f]ree disinterested play of thought" (162), a "stream of fresh thought" (151). (The language is reminiscent of Kant on the aesthetic, see Chapter 4.) Spontaneity of consciousness is aided by engagement with "the best that can at present be known in the world" (151). This is an open-ended process, in at least two senses. First, it's a never-ending striving, "a growing and a becoming" (62). Second, as Arnold himself practises it in *Culture and Anarchy*, it is non-systematic: he insists that he is "a man without a philosophy … a plain, unsystematic writer" (102). This open-ended way of looking at things (and English distrust of over-systematism or excessive rationalism) is, for Arnold, and this is an important point, "seeing things as they are".

Hellenism allows a transition, within anyone, from one's habitual and partial perspective to "culture", as Arnold understands it: "in each class there are born a certain number of natures with a curiosity about their best self, with a bent for seeing things as they are, for disentangling themselves from machinery" (109). Arnold's view of culture is ostensibly quite inclusive. Culture, he points out, is usually understood and used as "an engine of social and class distinction" (58). Culture à la Arnold, on the other hand, is primarily self-culture – "the development of [our] best self" (166) – and is open to everyone, for the benefit of all. And, importantly, it is secular. This is then Arnold's full definition:

> [Culture] is not satisfied till we *all* come to a perfect man … It seeks to do away with classes; to make the best that has been thought and known in the world current everywhere; to make all men live in an atmosphere of sweetness and light, where they may use ideas … freely, – nourished, and not bound by them.
>
> (78–9)

Arnold reaffirms the Enlightenment's emphasis on the critical spirit of ancient Greece, the spirit of Socrates, and on the value of an examined and reflective life, as a private but generalizable exercise contributing to social harmony. This private exercise is aided by familiarity with a canon, a body of writings that is "the best that has been thought and known in the world". Arnold doesn't see any problems in deciding upon what should be included and what should be excluded from such a canon (though the canon as he sees it is broader than sometimes represented, including, for example, the best of scientific writing). The combined effect of familiarity with the books of the canon and the open-minded free play of thought is proposed as the formula for a renewed social harmony and unity.

Culture, criticism and the canon are arguably Arnold's escape route from the rapid change and the becoming and multiplicity of modernity. (For

Nietzscshe on being and becoming, see Chapter 1.) Arnold might to an extent be willing to acknowledge them in external reality and in "all the multitudinous, turbulent, and blind impulses of our ordinary selves" (166–7) – indeed Arnold's free thought is a form of becoming. However, to show the viability of harmony, he has to move, at some point, away from the world of becoming in order to assume one world of being and stable essences: "our best self ... is not manifold ... and unstable ... and ever-varying, but one ... and the same for all mankind" (181). Arnold seems to assume that if two people think freely, they will see things in ways that are compatible rather than incompatible and antagonistic.

In "The Function of Criticism at the Present Time" (1864, 1875) Arnold substantially reiterates the value of the canon and of disinterested criticism. Arnold's contemporary, Flaubert, on the other hand, introduces formal innovations into his writing that question the value of the canon. Flaubert was simultaneously a realist and a "martyr of literary style" (Pater 1904, 27) who anticipated Aestheticism. The reader-response critic Hans Robert Jauss, in "Literary History as a Challenge to Literary Theory" (1969, 1970), describes Flaubert's *Madame Bovary* (1857) – particularly Flaubert's "formal innovation ... of 'impersonal narration'" – as a radical break with its contemporary readers' "canon of expectations" (hence the novel's initial lack of success), before its eventual incorporation into revised expectations (Jauss 1982, 27–8). Flaubert's comic masterpiece *Bouvard et Pécuchet*, published posthumously in 1881, describes the attempts of its eponymous heroes, two retired clerks, to find any sense of truth or coherence amidst the burgeoning knowledge of the nineteenth-century arts and sciences. Their experience of the period they spend studying literature and aesthetics in order to settle such questions as the true nature of the standard of taste results in them concluding, in the words of the narrator, that "the opinion of professionals was misleading and the judgement of the crowd was not to be trusted" (Flaubert 2005, 126).

While Arnold resists the idea of culture as a site of conflict, Friedrich Nietzsche and Walter Pater outline and embrace the fluidity and multiplicity of the modern world and the modern self. Nietzsche (1844–1900), the son of a Lutheran minister, lost his religious faith when he was 13 years old. His entire philosophical project can be described as an indefatigable effort to move Western thought away from the eternal and towards the temporal and historical. To put this in the language of philosophy, Nietzsche's thought attempts to move away from being towards becoming. The enemy is idealism as the belief in an eternal and immutable world that is the True and the Real world, not the mundane world we inhabit. Nietzsche's two great examples, and targets, are Plato's ideal world of Forms and Christianity's belief in an afterlife and the world to come. Unlike Marx and Baudelaire, Nietzsche does not see a link between his philosophy of becoming and certain aspects or tendencies in modern life; rather he stridently condemns modern life and seems to see modern society and the modern individual as everything he despises, the "weak" and "slavish" product of two millennia of Platonism and

Christianity. He sees his philosophy as an untimely philosophy of the future, speaking to those yet unborn.

In one of the most famous passages in philosophy, Nietzsche announces that "God is dead" (section 125 of *The Gay Science* [1882, 1887]; Nietzsche 1974, 181). What Nietzsche's announcement means is that there is no *one* Truth as to the nature of life – no Platonic ideal world of Forms (or being) – or as to how one should or should not live. Nietzsche's next step is to embrace multiperspectivism. In 1887 Nietzsche publishes *On the Genealogy of Morality*:

> There is *only* a perspective seeing, *only* a perspective "knowing"; and the *more* affects we allow to speak about one thing, the *more* eyes, different eyes, we can use to observe one thing, the more complete will our "concept" of this thing, our "objectivity," be.
>
> (Nietzsche 1989, 119)

If external reality, for Nietzsche, is becoming without being, or change and multiplicity without an underlying essence, so is internal reality a reality of becoming without being. He argues that the idea of the self has also been conceived in Platonic terms as, at heart, a stable and unified being. Christianity backed this up with the idea of the soul. With God and Plato gone, the human self also becomes a site of change and multiplicity without an underlying essence or stable core; we call this position (perhaps misleadingly) "anti-humanism". In his intellectual autobiography, *Ecce Homo* (1888), Nietzsche describes his internal reality thus:

> I shall … say a general word on my *art of style.* To *communicate* a state, an inner tension of pathos through signs, including the tempo of these signs – that is the meaning of every style; and considering that the multiplicity of inner states is in my case extraordinary, there exists in my case the possibility of many styles.
>
> (Nietzsche 1992, 44)

Nietzsche's influential theory of history is a rejection of at least three major philosophies of history. First, Nietzsche rejects the idea of history as *what really happened*. The first historian, in our sense of the word, is the ancient Greek historian Thucydides. The Athenian Thucydides (fifth century BC) distinguished between the *Histories* of his predecessor, Herodotus, containing entertaining and interesting, wonderful, but not necessarily true stories, and his own *The Pelopponesian War*, documenting the 30-year war between Athens and Sparta, as a laborious scientific project involving a meticulous search for facts. Second, Nietzsche rejects history as *origin*. This is the Christian view of history, as in the opening lines of the Gospel According to St John, "In the beginning was the word [*logos* in the Greek text], and the Word was with God, and the Word was God … All things were made by him; and without him was not any thing made that was made" (Bates n.d., 1007). The origin of history is God, history is the unfolding of God's cosmological plan, the Word of God contains within it a potential that is being fulfilled in history. History is a gradually drawn full circle: its end returns us back to its beginning, in that it is the completion, the full actualization of the Word of God. Following Nietzsche's rejection of origin, Roland Barthes in "The Death of the Author" argues that literary criticism has inherited this idea of origin in treating the author as the origin of the text and in having recourse to the author's intention in order to elucidate it. (See the poststructuralist turn to Nietzsche in the 1960s, discussed in Chapter 11.) Barthes rejects this literary reincarnation of God as origin. In this he is part of the general poststructuralist critique of origin. Derrida famously calls what he considers to be the Western emphasis on *logos* – the idea of a spiritual or metaphysical truth that is embodied in things, and which includes as a major instance the Word of God as origin – *logocentrism*, and he tries to expose it in its complex ramifications throughout thought and language.

Third, Nietzsche rejects history as *progress*. This is the Enlightenment view of history: history as a line, and in particular as an ascending line – this is the optimistic view of history. The history of humanity is the history of the progressive cultivation of the seed of reason, which is going to liberate us from superstition and political despotism and bring about enlightenment and democratization or "*liberté, egalité, fraternité*". As we saw, Hegel and Marx are the inheritors of – and two of the strongest believers in – history as rational and morally progressive. However, the Enlightenment placed the peoples of the world on different stages of the progressive line of history. Western Europe, which had its Scientific Revolution with Newton and others in the seventeenth century, was naturally seen as the vanguard of Reason and Progress, while the slaves, the colonized and those living in tribes rather than nation-states were seen as backward, or worse than backward, beyond the light of Reason in a darkness without History. After World War I, when Europe dragged the whole continent, and other parts of the world, into four years of appalling carnage, in which it was rather difficult to discern the light of Reason, Europeans found themselves less confident about the link between Europe, science and technology and progress. To return to Nietzsche, his rejection of history as *progress* includes rejection of history as having a rational and morally progressive *dialectical logic* of thesis, antithesis and synthesis, the Hegelian and Marxian view of history. (In Marxism the Hegelian-Marxist view of history is called *historical materialism*. For example, Fredric Jameson's *Late Marxism: Adorno, or, The Persistence of the Dialectic* [1990] discusses Adorno's historical materialism.)

In *On the Genealogy of Morals* (1887), Nietzsche rejects quite decisively all the above views of history. He argues that history has no logic, being governed by struggle and chance, not an underlying rationality; history is not a line, it is discontinuous; it does not progress, instead it is a discontinuous succession of struggles and dominations; it has no origin, in the sense of a seed containing within it all future development, instead it is steered in a new and temporary direction at every point, reappropriated and redefined anew at every point. Historical texts give us not fact but interpretations, as the historian himself struggles to re-appropriate and redefine history, being part of the forces struggling in history. Nietzsche rails against those historians (of course, most of them) who claim to be objective, calling them "lascivious historical ... eunuchs" and "rotten armchairs" (1989, 158). Nietzsche's views are so at variance with the historiography of his time that a word other than "history" is required, and he chooses the word "genealogy" for the new historical vision and writing he proposes. In examining the genealogy of an institution – such as the institution of punishment or the institution of literature – instead of seeking its origins, Nietzsche seeks to describe the struggles constantly redefining the institution and its ends:

> [W]hatever exists, having somehow come into being, is again and again reinterpreted to new ends, taken over, transformed ... by some power superior to it ... [A]ll subduing and becoming master involves a fresh interpretation, an adaptation through which any previous "meaning" and "purpose" are necessarily obscured or even obliterated ... [T]he entire history of a "thing" ... can in this way be a continuous sign-chain of ever new interpretations and adaptations whose causes do not even have to be related to one another but, on the contrary, in some cases succeed and alternate with one another in a purely chance fashion.
>
> (77)

For example Nietzsche conveys just how discontinuous, "how supplemental, how accidental the meaning of 'punishment' is" and sketches out the genealogy of the institution of punishment at different historical moments: "Punishment as a means of rendering harmless ... Punishment as recompense to the injured party ... Punishment as the isolation of a disturbance of equilibrium ... Punishment as a means of inspiring fear of those who determine and execute the punishment ... Punishment as a festival, namely as the rape and mockery of a finally defeated enemy ..." (80). Nietzsche's list takes up an entire page. (Obviously the chief target here is the "civilized" idea of punishment as the moral correction of the offender.) If this is the genealogical sketch of the institution of punishment, what would be the genealogical account of the institution of literature? Nietzsche's *On the Genealogy of Morals* is a major influence on Michel Foucault's view of history and genealogical method (for further discussion, see Chapter 11).

Late Victorian Aestheticism and Mallarmé

In 1873 Walter Pater (1839–94), a central figure in the Victorian Aestheticist movement – a movement emphasizing aesthetic form, critiquing conventional morality and valorizing multiplicity and becoming – anticipates Nietzsche in some respects, though Nietzsche would not have had much time for Pater and would have considered him decadent (as he certainly considered French contemporary writers). Pater begins his notoriously controversial conclusion to *Studies in the History of the Renaissance* (now known as *The Renaissance: Studies in Art and Poetry*) with an untranslated epigraph from Heraclitus, the one philosopher of becoming ancient Greece did produce (and much admired by Nietzsche): "πάντα χωρεῖ καὶ οὐδέν μένει" (everything is in motion and nothing at rest), which Pater translates in *Plato and Platonism* as "All things give way: nothing remaineth" (Pater 1909, 7). Oscar Wilde will later tell W. B. Yeats that Pater's *Renaissance* is his "golden book" (Yeats 2001, 455) and will describe Pater in "The Critic as Artist" as "the most perfect master of English prose now creating among us" (Wilde 1961, 50).

Pater begins the conclusion by stating: "To regard all things and principles of things as inconstant modes of fashions has more and more become the tendency of modern thought" (Pater 1986, 150). He then captures very quickly his own sense of modernity: "This at least of flame-like our life has, that it is the concurrence, renewed from moment to moment, of forces parting sooner or later on their ways" (150). We find this volatile situation intensified when we observe internal reality, the self. Pater writes, anticipating Nietzsche: "if we begin with the inward world of thought and feeling, the whirlpool is still more rapid, the flame more eager and devouring" (151). The task of the philosopher and the critic is to observe the flux, inside and out: "the service of … speculative culture, towards the human spirit, is to rouse, to startle it to a life of constant observation" (152), Pater writes echoing Baudelaire. He then adds, exaggerating his difference from Baudelaire: "Not the fruit of experience, but experience itself, is the end" (152), i.e. not "wisdom" but "life". Baudelaire believes that the modern artist must "distil the eternal from the transitory" (Baudelaire 1992, 402, quoted above). He titles his major work *Les Fleurs du mal* (The flowers of evil). *Les Fleurs du mal* is a brilliantly crafted collection of poems whose artistry did not deter Baudelaire's enemies from taking him to court for obscenity in August 1857. Pater in his reworking of Baudelaire stresses not the flowers of experience, but intense sensuous experience itself, causing a furore among the Philistines, as Matthew Arnold had called them, and creating an impression of himself as a corruptor of youth. The suggestion of "decadence" and "impropriety" was strengthened by a second infamous quote from the conclusion: "To burn always with this hard, gem-like flame, to maintain this ecstasy, is success in life" (152). So wrote the shy and retiring scholar whose rumoured homosexuality was lived very discreetly and behind closed doors. Pater censored his conclusion in the text's second edition.

Oscar Wilde, born in Dublin in 1854, died in Paris in 1900, disgraced, three years after his release from Reading Gaol, where he served a sentence of two years hard labour for the crime of sodomy. Wilde's parents were Anglo-Irish Protestants. His mother wrote Irish Nationalist poetry under the pen name "Speranza". Yeats's recollections capture the contemporary cultural myth of Wilde: "My first meeting with Oscar Wilde was an astonishment. I never before heard a man talking with perfect sentences" (Yeats 2001, 455).

Wilde was part of a second wave of the Victorian aesthetic movement. His essay, "The Critic as Artist: With Some Remarks upon the Importance of Doing Nothing" (1881), which we will be reading closely, shows the depth and breadth of his erudition. In some respects Wilde is a perfect example of the Hellenism announced by Arnold. Indeed *Culture and Anarchy* is a major influence on Wilde's "The Critic as Artist". My understanding of "The Critic as Artist", telegraphically, is this: critical spirit meets multiplicity and becoming, to anticipate the art of the future. Slightly less concisely, Wilde mixes the emphasis on the critical spirit in Plato and Arnold with the emphasis on multiplicity and becoming in Baudelaire, Pater and Nietzsche, so anticipating modernism and postmodernism in literature. To start with Wilde's use of Plato, "The Critic as Artist" is a dialogue modelled on the Platonic form, intertextually referring to Plato's dialogues; borrowing the authority of Platonic dialogues but also, on occasion, hilariously caricaturing their stylistic quirks, questioning Socrates's authority and undermining his gravitas. It is quite impossible to fix Wilde's exact relation to Platonic dialogues, as it keeps shifting: Wilde the Plato scholar, Wilde the Plato fan, Wilde undermining both Plato's authority and his own, Wilde seeking truth and prophetically announcing the art of the future are all on display. The role of Socrates is played by Gilbert, a man about town: is Gilbert an intellectual *flâneur*, an idler, or is he a serious thinker? Does the dialogue between Gilbert and Ernest take place from nightfall until dawn in order to point to the idler status of the two young men or to strengthen Gilbert's prophetic announcement of a new dawn for art and to allude to Plato's *Symposium*, the action of which similarly takes place at night and goes on until dawn?

Wilde's intertextual relation to Arnold is equally explicit and equally ambiguous. Up to a point Wilde shadows Arnold very closely. The starting point of the dialogue is this: "What is our primary debt to the Greeks? Simply the critical spirit" (Wilde 1961, 49). Pointing us to the subtitle, Gilbert asserts: "to do nothing at all is the most difficult thing in the world" (87). Contemplation, thinking, which is very different from acting, is the most difficult thing in the world. Gilbert puts this in context: "our fathers believed" (88); "[a]nything approaching to the free play of the mind is practically unknown among us" (117). In this context "the mission of the aesthetic movement is to lure people to contemplation" (105).

Then Wilde starts deviating from Plato and Arnold in the direction of Baudelaire, Pater and Nietzsche. When you delve into "the best that is known and thought in the world" (Wilde quoting Arnold), you find "gifts of strange temperaments and subtle susceptibilities, gifts of wild ardours and chill moods of indifference, complex multiform gifts of thoughts that are at variance with each other, and passions that war against themselves" (90). You delve into your self and you find a similar situation. The true critical spirit, the true "man of culture", instead of aiming to lift himself above this world of moods, passions and instincts in flux, aims to make "instinct self-conscious" (91). In other words, "the contemplative life … has for its aim not *doing* but being" – so far we could be listening to Plato and Arnold – "and not *being* merely, but *becoming*" (91). "[N]ot *being* merely, but *becoming*" encapsulates the new orientation of modern thought.

Wilde goes on to embrace a form of subjectivism. The "most perfect art is that which most fully mirrors man in all his infinite variety" (50), with one important proviso: both art and criticism mirror not their subject matter but the artist and the critic themselves – not as they are but as they are becoming, in their flux. Both art and criticism are subjective in this sense rather than objective: "To give an accurate description of what has never occurred is … the inalienable right of any man of parts and culture" (48). "Criticism is … both creative and independent" of its object (66), and in this sense "purely subjective" (69). The aim of criticism is not to see the object as it really is, as Arnold argued, but to record the critic's "spiritual moods and imaginative passions of the mind" (68). Gilbert anticipates Barthes's "death of the Author" and "birth of the reader" (Barthes 1977b, 148): instead of "discovering the real intention of the artist" (Wilde 1961, 70), the critic "*lends* to the beautiful thing its myriad meanings" (71, my italics). I am reading this text and it speaks to me of something, "But at other times it speaks to me of a thousand different things … Beauty has as many meanings" as the critic has "moods" (71).

The aesthetic critic can "give form to every fancy, and reality to every mood"; in doing so he can "exhibit the object from each point of view, and show it to us in the round … To know the truth one must imagine myriads of falsehoods" (99) – "myriads of falsehoods" in the sense that reality or the critical mind is multiperspectival and constantly shifting from one perspective to the next. Strongly reminiscent of Nietzsche's "the *more* eyes, different eyes, we can use to observe one thing …" (Nietzsche 1989, 119, quoted above), this is an early manifesto for modernism. In *A Room of One's Own* Virginia Woolf's narrator states: "Clearly the mind is always altering its focus, and bringing the world into different perspectives" (Woolf 2004, 112); "truth is to be had by laying together many varieties of error" (122). Wilde's Gilbert is more flippant and anti-authoritarian: truth is merely "one's last mood" (Wilde 1961, 100).

And yet Gilbert is only too serious and quite insistent that literature (and the category would now include the creative criticism he has endorsed) is "the highest art" (55). It is the highest art because its medium is language, "which is the parent, and not the child of thought" (60), Gilbert argues flatly contradicting Coleridge and Shelley (who viewed language as secondary to thought and as an inferior copy of thought). Also "Movement ... can be truly realized by Literature alone" (65).

Announcing that the "art of today will occupy" the critic "less than the art of tomorrow" (110), Gilbert goes on to imagine the art of tomorrow, especially the literature of tomorrow. These are to be the elements of the literature of tomorrow:

- Emphasis on form. Wilde returns to Théophile Gautier's doctrine of *l'art pour l'art* – translated by Pater as "art for art's sake" – to understand it as an emphasis on formal concerns. Attention to form, formalism, has been a tendency in aesthetic theory ever since Kant's aesthetics. "[T]he real artist is he who proceeds, not from feeling to form, but from form to thought and passion" (108), Gilbert announces, anticipating the modernist emphasis on form and formal experimentation.
- Emphasis on recording internal states. As Gilbert declares, "there is still much to be done in the sphere of introspection" (113). Romanticism spearheaded the exploration of interiority, inwardness, the "inner world" (Hegel's term) but valorized its essential unity as discussed in the last chapter. Aestheticism, on the other hand, valorizes and records flux, multiplicity and conflict within the self. In this it anticipates modernism, looking forward, for example, to D. H. Lawrence's recording of love turning to hate in *The Rainbow* or James Joyce's use of stream of consciousness in the final, Molly Bloom episode of *Ulysses.*
- Emphasis on a literature of "suggestion" or allusion. This is an idea Wilde shares with his near-contemporary Mallarmé and inherits from Baudelaire – an idea pointing back to the theorization of the sublime by Enlightenment and Romantic critics. For Wilde literature must seek the great "quality of suggestion" (73) and "avoid too definite a presentation of the Real" (74). Rather than a literary text "hav[ing] but one message to deliver" (74), Wilde announces a literary text that is open to many interpretations. The creative critic seeks the latter kind of literary text that "make[s] all interpretations true, and no interpretation final" (74). Wilde here anticipates Barthes's idea of the "text". (In "From Work to Text" Roland Barthes defines "text" as openness to many interpretations, contrasting it to *work*, which has a definite meaning.) This emphasis announces the coming shift from a stable and omniscient narrator to, for example, the self-consciously subjective, partially illuminated and illuminating, dislocated and dislocating narrator of Conrad's *Heart of Darkness,* Marlow. (On the "dislocations" in Marlow's language, see Said 1993, 32.)
- Not only does criticism need to be creative, but literature also needs to be critical (this shows that Wilde does not drop but continues to mix the Plato/Arnold line into his thinking): "if creation is to last at all, it can only do so on the condition of becoming far more critical than it is at present" (112); "critical" here means self-reflexive and self-conscious. Wilde here anticipates the strong metaliterary element in modernist and postmodernist

literature, that is, the way in which literature and the nature of literature become literature's subject matter for experimental writers in the twentieth century.

- Literature and criticism will become more intertextual. "[A]s civilization progresses ... the critical and cultured spirits ... *will seek to gain their impressions almost entirely from what Art has touched*" (80). Wilde inherits the particular texture of much of his intertextuality from Joris-Karl Huysmans's 1884 novel *À Rebours* (Against nature), whose hero, Des Esseintes, withdraws to his country estate and devotes himself to the contemplation of the aesthetic objects he has accumulated and to the indulgence of his hyper-refined sensibility. Going further back, Wilde's intertextuality engages with Arnold's canon, which itself points back to Kant. Once Kant posits the autonomy of the aesthetic – that the aesthetic phenomenon is distinct from the pursuit of knowledge (pure reason) and goodness (practical reason) – we find ourselves in a distinct realm of art (though the austere and unsensuous Kant would have been shocked by his hothouse Aesthete progeny). Tennyson imagines this as both a solution, in relation to worldly and spiritual turmoil, and a problem in his 1832 poems, "The Palace of Art" and "The Lady of Shalott" (both in Tennyson 2009). Aestheticism is, broadly, a flight from external reality and withdrawal into the aesthetic realm. This withdrawal in disgust is explicitly discussed in Coleridge's *Biographia Literaria* (1975, 110–11). Arguably, the Romantic flight from reality is implicitly just as critical of reality as campaigning literature with revolutionary or reforming intent. Intertextuality, already practised by Wilde in "The Critic as Artist", is taken up by T. S. Eliot in his most famous essay, "Tradition and the Individual Talent", advocating the need for the writer to immerse himself in the canon and is in evidence, explicitly, in Eliot's *The Waste Land*. It is also a defining element of postmodern literature.

While Wilde anticipates several poststructuralist ideas, the French Symbolist poet Stéphane Mallarmé (1842–98) is a direct and readily acknowledged influence on poststructuralist critics such as Barthes and Derrida, as well as on Wilde himself. In "Crise de vers" (Crisis in poetry) (1896) Mallarmé rejects both mimetic and expressive theories of literature: literature is neither mimetic of the world nor expressive of the author and his intention; in effect he rejects these formulaic versions of, respectively, realism and Romanticism. Literature, unlike all other forms of writing, does not report; instead, "where literature is concerned, speech is content merely to make allusions" – "*evocation*, or *allusion*, *suggestion*" (Mallarmé 1999, 231). Equally, literature is "anonymous" and "omit[s] the author"; the "pure work of art implies the elocutionary disappearance of the poet" (232). Mallarmé turns his attention to the centrifugal multiplicity of language in its materiality (e.g. as sound and rhythm), as revealed and brought about by the French Symbolists. In this literature the "entire language ... escaped, in a free disjunction of thousands of simple elements ... not unlike the multiplicity of cries in an orchestra" (228), literature turning into music, as Pater said (see Chapter 1). Literature releases the "polymorphous" (229): the dynamic and fluid multiplicity of language, its "volatile dispersion", the "break in the great literary rhythms ... and their dispersal into shivers" (231–3). Where Coleridge aspired to harmony and unity of form, Mallarmé valorizes "infractions" and "dissonances" (229).

For Mallarmé in literature language emerges as a dissemination of proliferating self-referential chains of material signifiers in mobile and open-ended relations to each other: the writer "yields the initiative to words, set in motion by the clash of their inequalities; they illuminate each other with reciprocal lights" (232). What matters is the "raw and immediate" materiality of words and the "ensemble of links", the differential relations between them (233). In other words what matters is sound and "silence" (233). Literary activity denaturalizes and defamiliarizes reality, "transposing a fact of nature into its almost vibratory disappearance according to the action of the word" (233).

Jacques Derrida turns to Mallarmé in *Dissemination* and in his 1974 essay "Mallarmé". In this essay, which we will now discuss, Derrida outlines Mallarmé's entire project. Derrida discerns in Mallarmé – "pass[ing] *through*" Mallarmé and "travers[ing]" him (Derrida 1992b, 112) – the big themes of poststructuralist criticism and of Derrida's own deconstructive work. First, in relation to the theme of the death of the author, Derrida quotes Mallarmé claiming that literary achievement is "always paid for by the omission of the author and, as it were, by his death as such" (Mallarmé quoted in Derrida 1992b, 113). Second, Mallarmé puts forward a "doctrine of *suggestion*" or "undecided allusion" according to which the chains of signifiers are cut off both from the "intention of the author" and from the referent, "the thing itself" (121). The decomposed particles of words and chains of words – the word for Mallarmé is "no longer the primary element of the language" (116) – "refer only to their own game" (121). The only form of reference in Mallarmé is intertextuality: he "nearly always writes on a text", including his own texts (121). Third, Mallarmé displays the infinite deferral of the signified (meaning), what Derrida elsewhere calls *différance*: "these chains ... are as if without support, always suspended" (120). The signifier does not lead to the signified but "remains, resists ... and draws attention to itself" in its materiality (113). The "spacing" (Derrida borrows Mallarmé's term, *espacement*) between the signifiers has "no determinate meaning" (115); the deferral of the signified is being brought about by "a certain play of the syntax" (114). In Mallarmé's texts, at their "strongest points, the meaning remains *undecidable*" (113).

Derrida understands Mallarmé's "crisis", as thematized in his essay "Crise de vers", as a crisis in criticism. If criticism uses "judgement to *decide* (*krinein*) on value and meaning", Mallarmé's texts – in their deferral of the signified, their avoidance and forestalling of a definitive meaning and their openness to interpretations – suspend criticism: "simple *decision* is no longer possible" and the "choice between opposing paths is suspended" (113).

Mallarmé builds chains on the materiality of sound, rhythm and rhyme as well as on the materiality of the page, graphic signs and page layout. To give an example, Derrida follows the proliferating chains and "semantic indecision" (124) of the signifier *or* in Mallarmé, as in *son or* (his gold), *sonore* (sonorous), *le son or* (the sound "or"), "meaning the empty phonic or graphic signifier *or*" (123).

What might be the psychological implications of such semantic indecision? Sigmund Freud, founder of psychoanalysis, made momentous contributions to the themes discussed in this chapter: from the fragmentation of the self to the polysemy and materiality of language. He will be the focus of the following chapter.

Conclusion

- Marx (with Engels) but also Owen, Carlyle, Ruskin, Morris and others critically addressed the Industrial Revolution, the poverty of the new industrial working classes and social division. Marxism, which will give rise to a vigorous school of literary criticism in the twentieth century, believes it has a unique insight into the meaning of history; it describes as "utopian" and "idealist" those critics of capitalist industrialism who do not share the Marxist theory of history as class conflict. George Eliot's realism aspires to truthfulness and social sympathy, anxiously attempting to convey the complexity of self and of the historical life of previously misrepresented "low" groups, while her narrative voice attempts an ideal synthesis of social perspectives.
- Baudelaire coins *modernité* (modernity) and defines modern life as life amidst the crowds on the city streets; the modern artist is a worldly figure who gives up his otherworldly aura to seek the eternal in the mud of ephemera and fleeting modern life. Arnold, alarmed by deepening class divisions and irreconcilable social perspectives, promotes literary studies as an antidote to this lack of a shared culture. An education based on a literary canon, high culture and disinterested criticism promises to lift the mind to a self-reflective life salutary to both the individual and the nation, Arnold argues. Nietzsche, by contrast, celebrates multiplicity and "becoming", embraces multiperspectivism and shares none of Arnold's public spirit. In keeping with his multiperspectivism, his theory of history (genealogy) reconceives history as non-progressive, without underlying rationality, and the site and outcome of the struggle for power.
- Pater similarly emphasizes becoming and sees the task of literature and criticism as the heightened experience and observation of the flux and multiplicity of reality, particularly the internal reality of the self. Wilde's prophetic criticism attempts to combine Arnold and Pater as well as Baudelaire and Mallarmé; his sketch of a literature of the future anticipates modernism and postmodernism. Mallarmé's already

modernist, even postmodernist, theorizing and practice announce the death of the author; the flux, the centrifugal multiplicity and indeterminacy of meaning; and "dissonances" rather than unity of form.

Further reading

In relation to primary texts discussed in this chapter, see especially: Arnold 1993b; Baudelaire 1992; Darwin 1996; George Eliot 1990; Mallarmé 1999; Marx and Engels 1985; Nietzsche 1989; Pater 1986; Wilde 1961. See also Benjamin 1992b; Derrida 1992b.

6 Freud and psychoanalytic criticism

The self in fragments

Freud, Woolf, Klein, Lawrence, Lacan, Bloom, Gilbert and Gubar, Brooks, Kristeva, Felman, Žižek, Rose, Ellmann

Sigmund Freud was born in Freiberg in 1856, a Jew within the multiethnic Austro-Hungarian Empire. His middle-class family moved to Vienna when he was three years old. His constantly revised writings – spanning from the late 1880s to the late 1930s – are a window into 50 years of Viennese and more broadly European history. Sharply increased industrial competition and imperialist competition for colonies since the 1870s (see Brantlinger 1988) were followed by World War I; the disintegration of the Austro-Hungarian Empire and founding of Austria; the rise of Nazism and official anti-Semitism in Germany; and the annexation of Austria by Nazi Germany in 1938. Freud was then forced to move to London, where he died in 1939 after a long illness, a few days following the invasion of Poland and the official beginning of World War II. Freud's exile was compounded, Richard Wollheim argues, by his estrangement both from Vienna – for which "he had always expressed intense dislike" – and from Judaism and Zionism (Wollheim 1973, 217).

The self in psychoanalysis

The previous chapter outlined modernity in its relation to multiplicity and "becoming". We focused on Marx, George Eliot, Baudelaire, Arnold, Pater, Nietzsche, Mallarmé and Wilde, sketching their aesthetic, critical and philosophical responses to a period of rapid change and fragmentation within society and within the sense of the self. Arnold, for example, envisaged "culture" in opposition to these tendencies and claimed our "best self" to be one and immutable; Pater, Nietzsche, Mallarmé and Wilde, on the other hand, celebrated the flux and multiplicity of the self and became important precursors of, and influences on, twentieth-century modernism. Freud, Wilde's contemporary, is a major thinker of European modernity and a transitional figure whose long writing life spans the nineteenth and twentieth centuries.

During the fifty years of Freud's writing career, European literature significantly displayed a post-Romantic turn to subjectivism, psychic reality and fantasy, for example in Aestheticism and the late-Victorian gothic. Freud, who had a very good classical and literary education, returned as far back as Sophocles in order to read literature as supporting his discoveries. Harold Bloom, on the other hand, reads Freud as an inheritor of literary Romanticism in his essay "Freud and the Sublime". Bloom's literary genealogy facilitates Freud's comparison with his contemporary literature and criticism. In relation to our theme of the multiplicity of the self, Freud's ideas are strongly resonant with those of Pater, Wilde and Nietzsche (whom Freud was familiar with, finding some of his ideas very compelling): the self is *not one* but multiple, fragmented, decentred and at war with itself. Wilde writes of "passions that war against themselves" (Wilde 1961, 90), while Bloom summarizes Freud's vision as one of "civil war in the psyche" (Bloom 1994, 181). Freud's ideas also resonate with *fin-de-siècle* Victorian gothic fiction, particularly Robert Louis Stevenson's *Dr Jekyll and Mr Hyde* (1886). Wilde's *The Picture of Dorian Gray* (1891) is another tale of split identity. However, Freud's influence is not yet felt in these novels.

In the twentieth century, the modernists are very much aware of Freud. They implicitly or explicitly engage with and respond to him as a major interlocutor. Though Virginia Woolf's attitude to Freud was ambiguous and critical, Woolf and her husband, Leonard Woolf, used their publishing house, Hogarth Press, to make Freud available in English, translated by Lytton Strachey's brother, James, and his wife, Alix. D. H. Lawrence contested Freud with his own theories of the unconscious, developed in intriguing texts such as *Fantasia of the Unconscious* (1921–2) and *Psychoanalysis and the Unconscious* (1923) (Lawrence 2004). W. H. Auden's fine poem, "In Memory of Sigmund Freud" (1939), responding to Freud's death, presents Freud as "serv[ing] enlightenment" (Auden 1979, 94): he is a self-examining benefactor of humanity "doing us some good", though he "knew it was never enough" (91). Auden, who was well-versed in Freud, attempts to capture his profound influence: "If often he was wrong and at times absurd,/ To us he is no more a person/ Now but a whole climate of opinion/ Under whom we conduct our differing lives:/ … / He quietly surrounds all our habits of growth" (93). Canonical twentieth-century criticism such as Virginia Woolf's *Three Guineas* (1938) and Walter Benjamin's "Theses on the Philosophy of History" (1940), both desperately contemplating the coming war, do not so much as mention Freud yet could not have been written without him. The "fragments" in the subtitle of this chapter points both to European aggression and war and to ideas of the fragmented self; the two were connected by Freud following World War I in *Beyond the Pleasure Principle* (1920), where he develops his new concept of the death instinct.

Where the Romantics Coleridge and Shelley turned to Plotinus and Neoplatonist idealism to support their belief in the unifying role of the imagination (discussed in Chapter 4), Freud posits a radical decentring of consciousness – that is, a demotion of consciousness from its traditional position as the highest part of the human self – and splitting of the self. If we position Freud's ideas within the context of modern European thought, it can be argued that the self was already split with Descartes, between the thinking self and the self as thought. In Émile Benveniste's more recent, linguistically inflected version there is a split between the "subject of enunciation" (the speaking self) and the "subject of the statement" (the spoken self) (see Benveniste 1971). In *The Unnamable* Samuel Beckett captures this self-alienation of the self with characteristic brilliance: "I, say I" (Beckett 1979, 267). The two "I"s of Beckett's formula are not the same and can never coincide: "I, say I. Unbelieving". However, since Descartes and before Nietzsche and Freud, modern thought had kept the "self" together by assuming the centrality of consciousness and related ideas, such as the power and clarity of reason, the availability of the self to introspection and free will.

In "The Mirror Stage" the French psychoanalyst Jacques Lacan (1901–81) stresses the irreducible "dehiscence" of the self as envisioned by Freud (Lacan 1977b, 4). He captures Freud's revolution in thought and philosophical importance as lying in this decentring of consciousness in favour of Freud's most important idea: the Unconscious. Freud brings centre-stage those parts of the self that remain forever inaccessible to reason, primitive drives and instincts, automatisms beyond one's conscious control. Everything that Plato feared in human nature and wished to check with the rule of Reason is claimed to have been in the driving seat all along. In brief, we come face to face with the self as a dangerous and threatening other. Emily Dickinson's poem, "One need not be a Chamber – to be Haunted–" (*c.* 1863), stages this intuition using gothic props: "Far safer through an Abbey gallop,/ The stones a'chase–/ Than Unarmed, one's a'self encounter–/ In lonesome Place–" (Dickinson 1975, 333). Dickinson here shares in a vision or nightmare more widely intuited by nineteenth-century literature.

I will now sketch the development of the psychoanalytic understanding of the human self. Displacing consciousness, the centrality of sexuality – defined very broadly and scandalously, at the time, well beyond normative genital heterosexual and reproductive sex – and sexual energy (libido) is one of Freud's lasting contributions. However, sexuality is accompanied by resistance and repression, as the "pleasure principle" (the human pursuit of pleasure) clashes with the "reality principle" (the internalized limitations of external reality, including social reality and social commands) within the psyche. Wollheim points out that the ideas of sexuality, resistance and repression emerged simultaneously in Freud's early thought. In trying to understand resistance and repression – what does repression repress? – Freud was reluctantly led to acknowledge the force of sexuality (Wollheim 1973, 32–40). The Unconscious is born out of repression; without repression there would be no

Unconscious. Freud's understanding of the war between pleasure and its repression resonates with the final chapter of Stevenson's *The Strange Case of Dr Jekyll and Mr Hyde*:

> the worst of my faults was a certain gaiety of disposition … such as I found it hard to reconcile with my imperious desire to … wear a more than commonly grave countenance before the public … It was thus rather the exacting nature of my aspirations that … made me what I was.
>
> (Stevenson 2002, 55)

Intriguingly, Stevenson suggests that a character less repressed than Dr Jekyll would not have been forced to unleash Mr Hyde, and that excessive repression is dangerous.

Freud's last phase, initiated by the transitional essay "The Uncanny" (1919) and the influential and controversial *Beyond the Pleasure Principle* (1920), tells a more complex story. In *Beyond the Pleasure Principle* and *The Ego and the Id* (1923) Freud develops a new hypothesis triggered by his experience of World War I and war-traumatized veterans. No longer serving only the pleasure principle and sexual aims and objects, instinct is now divided against itself. There are now two basic instincts warring against each other. There is "eros": love, life, preservation, "Eros, the preserver of life" (Freud 1991b, 327); and "thanatos": death, hate, loss, a "death instinct" unleashing aggression and destruction, a desire to return to inorganic matter, to purge excitations, stimuli and intensity, such that "we shall be compelled to say that '*the aim of all life is death*'" (Freud 1991b, 311). Freud's "second topography" of the psyche, developed in *The Ego and the Id*, divides the psyche into the "id" (the instinctual terrain of both eros and thanatos); the social commands of the "super-ego"; and the "ego", as a fragile mediation between the instinctual forces of the id and the social imperatives of the super-ego, or as an armour defending the psyche against both.

Late Victorian gothic novels, such as *Jekyll and Hyde* and *The Picture of Dorian Gray*, echo Freud's exploration of violent, evil, demonic parts of the self. D. H. Lawrence's modernist novels, *The Rainbow* (1915) and *Women in Love* (1920), can be read as studies of the relation between eros and thanatos. Chapter VI of *The Rainbow*, "Anna Victrix", on the honeymoon and early days in the marriage of Anna and Will Brangwen, is a minutely detailed psychic weather report of currents of love turning into hate and back into love, attraction turning into repulsion and back again, gentleness turning into rage and destruction. Love turns into an "unknown battle" or "some endless contest": "So it went on continually, the recurrence of love and conflict between them" (Lawrence 1949, 167–8). In *Women in Love* the coal-mine owner Gerald Crich can be read as a personification of the death instinct at work in modern industrial civilization. At the beginning of Chapter 9, "Coal-Dust", he is seen mistreating a "red Arab mare", a symbol of nature, next to a rail track as there passes a speeding train, a conventional symbol of modern life and industry (Lawrence 1960, 122). In Chapter 30, "Snowed-up", a "sudden desire leapt" in Gerald's "heart to kill" his lover Gudrun (518). But his attempt to strangle her is interrupted by the surfacing of a deeper desire for his own self-annihilation, which Lawrence associates with the "dead mechanical monotony and meaninglessness" (522), the "million wheels and cogs and axles" (525), of modern Western civilization. "[U]consciously climbing" the Alps, "[a]lways higher, always higher" (532), but in meaningless mechanical motion without end, symbolizing Lawrence's questioning of the modern ideology of progress, Gerald effectively kills himself when he falls asleep in the snow. In 1938, Virginia Woolf will examine the desire for war and destruction with great urgency in *Three Guineas*, as World War II, the second global conflict of the century, fast approaches.

Freud's new hypothesis of the death instinct as a power "beyond the pleasure principle" is supported by his seminal idea of the "compulsion to repeat" traumatic experiences, which makes its first appearance in "The Uncanny" and is discussed extensively in later works. The "compulsion to repeat" is foundational in contemporary trauma theory (see Chapter 1 of J. Brooks Bouson's *Quiet As It's Kept* [2000]). Unable to properly experience a traumatic loss at the time it happened, and unable to remember, represent and symbolize it "properly", we repeat the painful experience compulsively, stuck in unconscious repetition and the "return of the repressed". For example, in Toni Morrison's *Beloved* Sethe kills her daughter, Beloved, to save her from slavery, but Beloved returns. Her return, after her death and the transgenerational trauma of slavery, is the return of the repressed exactly because "proper" symbolization had been impossible at the time. Sethe then enters into the process of telling her story; she avoids the repetition of Beloved's killing, and Beloved is seemingly exorcized. However, the novel suggests that the representation of trauma is bound to be "improper", experimental in form, and only partially successful as it knocks against the limits of representation.

Freud's last phase has been especially important to contemporary psychoanalytic literary critics, as have been the slightly earlier essay "Mourning and Melancholia" (1917) and case history "Wolf Man" (1918). In "Wolf Man" Freud's minor concept of "*nachtrachlichkeit*", usually translated as "deferred action" (or "afterwardsness"), has been especially fruitful, as discussed by Lacan and especially as developed by Jean-Bertrand Pontalis and Jean Laplanche more fully in *The Language of Psycho-Analysis* (1967). Traumatic events, exceeding the self's powers of comprehension and representation, are not properly experienced when they happen. However, they find an indirect and partial expression in the future, when they are involuntarily reactivated through repetition compulsion; or they might be more fully recognized and experienced if and when they are more fully symbolized. In instances of "deferred action", time moves in loops rather than forwards, in the sense that the self experiencing the traumatic event is in-between the two selves separated by such temporal distance and cannot be exactly located in time. For an interesting use of "deferred action" in literary criticism, see Jean Wyatt's "*Love*'s Time and the Reader" (2008) on Toni Morrison's novel, *Love*.

In "Mourning and Melancholia" Freud describes melancholia as mourning for a lost object of love that is without end or issue. In melancholia the "ego wants to incorporate this object into itself" (Freud 1991d, 258): the self introjects the lost loved one and identifies with him or her. Freud defines the three preconditions of melancholia as "loss of the object", "ambivalence" – love and hate – towards the object, and conversion of the object into a part of the self (267). The melancholic, unable to accept the loss, keeps the lost other alive by incorporating him or her as part of the self, while the melancholic's violent self-reproaches are really disguised reproaches against the lost object. To return to the theme of this chapter, not only is the self multiple and fragmented, but it includes "external" fragments: incorporated others (as well as social norms, etc.). In Woolf's *Mrs Dalloway* (1925) the tête-à-tête between Clarissa Dalloway and Peter Walsh – conveyed through dialogue as well as their interwoven internal monologues – shows that an introjected version of Peter is part of Clarissa's self and vice versa (Woolf 1996, 45ff.). Julia Kristeva develops the connection between melancholia and literary production in *Black Sun: Depression and Melancholia* (1987). Her close textual reading of Gérard de Nerval's poetry shows the intricate connection between his poetic form and his melancholia, and suggests how his poetic activity is the momentary cure or lifting of his melancholia.

As well as including "external" fragments, the self, as viewed by psychoanalysis, also projects parts of itself onto "external" reality and onto others. Kristeva's concept of "abjection" develops Freud's concept of projection, cross-fertilized with the work of the psychoanalyst Melanie Klein (1882–1960). In Kristeva's *Powers of Horror* (1980), the very boundary between self and other, inside and outside, is fundamentally an imprecise and fragile construction. As infants we emerge out of an intense and affectively ambivalent dyadic relation with the mother, where self and other are not distinctly differentiated; and while the process of our socialization consists exactly in our symbolic differentiation from others, this original fluidity of relation between self and other remains with us. Melanie Klein "will make of this area her privileged field of observation", though "it is Freud indeed who blazes the trail" (Kristeva 1982, 60). In *Anti-Oedipus* (1970), Gilles Deleuze and Félix Guattari had already combined Freud and Klein and described this world of "partial objects" – Deleuze and Guattari's modification of Melanie Klein's "part-objects", referring for example to breastfeeding and the relation between the mother's breast and the infant's mouth – rather than complete and independent persons, and "inclusive" rather than "exclusive differentiations" between self and others (Deleuze and Guattari's terms). Deleuze and Guattari drew on D. H. Lawrence, Samuel Beckett and other writers as allies in their project of describing these primary processes; we will be discussing them extensively in Chapter 11.

To return to Kristeva's *Powers of Horror*, "abjection" is the opposite of melancholic incorporation; it is the projection of unacceptable parts of the self onto others, who function as scapegoats, phobic objects, objects of horror. However, Kristeva insists that the process of abjection is never fully completed; it remains discernible to the self that the horror is coming from within it, and as a result the distinction subject/object (or self/other) cannot be maintained. Due to this "non-separation of subject/object" (Kristeva 1982, 58) or the "frail identity of the speaking subject" (67), Kristeva concludes that the "abject is not an ob-ject" (1), "the ab-ject is … an impossible ob-ject" (154) because it can never be adequately constituted as split off from the self. According to Kristeva, who develops a distinctively feminist argument, the exemplary abject in most societies is women and particularly mothers. The "unsettled separation" (78) between men and women and the fear and abjection of women disguise men's projections onto women of their own horrifying mortality, "[i]ncompleteness and dependency" (88). However, the "[f]ragile threshold" or "impossible demarcation" between men and women, and men's "repulsion in relation to" women "in order to autonomize" themselves, bring about men's separation from their own bodies and the misrecognition of "man's particularity" as both "*mortal and speaking*" (85, 82, 88). Implicitly, Kristeva assumes that there is no difference between men and women, and that gender difference is a tool in the ongoing attempt to abject women (70ff.). As to literature and psychoanalysis, their roles are similar and highly important in Kristeva's view: to disclose the process of abjection and the horrors underlying it. Literature is "an unveiling of the abject … an undoer of narcissism and of all imaginary identity as well, sexual included" (208). Language makes distinctions and separates, but "the writer … is to be not only the one who separates … but also the one who touches … even taking the place of the feminine" (161). Finally, literature is "rooted … on the fragile border … where identities (subject/object, etc.) do not exist or only barely so" (205), while psychoanalysis witnesses acts of expulsion or "burst[ing out", "our dancing on a volcano" exploding (210). Appropriately, Kristeva is using a language of pregnancy and childbirth to describe the role of both literature and psychoanalysis. Her close readings of Louis-Ferdinand Céline's texts conclude that he "locates the ultimate of abjection – and thus the supreme and sole interest of literature" in "giving birth" (155).

We have seen that psychoanalytic thought greatly complicates the topography of the self and treats the boundary between self and other as permeable. Having opened and rendered unanswerable the question "where am I?" – the question of the *topos* (location), topology and topography of the self – the psychoanalytic concept of "*nachtrachlichkeit*" also problematizes the temporality of the self. To turn now to another aspect of the self, gender, Kristeva's *Powers of Horror* is one of many important texts posing the question of the relation of subjectivity and gender in psychoanalysis. Psychoanalysis has a prominent position in contemporary gender theory and vice versa. Most feminist critics would agree that, in contemporary societies, there are still two (unequally valued) gender norms, even though the content of these norms might vary greatly in different social contexts. However, psychoanalytic feminist theorists insist that assuming one's gender is (like Lacan's entry into the symbolic order to be discussed later in this chapter) simultaneously both inevitable and a never-completed process. As a result, one is never fully normalized, and the possibility for minor and major gender variations and deviations is ever open, though always under the threat of social censure. Similarly, in relation to sexual orientation, heterosexuality is still the norm. However, there is a gap between the social norm and the great variety of paths taken by human sexuality that Freud did so much to explore. As a result, distinctions between men/women and heterosexuality/homosexuality are far too simplistic and crude to capture the self.

Freud's work on the development of sexuality and gender is usually divided into two phases: before and after the mid 1920s. The context for this break is the 1920s grand debate on gender within psychoanalysis. Its contributors included Karen Horney, Ernest Jones and Melanie Klein; this was the context in which Virginia Woolf wrote *Orlando* (1928). Joan Riviere's contribution to this debate "Womanliness as a Masquerade" (1929) was discussed by Judith Butler in her important *Gender Trouble* (1990), exemplifying the continuing contemporary relevance of this debate. Freud himself seemed to equivocate throughout his work as to whether gender is biologically and anatomically determined or socially constructed (as is mostly thought today). On the one hand, the development of gender encounters many vicissitudes, and often never arrives at a socially acceptable form; on the other hand, until the mid 1920s Freud tells a simple universal story whose core is the "Oedipus complex" and "castration anxiety", which goes like this. In early infancy, during the short-lived and insignificant pre-Oedipal phase, boys and girls are indistinguishable (they are both boys, as it were) and both take the mother as their love-object. In the Oedipal phase, the girl notices her lack of male (external) genitalia, considers it a catastrophic loss, and suffers from what Freud terms "penis envy". The boy loves his mother and wants to kill his father to take his place, but he perceives the girl's lack of a penis as castration, fears retribution from the father in this form and suffers from "castration anxiety". In the meantime, the girl now loves her father and perceives her mother as rival. She hopes that her love for the father will give her the penis she lacks, in the form of a penis substitute, a baby. Feminists have pointed out that Freud's account only makes sense in societies where women are subordinate to men and where, therefore, lacking a penis is a sign of powerlessness. The overvaluation of the penis in Freud's account makes sense in the context of the social privilege enjoyed by men. (One might of course also point out that this primordial scenario rather seems to depend on large Victorian families where it would be unusual for there not to be both girls and boys.)

Freud's case history "Dora" (1901; 1905) has been especially relevant to feminist contentions that Freud skewed his account of development in favour of the acceptable norms of the day. Freud finds in Dora's account her early love for her father, her love for Herr K. and the reactivation of her love for her father in order to counter her love for Herr K., in keeping with his understanding of the normal path of development, and amidst Dora's vociferous denials. Finally Dora, a highly intelligent girl by Freud's account, ends her analysis abruptly. In a footnote in the postscript, written 20 years later, Freud is belatedly forced or willing to consider an additional factor, Dora's love for Herr K.'s wife, Frau K.: "I failed to discover in time and to inform the patient that her homosexual (gynaecophilic) love for Frau K. was the strongest unconscious current of her mental life" (Freud 1977, 162; see also Gyler 2010, 27).

Responding to the 1920s psychoanalytic debate on gender (Klein, Horney, Riviere, Jones) Freud's "Female Sexuality" (1931), while continuing to outline a "normal" path of development, also conveys his new understanding of female sexuality as overflowing on all sides his earlier description of normative adult female sexuality as heterosexual, genital, reproductive, and lacking in relation to male sexuality (Freud 2001b, 230). Freud now posits the great intensity and ambivalence of women's early love for their mother and the lifelong importance of the pre-Oedipal phase for women. Klein indeed insists on the lasting importance of the pre-Oedipal phase (dominated by the relation to the mother) for both men and women. Freud now also acknowledges the variety of paths and increased complexity of the process of genderization for women in relation to men. Even in "normal" development women are required to change primary erogenous zone, gender and sexual orientation in the transition from the pre-Oedipal to the Oedipal (from the clitoris to the vagina, from masculinity to femininity and from desire for the mother to desire for the father). He reiterates that these processes are little understood and remain obscure.

However, Freud continues to hold that woman suffers from penis envy and a sense of inferiority due to "the fact of her castration" (Freud 2001b, 230), her "organic inferiority" (233) and absence of a "proper penis" or "proper genital" (235). Horney argues that Freud's views are based on "the little boy's fantasy of the woman and repudiation of the pre-oedipal mother, and that this fantasy has its roots in men's envy and fear of women"; in other words, their primary "dread of infantile dependency and the denial of helplessness" (Gyler 2010, 34). Klein redefines vaginal eroticism in positive terms, as receptivity. Riviere defines conventional femininity as a reaction formation against a primary aggression shared by men and women, but also as a manifestation of women's "fear of retribution for masculine identifications" (Gyler 2010, 24).

The feminist reception of Freud, and his value, has oscillated between those who see Freud as a mystifying supporter of patriarchy (the subjection of women by men) and those who wish to emphasize the way in which Freud's work helps us to understand the nature of patriarchy. Juliet Mitchell, in particular, defended and rehabilitated Freud in *Psychoanalysis and Feminism* (1974). Whatever our view, the feminist engagement with Freud has been intensive and highly productive.

Jacqueline Rose, Julia Kristeva and, more recently, Louise Gyler have explored the potential Melanie Klein's account of subjectivity holds for contemporary gender theory, while rejecting her "biologistic and heterosexist" assumptions (Gyler 2010, 40). Kleinian subjectivity, up to a point, follows Freud from *Beyond the Pleasure Principle*: Klein emphasizes the role of aggression, negativity and the death instinct in the psychic life of both men and women. But Klein rejects the distinction between pre-Oedipal and Oedipal in favour of what she calls the "paranoid-schizoid position" and the "depressive position". While these positions initially follow each other, they keep recurring in later life, so that the self oscillates between them. In the paranoid-schizoid position, "fear and terror dominate subjective experience, and the predominant defence is splitting" into good and bad part-objects. For Klein the "good breast" and the "bad breast" are the "prototypical part-objects" (Gyler 2010, 44). While the infant's love for the mother is projected onto the "good breast" (as an endless flow of milk), the infant's destructive impulses towards the mother (perhaps due to its helplessness and the mother's less than infinite availability of milk) give rise to terrifying fantasies in relation to the mother, who is conceived as a bad breast, omnipotent, persecuting and life-threatening. But the infant's "hatred against parts of the self" is also projected onto the mother, through "projective identification" (Klein's concept, in Gyler 2010, 46). So Klein posits the infant's "envy of the mother's breast" (Klein quoted in Gyler 2010, 51), a mother-centred vision rather than Freud's father-centred "penis envy". For Klein the infant's inner world is "conflicted", "consumed with loving and hating, anxiety, loss, guilt and reparation" – both good breast and bad breast – in its relation to the mother (Gyler 2010, 48). In the depressive position, it is now perceived that the "good breast" and the "bad breast" are both aspects of one's relation to the same person, the mother, who emerges as a complete person, separate from the infant.

For Kristeva, Klein fruitfully combines Freud's (and later Lacan's) acknowledgement of negativity with a mother-centred – as opposed to Freud's father-centred – perspective: "Kleinian negativity, which … guides the drive to intelligence by way of fantasy, chooses the mother as its target" (Kristeva quoted in Gyler 2010, 55). Klein's and Kristeva's emphasis on the relation to the mother and the pre-Oedipal phase – a phase that precedes gender difference – lends itself to a perspective endorsing the evanescence of gender. Klein and Kristeva are fruitful in thinking about gender difference as a mirage on the surface of our common passionate psychic relation to the mother. Symbolization, thought and creativity are traced back to this psychic relation and the role of fantasy in psychic life.

Psychoanalytic literary criticism

In *Literary Freud* (2007), Perry Meisel recounts the fascinating history of Freud's reception by writers and literary critics. How do we understand today the relation between psychoanalysis and literature? Certainly *not* as one where psychoanalysis is applied to literature in order to speak its truth. Psychoanalysing authors and characters is currently considered particularly disreputable. Instead the attention of psychoanalytic criticism turns to the textuality of literature, as well as to the textuality of psychoanalysis itself. Psychoanalytic criticism sets outs to avoid an earlier assumption of a "relation of master to slave" with literature (Shoshana Felman quoted in Ellmann 1994b, 10); it attempts to divest itself of authoritarian claims to definitive readings and modestly assumes the incompleteness of interpretation.

Maud Ellmann's introduction to her landmark anthology, *Psychoanalytic Literary Criticism* (1994), repudiates earlier psychoanalytic criticism which concentrated on psychoanalysing author or characters, including texts by Freud. Ellmann stresses the contemporary consensus that psychoanalysis and literature, critic and literary text, are *not* in an unequal, unreciprocal, fixed relation of subject and object. On the contrary, the relation between psychoanalysis and literature is one of mutual and never-completed elucidation. Language and interpretation are fundamental to psychoanalysis, but language for Ellmann and others with a contemporary interest in psychoanalytic criticism is understood – within a poststructuralist, post-Lacanian frame – as endless substitution and *tropes* (metaphor, metonymy, synecdoche, etc.). For example, the texts by Julia Kristeva and Jacqueline Rose, anthologized in *Psychoanalytic Literary Criticism*, display these new assumptions, demonstrate their potential, but also test their limits from a psychoanalytic point of view. Rose, in particular, embraces metaphor but rejects a naïve endorsement of endless substitution as unliveable psychosis.

Within the poststructuralist, post-Lacanian frame, one of the significant shifts in contemporary psychoanalytic criticism is an opposition between older psychoanalytic criticism – assuming a fixed relation between signifier and signified, and fixing the text's meaning – and poststructuralist, post-Lacanian psychoanalytic criticism – supporting the sliding of the signified (the deferral of meaning and of interpretation) advocated by Lacan and thinkers such as Kristeva. Sue Vice also endorses this opposition between old and post-Lacanian psychoanalytic criticism in her anthology, *Psychoanalytic Criticism: A Reader* (1996). For example, in this anthology contemporary criticism is represented by Shoshana Felman's reading of Henry James's *The Turn of the Screw* (Felman 1996), while older psychoanalytic criticism is represented by Edmund Wilson's reading of the same text (Wilson 1996).

As Harold Bloom and others have pointed out, in "Freud and Literature" (1940) the American critic Lionel Trilling anticipates Lacan in understanding language as essentially figurative or tropic and in describing psychoanalysis itself as a "science of tropes" (Trilling 1970, 64; Bloom 1994, 176). However, Lacan's understanding of science – and of psychoanalysis as a science – is idiosyncratic: science neither possesses the Truth nor is opposed to literature and myth. (See Felman's account of Lacan in Felman 1994, 98–100.) Lacan, though not a literary critic, often seems to privilege literature over psychoanalytic investigation and to treat psychoanalysis as literature: "we can talk adequately about the libido only in a *mythic* manner" (Lacan quoted in Felman 1994, 95). Shoshana Felman's Lacanian reading of Sophocles's *Oedipus at Colonus* in "Beyond Oedipus" presents Oedipus as an exemplary narrator or author figure: as an itinerant, wandering, errant and "*erring*" story-teller (94). Literature transmutes repressed desires and aspects of reality into narrative "symbolisation" (86), into the metonymic chain of symbolic substitutions. Similarly, Felman understands psychoanalysis itself on this model of literature: as "*erring*" and "*self-expropriation*" without end, and *not* as a body of knowledge possessing the Truth (85, 94). Lacanian psychoanalytic criticism thus joins the nineteenth-century theorists of becoming (Pater, Nietzsche, Wilde, see Chapter 5).

Lacan, in Felman's account, favours myth or narrative as metaphorical *approximation*, rather than claiming for his theorizing a relation of correspondence (and adequation) with reality. However, is the assumption of an interpretive position of mastery and the closing of meaning ever fully avoided, even by those programmatically announcing the openness of their interpretations and the relation of equality – in mutual and open-ended elucidation – between psychoanalysis and literature? Barbara Johnson's "The Frame of Reference" raises this question in relation to Lacan's reading of Edgar Allan Poe's short story, "The Purloined Letter", and Jacques Derrida's reading of Lacan's reading of Poe. Derrida accuses Lacan's interpretation of ignoring the intertextual contexts of Poe's story and reducing the story into a single meaning – particularly into Lacan's idea of lack at the heart of being – against Lacan's programmatic commitment to open-ended and deferred interpretation. In the veiling and unveiling of the purloined letter, "What is veiled/unveiled in this case is a hole, a nonbeing (*non-étant*); the truth of being (*l'être*), as nonbeing[,] … veiled/unveiled castration" (Derrida quoted in Johnson 1996, 87). But Johnson argues that, in making this accusation, Derrida himself reduces Lacan's text into a "single unequivocal meaning" against Derrida's own similar commitment to following the complex and contradictory movement of a text rather than fixing its meaning:

> To cut out a text's frame of reference as though it did not exist and to reduce a complex textual functioning to a single meaning are serious blots indeed in the annals of literary criticism. Therefore it is all the more noticeable that Derrida's own reading of Lacan's text repeats precisely the crimes of which he accuses it.
>
> (Johnson 1996, 88)

Johnson concludes that "the author of any critique is himself framed by his own frame of the other" (97). However, having reiterated the "impossibility of any ultimate analytical metalanguage" (100), Johnson does *not* reject the moment of critique and the temporary assumption of mastery and closing of meaning that it involves. Rather, she inserts it within a wider movement, that of the "eternal oscillation between unequivocal undecidability and ambiguous certainty" (100).

***

In this chapter we have discussed the psychoanalytic theorization of the self, moving on to address the relation between psychoanalysis and literature as understood by psychoanalytic criticism. We will now turn to psychoanalytic theorizations of representation and fiction. What Lacan has called the "fictional direction" of the self in psychoanalysis emerges in Freud's work around the question of fantasy (Lacan 1977b, 2). In a 21 September 1897 letter to his colleague Fliess, Freud intimates that the childhood trauma of seduction by the father surfacing in the psychoanalysis of his patients might well be a fantasy in most instances. One of the reasons Freud gives to Fliess is that "there are no indications of reality in the unconscious, so that one cannot distinguish the truth and fiction that is cathected with affect" (Freud 1995, 112). In his "Wolf Man" case history Freud also gradually comes to a similar conclusion. Childhood scenes uncovered by analysis are fantasies: these scenes "are not reproductions of real occurrences" but rather "products of the imagination, which find their instigation in mature life" and "serve as some kind of symbolic representation of real wishes and interests" (Freud 1979, 282). In other words, the reality of a traumatic event might well be a psychic reality only, a fiction rather than the memory of fact. The "primal scene" is primarily a representation of the analysand's desire.

Psychoanalysis offers the promise of finally hearing the psychic *truth* long repressed. But the representation of psychic reality has to voice what is repressed, while also evading the forces of repression. In Freud's *The Interpretation of Dreams* (originally published in 1900 and often revised subsequently), Chapter VI, "The Dream-Work", describes the essentially substitutive – tropic, metaphoric, transferential – nature of representation in dreams. Freud starts with a medieval model of signs: he distinguishes between the dream's "manifest content" and its "latent content": this is a "shell and kernel" or depth model (Chapter 3). However, he soon develops a modern model whose basic concepts are *displacement*, *condensation* and *overdetermination*. One element in the manifest content of the dream might point to several elements in the latent content, and, conversely, one element of the latent content might manifest itself in several elements of the manifest content of the dream. Freud writes:

> Not only are the elements of a dream determined by the dream-thoughts many times over, but the individual dream-thoughts are represented in the dream by several elements. Associative paths lead from one element of the dream to several dream-thoughts, and from one dream-thought to several elements of the dream.
>
> (Freud 2001a, 284)

In the language of his contemporary, the originator of structuralism, Ferdinand de Saussure, Freud develops a model where one signifier has many signifieds and one signified many signifiers (see Chapter 7). The one-to-one relation between signifier and signified is broken in favour of open-ended substitution and continuing slippage or, in the terminology of Lacan, "sliding".

Lacan moves Freud's thought further along in a direction where it questions the idea of unconscious material *pre-existing* its representation, and therefore problematizes the very idea of truth, understood as correspondence with a pre-existing reality. For Lacan the unconscious is *already* representation. The unconscious is not a content, but the very processes of displacement, condensation and overdetermination described by Freud. Lacan's comment on the "fictional direction" of the self quoted above is made in the context of his essay on *the imaginary*, as part of an evolving Lacanian distinction between three orders: *the imaginary*, *the symbolic* and *the real*. We will now discuss this model of three interconnected orders or interlocking circles. (The model is complicated in Lacan's last work, with the introduction of the concept of the *Sinthome* and a fourth interlocking order, "the symptom". See Chapter 10 of Rabaté 2001).

Lacan outlines *the imaginary* in his early essay, "The Mirror Stage as Formative of the Function of the I as Revealed in Psychoanalytic Experience" (1949; an early version was delivered in 1936 and published in English translation in 1937). Lacan's starting point is a rereading of Freud that stresses the irremediable fragmentation and aggression of the self: Lacan outlines the "dehiscence at the heart of the organism" (Lacan 1977b, 4) and "lay[s] bare the aggressivity" (7). However, most of us misrecognize this condition. More importantly we set out to overcome it and to aim for an *imaginary* coherence, unity and autonomy, but with *real* and "formative effects" (3). In particular the "agency of the ego" transforms the self "in a fictional direction" of fixity and oneness which is just as "irreducible" as the primary fragmentation (2). In the "mirror stage" – which we never leave behind – through "*identification*", the subject "assumes an … *imago* [image, representation, likeness, statue]" of "permanence"; the subject "projects himself" onto a "statue" which is nothing but the defensive "armour of an alienating identity" (2, 4). This *imago* might be one's reflection in the mirror or the figure of the mother or any significant figure. In this sense, the self is an other: our identity is based on misrecognition – *méconnaissance* (6) – and psychic alienation.

Lacan accuses the Western philosophical tradition of taking part in this misrecognition – its very own particular *imago* is "consciousness" (the centrality of which we discussed above). He engages particularly with existentialism, the dominant philosophical paradigm in France at the time of writing; the central text of French existentialism, Jean-Paul Sartre's *Being and Nothingness* was published in 1943. On the one hand, Lacan endorses and shares existentialism's "negativity" (Lacan 1977b, 6), recognition of the mutual constitution of self and other – inherited from Hegel, another of Lacan's major interlocutors at this point – and theorization of "the look" (or "the gaze"). On the other hand, Lacan claims to expose existentialism's misrecognitions: the centrality of the "*perception-consciousness system*"; "self-sufficiency of consciousness"; its "illusion of autonomy" (6). Instead of privileging consciousness, Lacan proposes that we start from the role of the imaginary: the fictionality of the self, and the "*méconnaissance* that characterizes the ego" (6). Lacan's *imaginary* soon makes an impact on existentialist texts such as Simone de Beauvoir's *The Second Sex* (1949) and Frantz Fanon's *Black Skin, White Masks* (1952) (see Moi 1998, 80).

In "The Agency of the Letter in the Unconscious or Reason since Freud" (1957), Lacan concentrates on *the symbolic*, in response to his encounter with structuralism, particularly Saussure, Roman Jakobson and Claude Lévi-Strauss. In this essay Lacan returns to earlier themes and to Freud's *Interpretation of Dreams* in order to move beyond Freud, aided by structuralism, and beyond structuralism itself. In particular, Lacan here reiterates his earlier position that "the truth discovered by Freud" is that of "the self's radical ex-centricity to itself" or the "radical heteronomy … gaping within man" (Lacan 1977c, 171–2). However, while Freud discovers that "the unconscious is the discourse of the Other" (172), his work suffers from a misrecognition, a "*méconnaissance* of the constitutive role of the signifier" (162) and of "the signifying mechanisms" in the unconscious (165). Both Saussure and Freud (as discussed above) have left behind the model of language where the signifier "represent[s] the signified" (150) – where there is a one-to-one correspondence between signifier and signified. For Saussure a signifier acquires a signified out of its differential relations with other signifiers within syntagmatic and paradigmatic (or associative) chains of signifiers. Lacan emphasizes the way in which the space constituted by syntagmatic and paradigmatic chains of signifiers is multidimensional and polyvocal (rather than linear and univocal). For Lacan – in common with emerging poststructuralist thought and going beyond Saussure – the differential nature of signification means not only the primacy of the signifier over the signified but, importantly, the non-arrival of the signified: "an incessant sliding of the signified under the signifier" (154). In Freud's terminology, this is the incessant sliding of *displacement* and *condensation*: for Lacan "the letter [the signifier] … produces all the effects of truth" (158) rather than mirroring/masking a pre-existing truth. (That the signifier has no signified, that the letter has no content, that its "essence" is to circulate: this is how Lacan reads Edgar Allan Poe's short story, "The Purloined Letter", discussed above; see Lacan 1973.) For example, the signifiers "men" and "women" are purely differential but produce the effect of seemingly pre-existing men and women who "will be henceforth two countries" (152).

Lacan therefore rejects Freud's and Saussure's scientism in favour of those moments in Freud when he acknowledges that psychoanalysis is interminable. For example, in *The Interpretation of Dreams* Freud points to an uninterpretable kernel within the dream, figuring it as a navel connecting the dream to the unknown:

> There is often a passage in even the most thoroughly interpreted dream which has to be left obscure; this is because we become aware during the work of interpretation that at that point there is a tangle of dream-thoughts which cannot be unravelled and which moreover adds nothing to our knowledge of the content of the dream. This is the dream's navel, the spot where it reaches down into the unknown.
>
> (Freud 2001a, 525)

Lacan first outlines the relation between *the real*, *the imaginary* and *the symbolic* in a 1953 lecture (Lacan 1982) and continues to develop *the real* throughout his work, giving it increasing importance after 1972. *The real* is clearly a polysemous concept condensing a number of registers. Following Freud's metaphor of the navel connecting the dream to the unknown, *the real* can be understood as located in the navel of dreams (and other works of the unconscious). In *The Four Fundamental Concepts of Psychoanalysis* (1973), Lacan turns to Freud's *Beyond the Pleasure Principle* and "repetition compulsion" to describe *the real* "as trauma" (Lacan 1979, 53; see especially Chapter 5, "Tuché and Automaton"). The concept of *the real* is especially relevant in contemporary criticism, in large part due to its importance for the Slovenian critic Slavoj Žižek, Lacan's most prominent disciple. In view of Žižek's own contemporary importance, my discussion of *the real* will focus on Žižek's account of it in *Looking Awry* (1991).

In *Looking Awry* Žižek returns to Lacan's big themes. There is an "irreducible fissure" in man (Žižek 1991, 36). We are unknowingly dominated by *the real* of the death drive: "in the real of our desire, we are all murderers" (16). Žižek, like Lacan before him, sees himself as a Socrates-like figure confronting us with unpalatable truths and exposing the "utter nullity of our narcissistic pretensions" (64). However, the Socratic parallel can only be partial since Socrates claimed he knew nothing, let alone that he had grasped the truth of *the real.* Here Lacan and Žižek are caught in the paradox of having to occupy a position of mastery they have denounced, as Derrida's critique of Lacan (discussed above) points out. Unlike Lacan, Žižek is a post-Marxist who seems to resurrect the Marxist distinction between ideology as *doxa* and Marxist science as truth possessed by the Marxist critic – and this combined with Lacanian psychoanalysis.

Lacan and Žižek distinguish between *the real* and *reality*, and posit an oppositional and antagonistic relation between the two. The symbolic order produces *reality*: i.e. reality effects that appear "found" (Žižek 1991, 32–3), natural, already there rather than produced by us. (See Roland Barthes's similar analysis in *Mythologies*.) This semblance of the settled sense of reality – of *normality* – is constituted symbolically by us (or rather by our society's dominant forces) and cemented through our habitual automatisms of routine symbolization, though we misrecognize this. *The real* is the interruption of normality and of the reality of the status quo, when the "symbolic cobweb" is "torn aside by an intrusion of the real" (Žižek 1991, 17). *The real* is "lack, a hole in the midst of the symbolic order" (40); it is a limit to symbolization, a "meaningless leftover that cannot be integrated into the symbolic universe" (31). It is the moment when "trauma erupts" (17) and interrupts reality; the return of the dead when they cannot be symbolized and cannot find their place in the symbolic order. (See Beloved's return in Toni Morrison's *Beloved.*) Žižek continues that when *the real* erupts, objects dissolve and we become aware of "the pulsing of the presymbolic substance in its abhorrent vitality" (14), fleetingly, momentarily perceptible. Reality then loses its solidity and we become aware that normality is a façade or production. In a modern philosophical register, *the real* is radical or "pure contingency" (39); in an ancient Greek philosophical and tragic register *the real* is *tuchē* (pure chance): the fragility of luck.

Lacan had earlier delineated *the symbolic* in terms of the "incessant sliding of the signified under the signifier" (discussed above). This open and unfinished aspect of *the symbolic* is precisely the point where it connects with *the real,* allowing our "encounter with the 'impossible' real" (Žižek 1991, 58). *The real* for Lacan and Žižek is thus a safeguard against any form of dogmatism, a safety valve blocking any dominant view of reality from claiming finality and completion, including presumably Lacan's and Žižek's own views. Lacan and Žižek insist on the "irreducible gap separating the real from the modes of its symbolization" (Žižek 1991, 36), the barrier separating *reality* from *the real.*

To give some examples of literature in which such ideas are being explored, the Victorian gothic arguably attempts to render the amorphous, non-symbolizable real. Hence Bram Stoker's Dracula or Stevenson's Hyde are figures mixing incompatible elements and crossing symbolic differentiations and oppositions. Dracula, for example, interrupts the symbolic order in that he combines in his person stereotypical masculine *and* feminine characteristics. In Virginia Woolf's *To the Lighthouse,* Mrs Ramsay can be read as crossing the boundary between the real and the symbolic. On the one hand, she is busy knitting the symbolic cobweb of familial and social cohesion in her roles as mother and hostess, highlighted by her stocking knitting. On the other hand, she perceives herself as a hole in this symbolic cobweb, as a "wedge-shaped core of darkness" (Woolf 1964, 72).

Modernist "stream of consciousness" can be described, in Lacanian terms, as symbolic "sliding". Famously, Freud abandoned an initial interest in hypnotism to develop the "talking cure" of psychoanalysis and its method of "free association" (Freud's terms). The modernists experimented with the "stream of consciousness" technique aiming for enhanced psychic realism and trying to capture the mind's incessant sliding between observations, memories and desires – present, past and future. In Lacanian terms, they attempted to capture the symbolic sliding between multiple, heterogeneous signifying chains; the stereoscopic and multidimensional nature of psychic reality. Modernist experiments with "stream of consciousness" were influenced by Freud as well as by Aestheticism, the French philosopher Henri Bergson and the American philosopher William James. However, this literary project arguably goes further back. For example, in George Eliot's *Adam Bede* (1859), while Adam is walking, he is simultaneously observing the "objects around him"; thinking of his projects; having a "consciousness of wellbeing"; experiencing an "intense feeling" for Hetty, etc.: "But after feeling had welled up and poured itself out in this way, busy thought would come back with a greater vigour; and this morning it was intent on schemes by which the roads might be improved" (Eliot 1996, 392). Surrealism was the first modernist school to be programmatically committed to Freud and "free association", with André Breton directly inspired by Freud. Breton's first Surrealist Manifesto defined surrealism as: "Psychic automatism in its pure state, by which one proposes to express … the actual functioning of thought" (Breton 1972, 26). The surrealists translated "free association" into a method of "automatic writing", with limited success. Among the modernists, the paradoxical project of letting the unconscious speak beyond the author's conscious control – one of the origins of Roland Barthes's later critique of authorial intention – is encapsulated in D. H. Lawrence's "Never trust the artist. Trust the tale" (Lawrence 2003, 14). However, Lawrence's statement hugely downplays the role of extensive revisions, and therefore conscious design, in his writing.

Returning to Kristeva, and her appropriation of Lacan's schema of the imaginary, the symbolic and the real, Kristeva recasts this trio of concepts into a distinction between what she calls *the semiotic* and *the symbolic* in her early work, *Revolution in Poetic Language* (1974), which concentrates on the radical innovations of modernist writers. *The semiotic*, emerging in an early, pre-Oedipal phase of proximity with the maternal body, is a process that calls forth and mobilizes the material properties of language, such as sound and rhythm, in alliteration, assonance, rhyme, etc. *The symbolic* refers, denotes, makes propositions and judgements, takes up positions, leads to the "emergence of subject and object" as distinct and separate from each other, and is constrained by sociopolitical orders and structures (Kristeva 1984, 86). Kristeva calls the space of the semiotic *chora*, borrowing a polysemous term from Plato's *Timaeus*, whose many connotations include "womb" and "mothering" (see Chapter 1). (In the *Timaeus* the *chora* is: "receptacle"; "the nurse of all becoming"; "a kind of neutral plastic material"; "invisible and formless, all embracing"; "space, which is eternal and indestructible", inaccessible to the senses, "invisible and formless" but "intelligible"; it "provides a position for everything that comes to be" [Plato 1977, 49–52].) For Kristeva the semiotic is an open-ended *process* of signification, and "only certain literary texts of the avant-garde (Mallarmé, Joyce) manage to convey the infinity of the process" (Kristeva 1984, 88). In relation to Lacan, Kristeva's semiotic, often read as Lacan's imaginary, can also be read as the sliding of the signified under the play of signifiers that Lacan identified as an aspect of the symbolic itself – the symbolic in Lacan seems to oscillate between conventional signification/*doxa* and its undoing.

Kristeva's argument is that what is at stake is not to choose the semiotic against the symbolic, but to think and practice their interaction. While a purely semiotic writing might collapse into non-sense, the releasing of the semiotic into the symbolic and their co-existence is a source of aesthetic and even social renewal in literature. Jacqueline Rose's critique of *écriture feminine* (women's writing, as theorized by Hélène Cixous, Luce Irigaray and other French feminists, see Chapter 12) in "'Daddy'" (1991) is in this spirit: Rose cautions against a "feminist celebration of the breakdown or fragmentation of language" and "the psychic and political cost of that desire for fragmentation" (Rose 1994, 241, 249), in favour of a less anarchic version of feminism. (Rose doesn't name anyone. In relation to Freud, see especially the first section of Irigaray's *Speculum of the Other Woman* [1974], "The Blind Spot of an Old Dream of Symmetry".)

A good example of the application of Kristeva's ideas to the novel would be Makiko Minow-Pinkney's 1987 reading of Woolf's *Mrs Dalloway*, focusing on the relation between the semiotic and the symbolic in this novel, while also highlighting both Kristeva's Bakhtinian lineage and especially her feminist concerns. Minow-Pinkney argues that Woolf's "semiotic" use of free indirect discourse makes the voice "unindentifiable" – impossible to attribute either to the narrator or to one of the characters – and "suspends the location of the subject" (Minow-Pinkney 1996, 167). She draws the feminist conclusion that this works as a "denial of the unified subject which … is necessarily 'masculine'" (168). Another "semiotic" technique in this novel, working in the same direction, is the undermining of simple linearity by "simultaneity" (170); yet another is the extensive use of present participles in order to "loosen the binding function of syntax" (166). However, Minow-Pinkney reiterates the Kristevan point that Woolf combines use of the semiotic and the symbolic. Woolf does not set out to overcome the symbolic but to "minimize" its control and allow the semiotic "as much autonomy as possible" (168).

***

In this chapter we discussed psychoanalytic ideas of the self, of the relation between psychoanalysis and literature and of the nature of representation and fiction. We will turn now to the question of reading and interpretation in psychoanalytic literary criticism. Harold Bloom, in his influential and controversial *The Anxiety of Influence* (1973), advanced the theory that poetry and criticism, at their very best, work through creative misreading or "poetic misprision" (Bloom 1997, 7). (He rejected the distinction between poetic and critical activity, as Pater, Wilde and others did before him.) Bloom's psychoanalytic history of poetry avoids the Freudian concept of *sublimation* (investment of sexual energy in higher aims) and creatively misreads, instead, the Freudian concepts of *anxiety* and the *Oedipus complex*. The "strong" – the original – new poet (and critic) is a "son" in existential rebellion against his "father" and against life itself. He refuses to give up on infantile ideas, such as immortality and the omnipotence of thought: "poems arise out of the illusion of freedom" (96). However, his emergence as a strong poet involves, not inspiration and god-like creativity *ex nihilo*, but "anxiety", the anxious misreading of a "father" poet that Bloom calls the *anxiety of influence*: "Poetry is the anxiety of influence, is misprision … Poetry is a misunderstanding, misinterpretation" (95); "Every poem is a misinterpretation of a parent poem. A poem is not an overcoming of anxiety, but is that anxiety" (94). The new poet is caught in an Oedipal, father-and-son struggle with a strong precursor poet, which takes the form of a creative "misprision" of the precursor. The measure of the new poet's success is his ability to misread the precursor's work – to symbolically and creatively disfigure and kill the father. Bloom suggests that his theory is proven by the experience of strong critics like himself: "How do we understand an anxiety? By ourselves being anxious. Every deep reader [of poetry] … asks, 'Who wrote my poem?'" (96). Bloom's theory seems to be a translation, in psychoanalytic terms, and a misreading of T. S. Eliot's criticism, especially "Tradition and the Individual Talent" (Chapter 8), though Bloom is silent about this intertext, both in the first and in the second (1997) edition of *The Anxiety of Influence*. Paradoxically, the conservative critic Eliot is forward directed to the strong poet's (and critic's) *re*interpretation, not as erring in relation to the tradition, but as a better interpretation for his times. Bloom's "misprision" is backward directed, portraying the lack of independence of an essentially weak son who feels he is fundamentally wrong and inferior, and submits to his feelings of guilt in relation to the father.

In their groundbreaking *The Mad Woman in the Attic* (1979), Sandra M. Gilbert and Susan Gubar's feminist critique of Bloom is that his theory of literary history unintentionally makes visible the "patriarchal poetics (and attendant anxieties) which underlie our culture's chief literary movements" (Gilbert and Gubar 2000, 48). However, Bloom's story of conflict between fathers and sons is not suited to understanding the history of women's literary production. Women writers – producing in a social and literary context in which authorship had been considered unfeminine and antithetical to women's nature – have suffered from the absence or scarcity of female precursors desperately needed to authorize and "legitimize" their writing, and to "prov[e] by example that a revolt against patriarchal literary authority is possible" (49–50). The problem of the scarcity of women writers was compounded by their exclusion from the literary canon and the absence of a resistant counter-canon of women writers. All these factors contributed to a very different, socially induced experience for women writers; not an anxiety of influence, but an "anxiety of authorship": that "the act of writing will isolate or destroy her" (49).

While Gilbert and Gubar position their theory of the history of women's literary production in relation to – in Oedipal struggle with? – Bloom, their obvious precursor is Virginia Woolf's *A Room of One's Own* (1928). In *A Room of One's Own* Woolf's history of women's writing conveys a sense of the impediments that for much of literary history have worked to silence women and suggests the need for literary mothers. Woolf discusses the "lack of tradition" in women's writing (Woolf 2004, 28) and the importance of "thinking in common" (76) and "think[ing] back through our mothers" (88); a great woman writer is "an inheritor as well as an originator" (126).

Gilbert and Gubar wrote at a time when the inclusion of texts by women in the canon, the (re-)construction of a counter-canon of women's writing and the salvaging of forgotten texts were high priorities for feminist literary critics. For example, Cora Kaplan's 1977 Women's Press edition of *Aurora Leigh* (*Aurora Leigh and Other Poems*) salvaged Elizabeth Barrett Browning's epic from oblivion. See also Elaine Showalter's *A Literature of Their Own* (1977). These remain important feminist tasks, in response to the *anxiety of authorship* felt by women and other marginalized groups.

Particularly relevant to the contemporary psychoanalytic understanding of reading and interpretation is the psychoanalytic notion of *transference*. Freud's distinction between "manifest" and "latent" content in *The Interpretation of Dreams* initially points to a depth-model of reading, where we are required to go beyond the shell towards the kernel inside. Freud usually perceives himself as a scientist who aspires to bring his object fully to light (from dreams and symptoms to works of art): to interpret objectively and exhaustively, to fully expose the kernel and discard the shell. However, complications to Freud's model (such as "dream-thoughts which cannot be unravelled" or the "dream's navel" reaching "down into the unknown", quoted above) introduce something more akin to a modern theory of reading and interpretation emphasizing the incompleteness, provisionality and indeterminacy of interpretation we favour today. These margins of Freud's work have been strongly emphasized by Lacan and many contemporary psychoanalytic critics. One of the complications at work in the relation between psychoanalyst and analysand has to do with the role of *transference* – the analysand's unwilled replaying of repressed situations in their relation to the analyst – and the analyst's *counter-transference* – the analyst's replaying of their own repressed scenes in their relation to the analysand. Rather than elucidating signs in a scientific manner, the analyst relies on the analysand's transference and his or her own counter-transference. The analysand, unable to recollect properly and in the absence of full insight from the analyst, unknowingly repeats or *transfers* (hence "transference") a repressed scene in the analytic situation, casting the analyst in the role of the significant other in that repressed scene, and thus giving the repressed scene an indirect form of expression. In response the analyst, rather than simply witnessing this drama as an outsider and retaining his objectivity and non-involvement, repeats and plays out his own repressed scene, in counter-transference.

To understand literature and criticism as repetition, transference and counter-transference is to see literature and criticism not as cognitive but as symptomatic of repressed scenes and desires. Peter Brooks's *Reading for the Plot* (1984) is advancing such a view. Turning to Freud's *Beyond the Pleasure Principle*, Brooks defines literary narrative as "repetition": as "a form of remembering, brought into play when recollection properly speaking is blocked by resistance" (Brooks 1992, 98). For Brooks literary repetition has many aspects or manifestations. He recasts the Russian Formalist distinction between *fabula* (story) and *sjužet* (narrative, plot): *sjužet* is, in psychoanalytic terms, the repetition of *fabula*. Other aspects of literary repetition are: metre and rhyme; assonance and alliteration; the use of refrains; narrative return to earlier events and making connections between events; tropes, such as repeated motifs, running through texts. Brooks defines literary repetition broadly as a "shuttling" back and forth, a movement of "oscillation that binds" the text together (100). This "binding of textual energies" through formalization creates *sjužet* out of *fabula* (101). While binding, repetition also introduces delay, which Brooks describes in a sexual language. Narrative is delayed "erotic" tension, "arousal" and delayed gratification between two states of zero intensity, the beginning and the end (103). Brooks declares himself in favour of the "most delayed" and most "highly bound" texts (102). The reader participates in this "tumescence" (103) and delayed erotic tension. He or she reads for the end – which is also the end of the reader's erotic tension – but the end must not come "too quickly" (104).

Brooks attempts to clarify and defend his project in "The Idea of Psychoanalytic Criticism" in *Psychoanalysis and Storytelling* (1994). He argues for a "model of reading based on Freud's notion of transference" (Brooks 1994, 42). This model combines psychoanalysis, formalism and reader-response theory. In particular Brooks pays a formalist's attention to "the structure and rhetoric" (20) of texts, informed by the psychoanalysis-inspired insights that "aesthetic form harbors an erotic force" (26), and that the text's erotic force is "activated in its reading" (35). While Brooks hadn't mentioned Harold Bloom at all in *Reading for the Plot*, he now mentions Bloom disparagingly, as antithetical to his own project. Bloom's "psychomachia of literary history" resurrects the disreputable tradition of biographical psychoanalytic criticism (21), while Brooks allies himself with the poststructuralist attention to textuality: "texts and rhetoric rather than authors" (23). However, in Kristeva's poststructuralist terms, it might be argued that Brooks's theory of literature and criticism is completely semiotic, at the exclusion of the symbolic, with problematic consequences. Brooks claims to reveal the truth of literature and criticism as symptomatic semiotic repetition of repressed desires, but in making this claim his own theory presents itself as cognitive, exempt from semiotic repetition and completely symbolic. Brooks's psychoanalytic theory of literary interpretation is thus an odd combination of pretension to knowledge and claim that knowledge is not possible.

Conclusion

- Our discussion of Freud outlined his theorization of the self: the Unconscious; the relation between sexuality, resistance and repression; the relation between *pleasure principle* and *reality principle*; the role of fantasy and *nachtrachlichkeit* ("deferred action" or "afterwardsness"). In Freud's later work, the relation between *eros* and *thanatos* (the death instinct); the distinction between *id*, *ego* and *super-ego*; his theorization of melancholia; the 1920s debate on gender within psychoanalysis and the subsequent break in Freud's theorization of gender. In relation to the formation of dreams, we outlined the processes of *displacement*, *condensation* and *overdetermination*. We discussed *transference* and *counter-transference*, in the relation between analysand and analyst.

- Melanie Klein emphasized the relation to the mother and the role of aggression in the psychic life of both men and women. We discussed her distinction between the *paranoid-schizoid position* and the *depressive position*.
- We discussed Lacan's distinction between *the imaginary* (identifications, misrecognition, fictional direction), *the symbolic* (symbolic differentiations and the sliding of the signified under the signifier) and *the real*. We turned to Žižek's understanding of Lacan's real, and Žižek's distinction between *the real* and *reality*.
- We discussed Kristeva's distinction between *the semiotic* and *the symbolic* and its relation to Lacan; her theorization of the relation between melancholia and literary production; her concept of *abjection* (as it relates to Freud and Melanie Klein) and its relation to literature.
- We outlined Bloom's *anxiety of influence*, and Gilbert and Gubar's *anxiety of authorship*.
- We discussed Brooks's theorization of literary narrative, reading and interpretation as repetition and transference of repressed desire.

Further reading

See Freud 1977, 1979, 2001a, especially Chapter 6, and 2001c. See also: Bloom 1997; Breton 1972; Brooks 1992; Deleuze and Guattari 1984, Chapter 4; Ellmann 1994b; Felman 1994; Gilbert and Gubar 2000, Chapter 2; Kristeva 1982 and 1989; Lacan 1977b, 1977c and 1979; Lawrence 2004; Meisel 2007; Rose 1994; Wollheim 1973; Žižek 1991.

7 Defamiliarization, alienation, dialogism and montage

Saussure, Russian Formalism (Shklovsky, Jakobson), Bakhtin and German modernist Marxism (Brecht, Benjamin)

From Saussure's *semiology* to Bakhtin's *dialogism*: Saussure versus Du Bois, Woolf, Shklovsky, Jakobson and Bakhtin

Critics agree that the Swiss linguist Ferdinand de Saussure (1857–1913) provided one of the foundations of twentieth-century and contemporary literary theory. He did not contribute to literary theory directly, but he put forward a new science of linguistics, which became a model for literary theorists. It is often said, and with much truth, that twentieth-century literary theory originates in Marx, Nietzsche, Freud and Saussure – four white European men – and that twentieth-century and contemporary critical theory translates, critiques and imaginatively combines these thinkers. For instance, there are several Freudo-Marxisms, and we discussed Lacan's and Kristeva's mixing of Freud with Saussure in the last chapter.

Saussure's *Course in General Linguistics* is an elusive text and in this sense anything but a solid foundation. The book was not written by Saussure himself, but was put together posthumously by Saussure's colleagues, Charles Bally and Albert Sechehaye, and published in 1916. The text is constructed out of a collation of several students' notes, as Saussure, it seems, did not see fit to keep his lecture notes. Clarifying this intriguing attitude, Bally and Sechehaye, in their 1915 "Preface to the First Edition", comment that Saussure was one of those thinkers "who never stand still", claiming that his thought "evolved in all directions" without "ever contradicting itself" (Bally and Sechehaye 1960, xiv). They describe their own "main aim" as "draw[ing] together an organic whole" (xv).

In *Course in General Linguistics* Saussure announces and outlines a new semiology or science of signs. I will begin by sketching out the elements of his theory.

- *Semiology*. Saussure understands language as a "system of signs" (Saussure 1960, 15). While language is one of many systems of signs and linguistics is "only a part" (16) of semiology, language is *the exemplary* (68) and "most important" system of signs (16). Sign systems are thoroughly social – language, for example, is a "social institution" (15) – and semiology explicitly aims to study "*the life of signs within society*" (16).

- *Langue and parole.* Saussure distinguishes between *langue* (language) and *parole* (speech). He describes *langue* as an impersonal social structure – a synchronic (in one moment in time, as opposed to diachronic) and self-referential "system of interdependent terms" (114); *parole* as an individual instance (e.g. an utterance or a piece of writing) of the system of language. He claims that we "must start" from the "interdependent whole", *langue*, not from the individual *parole*, as "by himself the individual is incapable of fixing a single value [meaning]" (113). Within *langue* the meaning of each and every term is "determined by its environment" (116) of other terms. In other words, *langue* is a purely *differential* system, and the meaning of each term is determined negatively, through its differential relations to other terms: "*language is a form and not a substance*" (122). Though linguistic "values" (meanings) are always subject to "usage and general acceptance" by "[t]he community", they emerge from a differential and self-referential system and therefore "remain entirely relative" (113).
- *Signifier/signified = sign.* Saussure distinguishes between "signifier" (*signifiant*), the sound pattern of a spoken word, for example, and "signified" (*signifié*), the concept or meaning "associated with" that word (14). He calls the coupling or the "union" (15) or the "combination" of signifier and signified, the "sign" (*signe*) – sign "designate[s] the whole" (67). It is important to note that a signifier doesn't represent or mirror reality – it doesn't match "a thing and a name" (66). Instead it gives meaning to reality. Equally importantly, the signifier does not imitate or mirror the signified. On the contrary, there is "no natural connection" (69) between the two; the "bond" between the two is purely "arbitrary" (67). Even in cases of onomatopoeia the link between signifier and signified is arbitrary – hence the signifier of frog sounds is *ribbit* in American English, *croak* in United Kingdom English and *vrekekex kouax kouax* in modern Greek. (Of course, we might object that they are likely different species of frogs in these three countries, and we might wish to say that cats really do make a noise more like *meow* than *woof* or (the Greek dog) *gav gav*, but we must move on!) Furthermore, the bond between a signifier and a signified is far from "fixed" (69), given, unmediated or primary. Even more radically, "signifieds" – concepts, ideas, thoughts – do not pre-exist the differential system of language but are shaped by it. It is wrong to assume that "ready-made ideas exist before words" (65). Directly against the views of Coleridge and Shelley (discussed in Chapter 4), Saussure claims that "thought – apart from its expression in words – is only a shapeless and indistinct mass" (111); "Without language, thought is a vague, uncharted nebula" (112). A signified is primarily shaped by its differential relations with other signifieds: "concepts are purely differential and defined … negatively

by their relations with the other terms of the system … being what the others are not"; in this sense concepts "emanat[e]" from the linguistic system (117). Similarly a signifier is determined differentially by its relations with other signifiers; it is "constituted not by its material substance but by the differences that separate" it "from all others" (118–19). Any apparent solidity in the marriage of a signifier and a signified is only a temporary and belated effect of chains of signifiers and chains of signifieds and their relations: "in language there are only differences *without positive terms*. Whether we take the signified or the signifier, language has neither ideas nor sounds that existed before the linguistic system" (120). For example, the signifier "cool" has a certain signified in the chain "it's hot and I want some cool water"; a rather different signified in the chain "this is a cool t-shirt".

- *Syntagmatic and associative relations.* Saussure distinguishes between "syntagmatic" and "associative" (or "paradigmatic") chains of signifiers. "This is a cool t-shirt" is a syntagmatic chain or *syntagm*; the "ideal type of syntagm" is the sentence (124). Each syntagm has "a fixed number of elements" (126) which are "presented in succession" and thus "form a chain" (70). Each signifier in a syntagm acquires a signified through its relation with the signifiers that precede and follow it in that syntagm.

  You meet someone you are attracted to on the street and say, "That is a cool t-shirt". Instead of "cool", you could have selected: "nice", "wicked", "sick", "sexy", etc. "Cool", "nice", "wicked", "sick", "sexy", etc. are part of an "associative" chain, a virtual repertoire or "storehouse" (123) of associated terms. You speculate inconclusively – because of the inherent ambiguity of language – that "sexy" might have been too obvious, "nice" too bland. While you are asking yourself whether "cool" was the right word to use, all the terms you didn't select have been defining "cool" differentially.

  Associative chains link "words … that have something in common" (123); unlike syntagmatic chains they "occur neither in fixed numbers nor in a definite order" (126), and the same signifier can give rise to multiple series of associative chains: for example, "cool" can trigger a chain of words containing c– and –l or a chain of words ending in –ool. While syntagms are actual, associative chains are virtual and constructed by the interpreter of a syntagm; Saussure describes the former as "*in presentia*" and the latter as "*in absentia*" (123). Given an actual syntagmatic chain such as "this is a cool t-shirt", each one of its signifiers, for example "cool", triggers a virtual associative chain. The signified of "cool" in this particular syntagm is determined both by its syntagmatic chain and its associative chain.

Reading Saussure's *Course in General Linguistics* with W. E. B. Du Bois's *The Souls of Black Folk* (1903) and Virginia Woolf's *A Room of One's Own* (1928) might seem an incongruous juxtaposition. But the discussion of

Mikhail Bakhtin to follow will, I hope, allow us to retrospectively articulate their relation, while in turn the discussion of Du Bois and Woolf will demonstrate the significance of Bakhtin's critique of Saussure. Saussure's Copernican Revolution in language consists in viewing language not as a mirror of society, but as itself a central part of society, as a central social institution embodying and even constructing social perspectives and social meanings. But his revolution – and his vision of *langue* – cannot give a proper account of social fissures and the socially and economically marginalized. To be fair to Saussure, although he didn't discuss issues of class or gender in relation to language, he was part of a broad democratizing movement within French linguistics that began in the later nineteenth century. His insistence on the priority of the spoken word – which Derrida was later to critique as an instance of logocentrism (see Chapter 3) – was intended to give priority to ordinary everyday language over written literary texts when deciding what it was that constituted *langue*. Saussure also fiercely polemicized against racist linguistics.

The opening lines of Du Bois's *The Souls of Black Folk* boldly state the magnitude of the issue: "the strange meaning of being black here in the dawning of the Twentieth Century … is not without interest to you, Gentle Reader; for the problem of the Twentieth Century is the problem of the color-line" (Du Bois 1999, 5). Du Bois makes explicit the global dimensions of the problem: it concerns "the relation of the darker to the lighter races of men in Asia and Africa, in America and the islands of the sea" (17). Du Bois's analysis of the "strange meaning" of blackness shows up the limitations of Saussure as well as Freud. Freud theorized a conflict-ridden split within the self between unconscious desire and the conscious social commands of the super-ego (see Chapter 6). Du Bois, on the other hand, theorizes a fracturing, within both conscious thought and unconscious desire, along a societal fault line: "One ever feels his two-ness, – an American, a Negro; two souls, two thoughts, two unreconciled strivings; two warring ideals in one dark body, whose dogged strength alone keeps it from being torn asunder" (11). Du Bois calls this fracturing "double consciousness" (11). The African-American (male) self is projected onto American history and split across/along by the "race-line". Situating this self particularly within the American historical context of the failure of Reconstruction (the promise to give at least male former slaves full citizenship: the right to vote and stand for political office, access to education, economic opportunity) following the abolition of slavery in 1863, he outlines the hope of a successful bi-culturalism: "The history of the American Negro is the history of this strife, – this longing … to merge his double self into a better and truer self. In this merging he wishes neither of the older selves to be lost" (11). Simultaneously, and on occasion, Du Bois's "self" is not exclusively African-American but "darker", and its field is the global field of colonial empires. Writing in the very early years of the twentieth century, Du Bois prophetically announces the global decolonization movements and the US civil rights movement:

> So dawned the time of *Sturm und Drang*: storm and stress to-day rocks our little boat on the mad waters of the world-sea; there is within and without the sound of conflict, the burning of body and rending of soul. (15)

In *A Room of One's Own* Virginia Woolf records the fracturing of the self along another social fault line, the gender line:

> if one is a woman one is often surprised by a sudden splitting off of consciousness, say in walking down Whitehall, when from being the natural inheritor of that civilization, she becomes, on the contrary, outside of it, alien and critical. (Woolf 2004, 112)

Woolf turns this painful experience into a revelation of the true nature of thought – "Clearly the mind is always altering its focus and bringing the world into different perspectives" (112) – and declares the "fusion" of conflicting perspectives as a principle of artistic creation. She writes in praise of the "androgynous mind" of Shakespeare: "It is when this fusion takes place that the mind is fully fertilized and uses all its faculties" (113–14).

Viktor Shklovsky (1893–1984) was a leading member of the Russian Formalists. Russian Formalism is a movement in literary criticism associated with two inter-related groups of critics emerging around 1914: the members of *Opoyaz* (Society for the Study of Poetic Language) based in St Petersburg and led by Shklovsky, who published his first pamphlet, *The Resurrection of the Word*, in the same year; and the Moscow Linguistic Circle, led by Roman Jakobson and contributing their engagement with Saussure. The Russian Formalist Boris Eikhenbaum (or Eichenbaum) has given an insider's account of the movement, "Introduction to the Formal Method" (1927). According to Eikhenbaum, Russian Formalism is an "investigation of the specific properties of literary material" (Eichenbaum 1998, 8). In Jakobson's definitive formulation, quoted by Eikhenbaum: "The object of study in literary science is not literature but 'literariness'" (Jakobson quoted in Eichenbaum 1998, 8). In Eikhenbaum's view the movement coalesced around 1916; and Shklovsky's seminal essay, "Art as Technique", published in 1917 – the epochal year of the outbreak of the Russian Revolution, in the midst of World War I – is "a kind of manifesto of the Formal method" (11). Anxious to establish the absolute novelty of Russian Formalism – in a gesture repeated in many early-twentieth-century avant-garde movements valorizing newness – Eikhenbaum claims that already in 1914, in Shklovsky's *The Resurrection of the Word*, there is a "decisive departure from" *fin-de-siècle* Symbolism, and *fin-de-siècle* "'aestheticism' … had likewise been overcome" (10). In "The Theory of the 'Formal Method'" (1926, 1927) Eikhenbaum continues to define Russian Formalism as a new and "scientific investigation" directly opposed to the by-now canonical "subjectivism" of the Symbolist poetics of an older generation

(Eichenbaum 2001, 1065). By contrast, Peter Bürger, in his influential *Theory of the Avant-garde,* views Aestheticism and Symbolism as opening the way for the early-twentieth-century avant-gardes (Bürger 1984, 22, 27). On the other hand, Eikhenbaum freely acknowledges the Russian Futurists as the Russian Formalists' contemporaries and close allies. Paying tribute to the "startling innovations" of Russian Futurist poetry (of which Vladimir Mayakovsky was the leading example), he comments that "Formalism and Futurism seemed bound together by history" (1064). Both Bürger and Eikhenbaum were right. Eikhenbaum is referring primarily to the Russian Symbolists, Bürger to the French Symbolists, who are arguably much closer to the Russian Futurists in spirit. Bürger's case is stronger for the United Kingdom, if only due to the fact that although there was a Futurist-related movement called Vorticism (of which Wyndham Lewis was the principal figure), it had nothing like the impact of Futurism in Russia, where the movement was so connected with the historical moment of the Revolution. We are reminded that literary and critical history, like all other history, is rarely the clear-cut progression that we are tempted to try to make it. And we might also reflect that the Russian avant-garde was only a brief flowering. A few years would bring imprisonment, exile, lives lived in fear and silence and for some death, as Russian intellectual and artistic life was subjected to the brutal force of Stalinism, and the arts forced to comply with the deadly philistinism of the state-sponsored artistic style: Socialist Realism.

Futurism was initially launched in Italy in 1909 with F. T. Marinetti's "The Manifesto of Futurism". Addressed to men under 30, this is a self-described "erect" text with proclamations of the sort: "9. We intend to glorify war – the only hygiene of the world – militarism, patriotism ... and contempt for woman. 10. We intend to destroy museums, libraries, academies of every sort, and to fight against moralism, feminism" (Marinetti 2009, 53, 51). It seems unsurprising that Italian Futurists later gravitated towards Fascism. Russian Futurism developed independently, resisting Marinetti's attempts at leadership and moving in the opposite political direction, aligning themselves rather with the Left and in particular the Bolsheviks, later to become the Communist Party of the Soviet Union. Russian Futurism was launched in 1912, with the first publication of the manifesto "A Slap in the Face of Public Taste", cowritten by David Burliuk, Alexander Kruchenykh, Vladmir Mayakovsky and Victor Khlebnikov. "A Slap" announced "Word-novelty" and "the New Coming Beauty of the Self-sufficient (self-centred) Word" and polemically promised to "Throw Pushkin, Dostoevsky, Tolstoy" and other greats of Russian literature "overboard from the Ship of Modernity" (Burliuk *et al.* 1988, 51–2).

This is the fervently creative, experimental and innovative milieu in which Shklovsky published "Art as Technique", outlining his concept of *defamiliarization* in 1917. Shklovsky proposed *ostranenie* (usually translated as "defamiliarization"; also translated as "estrangement") as a general artistic technique that can be found at work throughout literature, though Shklovsky himself concentrated on prose. We might note immediately that in the use of the word "technique" there was a polemical resonance. Shklovsky sought to address what it was about literary writing that made it literary; this then can be seen as his "formalism". This approach Shklovsky and his fellow formalists considered in contrast with the criticism of the period which, like Symbolist literature itself, they thought to have neglected such questions in favour of over-much emphasis on psychological and historical content.

The Romantic poets Coleridge and Shelley defined their literary practice as a defamiliarization of reality. Theirs was a transformative view of literature akin to Hegel's own (see Chapter 4). Shelley in particular envisaged defamiliarization in its potential for *social* transformation that would bridge the widening gap between rich and poor. Shklovsky's "defamiliarization" also points (though not exclusively) to social transformation. In "Art as Technique" Shklovsky claims that art makes "the stone *stony*": "the technique of art is to make objects unfamiliar", to delay and impede perception (Shklovsky 1998, 18). This enables a critical attitude in the reader, as Shklovsky's examples show. To stay with Shklovsky's most sustained example, Tolstoy uses defamiliarization to question the institution of private property in his short story, "Kholstomer". An old horse, still trying to understand the world of humans after many years of observation and reflection, is having particular trouble figuring out the meaning of the words "my" and "mine". What does it mean when humans say, for example, this is "my" horse. Here the thoughtful horse concludes his meditation:

> They agree that only one may say "mine" about this, that or the other thing. And the one who says "mine" about the greatest number of things is … the one they consider the most happy … For a long time I tried to explain it to myself in terms of some kind of a real gain, but I had to reject that explanation because it was wrong. Many of those, for instance, who called me their own never rode on me … There are people who call a tract of land their own, but they never set eyes on it and never take a stroll on it. There are people who call others their own, yet never see them. And the whole relationship between them is that the so-called "owners" treat the others unjustly … I am now convinced that this is the essential difference between people and ourselves.
>
> (Tolstoy quoted in Shklovsky 1998, 19)

Du Bois and Woolf record the co-existence, within the self, of socially dominant and minority perspectives. Shklovsky's *defamiliarization* implies a critique of the socially dominant perspective and suggests a role for literature in displaying or constructing emergent social and political perspectives. Beyond the race line and the gender line, the humanitarian anarcho-communist horse speaks against an inhuman institution on behalf of those treated by it like animals.

History has rendered Shklovsky's choice of the loquacious horse speaking in the name of the ideals of the Revolution sharply ironic. The opening of possibilities around the time of the Russian Revolution that underpinned the efflorescence of Russian Futurism and Russian Formalism did not last. With a warrant for his arrest as a political enemy issued, due to his involvement with the Socialist Revolutionary Party, rivals to the Bolsheviks, Shklovsky had to flee Russia for Berlin in 1922. Deeply unhappy abroad he begged the authorities to allow him to return, and after Mayakovsky's intervention he was allowed to in 1923. He recanted his Formalism in a 1930 article. In 1936 Formalism was officially condemned. Shklovsky lived quietly in Moscow until his death, continuing to write academic books and novels and also developing a career as a screenwriter.

Shklovsky's notion of *defamiliarization* has been so influential because it captures an aspiration or mission shared broadly by very many writers and critics, one way or another. One might defamiliarize by reinterpreting the facts, by seeing things differently. Or very often – e.g. for Žižek, as discussed in Chapter 6 – there are special moments of access to the truth, moments of revelation, for which we may be able to prepare, but which are not in our power. Reality rents the veil of appearance and exposes us to the uncognizable glare of a familiarity-nihilating alien world. Or suddenly we are back there in the vanished moment, which is no longer "imagination", no longer object, but the subject of the past which reveals itself as a present irradiated with its full lived significance – e.g. for Benjamin, to be discussed shortly. Shklovsky of course focuses more narrowly on defamiliarization as a literary device or technique.

Roman Jakobson (1896–1982), also identified with Russian Formalism, migrated to Czechoslovakia in 1920 and was one of the founders of the Prague Linguistic Circle in 1926. After the Nazi invasion of Czechoslovakia in 1938, he fled to Scandinavia and finally migrated to the US in 1941. "The Dominant" (1935) belongs to Jakobson's Prague period, but positions itself explicitly as a post-Saussurean text within the tradition of Russian Formalism, following Shklovsky in thinking about literary language. Indeed Jakobson seems to close his text with a reaffirmation of the validity of Shklovsky's defamiliarization: the reader or viewer "has a vivid awareness of two orders: the traditional canon and the artistic novelty as a deviation from that canon", as "brought to light" by Russian Formalism (Jakobson 1987b, 46). Unlike Shklovsky, whose focus is prose, Jakobson focuses on poetic form or structure. Jakobson's starting point is a critique and a substantial reformulation of Saussure's understanding of structure as a synchronic system of inter-related elements.

First, Jakobson understands structure as a hierarchy articulating a dominant element – "the dominant" – and marginal elements. The dominant "rules, determines, and transforms the remaining components" and "guarantees the integrity of the work" (41). Jakobson defines the "poetic work" as "a verbal message whose aesthetic function" or "poetic language" is dominant; "aesthetic function" and "poetic language" are interchangeable and the latter is defined as language "directed precisely toward the sign as such", i.e. towards the signifier, the linguistic message itself, rather than the context, the referent, the addresser or the addressee (43–4). (Jakobson will later settle on the term "poetic function".) So, on the one hand, the poetic work displays several other functions (for example, emotive, referential, etc.); Jakobson defined these functions, including the poetic function, more precisely in "Linguistics and Poetics" (1960). On the other hand, the aesthetic or poetic function is "not limited to poetic works" (43). Finally, the linguistic functions of a poetic work by no means exhaust the elements of a poetic work (such elements might be musical, rhythmic, visual, etc.). Unlike Saussure but following Shklovsky, Jakobson addresses the formal features of literary language, his concept of "the dominant" introducing the world and power relations between different kinds of language, linguistic functions and extra-linguistic elements into Saussure's purely logical differential linguistic system. For example, a poem makes the stone stony by using the resources of language to evoke a sense of the stone. The poet may have a stone in mind, or in front of him, as he writes the poem. However, it is not this reference that makes it a poem, even though the poem will mean nothing to the reader if they do not have an extensive knowledge of stones in general, of the connotations of stones and finally of a shared world. Nor is making the stone stony reducible to Saussure's differential definition of the signified of the stone (not a rock, not a pebble, etc.).

Second, Saussure's understanding of structure as purely synchronic is too static and introduces a "gap" (46) between synchronic (in one moment in time) and diachronic (over time) analysis, which makes it impossible to address historical change. To bridge this gap, Jakobson posits a "shifting dominant" in an ever-shifting hierarchy whose "superior" and "inferior" elements (42) are constantly redefined: the "evolution of poetic form" is a "question of shifts in the mutual relationship among the diverse components of the system … a question of the shifting dominant" (44). For example, epic poetry might be dominant in one period, lyric poetry in another. (If Jakobson had limited himself to functions, given the definitional dominance of the poetic function, there would be little scope for change.) Jakobson boldly extends this mobile and dynamic model beyond the understanding of poetic form and towards an ever-widening circle of cultural interaction. In a ripple effect, a "shift" in the "hierarchy of poetic genres" leads to shifts in the relation of literature to the others arts (for example, literature might be dominant in one period, music in another), as well as the relation of literature to extra-aesthetic discourses: "Questions concerning changes in the mutual relationship between the individual arts also arise", as well as "changes in the mutual relationship between the arts and other closely related cultural domains …

especially … between literature and other kinds of verbal message" (44–5). This view of literary history anticipates the tenets of New Historicism in the late 1980s (to be discussed further in this chapter). Fredric Jameson will later take up Jakobson's idea of "the dominant", defining postmodernism as the cultural "dominant" during the new era of late capitalism (Jameson 1991, 4) (this will be discussed in Chapter 9).

Third, Jakobson acknowledges the historical "instability of boundaries", particularly the shifting boundary between what counts and doesn't count as literary or poetical (45). For example, "transitional genres" – such as "letters, diaries, notebooks, travelogues" – are, in some periods, "evaluated as extra-literary and extrapoetical, while in other periods they may fulfil an important literary function" (45).

Mikhail Bakhtin's (1895–1975) early milieu was the group that came to bear his name, the Bakhtin Circle, other notable members being the critics Valentin Voloshinov and Pavel Medvedev. The group was formed in 1918, originally meeting in the Belorussian towns of Nevel and Vitebsk (now in Russia and Belarus, respectively) before moving to Leningrad (now St Petersburg) in 1924. With the Soviet Union in the grip of Stalinism, the group was broken up in the late 1920s when a number of members were arrested. The intellectual bearings of the circle included Kant and contemporary German neo-Kantianism (of which Hermann Cohen was the central figure) and phenomenology, the Russian Formalists, Marx and Freud, who was discussed a great deal. Uncertainty continues to surround the authorship of texts attributed to Voloshinov (who died early in 1936) and Medvedev (a victim of Stalin, executed in 1938), which may have been (co)written by Bakhtin.

Bakhtin's now-canonical essay, "Discourse in the Novel", was begun in 1930 and was still in progress in 1936 (see Bakhtin 2012, 722–30). It continued his circle's intense engagement with neo-Kantian thought (see Holquist 2002, 3–7). We have already discussed Kant's aesthetics in Chapter 4. In the *Critique of Pure Reason* Kant distinguishes between *things-in-themselves* (what is real) and *phenomena* (things as they appear to us). He argues that things-in-themselves are completely beyond our grasp. The only world we can know is the world of appearances. Kant claimed that we must experience external phenomena in space, that we must experience things in time and that we must experience phenomena as caused. Space, time and causality are conditions without which no experience is possible. And if they made experience possible, they would always be true of experience. Therefore, without claiming to know reality, Kant claimed to establish truths that would always and everywhere be true for us. German neo-Kantianism put even more emphasis on the way in which our minds produce experience, and so the world, thereby further de-emphasizing any sense of the world "out there". In connection with this it was also relentlessly rationalistic in its conception of human knowledge and experience, which is to say that it de-emphasized exactly those very carnal and earthy aspects of human life that captured Bakhtin's attention in Rabelais's world (Chapter 3): the world of Kant and the world of Rabelais are dramatically different places! (Bakhtin's book *Rabelais and His World* was published in 1965, though an earlier version was completed in 1940.) But this brings us to a key point. At the heart of Kant's philosophy is the idea that we cannot know reality – it is forever beyond us – yet there is truth (beginning with the necessary truths of experience). There is only appearance – representations, interpretations are other words we have used – but there is still truth. And finally, with regard to Kant's necessary truths of experience, the truth is, in a way, our creation; it is our minds that introduce the necessary conditions of all our experience into the unknowable "outside" of reality. Bakhtin rejects Kant's universalism and embraces multiperspectivism, celebrating literature as a force exploring and intensifying the pluralism of social groups, voices and points of view. But the connection with Kant is that the languages and perspectives of these groups speak their truth of the world and embody the world for them; they are not interpretations or representations for them: they are the truth, the way it is. This is the Bakhtinian world, the world of many worlds, many languages, many truths.

We discussed the emergence of multiperspectivism in the works of Walter Pater and Friedrich Nietzsche (see Chapter 5). But Bakhtin developed his own version of multiperspectivism and championed the novel as the best place for the orchestration of multiperspectivism. There is some evidence of Bakhtin's familiarity with Nietzsche and there are parallels beyond their multiperspectivism. However, the tenor of Nietzsche's work is inescapably individualist, while, from his very earliest thinking, the basic tenor of Bakhtin's work is social and collective. According to Bakhtin, there is (or should be) in society an ineradicable "heteroglossia" (in ancient Greek, "diversity of languages", "glossa" meaning language and "heteros" meaning different or other; *raznorečie* is Bakhtin's original term): "a multiplicity of social voices and a wide variety of their links and inter-relationships (always more or less dialogised)" (Bakhtin 1981b, 263). Bakhtin continues: "all languages of heteroglossia ... are specific points of view on the world, forms of conceptualizing the world in words ... each characterized by its own objects, meanings and values" (291). These languages cannot be counted – instead "[e]ven languages of the day exist" (291). Bakhtin calls "dialogism" the complicated and constantly shifting relations of "harmonizing" and "dissonance" (277) between different languages; relations ranging from a "trace" (anticipating Derrida's use of "trace") of the other's language in my language (276), to "unresolvable dialogues" (291) and irreconcilable struggle between languages. The task of literature is to intensify and orchestrate heteroglossia, i.e. to dialogize it, as Bahktin keeps insisting. The novel is a major force of dialogism, and the novelist actualizes and even produces polyphony and dialogism which are virtual or even lacking in society, endowing the language around them with a forward motion it doesn't inherently possess. The novelist might pursue polyphony and dialogue through linguistic heteroglossia or might explore other means – e.g. interaction between different characters as representing different ideas and different attitudes to life – as the stylistically homogeneous Dostoevsky does, according to Bakhtin (Bakhtin 1999).

Bakhtin wrote "Discourse in the Novel" in enforced internal exile. In 1929 he was accused of participating in the underground activities of the Church, under savage repression at the time, and sentenced to six years in a labour camp. His sentence was commuted to internal exile on health grounds. Life in the Soviet Union left Bakhtin, as so many others like him, unemployed, poor and unpublished for large parts of a long and very productive writing life. In "Discourse in the Novel" Bakhtin sees both society and literature as swept, on the one hand, by centralizing, dominant forces trying to impose their own perspective (Bakhtin calls them the forces of "monologism") and, on the other hand, the decentralizing forces of heteroglossia and dialogism. The task of literature is to "activate and organize" (Bakhtin 1981b, 277) the forces of heteroglossia and dialogism.

Before Bakhtin, Du Bois and Woolf already recorded the co-existence, within the self, of socially dominant and socially marginal perspectives, as discussed above. Bakhtin's heteroglossia and dialogism – anticipated by Pater, Nietzsche, Wilde and especially Du Bois and Woolf – can be usefully contrasted both to orthodox Marxism (and of course to the Soviet Union's drive for ideological purity) and also to facile pluralism. Bakhtin, as a Russian writing in the aftermath of the Russian Revolution, is substantially engaged with Marxism. He adopts Marxism's emphasis on struggle, conflict or, to use a Bakhtinian word, "dissonance". However, this is where Bakhtin parts ways with orthodox Marxism. Orthodox Marxism only recognizes two groups and one kind of conflict. In *The Communist Manifesto* Marx and Engels announce:

> The history of all hitherto existing society is the history of class struggles ... Our epoch, the epoch of the bourgeoisie, possesses, however, this distinctive feature: it has simplified the class antagonisms. Society as a whole is more and more splitting up into two hostile camps, into two great classes facing each other: Bourgeoisie and Proletariat.
>
> (Marx and Engels 1985, 79–80)

Bakhtin, on the other hand, recognizes many groups rather than two; he recognizes many fissures, conflicts and struggles – some very large scale, others microscopic – and resonances as well as dissonances between those groups.

Bakhtin anticipates our own globalized world, where distance is truncated and where diverse cultures are transported into uneasy co-existence. He also anticipates the current state of literary theory and criticism: today we find ourselves in the midst of many critical schools and movements, in relations of resonance as well as dissonance. Anticipating what is for us the "fact" of pluralism, Bakhtin is not a facile pluralist simply acknowledging that there are many perspectives, as the concept of "internal dialogism" shows. According to Bakhtin, a perspective constructs its object in dialogue with other perspectives, which it therefore already bears within itself in a variety of ways. In this sense there are no pure, only hybrid, perspectives. Echoing some of Bakhtin's earliest writing, we might say that our sense of our own identity is going to be influenced by the understanding we have of the alien view other people have of us. An anti-authoritarian enemy of dogmatism in all its forms – including of course the Soviet Union's ideological monologism – Bakhtin highlights the unresolvable tensions within each perspective or internal dialogism.

This is why Bakhtin is especially keen on free indirect discourse (mixing the perspectives of narrator and character) and discusses several examples of free indirect discourse in Dickens's *Little Dorrit* (Bakhtin 1981b, 302ff.), such as the following passage about the swindling financier Murdle:

> It was a dinner to provoke an appetite, though he had not had one. The rarest dishes, sumptuously cooked and sumptuously served; the choicest fruits, the most exquisite wines; marvels of workmanship in gold and silver, china and glass; innumerable things delicious to the senses of taste, smell, and sight, were insinuated into its composition. *O, what a wonderful man this Murdle, what a great man, what a master man, how blessedly and enviably endowed* – in one word, what a rich man!
>
> (Dickens quoted in Bakhtin 1981b, 304; the italics are Bakhtin's)

Bakhtin comments on the last, italicized sentence of the quotation: "We have before us a typical double-accented, double-styled *hybrid construction*" (304). Within the same sentence and as if coming from the same speaker, there are "two utterances ... two 'languages,' two semantic and axiological belief systems" – that of Murdle's admirers and that of the narrator (304). Bakhtin adds the italics so as to help us spot one of the two languages at a glance, but the separation between the two languages is not as clear as that. For example, the word "master": does it come from Murdle's admirers or does it mock their point of view? Bakhtin concludes:

> So it is throughout Dickens's whole novel. His entire text is, in fact, everywhere dotted with quotation marks that separate out little islands of scattered direct speech and purely authorial speech, washed by heteroglot waves from all sides. But it would have been impossible actually to insert such marks, since, as we have seen, one and the same word often figures both as the speech of the author and as the speech of another – and at the same time.
>
> (307–8)

I will now turn to the question of Bakhtin's engagement with Saussure. Bakhtin only mentions Saussure once in "Discourse in the Novel" and his familiarity with *Course in General Linguistics* in the 1930s is a matter of speculation. Internal evidence suggests to me that Bakhtin is critical of Saussure. Saussure brings about a revolution in thought by claiming that words are essentially turned not towards their object but towards other words. However, Bakhtin writes: "no living word relates to its object in a *singular* way: between the word and its object, between the word and the speaking subject, there exists an elastic environment of other, alien words" (276). Bakhtin's "alien words" have nothing to do with Saussure's purely differential understanding of meaning (that stone is not rock, not pebble, etc.) and everything to do with the experience also captured by Du Bois and Woolf: the experience of a materially (socially and economically) marginalized group whose perspective of the world, whose truth, sense of the world and sense of self-worth is under attack by an alien, socially dominant perspective. The point is not that white and black, man and woman, worker and capitalist are differentially defined, but that the truth of the black working-class woman is negated by an alien, contemptuous, socially powerful truth of which she is painfully aware, in the midst of which she lives and against which she might voice her own truth in antagonism. Hence the difficulty but also the high social value of the task of the novelist, as Bakhtin understands it: dialogizing different languages, all of which are true in that they express (albeit antagonistic) worldviews.

Bakhtin argues that "an artistic representation" is not a ray of light that falls directly on its object and illuminates it; instead it is the refraction of the ray of light, "its spectral dispersion in an atmosphere filled with alien words, value judgments and accents through which the ray passes" (277). In this passage, we witness the emergence of the poststructuralist theory of intertextuality, elaborated by Julia Kristeva and others. Graham Allen, in *Intertextuality*, tells the story of Kristeva's turn to Bakhtin in the 1960s – unknown in France at the time – in order to address the limitations of structuralism. At the end of 1965 Kristeva, a student at the time, started attending Barthes's seminar. She had read Bakhtin in Russian, discussed Bakhtin with Barthes in private and then presented a paper on Bakhtin to Barthes's seminar in the academic year 1966–7 (Calvet 1994, 155–7). In subsequent essays such as "Word, Dialogue and Novel" Kristeva introduced Bakhtin to a French audience. Her concept of intertextuality, developed out of her rewriting of Bakhtin, was then taken up by others.

Bakhtin's theory of literature rejects Saussure's distinction between "language" (*langue*) and "speech" (*parole*) and instead proposes a third term, "utterance". Bakhtin's first objection to Saussure is that language is not one but many. His second objection is that ostensibly individual speech, for example the ostensibly unique text and language of an author, is actually both collective and dialogic. With his second objection Bakhtin inaugurates his critique of the author as origin or "father" of their work, stressing instead the author's role as orchestrator of collective voices that precede him. Hence

Barthes's famous critique of the author in "The Death of the Author" (1968) involves a rewriting of Bakhtinian heteroglossia, among other elements:

> a text is ... a multi-dimensional space in which a variety of writings, none of them original, blend and clash. The text is a tissue of quotations drawn from the innumerable centres of culture ... [The writer's] only power is to mix writings, to counter the ones with the others, in such a way as never to rest on any of them.
>
> (Barthes 1977b, 146)

According to Bakhtin, literature is an "utterance" turned to other utterances – utterances past, utterances present, but also surprisingly utterances to come: "every word is directed toward an *answer* and cannot escape the profound influence of the answering word that it anticipates" (Bakhtin 1981b, 280). Bakhtin distinguishes between an utterance's "*neutral signification*" and its "*actual meaning*" (281). Grasping an utterance's neutral signification requires passive understanding, but "passive understanding ... is no understanding at all" (280). What really matters, an utterance's "actual meaning", requires *active* understanding because the meaning is not given, it is not a core within the text, but lies on the side of the reader's response: "primacy belongs to the response, as the activating principle: it creates the ground for understanding, it prepares the ground for an active and engaged understanding", which introduces something new to the utterance (282), either "as resistance or support enriching the discourse" (281). Bakhtin is an early example of a modern literary critic emphasizing the role of the reader and the creativity of reading: the reader as actively participating in the making of meaning rather than the passive receiver of it. It is an idea that seems very consistent with Bakhtin's dialogical, heteroglossic vision.

By contrast, the American critic E. D. Hirsch, Jr., draws on a more objectivist or scientific trend in German phenomenology. In "Objective Interpretation" (1960), he distinguishes between a text's "meaning", which remains constant and is intended by the author, and its "significance", which changes from one reader to the next (Hirsch 2001, 1686, 1688). Unlike Bakhtin, he valorizes the text's authorial meaning or neutral signification against its significance for the reader, its *active* or "actual" meaning. Certainly Hirsch's view is against the grain of much postwar literary theory. Barthes in the essay quoted above, "The Death of the Author", and following Bakhtin again, makes it explicit: "to give writing its future, it is necessary to overthrow the myth [of the author]: the birth of the reader must be at the cost of the death of the author" (Barthes 1977b, 148). Barthes was joined by other major figures with similar pronouncements. It should be noted that Barthes and other French writers also saw themselves as applying Nietzsche's proclamation of the "death of God" (Chapter 5) to literature. With God gone, the world no longer had a metaphysical meaning. There was no more truth, in the metaphysical sense, leaving, as we know, interpretation, multiperspectivism. In the name of critical and readerly freedom, and generally informed by the sense that the autonomous, conscious subject was a highly contestable idea – derived from all the major sources of twentieth-century literary theory (Nietzsche, Marx, Freud, Saussure) – the God of the text was also declared dead.

Stephen Greenblatt and other Anglo-American critics identified with the so-called New Historicist school of critical theory and practice explicitly acknowledge their debt to Bakhtin. In 1982 Greenblatt, sounding very Bakhtinian, differentiated his approach in this way: where old historicism assumed that a text has "a stable core meaning", New Historicism sees a text as composed of "disparate and even contradictory parts" (Greenblatt 2001, 2253). Where old historicism "tends to be monological", New Historicism is dialogical (2253). Where old historicism views a text as an "organic unity", New Historicism views a text as an occasion "for the jostling of orthodox and subversive impulses" (2254). In 1989 Louis Montrose pays his own tribute to Bakhtin, while summarizing New Historicism: "On the one hand, the social is understood to be discursively constructed; and on the other, language-use is understood to be always and necessarily dialogical, to be socially and materially determined and constrained" (Montrose 1998, 777) – i.e. the sense that social groups make of the world depends on their material (socioeconomic) situation. New Historicism rejects the conception of literature as "an autonomous aesthetic order" (782), instead placing literary texts in relation to other kinds of discourse in a culture: the discourse of law, the discourse of economics, etc. Finally, New Historicism accepts that "representations … are engaged in constructing the world" (778) – representations do not mirror the world but shape it as well as being shaped by it. We will be discussing another major source for New Historicism, Michel Foucault's development of Nietzsche's idea of history as "genealogy", in Chapter 11.

Today Bakhtin is perhaps more influential than ever. Ken Hirschkop, in his *Mikhail Bakhtin: An Aesthetic for Democracy* (1999), demonstrates the diversity of this influence, outlining contemporary American liberal and also Russian religious readings of Bakhtin, as well as the democratic socialist reading to which Hirschkop's book makes a substantial contribution.

An aspect of "Discourse in the Novel" one might critique or qualify is Bakhtin's polemical opposition between poetry and the novel. Bakhtin here argues that the novel tends to be heteroglossic and dialogic (and that it sides with the forces of dialogism in society) while poetry tends to be monologic, aspiring to express the poet alone in a language uniquely his own. In "From the Prehistory of Novelistic Discourse" Bakhtin also insists that there is a "fundamental" and "categorical" difference between "the novel (and certain forms close to it)" and the "*poetic* genres in the narrow sense" (Bakhtin 1981c, 43). However, he understands the "novel" very expansively to include long narrative poems, giving as an example Pushkin's *Eugene Onegin* (Pushkin 1975). Since the first version of his *Problems of Dostoevsky's Poetics* (1929), Bakhtin obviously considered the novel the exemplary genre of heteroglossia, but there is no reason why poetry should not be heteroglossic, and possibly the most famous piece of heteroglossia and intertextuality is T. S. Eliot's *The Waste Land*. Eliot himself, in "Tradition and the Individual Talent" (1919), advocates a theory of the writer's impersonality – as does Mallarmé before him and Woolf after him in *A Room of One's Own* – that resonates with Bakhtin. Eliot writes about the poet's immersion into the canon of literature, the medium of his art and his "process of depersonalization":

> What happens is a continual surrender of himself as he is at the moment to something which is more valuable. The progress of an artist is a continual self-sacrifice, a continual extinction of personality ... the more perfect the artist, the more completely separate in him will be the man who suffers and the mind which creates ... the poet has, not a "personality" to express, but a particular medium ...
>
> (Eliot 1997b, 43–6)

While Eliot advocates the writer's immersion into the literary tradition, Bakhtin advocates the writer's immersion into his contemporary social heteroglossia. In recent years, no doubt in part as a result of Bakhtin's work, poets have explicitly set out to be heteroglossic – problematizing the idea of a self-expressing author – and have also emphasized the reader in the making of meaning. One very significant example of this would be the American (and international) Language school of poets, dominant experimental school of poetry in the US since the 1970s (e.g. Charles Bernstein, Ron Silliman, Lyn Hejinian).

It can be argued that "Discourse in the Novel" is itself internally dialogic and that Bakhtin implicitly critiques his own distinction between poetry's monologism and the novel's heteroglossia when he writes, "every concrete utterance ... serves as a point where centrifugal as well as centripetal forces are brought to bear. The processes of centralization and decentralization, of unification and disunification, intersect in the utterance" (272). It follows from this that there are both monological or centralizing and heteroglot or decentralizing forces within a poem as well as within a novel – they are both internally dialogic. However, Ken Hirschkop clarifies the historical connection between dialogism and the novel. He argues that the 1929 version of *Problems of Dostoevsky's Poetics* already made clear that dialogism "was in fact a creature of modern Europe" (Hirschkop 1999, 12); and that "Discourse in the Novel" and Bakhtin's other essays on the novel theorize the novel as a genre "born of this modern world", a dynamic genre still "in a state of becoming" and best "reflect[ing] the tendency of the modern world to become" (Bakhtin quoted in Hirschkop 1999, 12). The novel embodies "contemporaneity" and modern dialogism, and "anticipate[s] the future development of all literature" (Bakhtin quoted in Hirschkop 1999, 12). The historical development that underpins Bakhtin's distinction between monologism and heteroglossia is the modern European emergence of national cultures and the "creation of a national 'culture of print', where a new printed standard language, accessible to every literate person", could portray the "multitude of dialects and styles which flourished at the oral and informal written level of the language" (22). Hirschkop concludes that Bakhtin views the novel as both exemplary modern "symptom" and, in Bakhtin's anti-authoritarian and democratic hope for the novel, exemplary modern "cure" (14).

From organic unity to alienation and montage: modernist German Marxism

> In the Germany of the 1930s a loosely connected group of largely Jewish-German Marxist critics were debating modernism and realism: the group included the Jewish-Hungarian György or Georg Lukács, the Jewish-Germans Ernst Bloch, Walter Benjamin and Max Horkheimer, Theodor Adorno, who was Jewish on his father's side, and the German Bertolt Brecht, married to a Jewish actress and close collaborator, Helene Weigel. They wrote in the traumatic context of the rise of Nazism, as the threat to Jewish lives was daily increasing. Almost all (with the exception of Benjamin) escaped the fate of many millions of Jews, and also many millions of non-Jews, in the Nazi death camps. Fleeing Germany they worked to oppose Nazism and to try to understand and bear witness to the Holocaust.

The concerns of this influential debate about modernism and realism were both aesthetic and political, addressing a desperately urgent question: how to use literature and art to create an international anti-fascist popular front, and what kind of literature would best accomplish this? As mentioned above, realism as an artistic model acquired a significant new political meaning in the early twentieth century when the Soviet Union declared Socialist Realism to be its official artistic style in 1932. It was to be populist and accessible and to devote itself to the aims of the Revolution and the celebration and heroization of the life of the Soviet worker. Experimental and avant-garde art was condemned as bourgeois, elitist and degenerate. In 1938 the close friends Lukács and Bloch came to diametrically opposed conclusions in relation to the historical significance and political potential of the European modernist avant-gardes and the modernist German Expressionism (a broad movement of the 1920s and 1930s across the arts in Germany, often emphasizing the exploration of extreme emotional and psychic states in an exaggerated and anti-realist style). Lukács rejected Expressionism and modernism more broadly in favour of realism, prompting Bloch's defence of Expressionism and critique of Lukács, in turn spurring Lukács to clarify his position.

In "Discussing Expressionism" (1938) Bloch defends the Expressionists' project of making visible and illuminating social fragmentation and its political relevance; modernist art "strives to exploit the *real* fissures ... and to discover the new in their crevices" (Bloch 1977, 22). If the Expressionists "tried to plaster over the surface of reality", would they not have been "play[ing] doctor at the sick-bed of capitalism?" (23), Bloch asks. For Bloch Lukács's desire for a literature that portrays reality as an organic whole is in danger of simply taking for granted that reality is "closed and integrated" (22). He argues that Lukács unwittingly inherits this desire for a "seamless totality" (22) from idealist philosophy (e.g. Hegel), a stinging accusation indeed for the dialectical materialist Lukács!

In "Realism in the Balance" (1938) Lukács restates his faith in the tradition of classic realism – the nineteenth-century realist novel represented in exemplary fashion by Balzac – which, in Lukács's long-held view, represents reality as a totality. Espousing the mimetic theory of literature as reflection of a single reality and a truth for all – critiqued by Bakhtin (and of course by very many others in recent times) – he argues that "[i]f literature is a particular form by means of which objective reality is reflected", then it must "grasp that reality as it truly is" (Lukács 1977, 33). And for Lukács and other Marxists it is of great importance to understand that reality, the reality of capitalism, forms "an objective whole" (31). For Lukács the ultimate truth of Marxism is that all aspects of human life, or reality, are governed and determined by the economic base and its social (class) relations; there are no other factors and nothing escapes the totality. Therefore all aspects of life under capitalism are determined by capitalist economics and social relations, and capitalism constitutes the truth of the whole of reality. For Lukács to question this is to question Marxist truth. And naturally it is the duty of literature to attempt the realist totality, because in this way the inhumanity of capitalism and the need for its total overthrow is most powerfully brought home and the Revolution advanced. Therefore, authentic modern literature is contemporary literature in the classic realist tradition. By contrast, "[s]o called avant-garde literature ... from Naturalism to Surrealism" is not "authentic modern literature": its "main trend is its growing distance from, and progressive dissolution of, realism" (29). Lukács will continue in his opposition to the modernists, including such major figures as Joyce and Kafka.

The editors of *Aesthetics and Politics,* Rodney Livingstone, Perry Anderson and Francis Mulhern, critique Lukács in the name of the Marxian principle of conflict or "contradiction": while "emphasiz[ing] the *unity* of the social whole", Lukács "failed to register ... that this unity was irreducibly *contradictory*" (that is, marked by class struggle) (Livingstone *et al.* 1977a, 14). Brecht (1898–1956), in "Against Georg Lukács", written in 1938 but only published posthumously, speaks up as a left-modernist writer aiming for a revolutionary popular theatre. He argues that "[w]ere we to copy the style" of Balzac, Tolstoy and other great nineteenth-century realists, "we would no longer be realists" or truly popular writers (Brecht 1977, 82). Citing his "own experience", Brecht points out that workers "did not object to the fantastic costumes and the apparently unreal mileu" of his *Threepenny Opera* (84).

Essentially claiming a new left-modernist popular realism, he argues that the "criteria for popular art and realism" must not be "drawn merely from existing" works in the classic realist tradition (85).

By late 1935, Goebbels, the minister for propaganda, had formulated an antimodernist arts policy and in late 1936 he abolished art criticism. All modernist movements were condemned and forbidden, and in their place a state-approved heroic-realist art promoted Nazi values and the "true spirit" of the German people (Clinefelter 2005, 91). In 1937 the regime organized an exhibition of modernist works entitled *Degenerate Art*, intended to ridicule modernist art. In July 1937 Hitler publicly denounced modernism as "artistic lunacy" and "cultural destruction of our people", declaring "a relentless cleansing campaign" against it (Hitler quoted in Clinefelter 2005, 91).

In his theatrical practice and theory, Brecht developed a Marxist version of Shklovsky's defamiliarization. (On the relation between the two, see Brooker 2006, 216.) Brecht's "alienation effect" (*Verfremdung*) is envisaged as socially transformative defamiliarization. The "alienation effect" is a technique that Brecht developed in his theatrical practice in the period from the end of the First World War through to the rise of Nazism and the Second World War. Brecht condenses and theorizes his ideas in "A Short Organum for the Theatre" (1949). Brecht explains here that this theatrical technique became increasingly necessary, as more direct political intervention became impossible. "A Short Organum" addresses primarily actors; it is a manual for actors outlining Brecht's "theory of theatrical alienation" (Brecht 1964, 180).

What then is the "alienation effect"? Brecht wanted a theatre that enables the audience to analyse their own situation, to think critically about it and ultimately to change it, but he finds that his contemporary theatre and acting style are not conducive to this. Brecht argued that modern theatre, unlike for example ancient Greek or Chinese theatre, relies too heavily on character and the character's emotions, on the actor's identification with the character, as well as on the audience's identification with the character. In short, contemporary theatre relies too heavily on "empathy" (183) of a passive kind. Characters, actors, spectators are "like sleepers", they are in the throes of something they can't control, "relieved of activity and like men to whom something is being done" (187). Brecht complains that we are encouraged to treat the situation represented on stage as a permanent fact that cannot be questioned, understood and altered, only felt and endured.

If this is implicitly a critique of Naturalist theatre and Naturalism more generally, in its emphasis on the weight of environment, it would be a very questionable reading of Ibsen's *A Doll's House*, for example, which certainly does not invite women to endure their situation. As a potential critique of nineteenth-century classic realism, we discussed George Eliot's emphasis on historical context and her advocated response of sympathy (Chapter 5). Does sympathy with the socially deviant Maggie Tulliver, Eliot's heroine in *The Mill on the Floss*, go hand in hand with a figuring of historical change as beyond her control? Or does Eliot allow Maggie agency and demand thinking and active empathy from her readers?

For Brecht a theatre that alienates frees "socially-conditioned phenomena from the stamp of familiarity which protects them against our grasp" (Brecht 1964, 192). Actors must "make it harder for our spectator to identify himself with them" and must leave his intellect free from affects (190–91). How? The actor must appear on the stage both as the character and as the actor playing the character and must constantly show both. When this happens, *I am Hamlet*, for example, becomes *Hamlet does this* becomes *Hamlet did this and he could have done something else.* Plot must not flow naturally but must be visibly knotted together to "give us a chance to interpose our judgement" (201). The spectator should be helped to behave like a scientist: for example, a geologist who can simultaneously see a river's present course, together with other possibilities for the course it might have taken "if there had been a different tilt to the plateau or a different volume of water" (191). The spectator should be helped to critically observe society as a dynamic and moving structure, to "develop that detached eye with which the great Galileo observed a swinging chandelier" (192) while its candles were dangerously ablaze over his head.

It is clear that Brecht's "scientist" is a figure discerning the dynamic and contradictory and, in this sense, the dialectical nature of reality. Peter Brooker stresses that while Brecht "began to think through" his terms in the late 1920s and early 1930s, he kept revising them throughout his life (Brooker 2006, 209) and increasingly described his theatre as a "dialectical" theatre (210). In Hegel's dialectical logic, thesis and antithesis lead to synthesis and reconciliation, but this is the very opposite of Brecht's sense of the dialectical, which involves montage, defamiliarization of the norm and introduction of marginalized alternatives. Brooker clarifies this important point: against Lukács's Hegelian Marxism, Brecht practised "a 'separation of the elements' rather than the traditional, organically fused work of art"; his narratives moved dialectically or contrapuntally, "not in a continuous linear direction, but in a montage of 'curves and jumps'" (213). The dual aim was, on the one hand, to denaturalize the dominant "taken-for-granted" (210), "conventional" social perspective (214) and, on the other hand, to "reveal a suppressed or unconsidered alternative" (218) and thus to "prise open social and ideological contradictions" (210).

Walter Benjamin (1892–1940) did more than anyone else to theorize "montage" as a defamiliarizing and politically radical form of aesthetic experimentation with the disjunctive composition of fragments, opposed to traditional ideas of integrated aesthetic wholes and their disinterested aesthetic contemplation. We will be focusing on his two most famous essays – "The Work of Art in the Age of Mechanical Reproduction" and "Theses on the Philosophy of History" – but a theory and practice of montage is running throughout his work. Benjamin's "montage" (and his related concept of "constellation") is indebted to Dadaist (e.g. Kurt Schwitters) and Surrealist collage – described by the painter Max Ernst as a "linking of two realities that by all appearances have nothing to link them, in a setting that by all appearances does not fit them" – and Russian film director Sergei Eisenstein's disjunctive and disruptive use of montage since the 1920s. Benjamin's "montage" is a spiritual heir of Baudelaire's *flâneur*, wandering between disjunctive, often marginal, modern urban sites, with a certain critical distance and flashes of critical insight. It is akin to nineteenth-century multiperspectivism (Chapter 5) and Bakhtin's theorization of dialogism, as dissonant orchestration of dominant and marginal voices.

Michael Jennings, in "Walter Benjamin and the European Avant-Garde", illuminates the genealogy of Benjamin's aesthetic thinking. His early criticism (up to 1926) emerges out of a critical engagement with German Romanticism and already "entails the demolition or demystification of the unified work of art" and its "disenchantment"; he "reduces the apparently coherent, integrally meaningful work to the status, to name but a few of Benjamin's figures, of ruin, of torso, of mask" (Jennings 2004, 18). From about 1926 his participation in the cosmopolitan avant-garde G-Group in Berlin and his visits to Paris after 1924, the year of André Breton's first *Surrealist Manifesto*, reoriented Benjamin towards Dada, Surrealism and the Russian avant-gardes. He adopted their shared predilection for montage and practised it in *One-Way Street* (1928), a "montage-book" (Jennings 2004, 25) whose prose pieces, very self-consciously, "differ wildly" (23). Benjamin described it as capturing "something heterogeneous" so that "certain flashes" (allusive of Baudelaire) emanate from its tensions (Benjamin quoted in Jennings 2004, 24). As to the materials he introduces into his montage, he shows a Dadaist propensity for the concrete, the industrial, the expendable and the marginal. Sharing the Dadaist "conviction that it is only that which lies unused or already discarded that is free of the ideological contamination of the ruling formation" (30), his building blocks are the "overlooked or misused" (31). *One-Way Street* is a work of contemporary cultural criticism in fragments that captures street signs, shop signs, public announcements, advertisements, newspaper titles, fragments of the language of modern technology, commerce and consumerism, new technological inventions, luxury products, expensive hobbies and cheap amusements, urban sites. For example: a construction site with its detritus and waste products; shooting ranges in fairground booths; a betting office; Madame Ariane, fortuneteller, second courtyard on the left; coiffeur for fastidious ladies; travel souvenirs; airtravel; a filling station; Germans, drink German beer; underground works; dreams (Benjamin 1997). What Benjamin takes from Surrealism (an art movement drawing heavily on Freud) is the project of liberating the Unconscious, understood as a political liberation.

Benjamin's montage-aesthetic was political: the "unstable" form would "bring to consciousness the 'true history' which lay embedded in cracks and fissures" (Jennings 2004, 29).

Benjamin's montage brings together and articulates marginal fragments previously unrelated and, in their newly apprehended inter-relation, mutually illuminates them and sheds new light on an entire historical field. Benjamin's fragments, in their inter-relation, construct a social field that brings social reality into view in a new way. We are reminded of Shelley's revolutionary role for poetry, which is to mobilize the imagination in order to discern previously unapprehended relations (see Chapter 4). On such principles of montage, between 1927 and his untimely death in 1940, Benjamin was composing his palimpsestic *The Arcades Project*, on the consumer culture of nineteenth-century Paris, capturing its language and objects of fashion, advertising and consumption, and focusing on Parisian steel-and-glass-roofed shop arcades. Benjamin delivered it, unfinished, to his friend the French thinker Georges Bataille, and it was eventually edited and published (Benjamin 2002).

In his seminal 1936 essay, "The Work of Art in the Age of Mechanical Reproduction", Walter Benjamin theorizes montage and critiques aesthetic "aura", which he considers politically suspicious. Benjamin explores the thesis of the historical decline of aesthetic "aura" in modernity. If aesthetic objects had a ritual function in the Middle Ages, they are now increasingly desacralized and have lost much of their otherworldly nimbus. This will of course affect the reception of aesthetic objects and their potential impact on reality. Baudelaire, acutely aware of the poet's loss of *his* aura in the midst of Parisian modernity, embraces this loss as the very condition of his art, for which Benjamin praises him (see Chapter 5). However, only a generation earlier the German philosopher Arthur Schopenhauer, in *The World as Will and Representation* (1818), had valorized aesthetic experience as the individual's passive contemplation of an artwork (for Schopenhauer music was the highest art) in which the contemplator is rescued from the suffering that attends his will, and indeed is relieved, for a brief time, of all sense of himself (Schopenhauer 1969). If Schopenhauer is an extreme version of ideas of aesthetic experience as abstraction and withdrawal from our normal experience, an exemplary image of aesthetic experience is the visitor in the museum or gallery, uncrowdedly and peacefully absorbed in a painting. In contrast with this sense of the aesthetic, and in the spirit of Baudelaire, Benjamin's focus in this essay is the new, worldly, collectively produced and consumed medium of film. Benjamin singles out two aspects of film that he believes have revolutionary potential: the technique of montage and the collective reception of film. These aspects encourage a response which is the opposite of Schopenhauer's experience of art: what Benjamin calls *distraction* (*Zerstreuung*, note the resonance with Brecht's *alienation*). Instead of losing oneself in the work of art, the speed and suddenness of montage jolts and assaults the audience into a distracted response of "heightened presence of mind" (Benjamin 1992c, 232). Similarly, film makes possible a "simultaneous collective experience" and invites a co-ordinated and organized collective response (228), such as an anti-fascist response, though Benjamin doesn't spell this out.

Benjamin is one of the first critics to take an unsnobbishly positive view of the new and, at the time, still aesthetically suspect medium of film. Béla Balázs published *Der Sichtbare Mensch* (Visible man), celebrating the way film allows new access to the human face in 1924, while the art historian Rudolf Arnheim published *Film als Kunst* (Film as art) in 1932. However in 1936 Benjamin had already become painfully aware that film was being used by the Nazis for propaganda and to fuel the cult of Hitler. The most famous of these films is Leni Riefenstahl's *Triumph of the Will* (1935). Nevertheless, he claimed that this new reincarnation of aesthetic passive contemplation – in that Nazi propaganda invited a loss of all presence of mind and ecstatic identification with Hitler and his mission – goes against film's potential for *distraction*. Michael Rosen writes that it is important to "emphasize that Benjamin does not disapprove" of the "desacralising process" in this essay; on the contrary, the decline of aura is envisaged to "open the way to a political form of art" (Rosen 2004, 48). (Benjamin's "On Some Motifs in Baudelaire" is more ambivalent, while "The Storyteller" seems to narrate desacralization as decline. All three essays were written in the mid 1930s.) However, Rosen remarks on Theodor Adorno's reservations regarding these ideas of his friend and colleague. In *Aesthetic Theory* (1970), perhaps with the benefit of hindsight, Adorno argues that post-auratic art is open to the "abuse of aesthetic rationality for mass-exploitation and domination" (Adorno quoted in Rosen 2004, 48).

Benjamin wrote "Theses on the Philosophy of History" in Paris in January 1940. He had moved to Paris in 1933 and had written "The Work of Art in the Age of Mechanical Reproduction" in French in 1936, after two drafts in German. In June 1940 France surrendered to the Germans, and Benjamin fled, with a Jewish group, across the Spanish border to avoid arrest. However, the Spanish authorities were under instructions from General Franco's fascist government to return those fleeing the Nazis to France. On 25 September 1940, in response to his imminent repatriation to German-occupied France, Benjamin killed himself.

In *The Arcades Project* and in "Theses on the Philosophy of History", Benjamin introduced the concept of "constellation" (*Konstellation*) to capture his particular practice of montage. What he considered particularly urgent was the task of constellating the present with repressed fragments of the past. "Theses on the Philosophy of History" (also translated as "On the Concept of History") is a dense, elliptical and groundbreaking essay. Benjamin argues that only from the point of view of the victors, the ones in the ascendant, the "ruling class" does history look like an *ascending line* culminating in themselves: "as flowers turn toward the sun, by dint of a secret heliotropism the past strives to turn toward that sun that is rising in the sky of history" (Benjamin 1992d, 246). When we see history in this manner, without quite realizing it, we identify with the victors, we feel empathy for the victors rather than the vanquished, and this "empathy with the victor invariably benefits the rulers" (248). Benjamin distinguishes between two histories: the history of the victors, which is fully present; and what he calls "the tradition of the oppressed" (248), which is not available. In psychoanalytic terms, the tradition of the oppressed is repressed and has become unconscious. While the past of the victors is a "chain of events" (249) or a line, the past of the oppressed is a collective unconscious to which at best we can have the most fleeting access. Thinking about this other past, Benjamin writes: "The true picture of the past flits by. The past can be seized only as an image which flashes up at the instant when it can be recognized and is never seen again" (247). While for the victors History is "homogeneous, empty time" (252), Benjamin describes what he calls the "now" (*Zetztzeit*; 253) as the shattering of the continuum of History; a shattering of the smooth flow of the river of history that momentarily brings fragments of the unconscious depths of the tradition of the oppressed to the surface, *constellating* them with the present. The "now" is a revolutionary event suspended undecidably (prior to victory or defeat). It is also a fleeting revelatory event, a flash, the sudden "return of the repressed" moment, *as it was*, before its effacement by history. It causes "the continuum of history to explode" (263) and, just for an instant, we glimpse the vanished and silenced as it was, before historical catastrophe and crushing defeat and history as told by the winners. The task Benjamin sets himself and others is to develop "a conception of the present as the 'time of the now'" and to grasp its "constellation" with the past (255).

Benjamin seems to outline at least three sorts of constellation: a revolutionary political constellation of the *now* with past moments of special affinity (see above); an aesthetic constellation (e.g. avant-garde montage and collage); and a historiographic constellation (e.g. Benjamin's own ongoing critical history of the nineteenth century in *The Arcades Project* and elsewhere). He doesn't fully define how they relate to each other. All kinds of constellation depend on a flash which, in aesthetic and historiographic constellation, is something that must be evoked or provoked in the reader/viewer, rather than the author writing about it; this flash might have to do with the past or with a critical awareness of the present. Kaufman argues that the "effort to constellate" is an effort to achieve critical *distance* from the present, a distance which is a new and positive form of aura (Kaufman 2005, 142, 144–5). This is still disruptive of traditional aura as passive absorption and of the history and reality of the victors. In attempting to clarify "constellation", Kaufman claims that aesthetic constellating "illuminates the larger social reality whose elements have been brought together in affinity and tension (rather than in a falsely integrative, positivistic totalization)" (Kaufman 2004, 366).

Howard Caygill usefully clarifies Benjamin's ideas and their methodological implications for criticism:

- Attention to "excluded" and un-canonical periods and genres and questioning of "canonicity itself" (Caygill 2004, 82).
- Attention to "artistic 'failures'" and valorization of the "incompleteness" of texts (82).
- Art (and criticism) not as "therapeutic liberation" but as acts of "witness and mourning" (89).
- In art and criticism, the "modernist 'montage' narrative form" constructs a "unique and transient constellation" of past and present (89). This is not a moment of synthesis or integration but an "experience of shock in which neither present nor past can contain each other" (90–91).
- The past is not "eternally present" (89) or even completed, nor does the present complete the past but is rather unsettled by it. In a constellative act of art or criticism the past works to unsettle established "conceptual frameworks" (94), to force "the present to face its own fragmentation" and to question the "invincibility" of the forces dominating the present (95). In other words, constellative art and criticism are acts of resistance.

After World War II Adorno and Horkheimer will attempt to come to terms with the scale of "suffering" (Adorno's term) inflicted and the kind of art that could best witness it. We will discuss them in Chapter 10.

Conclusion

- This chapter traced developments in Russia and Germany from the Russian Revolution to the rise of Stalinism and Nazism. Writers and critics put forward and theorized democratic and pluralist aesthetics of *defamiliarization*, *alienation*, *dialogism* and *montage*, in their efforts to resist totalitarianism in all its forms – political, artistic, theoretical, critical, etc.
- We outlined Saussure's *semiology* (science of signs); his distinction between *langue* and *parole*; the arbitrariness of the bond between signifier and signified and their combination in the sign; the syntagmatic and associative (or paradigmatic) chains in relation to which the signified is defined, negatively or differentially. Saussure's *langue*, as a static structure of inter-related elements, fails to register change, social fissures and the voices of the socially marginalized.
- We discussed Russian Formalism, focusing on Shklovsky and Jakobson. Shklovsky's literary technique of *defamiliarization* sought to address what it was about literary writing that made it literary. *Defamiliarization* impedes a routine and formulaic view of reality, introducing a renewed and novel perception of the world. Jakobson's concept of *the dominant* allows him to analyse literary language into a number of constituent elements. The poetic function (or *literariness*) is not exclusive to literature

but is the dominant element within the literary text, understood as a mobile and dynamic hierarchy of many functions, while the boundary between literary and extra-literary texts is ever shifting.

- For Bakhtin the democratic and pluralist role of literature is to mobilize and intensify the *heteroglossia* of social groups, its *dialogism* resisting *monologism* and totalitarianism. We outlined Bakhtin's concept of *internal dialogism* anticipating *intertextuality*, the collective nature of *utterance* and the active role of the reader.
- We discussed German modernist Marxism, focusing on Brecht and Benjamin. We outlined Brecht's theory and practice of the *alienation effect*, envisaging an actively critical role for literature. We sketched out Benjamin's critique of aesthetic *aura.* His theory and practice of montage or *constellation* attempts to capture and bear witness to socially heterogeneous, marginal and forgotten voices, connecting them with the present.

Further reading

See especially Bakhtin 1981b; Bloch 1977; Benjamin 1992c, 1992d; Brecht 1964; Jakobson 1987b; Lukács 1977; Saussure 1960; Shklovsky 1998. In relation to Bakhtin, see Allen 2000; Hirschkop 1999; and Holquist 2002. In relation to German Marxism, see Adorno *et al.* 1977a; Brooker 2006; Caygill 2004; Jennings 2004; Kaufman 2004 and 2005; Rosen 2004; Rush 2004b.

8 Decentering modernisms

Newness, tradition, culture and society

T. S. Eliot, Richards, Woolf, Empson, Leavis, Williams, Ngũgĩ, Achebe, Hebdige, Eagleton, Hall

This chapter outlines a dynamic British *and* transnational twentieth-century critical tradition, involving both continuity and conflict, and including modernists (Eliot, Richards, Empson, Leavis, Woolf's feminism), Marxists (Williams, Eagleton, Hall, Hebdige) and postcolonial critics (Ngũgĩ, Achebe). The overarching question in this critical tradition is the role of literature and literary criticism in society. Key terms and issues include: modernism; the new, tradition and the canon; culture and society; literature, criticism and education; cultural studies; the institutionalization of literary studies and cultural studies; literature, criticism and science; literary-critical analysis, synthesis and evaluation; the specialization of knowledge, globalization, democracy and the mass media; class, gender and empire; decolonization and "decentering the centre". The chapter concludes with an appendix on transnational modernist studies today.

T. S. Eliot

T. S. Eliot (1888–1965) was born in St Louis, Missouri. Highly academic, he studied philosophy at Harvard University from 1906, spent a year in Paris attending lectures at the Sorbonne, returned to Harvard to study Indian philosophy and embarked on doctoral research. In 1914 he went to Britain, attending Oxford University while pursuing his PhD. The doctoral thesis, on the English idealist philosopher F. H. Bradley (1846–1924), was completed but Eliot did not return to the US to do the required spoken defence.

In addition to his reputation as a poet, Eliot is one of the most important literary critics of the twentieth century. It is difficult to overstate the extent of his influence, of his early criticism in particular, in the middle decades of the last century. In England Leavis's 1932 *New Bearings in English Poetry: A Study of the Contemporary*

Situation proclaimed Eliot the modern poet *par excellence*, Leavis's outlook and language deeply marked by Eliot's critical writings. In the US Eliot's early essays were foundational for the New Critics (Chapter 9) as they rose to prominence in the 1930s. In the 1920s and 1930s Eliot's place as foremost critic of his time was consolidated by *The Criterion* literary magazine (1922–39), which Eliot founded and of which he was editor throughout its life (*The Waste Land* was published in the first issue). In addition, as editor and a little later as a director, from 1925 until his death Eliot occupied what he would establish as the most important position in British poetry publishing at the company of Faber and Faber.

Readers new to Eliot's criticism may find his tone in *The Sacred Wood* (1920), his first collection of criticism, somewhat superior or rigid, at least in some of the essays. Early reviewers commented on this, though they were by no means always disapproving. Leonard Woolf (husband of Virginia) found invigorating "the satisfying, if painful, hardness of the intellect" that the book exhibited (Spears Brooker 2004, 59), and others joined in welcoming Eliot's championing, in both creative and critical writing, of the anti-Romantic and anti-sentimental, the impersonal, disinterested and scientific. Even those disturbed by these new values and the short shrift Eliot often appeared to give "distinguished reputations" (Eliot 1997b, 42), or otherwise not entirely convinced by his "rather congested style" and "disembodied voice", in the words of a perceptive anonymous early reviewer of *The Sacred Wood*, usually saluted his evident critical powers; in the words of the same unnamed writer, his "[s]cholarship, acuteness of mind, delicacy of perception" (Spears Brooker 2004, 67).

By the time Eliot came to write the preface to the second edition of *The Sacred Wood* (1928), he was the author of *The Waste Land* (1922) and an established figure as poet and critic. Nevertheless he took the opportunity to apologize for his "faults of style" and particularly for its "[s]tiffness and an assumption of pontifical solemnity" (Eliot 1928, ix). But we should pause at this rather verbose expression. First, surely it is an apology that repeats the fault. Second, Eliot is punning: the Catholic and Anglo-Catholic Churches celebrate a Solemn Pontifical Mass at Assumption (it is the celebration of the Virgin Mary being taken up into heaven). Third, there is biographical significance: Eliot had converted to Anglo-Catholicism the previous year. In fact there are a number of styles in *The Sacred Wood.* It is in part a parodic book, parodying literary criticism and particular critics. (See the short pieces that comprise "Imperfect Critics" in *The Sacred Wood*, following Eliot's outline of types of literary criticism in "The Perfect Critic" [Eliot 1997c, 1997e].)

"Tradition and the Individual Talent" (1919; reprinted in *The Sacred Wood*) is Eliot's most famous essay, the most famous poetics essay of the twentieth century. It was first published in two instalments in *The Egotist* magazine. In it Eliot develops the idea of the writer's need for a tradition, with the important qualification that it be the *right* tradition, though Eliot refrains from defining it. The essay at points applies itself more generally to all art or to all literary writing, but the focus is poetry, and the (singular) poet in his relation to the dead poets (oddly excluded is the poet's relation to other living poets). The essay uses an English persona addressing an English audience and refers to European literature. Authors referred to, or whose works are referred to, are Homer, Aeschylus, Seneca, Brunetto Latini, Dante, Petrarch, Shakespeare, Thomas Middleton and Keats. However, Eliot's references are deliberately difficult to determine and marked by doubleness. He refers to *Agamemnon* but does not specify whether he is referring to Aeschylus's *Agamemnon* or Seneca's. Nor does he clarify which ode about a nightingale by Keats he is alluding to: "Ode to a Nightingale" or "Ode: 'Bards of Passion and of Mirth'" (Keats 1998, 146–7, 174–7). Following Eliot's references will reveal much. Eliot presents his impersonal theory of poetry and illustrates the poetic process with the famous analogy of a chemical reaction.

The first sentence of "Tradition and the Individual Talent" is: "In English writing we seldom speak of tradition, though we occasionally apply its name in deploring its absence" (Eliot 1997b, 39). The style is unpretentious, perhaps even a little dull (despite obscure mentions of the "science of archaeology"); a contrast is drawn between the "'more critical'" French (overwrought, rationalistic, etc.) and the English, who "plume" themselves "with the fact" of their spontaneity (39). (But are the English stereotypically known for their spontaneity?) The man behind his parodic English persona's first woolly sentences and the unhesitating use of the inclusive "we" of the "nation" or "race" had been in England for about five years at the time (Eliot became a British citizen in 1927). Under the impression of determinate meaning, Eliot practises a relentless imprecision. For example, what is "English writing"? Is it not rather odd that the essay's second sentence – "We cannot refer to 'the tradition' or to 'a tradition'; at most, we employ the adjective in saying that the poetry of So-and-so is 'traditional' or even 'too traditional'" – denies we can, yet refers a number of times to both the word "tradition" and also a traditional poetic style, which entails the existence of a tradition.

Among the huge number of influences alluded to in "Tradition and the Individual Talent" is the philosopher Henri Bergson (1859–1941), whose lectures Eliot attended during his student days in Paris. For Bergson the past is not finished and over with; it is a living past, revivified by and revivifying the present. Similarly, in "Tradition and the Individual Talent", the writer's realized "historical sense involves a perception" that the "pastness of the past" is also present, "a feeling that the whole of the literature of Europe from Homer and within it the whole of the literature of his own country has a simultaneous existence and composes a simultaneous order" (Eliot 1997b, 40–41). This simultaneous relation of past and present "in his bones", "compels a man to write" and is "what makes a writer most acutely conscious ... of his contemporaneity" (41).

Tradition, or the sense of it, must be obtained "by great labour" (Eliot 1997b, 40). The poet must read a great deal (however, Shakespeare did not have to work as hard as "the more tardy") (43). As the "dead poets, his ancestors" (40) nourish the living poet's work, so the poet's work causes the tradition to be "modified", "adjusted" (41). Criticism must have the same sense, to some degree, of past and present; the writer will be judged in "relation to the dead poets and artists", "for contrast and comparison"; the criterion of judgement is whether the new work conforms to or coheres with the tradition. Criticism does not judge works as "worse or better than the dead" or according to "the canons of dead critics" but is a "test of … value" which must be "slowly and cautiously applied, for we are none of us infallible judges of conformity" (42). We feel perplexed. What is the comparative test of value if not in terms of worse or better? The poet is judged in relation to dead poets, but the critic disregards dead critics.

Eliot is arguing for some kind of difference within conformity in the individual artist's relationship to the tradition: originality as variation or interpretation of tradition rather than break with tradition; "the most individual parts" of a poet's work "may be those in which the dead poets … assert their immortality most vigorously" (40). Through conforming we will become richly individual artists. But "blind or timid adherence" to the tradition, particularly "the immediate generation before", would mean that "'tradition'" should be positively discouraged, as it will result in "repetition" or mere "novelty" (40). We might accept that we have to read beyond the last generation and that copying can't be good conforming to the tradition, but we're not told more about what we should or should not be reading or how to conform in a good way. The air is thick with paradox. We're told that we have to be "conscious of the major current, which does not at all flow invariably through the most distinguished reputations", but we do not know how to discriminate the main current (42). A clue comes with the description of the tradition as "the mind of Europe" (42), a mind the poet will learn is "more important than his own private mind" (42). And further that the poet must continue to develop his "consciousness" of the past, which "progress" is one of "self-sacrifice, a continual extinction of personality" (43–4).

Eliot's critical writings might give the impression of, and have certainly been understood (and emulated) by other critics to be, aiming to re-evaluate and modify the canon of great literature. He is in dialogue with Matthew Arnold (Chapter 5), who argued for the role of a canon of "the best that can at present be known in the world" (Arnold 1993b, 151), though deviating from Arnold in important respects. In relation to English literature, Eliot appears to promote the neglected seventeenth-century poets and dramatists; to devalue Victorian poetry on the whole; to criticize English Romanticism, in spite of his acknowledgement of Coleridge as the greatest English critic and his equivocal admiration for Blake. He also seems to "readjust the relative ranking" of Shakespeare's plays, in favour of the later ones (Materer 1994, 52). He seems intent on dissociating newness from subjectivism, fancy and personal fragmentation, as flaunted dangerously by his immediate ancestors, Pater and Wilde (discussed in Chapter 5), apparently failing to acknowledge the extent to which he is their heir. By contrast he is happy to acknowledge his debt to French Symbolism, to Baudelaire (Chapter 5), Rimbaud, Laforgue. There often seem to be veiled personal and idiosyncratic reasons for Eliot's promotions and relegations, and one should be very attentive to the grounds, if any, Eliot gives for his literary judgements.

"Tradition and the Individual Talent", far from spelling out a new canon, is packed with allusions. A mirage of sense rather than the surgical precision of language, indefiniteness, equivocation, indirection and even misdirection seem more appropriate descriptors of the writing. Eliot might seem to advertise his opposition to Wordsworth's description of poetry as "emotion recollected in tranquillity", calling this inadequate clipping from Wordsworth's definition an "inexact formula" (Eliot 1997b, 48) – surely a deliberate irony that subtly satirizes the pretensions of modern science. But he implicitly endorses many aspects of Romanticism without acknowledgement: for example, the Romantics' interest in Plato's, Aristotle's and the Neoplatonists' understanding of instantaneous intuitive contemplation or insight (see Chapters 1–3), Coleridge's organicism, etc.

Eliot aims to counterbalance or fit together or sustain a dialectic between "tradition" and newness, in a mutual "conformity between the old and the new", "the timeless and … the temporal together" (Eliot 1997b, 41), the abstract/ideal and the concrete, visionary insight and critical thinking. Eliot is, in this sense, a follower of Aristotle, the philosopher of the mean, the medium, the middle way; and *The Sacred Wood* is imbued with him. Eliot's poetic credo of "impersonality", as outlined in "Tradition and the Individual Talent" (49), though perhaps indebted to Mallarmé (see Rabaté 1994, 221), is to be understood in these terms. It is anti-expressive, and in this sense anti-Romantic (according to a very reductive definition of Romanticism), but it will be remembered that Coleridge and Shelley also see the petty self or ego as an impediment to visionary insight (Chapter 4). However, while the Romantics are turned towards the Neoplatonist Ideal World, the Aristotelian Eliot is keen to combine the transcendent and the worldly.

Eliot now introduces a "suggestive analogy" (Eliot 1997b, 44) in order to "define this process of depersonalization and its relation to the sense of tradition. It is in this depersonalization that art may be said to approach the condition of science" (44). The analogy is the reaction that takes place when a "bit of finely filiated platinum" is put into a "chamber" containing the gases "oxygen and sulphur dioxide" (44). The platinum catalyses the reaction but remains unaffected by it. This famous analogy has been understood to invite the reading that poetry should aspire to being like modern natural science. However, closer attention suggests otherwise. Very briefly, the idea of poetry as a "species of reaction" appears in Wordsworth's Preface to *Lyrical Ballads*, in the same sentence containing Eliot's quotation ("emotion recollected in tranquillity") (Wordsworth 2012, 514). So Eliot's analogy is not original as a metaphor for poetic inspiration. Eliot's use of the term "filiated" alludes to further connections: not a word employed in contemporary natural science, it is a Catholic doctrine explicated by Thomas Aquinas (Chapter 3) and others. God created Christ, his son, with the utterance of his Word, thereby incarnating the divine as man, the infinite as finite. Incarnation, celebrated as Holy Communion, is the spiritual expression of Eliot's aesthetic and philosophical position.

The strikingly novel part of Eliot's famous analogy is the poet's mind as a "catalyst" (44), but Eliot quickly abandons it. His description of the poet's mind keeps changing: from a "more finely perfected medium", to a "catalyst" of gases, to the "combination" of elements in liquid "suspension" (precipitating out the poem as a solid substance), to a "receptacle for seizing … particles" until they unite, to "the pressure … under which the fusion" of elements "takes place", to the "medium" in which elements "combine", to the combination of "floating" elements, to a "working … up" of elements, to an unwilled "concentration" of elements (44–48). It is unsurprising that Eliot drops the "catalyst" because the poet's mind enables rather than triggers or speeds up the poetic reaction. Indeed Eliot's description adds nothing to Wordsworth's "reaction".

Eliot begins the final section of "Tradition and the Individual Talent" with an untranslated and unattributed ancient Greek quotation. The quotation is from Aristotle's *De anima* (On the soul) and can be translated as follows: "But this leaves open the possibility that the mind is something more divine and unaffected" (Aristotle 1986, 146). In crude summary, Aristotle distinguishes between *noesis*, as instantaneous intuition of truth; *dianoia*, as progressive critical reasoning; and *phronesis*, as translation of an abstract principle into practice according to the mean (e.g. acting courageously involves avoiding both cowardice and foolhardiness). *Noesis*, though "divine", is not exclusive to poetic vision but is also a part of science, broadly understood, and ordinary experience. For example, Aristotle's general definition of tragedy in the *Poetics* (see Chapter 2) or inductive hypotheses in science are examples of *noesis*. *Noesis* synthesizes experiences, observations, etc. and produces truth or a strong sense of truth. Similarly the poet in "Tradition and the Individual Talent" combines "numberless feelings, phrases, images" in the creation of a vision (Eliot 1997b, 45). This vision has prophetic power. *The Waste Land* is a vision of Western civilization, its essence or spiritual truth. It is not a truth of science, fact or the product of critical consideration; it is a revelation. For Aristotle too the intellect intuits the first principles of science. But *noesis* has also to be counterbalanced and grounded by *dianoia*, immersion in the critical tradition and the "great labour" (quoted above) it involves. (Eliot's term, *intelligence*, partly refers to this dialectic.) The poetic image is powerful but it might be mistaken.

In "Tradition and the Individual Talent", against a carefully constructed impression of making sense and intellectual authority, Eliot painstakingly avoids the definition of his terms, keeps multiplying them and subtly alludes to a huge number of references in the Western tradition since Plato and beyond. Against modern specialization, Eliot mixes the language of modern science with classical philosophy, theology, alchemy and hermeticism (all claiming the name "science"). He thus suggests that the literary tradition and modern science be understood within a greatly amplified, if undefined, sense of "tradition". His core critical idea, the mutual conformity of tradition and poet, is Aristotelian, attempting to ground the Romantics, his ancestors, in the same manner that Aristotle attempted to ground and temper Plato's idealism. This dialectic between insight and critical consideration or empirical testing or common sense is the scientific method as old as thought itself, and Aristotle is a fountainhead and central figure of the tradition.

We might understand Eliot's other well-known critical terms – the "objective correlative" and the "dissociation of sensibility" – as variations of Eliot's core critical idea, in Aristotelian terms. Eliot invents the expression "objective correlative" in his 1919 essay, "Hamlet and His Problems" (Eliot 1997d, 85). I will venture a definition. To find an "objective correlative" is to find or devise objects of sensation or experience as external manifestations for immaterial things – in Aristotelian terms to bring together the abstract and the concrete. For example, Dante was a great poet of the "objective correlative" because of the vivid sensuousness of his depiction of hell (Chapter 3). By contrast, Eliot claims, *Hamlet* is a failure because Hamlet, in his inability to act, fails to find an "objectivity correlative" for his emotions. (Against Eliot one might object that his inability to act is a perfect "objective correlative" of the very idea of failing to find an "objective correlative".) Eliot uses the expression "dissociation of sensibility" in his 1921 essay, "The Metaphysical Poets" (Eliot 1951b, 288). Eliot claims that the Metaphysical Poets are great because they lived in an age before "a dissociation of sensibility set in, from which we have never recovered" (288). Though Eliot refrains from clarifying this dissociation, we might define it as a failure to connect the sensible and the intelligible, experience and abstract conception, science and theology.

Eliot's 1923 essay, "The Function of Criticism" (recalling Matthew Arnold's essay, "The Function of Criticism at the Present Time"), is a variation on "Tradition and the Individual Talent". Eliot revisits the idea of literature – world, European and national – "as 'organic wholes'" in the sense of "systems in relation to which" literary texts "have their significance" (Eliot 1951c, 23–4). (Eliot adopted this organicism from Coleridge, but also from Bradley's idealism.) He also reiterates his criticism of Pater's and Wilde's legacy of subjectivism and individualism – once again without acknowledgement of his debt to them – in favour of "fact": "*fact* cannot corrupt taste", so one should pursue "data" and avoid "opinion or fancy" (33). Behind the matter-of-fact modern-scientific or analytic-philosophical language, it seems that he is revisiting the broadly scientific Aristotelian idea of the need to bring together *noesis* and *dianoia*, induction and deduction, poetic insight and critical rationality, the abstract and the concrete. This would allow us to understand Eliot's double emphasis in this essay: on "facts" but also on consensus, i.e. on what we collectively agree upon as true (see Shusterman 1994, 38). In relation to the latter, Eliot calls for an "attempt" to pursue "*common* principles" for criticism (Eliot 1951c, 29, my italics). Yes, criticism ought to be the "elucidation" of texts and "correction of taste" in a broadly scientific spirit, but this needs to be combined with a *collaborative* "articulation" and composition of the critics' "differences" in "*common* pursuit of true judgement" (24–5, my italics). Whatever these common principles might be – Eliot is typically vague – he cannot stress enough the value of criticism and claims to be going further than Arnold in acknowledging the "capital importance of criticism in the work of creation itself" and the necessary "critical toil of the artist" against the overvaluation of "inspiration" (30). This can be understood as the need to combine *noesis* and *dianoia*. The emphasis on common principles might be read in relation to Aristotle's idea of *common law*, i.e. that certain values (e.g. the burial of the dead) are shared by all. What is suggested is the need for conformity between the new critic and the critical tradition.

In *The Use of Poetry and the Use of Criticism* (1933) Eliot might be understood to move towards cultural specificity, cultural authority, the master critic who uniquely accomplishes the feat of voicing his time and place. The individual talent, critical and artistic, gains his authority by claiming to truly represent his community, thus bypassing both subjectivism and the need for actual critical collaboration. Once every century or so a strong critic or "master of criticism" (Eliot 1964, 109) – such as Dryden, Johnson and Arnold – emerges and, "armed with a powerful glass", accomplishes a "new order" of past literature (108). This master, unlike both those who follow critical *doxa* and those who proliferate subjectivist "heterodoxies" (108), is an authoritative representative of an entire new generation and its own relation to the tradition. Therefore literary appreciation is not universal but culturally specific: "each generation prefers its own alloy" and each critical master has different "errors" specific to his generation (109). Eliot is as vague in his use of "generation" as he was in his use of "tradition". However, to deny that the master critic's truth is not universally true for other generations and cultures is not at all to deny that he is the true voice of his culture and time.

In *Notes towards the Definition of Culture* (1948) Eliot distinguishes between three senses of "culture": the culture of an individual, the culture of a group or class and, most "fundamental" (Eliot 1962, 21), the culture of a whole society or "the pattern of the society as a whole" (23). The culture of the individual is "dependent upon" the culture of a group and a "whole society" (21). Against Arnold, who associates perfection with individual cultivation and high culture, Eliot claims that "our notion of 'perfection'" should include all these senses of "culture" (24). Eliot envisages this as resistance towards an age of increasing specialization and as promotion of "overlapping and sharing" (24). He declares his age a period of cultural decline and malaise (19). However, as culture, in all three senses, is what "makes life worth living" (27), literature is given an urgent if near-impossible task: having derived nourishment from its roots in society, it needs somehow to feed and revive the exhausted ground from which it sprang.

We can discern in Eliot's later work a shift of emphasis from literary culture to culture anthropologically understood as a whole way of life. However, there is little consensus as to the nature and relative value of Eliot's earlier and later periods. It is indicative of Eliot's elusiveness that Timothy Materer and Richard Shusterman (to be discussed shortly) have opposing characterizations of the later Eliot, Materer reading him as too respectful of authority and politically conservative, Shusterman praising him for his pluralism. In 1928 Eliot famously declared himself "classicist in literature, royalist in politics, and anglo-catholic in religion" in the Preface of his *For Lancelot Andrewes: Essays on Style and Order* (Eliot 1928, ix). But what Eliot means by "classicist" and "royalist" is not obvious. Eliot's literary taste was not "classicist" nor his poetry or prose style, but he was immersed in the classical philosophical tradition. Immediately having issued this neat if perplexing self-definition Eliot, on the pretext of obliging us with a clarification, effaces it: the first term is "completely vague", the second "at present without definition" and the third "does not rest with me to define" (ix). Materer argues that conservative politics increasingly underpins Eliot's literary judgements. Eliot sides with authority and order. For him classicism "connotes order and rationality", while Romanticism "connotes individualism and emotionalism" (Materer 1994, 56) symptomatic of social disorder, fragmentation and the "dissociation" discussed above. Poets of "an entire age tend to be superior to those of another" (53), depending on whether the age was one of order or disorder. Materer concludes in favour of Eliot's earlier period: when Eliot was an "experimental poet, rebelling against literary convention, his respect for tradition generated a creative dialectic in his work … As he leaned more and more to the authority side of this dichotomy, this creative tension was lost" (58). We might ask Materer a few questions. Isn't Eliot's time one of disorder and is he therefore not bound to display "dissociation", to fail in the connection of dichotomies, the synthesis of fragments? Isn't Eliot in *The Waste Land* thematizing fragmentation and the difficulties of synthesis? For example, "On Margate Sands./ I can connect/ Nothing with nothing" (Eliot 1969b, 70). Isn't the expression of fragmentariness in an age of disorder a fitting "objective correlative" for this age?

Shusterman, by contrast, favours Eliot's later criticism as a clear advance, claiming that he broadly progresses – in a Hegelian fashion of thesis, antithesis, synthesis (see Chapter 4) – from idealism to empiricism to pragmatist pluralism. Eliot is initially under the influence of the idealist Bradley. Supporting Bradley, Eliot's doctoral thesis argued that the "existence of our common world relies on our sharing a stable consensus" (Shusterman 1994, 33), a lasting aspect of Eliot's thought. A related theme in his thesis, and as we have seen a major one for Eliot, is the "painful task of unifying … jarring and incompatible perspectives" (Eliot quoted in Shusterman 1994, 35), which points not only to the "fragmentation and synthesizing efforts" of *The*

Waste Land but to a lasting preoccupation with unity (35). However, Shusterman claims, Eliot's early literary criticism revolts against Bradley's "repudiation of empiricist thought" and facts (33). While Eliot's Bradleyan doctoral thesis asserts that "all truth is 'only an interpretation'", his early literary criticism shows an empiricist insistence on facts and analysis (34). This "striking reversal" is accompanied by a "reversal of the valencies of the private, the subjective, and the internal versus the public, objective, and external", in favour of the latter (34). Shusterman claims that this "radical" break (34) is attributable to Bertrand Russell's influence: Russell's "scientific empiricism" and emphasis on "facts", analysis and linguistic "precision" (36); for Russell and for Eliot's early criticism, words refer primarily to "sensations or 'sense-data'", hence the superiority of science and "empirical facts" over "speculation and interpretation" (37). But the Aristotelian Eliot was not a follower of Russell. Against Shusterman we might argue that induction and deduction, intuition and attention to facts, are both aspects of modern science and of science broadly understood, for example by Aristotle and even Plato. Eliot seems to be calling this to attention in "Tradition and the Individual Talent".

Shusterman argues that by 1927 Eliot was critical of Russell, came to view his narrow objectivism as both impossible and undesirable, and moved towards a third phase: a "hermeneutic historicism" that acknowledges the "inevitable role and value of the subjective" (38). Shusterman claims that Eliot's "hermeneutic historicism" was also a "pluralism" (40); that it anticipated the work of Hilary Putnam, Bernard Williams and Richard Rorty in arriving at the "value of pluralism" and the "plurality of interpretive perspectives" (41). In relation to Continental philosophy, Eliot's turn towards a "hermeneutic historicism" (44) brings him close to his contemporary Martin Heidegger and Heidegger's student Hans-Georg Gadamer (42) (see Chapter 10). In response to Shusterman we might argue that, though Eliot seems uninterested in adopting a precise position, "hermeneutic historicism" is not necessarily a pluralism (e.g. Heidegger's and Gadamer's wasn't) and might be conformist and authoritarian. It seems doubtful that Eliot's critical writing divides into phases so sharply. Throughout his career Eliot sustains a commitment to – but also awareness of the danger of – transcendent moments, from the "hyacinth garden" in *The Waste Land* (Eliot 1969b, 62) to the garden and "the still point of the turning world" in *Four Quartets* (Eliot 1969c, 173). These moments of insight, however, are wedded and only make sense in relation to the non-transcendent, the critical common-sense world we inhabit with others. Eliot's classicism, his classical tradition, from the Greeks through Catholic thought, is the tradition of this wisdom, the combination of insight and criticism, of knowledge as understanding and knowledge as contemplation, of the individual and the social. Modernity, modern science and philosophy, challenges this tradition with its individualism and materialism, but it is still alive with Coleridge, who invests, doubly, both in Neoplatonist Unity (the One) and in culture and cultural critique (Chapter 4). Eliot is a thinker in this tradition and has been criticized for his conservatism and authoritarianism. But any assessment of his ideas must take into account the insistence on balance he feels modernity has lost.

I. A. Richards

I. A. Richards (1893–1979) is a key figure in the development of twentieth-century literary studies in the English-speaking world. He was appointed to teach literature at Cambridge University in 1919. He had himself studied Moral Sciences (ethics, logic and psychology) at Cambridge. The study of English literature as the appreciation of literary art was something new to higher education in the United Kingdom, as was the study of English literature after Chaucer. Traditionally Classics had been studied, in a combination of literary and linguistic approaches, and Old and Middle English (English of the middle ages), but with a philological approach – and significantly, as the United Kingdom emerged from World War I, an approach heavily influenced by German scholarly methods. Although literature had been taught at Cambridge before, it was something that existed on the sidelines and had a distinctly amateurish air. It was only in the year of Richards's appointment, 1919, that the Cambridge English Faculty was established (1894 at Oxford University). Richards was a pioneer. And he was under pressure to prove the worthwhileness of the upstart faculty. For there were those who questioned that literature could be a rigorous academic discipline. How, they asked, could literary appreciation be evaluated or examined? Was it not finally a mere matter of taste? And if a mere matter of taste, what were the ethical implications, for the individual and the nation, of promoting its study? This explains a great deal about Richards's work at Cambridge. But help was on its way in the form of the Newbolt Report on the Teaching of English in England (1921), to which we will return in this chapter.

Richards and Eliot were friends, and together they were both very influential on the New Critics in the US (whom we will discuss in Chapter 9). Richards admired and defended Eliot's poetry and called it "the music of ideas". There are similarities between their critical ideas, though Richards was a man untroubled by "old-fashioned" religious and moral notions. One can draw a parallel between Eliot's critique of the over-emotional or the over-intellectual poet or critic and Richards's attempt to develop a literary criticism of "close reading". Readers must concentrate on the words on the page, extracting the meaning from them alone. If we maintain this discipline, perhaps the cloud of subjectivism, of personal taste, would clear, leaving in its place shared meaning, shared response. On this basis Richards will move to claim an important role for the new literary criticism in that troubled place known as "modern society".

In *Principles of Literary Criticism* (1924) Richards launches a staunch defence of the arts and humanities, most particularly literature, for their great serviceableness in the cause of psychic wellbeing. He develops a psychological theory which is certainly distinct from psychoanalysis, but which can be usefully compared to it, for example to Freud's *Civilization and Its Discontents* (1930) (Chapter 6). For Richards the mark of "high civilization" is the avoidance of repression in favour of the harmonious co-ordination and integration of a large number of very different and usually opposed and conflicting impulses, and literature plays a crucial role in the transition from a "chaotic" to a "free, varied" but highly organized psychic state (Richards 1967, 43). Richards advocates a "naturalistic morality" (45) whereby "[a]nything is valuable which will satisfy an appetency without involving the frustration of some equal *or more important* appetency" (36). The highest possible co-ordination of our instincts, needs and desires promises the least degree of their "curtailment, conflict, starvation and restriction" (45). The good life involves the widest possible array of varying, obscure, hidden, unconscious impulses and their refined co-ordination – too fine to be adequately described by the psychologist. Literature and criticism are defended as central in the development of a free and harmonious life.

Richards reconstructs a tradition for his own thinking, a line of predecessors: Coleridge on social and poetic unification; Shelley on the socially synthetic role of poetry; Arnold on anarchy versus harmonious development, free thinking and disinterestedness. Even Pater's descent to warring instincts and moods re-emerges transformed in Richards's criticism. Richards rejects the artistic autonomy of *l'art pour l'art*, insisting that Pater must not be reduced to such a version of Aestheticism. He is also a crucial early defender of Eliot and modernism (Richards's book appears two years after *The Waste Land*). He sees Eliot's poetry as working to produce a harmonization of opposed impulses. He praises Eliot's "conjunction of feelings which, though superficially opposed … yet tend as they develop to change places and even to unite" (235); the "interaction" of the "emotional effects" of the fragments in turn enables a "unified response" in "the right reader" (231).

In relation to science, scientific objectivity and verifiable truths, Richards is by no means opposed to science, indeed his psychology relies on emerging knowledge about the "higher … co-ordinating parts" of the nervous system (Richards 1967, 64) and the gap between stimulus and response (63–7). However, he distinguishes between the narrow "scientific use of language" or "reference", which is either true or false, and "the *emotive* use of language" (211), whose "supreme form" is poetry (215). The two are independent, and it would be "very foolish" to attempt to verify the statements of poetry (214).

The narrow world of reference is constantly "interfered with" (208) by our various impulses, and the role of the *emotive use* is to involve our impulses as "*completely*" and coherently as possible; this is Richards's understanding of Arnold's call to be disinterested and to see things "'all round' ... as they really are" (197–8). The emotive involves an "amplitude and fineness" of response whose authority is free from "actual assertion" (218). The value of *King Lear* is unrelated to verifiable truths, and tragedy is Richards's great and recurring example of harmonization of incompatible impulses (Aristotle's pity and terror discussed in Chapter 2). The union of these "discordant impulses" is the *catharsis* of tragedy; at the same time, we must face reality with "no suppression" and "without ... the innumerable subterfuges" of which we are capable, Richards writes, echoing Nietzsche (193). What Richards calls emotive is effectively his naturalistic morality and needs to be distinguished clearly from conventional morality, understood by him as the blind following of commands. (We have recently seen Nietzsche, Pater and Wilde reject morality in similar terms in pursuit of alternative values [Chapter 5]. But Eliot will not be assisting Richards in "clearing away from moral questions ... all ethical lumber and superstitious interpolations" [45].) Richards's naturalistic morality thus forms the basis of his defence of the distinctive and irreplaceable valuableness of literature and literary criticism, establishing the central need for it in education.

Richards is intent on elaborating the manner in which great literature brings about psychic integration. While usually the "ordinary man suppresses nine-tenths of his impulses" (191), good poetry is an exemplary apprenticeship, for the reader, in the fine co-ordination of a whole spectrum of impulses: "remote relationships between different systems of impulses arise" and previously "unapprehended and inexecutable connections are established" (187). The "imaginative moment" is this free and "untrammelled response", in contrast with the constrained and automatic responses of "ordinary life" (187). Recasting Coleridge's ideas of defamiliarization through the synthetic imagination (Chapter 4), Richards argues that the reader's "responses, canalized by routine ... break loose and make up a new order with one another" (191). By contrast, bad culture – for example, "the average super-film" (cinema) – disorganizes its audience (182), harms it by "fixing immature" attitudes and "stock responses" (Arnold's term, the stock is the familiar, the automatic) (159) or offers "appeasement" of "inadequate" impulses at a low "level of organization" (158). (As we saw in the last chapter, Benjamin feels rather that film has exciting potential for generating fresh response.) Thus good literature contributes to "freedom and fullness of life" (101), and the complex and full "balance" it brings about is the true meaning of aesthetic disinterestedness, as advocated by Arnold and aestheticians since Kant (195).

In *Principles of Literary Criticism* Richards registers in passing (Richards 1967, 165) his awareness that response to great literature takes place at very different levels depending on the reader. This issue takes centre stage in *Practical Criticism* (1929). Its starting point was Richards's famous experiment with university students, where he gave them poems to read but without providing the author's name or any other contextual information. To Richards the experiment revealed the extent of bad reading among even the most educated and privileged readers – a "widespread inability to construe meaning" (Richards 1929, 312). Hence the urgent need for educational reform: "better methods of instruction" (313) and a "better technique" of reading (309) were needed in order to train readers to read great literature properly. *Practical Criticism* provides elements towards a new method of reading that promises genuine access to literature for all, as currently "not a thousandth part" of the "power of poetry is released for the general benefit" because of our "ineptitude as readers" (321).

First, in a negative vein, bad reading needs to be analysed and properly understood. Readers need to avoid: "*mnemonic irrelevancies*" (irrelevant personal associations), "*Stock Responses*", sentimentality, inhibition, "*Doctrinal Adhesions*", "*technical presuppositions*" and "*general critical preconceptions*" (Richards 1929, 15–16). For example, in a spirit alien to Eliot, Richards argues that the "authority" invested in the literary canon and our "blind obedience" to the canon make great literature practically unreadable because we accord our admiration to an "idol" rather than thinking for ourselves in the spirit of the Enlightenment (361). One could argue that it is impossible to read without any "critical preconceptions" and that the distinction to be made is between those who are aware of their critical preconceptions and those who believe they have none. Second, in a positive vein, Richards asks readers to assume – obviously a critical preconception of a sort – that poems combine several kinds of meaning. In this sense, ambiguity is "systematic" and unavoidable, and readers need to develop "a 'perspective' which will include and enable us to control and 'place' the rival meanings that bewilder us" (10).

To facilitate the reader's core critical task of "*making out the meaning*" – understood as a "combination of several contributory meanings of different types" (180) – Richards distinguishes the following four kinds of meaning: sense or what the speaker says; feeling or the speaker's "nuance of interest" and affective "attitude to what he is talking about"; tone or "his attitude to his listener"; and intention or "the speaker's … aim, *conscious or unconscious*" (181–2). Richards is very far from proposing "stricter definition of leading terms and a more rigid adherence to them" as the answer to the task (343). On the contrary, this distinction is only a beginning, and "'[m]aking up our minds about a poem' is the most delicate" and difficult undertaking (317). To hazard a comparison, Aristotle points out that moral and political deliberation is difficult and requires the full exercise of the citizen's faculties, not because he does not know the principles (that he should be brave, generous, kind, etc.) but because of the gap between general principles and the unique situation one is judging (e.g. what is the brave thing to do in this *particular* situation?). Similarly, even armed with these four distinctions, the reader of a particular poem needs to grasp the "[i]nnumerable cross influences and complications between these four kinds of meaning" and the "*internal order* among" them (332). Identifying the four meanings, as a breakdown of the functions of language that constitute "Total Meaning" (180), is an aid to fuller appreciation of the poem, "greater suppleness" (343).

In *Practical Criticism* Richards translates the ideas he developed in *Principles of Literary Criticism* – of literature as a means to balanced and harmonious development of the personality – into a defined method of reading, and connects his earlier commitment to psychic integration to current social and political concerns. The supple and free ordering cultivated by proper training in reading literature is "the most serviceable" path (320) to democratic citizenship, and will make us "more reasonably self-reliant" and capable of thinking for ourselves (315) and "less easily imposed upon by our fellows and by ourselves" (350). This is especially urgent today, Richards argues (1929), because "[m]echanical inventions, with their social effects, and a too sudden diffusion of indigestible ideas, are disturbing … the whole order of human mentality"; "the burden of information and consciousness that a growing mind has now to carry may be too much for its natural strength" (320). We are facing the dissolution of family and local community (321), while "the mixtures of culture that the printed word has caused" have had the consequence that our "everyday reading and speech now handles scraps from a score of different cultures" (339). This situation will escalate as "world communications … improve" (340). (Bakhtin, theorist of *heteroglossia,* would have seen this in more positive terms than Richards, see Chapter 7.)

In response to this growing chaos, Richards sees a temptation to "defend ourselves … by stereotyping and standardizing" (340), but exactly the opposite is required. Rather, "in the interests of our standard of civilisation", the "best of all possible means" we have for countering the situation is "[p]oetry, the unique linguistic instrument by which our minds have ordered their thoughts, emotions, desires … in the past" (320). Are you reading this on-screen? One wonders what Richards would have made of the "information burden" on the "growing mind" today. I have quoted at some length to illustrate that the cultural concerns, anxieties, of Richards have clear parallels with Eliot, with F. R. Leavis (whom we will come to shortly) and with Matthew Arnold (see Chapter 5). (And of course, in updated form, we still hear them.) The social mission for literary studies within modern societies that Richards (and others) argues for becomes an important way in which literary studies in higher education understands itself in the twentieth century and beyond. The nature of literary studies and its social mission will, of course, be hotly contested.

I. A. Richards left Cambridge in 1929, the year *Practical Criticism* was published. He moved to Harvard and China (where he met up with his brilliant if wayward pupil Empson) before taking up an appointment at Harvard in 1941, the year of publication of John Crowe Ransom's *The New Criticism,* the book that lent the American critical movement its name. Back in the United Kingdom Cambridge would take a new turn to "value".

Virginia Woolf

Virginia Woolf (1882–1941) was one of the major British modernist writers of the twentieth century. The novel *To the Lighthouse* (1927) is her single most famous work. She was a prolific and boldly experimental novelist, short-story writer, essayist, biographer, autobiographer and diarist. She was a member of the famous Bloomsbury Group, a circle of artists and intellectuals who took their name from the Bloomsbury area of London where many of them lived in the early years of the last century. Many of the men had been at Cambridge University. Upper middle class, bohemian and unconventional, they attracted controversy. They espoused pacifism, love (including a good deal of "free love"!) and the pursuit of art and knowledge as central values of life. Woolf was friends with Eliot from the 1920s. Eliot was occasionally to be found among the Bloomsbury Group, but Eliot in his "*four*-piece suit", as Woolf once quipped, was definitely not Bloomsbury! Woolf suffered from mental illness for most of her life, with a manic-depressive condition. In 1941, in the midst of severe depression, she drowned herself. We will be looking further at her feminist classic *A Room of One's Own* (1929).

Interestingly, just as Richards was about to advance practical criticism as the solution to society's ills, Woolf gave what would become *A Room of One's Own* (1929) as lectures to the two women's colleges at Cambridge University, Newnham and Girton. By that time they had been established for about fifty years. However – it does seem amazing – women were not made *full* members of the University (granted the same sort of degrees as the men) until 1948! Oxford University, the other "ancient" university in Britain, did little better: 1920 for full membership. Woolf's brothers went to Cambridge, but Virginia and her sister were not allowed to by their father.

Published in the same year as Richards's *Practical Criticism*, Woolf's *A Room of One's Own*, in some contrast, voices the hope for a more pluralistic and multicultural world and literary canon, and is thus closer to the spirit of Bakhtin, who in 1933 called on literature to intensify *heteroglossia*. Richards claims Coleridge as his great predecessor in calling for psychic integration, but Woolf counter-claims him, seeing Coleridge as the originator of her call for the "androgynous mind". For Coleridge "a great mind is androgynous", writes Woolf, and continues, "when this *fusion* takes place … the mind is fully fertilized and uses all its faculties", becoming "incandescent and *undivided*" (Woolf 1929, 148, my italics). Thus Woolf proposes a form of "gender-bending" as the synthesizing solution to the multiform modern problem of psychic conflict and alienation outlined by Richards and Freud. Woolf recruits Shakespeare, Sterne, Coleridge, Keats and Proust as belonging to an alternative literary canon of androgynous minds. She is thus considerably at odds with T. S. Eliot's canon-forming and his criteria for inclusion! (But one could mention the androgynous Tiresias, prophet-narrator of *The Waste Land*, as a possible point of comparison. It can also be argued that Woolf implicitly suggests androgyny as an overcoming of the "dissociation of sensibility" lamented by Eliot.)

However, more than simply redefining *the* canon of literature, Woolf's aim is to reconstruct *an other* canon of women's writing, for women writers, and to situate her own literature in relation to it. Furthermore, *A Room of One's Own* is narrated by female first-person narrators, but also explicitly addresses a female audience. Chapter IV is Woolf's brief alternative history of women's writing in English. It made a great impression on Simone de Beauvoir, who returned to it in *The Second Sex* (1949) (Chapter 10), and has influenced successive generations of feminists. But it has also inspired the construction of other alternative literary canons – for example, an African-American canon. Woolf views women's writing in English as a submerged or repressed tradition – comparable to Benjamin's "tradition of the oppressed" (Chapter 7) – that requires an alternative form of literary history. Jane Austen, Charlotte and Emily Brontë, George Eliot, *et al.* must be understood in relation to "books that were not there" (68) and "empty shelves" (79). In response to the unavailability of writing by Elizabethan women, the narrator must enlist the imagination to evoke the conditions that were bound to drive Shakespeare's gifted sister – Woolf calls her Judith – to destruction (Shakespeare did in fact have four sisters, though only one, Joan, lived to maturity). The mixed genre of *A Room of One's Own* – criticism and fiction – is merely a consequence of the subject. A history of women's writing is going to be half made up, untrue, but that is its truth. (We will continue to address Woolf's understanding of a women's tradition.)

Understanding the social conditions enabling or rather disabling literary production is, argues Woolf, hugely important. Woolf must use her imagination, but she also wants to think about basic requirements, the basic practicalities. To start with texts are "attached to grossly material things", such as money (Woolf 1929, 63). She therefore pays considerable attention to money and women's lack of it: "a woman must have money and a room of her own if she is to write fiction" (6). And of course (in what must be one of the earliest uses of the term by a feminist) there is explicit discussion of the specific and overarching social condition that feminists, literary or otherwise, seek to challenge: "England is under the rule of a patriarchy" (50).

Woolf's discussion of patriarchy addresses wider debates and claims broad relevance, in that it incorporates discussions of aggressive instincts (implicitly addressing Freud's later work – see Chapter 6), British colonialism and literary criticism. The patriarchs are prey to their "instinct for possession, the rage for acquisition" (58), whether it is exercised on "a piece of land or a man with curly black hair" (76). A patriarch is "concerned … with his own superiority" (52) because he "has to conquer" and "rule" (53). Women have "served" as "looking-glasses … reflecting the figure of man at twice its natural size" (53). However, if she "begins to tell the truth" about man, inevitably deflating his exaggerated sense of his superiority, "[h]ow is he to go on … civilizing natives" (54)? The colonial ideology of the civilizing mission will be exposed as a lie. Provocatively Woolf singles out mainstream literary critics – "the professors" – from among the patriarchs (58). She imagines the patriarchal critic "measuring" books in order to pronounce them too long or too short (160). She urges the woman writer not to submit to the "decrees of the measurers": write "what you wish to write" (160)!

Woolf explores why it is women writers need a women's tradition rather than the male tradition. One of the many, often contradictory, lines pursued in *A Room of One's Own* is the way in which the "values of women differ" often from the prevailing "masculine values" (110). For example, it is suggested that allusiveness, the "power of suggestion" (152), is a female value lacking in Kipling (154), but manifesting itself in Coleridge and in deservingly canonical literary texts, as suggestion "has the secret of perpetual life" (153). Because of this difference of values, the early-nineteenth-century pioneers of women's writing had "no tradition behind them" (114). Formally, the woman writer had "no common sentence ready for her use" (114) – Jane Austen had to "devise" her own sentence (115) – and Woolf feels the poetic tradition could not easily be bent to her values. The relatively new genre of the novel "alone was young enough to be soft in her hands" (116).

Woolf shares with her contemporaries (both the conservative Eliot and the liberal Richards) a fear of political anger and conflict: "It is fatal for a woman to lay the least stress on any grievance … There must be freedom and there must be peace" (Woolf 1929, 157). But her awareness of the oppression of women leads her to take a critical distance from dominant norms in favour of an anti-authoritarian pluralism and multiperspectivism. If it is undesirable to be "locked out" as an outsider, it is "worse perhaps to be locked in" (37); Woolf's desideratum is the Outsiders Society she outlines in 1938 in *Three Guineas* (Woolf 1991, 122ff.). The narrators of *A Room of One's Own* praise their female audience for their "unconventionality" (167–8) and free-thinking critical spirit. If "[y]ou have been contradicting" one of the narrators this is good because "truth is only to be had by laying together many varieties of error" (158). In relation to literary criticism, the narrators argue against the self-important style and scientific aspirations of literary critics in highly ironic prose, and even cast doubt on the value of contemporary university education – poking fun at the university-trained male student "extracting" from a book "pure nuggets of the essential ore" of truth (42) rather than thinking for himself.

William Empson

Meanwhile, the institutionalization of contemporary literary studies continued apace in Cambridge, and Richards's work was becoming known and influential. Although he left Cambridge in 1929, his ideas in *Practical Criticism* would bear their most brilliant fruit in the book of his student, the poet and critic William Empson (1906–84), *Seven Types of Ambiguity* (1930), published when he was only 24. It was a foundational text for the New Critics in the US, more important than Richards and Eliot. In his 1947 preface to the second edition, Empson describes his method as "verbal analysis" of a literary text (usually a short poem) concerned with ambiguity (Empson 2004, vii): the poem is viewed as a "puzzle as to what the author meant" because of the inherent multiplicity of meanings (x) and of relations between them. The main text, discussed here in its third, 1953 edition, clarifies the method and distinguishes it from rival approaches. First, Empson rebuts the criticism that his emphasis on meaning leads to a "fallacy of pure Meaning" as problematic as the Aestheticist or Symbolist fallacy of "Pure Sound" (10). Second, following Richards's wish to de-emphasize the idea of a truth to be searched for in the text by his practical readers, Empson takes his distance from a "'scientific' mode of literary criticism" (11). He is not concerned with "what is really there" in a poem (245) – not "concerned with science" – but with the "effects" of that poem, aiming to expose "how a properly-qualified mind works" in the act of making sense of it (248). This includes one's emotions, as with poetry, unlike science, "the act of knowing is itself an act of sympathising" (248). Third, again following Richards, Empson insists that his is a purely empiricist method without theoretical presuppositions. There is both a "great variety of different styles of poetry" and a "great variety of critical dogmas", but what he offers is a neutral "machinery for analysis" (255) as a common ground for criticism. More broadly, now that specialization and globalization are turning English into an "aggregate of vocabularies only loosely in connection with one another" (236), this "machinery" promises to "keep the language under control" (237), argues Empson, sounding very similar to his teacher.

Empson redefined his method in his 1950 essay, "The Verbal Analysis". He reiterates his claim that his method is purely empiricist and avoids all theoretical assumptions: the critic "ought to trust his own nose" and scrupulously avoid the distractions of "any kind of theory or principle" (594). Poems and theories alike need to be individually "masticated and brought up to the taste buds" (595). However, Empson's method does not concern itself with evaluation or comparison. Its core task is expository: "to show how the machine is meant to work", in all its parts, in the "mind of a fit reader" (597–8). Empson's vivid and witty rejection of evaluation – his "machine" does not aim to decide "whether marmalade is better than sausages" (598) – is a dig perhaps at those arch discriminators, Eliot and Leavis, for whom evaluation was key. Empson was being provocative with his "machine" also, as Eliot and Leavis were both in favour of the organic (i.e. social and literary organicism) and positively anti-machine (industrial society, modern technology).

F. R. Leavis

F. R. Leavis (1895–1978) is the central figure of Cambridge English in the twentieth century. Storer describes Leavis's "psychological hold" over "generations of students, teachers and writers", especially in Britain (Storer 2009, 1–2). Leavis was born and raised in Cambridge, but as the son of a shopkeeper he was of a different background from most of those who taught at the University in the first half of the last century. He went to Cambridge as a student in the momentous year of 1919, initially to read history. He switched to English in his second year and bought Eliot's *The Sacred Wood* (1920) as soon as it came out. Leavis's early work would be dominated by Eliot. He completed a doctorate in 1924 and began teaching at the University in 1927.

Leavis always felt himself to be an outsider at the University. His work is characterized by a severity and moral earnestness which is often related to his Protestant Nonconformist sympathies; this seriousness along with his conviction (supported by Arnold, Eliot and the Newbolt Report) of the central importance of literary studies in higher education and national culture naturally had strong appeal for students and teachers. But Leavis's belief in the importance of literary studies is accompanied by his touchy and insistent self-importance as master critic and voice of true culture. This often results in self-righteousness and over-combativeness. In addition, as he made clear at the very outset of his career with the pamphlet *Mass Civilisation and Minority Culture* (1930), in contrast to the Newbolt Report, and more so than Arnold, Leavis is an elitist who believes that most people are not capable of worthwhile judgements about art and literature and are therefore, in his estimation, set outside the possibility of "fine living" (Leavis 1933, 14). Literature appears as the preserve of a Platonic spiritual elite, who are "the consciousness of the race" (15). This snobbery and self-importance is reflected in Leavis's style of criticism, which, particularly in the earlier writings, can be very pompous and condescending. Leavis therefore felt himself both an outsider at Cambridge, but also the true spirit, or the leading representative of the true spirit, of not only the University of Cambridge, but of British university education. But if there is in Leavis a tendency to see plots and persecutors, his sense of embattledness and of being insufficiently recognized by his university was not groundless, as his slow progress up the academic hierarchy indicates. He was not given a full employment contract until 1947 and was never made a professor.

Q. D. Leavis, Leavis's wife, was also a distinguished critic, though raising the couple's children she was much less prolific than her husband. In addition to her sole-authored writing, she co-wrote a number of texts with her husband. In 1933 the Leavises and others founded an important literary magazine, *Scrutiny*, of which F. R. Leavis was principal editor until its close in 1953. The journal published the major literary critics of the day, including Eliot, Empson and Richards, and was well known and widely read.

Leavis is often criticized for his antitheoretical stance. This is an unsatisfactory characterization, because Leavis of course made theoretical statements about literature and literary criticism and about history and culture, just as the antitheoretical New Critics did (Chapter 9). In the late 1930s the critic René Wellek called on Leavis to make his critical principles and assumptions explicit. In "Literary Criticism and Philosophy" (1937), in response to Welleck, Leavis writes: "Philosophy, we say, is 'abstract' ... and poetry 'concrete'. Words in poetry invite us, not to 'think about' and judge but to 'feel into' or 'become' – to realize a complex experience that is given in the words" (Leavis 1964, 212–13). What Leavis resists is a statement of principles abstracted from engagement with literary texts and pretending to general validity, or at least premature abstraction and generalization. The essay shows the influence of "Tradition and the Individual Talent", Eliot's ideas of the dialectic between insight and criticism, his emphasis on the concrete image in poetry and the critic who remains strenuously engaged with the text. However, the example that Eliot gives of the perfect critic (in "The Perfect Critic") is a philosopher, Aristotle, and the example of his literary-critical genius is of course the *Poetics*, a work of literary theory.

Leavis's emphasis on valuation in the essay manages to avoid the word "meaning". It is used four times, two of which are quoting Welleck. But literary critics spend more of their time interpreting the meaning of literary texts than evaluating them and to value them requires an understanding of their meaning. In addition, literary texts themselves are the products of "thinking about" and are themselves engaged in the act of "thinking about". This does not make them abstract or lacking in concreteness, nor does concreteness preclude philosophical interest. Leavis sets up an opposition between literature, which we "feel into", and philosophy, which we "think about", but it is a false opposition. Perhaps Leavis would agree if pressed, for in fact what he is attacking in criticism is what Eliot vaguely characterizes as the "dissociation of sensibility" in poetry, taken to mean a dissociation of thought and feeling. A key term for Leavis, also inherited from Eliot, in his evaluation of both literature and criticism, is "intelligence", a word that he uses throughout his career, even after the cooling of his early enthusiasm for Eliot. For Leavis it is the capacity for unified response of feeling and understanding. But a more constructive conversation would have resulted had Leavis "thought about" his terms more. However, it is clear that we are here given a theoretical statement.

The writer puts into words "complex experience" and the reader seeks to respond fully to the language and so "realize" the experience. Surely the experience that George Eliot puts into words in *Middlemarch* and embodies in the fictional characters, their world and the events of the novel is the product of much "thinking about", much reading as well as her own observations and, in the case of the intensely intellectual Eliot, much reading of philosophy. The reader's "feeling into" – in order to apprehend, organize and criticize their response to the literary work, interpretively, aesthetically, morally, and to assess it comparatively in relation to other literary works – will also include "thinking about" and will bring to bear all their resources of knowledge and experience. There is no space to discuss whether *Middlemarch* puts into words a "complex experience" in the same way that Shelley's "Mont Blanc" or Keats's "Ode to a Grecian Urn" does, or my recounting of what I did on my summer holiday. The activity of literary study will enrich our understanding of ourselves and others and all aspects of our lives, and conduce to the development of intellectually, emotionally and morally sophisticated people. As Arnold and Eliot, Leavis believed that the canon was a kind of repository of the authentic values of a nation or civilization. The writer and the critic work in their different ways to conserve those values which have come to be considered constitutive of "fine living" and to respond critically to changing conditions.

The openness of approach I have indicated is what Leavis values, whether the artist's openness to life and experience or the reader's openness to the literary work. His so-called antitheoretical attitude can perhaps be more accurately characterized as antidogmatic. The years after World War I saw the growing popularity of Marxism among Western intellectuals and the development of Marxist literary theory. Though sharing Marxist views about the alienated and fragmented nature of modernity, it seems fairly clear that Leavis had little political sympathy for Marxism; he might be described as a Romantic conservative in the tradition of Coleridge (see Williams below). Leavis's critical objection to Marxism is that Marxist literary criticism could seem crudely reductionist and with little interest in the literary work other than its function as yet another document confirming the truth of Marxism. In turn the Marxist idea of "false consciousness" problematized Leavis's emphasis on lived experience, for lived experience could be distorted by capitalist ideology.

Another keyword for Leavis is "life" (adopted from Lawrence). His judgement of writers goes beyond an attitude of openness or breadth and complexity of response to life in the sense of existing conditions; it addresses the degree to which writers seek to intensify and refine life, to live more fulfillingly, with a greater sense of the value and significance of life, and to pass their discoveries to their readers. The writer is therefore, for Leavis, in a critical position with regard to existing conditions and combats those forces, material and intellectual, antithetical to the desire for richer and more fulfilling lives. In this regard Leavis became critical of Eliot (to be discussed further below), seeing his stance as world-weary and insufficiently affirming. D. H. Lawrence, whom Leavis had first written on before Eliot, came to occupy in Leavis's view the position of the greatest modern writer, in his restless quest for more "life" and his criticism of Western industrial, rationalistic civilization. Leavis agreed with Lawrence in his rejection of Western modern life, with Leavis coining the term "technologico-Benthamite" age (Storer 2009, 52) to describe what he considered our spiritually impoverished civilization following the rise of a reductive scientific worldview whose bland promises of technological utopia disgusted Leavis. (Dickens famously attacked Bentham and his Utilitarian philosophy of facts in *Hard Times*, the only novel by Dickens Leavis praised in *The Great Tradition* [discussed below].) Leavis made his view very clear in his 1962 *The Two Cultures? The Significance of C. P. Snow* (Leavis 2013), in response to the scientist and novelist C. P. Snow's 1959 lecture "The Two Cultures and the Scientific Revolution" (Snow 1993). Leavis is at his most unrestrainedly scathing in this exchange.

Leavis's first major publication, *New Bearings in English Poetry* (1932), is clearly influenced by T. S. Eliot's criticism and commitments and was a significant early statement from the academy in defence and promotion of modernism. But it is Eliot who is the central figure: the book can be said to be written around him as poet and largely according to his valuations and in his language as critic. The Victorian poets are criticized (following Eliot) for retreating from modernity into dream and nostalgia, as is W. B. Yeats before his 1912 collection, *The Green Helmet*. Yeats's later work is applauded for residing in the "actual waking world" and for using "the idiom and movement of modern speech" (Leavis 1972a, 36). Instead of escapism it is attuned to modern disillusionments, to the impossibility of the "Unity [of Being]" in a civilization in which the "Unity of Culture ... is no longer possible" (Yeats quoted in Leavis 1972a, 40).

The great poet is "at the most conscious point of the race in his time" (Leavis 1972a, 16). Eliot, with the broken myth of *The Waste Land*, has distilled the spirit of the time, in the language of the time. He, more than anyone else, is deemed "fully alive in our time", in his "unmistakable newness of tone, rhythm, and imagery" and "utterly unfamiliar 'feel'" (24). Eliot is "more aware" of his age than anyone else, and it is due to his "very strong originality", which has "triumphed over traditional habits" (62), that Ezra Pound and Gerard Manley Hopkins (the two poets given their own chapter in addition to Eliot) find their place in a "revised tradition" for the new century (144).

New Bearings sees Leavis exhibiting the heroic ideology of the new that is so strongly associated with modernism. The critical values, language and tone of his criticism follow Eliot. However, Leavis's pomposity exceeds his master. While Eliot has "a mind unquestionably of rare distinction" (Leavis 1972a, 25), "so inferior a mind and spirit as Browning's could not ... bring back into poetry the adult intelligence" (21), and for Tennyson to fulfil his ambition "would have taken a much finer intelligence and a much more robust original genius ... much greater strength and courage" (18)! Victorian women poets are not even mentioned. Such pomposity and condescension invite ridicule and display an attitude unattractively close to class arrogance. In addition to a dismissive attitude towards Romanticism (though sharing Eliot's admiration for Blake) and certainly towards the Victorians, Leavis also falls into line with Eliot's insinuations regarding Milton. In "The Metaphysical Poets" Eliot describes Milton as "aggravating" the dissociation of sensibility (Eliot 1951b, 288). In what sense he did this is not specified, Eliot making no claim that Milton's poetry is characterized by this dissociation. However, Leavis is confident in declaring of Milton that his words "have little substance or muscular quality" (Leavis 1972a, 64). The reader might like to remind themselves of the vast desolation of hell in *Paradise Lost*, and of Satan's annihilating despair and titanic upsurges of renewed power – a vision unique in its sustained intensity and primordial mythic force in English literature.

Later Leavis would question how "fully alive in our time" Eliot was, at least in the sense of the affirmation of "life" that Leavis approved. It is impossible to avoid the dispiritment and sense of nullity in Eliot. Leavis commented on this in *New Bearings*, but nevertheless considered that Eliot's originality as poet was so vital and vitalizing that it outweighed the shrinking from life to be found in Eliot's poetry, and also Eliot's unfortunate attraction to Christianity (a point on which Leavis's distaste is clear). But while Leavis retained great respect for Eliot as poet as well as critic, later years saw an increasingly critical attitude towards Eliot's outlook, as Leavis understood it, and an emphatic shift in allegiance to D. H. Lawrence. Leavis's last engagement with Eliot, a lengthy essay on *Four Quartets* in *The Living Principle* (1975), takes up again Eliot's distaste for the temporal world, in favour of moments of escape from time and mystical experience. It is true that Eliot expresses distaste for the experience of the mundane or temporal world – in much the same way that Leavis indulges in relentless gloom and pessimism about every aspect of the contemporary world – and longs for the eternal moment. As discussed earlier, in so doing Eliot adds his voice to a tradition stretching back to Plato, Aristotle and beyond. The final words of Leavis's last book express this longing, as amidst the dreary mundanity of the modern world he beseeches that "the decisively new and unforeseen may yet reward us" (Leavis 1976, 156). However, *Four Quartets* is Eliot's culminating statement on the conformity between the visionary/creative and the rational/critical, already to be found in "Tradition and the Individual Talent": "only in time can the moment in the rose-garden … be remembered" (Eliot 1969c, 173). So there is no good reason, with regard to *Four Quartets*, for Leavis in his last essay on Eliot to change the view he argued in *New Bearings* that the meaning of Eliot's poetry was by no means confined to a religious interpretation.

In his 1950 "Retrospect", included in the second edition of *New Bearings*, Leavis looks back, very critically, on the intervening canonization of the "revolution" of modernism and of T. S. Eliot as well as the canonization of his own book, which became a significant "historical fact" in "literary history" (Leavis 1972a, 158). He claims that it resulted in the neutralization of disturbingly mould-breaking new literature. The initial "punitive opposition" to Eliot, among the educated public but also the "advanced academic" world, which Leavis fought hard to combat, gave way to a bland and even misunderstanding kind of acceptance (160–61). Pledging to remain an antiestablishment figure (and reaffirming the role of strong master critic for himself), Leavis argues that his book initially provoked "indignation" (173) but its evaluations were later much copied by others, who replaced his genuine "pioneering" with vacuous and undiscriminating "deference" (159). Thus Leavis's "championship" of the neglected Hopkins led to his canonization into "a glory of the establishment" (174) and Eliot is now a "public institution" (161). But Eliot's false admirers fail to see how "disturbing" he really is (164) and are only interested in making the world "safe again" (159). Leavis deplores the sort of canonization that is working to "deny the genius" while ostensibly "acclaiming it" (164). His very sharp response to Empson's defence of exposition against evaluation is that "exegesis" is contrary to Leavis's pioneering spirit. The bold evaluations of others are simply taken for granted and reproduced, and the poem is assumed to be a "presentment of familiar doctrines" and thus neutralized (164).

Turning to poetry since Eliot, Leavis is unimpressed by the poets emerging in the 1930s: W. H. Auden, Stephen Spender, Louis MacNeice, Dylan Thomas. He accuses Auden of arrested artistic development and blames it on the institution of literary criticism (primarily newspaper critics but by no means excluding academic critics). He claims that Auden was damaged by his membership of an Oxford University "coterie" protecting "its members … from the severities of criticism" (Leavis 1972a, 169), exemplary of an "international" system operating in the field of literary production and criticism throughout Europe and America; the purpose of this system is to instil conformist "social values" and maintain class prestige, with inclusion in the canon denied to anybody not willing to fall into line (171–2). Leavis had expressed this criticism of Auden in a 1936 review article for his journal, *Scrutiny* (Leavis 1968). However, whether or not his comments were justified in 1936, by 1950 Auden is surely a very different poet, and 15-year-old opinions are in need of revision. Leavis's alternative to a literary establishment run by Oxford graduates and university literary studies increasingly populated by Marxists is *Scrutiny*. Against mass civilization, coteries and dogmatists, *Scrutiny* is a genuinely critical voice "vindicating the Idea of a University" (that is Leavis's idea of it) (Leavis 1972a, 170).

In *The Great Tradition* (1948) Leavis pioneers a "drastically revised" tradition and canon of great novelists in English, acknowledging the substantial contribution of Q. D. Leavis, his wife, to the work. Leavis follows Woolf in declaring Jane Austen and George Eliot the first great novelists, in his very exclusive canon of five, followed by Henry James, Joseph Conrad and, of course, Lawrence. The book is essentially a genealogy of Lawrence. What then are Leavis's criteria for evaluation? Formal inventiveness as inseparable from "awareness" of "life" (Leavis 1972b, 10); "interest in life" in all its aspects and "intense moral interest" as opposed to narrow moralizing (16); "vital capacity for experience" or "reverent openness before life" (18); and "seriousness" (19).

T. S. Eliot championed James Joyce and the Joyce-influenced Djuna Barnes, Henry Miller and Lawrence Durrell (Leavis 1972b, 37). Leavis accuses Joyce *et al.* of aiming, "in Laurentian phrase, to 'do dirt' on life", without offering any clarification (38). As he had done with Eliot, he champions Lawrence, in Lawrence's own "disconcertingly original" (38) terms, as a Nietzschean seer "receiving the hidden waves that come from the depths of life" and "transferring them to the unreceptive world" (Lawrence quoted in Leavis 1972b, 36).

Leavis's *The Great Tradition* and *D.H. Lawrence: Novelist* (1955) are windows into the early battles for the modernist canon: "if you took Joyce for a major creative writer ... you had no use for Lawrence" and vice versa (Leavis 1967, 10). Eliot, followed by the majority of critics, championed Joyce, while a minority including Leavis, Aldous Huxley and E. M. Forster championed Lawrence. In *D.H. Lawrence* Leavis greatly elaborates on earlier attacks on the institution of literary criticism. He also claims that Eliot's rejection of the working-class Lawrence for being "rotten and rotting others" (Eliot quoted in Leavis 1967, 311) was wholly due to Eliot's failure to emancipate himself from "disabling" class "prejudices" (304). Eliot's class-bound misunderstanding was that Lawrence was an untrained genius lacking "critical faculties", as a result of "not having been brought up in the environment of a living and central tradition" (305–6; see Eliot 1934, 58–62). Leavis's counter-claim is that Lawrence's "supreme intelligence" (14) grew out of his participation in the lowly, in class terms, but vital English tradition of Nonconformity (the broad spectrum of Protestant religious denominations and movements outside the Anglican church), a tradition of "moral seriousness" and "strenuous intellectual inquiringness" (Leavis 1967, 307). Furthermore, as the son of a miner, Lawrence had "intimate experience" of the realities of industrial England (307). Decentering the centre, Leavis concludes that Lawrence "*was* brought up in a living and central tradition" (308), if one invisible to the institution of literary criticism.

Raymond Williams

> Raymond Williams (1921–88) was born in a village in Wales to working-class parents. His abilities won him a place at Cambridge University to study English, at the time an exceptional achievement for one of his background. At Cambridge he joined the Communist Party of Great Britain, having first read *The Communist Manifesto* as a schoolboy. During World War II he saw action as a member of an anti-tank regiment. After the war he taught at the universities of Oxford and Cambridge, and became Cambridge's first Professor of Drama in 1974. The first book of this prolific writer appeared in 1950. His range of interests was broad and integrative: cultural and media theorist and literary theorist, he was also a novelist. Williams is recognized as a major founder of cultural studies as a discipline.

Williams was the first major working-class British (Welsh) literary critic. We already discussed his work on tragedy in Chapter 2. In his *Culture and*

Society, 1780–1950: Coleridge to Orwell (1958), our focus here, we can see him drawing on yet radically revising ideas to be found in Leavis, Richards and Eliot. The concept of "cultural materialism" that he introduces in the book has been very influential in literary studies, where today it defines an approach similar to that of New Historicism in the US (see Chapter 11); it was also a key concept for the new academic field of cultural studies that emerged in the 1970s and established itself in the 1980s. Williams argues that literature can only be properly understood in relation to culture, where culture is, in Eliot's definition, "a whole way of life" – an entire society – and he pays tribute to Eliot for advancing this view (Williams 1987, 232). For Williams "cultural materialism", with regard to literature, is the recognition that literature is embedded in society, affected by economic, social, institutional, technological, political reality. These aspects of social life interpenetrate one another. Culture is Williams's name for the totality of all these factors as they shape our literary experience and the meaning of all our literary practices: writing, performing, publishing, selling and buying, reading, interpreting, criticizing, theorizing, institutionalizing, forming a canon, banning and burning literature. However, "materialism" signifies Williams's belief that a particular aspect of social reality is more significant than others: the mode of production. In the case of the UK since the eighteenth century, this is industrial capitalism. For Williams, following Marx, industrial society is divided into two antagonistic social classes (Chapter 5), the bourgeoisie and the working class, each with its own culture, though the culture of the bourgeoisie is dominant in industrial society. "Cultural materialism" is a political approach to literature, seeking the ways in which literature expresses class struggle. If Williams therefore adopts Eliot's definition of culture, he adopts it in a very different sense.

But Eliot is only the most recent in what Williams claims is a "continuous" (Williams 1987, 233) line of literary figures to have taken a similar view in their social thought. Eliot's great predecessors are the Romantics who, deeply involved in the "study and criticism of the society of their day" (30), inaugurated the critical attention to culture as a whole in response to the Industrial Revolution and emerging industrial society. Williams points out the irony of this, given Eliot's antipathy for Romantic poetry. He provides an overview of the key figures: Coleridge (whom we discussed in Chapter 4), Carlyle, Ruskin, William Morris (Chapter 5) in the nineteenth century, Eliot, Richards and Leavis in the twentieth. Having fleshed out this tradition, Williams then aims to "reinterpret" it "in terms of the experience of our own generation" (iii), particularly the experience of the new mass media. One of Leavis's important contributions, for Williams, was his insight into and attack on "the *domination* of the world of English letters" by a "minority" that "coincide[s] with a particular social class" (262, my italics).

Shadowing Leavis but radicalizing his insights Williams argues that the wide diffusion of the arts has been "*dominative* in character": disseminating the "ideal of an existing class" (the bourgeoisie) and "leading the unenlightened to the particular kind of light the leaders find satisfactory for themselves" (Williams 1987, 238, my italics). To outline his vision for the future, Williams develops a distinction between the "dominative mood" (336) and democracy. The dominative mood was one of the "mainsprings" of the Industrial Revolution. But man's "mastering of and controlling his natural environment" also "extends to man himself" (336). (Williams's call to "unlearn" this mood is not only a critique of the exploitation of man by man, but also an ecological critique [vii].) For Williams, the dominative mood is supported by "individualism", which is fundamental to bourgeois culture, the culture of capitalism (325). Williams's critique of the dominative mood and of individualism occasionally recalls Heidegger (see Chapter 10), but his political analysis and democratic alternative are distinctly un-Heideggerian. Williams claims that the entire post-Coleridge British tradition he has identified has been engaged in a sustained "criticism of … the bourgeois idea of society", particularly its individualism, broadly in favour of community, which Williams applauds (328). However, Williams's "democratic" alternative has to be carefully extricated from certain problematic aspects of this tradition. He criticizes Eliot's "complacent conservatism" (243) and rejects Richards's view of literature as a "training-ground for life" as uncritical (251), discerning an "element of passivity" in the reader's relation to the text as described by Richards (250). More broadly, the organic community valued by so many in this tradition is an idealized version of rural communities, blind to all the real disadvantages of rural society (poverty, disease, ignorance) and surrendering to a "characteristically industrialist, or urban, nostalgia" (259–60). Williams calls on readers to reject the myth, within this tradition, that history is "almost wholly decline" (262) leading to a "disintegrated and dissatisfying present" (for example Eliot's view of English history since the seventeenth century) (263). He similarly rejects the tradition's elitist idea of a cultivated minority who are the bearers of true culture amidst the benighted masses (for example Leavis, whose sense of a minority literary culture amidst a majority debased by modern consumer culture amounted to a pessimistic elitism) (263). The tradition's "pseudo-aristocratic authoritarianism" and "scepticism … intolerant of any contemporary social commitment" must be replaced by a "training in democracy" (263) and a more constructive sense of the possibility of change.

The British tradition of literary thinking about culture as a whole way of life (as opposed to merely the high culture of the literary canon, high art, etc.) and their criticism of existing society provides a valuable model, but it is, in large part, a conservative tradition fearful of democracy and the working classes. Williams desires to promote democratization and working-class values as an alternative to elitism, paternalism, authoritarianism and individualism in literary and cultural matters. He defines the core working-class values as "solidarity" (Williams 1987, 328), a "collective and mutual" perspective (325) and "active mutual responsibility" (330), and identifies them as the bases of democracy. Democracy involves active citizenship – ensuring "multiple" voices that all have "access to the common channels" (316) – and "even dissidence", as "we need to listen to others who started from a different position" (334). Rejecting both "romantic individualism" and "authoritarian training" (337), Williams values active "response" (313) and "common government" freely "made and remade" (337).

Culture and Society came to be widely viewed as one of the inaugural documents of the "new intellectual and political tradition" of the Anglo-American New Left, as Williams acknowledges in the 1987 foreword. Williams was unwaveringly committed to working-class values and politics, but though he remained politically close to Marxism his relationship to orthodox Marxist theory was critical. In particular he was critical of the determining role of the economy in orthodox Marxism – the base/superstructure model – which reduces culture and society (superstructure) to mechanical reflections of the economy. To Williams this was a "rigid methodology" involving "forcing and superficiality" (281). His "cultural materialism" and the British tradition he critically reconstructed countered Marxist reductionism with an elaboration that would make plain that culture was not a chimera, but the medium in which we lived, and in which politics is conducted, "mak[ing] impossible the mechanical procedures" of the orthodox view (282). In this way Williams established the legitimacy, that is to say the political value, of thinking about culture from the point of view of Marxism, in regard to any aspect of culture and on a definition of culture that was unlimited (for what is there that can be excluded from "a whole way of life"?). On all of it, useful political work could be done and the struggle advanced. No doubt this was a particular service to literary studies.

Williams's antielitist and inclusive view of culture has been triumphant, and cultural studies, the discipline of which he is one of the major founders, has flourished and had a major impact on literary studies and throughout the humanities and the social sciences. However, the years since his death have also seen the continued waning of working-class politics in Britain. That politics was for Williams the expression of his culture, working-class culture. Many have lamented this as the loss of the only hope for real social transformation. However, others have welcomed a situation in which personal and political identities and struggles are freed from the reduction to social class and class politics alone. This is one of the major developments in literary and cultural theory in the English-speaking world since the 1980s, and therefore one of the major themes of this book.

Postcolonial canons, postcolonial critiques

The internationally acclaimed Kĩkũyũ Kenyan writer and critic Ngũgĩ wa Thiong'o (1938–), the well-known Ugandan writer and critic Taban lo Liyong (1939–) and the now deceased Kenyan critic Henry Owuor-Anyumba (1933–92) were teaching at the University of Nairobi, Kenya in 1968, five years after the independence of Kenya in 1963. Their "On the Abolition of the English Department" (1968) was primarily intended to reform the study of literature at the University of Nairobi, but boldly claimed a global relevance by outlining new programmatic assumptions for the (re)construction of canons of East African literature, modern African literature and even world literature. *Contra* Arnold, Eliot and their legacy, they argue against a canon of so-called *great* literature and "classics". Judgements of "literary excellence" inevitably impose a particular perspective rather than being objective, it is therefore better "[f]or any group ... to study representative works which mirror their society" (Ngũgĩ *et al.* 2001, 2096). This may be a valuable critique, but arguably creates its own problems as to what is and isn't deemed representative of a society; for example, are dominated, minority or emergent perspectives going to be deemed unrepresentative? (We've just witnessed some ugly scenes between different classes and religions in the form of Leavis and Eliot.) Be that as it may, the writers affirm the general point that the practical purpose of any university literature department anywhere is to "illuminate the spirit animating a people, to show how it meets new challenges, and to investigate possible areas of development and involvement" (2094). In other words, the study of literature is a people's "means" of "knowledge about ourselves" (2096). What counts as a "people", however, is far from obvious or even stable: the writers avoid both national identities and tribal identities, focusing instead on the need to develop broader and interlinked East African, African and black perspectives.

Of course in order to even begin to develop any of these perspectives, an initial reversal of the colonial distribution of the positions of centre and periphery needs to have taken place. To continue to assume that the English literary tradition, and its language, is central to African literature is to continue to assume that Africa is an "extension of the west" (Ngũgĩ *et al.* 2001, 2093) – "Why can't African literature be at the centre" (2093)? The writers thus propose to proceed on the assumption that the African oral tradition is the "primary root" of modern African literature and its "most significant" source (2094). This assumption gives substance to the reorientation and calls on African writers to take appropriate action. For example, the manifesto contributed to Ngũgĩ's later decision to decolonize his name, changing it from James Ngũgĩ to Ngũgĩ wa Thiong'o, and, importantly, to write first in his native Gĩkũyũ and then translate his own work into English, beginning with *Devil on the Cross* (1980). The assumption of the centrality of African oral literature is intended to have vital formal, critical and methodological consequences. For example, unlike canonical Western literary practice, in "traditional practice" literature is inextricably linked with dance, music and other art forms; the border between poetry and prose is either "absent or very fluid" (2094); literature aims towards both aesthetic pleasure and "social purposes", being in "intimate ... involvement" with society; but the "Spontaneity and liberty" of oral transmission encourage a "willingness to experiment" with new forms and re-evaluate neglected and devalued forms (295). The intrinsic populism of African traditional literary practice – in contrast to the varieties of elitism that we have seen from Western theorists – promises to lead to "fresh approaches" (2094) and become a source of innovation of Western literary genres such as the novel in the hands of contemporary African writers. In addition, modern African literature cannot be understood as part of an autonomous order of literature (as espoused by T. S. Eliot's early and most influential criticism), but requires "understanding of social and political ideas in African history" (2096).

In addition to the emphasis on the African oral tradition, a Department of African Literature and Languages in Nairobi – thinking now more specifically of Kenya – should develop an East African perspective. European literatures are "sources of influence" but, in East Africa, so are Swahili, Arabic and Asian literatures (2094), and Western literatures should therefore be taught for their "relevance to the East African perspective" (2095). Further, cultural alliances and political solidarity with the black diaspora need to be strengthened, by pursuing the "sister connections" (2093) of modern African literature with Caribbean and African-American literatures. The African-literature syllabus should include both Caribbean and African-American literature, and critical themes such as the Caribbean "involvement" with Africa or the Caribbean "roots" of the African poetry of the *négritude* movement (discussed in Chapter 10) cannot be "over-emphasized" (2093, 2096). Ngũgĩ went on to develop some of these themes in *Decolonising the Mind* (1986).

The Igbo Nigerian writer Chinua Achebe (1930–2013), perhaps the most widely read and influential African author, produced a substantial and influential body of criticism over the years, but "An Image of Africa: Racism in Conrad's *Heart of Darkness*" (1975) remains his most widely read and controversial essay. It is a reading of *Heart of Darkness*, articulating an explicitly African postcolonial perspective on a canonical text of Western literature, and, more broadly, a meditation from this point of view on the criteria for inclusion in canons of great literature. Does racism disqualify a text from inclusion in a canon? Achebe's argument is that, although Conrad "condemned … imperial exploitation", he was blind to his own racism (Achebe 1990, 19). Achebe begins by defining what constitutes racism in *Heart of Darkness*. Conrad is unwittingly reproducing a "dominant" image of Africa in the "Western imagination": in an act of projection, "the master uploads his physical and moral deformities" onto his image of Africa, in order to "go forward, erect and immaculate" (17). With "preposterous and perverse arrogance" (12), Conrad reproduces "myths" that are "comforting" to his European readers (5), but which deny Africans their humanity, language, culture and history. For example, Conrad bestows language on Kurtz's white fiancée, his "Intended", but withholds it from his black mistress and, more generally, refuses to "confer language" on his African characters (8). The rare exceptions where Conrad gives speech to Africans are used to confirm African bestiality, as when cannibals exclaim "Eat 'im!" (Conrad quoted in Achebe 1990, 9). Particularly damaging is Achebe's argument that Conrad actively attempts to impose this image of Africa on the reader by formal means: for example, Conrad's repetitive conjunction of "silence" and "frenzy" as descriptors of the

African characters is "engaged in inducing hypnotic stupor in his readers through a bombardment of emotive words and other forms of trickery" (4–5). Conrad is accused of dishonourable manipulation of the reader. Achebe rebuts the possible objection that the racist attitude belongs to the narrator, Marlow, and not necessarily to Conrad, arguing that Marlow is legitimated by the text itself as "a witness of truth … holding those advanced and humane views appropriate to the English liberal tradition" (10). Achebe concludes that Conrad, in a way typical of others of his liberal cast of mind, will give no clear answer to the "question of equality between white people and black people" (10), but the words and actions of his spokesman reveal the author's belief in the status quo.

Achebe's thesis is that Conrad's "dehumanization" of Africans is unequivocal, even when he/Marlow seems to equivocate (Achebe 1990, 12). Others have responded that *Heart of Darkness* supports a reading at least to some degree critical of Western racist stereotyping. For example, from among passages quoted by Achebe: "what thrilled you was just the thought of their humanity – like yours – the thought of your remote kinship with this wild and passionate uproar … [I]f you were man enough you would admit to yourself that there was in you just the faintest trace of a response … a dim suspicion of there being a meaning in it which you … could comprehend" (Conrad quoted in Achebe 1990, 6). Such passages may suggest the possibility of a double reading of *Heart of Darkness* as both racist and critical of racism. Achebe plausibly concludes that the kinship sensed "worries" Conrad (4). Edward Said, however, offers a double, "contrapuntal" reading of *Heart of Darkness* in his *Culture and Imperialism* (see Chapter 12).

The New Left and cultural studies

The New Left was a political and intellectual movement critical of the more reductive aspects of Marxist theory, with a particular interest in the cultural sphere and drawing strongly on so-called Western Marxism. Western Marxism is an umbrella term including a variety of Western European thinkers: the Italian cultural theorist Antonio Gramsci (1891–1937), the German modernist Marxists (Chapter 7), the French existentialist Jean-Paul Sartre, the Frankfurt school (Chapter 10) (including Herbert Marcuse's work in America), French structuralism (Chapter 11), of course the 1950s work of Raymond Williams, etc. What they had in common was a rejection of a narrow economism, where culture is understood as determined by and mirroring the economic base (Chapter 5), assuming instead the relative autonomy and freedom of cultural production. Gramsci argued that the bourgeoisie is the dominant class through "hegemony" (leadership): rather than ruling by force, it rules by cultural persuasion and consensus, by successfully establishing its perspective on the world as reality itself, in the cultural sphere. The British New Left was involved in the further theoretical elaboration of culture and the creation of the first institutional bases for a new discipline, cultural studies. While drawing on literary studies, cultural studies is in some sense also its rival.

While Ngũgĩ and Achebe were thinking about postcolonial canons and critiquing the racism of the former colonizer's great literature, the British New Left was gathering momentum in the 1960s. In 1964 Richard Hoggart founded the Centre for Contemporary Cultural Studies at the University of Birmingham, staffed by Stuart Hall, Paul Gilroy and others. Dick Hebdige studied at the Centre, and his widely read *Subculture: The Meaning of Style* (1979) traced the theoretical emergence of cultural studies out of the work of Raymond Williams and early Roland Barthes (see discussion of Barthes's *Mythologies* in Chapter 11). Williams's cultural theory involved a "new theoretical initiative" shifting emphasis "from immutable to historical criteria, from fixity to transformation" (Hebdige 2003, 7). However, Williams's cultural studies oscillated between culture and literature, between interpretation and evaluation: between a more democratic and antielitist view of cultural value and the desire to discriminate, like an Eliot or a Leavis, between the "excellent" and the rest. For example, Williams was sympathetic towards working-class culture but showed "a strong bias towards literature and literacy and an equally strong moral tone" (8). Though Williams was not hostile to the mass media and to popular culture, as Leavis had been, his approach was to search for "aesthetic and moral criteria for distinguishing" the good – such as jazz and football, in Williams's view – from "the 'trash'" (8). Barthes's early work shared Williams's assumption that it "required a literary sensibility to 'read' society with the requisite subtlety" (8). However, unlike Williams, Barthes was not concerned with the evaluation of mass culture, but rather sought to interpret its meaning. Hebdige declares himself free from Williams's high-cultural literary prejudices and interested in the meaning rather than the value of youth subcultures.

For Hebdige youth subcultures are signs of a "breakdown of consensus" – a breakdown of the bourgeois hegemony – after World War II, but their particular "challenge" to the failing hegemony of the bourgeoisie is "expressed obliquely, in style" (Hebdige 2003, 17). The role of the critic, modelled on the "mythologist" (the critic decoding myths) in Barthes's *Mythologies*, is to discern and spell out the "'secret' meanings" and "hidden messages" behind signs that "obscurely represent the very contradictions they are designed to resolve or conceal" (18). For Hebdige the message to decode and spell out is an expression of resistance, by subordinate groups, against "the order which guarantees their continued subordination" (18). Style has been used by the

British working-class subcultures of the Teddy Boys (1950s), the Mods (1960s) and the punks (1970s) as a gesture that "challenges the principle of unity and cohesion" and the "myth of consensus" (18) at the level of signification. Closely following Barthes's argument that the bourgeoisie immortalizes its views as the nature of reality, and Barthes's call to denaturalize it, Hebdige praises subcultures for their "alienation from the deceptive 'innocence' of appearances" and "false nature" (19). He also praises them for being "genuinely expressive" (19).

Obviously, having rejected evaluation, Hebdige is in practice as strongly evaluative as T. S. Eliot and Leavis. Barthes was soon to acknowledge and critique the authoritarianism of his model of the critic in *Mythologies*, which Hebdige uncritically inherits. The claim that the only true meaning of subcultures is resistance matches Eliot and Leavis in high-handedness, and could benefit from Williams's pluralism. This claim is undermined by Hebdige's needlessly restrictive Marxist terms of analysis and evaluation, which cause him to ignore one particular subculture which was very clearly resistant to mainstream culture but which cannot be easily identified with the working class: the hippies and the flower-power subculture of the 1960s.

Nevertheless, Hebdige's *Subculture* is a pioneering work in its serious academic attention to popular music. Inaugurating a new academic field, it is enabled by the new serious music journalism of the mainstream British music press in the 1970s – such as the dense and theoretically informed pieces of Paul Morley, Ian Penman and others for *New Musical Express*.

It is exactly Williams's pluralistic and anti-authoritarian ethos that Stuart Hall (1932–), one of the founders of British cultural studies, inherits. In "Cultural Studies and Its Theoretical Legacies" (1990, 1992) Hall offers a Foucauldean genealogy (Chapter 11) of cultural studies: its multiple origins and sites, ruptures and discontinuous history since the 1960s. Paying tribute to the role of Raymond Williams, he turns to the history of the Birmingham Centre for Contemporary Cultural Studies, mapping relations between the "unstable" discursive formations (Foucault's term) of Marxism, feminism, postcolonial theory and poststructuralism within that institution (Hall 2001, 1899). In relation to Marxism Hall argues that, in keeping with New-Left thinking as he understands it, cultural studies and Marxism never "represented a perfect theoretical fit" (1901) and that Marxism was viewed as "a problem … not as a solution" (1900). Hall had been critical of Soviet policy since the Hungarian Uprising of 1956 (which resulted in military suppression by the Soviet Union, with much loss of life, followed by severe repression); born and raised in Jamaica, a society where capitalism was "imposed by conquest and colonization", he was also critical of the "profound Eurocentrism of Marxist theory" (1901). Hence Antonio Gramsci was important to Hall, exactly because of Gramsci's atypical Marxism and responsiveness to the irresolvable "conundrums" of theoretical work and the questions that Marxism "couldn't answer" (1902). Gramsci's figure of the *organic intellectual* is central to the educational aim of British cultural studies, as Hall sees it: to produce intellectuals who are both "at the very forefront of intellectual theoretical work" and committed to "transmitting those ideas" widely (1903). This is not at all a question of popularizing *the* truth. It is rather a question of living with the "tension" between the "dialogic", open-ended and unresolved nature of theory (1899) (i.e. without some final truth) and the political need to "stake out some positions" in moments of "arbitrary closure" or "worldliness" (the need in other words to decide and act). Hall sees himself as both theorizing and being this kind of intellectual, and he mentions also the postcolonial theorists Edward Said and Homi K. Bhabha as figures he feels an affinity for in this. Hall's preferred metaphor for theoretical work is that of "struggle" (1901), as a "refusal to close" and "police" theoretical work (1899).

In relation to feminism and postcolonial theory, emerging strongly in the 1970s, Hall argues that their role within the Centre for Contemporary Cultural Studies was "ruptural", leading to struggles – for example, around revising the syllabus – and injecting discontinuity and renewal (Hall 2001, 1904–5). Feminism, particularly, led to several inter-related important theoretical reorientations. These included a new understanding of power: the new "centrality of questions of gender and sexuality" in relation to "power", rather than exclusive attention to questions of class; the "radical" extension of the scope of "power" beyond the "public domain" (i.e. power relations between the sexes as pervading private life) and the related "question of the personal as political" (1904). Feminism advocated a new emphasis on the "dangerous area of the subjective and the subject", rather than the economy – e.g. female masochism or the role of pornography – attempting to understand its connections to social relations and pioneering a renewed interaction between psychoanalytic concerns and social theory (1904). Poststructuralism, since the 1970s, similarly "decentred and dislocated" cultural studies, particularly in its "discovery of discursivity" or "textuality" (1906). "Textuality" (with the meaning we have seen before in discussion of Lacan, Barthes, *et al.* of an interpretability or production of meaning that never arrives at finality) captures well for Hall his conception of the endlessly deferred or unresolved nature of theoretical work, in tense relation with "'worldly' vocation" and urgent political tasks (1907). Hall keeps returning to this tension as definitive of cultural studies.

Finally Hall addresses what he sees as the "problems" and dangers inherent in the "enormous explosion" of cultural studies in the US and its attendant "rapid professionalization and institutionalization" (Hall 2001, 1908). Hall warns against discarding this valuable tradition of tension between dialogical theory and political commitment, and against the adoption of an intellectually immodest scientific-truth model purporting to offer "achieved" knowledge; cultural theory must not be understood as "the will to truth", but as a "set of contested, localized, conjunctural knowledges, which have to be debated in a dialogical way", and with an eye on making "some difference" in the world (1909–10).

A classic of the British New Left, *Literary Theory* (1983; revised 1996; 25th anniversary edition 2008) by Terry Eagleton (1943–), the first and the most-read guide to twentieth-century literary criticism and theory, delights and/or unnerves the reader with its hard-boiled wit and debunking zest. Eagleton offers a disenchanted historical account of the institutionalization of English Studies in Britain since the latter part of the nineteenth century, and argues that its role has been socially repressive: "If the masses are not thrown a few novels, they may react by throwing up a few barricades" (Eagleton 1996, 21). That English Studies targeted primarily the working classes is supported, according to Eagleton, by the evidence that "'English' as an academic subject was first institutionalized … in the Mechanics' Institutes, working men's colleges and extension lecturing circuits", functioning as "the poor man's Classics" (23). Women were also targeted, and English was the ideal university "non-subject to palm off on the ladies" at a time when they were grudgingly being allowed a university education (24).

So what then was the repressive ideology propagated by English Studies? Eagleton discusses three elements of this ideology. First, literature conveys "*timeless* truths, thus distracting the masses from their immediate commitments" (Eagleton 1996, 23). Second, literature "rehearse[s] the masses in the habits of pluralistic thought and feeling … nurturing in them a spirit of tolerance and generosity, and so ensuring the survival of private property"; the aim was "solidarity between the social classes, the cultivation of 'larger' sympathies'" (22–3). Third, literature conveys British national superiority: the institutionalization of English coincided with "high imperialism" and English literature was meant to prop it up; "the servants of British imperialism could sally forth overseas" armed with a sense of national "cultural superiority" (24–5). Eagleton argues that the "final victory of English Studies at Oxford and Cambridge" coincided with the "imperialist" First World War; English Studies "rode to power" on a wave of "wartime nationalism" (25–6). Eagleton treats these elements as compatible, interchangeable and equally suspect, while they seem to me antagonistic, some elements potentially radical. Surely pluralism and multiperspectivism are not easily reconciled with belief in eternal truths and nationalism. Pluralism and solidarity, in particular, are potentially radical, and indeed formed the basis of Raymond Williams's New Left ethics and politics. For example, in *Culture and Society* Williams is explicit that his investigation does not claim to tell *the* truth or to state facts, but "involves … the proposition of values which are quite properly the subject of difference" (Williams 1987, xix–xx), thus anticipating Foucault's perspectivist "effective historian" (discussed in Chapter 11). Eagleton by contrast, like Hebdige, claims to tell the truth and unmask ideological lies. From Hebdige's cultural studies point of view Eagleton shares Williams's literary prejudice, in that he remained a literary critic, but Eagleton's continuing commitment to literary studies is a mystery, in view of his account of its role and function. Why has he spent a lifetime on this non-subject for the ladies?

If we look at one of the documents that Eagleton will have drawn on, the Newbolt Report on the Teaching of English in England (1921), the advisory document commissioned by the Board of Education and the document which invented English Literature in the United Kingdom as the subject we know today, we will certainly not find any evidence that the authoring committee think of it as a "non-subject". In fact it's a document frequently brimming with Arnoldian passion for its subject: the English language, but more particularly English Literature. Here is the description of the Professor of English Literature:

> The Professor of Literature in a University should be … a missionary in a more real and active sense than any of his colleagues. He has obligations not merely to the students … , but still more towards the teeming population outside the University walls … The fulfilment of these obligations … first, and above all, … means a right attitude of mind, a conviction that literature and life are in fact inseparable, that literature is not just a subject for academic study, but one of the chief temples of the human spirit, in which all should worship.
>
> (Board of Education 1921, 259)

So it goes on, going further than Arnold and warning against any Arnoldian tendency to elitism. However, we *do* find that English Literature was a subject popular with some of the ladies during the period in question. The "extension lecturing circuits" referred to by Eagleton, the University Extension Programmes (which were run at Oxford, London and Cambridge from the 1870s) were not aimed at the working classes, as Eagleton claims, but at both working and middle classes. During the course of World War I the majority of attendees of the English Literature courses were middle-class women (268). Attendance by working men, however, was disappointing.

In fact the failure of the working man to take more interest in the world of sweetness and light is a stubborn one, the report reveals. The worthy gentlemen of the advisory committee lament that

> [l]iterature, in fact, seems to be classed by a large number of thinking working men with … fish-knives and other unintelligible and futile trivialities of "middle-class culture", and, as a subject of instruction, is suspect as an attempt "to side-track the working-class movement."
>
> (252)

The youngest and best educated of the workers "see education mainly as something to equip them to fight their capitalistic enemies. In the words of one young worker: 'Yes, what you say is all right – but will that sort of stuff bring us more bread and cheese?'" (254). This type of worker "is very much alive; he is a student – especially of economics; yet he takes no interest in literature, because he feels that it has nothing to contribute towards the solution of 'the social problem' in which all his thoughts are centred" (254).

The prospects for using literature to quell the revolution are looking bleak. And it's not as though the exploiters can find any use for the stuff: "we are unable to subscribe to the dictum that literature … is a part of 'middle-class culture'. We sincerely wish it were. We find on the contrary, an indifference among middle-class persons to the claims of literature, even more disheartening than the open hostility which we are told exists among certain circles of working-class opinion" (256).

Alas. But then the implacable agents of capital alight on another ruse to lure the male masses into the eternal plural befuddlement of the non-subject of literature: "perhaps the easiest route" would be "one that started with economics and then went on to the study of social philosophy, which would introduce the students to 'the work of writers who have endeavoured to interpret the life of their time, such as Carlyle, Ruskin, Morris and the modern school of social dramatists and writers. The step from work of this type … to the study of literature is but a small one'" (274). The advisory committee resort to a Raymond Williams reading list to entice the workers into the snare of the literary! I'm afraid the comic distress of the well-meaning gentlemen of the Newbolt Report utterly fails to communicate to me the sinister intent that is attributed to them by Eagleton.

With regard to higher education, Eagleton's description of literature as "the poor man's Classics" hits on an important truth. The Newbolt Report firmly moves Classics aside for English Literature. Part of the stir caused by the full introduction of literature at Cambridge was the perceived downgrading of Classics, the traditional basis of the liberal education of the English gentleman (it was on Classics that the Empire had been built). This class character of the establishment of English Literature and the central place that the report urges for literature at the heart of education in Britain at all levels struck home, I believe, with a young man in his second year at Cambridge when the report came out: Leavis. Leavis had just switched from History to English. How much he knew about the report when he switched I don't know; Arthur Quiller-Couch, Cambridge's Professor of English and Leavis's future PhD supervisor, was on the committee. But whenever it was that he did learn the contents of the report, it seems clear that Leavis heard a call in passages such as the description of the Professor of English above, particularly given the class aspect.

Is there truth in Eagleton's claims about nationalism, imperialism, worries about the workers, etc.? Yes, there is some truth. Is it true that the institutionalization of literature in the late nineteenth and early twentieth centuries, indeed the definition of English Literature as that body of work stretching from Chaucer to the present time, was some kind of capitalist imperialist plot to (with apologies to Marx and Keats) drowse the sense of the masses with the opiate of poesy? Of course not.

Decentering modernisms: modernist studies today

Critical thinking in the first decades of the twentieth century in Britain, as mapped in this chapter – and with the addition of Ezra Pound as critic, promoter, editor, publisher, organizer – had close personal and intellectual links with major modernist writers. In Eliot critic and writer were combined of course, to unprecedented effect. Eliot, Richards, Empson and Leavis, despite differences and changing alliances, created a core canon of high modernism with the two 1922 works, *Ulysses* and *The Waste Land*, a canon supported by aesthetic and critical ideas that gained widespread acceptance both in Britain and – through Eliot's, Richard's and Empson's influence on the New Critics – in the US. (The close identity between the aesthetic ideas of Eliot and Joyce lay in their shared Catholicism and the philosophy of Thomas Aquinas, itself deriving its ground from Aristotle, but you didn't need Aquinas to use the ideas – and Eliot as critic was wise not to be too explicit.) Others we have discussed, who were also more or less a part of this nexus of artists and critics at the time – Yeats, Woolf, Lawrence, Pound – join the canon as major modernist writers (Pound's status is troubled of course), but not at the 1922 core. Everybody knew that what was called modernism was a complex, differentiated, international movement. But the straggling and very various army of English-language "modern classics" gathered and continued to burgeon around the two towering monuments of 1922. The New Criticism began to fade in the 1950s. By the mid 1960s, Leavis, though still active and writing (and getting increasingly negative about Eliot), was for many a figure of the past. Eliot's reputation began to fade after his death in 1965. But the modernist canon maintained its position in the 1970s and 1980s.

However, modernism and the modernist canon were understood in increasingly narrow terms in the 1970s and 1980s. Modernism was thought to begin around 1910 and last 20 or 30 years (Shiach 2011, 23), with "late modernism" beginning broadly after 1930 (28). And it was canonically understood as "short-lived", "iconoclastic, revolutionary" (28), a "radical break from the past" (21) – particularly in its "radical commitment to new forms of cultural expression" (19). The modernists were increasingly formulaically defined as Western metropolitan heroic male rebels, literary innovators making the new, breaking with the past, uncompromisingly aloof from society and their audience. As Tim Armstrong elaborates, Anglo-American critics usually periodized modernism into three phases between 1900 and 1940:

- an early "politically-engaged, radical avant-garde" modernism before 1918 (e.g. Dada or Gertrude Stein);
- a central, "more conservative 'high' modernism" of the 1920s (Eliot, Joyce, etc.);
- a "late" modernism, including W. H. Auden's "politicization" of literature in the 1930s (24), as well as texts – by Wyndham Lewis, Djuna Barnes,

> Samuel Beckett – whose relation to "high" modernism involves "direct attack and satire or parody" (Tim Armstrong 2005, 36–7).

Hugh Kenner's *The Pound Era* (1971), on Pound and the other "Men of 1914" (Wyndham Lewis's term, that is Eliot, Pound, Joyce and Lewis himself), is exemplary of the heroizing approach adopted by much criticism and biography. Kenner, highlighting Pound's enabling role in relation to "the monumental works of 'high modernism'" (Kenner 1971, 25), typically emphasizes "high modernism", emerging in 1922 – by critical consensus the *annus mirabilis* of English-language modernism – with the publication of *The Waste Land* and *Ulysses*, with both of which Pound was substantially involved (33). Kenner and other critics duly noted the influence of Italian Futurism on Pound and Yeats and the influence of European Surrealism on American late modernism (28, 37–8).

In the 1990s, every single aspect of the canonical critical definition of modernism just discussed began to be questioned. Modernist studies entered a strongly revisionist period, under the combined impact of Marxism and cultural studies, poststructuralism, feminism, postcolonial theory, race studies, African-American studies and of course the postmodernism debate (see Chapter 9). Thus it finally came about, some 60 or more years after the establishment of the modernist first-generation canon, that modernism was opened up, and the story retold to capture the distinctiveness and originality of (now plural) modernisms previously viewed as peripheral, belated and derivative. Modernist movements in little-considered locations were (more seriously) researched, and patterns of influence between them and movements elsewhere explored; different periodizations were introduced; new and revised canons put forward. The work continues and the field remains in flux, but the summaries below of some of the more notable introductions and anthologies give a sense of the variety of work done in the last 20 years. The material is largely in chronological order, but there has been some integration of material from different dates to better bring out themes and critical approaches.

From the perspective of the new field of cultural studies, the critical dogma of the modernists' aloofness is highly questionable, opening the way for the exploration of the modernists' un-heroic cultural and institutional embeddedness and degree of complicity. So Tim Armstrong's *Modernism: A Cultural History* (2005) traces an American genealogy of modernism back to Edgar Allan Poe. Armstrong's de-heroizing story emphasizes the links between modernism and nineteenth-century consumer capitalism. Poe, in an 1844 letter, situates his short-story writing in relation to the "rapidly expanding American print market", the "commodity status" of literature and the "limited" attention span of the audience (23). Not the kind of consideration that preyed on the mind of the author of *Ulysses*!

The canon of modernism has been changing and expanding, and Armstrong greets the rediscovery of Herman Melville as an "important moment for modernism" (Tim Armstrong 2005, 23). Armstrong, more generally, registers recent attention to "neglected areas", such as the Harlem Renaissance and women's modernism (23). The recent "canonical 'promotion'" of Mina Loy (46) is further evidence of new attention to an "alternative 'women's modernism'" that includes Zora Neale Hurston, Nella Larsen, Laura Riding and others – redressing women's earlier "exclusion from the canon" of modernism (41). Armstrong also registers the ongoing geopolitical decentralization of modernism. He argues that modernism has significant associations with the new nation-states emerging out of decolonization – for example, Yeats's "nation-building and its plot of struggle, violence, identity and disillusionment" (44) – thus reappraising and reinterpreting this canonical modernist in a postcolonial key. And modernism is importantly connected, Armstrong continues, to regionalism, as in Faulkner, and to cultural nationalism, as in African-American modernism. There is now renewed attention to "delayed" modernisms – Scottish, African-American, Native-American, New-Zealand, Australian, Caribbean modernisms – linked to "forms of local epic in which geopolitical struggles are enacted" (45). For example, Aimé Césaire's *Notebook of a Return to My Native Land* (1939) engages with Guillaume Apollinaire and Surrealism in order to address colonialism.

Michael Levenson, in his 2011 introduction to *The Cambridge Companion to Modernism*, like Armstrong, adopts the new assumptions of cultural studies, but also complicates them, presenting the canonical Anglo-American high modernists as consciously occupying a contradictory position in relation to their society and culture, both above it and complicit with it. He argues that, against Oscar Wilde's critique of Victorian moral earnestness, they were "distinguished precisely by the earnestness of their resolve" and "high-minded conviction" (Levenson 2011b, 5). In this sense, after the Victorian crisis of religious faith, they represented a re-enchanted "religious imagination" (6) – a reincarnation of religion or its continuation by other means. Their professed aim was to "challenge an unfreedom", variously defined as journalism, political orthodoxy, etc. (2). However, the high modernists were "closely wound in transactions with the commercial market" and "sharply conscious of their historical entanglements" with "accelerating social *modernization*" (2). (In relation to Wilde, I would argue that Wilde, Joyce and Eliot actually share an engagement with the Catholic theological tradition, as a comparison of Stephen's aesthetic ideas in Joyce's *A Portrait of the Artist as a Young Man* [1916] with Wilde's essay "The Author as Critic" [1891] would show.)

To turn now from cultural studies to feminist revisions of modernism, *The Cambridge Companion to Modernist Women Writers* (2010) is the joint outcome of feminist scholarship on modernism since the 1980s and recent more widespread opening up of the canon of modernism by criticism more generally. As Maren Tova Linett argues in her introduction, in "the new modernist studies", the old canon of "the men of 1914" accompanied by Woolf is being overtaken by a greatly expanded canon "along axes of location and time" (Linett 2010, 10). We are moving towards a "transnational account" of modernism (10) which covers, at least, the period 1890–1945. Linett's canon of women's modernism includes Woolf, Stein, Cather, H. D., Barnes, Hurston, but is elastic enough to find space for even contemporary writers such as Ama Ata Aidoo. Linett describes the project of *The Companion* as one of demonstrating the "major role played by women writers in producing modernism: conceptualizing, debating, writing, and publishing the critical and imaginative work that resulted in the tilling of 'fresh fields' in literary culture" (14).

However, the reappraisal of women modernists by no means exhausts the feminist revision of modernism. For example, Peter Nicholls's *Modernisms: A Literary Guide* (1995, new edition 2009) proposes a feminist reappraisal of Baudelaire. Nicholls revises the story of modernism in two respects. First, he offers a feminist psychoanalytic reading of Baudelaire and modernism, engaged with the work of Jessica Benjamin and others. Nicholls reads Baudelaire's poem, "To a Red-haired Beggar Girl" (*c.* 1845–6) in the context of his exploration of the connections between modernist formal experimentation, style and politics. The poem, he argues, performs an exemplary modernist "'elimination' of the feminine" – the feminine being a "suitable surrogate for social relations" – or a "triumph of form over 'bodily' content" (4). This suggests that form and irony are "*defences* against the other"; the aesthetic is grounded in an "objectification of the other" to "protect the poet's self from full recognition of identity with other people" (4). Nicholls thus posits that irony is the modern poet's "defence against modernity" (5). Needless to say, his story seriously deflates the critical dogma of heroic modernism. Second, Nicholls amplifies and diversifies the story of modernism. He dates modernism back to Baudelaire and the early 1840s, in Baudelaire's "new urban scene" and "complexity of *tone*" (vii). Of course Eliot explicitly acknowledged the influence of Baudelaire and French Symbolism, and Walter Benjamin gave Baudelaire a central role in thinking about modernity and literary modernism, but Nicholls' target is the subsequent critical dogma of the radical newness of high modernism. He also looks at all the avant-garde movements and the different European and American modernisms, adding a chapter on the Harlem Renaissance in the second edition.

The revision of modernist studies led to a reappraisal of canonical modernist authors. Kevin J. H. Dettmar's 2005 introduction to *A Companion to Modernist Literature and Culture*, while not explicitly revisionist, undertakes to re-examine canonical theorizations of modernism by returning to high priests and priestesses themselves – Yeats, Pound, Eliot, Joyce and

Woolf – and rereading them anew. Pound's modernist motto, "Make it new", can be understood not as a call for radical newness, "originality" and "innovation", but for the "renovation" of tradition (Dettmar 2005). (It certainly requires the qualification that in fact some of the work, principally Eliot's, if formally unprecedented, is markedly conservative and Pound's racist remarks in the *Cantos* are hardly progressive.) In support of "renovation" rather than "innovation", the explicit exaltation of "moments of artistic transcendence" in Yeats, Joyce, Woolf is "going back" to Wordsworth (Dettmar 2005). This tendency towards transcendence co-exists, among the modernists, with an apparently contradictory tendency towards realist "precise description" of the "ordinary – even the sordid", which becomes the "royal road to the extraordinary" (Dettmar 2005) (and Dettmar might have added that this, also, is an instance of "renovation" rather than "innovation", equally describing Baudelaire and Wordsworth). Also, canonical theorizations have described modernism as tending towards centralization, unity and order – and Yeats's and Eliot's pronouncements seemed to support this view. However, under the impact of the ongoing decentering of modernism(s), the "opposite", multiperspectivist tendency is now discernible in canonical modernism itself, for example in Pound's suggestions that "genius consists in the ability to see a dozen different things where the ordinary man sees just one" (Dettmar 2005).

To turn now to postcolonial and transnational revisions of modernism, Elleke Boehmer and Steven Matthews, in their contribution to the 2011 *Cambridge Companion to Modernism*, "Modernism and Colonialism", direct attention to colonial modernisms, against the "long-dominant Anglo-American or Euro-American axis" (Boehmer and Matthews 2011, 284). They propose a rejection of the canonical critical "assumption" that other modernisms were "merely reflective and derivative" of dominant modernisms, in order to "investigate whether" there was a "'two-way dialogic process' between the so-called center (London, Paris, New York) and its peripheries (Calcutta, Kingston, Sydney)" (285).

"Modernism", now more than 100 years old, is currently undergoing a major temporal and transnational amplification, and Levenson in the second edition of *The Cambridge Companion to Modernism* establishes a temporal span of 50 years (1890–1939). In Levenson's controversial view the commonly shared elements of transnational modernisms include the "willingness to make radical" and the "recurrent act of fragmenting unities" (of "character or plot", etc.) (Levenson 2011b, 3). Levenson echoes Woolf in *A Room of One's Own* that new women's writing first "broke the sentence" and "now … has broken the sequence" (Woolf 1929, 122). Nevertheless, however commonalities are to be defined, theoretical/critical emphasis at the beginning of the twenty-first century is on "irreducibly local ambitions" and "localized experiments"; modernisms as both "opposed" to each other and internally "contradictory" (Levenson 2011b, 3–4). For example, the modernism of the Harlem Renaissance is viewed as a "challenge" to the hegemonic modernism of the "men of 1914" and its "emerging norms" (3).

Morag Shiach's contribution to *The Oxford Handbook of Modernisms*, "Periodizing Modernism", discusses the impact of recent revisionism on the periodization of modernism. Canonical accounts, argues Shiach, were blind to the multiplicity and uneven development of modernism. For example, as Bonnie Kime Scott argued influentially, they "had the effect of marginalizing" modernist women's writing (Shiach 2011, 28). New theorizations of modernism are increasingly going back beyond 1910 to the nineteenth century, with Nicholls, as we saw above, going back to Baudelaire and other critics *c.* 1890 to explore the modernist "characteristics" of Wilde, Conrad, James, and the so-called "New Woman" novels (25). In terms of modernism's endpoint, the tendency is now to push it forward to the 1950s and 1960s, to include Beckett.

In the editors' introduction to the monumental *Oxford Handbook of Modernisms* (2011), Peter Brooker and his co-editors summarize recent developments, such as the nexus of "feminist, postcolonial, lesbian and queer" critiques (Brooker *et al.* 2011b, 1). Both modernity and modernism are now viewed as multiple, hence the currency of the term "modernisms". The editors affirm that, as a result of postcolonial theory, the study of modernism has taken a strong "transnational" direction (1), so that Western modernisms "beyond any doubt … can no longer be regarded as hegemonic" (12). The tendency now is to reverse the canonical distribution of centre and periphery/margins, and reject the canonical story that metropolitan Western modernism was belatedly copied by derivative peripheral modernisms. Modernism is now viewed by some as "the *product* of colonialism" and as "completely overhauled" by (post)colonial writers who "re-create and redeploy" it "in their own culturally specific terms and for their own distinctive purposes" (12) – a practice that I suppose would be approved by the author of *The Waste Land* and theorist of the new as recreation of the traditional for the present time.

Theorists are divided over the critical and oppositional potential of modernism: some view it as conducting a "partial, elliptical, and intermittent critique" of modernity, while others – "both leftist and neo-conservative" – argue that it is the "cultural embodiment of capitalism itself" (Brooker *et al.* 2011b, 8–9). It is a relief to find the editors retreat from such reductionism: this handbook takes the view that modernism does *both*: it is an "overdetermined … and multiply networked range of practices that were always caught up in a dialectic process of affirmation and negation" (10). A recent tendency is to embed modernism within a culture and society – though, as discussed above, this understanding of literature is already strongly present in later Eliot, Leavis, Williams and the cultural studies approach. Thus recent scholarship is exploring modernism's "multiple connections" to institutions as well as to "non-modernist" and "non-aesthetic" practices, and paying attention to the "material, economic and institutional forging" of modernism (2).

The ongoing revision of modernist studies we have been discussing echoes Bakhtin's ideas of the dialogical and heteroglossic (Chapter 7) and the other theorists of multiperspectivism we have encountered in previous chapters (Chapters 5 and 7). In the emphasis on the multiple and the local – Levenson's "localized experiments" (above) – there is also a strong resonance with the ideas of Jean-François Lyotard, whose book *The Postmodern Condition* (1979) was a major stimulus, during the 1980s and 1990s, to the debate on postmodernism and the revision of modernism. It is true to say that Lyotard's conception of postmodernism was in large part a reaffirmation of the experimental spirit of the early avant-gardes, but there were many ideas about what postmodernism was, and in the next chapter we will be encountering some of them.

Conclusion

- We discussed Eliot's dialectic of newness and tradition, and his recasting of the canon of English literature. We outlined his critical terms, such as "impersonality", "objective correlative" and "dissociation of sensibility".
- Since the 1920s Richards defended the value of literary studies as an apprenticeship in fine co-ordination of multiple contradictory impulses, promising a balanced inner life and free citizens able to combat the modern chaos of globalization.
- In the late 1920s Woolf calls for pluralism and multiperspectivism and sketches a history and canon of women's writing. Proposing a history not just of those forgotten by History (as Benjamin) but of those who had never existed or were not allowed to exist, she mixes criticism and fiction. She stresses the role of social conditions in enabling or disabling literary production, outlining patriarchy in its relation to empire.
- Since the 1930s Empson lays claim to a neutral empiricist method of textual analysis, without any presuppositions and distinct from scientific method, showing how a trained mind makes sense of the multiple meanings and inherent ambiguity of literature; he avoids comparison and evaluation.
- Since the 1930s Leavis stresses evaluation, the main criteria of his early championship of modernism being heroic newness and consciousness of the modern age. He criticized the institution of criticism for its class-bound canonization and neutralization of modernism. In the late 1940s he proposes an exclusive canon of the English novel championing D. H. Lawrence as the voice of a marginalized tradition of Protestant Nonconformity and the champion of "life".
- Williams's cultural materialism seeks to articulate the relation of literature to society and culture. In the late 1950s he reconstructs a democratic tradition of literature since Coleridge as critique of modern industrial culture and brings it to bear on the new mass media. He contrasts "democracy" (solidarity, collective mutual responsibility, pluralism,

dissidence) and "democratic" literary studies to the "dominative" mood and "dominative" literary studies.

- In the 1960s and in an East African context of decolonization, Ngũgĩ *et al.* propose reconstruction of literary canons and assume the centrality of the African oral tradition and importance of Caribbean and African-American literatures. Rather than strengthening existing tribal or national identities, Ngũgĩ *et al.* assign to literary studies the construction of a future-oriented innovative transnational black perspective; the return to African oral literature – its traditional links with other art forms, its social purpose and its valuing of improvization – is envisaged as a source of renewal and distinctiveness for African literature. In the 1970s Achebe, for his part, accuses the Western canon of dehumanizing Africans.
- In the context of the British New Left and as cultural studies takes off as a discipline, Hebdige takes theory onto the streets in the late 1970s, writing about popular culture and music; he eschews "evaluation" in search of the "meaning" of subcultures. For Hall, looking back in the 1990s, cultural studies is substantially informed by Marxism, feminism, postcolonial theory and poststructuralism, existing in productive tension between the dialogic and open-ended nature of theory and the need for political commitment. Hall fears this creative openness may be a victim of cultural studies' institutional success. In the 1980s Eagleton argues that the institutionalization of English studies in Britain was socially repressive, propagating an ideology of timeless truths, political quietism and nationalism in defence of the British Empire.
- Since the 1990s, a critical return to modernism revises and decentres embedded views of the movement. Under the impact of cultural studies, feminism, postcolonial theory and other recent critical approaches, canonical authors are reappraised and the canon opened up to peripheral modernisms previously considered belated and derivative.

Further reading

See especially Achebe 1990; Eagleton 1996; Eliot 1997b; Empson 2004; Hall 2001; Hebdige 2003; Leavis 1972a and 1972b; Ngũgĩ *et al.* 2001; Richards 1967; Williams 1987; Woolf 1929. In relation to modernist studies today, see especially Boehmer and Matthews 2011; Brooker *et al.* 2011b; Dettmar 2005; Levenson 2011b; Linett 2010.

9 Twentieth-century North American criticism

Close reading to interpretation, modernism to postmodernism, History to histories

Harlem Renaissance (Hughes, Hurston), New Criticism (Ransom, Wimsatt and Beardsley, Brooks), Northrop Frye, Black Aesthetic Movement, feminist criticism (Showalter, Gilbert and Gubar, Walker, Spivak), reader-response theory (Fish), postmodernism (Lyotard, Jameson, Hutcheon, hooks)

Harlem Renaissance

Slavery was abolished in America in 1863, but the failure of Reconstruction, the process of giving African-Americans full civil rights, in the 1870s was a sign of continuing racism. Gradually, effective disenfranchisement was legislated, mainly through property and educational requirements that the great majority of African-Americans didn't meet. From the 1870s laws for racial segregation were passed in the South, leading to a black exodus from the rural South to the urban North. After Reconstruction African-Americans focused their energies on education, Booker T. Washington advocating vocational training, while W. E. B. Du Bois in *The Souls of Black Folk* (1903) argued for liberal black university education, but also praised the African-American oral tradition (e.g. spirituals) as an important cultural resource, so advocating biculturalism (Chapter 7). Du Bois also called for political activism to address continuing discrimination and violence against black people. During World War I (1914–18), due partly to employment opportunities in the Northern munitions factories, black migration North greatly intensified, but so did Northern racism. The end of war and the return home of black veterans only intensified white race rioting, and historians have called the summer of 1919 "the Red Summer": there were 26 white riots against blacks, with blacks fighting back. In the course of World War I a new working-class black leader had emerged, the Jamaican Marcus Garvey, whose message was black pride. In 1920, Garvey organized a march of 50,000 African-Americans through Harlem (in New York), the pre-eminent black urban location in America at the time. Garvey's populist message of black pride was an influence on the high-brow Harlem Renaissance. The Harlem Renaissance (postwar to *c.* 1930) or the New Negro Movement is a black modernist movement whose members include Du Bois, the philosopher Alain Locke, the writers James Weldon Johnson (perhaps the central figure), Jean Toomer, Countee Cullen, Langston Hughes and the Jamaican Claude McKay, also the latecomer, Zora Neale Hurston, a writer and anthropologist trained at Columbia University, who collected Southern folklore. Alain Locke's edited anthology, *The New Negro* (1925), and other Harlem Renaissance texts define the "New Negro" as urban, proud to be African-American, defiant, self-inventing. However, texts such as Alain Locke's introduction to the 1925 anthology, James Weldon Johnson's *Black Manhattan* (1930) and Langston Hughes's *The Big Sea* (1940) were perhaps over-optimistic about the future for black people in the urban centres of the North. The milieu of the Harlem Renaissance in the 1920s was that of a glamorous cosmopolitan elite satirized by Zora Neale Hurston as "the glitterati", but the economic Depression of the 1930s savagely ended the movement, a stark reminder of the American civil rights deficit.

Discussing the ongoing revision and decentering of modernist studies in the last chapter, we saw that peripheral modernisms such as that of the Harlem Renaissance, previously viewed as belated and derivative in relation to canonical modernism, are now seen as local experiments serving important and often radical local purposes and significantly deviating from or even fighting against canonical modernism. In 2011 Michael Levenson wrote that the Harlem Renaissance represented a "challenge" to the hegemony of Euro-American modernism, as discussed (Levenson 2011b, 3). But it is important to add that the Harlem Renaissance also reoriented African-American literature towards the cultural resources of traditional oral African-American forms, pursuing the double, bicultural direction Du Bois hoped for. Du Bois's 1903 positive re-evaluation of spirituals in *The Souls of Black Folk* opened the way.

Langston Hughes (1902–67) outlines the new aims in his 1926 essay, "The Negro Artist and the Racial Mountain" (his response, in *The Nation*, to George Schuyler's controversial article, "The Negro-Art Hokum", published in the same magazine). Hughes addresses the cultural self-whitening of the black middle class, which condemns it to mimic white norms and culture and devalue black folk art, as a major obstacle to the flourishing of black writing. Black "common people will give to the world its truly great Negro artist" because, unlike the middle class, they are "not afraid of spirituals" and "jazz is their child" (Hughes 2001, 1314). Authentic black originality will sprout from a collective oral heritage that includes "incongruous humor" and "ironic laughter", and of which blues music is an existing example (1315). Turning to his own aesthetic practice, Hughes describes his efforts to "grasp and hold some of the meaning and rhythms of jazz" – considered disreputable at the time – both in its formal aspects and as a "revolt against weariness in a white world" (1316). Against black internalized racism and self-loathing, he declares plainly "I am a Negro – and beautiful" (1316). Embracing Bessie Smith, the blues singer frowned on for her scandalous life, and the developing jazz scene, Hughes calls on black artists in racist segregation-era America to draw on a rich folk heritage and contemporary popular culture and to write "without fear and shame" (1317).

Zora Neale Hurston (1891–1960) and other black modernist women writers were seen as marginal to the Harlem Renaissance but their importance has recently been re-evaluated. While the Harlem Renaissance focused on Northern urban oral traditions, Hurston (who grew up in an all-black town in Florida) pioneered the study of Southern dialects and published important collections of Southern folktales. In her essay, "Characteristics of Negro Expression" (1934) Hurston describes in detail the aesthetic elements of black expression – dialects, folktales, songs, poetry, prose, dance, visual arts, etc. – as living traditions. Black folktales are "not a thing of the past" but "still in the making" within contemporary collective African-American life, and Hurston draws attention to the way in which traditional forms such as "asymmetry" (an intentional lack of symmetry and regularity) are being practised by Langston Hughes and other writers (Hughes 2001a, 1149–50). But beyond such formal analysis Hurston came to feel that black writers (and critics) needed to go more deeply into the social conditions of their writing in order to understand themselves and black experience better. In 1950 she confronts social impediments to this fuller engagement with black experience in "What White Publishers Won't Print" (Hurston 2001b). She implies that the very modernist project of describing the self more fully was closed to black writers describing black characters because of the racism of the American reading public, who were unable to grant black characters full selfhood and humanity. She argues that the American audience was strongly inimical to the exploration of black interiority in its full complexity, and that black writers were actively discouraged from pursuing this route if they wanted to get published. Hurston further claims that other minorities were facing a similar situation in America at the time. She argues for the urgent need for such books, promoting fuller knowledge of minorities in the national interest. Hurston was describing her own experience with publishers and was no doubt aware that such books did get written and published in small editions, but this doesn't undercut her argument. On the contrary, her argument illuminates the conditions under which many writers of the Harlem Renaissance were unable to sustain their literary careers, including Hurston herself (see "Looking for Zora" in Walker 1983b). We will be returning to Alice Walker's literary rescuing of Hurston and will be addressing subsequent African-American literary and critical movements in this and other chapters (e.g. Chapter 12).

Both Hughes and Hurston stress the connections of African-American literature with other art forms and with culture, understood as a whole way of life. In their view, the literary tradition is not to be reduced to the canon of written single-authored "great" literature, but includes the African-American heritage of collectively authored and oral aesthetic forms, in whose context the African-American written tradition has to be situated. Simultaneously, African-American literature cannot be properly understood without reference to American history and society: from the institution of slavery to continuing racism, including the racism of the literary institution and reading public. (These critical orientations resonate with many aspects of British modernist criticism, see Chapter 8.)

From close reading to interpretation: New Criticism, Northrop Frye, reader-response theory (Stanley Fish)

New Criticism or American Formalism (John Crowe Ransom, Cleanth Brooks, William K. Wimsatt, Jr. and Monroe C. Beardsley) can be described as the deliberate excision of the above concern with the extra-textual from literary criticism. For the New Critics the core task of criticism is "close reading": originating in Coleridge's "practical criticism" (Chapter 4) and developed by I. A. Richards and in T. S. Eliot's early criticism (Chapter 8), it becomes central to New Criticism, to the exclusion of all the social and psychological concerns that preoccupied Coleridge and Richards. A younger generation of American critics, such as Stanley Fish, brought up on New Criticism, will later reject the exclusive emphasis on close reading, in favour of interpretation. However, close reading remains today a central skill in the view of many. If there are few who would now argue that it can be considered a value-free exercise, as Richards hoped to establish it, it is nevertheless regarded by many as an essential basic discipline.

The poet and critic John Crowe Ransom (1888–1974) first announces New Criticism in his manifesto, "Criticism, Inc." (1938). Ransom's early criticism, written in the context of the American South, combined attention to the techniques of poetry with social critique and ethical concerns, particularly a commitment to Southern anti-industrial agrarianism and regionalism. In "Criticism, Inc.", however, Ransom announces his commitment to a literary criticism (with a particular emphasis on poetry) that excludes all such concerns and commitments, and the decision to limit himself to the text alone – to the words on the page. Programmatically, New Criticism is narrower – more doctrinaire or dogmatic, as some critics have argued – than Practical Criticism. Ransom's essay identifies the following four principles. First, as we have seen, the core task of literary criticism is rigorous close reading of the text itself. What does this mean concretely? Ransom elaborates close reading as excluding the following: the habit of "paraphrase"; history and ethics (e.g. Marxist and "humanist" criticism); amateurs and the subjectivity of the reader. In summary, the "first law to be prescribed to criticism … is that it shall be objective, shall cite the nature of the object rather than its effects upon the subject" (Ransom 2001, 1115–16). Second, New Criticism will work towards a scientific literary criticism: "Criticism must become more scientific, or precise and systematic" (1109). This will be achieved through formalist attention to poetry's "technical devices" (1118). Third, Ransom calls upon literary critics to become "professionals" (1109). Fourth, he proclaims the institutional autonomy of English departments: English must not be "a branch of the department of history" or "a branch of the department of ethics" (1112). Ransom attempts to autonomize literary studies from other fields in the humanities, and he turns to the sciences for his model of critical objectivity. This is close to the language of T. S. Eliot's early criticism.

"The Intentional Fallacy" (1946), by William K. Wimsatt, Jr. (1907–75) and Monroe C. Beardsley (1915–85), is considered a thought-provoking classic, in spite of its problematic aspects. The essay's objection to "consulting the oracle" of the author as a basic approach to literary interpretation (in Wimsatt and Beardsley 2001, 1387), that is its "anti-intentionalism", is in keeping with statements by Eliot, Lawrence, Woolf, the New Critics (with whom Wimsatt and Beardsley are closely associated) and others against authorial intention and against the relevance of the author's biography. Wimsatt and Beardsley position themselves against both "classical 'imitation' and romantic expression" (1375). In other words, literature neither imitates external reality nor expresses the author's internal reality; it is the work itself that must be focused on. They claim that "the intentional fallacy is a romantic one" (1377), implicitly following Eliot's devaluation of Romanticism (as discussed in Chapter 8). However, their view of Romanticism is formulaic and they explicitly refrain from engagement with the criticism of Coleridge and other Romantics. The essay's main argument is that "[t]he design or intention of the author is neither available nor desirable as a standard for judging the success of a work of literary art" (1375). Therefore "even [in] a short lyric poem … [w]e ought to impute the thoughts and attitudes of the poem immediately to the dramatic *speaker*" rather than the author (1376). Following Ransom, Wimsatt and Beardsley stress the nature of the literary text as an "object" (1376) or "linguistic fact" (1381) and repeatedly describe their criticism (and New Criticism) as "objective": "objective criticism" (1376–7); "science of objective evaluation" (1380); "the true and objective way of criticism" (1387). The core task of objective criticism is to focus on what is "internal" to the text, disregarding its contexts (1384). For example, they make the curious claim that Eliot's allusions "work when we know them – and to a greater extent even when we don't know them" (1384). However, the distinction between what is "internal" and "external" to the text is problematic, as many have pointed out. Wimsatt and Beardsley themselves seem to acknowledge that what they take to be "internal" focus on the *work itself* assumes and presupposes the critic's prior knowledge of "the external": the language and its history, the literary tradition and the culture within which the work, as "linguistic fact", exists (1384). By all means we may argue for the usefulness of the distinction between the internal and the external, but this will be a matter of degree or emphasis; attempts at rigorous separation are misconceived.

Cleanth Brooks's (1906–94) major contribution to New Criticism is *The Well Wrought Urn* (as other New Critics, concentrating on poetry) (1947), particularly the chapter, "The Heresy of Paraphrase". He offers a retrospective account of New Criticism in his essay, "The Formalist Critics" (1951). Brooks's work can fruitfully be situated in relation to Ransom, his teacher, and Richards. In keeping with Ransom, Brooks rejects an earlier historical and biographical criticism as well as subjective impressions in favour of "the work itself" (Brooks 2001, 1366). Brooks's debt to Richards is more substantial and his relation to him more creative. In keeping with Richards (and Empson), Brooks emphasizes poetry's ambiguity, irony, paradoxicality. His criticism looks for the poem's "inner" or "essential" *structure* (Brooks 1968, 162). His understanding of "structure" reiterates Richards's Coleridge-inspired description of poetry as complex "equilibrium" and "conciliation" of opposites (Richards's terms). Poetry for Brooks is a "pattern of resolutions and balances and harmonizations" (166). *The Well Wrought Urn*, each chapter devoted to a reading, discerns this pattern in ten poems from all periods of English literature from Donne to Eliot. The poet "triumphs over the apparently contradictory and conflicting elements of experience by unifying them into a new pattern" (174). Brooks creatively rewrites Richards's distinction between the *referential* function in science and the *emotive* function in poetry: science uses "strict denotations", while "the poet's tendency is by contrast disruptive" (6) of all statements because of the poem's complex unity of opposites – hence the "resistance which any good poem sets up against all attempts to paraphrase it" (160). In sum, for Brooks a poem's "meaning" is this "structure", and thus "*form is meaning*"; form and meaning are the dynamic "*unity*" which the poem forms out of "recalcitrancy" (Brooks 2001, 1366 and 1371).

Brooks sheds Richards's concern for the psychic integration of contradictory impulses in order to focus more narrowly on "well-wrought" aesthetic unity, a well-formed balance of aesthetic tensions. In "The Heresy of Paraphrase" his proposed transhistorical criterion for literary greatness is achieved "organic" unity (Brooks 1968, 163), and this primary criterion will therefore be the critic's primary concern, as we find stated in "The Formalist Critics": "*the primary concern of criticism is with the problem of unity – the kind of whole which the literary work forms or fails to form*" (Brooks 2001, 1366). Brooks calls this the "basic" meaning of the text (1371) and so denies that his view is one of many interpretations of literature; at least finally, for literature as a whole and in the appreciation of the individual work, meaning, value, form, content are formalized and made synonymous as dynamic, balanced unity. The later critical counter-tendency of searching for unreconciled tensions within the text as a criterion of its value is partly in response to this New Critical dogma.

In *Anatomy of Criticism* (1957) the Canadian literary critic Northrop Frye (1912–91) calls on critics to "stand back" from the text (Frye 1973, 140), countering the New Critical emphasis on "close" reading. *Anatomy of Criticism*, widely influential, outlines a scientific literary criticism as both a distinct academic discipline autonomous from other academic disciplines and boldly drawing on other fields, including medieval scriptural criticism, anthropology, psychoanalysis and even pure mathematics. However, Frye critiques and redefines the model of scientificity in Ransom and Wimsatt and Beardsley. Frye argues that literary criticism under the reign of the New Critics was in a "state of naive induction" comparable to "a primitive science" (15). New Critical *close reading* attends only to "discrete works", lacking a "conceptual framework" and "central hypothesis" (15–16), the progressive development of which would aim to make "the whole of literature intelligible" (9).

New Criticism, to use philosophical language and the language of science the New Critics use, is *empiricist* in spirit; they feel themselves opposed to *metaphysical* or theoretical approaches to literature – those that seek or find in the literary work meanings or evidence for readings of the work, or parts of it, that depend for their claims to truth on interpretative resources that *exceed* the "words on the page" and the skills and competencies of the close reader. For the New Critics these "external" approaches cannot support their interpretations with "objective" evidence from the individual text and they take one away from the literary object and from literary value to make literature into, or reduce it to, the univocal expression or effect of the determining truth (as theorized by the "metaphysicians") of social, economic, historical or psychological reality, etc. Frye does not object to New Critical empiricism in the sense of close reading. Nobody is going to advocate inattentive reading! He also joins the New Critics in his belief in the fundamental autonomy and irreducibility of literature. His problem is, first, that the New Critical distrust of grand theory, while emphasizing the literary, in fact reduces literary value and meaning to a formalist aestheticism. Frye does not want to reduce literature to class struggle or the occult dramas of the psychoanalytic Unconscious, but his huge project seeks to articulate – in a way that attempts to combine analysis with the unreduced play of complexity – literature as the immaterial world of meaningful collective human experience as myth. However, his desire to make "the whole of literature *intelligible*" (my emphasis) – to make literature "understood", yes, but also the strong connotation the word still carries of the anagogical revelation of higher intellectual or spiritual meaning (Chapter 3) – is not going to be possible with a "correspondence" model of truth, such as the New Critics had: "objective" evidence explicated in regard to the discrete work under examination. Frye's desire to produce a "metaphysical" theory of all literature as mythic expression, coupled with the great variety of ways in which fundamental mythical meanings are refracted in literature synchronically and diachronically, means that the evidence and analysis must be developed together across texts and across or between different levels of categorization. The reader is asked to allow Frye to develop his account or "hypotheses" and to suspend judgment until such time as the account assumes coherence sufficient for authorial assertion. Frye seeks to inaugurate a new "scientific" (7), "systematic" and "progressive" (8) search for what he variously calls the "laws" or "patterns" (26) or "structural principles" (134) of literature. "[I]nductive survey" (6) across literature and through the ages will be the medium for the development and testing, in a process of hermeneutic closing in and standing back, of an analysis that seeks, and assumes from the beginning, the intelligibility of the whole as differentiated totality. But if the intelligibility of the whole is assumed from the beginning, truth will emerge not as an accumulation of building blocks of fact, but rather as a complex process of provisional judgements, until ultimately Frye stands back and presents his work to us as complete. *Anatomy* offers a deliberately schematic "classification" (29) of literature, arguing that – against the New Critics who "stand close" and "analyse details" of a particular text – we "have to 'stand back'" to perceive the "archetypal organization" of all literature (140).

What has no place in this project is evaluation, and Frye is uninhibited in rejecting evaluation since Matthew Arnold (though he doesn't name Eliot or Leavis). In pursuing a "unified structure" (11) or "central expanding pattern" (12) of all literature, Frye models literary criticism on pure mathematics, which works with a coherence-model rather than correspondence-model of truth – i.e. truth is judged by criteria of internal coherence rather than correspondence to an external object. (This is an acceptable model in science and philosophy more generally.) Pure mathematics – and Frye's scientific literary criticism – is an "autonomous language" progressing according to criteria of "inner integrity" and reliant on "hypothetical possibilities" and "postulates, not facts" (350–51). In other words scientific literary criticism is "constructive" rather than "descriptive" (353). It is imperative, therefore, that it distances itself from the still-dominant view of literature as "representation or 'lifelikeness'" (134) towards a non-mimetic view of literature as a "self-contained" structure (135).

According to Frye, New Criticism, historical criticism, ethical criticism, etc. are all limiting, partial and in conflict with each other, while his project – "archetypal criticism" – promises to play the role of critical common ground (Frye 1973, 346). Archetypal criticism explicitly points to the psychoanalyst Carl Gustav Jung's work on the "collective unconscious" and "primordial images" or "archetypes" in their relation to literature, and to the anthropologist Sir James Frazer's *The Golden Bough* (1906–15, in 12 volumes, a work influential for Eliot and for many other twentieth-century authors). Frye's project is strongly resonant with aspects of Russian Formalism (for example, Vladimir Propp's 1928 *Morphology of the Folktale*) and especially early structuralism, though Frye seems unaware of Saussure, Propp, Roman Jakobson or his contemporary Claude Lévi-Strauss, who published *Tristes Tropiques* in 1955. However, perhaps Frye's greatest affinity is with medieval scriptural and literary criticism (Chapter 3), the essence of which is allegorical interpretation. Frye laments that allegorical interpretation is now commonly regarded as "fantastic nonsense" (341). He asks the reader to consider medieval scholasticism as a path to a genuine science of criticism, and to consider the "symbolism" of the Bible and of classical mythology as "a grammar of literary archetypes" (135). (Eliot's and Joyce's engagement with medieval theology and revision of classical mythology – indicative of a broader modernist relation to myth – connect Frye's project with modernism.) Having outlined this typology in the essay "The Archetypes of Literature" (1951), Frye develops a revised, detailed, but by no means final version in *Anatomy of Criticism*, which we will now discuss, though this will necessarily be no more than a quick overview.

For Frye the two central, inter-related archetypes of literature are heaven and hell: "two contrasting worlds ... one desirable and the other undesirable"; he calls them "the apocalyptic and the demonic" (139). These are "undisplaced" (139), undistorted, pure expressions of "human desire" (136). The apocalyptic imagination views things "as though it were all inside a single infinite body" (136): what we most desire is oneness, the sense of our participation in this one infinite spiritual body, death as separateness, fallenness, alienation giving way to a renewed sense of our oneness with the universal whole. The demonic, by contrast, is "the world that desire totally rejects" (147): "the state of chaos or dissolution" (146). Frye's understanding of desire has little in common with Freud. Frye's idea of heaven as oneness is, rather, a Christian Neoplatonist desire for spiritual communion with ultimate spiritual reality (see Chapters 3 and 4), though he acknowledges that the ideal world is a product of the human imagination. For Frye the Bible is "the main source for undisplaced myth" or pure archetypes in the Western tradition (140). His emphasis on the imagination, his orientation towards an immaterial world and his unifying drive indicate Frye's situatedness in the orbit of Romanticism, and particularly William Blake. Frye's first book, *Fearful Symmetry* (1947), was a groundbreaking study on Blake. As such, though the relationship is by no means purely oppositional, Frye is a major counter to T. S. Eliot's influential devaluation of Romanticism (Chapter 8).

Basic symbols of the apocalyptic in the Western literary tradition include the rose, the tree, the garden, the sheepfold, the city, the straight road, geometrical and architectural patterns such as ladders and towers, though Frye insists on the flexibility of such "communion symbols" and of all symbols (Frye 1973, 144). For example, sheep and the sheepfold are established images conveying the apocalyptic "metaphor that we are all members of one body" (142), but "any other animal would do" (143) if the audience is sufficiently prepared for it. Demonic imagery includes: water, the sea, the desert, the waste land, the wilderness, the sinister forest, the labyrinth; monsters and beasts of prey; hermaphroditism, *sparagmos* (ritual dismemberment of a living creature; Frye makes use of a number of such Greek terms and we will include some of them below), cannibalism; demonic perversions of apocalyptic images, such as the tree of death, the sinister enchanted garden, the ruined tower; the harlot, the witch, the siren, the black man. (The last group raises the issue of the inherent misogyny and racism of Western imagery.)

Frye argues, in Freudian terms, that when desire meets the "reality principle" (social prohibitions), the expression of the apocalyptic and the demonic takes a "displaced" form; in psychoanalysis "displacement" can be understood as a compromise formation in response to the conflict of desire and the reality principle (Chapter 6). The apocalyptic then takes the displaced form of what Frye calls – recalling Blake's *Songs of Innocence and of Experience* (1789) – the "*analogy of innocence*" (Frye 1973, 151) while the demonic is displaced into the "*analogy of experience*" (154). Innocence is figured as chaste and "matrimonial or virginal" imagery (156), as for example in the figure of the sleeping beauty. Experience is figured as work (e.g. the farm) or the volatile fortunes of common people (e.g. the capsizable boat). However, images can only be properly interpreted in context: "Any symbol at all takes its meaning primarily from its context" (156). For example, Frye interprets the innocent serpent in Shelley as a "deliberate reversal" of the conventional demonic use of the serpent (156). Having named two poles of desire (apocalyptic and demonic) and two poles of reality (innocence and experience) for the interpretation of literary imagery, Frye then proposes a fourfold schema for the interpretation of literary genre. He distinguishes between four categories "broader" and "prior to" literary genres: comedy, romance, tragedy and satire/irony (162). As understood by Frye, comedy and romance tend towards the apocalyptic and towards innocence, respectively; tragedy and satire/irony tend towards the demonic and experience, respectively. In addition, while comedy and tragedy are mutually exclusive (and cannot combine), they both oscillate between the poles of romance and satire/irony. Similarly, romance and satire/irony are understood as mutually exclusive, but oscillating between the poles of comedy and tragedy. Frye will then distinguish six degrees, as it were, for each of the four *ur*-genres of tragedy, comedy, romance and satire/irony. Among these six variations, the "dominant" is the genre combined with an equal mixture of the other two genres with which it can combine. Therefore the "dominant" for comedy is the comic element combined with an equal mixture of romance and satire/irony, and so on for the other three genres. Frye thus creates a matrix for classification and a typology of 24 (4×6) genre variations, which he feels is differentiated enough to usefully capture and describe all of literature from his mythic/archetypal point of view.

Each genre is associated with one of the four seasons and with an archetypal plot-form called a "mythos" (myth). Comedy, in its "dominant" variation, is what Frye calls the "[m]ythos of spring" (Frye 1973, 163). The mythos of spring will represent the revival and restoration, by the comic hero, of a "stable and harmonious order" (171) following disruption by "blocking characters" and their temporary disordering or dissolution of society (166). It combines, in equal measure, dissolution (an element of satire/irony) and restoration (an element of romance). Romance, in its dominant variation, is a "mythos of summer": it represents the "adventure" of an innocent young hero and his conflict with a demonic/experienced enemy (Frye 1973, 186). At its core is a "quest" involving struggle (*agon*) (187) against this enemy. Tragic elements of the hero's suffering (*pathos*) or dismemberment (*sparagmos*) will be followed by a comic "reappearance and recognition of the hero" (191). Compared to comedy and romance, tragedy – the mythos of autumn – is understood by Frye, in its positive aspect, as the genre-archetype concerned with the individual's emancipation from desire and dream and his or her coming face-to-face with reality, nature or the law. For Frye tragedy is neither heroic nor fatalistic, eluding the "antithesis of moral responsibility and arbitrary fate" (211). Negatively, tragedy's confrontation with reality involves the "narrowing" of an individual's "comparatively free life" (212). Its dominant variation is the tragic hero's fall due to *hybris* (excessive pride) or *hamartia* (tragic error or tragic flaw) (221). Lastly, satire/irony as "mythos of winter" displays the greatest realism. Frye now distinguishes between the two (223). Satire is "militant irony" with clear "moral norms"; irony, on the other hand, is characterized by ambiguity: "a reader is not sure what the author's attitude is or what his own is supposed to be" (223).

The reader of *Anatomy of Criticism* is bound to spot many minor inconsistencies, but it seems unfair to linger on them when Frye himself so openly admits incompleteness and commits to ongoing revision. It is built on a central hypothesis of undisplaced human desire which is not asserted as universally true, but which enables a number of new statements that follow from it. (One of the thrilling aspects of reading *Anatomy* is that the most remote texts find themselves side by side, discussed by Frye as examples of one of the 24 genre variations of his typology.) It is not difficult to see why a new generation of mostly European structuralist thinkers of intertextuality, such as Tzvetan Todorov and Julia Kristeva, recognized Frye as a predecessor. In structuralist terms, *Anatomy*'s complex and highly differentiated typology understands literature as an autonomous intertextual order, a differential structure or a system of differences (see Chapter 7). Five years after the publication of *Anatomy* the American philosopher of science Thomas Kuhn published his pathbreaking structuralist history of science, *The Structure of Scientific Revolutions* (1962). Kuhn argues that science, historically, has moved from one *paradigm* (model built on a central hypothesis or set of postulates) to the next without progressing, as paradigms are neither strictly comparable nor true/false. (A geometry based on the central hypothesis that two parallel lines never meet allows certain truth-statements that follow from it, but is not necessarily truer than a geometry that assumes that they meet.) In spite of affinities between Frye and structuralism, Frye, by contrast, seems to believe that the progressive revision of his typology will lead to an increasingly more coherent, truer model and thus to an increasingly scientific or objective literary criticism.

The close reading practised by New Critics, the standing back advocated by Frye and the claims to scientific objectivity underlying both remained central in American literary criticism. In 1961 Wayne C. Booth published *The Rhetoric of Fiction*, following Frye in standing back to outline a clear, exact and detailed language for the analysis of fiction and claiming to be more objective than the New Critics. *The Rhetoric of Fiction* went into a second edition in 1983 and remains a canonical textbook in Anglo-American curricula.

Just how powerful the model of scientific objectivity was can be seen in the work of Stanley Fish. From the beginning Fish was explicitly engaged in a comprehensive critique of the New Critics. However, by his own account, it took Fish from the mid 1960s to his 1980 *Is There a Text in This Class? The Authority of Interpretive Communities* to move away from his early claim that his reader-response theory was even more objective than New Criticism to his well-known claim that an objective, "value-independent" position is "unavailable" (Fish 1980, 22). Fish mentions Roland Barthes's 1970 *S/Z* as enabling this change of direction (21), a text in which Barthes rejects his earlier distinction between denotation and connotation, arguing that all we have is the open-ended chains of connotation (Chapter 11). However, it can be argued that Fish's emerging pluralism is an early response to the proliferation of models of literary criticism brought about by feminism, postcolonial theory, African-American studies, etc., which new social movements and critical developments we will move onto next.

In his introduction to *Is There a Text in This Class?* Fish highlights the "spatial rather than temporal" emphasis of the New Critics' model (Fish 1980, 147). If the New Critics understand the text as an autonomous, unified, spatial object – the exemplary figure being Brooks's "well wrought urn" – Fish proposes to understand the text as a temporal process of reading. In the 1980 revised, book version of "Interpreting the *Variorum*" Fish dramatizes, from section to section, the reconfiguration of his critical views. In the section entitled "The Case for Reader-Response Analysis" Fish makes a partial break with New Criticism. Where Brooks discerned "resolutions" and "harmonizations" (Brooks's terms), Fish's model emphasizes failures, gaps, aporias (impasses) of interpretation, irresoluble slides of signification: "without the satisfaction" of a "firmly conclusive ending" the reader/critic lacks a "firm perspective", "can't tell" and experiences "uneasiness" (157–8). Fish proposes to replace the New Critical text (understood as a structure "available on the page") with another "object of description": the critic's self-reflexive understanding of the "structure of the reader's experience" (152). At this point, Fish's project remains one of objective description.

In the section entitled "Undoing the Case for Reader-Response Analysis" Fish overturns the objectivism of the earlier section: "the choice is never between objectivity and interpretation but between an interpretation that is unacknowledged as such and an interpretation that is at least aware of itself" (167). There are no objective "formal features" of the text, pre-existing one's interpretative model: "formal units are always a function of the interpretive model one brings to bear: they are not 'in' the text" (164). In other words, "I 'saw' what my interpretive principles permitted or directed me to see, and then I turned around and attributed what I had 'seen' to a text and an intention"

(163). Similarly, the reader's experience is not an objective fact pre-existing one's own model but is shaped by that model. For example, Fish highlights reader activities that have to do with sense-making in the face of aporias and solving interpretive "puzzles" (159), but now insists that this is one model among many: "you make a sense (or so my model claims) as soon as you can" (164). In short, he now rejects the "assumption that there *is* a sense, that it is embedded or encoded in the text" (158) or in *the* reader or in *the* act of reading. However, Fish seems caught in the liar's paradox (I am a liar). He appears to be asserting as true that everything is interpretation and there is no right interpretation or truth. If he is right that everything is interpretation and there is no truth or right interpretation then he is wrong.

In a final section entitled "Interpretive Communities" Fish reaches the conclusion that there is a multiplicity of "interpretive communities" (communities of critics sharing interpretive strategies) and that an act of reading and interpretation needs to be understood in relation to one or more of these communities. As a result, interpretation is neither objective nor subjective, but situated in a complex manner. Fish doesn't name and specify interpretive communities, but claims that they "grow larger and decline", and readers/critics "move from one to another" or belong to different communities simultaneously (Fish 1980, 171–2). We will be returning to Fish's theme of the diversity of critical/theoretical communities in this chapter, discussing the pluralism of literary criticism in the second half of the twentieth century.

The new social movements, the Black Aesthetic Movement and feminist criticism

In the 1950s, while American literary critics were building their models of scientific objectivity and paying great attention to Frye's "apocalyptic" dream of an ordered and unchanging society, the American civil rights movement was unfolding, aiming to extend equal civil rights to all Americans and end the institutionalized racial segregation of public spaces.

In 1955 in Montgomery, Alabama, Rosa Parks refused to give up her seat to a white male passenger and move to the back of the bus. After her arrest, African-Americans boycotted Montgomery's public transport for 381 days, supported by the local branch of the National Association for the Advancement of Colored People (NAACP) until the city changed the segregation law for public transport. The boycott occasioned the emergence of the 26-year-old Martin Luther King, Jr. as a political leader. Purer considerations aside, American national interest required that the civil rights deficit be addressed: after World War II, and while Africa and other European imperial territories were decolonizing, America's new role as a global superpower claiming to embody freedom in the Cold War with the Soviet Union was undermined by its legally embedded racism. However, the civil rights movement encountered serious resistance, and by the mid 1960s sections of it, such as the Black Power movement, had become more militant.

The Black Aesthetic Movement or Black Arts Movement (1965–75) responds to the civil rights movement, but there is a particular correspondence with Black Power. Like the Harlem Renaissance (discussed above), it was connected to political activism and the assertion of black pride. Amiri Baraka (LeRoi Jones), Lary Neal and Addison Gayle, Jr. are among the major figures in the movement. *Black Fire* (1968), edited by Baraka and Neal, and *The Black Aesthetic* (1971), edited by Gayle, are core documents. The movement advocated artistic and critical resistance, autonomy and difference, emphasizing the need for an independent black press. It revived and radicalized a tradition, stretching back to the early nineteenth century, of African-American writers claiming the right to speak for themselves and address not society at large – i.e. white society – but each other. The Black Aesthetic Movement rejected universalism and called for the representation of black experience by African-Americans for African-Americans. It renewed the call of the Harlem Renaissance for distinctively black art forms, emerging out of African-American oral folk traditions, discussed above (nineteenth-century writers such as Frederick Douglass and Charles Waddell Chesnutt had already made use of black folklore in their work). The movement further argued for specifically black criteria by which to evaluate black art forms. Du Bois, in "'Krigwa Players Little Negro Theatre': The Story of a Little Theatre Movement" (1926), had already argued that black art forms must be judged by black standards and by black critics. In this way the Black Aesthetic Movement self-consciously formalized earlier African-American aesthetic traditions and debates into principles of a black art.

Simultaneously, the movement seems to have adopted the black essentialism – the belief in a fixed black human nature – of the Francophone *négritude* movement (see Chapter 10). Whereas white racism spread inferiorizing black stereotypes, *négritude* polemically asserted the superior value of blackness, grounding positive black stereotypes in a black human nature (or essence) originating in Africa. One of the limitations of black essentialism, in its use of positive black stereotypes, is that it is just as reductive as white racism, impoverishing the complexity and heterogeneity of African-American experience into a narrow repertoire of types. Some critics viewed the Black Aesthetic Movement as sexist and homophobic. The 1970s generation of self-identified black women writers – Alice Walker, Toni Morrison, Toni Cade Bambara, Gayl Jones, Gloria Naylor – while endorsing several aspects of the movement, rejected its essentialism, specifically representations of black women associated with it, and set out to present African-American women in their complexity and diversity.

The civil rights movement initiated a period of broader political activism involving a spectrum of so-called new social movements, such as the women's movements of the 1960s and 1970s. American feminist literary criticism as an academic field emerged as a part of the women's movements. Mary Ellmann's *Thinking about Women* (1968), Kate Millett's much-maligned *Sexual Politics* (1970), Ellen Moers's *Literary Women* (1976) and perhaps especially Elaine Showalter's *A Literature of Their Own* (1977) and Sandra M. Gilbert and Susan Gubar's *The Mad Woman in the Attic* (1979) constructed a new field and a new literary canon. Elaine Showalter's *A Literature of Their Own: British Women Novelists from Brontë to Lessing* announces the new academic field of feminist literary criticism. Showalter figures the feminist literary critic as an intrepid explorer discovering the "lost continent of the female tradition" and making Atlantis rise "from the sea of English literature" (Showalter 1982, 10). Virginia Woolf began the reconstruction of a tradition of British women's writing in *A Room of One's Own*, and Showalter continues this reconstruction, adopting the terms of British twentieth-century criticism (from T. S. Eliot to Woolf to Leavis and Williams): tradition, the canon, the relation of literature to culture and society, evaluation and agonistic re-evaluation (Chapter 8).

Showalter's project is broadly descriptive. She offers a survey of about two hundred British (including colonial) women writers and periodizes them into three phases: "feminine", "feminist" and "female aestheticians" (to be discussed shortly). She combines close reading of "great" texts and authors, including previously devalued and "'lost' works", with attention to minor writers, women's history, literary history and literary biography, partly as salutary "documentation" of silenced voices, "lives and careers" (Showalter 1982, 36, 8). Further, she argues that new insight will be gained when women writers – previously "misread and underrated by male-oriented criticism" (112) – are considered in relation to women's history (the conditions of women's lives and gender ideology of their time) and in relation to each other. She claims that she is describing *the* female tradition (rather than constructing *a* female tradition and canon) and that *the* female tradition begins in 1840 because there is "almost no sense of communality and self-awareness" as women among women writers before 1840 (18); that *the* tradition is objectively "unified by values, conventions, experiences, and behaviors" commonly shared (11); and that women writers were all middle and upper class and therefore an objectively homogeneous group. As a result she elides differences under the guise of objectivity; for example, she allows herself to discuss colonial writers such as Olive Schreiner, Jean Rhys and Doris Lessing without any attention to race or imperialism.

Showalter's large survey allows for significant common features to emerge – widely shared plots, endings, character types, themes and figures – thus providing further proof of a tradition of women's writing. For example: the theme of conflict between "womanhood" and writing (72); the figure of the enclosed private room or a *secret* room of one's own; the projection of socially unacceptable aspects of the female heroine onto demonic female characters like Bertha Mason, the mad woman in *Jane Eyre*; the projection of female "personal ambition" (28) and other socially unacceptable qualities onto male characters like Rochester and Heathcliff; the "blinding, maiming, or blighting" (150) of a male character (127); plots of female adventure and freedom circumscribed by endings exacting "terrible punishment" (172) for that freedom. As we can see, there is little left in this of New Critical anti-mimeticism, anti-expressivism, anti-historicism. Showalter tends to psychoanalyse authors (a tendency at odds with contemporary psychoanalytic literary criticism, see Chapter 6) and to assume that, because of their self-repression, women writers have expressed inauthentic female identities.

Showalter's project includes a strong normative element: evaluating each one of the three phases of the female tradition according to criteria that the New Critics would have rejected as external to the analysis of literary form. The mid-nineteenth-century "feminine" phase, exemplified by Charlotte Brontë and George Eliot, involves internalization of the values of "dominant tradition" (13), "veneration of male culture" (44) and pursuit of the "educational standards of the male establishment" (42). Showalter clearly rejects George Eliot's "self-sacrificing masochism" (162) and concludes that this generation's "self-abasement backfired" (86). She praises a transitional generation of so-called "sensation novelists" – exemplified by Mary Braddon's *Lady Audley's Secret* – for expressing "female anger" (160), "self-assertion and independence" (161), and for their entrepreneurialism and professional involvement in the business of publishing. The late-nineteenth-century "feminist" novelists, whose exemplary figure is the "underambitious" Olive Schreiner (203), are criticized for their "revulsion from" sexuality (29) and separatism. Finally, the early-twentieth-century "female aestheticians" are exemplified by Virginia Woolf. Showalter argues that Woolf's disappearing or unlocatable narrator (and other formal experiments) is "another form of self-annihilation" rather than "self-realization" (240). Woolf and her generation are severely criticized for their "disturbing … retreat" from their feelings, bodies, sexuality, the world, political engagement – "how much better it would have been … if they could have faced the anger instead of denying it" (258). Woolf's *A Room of One's Own* is read as expressing Woolf's repression of her "anger and ambition" (264). Showalter claims that Woolf's aesthetic stifled her artistic "development" (264) and led to a failure of realism: her increasing "technical inability to accommodate the facts and crises" of life in her writing (291). In response to Woolf's call, in "Professions for Women" and *Three Guineas*, to kill the Angel in the House, she argues that Woolf is the Angel female novelists now need to kill (265). Greeting Doris Lessing's *Golden Notebook* (1962) as a "monumental achievement" in the authentic expression of women's subjectivity, Showalter defines the "task" of a "radical" contemporary women's writing as follows: "to replace the secondary and artificial images women receive from a male chauvinist society with authentic and primary identities" (314–15). Showalter's values, though not explicitly stated, can be deduced from her above evaluations: self-expression, self-assertion, self-realization (understood as expression and fulfilment of women's anger, worldly ambition and sexuality) and rebellion to overcome obstacles to such expression and fulfilment. With the benefit of hindsight, these individualist values seem disturbingly close to the emerging yuppie culture of the Thatcher and Reagan years.

Sandra M. Gilbert and Susan Gubar's *The Madwoman in the Attic: The Woman Writer and the Nineteenth-Century Imagination* (1979) was discussed in Chapter 6. I will limit myself here to discussing Gilbert and Gubar's definition of their project in their original preface and their extraordinary map of feminist critiques of *Madwoman* in their 2000 "Introduction to the Second Edition: The Madwoman in the Academy". In 1979 Gilbert and Gubar aimed to construct a broader nineteenth-century canon of British and American women novelists and poets. Instead of assuming their homogeneity (as Showalter had), they sought to show their heterogeneity, yet still discovered "a distinctively female tradition" of "striking coherence" (Gilbert and Gubar 2000, xi–xii). Gilbert and Gubar's definition of this tradition is quite similar to Showalter's, and they explicitly recognize their debt to her and to Moers (Gilbert and Gubar 1979). In particular they discern common "[i]mages of enclosure and escape" and "metaphors of physical discomfort manifested in frozen landscapes and fiery interiors"; female "maddened doubles" as "asocial surrogates of docile selves" as well as "act[ing] out" of "male metaphors"; and "obsessive depictions of diseases like anorexia, agoraphobia, and claustrophobia" (xi–xii). To explain this commonality Gilbert and Gubar argue that, in spite of their differences, women writers shared an impulse to "struggle free … through strategic redefinitions of self, art, and society" (xi–xii). Unlike Showalter's very broad survey of writers, Gilbert and Gubar focus on a select group of white "great" authors, arguing that they were previously neglected or misunderstood. However, the exclusivity of their female canon is problematic. Had they focused on nineteenth-century African-American writers such as Harriet Jacobs or Frances Harper, might not new images and themes, for example, have been discerned? Gilbert and Gubar explicitly value feminist collaboration and practice it in their life-long work together, but do not *initially* extend it across divides of race, sexual orientation and geopolitical location. (By contrast, their preface to the third (2007) edition of their *Norton Anthology of Literature by Women* (1985) promises ever-greater diversity.)

In their 2000 "Introduction to the Second Edition: The Madwoman and the Academy", written as a dialogue between the two, Gilbert and Gubar describe the disjunction between their own initial perception of their project and the critiques from other feminists over the years, as feminist literary criticism diversified. Borrowing Showalter's language, Gilbert claims that they imagined themselves as "*explorers* – geographers trying to map the newly risen Atlantis of women's literature" (Gilbert and Gubar 2000, xxiv). The project of defining "*a* (if not *the*) female literary tradition" was, as Gilbert recollects, a "transformative" Pauline conversion, an experience of "revisionary transport" (xx, xxv). However, Gilbert then goes on to describe how new feminist literary critics working within the then-emerging theoretical frameworks of poststructuralism, New Historicism, African-American studies, postcolonial theory, queer theory, etc. attacked the book on several fronts in the years following the 1979 first edition. They critiqued its "essentialism" (belief in a fixed female human nature), "phallologocentrism" (a term from Derrida, manifested here in Gilbert and Gubar's construction of a "monolithic 'plot'" for women's writing) and reliance on the figure of the "author" as creator of the text (Chapter 7), its racism, "heterosexism" and unacknowledged position of "middle-class, white, heterosexual privilege" (xxv).

Gubar offers her own analysis of the development of feminist literary criticism from the late 1970s to the beginning of the twenty-first century. Feminist literary theory has questioned and redefined all the categories underpinning the 1979 book: literature, woman, self, author, women's writing, gender (Gilbert and Gubar 2000, xxxiii, xxxvii, xxxviii). Gubar now sees a feminist literary criticism that has shifted: from "gender as a privileged lens to gender combined with sexuality, nation, race, class, religion", etc.; "from authors to texts" (xxxiv) and to a critique of the "myth of the autonomous subject" (xxxviii); from exclusive focus on literary history to extra-literary discourses and a "thickened" sense of history inspired by cultural studies and New Historicism (xxxv, xxxvii).

Since the 1980s Barbara Christian, bell hooks, Audre Lorde, Barbara Smith, Alice Walker and many others have articulated an African-American feminist literary criticism with its own changing canon of black women writers and its own themes and priorities. For example, the enforced privatization and entrapped idleness of white middle-class women, thematized in women's writing (as discussed in Gilbert and Gubar above), was historically made possible by the hard labour of black women, as house or field slaves and later as domestic servants (who in addition often headed single-parent households). The writer and critic Alice Walker (1944–), author of *The Color Purple*, alludes to the divergent historical experience of black women in her very definition of black feminism as "womanist": "From the black folk expression of mothers to female children, 'You acting womanish,' i.e., like a woman. Usually referring to outrageous, audacious, courageous or *wilful* behavior" (Walker 1983b, xi). Walker's critical work, *In Search of Our Mothers' Gardens: Womanist Prose* (1983) subtly points to a black lower-class tradition of resistant women. Further, she highlights the collectivism of this black tradition and of black feminism (in contrast with Showalter and Gilbert and Guber): the "womanist" is "[c]ommitted to survival and wholeness of entire people, male *and* female" (xi). The question of survival, literal and cultural, is paramount. In relation to literary tradition, Walker points out that the fate of the black writer, especially the black woman writer, has been a pauper's unmarked grave, such as the grave of Zora Neale Hurston (who died in 1960).

In "Looking for Zora", initially published in *Ms.* magazine in 1975, Walker begins to reverse the near-total oblivion surrounding Hurston at the time, and asks why Hurston was unable to publish in her later years. Walker's campaign for Hurston soon led to renewed interest in her work (interest in other black women writers of the Harlem Renaissance, such as Nella Larsen, is much more recent).

Gayatri Chakravorty Spivak and others developed a postcolonial feminist literary criticism since the 1980s. Edward Said's *Orientalism* (1978) launched North American Postcolonial Studies (see Chapter 12). Postcolonial theory remains today a vibrant part of literary studies in America, as represented by Gayatri Chakravorty Spivak, Homi K. Bhabha and Robert J. C. Young. Spivak's complex critique of Gilbert and Gubar in "Three Women's Texts and a Critique of Imperialism" (1985) delineates core issues for a combined postcolonial and feminist critique. Gilbert and Gubar, argues Spivak, unwittingly reproduce the "axioms of imperialism" (Spivak 1985, 243). They read Bertha Mason "only in psychological terms" as Jane Eyre's "dark double" (248). However, the animalization of Bertha, a dark colonial woman, also raises other issues. The plot of *Jane Eyre* requires Bertha to "act out the transformation of her 'self'" into a demonic other, to "set fire to the house and kill herself, so that Jane Eyre can become the feminist individualist heroine of British fiction" (251). Spivak therefore reads *Jane Eyre* as an "allegory of the general epistemic violence of imperialism, the construction of a self-immolating colonial subject for the glorification of the social mission of the colonizer"; Bertha, the dark colonial woman, is "sacrificed as an insane animal for her sister's consolidation" (251). Jean Rhys's rewriting of *Jane Eyre* in *Wide Sargasso Sea* (1966) makes this process visible and enables Spivak's own critique. By allowing Bertha to tell her story Rhys keeps Bertha's "humanity, indeed her sanity as critic of imperialism, intact" (249). Because it is the case that "so intimate a thing as personal and human identity might" nevertheless "be determined by the politics of imperialism" (250), Spivak, drawing on Rhys, argues that the issue of female personal identity that preoccupied 1960s and 1970s feminist literary criticism cannot be considered in isolation from the colonial and postcolonial dimensions.

American feminist literary criticism inherited and initially reproduced the lack of pluralism that characterized mainstream canon-building in the first half of the twentieth century in the English-speaking world. Thus Showalter and Gilbert and Gubar initially claimed to be unearthing *the* female tradition. No doubt in the case of these early feminist efforts the idea of a unified tradition served a strategic purpose in staking out the new field, even if many significant differences and complicating conditions were neglected. If Gilbert and Gubar's groundbreaking book suffered harsh criticism, there is no reason to doubt the validity of their sense of revelation as, in a Benjaminian moment, a significant unison of voice sounded out of literary history. It is just that the truth in its simplicity, as is usual, was less than the whole and too simple.

Postmodernism

In the 1960s and the 1970s, the term "postmodernism" entered American critical debates to describe an emerging movement in the arts (literature but also architecture and the visual arts) dating back to the late 1950s, often defined in opposition to modernism. Ihab Hassan's *The Dismemberment of Orpheus: Toward a Postmodern Literature* (1971) or Robert Venturi and Denise Scott Brown's *Learning from Las Vegas* (1972) perhaps best capture this period. During a second, explosive phase in the 1980s and early 1990s, "postmodernism" and "postmodernity" were the focus of a *gigantic* interdisciplinary and international, if largely English-speaking and American-led debate. As a result, there has been very little agreement on what postmodernism was. Indeed, as Judith Butler pointed out, "[t]he question of postmodernism is surely a question, for is there, after all, something called postmodernism?" (Butler 1995, 35). However, the accounts of postmodernism by the French poststructuralist philosopher Jean-François Lyotard (1924–98) and by the American Marxist literary critic Fredric Jameson (1934–) soon came to dominate discussion. Its unprecedented scale and proliferation was therefore countered through the ritual repetition in the debate of a small number of texts working as anchorage points, of which Lyotard's *The Postmodern Condition* (1979; English translation 1986) and Jameson's essay "Postmodernism, or, The Cultural Logic of Late Capitalism" (1984, 1991) were the principal.

Critics were producing charts *opposing* modernism and postmodernism, though there was no agreement on the definition of modernism either (Chapter 8). Jameson summarized this critical tendency as the "hypothesis of some radical break or *coupure*, generally traced back to the end of the 1950s or the early 1960s" (Jameson 1991, 1), and contributed to it with his own mapping opposing modernism and postmodernism. He influentially described postmodernism as the "cultural dominant" of the period (4), borrowing Roman Jakobson's concept of "the dominant" (Chapter 7), and the cultural expression of a new phase of socioeconomic development in the West: "late capitalism".

However, there is now a strong critical shift from *discontinuities* towards *continuities* between modernism and postmodernism, as I argued in my editorial introduction to *Postmodernism. What Moment?* (2007), a collection asking the protagonists of the postmodernism debate to assess its legacy. Many of the contributors to this collection sought to map out these continuities. It is also true to say that from the beginning of the debate postmodern traits were identified in certain literary works produced long before the 1950s, or indeed literary modernism. For example, Laurence Sterne's *Tristram Shandy* (1759–67) has often been cited as postmodernist or as a precursor of postmodernism: written at a time when the novel was a new genre still developing its conventions, it self-consciously exposes and displays these conventions, a self-referentiality often identified with postmodernist literature and art. While many critics saw realism, modernism and postmodernism as following each other in a chronological succession, others rejected the very idea of periodization as suspect and undesirable. Lyotard in his essay "Answering the Question: What Is Postmodernism?" (1982; English translation 1986) theorized realism, modernism and postmodernism as co-existing and recurring tendencies in the arts. He argued that there are two recurring moments within the modern: the postmodern and realism. The postmodern is the moment of experimentation and innovation, when one breaks from the existing rules of art to create a new paradigm. Once a new paradigm is established and literature and art operate within it, conventionally reproducing it, this is what Lyotard calls the moment of realism; output within an established paradigm, because we are so used to it, appears like a mirror of reality. With this view Lyotard in fact critiqued his own earlier periodizing definition of postmodernism in *The Postmodern Condition* as a post-1950s phenomenon. Other critics agreed with Lyotard in seeing postmodernism not as a period, but as a recurring tendency (style or even disposition or frame of mind, such as scepticism).

With regard to the characteristics of postmodern literature, critics have often identified *intertextuality* (Chapter 7) and *self-referentiality* (or *metaliterature*) among its constitutive features. Postmodern *intertextuality* is an overt and explicit engagement with and *resignification* of canonical discourses and texts, including canonical literary texts; oral, anonymous, collectively authored texts such as myths and folktales; and contemporary cultural icons and stereotypes. Examples are Jean Rhys's *Wide Sargasso Sea* (1966) in its intertextual relation to *Jane Eyre*, Tom Stoppard's *Rosencrantz and Guildenstern Are Dead* (1966) in relation to *Hamlet*, J. M. Coetzee's *Foe* (1986) in relation to *Robinson Crusoe*, Toni Morrison's *Beloved* (1987) in relation to nineteenth-century abolitionist and anti-abolitionist discourse, Derek Walcott's *Omeros* (1990) in relation to the *Iliad*, Margaret Atwood's *The Penelopiad* (2005) in relation to the *Odyssey*. Some critics have identified and applauded an agonistic, contestatory, critical relation to the canonical text (see Spivak's discussion of Rhys's rewriting of *Jane Eyre* above); Jameson (and others) lamented the flat and uncritical "pastiche" of the original in postmodern literature (Jameson 1991, 16).

Angela Carter revised European folktales in several of her short stories. For example, "The Courtship of Mr Lyon" and "The Tiger's Bride" (both in her 1979 *The Bloody Chamber and Other Stories*) both revisit "Beauty and the Beast". Arguably the former is a pastiche while the latter is contestatory of the "original". Toni Morrison, in an affirmation of cultural doubleness and hybridity, critically revises *both* African-American folktales marginal to dominant culture – the tale of the flying African slaves in *Song of Solomon* (1977) and Brer Rabbit and the tar baby in *Tar Baby* (1981) – *as well as* ancient Greek myths and European folktales. Salman Rushdie's *Midnight's Children* (1980) refers to Indian myths *and* canonical Western texts, its opening page alluding simultaneously to *The Arabian Nights*, *Tristram Shandy* and

Dickens's *David Copperfield.* Morrison and Rushdie invite readers to open themselves to hybridization, enter a process of cross-cultural apprenticeship and develop an awareness of the contemporary multiplicity of canons, cultures and traditions. This attitude to cultural multiplicity and mixity characterizing the literature of the last quarter of the twentieth century seems in contrast with the anxieties about cultural fragmentation, incoherence and overload that characterized English-speaking literary criticism and much of the literature of the first part of the twentieth century.

Angela Carter's short stories often engage with cultural icons and stereotypes: "Black Venus" engages with a cultural icon, Baudelaire, while "The Loves of Lady Purple" engages with gender stereotypes. Feminist critics have pointed out two opposing stereotypes of woman: the angelic woman, self-sacrificing and chaste; and the demonic woman, dangerous and sexually promiscuous. "The Loves of Lady Purple" (first published 1974) investigates the stereotype of the demonic woman as well as the limitations of feminism. The over-sexed and murderous Lady Purple is not a real woman but a puppet lovingly created by an old man. But when she comes miraculously to life she lacks the freedom and imagination needed to break with the stereotype: "But whether she was renewed or *newly born* … the brain beneath the reviving hair contained only the scantiest notion of the possibilities now open to it … She walked rapidly … towards the town, making her way like a homing pigeon, out of logical necessity, to the single brothel it contained" (Carter 1987, 37–8, my emphases; see *The Newly Born Woman* [1975; English translation 1986] by Hélène Cixous and Catherine Clément).

Pop Art (particularly Andy Warhol and Roy Lichtenstein) offers perhaps the most famous examples of postmodern engagement with cultural icons. For example, Warhol's images of Jackie Kennedy Onassis, Marilyn Monroe, the Mona Lisa and Botticelli's Venus are often doubled or in a series of variations. Many Warhol and Lichtenstein silkscreens are representations of representations: either of mass-media images (Jackie O, comic-book heroes) or of masterpieces made iconic by the mass media (the Mona Lisa). In this sense, there is no difference between canonical texts and cultural icons/stereotypes. With obvious critical intent, unlike Pop Art, Roland Barthes's *Mythologies* (1957) engaged with iconic texts, such as the photo of a black soldier saluting the French flag on the cover of the French magazine *Paris Match* in the summer of 1955, in the midst of decolonization struggles within the French Empire (the Algerian liberation movement emerged in 1954). Barthes's reading exposes the role of this icon in legitimizing the French Empire (Chapter 11).

If postmodern intertextuality is a kind of re-presentation of representations, why are literature and the arts representing representations rather than representing reality? Plato's answer (Chapter 1) was that poetry and the arts represent a world which is itself a (bad) representation of reality, a representation corrupted by un-truth and non-being, a world of seeming and becoming in which all that is solid melts into air. Poets and artists are for

Plato ideologues of this false world: the whispering, flickering, chain-bound shadow-world of the cave. Perhaps contemporary answers to the question are not as different as we might think given the two millennia that separate classical Athens and postmodern thought, and this despite so many thinkers wishing to oppose themselves to Plato. To turn now to postmodern answers or stories, in 1967 in the book of the same name Guy Debord described the emerging postwar order as "the society of the spectacle" – life taken over by the explosion of contemporary mass media. For Debord our life is one of conspicuous over-consumption of representations. The artist Nam June Paik captured such postmodern landscapes with his installations comprising multiple television screens, such as his "TV Garden" (1974): a large installation of 31 TV screens bombarding us with images in the midst of tropical vegetation. A second story is Jean Baudrillard's theory of the "precession of simulacra" (Chapter 1). In influential texts such as *Symbolic Exchange and Death* (1976) and *Simulacra and Simulation* (1981), Baudrillard argues that our age is the age of the "precession of simulacra": representations today precede reality. Rather than following reality and attempting to copy it, simulacra are copies without an original. Dickens and George Eliot valued *truthfulness* and aspired to a mimetic relation with reality – they wanted to hold a mirror to reality. Instead of engaging with reality, has postmodern intertextuality withdrawn irresponsibly into a hall of mirrors? Fredric Jameson thought so and deplored what he called the loss of the historical "referent" and the "waning of historicity" (Jameson 1991, 18, 6).

It can be argued that the omnipresence of representations, the saturation of reality with representations from the new mass media is such that reality has to be redefined to include representations. Postmodern engagement with representations, then, would be a new realism; and a postmodernist literature intertextually engaging with canonical texts would be, in a new sense, mimetic. However, there are differences from Plato's literature as mimesis and from nineteenth-century realism. For the postmodern writer, in the age of "simulacra" reality is reaching us already shaped and interpreted in a certain way, and his or her re-presentation of representations is an *intervention* or, to use a poststructuralist term, a *resignification*: it contests a canonical shaping and interpretation of reality and sets out to shape it and interpret it anew. Postmodern realists are much more acutely aware than the nineteenth-century realists that representations – including their own – shape and give meaning to reality rather than simply mirroring it. (Plato was all too aware that our reality is shaped by false representations, but included literature in these.) It can be argued that postmodernism engages with historical actuality, the world, *understood to include* dominant representations circulating in our world *as part of it*. Hence the worldliness of postmodern literature – for example, often mixing *historical* events with fictional ones. It could then be argued that postmodernism is a return to the world and a reaction against late modernist developments – Beckett (and his double significance, as modern poet of the impossibility of the word of truth and postmodern poet of the ever-fecund word of story) or Adorno's aesthetic theory (which we will discuss in Chapter 10) or Schoenberg in music and the abandonment of traditional melody or abstraction in painting or the austerity of international modernist architecture. This kind of art was inward looking, a kind of spiritual austerity and spiritual discipline for a post-theological, industrial, materialist age, in which the Gnostic moments of insight were few and far between. Postmodern literature and art, self-reflexively aware of the limitations of this project, returns to storytelling (though not storytelling as opposed to the truth), to ideas of melody in music, to embellishment in architecture and to a more expansive attitude to "the world". Derek Walcott, though intensely engaged with modernism, nevertheless commented that he wrote an epic of sorts, *Omeros*, because he felt that literature had narrowed its focus too much, focused too much on interiority: "poetry has surrendered too much of what it used to do. The novel used to be an epic poem, and it's sort of withering and withdrawing into small, personal, diaristic considerations" (Walcott 1996, 191).

However, postmodern intertextuality is very much anticipated by modernism and, further back, by *fin-de-siècle* Aestheticism (for example, Wilde's critical writings). In 1919 in "Tradition and the Individual Talent" T. S. Eliot calls on the new poet to immerse himself in the literary tradition. The new poet will be erudite, aware of his belatedness and yet not shackled by it. Eliot's *The Waste Land* (1922) is explicitly intertextual; so is Joyce's *Ulysses* (1922), not only in its Homeric patterning but also in its mimicry of a great variety of discourses and literary styles. As to the value of intertextuality as a literary strategy, Jameson and Spivak disagree but do not discuss the same works. Jameson seems too busy complaining about Andy Warhol to acknowledge Rhys or Morrison and their use of intertextuality. Intertextuality is not inherently valuable, but instead of generalizing for or against it, it would be best to keep the question of its value open.

Another trait of postmodern literature, according to many critics, is self-referentiality or metafiction. Linda Hutcheon's (1947–) *The Politics of Postmodernism* (1989, 2002) describes postmodern literature as "*historiographic metafiction*". This is literature that takes a critical distance from itself and explicitly so, mixing literature and criticism, the aesthetic and the critical, and crossing the boundary between the two. This can take a variety of forms. For example, the narrator is explicitly aware of the particularity and interestedness (rather than disinterestedness) of their perspective, and the obstacles to objectivity in narration. The narrator of Salman Rushdie's *Midnight's Children*, Saleem Sinai, is trying to narrate the Indo-Pakistani war of 1965, caught between the conflicting accounts of the war given by the Voice of Pakistan and All-India Radio, and thinking about the limits of objectivity in narration (Rushdie 1995, 340–41). Metafictional awareness is not enough, however, to turn Saleem into a reliable narrator and he self-consciously exhibits his unreliability (338–39). Having inherited a pickling factory, Saleem theorizes his narrative practice using a metaphor that is close at hand. His narration is a "pickling process": he pickles historical facts and memories, and the chapters are his jars; he calls this his pickling or "chatnification of history" (459). Saleem refers to himself in the third person as a persona he has constructed, in a passage that is both metaliterary and metatheoretical (460). He winds down his narrative by exclaiming "yes, I should revise and revise … but there is neither the time nor the energy" and openly acknowledging the "inevitable distortions of the pickling process" (461). Another example of the metaliterary use of a self-consciously unreliable narrator is Toni Morrison's novel, *Jazz* (1992): "How could I have imagined him so poorly? … I have been careless and stupid and it infuriates me to discover (again) how unreliable I am" (Morrison 1993, 160). The character imagined poorly is a mixed-race character, a notoriously problematic character in African-American literature. One of the effects of this literary strategy is to alert the reader to his or her own situated-ness, interested-ness and unreliability – and to create a horizon within which to think of an ethics of reading. Once again, this is not absolutely new and continuities need to be acknowledged, in modernist literature but even in realist fiction. For example, in George Eliot's *Adam Bede* the authorial persona states: "The mirror is doubtless defective" (1996, 175).

The mixing of literature and criticism/theory, and the crossing of the boundary between the two in postmodern literature, is replicated in contemporary criticism, for example in Roland Barthes's *Roland Barthes by Roland Barthes* (1975). The title is an intertextual reference to a well-known French book series on famous authors; Barthes himself had written the volume on the historian Michelet in 1954. Is this a theoretical text, is it literature, is it Barthes's autobiography? The text is generically mixed and undecidable. For example, it moves from a childhood memory to a metafictional critical passage on pleasure (Barthes 1993b, 415–16). Pleasure was the main concept in Barthes's theoretical text of 1973 *The Pleasure of the Text*, and it continues to preoccupy this 1975 text. Another example would be Baudrillard. Is Baudrillard's dystopic vision philosophy or literature, social theory or science fiction?

We will now turn our attention to the phenomenon in world history variously called "postmodernity", the society of the spectacle (Debord), the age of simulacra (Baudrillard), consumer capitalism, multinational capitalism, late capitalism (Jameson), etc. Lyotard's and Jameson's accounts of postmodernity provide us with a useful entry point into their hugely influential work on postmodernism. Jameson and Lyotard describe postmodernity in very similar terms, in spite of the apparent great difference in language. They both equate postmodernity with cultural fragmentation and pluralization in an increasingly globalized world. However, their evaluations of the phenomenon are diametrically opposed. Jameson laments it and calls for *totalization* (Jameson's term), while Lyotard finds great promise in it.

In *The Postmodern Condition* (1979) Lyotard argues that today society, the arts and even science can best be described as a multiplicity of "language games" (Lyotard 1984a, 10) (appropriating a term from Wittgenstein). These "language games" are incommensurable: they are not parts of an organic whole where they find their proper place. Each language game is based on its own rules, discursive presuppositions and narrative, which Lyotard calls *petit récit*, "little narrative" (60). Until recently a small number of "grand narratives" (such as the advance of human knowledge or the political emancipation of humanity) dominated, but this is no longer the case. We witness, he argues, a decline of grand narratives in favour of a proliferation of *petit récits.* If we use Lyotard's conceptual framework to read English studies today, we might argue that Caribbean literature, African-American literature, women's writing, etc. are now constituted as new language games, each with its own *petit récit*. Constituting these language games is the result of bold resignification by critics and writers: constructing a new canon, a new critical language, etc. For example, the *petit récit* of Jean Rhys as foremother of Caribbean literature has been important to Caribbean writers and critics. When Achebe is defining the African novel in his essays (Achebe 1990) or when Toni Morrison is defining the formal and thematic constituents of black art (Morrison 1984), they are trying to redefine the canon and the critical language through which their texts will be read. To return to Lyotard his model is essentially "agonistic" or contestatory: as he makes clear, "it is now dissension that must be emphasized" (Lyotard 1984a, 61). Repeating old moves and reaching consensus are both undesirable. What is important for Lyotard is what he calls an ethics of "paralogy": an experimental ethics involving the invention of new and surprising moves, and initiating new language games (65–6) ("paralogy" alluding to Kant's "paralogisms" in the *Critique of Pure Reason*).

As discussed above, in "Answering the Question: What Is Postmodernism?" (1982) Lyotard uses this set of concepts to reinterpret the distinction between realism, modernism and postmodernism. "Realism" is the repetition of old moves, whose familiarity lends them a reality effect, an appearance of mirroring reality. Both modernism and postmodernism offer new moves and language games which undo established representations and their reality effect: "the painter and novelist … must question the rules of the art of painting or of narrative as they have learned and received them from their predecessors. Soon those rules must appear to them as a means to deceive, to seduce, and to reassure" (Lyotard 1984b, 74). Lyotard concludes that the "artist and the writer, then, are working without rules in order to formulate the rules of what *will have been done*" (81). For Lyotard, both modernism and postmodernism are anti-representational and anti-mimetic, presuppose that reality is sublimely unrepresentable and set out to present the unpresentable in its unpresentability. Lyotard situates the difference between modernism and postmodernism in their attitude towards the loss of unity and proliferation of language games discussed above. He describes modernism as melancholic, still mourning the loss of unity and totality; postmodernism as embracing the "increase of being and the jubilation that results from the invention of new rules of the game" (80). (In these terms, Baudrillard's dystopian vision of contemporary reality would be modern rather than postmodern.) Postmodern art and literature, in this view, do not mirror the world: they are already of the world.

In that postmodernism in general is new, surprising and agonistically related to previous moves, Lyotard highlights and endorses the *intertextuality* of postmodernism. Originality in Lyotard's model involves an agonistic relation to previous significations and a surprising resignification. Lyotard's model resonates with other poststructuralist models, for example with resignification in Barthes and Kristeva, Foucault and Judith Butler. In that postmodernism interrogates existing rules of the games – interrogates art, what counts as art, etc. – Lyotard highlights and endorses the self-referential and metaliterary practices of postmodernism.

Finally, Lyotard connects this ethics of paralogy with an aesthetics of the sublime: presenting the unpresentable in its unpresentability. An allusive aesthetic is appropriate for presenting catastrophic events in human history or voicing those irreparably silenced by history without appropriating their silence. Lyotard links the postmodern sublime with the acute problems of presentation posed by the Holocaust. How can writers and artists present an overwhelming event such as the Holocaust in such a way that its terror is not reduced and domesticated, and so as to make its repetition less likely? Postmodernism puts formal innovation in the service of an ethics/aesthetics of presenting the unpresentable in its unpresentability: this is the motto of postmodernism for Lyotard (obviously highly familiar modern territory, see Chapters 4 and 5). The alternative, an art that claims an adequation between itself and its object, is a totalitarian "fantasy to seize reality" (Lyotard 1984b, 82). Lyotard claims a connection between the aesthetics of a naïve realism and the politics of totalitarianism. In his view, to avoid a return to totalitarian terror, here is the task of the postmodern: "not to supply reality but to invent *allusions* to the conceivable which *cannot* be represented … [L]et us be witnesses to the unpresentable" (81–2, my italics).

The novels of Toni Morrison or Salman Rushdie, for example, attempt to rewrite history from below, from the perspectives of the ex-slave and the ex-colonized. However, writing from the point of view of the silenced, in a way that respects their alterity, poses difficult problems of presentation, and this is why postmodern literature has a strong metafictional element, and why it self-reflexively addresses its own limits. In *Playing in the Dark* (1992), Toni Morrison describes her task as one of familiarizing the unfamiliar, that from which we are estranged, without either demonizing it or translating it to the familiar:

> I have to place enormous trust in my ability to imagine others and my willingness to project consciously into the danger zones such others may represent for me … I am interested in what prompts and makes possible this process of entering what one is estranged from – and in what disables the foray, for purposes of fiction, into corners of the consciousness held off and away from the reach of the writer's imagination … imagining is

> not merely looking or looking at; nor is it taking oneself intact into the other. It is, for the purposes of the work, *becoming.*
>
> (3–4)

The difficulties involved in this process come into sharp relief in a project such as Morrison's *Beloved* (1987). The enigmatic epigraph of *Beloved*, "Sixty million and more," refers to the victims of slavery, the American Holocaust, as it is being called, and particularly the victims of the Middle Passage (the transportation of slaves across the Atlantic, under conditions leading to enormous suffering and loss of life). *Beloved*'s aesthetic is self-reflexively sublime. The narrative focuses on an escaped female slave, Sethe, just before the abolition of slavery. When the slave-catcher comes to return her and her children to their owner, Sethe kills her baby daughter, Beloved. Seventeen years later Beloved comes back to life as a young woman, furious with her mother. She brings with her not only personal memories but fragmented collective memories of the Middle Passage, so that she is not just Beloved but the channel of a spectral community of innumerable dead whose suffering is not only unvoiced but sublimely unvoiceable. Sethe opens herself to this encounter with Beloved to make amends and redeem herself, but making amends is impossible and sustaining the encounter with a force so enormous is beyond the individual. The encounter with Beloved is too much for Sethe, but the community, like a Greek chorus, conveys the following *anagnorisis* (recognition). The "Sixty million and more" concern all of us. One must seek to remember what *cannot* be remembered, for how can an individual with justice remember the suffering of millions? The work of mourning and commemoration is therefore always incomplete, never completed, and justice means that justice can never be done or never be done with.

Linda Hutcheon argues that postmodern literature is intensely preoccupied with history. However, instead of addressing history with a capital H (what Benjamin calls the "history of the victors", see Chapter 7), postmodernism attempts to write the minor and plural histories of the silenced many: "we now get the histories (in the plural) of the losers as well as the winners, of the regional (and colonial) as well as the centrist, of the unsung many as well as of the sung few, and I might add, of women as well as men" (Hutcheon 2002, 66). According to Hutcheon, postmodernism derives "its historical consciousness (and conscience) from the inscription into history of women and ethnic/racial minorities" during the 1960s (as I have attempted to sketch above) (10). If postmodernism is "typically denounced as dehistoricized" by some critics, this is because the "problematized histories of postmodernism have little to do with the single totalizing History" such critics have in mind (57). Hutcheon is implicitly addressing Jameson's lament about the waning of historicity in postmodern literature, but counter-arguing that what is perceived as a loss is a very welcome transition from History to histories.

Let's now turn to Fredric Jameson's *Postmodernism, or, The Cultural Logic of Late Capitalism* (1991), particularly the first chapter, initially published as

"Postmodernism, or, The Cultural Logic of Late Capitalism" in *New Left Review* (1984), to look at his claims more closely. Jameson considers the "view of present history as sheer heterogeneity, random difference, a co-existence of a host of distinct forces" (Jameson 1991, 6) to be an important distinguishing feature of postmodern literature as well as of contemporary theory: "contemporary theory ... is also, I want to argue, itself very precisely a postmodern phenomenon ... a very significant symptom of the very post-modernist culture which is our subject here" (12). Jameson argues that the shift from History to histories in literature and criticism is not empowering or freely chosen; it is instead a paralyzing *symptom* of late, globalized, multi-national, consumer capitalism: "this whole global, yet American, postmodern culture is the internal and superstructural expression of a whole new wave of American military and economic domination throughout the world" (5). In his view, global capitalism produces fragmentation, and postmodern literature and theory are exacerbating symptoms of it, and complicit with it. The cure for Jameson would be to return to History. This History with a capital H, in Jameson's case, is Marxist history: the history of capitalism, contemporary global "late capitalism", and Marxism as the one true critique of capitalism and capitalism's inevitable successor, according to the iron logic of History (see Chapter 5). He advocates a literature and literary theory that aim to synthesize or totalize all the voices and perspectives within the frame of global capitalism. He calls for an "aesthetic of cognitive mapping" (51), whose task it is to represent global capitalism in its ever-increasing complexity. Giving as an example one of Nam June Paik's chaotic TV-screen installations, what Jameson requires of us is "the impossible, namely, to see all the screens at once" (31). The sublime for Jameson is late capitalism. Can the impossible be done? Effectively, yes. You cannot see all the screens at once, but you can *know* what is on them fundamentally. For Jameson what all screens will testify to is the truth of Marxism. Why? Because Marxism is true. Therefore on all channels, 24/7, essentially one thing will be showing: global capitalism.

Central to Jameson's argument is a distinction between *the symptomatic* and *the cognitive*. He divides both literature and theory/criticism into two groups: symptomatic of the economic system within which it is produced (and therefore unconsciously reproducing it); and cognitive of this system (and therefore exposing this system and enlightening the readers). Needless to say, he endorses the cognitive. He calls for a return to the "age-old function of art – the pedagogical and the didactic ... the cognitive and pedagogical dimensions of political art and culture" (Jameson 1991, 50). Jameson rejects existing postmodernism and calls for a cognitive postmodernism, to be brought about by his proposed aesthetic of cognitive mapping. Each one of us, he argues, has an experience of late capitalism; economists and sociologists have provided us with abstract knowledge of it. However, we have been incapable of fashioning *representations* of late capitalism, i.e. incapable of cognitive mapping. There are two requirements: first, cognitive mapping needs to articulate individual experience and abstract knowledge of late capitalism; second, formal innovation is required in order to find representational codes or language adequate to the impossible task of representing multinational capitalism (21 throughout): "the whole new decentered global network of the third stage of capital" (38). Such a postmodernism would be truly political art and would achieve "some new and more comprehensive socialism … an internationalism of a radically new type" (50).

As we have seen, the essential "cognitive" content of everybody's experience will be only one thing for Jameson: global capitalism, which is to say the truth of Marxism. The question then remains, what will this generate in terms of worthwhile things to say about specific literary texts? Let's take two examples: Chinua Achebe's *Things Fall Apart* (1958) and Toni Morrison's *Beloved* (1987). Achebe's novel addresses the colonialization of the Igbo people and is written against – or in intertextual engagement with – Conrad's *Heart of Darkness.* Morrison's novel addresses slavery in America and is written in intertextual engagement with the American nineteenth-century discourses of abolitionism and anti-abolitionism. If we apply Jameson's criteria we would have to denounce both as symptoms of late capitalism and as cognitive and political failures. They are not addressing contemporary capitalism and they are intertextual engagements with representations of the past.

Jameson denounces postmodern intertextuality for its "depthlessness" and "weakening of historicity" (Jameson 1991, 6); lack of critical distance and "waning of affect" (10); "unavailability of the personal style" (16); "imitation of dead styles" and "complacent eclecticism" (18). He argues that the postmodern "historical novel … can only 'represent' our ideas and stereotypes about that past … it can no longer gaze directly on some putative real world … [W]e are condemned to seek History by way of our own pop images and simulacra of that history, which itself remains forever out of reach" (25). Postmodern intertextuality might display all the above or, on the contrary, might be part of a vibrant political project. To show this I will compare Angela Carter's "The Courtship of Mr Lyon" and "The Tiger's Bride", both renditions of "Beauty and the Beast". In the canonical fairytale, Beauty is an archetypal angelic woman: dutiful daughter to her father, pure of heart and of course of body. "The Courtship of Mr Lyon" stays close – arguably too close – to the canonical fairytale and Beauty retains these characteristics; "The Tiger's Bride" on the other hand is boldly innovative. In the canonical fairytale, the Beast was really a prince under an evil spell. In "The Tiger's Bride" the Beast wears a human mask and clothes, but underneath the mask he is really a furred animal – and so is Beauty, as she finds out when he licks her hand: "And each stroke of his tongue ripped off skin after successive skin, all the skins of a life in the world, and left behind a nascent patina of shining hairs. My earrings turned back to water and trickled down my shoulders" (Carter 1981, 67). Jane Austen, Charlotte Brontë, George Eliot, Virginia Woolf had little to say on the sexually desiring woman, and Carter is also writing against them, rewriting female sexuality as a potentially liberating force. Thus Carter makes a vibrant contribution to the 1970s feminist movement and resonates especially with French difference feminism, particularly Hélène Cixous and Luce Irigaray. To return to Jameson, should Achebe, Carter and Morrison have been writing on late capitalism instead?

Fragmentation (he calls it "schizophrenia") is the spectre haunting Jameson's work: "the links of the signifying chains snap, then we have schizophrenia in the form of a rubble of distinct and unrelated signifiers" (Jameson 1991, 26). Where Lyotard sees an exuberant proliferation of language games, Jameson sees fragmentation and the decline of great collective projects. Jameson objects to the multiplicity of language games in literature and literary criticism, and yearns for a time when Marxism was the dominant oppositional model. More broadly, Jameson is addressing the proliferation of new forms of political activism in the United States and Europe in the 1960s and 1970s. Foucault called these new forms of activism *micropolitics*. For example, May 1968 in Paris, the civil rights movement in the United States and the feminist movements of the 1960s and 1970s are all assemblages of semi-autonomous mobilizations irreducible to traditional political categories, particularly the category of class, and resistant to the leadership of traditional political actors, such as political parties and trade unions. These new political and theoretical movements are at the very heart of the postmodernism debate of the 1980s and 1990s, many participants designating them somewhat obliquely as "difference" or "Otherness". However, in "Postmodern Blackness" bell hooks argues that there is an attitude of exclusion underlying this apparently positive language in the rhetoric of the postmodernism debate. Many theories of postmodernism promise openness and unprecedented participation for marginal groups, but "are often exclusionary even as they call attention to, appropriate even, the experience of 'difference' and 'Otherness'" (hooks 2001, 2478). In this respect Jameson is closer than Lyotard to the spirit of the postmodernism debate.

Jameson positions and legitimizes Marxist literary criticism as cognitive, while delegitimizing rivals – from poststructuralism to feminist literary theory – as symptomatic, including Lyotard, his main rival in the postmodernism debate. In spite of Jameson's obvious familiarity with poststructuralist thinkers, he gradually came to insist that poststructuralism is symptomatic of late capitalism (Goulimari 2004) and to give a reductive account of it. For example, it is reductive to view Lyotard's model of incommensurable language games as exemplary of poststructuralism. Within poststructuralism Gilles Deleuze and Félix Guattari propose a *rhizomatic* model of incessant lateral connections among the local elements of decentred, non-totalizable multiplicities – an alternative to both Lyotard and Jameson. But at the heart of Jameson's work there is circularity and mere assertion: Marxism is true. From this prior truth or simple faith, the rest of his analysis follows. The result is a theoretical despotism blind to the value of the most significant developments in progressive politics since the 1960s and to the thinking that has accompanied those developments. We will turn to poststructuralism in Chapter 11.

Conclusion

- In the 1920s Hughes called on the African-American modernists of the Harlem Renaissance to turn towards African-American oral collective forms, Hurston pioneering the study of Southern rural forms. They situated black modernism in relation to American *and* African-American culture.
- Since the late 1930s New Critics focused on *close reading* of the text, to the exclusion of contexts and other concerns. For Ransom close reading was the path towards an objective and scientific criticism. Wimsatt and Beardsley's anti-mimetic and anti-expressive theory of literature bypassed authorial intention, advocating an objective criticism internal to the text. Brooks's Richards-inspired theory attended to the *structure* of the text, understood as organic unity and conciliation of opposites, claiming that the text's meaning is its structure.
- In the 1950s Frye called on critics to "stand back" from the text and developed a scientific hypothesis of the fundamental archetypes of all literature. He situated literary imagery in relation to two interconnected couples: apocalyptic and demonic, innocence and experience. He outlined two interconnected couples of *ur*-genres: comedy and tragedy, romance and satire/irony.
- In 1980 Fish argued, against models of scientific objectivity, that critical objectivity is unavailable – objectivity is unacknowledged interpretation. The text is not a spatial object but a temporal process of reading, fraught with aporias of interpretation. There is a multiplicity of interpretative models and interpretative communities.
- In the 1960s the Black Aesthetic Movement implicitly questioned the dominant scientific model of criticism in favour of explicitly political criticism; it called for black art-forms and criteria of evaluation, addressed primarily to a black audience.
- Since the 1970s feminist criticism reconstructed traditions and canons of women's writing. Showalter's account of British women's writing outlined its distinctive figures, themes, plots and characters, proposed a periodization specific to this tradition and evaluated texts in relation to feminist liberation. Gilbert and Gubar outlined a canon of Anglo-American women's writing, which they later critiqued for its unexamined white, middle-class, heterosexual assumptions. Black feminist critics reconstructed a canon of black women's writings, Walker stressing traditions of collectivism and resistance. Spivak critiqued Gilbert and Gubar for their individualism and blindness to race and imperialism.
- In the 1980s and 1990s the postmodernism debate addressed the explosion of the mass media and the globalization and pluralization of culture. In relation to literature, critics disagreed on the value of postmodern *intertextuality* and its relation to the "original" text(s), to literary history (realism and modernism) and contemporary mass-media culture, Jameson seeing postmodern intertextuality as ahistorical and uncritical

pastiche. Hutcheon connected postmodern *self-referentiality*, particularly metafiction, to a welcome transition from History to histories, but Jameson lamented the loss of History. Lyotard described and endorsed a postmodern plurality of incommensurable language games, advocating an agonistic, intertextual and self-referential postmodern ethics of paralogy and aesthetics of the sublime. But Jameson considered the pluralization (and pluralism) of postmodern literature and theory as symptomatic of late capitalism. hooks, by contrast, identified a continuing lack of genuine attention to marginalized voices in the postmodernism debate, in spite of its rhetoric, and called for more pluralism.

Further Reading

See especially Brooks 1968; Fish 1980; Frye 1973; Gilbert and Gubar 2000; hooks 2001; Hughes 2001; Hurston 2001a; Hutcheon 2002; Jameson 1991; Lyotard 1984a and 1984b; Ransom 2001; Showalter 1982; Spivak 1985; Walker 1983b.

10 Poetry and hermeneutics, critique and dissonant composition, freedom and situation

Heidegger, the Frankfurt School (Horkheimer, Adorno), the Constance School (Jauss, Iser) and existentialism (Sartre, Beauvoir, Fanon)

After the Holocaust: Heidegger, the Frankfurt School and the Constance School

Martin Heidegger (1889–1976) is the most controversial twentieth-century thinker. His *Being and Time* (1927) is considered a pathbreaking text, its contemporary influence unwaning. Yet during the 1930s and 1940s he supported the Nazis, never explicitly rejected the substance of the Nazi ideology of National Socialism and never denounced the Holocaust. After the war much of his best-known work is in the form of major essays. Many of them are of great interest to the literary critic, but we must limit ourselves to the consideration of two of them: "What Are Poets For?" and "Language".

"What Are Poets For?" was delivered as a lecture in 1946, in "commemoration" of the twentieth anniversary of the German-language poet Rainer Maria Rilke's death, then revised and published in 1950 (Heidegger quoted in Hofstadter 1975, xxiv). Heidegger here continues to deepen his critique of Western thought, modern reason and modernity, first initiated in *Being and Time* (though his later thought also implies a critique of *Being and Time*, as I hope to make clear). Heidegger argues that Western man's assertion of his "dominion" over the natural world has culminated in modernity, with disastrous consequences for the natural world as well as for humanity (Heidegger 1975b, 111). (See Heidegger 1993b and 1993c for major statements on this theme.) Poets have the momentous task of undoing the damage, finding a way out of modernity and reconnecting us with the earth and also with the true nature of our own being. (Heidegger provides a powerful philosophical resource for ecological thought.)

For Heidegger Western thought and science are not only complicit with the exploitation of nature, but have developed the very epistemology that underpins it. The division and the distance between the human knowing subject and the object of knowledge, as old as Plato, is fundamental to modern science. Heidegger unequivocally rejects this distinction, arguing that it legitimizes the "objectification" of the world (Heidegger 1975b, 110). He effectively rejects the very idea of representation, where "Man" stands as if apart from the world and "places before himself the world" as if it were something objective (110); he would strenuously reject any version of realist literature or objectivist literary criticism (e.g. New Criticism, Chapter 9).

Further, Heidegger rejects what we commonly understand as production, whether economic or literary. Comparison with Marx (Chapter 5) highlights the radicalism of Heidegger's critique. Like Marx, Heidegger is a vocal critic of alienated labour, and praises Marx for recognizing the "estrangement" and "homelessness of modern man" in his 1946 "Letter on Humanism" (Heidegger 1993b, 243). However, Heidegger is equally critical of Marx's conception of unalienated labour, understood by Marx as an expression and externalization of man's authentic productive activity through the mediation of the external world. While Heidegger's valorization of an authentic productive relation with the world in *Being and Time* can be interpreted as akin to Marx's unalienated labour (in spite of Heidegger's personal strident anti-communism), in "What Are Poets For?" Heidegger rejects the very possibility of authentic production and the presupposed distinction between an active human producer and a passive material object transformed by the encounter. Consequently, Heidegger would firmly reject any understanding of literature and literary criticism as a human productive *activity*. Such ideas of the active subject and the passive object – since Plato but particularly since the triumph of the modern subject with Descartes – are, for Heidegger, the ideological ground out of which modern technological civilization has grown. Modern technological man "rises up as the producer", while the "whole objective inventory in terms of which the world appears is given over to … self-assertive production" (Heidegger 1975b, 111). Things are produced only to be "used up" (130), hastily consumed and discarded.

Modern man's productive self-assertion has the "character of command … forcing everything under its dominion"; the earth becomes "raw material" (130) and all "living things" are "technically objectivated in … exploitation" (112). The irony of modern technology is that even "Man becomes human material" (111). Man is "exposed" (i.e. subject) to the will of others to exploit him and turn him "into mere material and into a function of objectification" (115): "Self-willing man everywhere reckons with things and men as objects" (135). But should he become willful and assertive himself – imposing himself "on the unprotected market of the exchangers" (136) – he is still nothing but a "functionary of technology" (116). His sense of power illusory, he is "exposed" to a sense of things and humans that all is for exploitation. According to Heidegger, the modern technological world and the "world market" (115) necessitate the "total state" (112) and "total organization" (117). However, Heidegger is anything but a defender of freedom in the Enlightenment sense, puncturing Enlightenment optimism and discarding the liberal, individualist and democratic model of man as "self-reliant" and "purposeful self-assertion" (116). What is more threatening than the atomic bomb – Heidegger writes in the aftermath of America's use of the atomic bomb against Japan, and in the midst of the onset of the Cold War and the nuclear balance of terror between America and the USSR – is the Enlightenment dream that man, "by the peaceful ... transformation ... of the energies of physical nature", could "render the human condition ... tolerable for everybody and happy in all respects" (116).

So what is Heidegger's alternative? In "What are Poets For?" Heidegger affirms humans' belonging to nature and praises Rilke for "surpassing" the technological view of the world in poetry which evokes "experiences ... [of] the non-objective character" of nature – what Rilke calls "the Open" (112). The relation between humans and the world is redefined as an interaction or a communication, initiated by the world: the world calls or "touches us" (125) and the authentic poet turns to the world, receiving its call or touch. Heidegger therefore finds in Rilke a reversal of the technological relation between man and the world. As antidotes to reason and modern subjectivist rationalism (e.g. Descartes, mentioned above), we are asked to consider the value of the "immediately perceptual" (126), the "intuitive image" and "the heart" (127). Heidegger privileges in particular poetry (but also art more broadly) for its authentic attitude to the world, and characterizes his own thinking as poetical, instead of conventionally philosophical. (Two German-language poets, the Romantic Friedrich Hölderlin – Heidegger's major poetic muse – and the modern Rilke, are the heroes of this essay.) Heidegger is a thinker whose understanding of the world includes a spiritual realm of deities, as well as "the forefathers, the dead, ... those who are to come" (128). His metaphor for humanity, "*We are the bees of the invisible*" (130), recalls Plato's description of poets in *Ion* (see Chapter 1), beloved of European Romantic idealism. Heidegger describes poets as those who "answer" to the call and "the will" of the world (141), understood as "the Open"; unlike the producers who will their domination of the world, poets display a different kind of willing – that of receiving the call of the world – which is "imperceptible" (119). Heidegger uses a quasi-religious vocabulary to find a way of formulating a position beyond instrumental and objectifying habits.

The role of poets is to use language in such a way as to reveal and performatively bring about "the healing whole" (140). Heidegger insists that poets do not use language to signify or represent a reality assumed to be external and separate from it. On the contrary, "Language is ... the house of Being" (132). This authentic speaking is the opposite of "purposeful self-assertion" (138) or willful production because the authentic poet, Heidegger claims, is a selfless medium voicing the world rather than himself. Inspired largely by the Romantic Hölderlin, this is a theory of impersonality comparable to T. S. Eliot's (Chapter 8), though Eliot contrasted his theory with what he characterized as Romantic self-expression.

Heidegger develops these themes further in his essay "Language" (1950). He sets out to critique current theories of language by showing their similarity with the technological model discussed above and to propose an alternative derived from German-language poetry, particularly in the case of this essay the Expressionist Georg Trakl. Heidegger's critique of contemporary theories of language has three related strands. He argues against language as 1. "audible utterance of inner emotions"; 2. as "human activity"; and 3. as "representation by image and by concept" (Heidegger 1975c, 193). First, Heidegger rejects the idea of language as expression of the self, as part of his rejection of Cartesian subjectivism, i.e. the self as willful and active and a source of meaning and knowledge. Heidegger rejects language as expression because it presupposes "something internal that utters or externalizes itself" and turns language to an "external, surface notion" (192). Second, Heidegger denies human agency in language and, reversing the relation (as with poet and world in "What Are Poets For?"), attributes agency to language: "language will call to us … and grant us its nature" (191). Language "first brings man about, brings him into existence", so that man is "bespoken by language" (192). Third, Heidegger rejects the idea of language as representation, in that it presupposes a division and separation between representation and its object. It is not enough to avoid the "exclusive" use of concepts, typical of philosophy and criticism, and include the "figurative and symbolical character of language" (193) characteristic of literature. Neither concepts nor figurative language must be understood as separate from their putative object. Heidegger rejects the scientific model generally, as well as the possibility or desirability of a science that would take language as its object (such as Saussure's science of signs, discussed in Chapter 7): "Reflection tries to obtain an idea of what language is universally … its essence or nature" (189), but "[w]e do not wish to reduce" language to this (190). Instead, Heidegger places humans within language: language is our home, "dwelling-place", "abode" (192) – or, famously, "Language is the house of Being" (Heidegger 1993b, 217). According to Heidegger, Western man, especially modern man, has condemned himself to a self-inflicted existential homelessness and destitution brought about by his technological worldview, and Heidegger's positioning of language, properly understood, as the medium or matrix of our being or primal home is intended as a cure. It is the poets' task to call us back out of the cold and "into the word" (Heidegger 1975c, 198).

Poetry is "spoken purely" in the sense, to use one of Heidegger's many neologisms, that it "presences" exactly what modern technological man has alienated himself from. The authentic and "masterful" poem presences a reality that exceeds encapsulation in the poem or the mind of the poet, and thus "can deny the poet's person and name"; the author is "unimportant" except as a medium (Heidegger 1975c, 195). Heidegger seeks to open us to this more expansive sense with his close reading and interpretation of Georg Trakl's poem, "A Winter Evening" (quoted in Heidegger 1975c, 194–5). As interpreted by Heidegger, Trakl's poem names two realms that are distinct but turned towards each other and interacting rather than separate: things and world. The world is itself comprised of four distinct but non-separable entities that are "being toward one another": sky, earth, mortals and divinities (199).

All these distinct elements are equally and mutually supportive, providing hospitality to each other. Each element is simultaneously figured both as a homeless wanderer and as a hospitable abode gathering the other elements under its roof. However, Heidegger suggests that all these elements – effectively the entire cosmos – are housed within the poet's language and within the poem. The poem *calls* these elements, visits them upon each other and entrusts them to each other (200–202). Heidegger seems to be suggesting that without authentic poetry this cosmos has no existence.

The essay introduces themes of absence and difference that strongly anticipate and influence Derrida's work: "dif-ference", and the mutual constitution of presence/absence and inside/outside, which therefore cannot be understood as binary opposites (mutually exclusive terms, where the one term is what the other is not and where one of the terms is valued at the expense of the other, for example presence valued at the expense of absence). Heidegger introduces the notion of "dif-ference" or "*diaphora*" ("difference" in ancient Greek) in response to the figure of the "threshold" of the house that appears in Trakl's poem (Heidegger 1975c, 199). The neologism "dif-ference" attempts to capture the relation between world and things as an "intimate" one but "not a fusion" (199). Yet the "dif-ference" between world and things constitutes them, as world and things do not pre-exist their "dif-ference"; "dif-ference presences" (205). The presence of things and world – the "brightness of world" and "gleaming of things" – is the effect of the presencing role of difference (205). This relation of (non-living and material) things and (living and spiritual) world undermines the binary opposition outside/inside. Instead, "the two, the outside and the inside, penetrate each other" (204).

Returning to poetry, Heidegger now answers the question "What are poets for?" more fully. First, poets performatively bring about or *presence* what remains absent in our modern technological times, the interdependence and "intimacy" (Heidegger 1975c, 206) of things and world, thereby pointing the way to a future beyond modernity. The poem "brings the presence of what was previously uncalled into a nearness", calling "[i]nto the distance in which what is called remains, still absent" (198). Second, "human speech", whose purest form is poetry, is "not self-subsistent": it "rests in its relation to the speaking of language" itself (208); it "listen[s] to" and "respond[s]" to a higher "command"; it "accepts" and "follow[s] the call" (209). This "primal" (206) calling that is "not anything human" (207) is not the *logos* (word) of God but language as *dif-ference*: "Language speaks in that the command of the dif-ference calls world and things into the simple onefold of their intimacy" (207); "the speaking of language … appropriates mortals by the command of the dif-ference" (209); "Language speaks. Its speaking bids the difference to come which expropriates world and things into the simple onefold of their intimacy" (210). Heidegger is a difficult writer, but this difficulty is a part of his project of articulating a thinking and a language critical of and alternative to the dominant way in which we frame our understanding of things in general – the framing of modern science that has increasingly cut us off, Heidegger feels, from a richer and more expansive sense of things. In his attempt to express this other sense of things and human life, poetry comes to play a very important role for him, as texts for interpretation in his essays, as models of authentic language, and therefore of authentic thinking and being.

Heidegger's critique of modernity and proposed alternative have been highly influential, but his thought and personal behaviour have attracted considerable criticism. For many he looks back to an imagined preindustrial, premodern rural past. Heidegger's critique of modern scientific and philosophical ideas of truth in favour of a model of revelation ("disclosure") or "call" has also troubled critics. The authentic poet obeys a higher call that comes from a beyond that is not graspable by mundane rationality, and potentially justifies himself by claiming access to a voice which others fail to hear. Heidegger is very far from alone in privileging this idea of truth. But his closeness to a regime led by men convinced of their superiority and higher calling, who caused world war and ordered the calculated murder of millions of civilians (administered by those who were "only obeying orders"), compels us to question theories of truth or ethics that privilege revelation at the expense of reason, individual and collective decision-making and critical consideration. Heidegger leaves no space for debate or disagreement, conflicts of perspective, social heterogeneity, power inequalities. Perhaps the higher command or the moment of revelation is diabolic, the product of one's own delirious imagination? If the authority that Heidegger favours is that of the call or the revelation of Being, as transmitted to the people by the poet-prophet, the people are a homogeneous, single-ethnicity, monolingual group. This sense of Heidegger's world does not change after World War II. Few would argue that Heidegger's thought taken as a whole is a Nazi philosophy, but it is certainly a philosophy that sits very uneasily with democratic political ideas and modern multiethnic, multicultural states, just as it does with every other aspect of modernity.

Heidegger holds out the vision of a home to those who will follow the higher command of Being and condemns unbelievers to homelessness. There is no room in Heidegger's universe for the critical theorists of the Frankfurt School. In their emphasis on disobedience and negation, they are neither poets nor people. Indeed, as many of them were Jews, the world of 1930s Germany, in which Heidegger entertained brief dreams of being the philosopher-prophet of the new regime, became an increasingly dangerous place to be.

The Frankfurt School group of thinkers worked for, or were affiliated to, the Frankfurt-based Institute for Social Research (founded in 1923) and were publishing in the *Zeitschrift für Sozialforscung* (*Journal for Social Research*) and its American incarnation, *Studies in Philosophy and Social Science*, when the institute relocated in New York to escape the Nazi regime in the 1930s. The first generation included

Max Horkheimer as director since 1930, Theodor W. Adorno, Herbert Marcuse, Otto Kirchheimer, Franz Neumann, Friedrich Pollock, Leo Löwenthal and Walter Benjamin as a marginal figure in dialogue with them but not finally working for the institute. The mantle was passed to a second generation of which the leading figure was Jürgen Habermas and to a third generation led by Axel Honneth.

Having discussed the modernist German Marxists (Benjamin, Brecht) in Chapter 7, we will now turn to the Marxism of the Frankfurt School, particularly to the work of Horkheimer (1895–1973) and Adorno (1903–69). The Frankfurt School after the war shares with Heidegger's later work a focus on aesthetic phenomena, a hermeneutic approach, a strong critique of science and objective (or objectivist) interpretation and a style of writing that is closer to poetry than conventional philosophy. However, their diagnosis of contemporary cultural and social malaise is substantially different, if equally bleak, and their proposed solutions move in a direction of critique, negation and contradiction, antithetical to Heidegger's.

Fred Rush elucidates both what Horkheimer and Adorno share with Heidegger and their respective critiques of him. As Rush explains, Adorno's "aestheticized" version of Critical Theory, influenced by Walter Benjamin, dominated the Frankfurt School after the war, and Horkheimer "migrate[d] over" to this version and co-wrote with Adorno what many consider the "principal" text of the Frankfurt School, *Dialectic of Enlightenment* (1944, revised 1947) (Rush 2004b, 8). Theirs is an "interpretative venture" (17) refusing to claim objectivity for itself (yet prone to grand statements), committed to self-reflexive awareness (though not always practising it) and prepared to acknowledge the limits of self-awareness. Critical Theory does not claim to reveal "meanings that are already there" *in* the text. Instead, no interpretation is definitive, and one's own interpretation is itself subject to interpretation: "To stop interpretation is to settle on a meaning", and Adorno "equates this … with making life meaningful *qua* status quo and to that extent justifying it" (34). Also, following Benjamin, Adorno argues that our experience and interpretation of texts includes "unconscious elements" that cannot be ever fully brought to the surface (34). Adorno – anticipating Barthes's "text" – describes interpretation as the spinning of a fragile textual web (a textual *constellation*, in Benjamin's sense) out of the slightest threads. In "The Actuality of Philosophy" (1931) he claims that philosophy "must proceed interpretively without ever possessing a sure key to interpretation; nothing more is given to it than fleeting, disappearing traces within the riddle figures of that which exists and their astonishing entwinings" (Adorno 2000b, 31). Adorno adopts an "intentionally obscure style" that attempts to perform a fragile "mosaic" or modernist montage and embody the "negative dialectic" he advocates (Rush 2004b, 35). Privileging distance, defamiliarization and the fleeting nature of insight, Adorno's 1931 critique of Heidegger is that he relies on "immediacy" and "covert essentialism" (33; see Adorno 2000b, 27–9). In "Why Philosophy?" (1961) Adorno adds that "[w]ith Heidegger ... thought, in its character of reverent ... listener" of being, would "lose its right to criticize and would be forced to capitulate" to reality (Adorno 2000c, 46).

Horkheimer, for his part, is concerned to distinguish between interpretation as practised by Critical Theory, always in relation to "historical circumstance" (Rush 2004b, 17), and the alienated and "instrumental" interpretation practised by others, which is too conditioned by their "desires and the interests they implicate" (15). The question then becomes "whether and how it is possible to eliminate" the social alienation underlying "instrumental" thinking (16). Horkheimer is especially keen to distinguish between Critical Theory hermeneutics and Heidegger's hermeneutics. He positions Critical Theory as a materialist rationalism, Heidegger's thought as an idealist irrationalism. Horkheimer critiques both instrumental rationality that debases reason and idealist irrationalism. His critique of Heidegger's hermeneutics is that it "advocates a return to an atavistic, authoritarian, prerational conception of human life" where "the individual has no essential role and the perceived disintegration of modern culture is replaced with a mythical unity of being" replicating the "supernatural ground of existence that is the hallmark of idealism" (23). Heidegger sacrifices "critical individuality to unthinking and mythic absorption in the *Volk*" (25).

"The Culture Industry: Enlightenment as Mass Deception" is a seminal chapter of *Dialectic of Enlightenment*, disturbingly mixing rare insight and foresight with unpalatable views and clearly erroneous predictions. Horkheimer and Adorno describe a 1930s and 1940s world order in which cultural production is controlled by a few large corporations whose political agenda is to reproduce the *status quo*: to reconcile people with the reality of exploitation and pre-empt resistance. Horkheimer and Adorno claim that this is a form of fascism by other means, which it will take more than the defeat of Germany to combat, and the Nazi regime is conversely seen as a form of capitalism. (Heidegger similarly saw no essential difference between Western capitalism and Soviet communism; both were for him technological civilizations.)

Horkheimer and Adorno describe the culture industry or the entertainment business as a global "iron system" encompassing films, radio, magazines and television (Horkheimer and Adorno 1998, 120). Underlying the postwar Cold War between the West led by the US and the Communist bloc led by the USSR is the global triumph of a culture industry producing "identical goods" (121). *Across* the global political divide, industrial processes of "standardization and mass production" have come together with a political will to "central control" (121). For example, Hollywood dominates film production and is in turn dominated by studio bosses who appease the "real holders of power" to avoid interference and "purges" (122–3), Horkheimer and Adorno argue, anticipating McCarthyism. (The first Hollywood blacklist dates back to October 1947 and included Brecht.) While focusing on the West, Horkheimer and Adorno seem equally critical of both sides of the Cold War, in spite of their Marxism. They attempt to bypass the Cold War divide, a divide further intensified after the Communist Chinese Revolution of 1949, to expose a postwar global continuation of totalitarianism by other means.

Horkheimer and Adorno's argument is that the culture industry only offers the "semblance ... of choice" (Horkheimer and Adorno 1998, 123). Like the car industry, it imposes differentiations between A-movies and B-movies or between "stories in magazines in different price ranges" (123). This is essentially an exercise in "labeling", "classifying" and dividing consumers, who appear as "statistics" on marketing charts, an exercise shared by "any type of propaganda" (123). However, they claim, the products are identical and A-movies are by no means genuine art. For example, the Hollywood dramatization of a Tolstoy novel or use of a Beethoven symphony is just a "cheap imitation" (122). The culture industry does allow for several styles, but requires from its products a formulaic obedience to one of these styles, indissociable from "obedience to the social hierarchy"; "schematization ... cataloguing ... classification ... bring culture within the sphere of administration" (131). The "studio hierarchy" is actively "suppressing" projects that do not "conform" to a formula (127). Yet formulaic repetition leads to "inferior" aesthetic production: "the great artists have retained a mistrust of style ... What Dadaists and Expressionists called the untruth of style" (130–31). Positing a link between aesthetic innovation and political radicalism, Horkheimer and Adorno argue that aesthetic value lies in "those features" of a work of art in which "discrepancy appears" – and which simultaneously enable it to "transcend reality", the reality of the status quo (131). Jean-François Lyotard's influential distinction, within modern art, between "realism" that formulaically repeats a style and "postmodernism" that creates new styles and so resists any totalizing style and indeed totalitarianism (e.g. fascism) (as discussed in Chapter 9) is indebted to Horkheimer and Adorno. (Of course those critical of Adorno and Horkheimer's totalizing vision of Western popular culture may feel they have reproduced the very totalitarianism they denounce and seek to escape.)

Against Walter Benjamin's insistence on the critical and radical potential of film (see Chapter 7), Horkheimer and Adorno claim that films leave "no room for imagination or reflection on the part of the audience" (Horkheimer and Adorno 1998, 126). For example, the "relentless rush of facts" in action films (127) inhibits reflection. The reliance on the "simple horror of situations" in thrillers, detective films and adventure films effectively justifies the unjust world such escapist films falsely promise to help the audience escape (138). Culture is the "prolongation of work" in that it is mechanized, industrialized and unthinkingly repetitive: any "mental effort" on the part of the audience is "painstakingly avoided", while plot is driven by "the most striking effect" and "[b]anal" surprise (137). Culture is "pornographic and prudish" (140). For example, in dramas it is "strictly forbidden for an illegitimate relationship to be admitted without the parties being punished" (141). (Is Tolstoy's

Anna Karenina, for example, so very different?) Even tragedy has been degraded into a "carefully calculated" acceptance of the world as it is, a spectacle of "exemplary behavior" in response to an ostensibly "inexorable" world where resistance is futile (151–2). However, this is a "liquidation" of tragedy and "abolition" of the individual; it creates a mirage of capitulation and social integration that "signifies Fascism" (154). By contrast, Horkheimer and Adorno understand tragedy as the irreconcilable conflict between individual and society, indeed understand "individuation" as deviation (or dis-identification) from society (156). A compliant individual is not an individual at all, but non-compliant individuality no longer exists, they grandly state, replicating philosophy's tendency, since Plato, to declare the great mass of humanity as living entirely in the realm of *doxa* (received opinion). Would not a more nuanced view be closer to the truth?

According to Horkheimer and Adorno, within the culture industry all genres and styles share the creation of a fictional reality where power is "inescapable" (Horkheimer and Adorno 1998, 140) and pleasure is "flight … from the last remaining thought of resistance" and "negation" – "not to think about anything, to forget suffering" (144). Further, they argue that the culture industry cultivates the illusion that the "outside world is the … continuation of that presented on the screen … Real life is becoming indistinguishable from the movies" and other products of the culture industry (126). Here Horkheimer and Adorno anticipate Baudrillard's analysis that we are now in the epoch of the "simulacrum": a postwar era of consumer capitalism when simulacra (fabricated cultural representations) precede reality and deter resistance (discussed in Chapters 1 and 9).

Horkheimer and Adorno build a distinction between the culture industry and pure art, using the notion of "contradiction". They begin with the familiar argument that, historically, the autonomy of art (as theorized since Kant) is a modern phenomenon whose condition of possibility is "bourgeois society", and draw out the contradictory nature of art: "Pure works of art" (from literature to music) are *both* autonomous, "obey[ing] their own law", *and* exchangeable commodities (Horkheimer and Adorno 1998, 157). This contradiction – if indeed it is a contradiction – can be resolved in two ways, both of which Horkheimer and Adorno reject. *Either* art is completely commodified and becomes indistinguishable from other commodities whose only value is their exchange-value (price-tag) on the market *or* art is seen as completely autonomous and fetishized. Against these options, which equally "cover up the contradiction", Horkheimer and Adorno favour making the contradiction conscious, as in their view Beethoven did (157).

Horkheimer and Adorno have been criticized in several respects. Their description of a ubiquitous "iron system" is greatly exaggerated and has the paralysing effect of making resistance seem near futile. Given their commitment to dialectical thinking, should they not be seeking for contradictions within the culture industry? The counter-argument would be that their hyperbolically exaggerated description of a total system is a rhetorical and performative choice intended to trigger a will to resistance. Adorno discusses the limits of the culture industry in his essay "Free Time" from the 1960s. The enormous media hype surrounding a royal wedding was met with contradictory responses: having "drooled over" it "breathlessly", viewers then "evaluated" it "critically" (2001b, 196). Another criticism would be that what counts as resistance, for Horkheimer and Adorno, is aesthetic resistance in the form of aesthetic innovation, and that they fail to give politics attention. Further, their view of art is elitist and assumes a problematic modernist distinction between pure art and popular culture. Adorno's willingness to turn even his own assumptions on their head is perhaps more evident in his 1942 "The Schema of Mass Culture": "There is no longer either kitsch or intransigent modernism in art"; the "difference between 'serious' and 'light' culture is either eroded or expressly organized and thus incorporated into the almighty totality" (Adorno 2001c, 67–8). If Benjamin rhetorically exaggerated the revolutionary and critical potential of film, their dismissal of mass culture (film, radio, television, popular music, etc.) as devoid of contradiction seems misguided and defeatist. Instead, mass culture can be counter-cultural (e.g. music in the 1960s), as Adorno himself discusses in the later essay, "Transparencies on Film" (Adorno 2001d). Horkheimer and Adorno are at their least palatable when they are deriding jazz or women's organizations (e.g. Horkheimer and Adorno 1998, 154). Horkheimer and Adorno's comment on the way that Orson Welles as rebellious figure is part of the Hollywood plan can be turned against their main thesis: late capitalism, it might be argued, does not require or deliver uniformity, but – more ambiguously – tolerates and feeds on innovations, new styles and niche audiences.

Equally, it seems presumptuous to assume the radical potential of high art in general and modernism in particular (and Adorno at times acknowledges that Stravinsky and Schoenberg are not politically progressive).

Peter Bürger's influential *Theory of the Avant-Garde* (1974) is a critique of Adorno, pertinent to *Dialectic of Enlightenment.* Bürger argues that while Adorno endorses aesthetic avant-garde movements as "the most advanced stage of art in bourgeois society" (Bürger 1984, 1), he fails to grasp their "twofold" project: to bring about the "nonorganic work of art", as Adorno argues, and also *simultaneously* to generate an "attack on art as institution", to be discussed shortly (86). For Adorno only the non-organic avant-garde work is an "authentic expression of the contemporary state of the world" and of "alienation in late-capitalist society" (85). The rejection of organic unity and the non-organic, montaged work, as theorized by Benjamin and Adorno, are crucial tasks for the avant-gardes, argues Bürger. For Bürger, following Benjamin and Adorno, montage assumes the "fragmentation of reality" (73) and "proclaims itself an artificial construct" (72) that "joins the isolated reality fragments and thereby creates meaning" (69), including the "message that meaning has ceased to exist" (70). Instead of the subordination of parts to a single "pervasive intent" (80), the montaged composition is assembled through the "contradictory relationship of heterogenous elements" (82). The recipient's attention turns away from meaning and towards the "construction" of the work (81). At the same time, the refusal to provide meaning is "experienced as shock by the recipient" and might be intended as "stimulus" towards "change in the recipient's life praxis" (80). However, Bürger rejects Adorno's assumption that the non-organic work is necessarily politically radical.

In relation to the second part of the "twofold" project of the avant-gardes, Bürger claims that Adorno fails to register the avant-garde attack on the institution of art because he lacks recognition of art as an institution. Bürger positions himself as an inheritor of Adorno's dialectical criticism that assumes the "contradictory nature" of reality (Bürger 1984, 9). However, Bürger's Adornean claim is that Adorno's view of avant-garde art is not dialectical (contradictory) enough. Adorno greatly values the autonomy of art (for example, as an antidote to the culture industry) but fails to appreciate that this autonomy is both a heroic project and a social condition: the autonomization of art is part of the "developmental logic of bourgeois society" (32). For Bürger French Aestheticism (Mallarmé, Valéry, symbolism, art for art's sake) is the "apogee" of an intensifying modern division of labour that turns the artist into a specialist (32). This process predates the French Revolution and leads to art as an "institution ... whose functional mode is autonomy" and thus detachment from the "praxis of life" (26). This is a deeply "contradictory role" for art (50) as both protest and safety valve. This "apartness" from the instrumental rationality of bourgeois society "already implies the claim to a happiness society does not permit" (25). Aestheticism breaks art's ties with the "society of Imperialism" (33), but simultaneously admits art's "social ineffectuality" and thus makes possible art's self-criticism by the early-twentieth-century avant-gardes (27). This self-criticism, in Dada for example, takes the form of a critique of the institution of art and its "lack of social impact" and the Dadaist aim to "reintegrate art into the praxis of life" (22).

Dada and the other avant-gardes failed in their attempt to liquidate the institution of art and were themselves, ironically, institutionalized as art. (The institution of art includes the universities, publishing houses, museums, etc. that canonized modernism.) Explicitly writing after another historical failure – "after the events of May 1968 and the failure of the student movement in the early seventies" – Bürger conveys his acute and painful sense that the institution of art neutralizes the effect of radical texts, which might strike one as an unsupported generalization (Bürger 1984, 95). He also highlights the contradictory and potentially compromised nature of Adorno's modernist aesthetics. In relation to Adorno's major but unfinished and posthumously published *Aesthetic Theory*, Bürger argues that the centrality of the category of the new in this text is problematic, as the aesthetic of the new – while potentially radical – is nevertheless "grounded in the hostility to tradition typical of the bourgeois-capitalist society" (59) and duplicates "commodity society" (61). As to Adorno's emphases on aesthetic autonomy and the individual, these had been criticized by the avant-gardes. Avant-garde artists sought to abolish exactly what makes art autonomous: the "disjunction of art and the praxis of life", e.g. politics (Tzara, Breton), "individual production" (Duchamp) and "individual reception as distinct from" production (51, 53). Against Bürger, it can be argued that Adorno also criticized aesthetic autonomy: "no authentic work of art … has ever exhausted itself in itself alone, in its being-in-itself. They have always stood in relation to the actual life-process of society from which they distinguished themselves" (Adorno 2000d, 200). In the "antinomies" in a work of art, "criticism perceives" the antinomies of "society" (208).

Adorno, who intended to dedicate *Aesthetic Theory* to Samuel Beckett, addresses here the significance of modernism. J. M. Bernstein situates Adorno as a post-Holocaust thinker for whom modernism holds the only hope of bearing witness to the enormities of human-inflicted human suffering, particularly for Adorno the Holocaust: "it would be preferable that some fine day art vanish altogether than that it forget the suffering that is its expression and in which form has its substance" (Adorno quoted in Bernstein 2004, 161). The proper object of art is "suffering that escapes both experience and sublimation" (Adorno quoted in Bernstein 2004, 155), a shameful and impossible object only experienced by the guilt-ridden survivor as beyond assimilation (see also Toni Morrison on the Middle Passage, discussed in Chapter 9). For the sake of this object, new formal means have to be found: committed art "looks crude" (158), the expressive lyric "I" is inappropriate and concepts fail. The new aesthetic is one of "sublimity or dissonance" (157). For example, the poems of the Romanian-Jewish German-language poet Paul Celan, whose parents were Holocaust victims, attempt to witness "the most extreme horror through silence" (155) and the "self-relinquishment of the lyric 'I'" (158). Celan attempts to voice the unreachable sensuousness and particularity of suffering through formal "dissonance or decomposition" (157). Through "syntactic and semantic decomposition", he performs a "disintegration" of language and "intended meaning" into fragments alluding to a reality that escapes cognition (156). For Adorno this is exemplary of modernism (and art more generally), hence his motto: "Only what does not fit into this world is true" (Adorno quoted in Bernstein 2004, 156). Modernist texts "emancipat[e] the elements of the medium as elements (words as words, paint as paint, etc.)" (156) to witness a "sensuous particularity" threatened with extinction and to prevent its (and their own) "conceptual appropriation" and "neutralization through interpretation" (156). For Adorno, art's role is to attempt to expose itself to the sublimity and alterity of truths repressed by modern "instrumental reason" (the "villain" in Adorno's theory of art) or to which instrumental reason is blind (157).

Bernstein seems to offer a post-Habermasian defence of Adorno's contemporary relevance. Habermas's alternative to "instrumental reason" is "communicative reason", but Bernstein claims that the "communicative" model of "truth would … disallow the truth-claim of the work of art" (Bernstein 2004, 159). Bernstein's central claim is that Adorno's aesthetics (and art for

Adorno) holds the promise of a new form of reason: an "integral" and "sensuously bound reason against its desiccated, instrumental form" (145), but also as an alternative to Habermas's communicative reason. This is poetry's promise for Heidegger too. For Adorno, modern instrumental reason excises sensuous particularity, which is thereafter a "split off" and repressed "part of reason itself" (141). In this context, art is (in the psychoanalytic language adopted by Bernstein) the return of the repressed, pressing the claims of modernity's "sensory/libidinal unconscious" (141); the art of Baudelaire, Mallarmé, Joyce and Beckett is the "last *systematic* hold-out against the self-destruction of enlightened reason" (145). In this sense, "Art is rationality that criticizes rationality" (Adorno quoted in Bernstein 2004, 139). While Heidegger lacks Adorno's moral sensitivity, Adorno and Heidegger share anti-subjectivism and anti-objectivism (favouring instead an ecstatic or sublime experience) as well as similar critiques of instrumental reason, communicative reason (language or art as communication) and conventional rationality.

Bernstein's exposition effectively counters Peter Bürger's critique of Adorno's aesthetic of the new, understanding this aesthetic in the context of art's revolt against its commodity status and easy consumption by its readers. Art works claim to be "cognitively nonsubsumable, unique objects of attention" (Bernstein 2004, 148). For example, in modernism the "destruction of genre" is the refusal of "genre assumptions" as "heteronomous conceptual determinations of what a work of art ought to be" (154). In Kantian language (see Chapter 4), the new in modern art presents itself as "a claim to art with which no knowledge is equal" (154).

Relations between text and context, innovation and the status quo, formal experimentation and dominant norms are among the issues addressed by the Constance School. Hans Robert Jauss (1921–97) and Wolfgang Iser (1926–2007) initiated a new school of criticism *c.* 1970, while working at the University of Constance. They developed Heidegger's and Gadamer's hermeneutics (Heidegger's pupil, Hans-Georg Gadamer published his *Truth and Method* in 1960) in the direction of a literary theory and history of reading and reception. Jauss's "Literary History as a Challenge to Literary Theory" (1969, 1970) is one of the inaugural texts of the school. His "aesthetics of reception" (Jauss 1982, 19) considers a hitherto neglected aspect of literature, the "dimension of its reception and influence" (18). The new literary text makes its entrance into the world in relation to a "horizon of expectations" (22): literary norms and "rules familiar from earlier texts" (23). Often it "evokes" this horizon of expectations, which it will then either reproduce or alter (23). In this manner the text "predisposes its audience to a very specific kind of reception", so that interpretation is determined as "the carrying out of specific instructions in a process of directed perception" (23). Some texts "break through" their contemporary horizon of expectations "so completely" that a readership "can only gradually be found for them" (26). Having reconstructed the horizon of expectations at the time of the production of a literary text, the critic can measure its "aesthetic distance", its "disparity" from that horizon of expectations. Aesthetic distance can be to some degree "objectified historically" in terms of readers' and critics' reactions at the time of publication (25). The aesthetic distance with which a text "opposes the expectations of its first audience" is an important "criterion for the determination" of its "aesthetic value" (25). However, this distance will "disappear for later readers" – their horizon has already been changed by this text; novelty has become familiarity (25). The reconstruction of the initial horizon of expectations, to the extent that it is possible, "brings into view the hermeneutic difference" between "former and current" understandings of a text, questioning the idea that the text's "objective meaning" is "determined once and for all" (28).

Far from aiming to understand a text "properly" by reconstructing its original horizon of expectations, Jauss argues that this is impossible because the original "historical horizon is always already enveloped within the horizon of the present" and merges with it (Jauss 1982, 29–30). Jauss's aim is the dynamic reconstruction of the entire history of a text's reception as the "successive unfolding" and actualization of a text's "potential for meaning" and, "in a controlled fashion[,] the 'fusion of horizons'" (30). Such analytical separation of horizons of expectation followed by their new, controlled synthesis does not claim to be definitive, acknowledging instead the "historical standpoint" of the "literary historian" doing the reconstruction (34). Complexity is enhanced by combining diachronic mapping of a text's reception over time and synchronic mapping of the "system of relationships in the literature" of this text's "historical moment" (36) and by treating literary history as "a 'special history' in its relationship to 'general history'" (39). For Jauss literature has a "*socially formative*" role "in the emancipation of mankind from its natural, religious, and social bonds" (45). Attention to literature's moral (as well as aesthetic) distance will reveal this history, but questions of reception are paramount. For example, at what point(s) of reception is the novelty of a literary text actualized?

Iser's "Interaction between Text and Reader" (1980) outlines his phenomenology of the reader's experience. He focuses on *gaps*, *blanks*, *vacancies* or *vacant positions* in the text, arguing that they have the vital role of directing and organizing the reader's experience. A textual gap in its simplest form is a lacuna inviting and even pressing the reader to step in and complete the text: for example, in Thomas Hardy's *Tess of the d'Urbervilles* is Tess raped or does she consent to sex with Alec? But Iser is more interested in gaps arising out of juxtapositions of different perspectives and themes. There are "four main perspectives in narration: those of the narrator, the characters, the plot, and the fictitious reader", and Iser attends to their juxtaposition and to further juxtapositions – for example, among characters, when the "hero's perspective" is "set against that of the minor characters" (113). According to Iser, the reader is directed by the text to synthesize the different perspectives, thus filling in the gap between them: the reader's "wandering viewpoint travels between all these segments" and "intertwines them"; the meaning of the text "is brought about by their constant intertwining through the reader in the reading process" (113). The reader thus composes the meaning of the text in a two-way dialogic interaction between text and reader, so that the text has two poles: an "artistic pole" – "the author's text" – and an "aesthetic pole" – the text's actualization by the reader (106). The text is "virtual" and "situated somewhere between the two" poles (106). Iser is anxious to stave off subjectivism and relativism, stressing that gaps are "guiding devices" that "control" the communication between text and reader (110, 112). The reader's activity is "to a great extent regulated" by them (113). The reader's wandering is directed, so that "the reader's viewpoint cannot proceed arbitrarily" (118). Iser insists that reading "produce[s] a determinate relationship" between the "interacting segments" (114), leading to a "determinate meaning" (116). However, is meaning determined in the same manner by each reader, irrespective of their widely differing determinations? Iser determines meaning at the cost of leaving the reader indeterminate. What is lacking is a sense of the reader's situation.

Existentialism (Sartre, Beauvoir, Fanon): freedom and situation

Existentialism was a Francophone movement led by Jean-Paul Sartre (1905–80) in the 1940s and 1950s: his major philosophical work, *Being and Nothingness*, was published in 1943. Another major figure was his close collaborator and life-partner Simone de Beauvoir (1908–86). Important precursors are Søren Kierkegaard, Fyodor Dostoevsky, Friedrich Nietzsche and Franz Kafka. Sartre's contemporary, Algeria-born Albert Camus, considered an existentialist by many critics, distanced himself from the term, possibly to highlight his differences from Sartre. The Martinican Frantz Fanon (1925–61), two decades younger than Sartre and Beauvoir, was strongly influenced by, and in turn influenced, the existentialists and collaborated with Sartre. Existentialism is a movement both artistic and theoretical, Sartre and Beauvoir's enormous combined output of writing including philosophy, literary theory and criticism, feminist theory, novels, plays and life-writing.

I will outline Sartre's main concepts and distinctions – freedom; existence and essence; immanence and transcendence – and his analysis of the complementarity of the writer's and the reader's freedom (the writer synthesizing the world and the reader synthesizing the literary text). Beauvoir, one of the founders of contemporary feminist theory, analyses patriarchy and calls on her women readers to resist their complicity with it; her reading of D. H. Lawrence engages with the relation of literature and patriarchy. Fanon, one of the founders of contemporary postcolonial theory and criticism, addresses the colonized in their struggle against the French Empire and analyses colonial and decolonizing culture. "Freedom" is perhaps the central existentialist term: we act in a distinctly human way only when we choose to embrace the freedom that defines our existence and characterizes all our acts.

Intensely preoccupied with politics, the existentialists lived in traumatic times: two world wars, the occupation of France, a collaborationist French government, the revelation of the Holocaust, the rise of the superpowers, the Cold War and anticolonial struggles. After World War II they struggled to come to terms with the barbarism of the Holocaust and with the French Empire as a system of domination and oppression. They condemned both unequivocally. As reported by Hannah Arendt in *Eichmann in Jerusalem: A Report on the Banality of Evil* (1963), during his trial in Jerusalem in 1960, the high-ranking Nazi officer Adolf Eichmann, Gestapo Head of Jewish Affairs, infamously made this defence for the crimes against humanity of which he was accused: "I obeyed orders". Eichmann's response denies his freedom and therefore his responsibility, his guilt. His defence was made by many, those prosecuted in the trials after World War II, but by very many others: politicians, military personnel, administrators, civilians, in Germany and France (and of course other European countries) who escaped or were not called to justice and who played an active role in the Holocaust. Those who were not active but knew of human rights abuses and did nothing had to find other excuses if challenged by themselves or others, but excuses they would be, or lies. (French collaboration with the German occupation remained a taboo subject until recently. I must acknowledge here that human rights abuses were not exclusive to the Nazis and their allies.)

In *Existentialism and Humanism* (1946), Sartre's answer to the attitude represented by Eichmann is: we always have a choice; we are, as humans, free to choose. Humans are "condemned to be free" (Sartre 1948, 34) – "Man is nothing else but that which he makes of himself" (28). When you treat reality and yourself as something that makes it impossible for you to choose, you choose not to choose, you turn yourself into an object, you are in "bad faith" (*mauvaise foi*). But you are not a being characterized by an essence that determines who you are or what you do. "*[E]xistence* comes before *essence*" (26), Sartre declares. He gives the example of a tool. The tool has an essence – its function – which precedes its existence. Human beings, collectively and individually, have no such function that determines their nature and what they will do. There are any number of facts or purported facts about humans, and with regard to each of us there are facts that constitute our individual identity (gender, race, social class, sexuality, character and abilities, etc.). But these facts do not amount to a function, an essence. We wish they did, as Sartre points out. Our great desire is to feel full of an unassailable sense of ourselves, to be quite sure of who we are and what we should do with our lives. But there is something in us which makes this impossible: "consciousness". For Sartre consciousness is a kind of nothingness that negates determination. We desire to be able to derive what we should do, how we should behave, as a kind of logical consequence of who we are, but we are unable to do so because consciousness negates any sense of sure identity or sure grounds for decision. Sartre's ideas have clear connections with Descartes and his dualism between spirit (mind) and extension (matter), Kant's moral philosophy and Nietzsche's atheism. For Sartre and for Nietzsche, perhaps once we had a sense of essence, derived from belief in a creator god, but God has gone, and also all gods, all sense of some one final metaphysical truth of ourselves and the world. In the Sartrean universe we are condemned to be free, never to be excused from the responsibility of choice, yet never to be able to feel justified as we desire to be, in our choices or in our sense of our being.

In *What Is Literature?* (1948) Sartre offers an existentialist interpretation of the tasks of the writer and the reader. He argues that the world in itself is meaningless; it is a mute mass of unrelated elements. The task of the writer is to synthesize the world. Writing is exemplary as an activity synthesizing the world, though we all do this synthesizing constantly without being aware of it. Here is an everyday example. You are about to meet your friend Jean-Paul in the pub. When you walk into the crowded interior, the pub is an infinite mass of details. You synthesize it by asking some questions. Where is the bar so that I can get a drink and quench my thirst? Is this animated voice behind my back my friend Jean-Paul? Here is an aesthetic example. You are looking at an ostensibly photorealist landscape painting by Gerhard Richter, his 1987 "Apple Trees". You perceive an aesthetic relation between this tree and this road or between this bit of green, this bit of blue and this bit of white. These relations are not inherent in the landscape, but are synthesized by Richter and then resynthesized by the viewer. Lily Briscoe, the painter in Virginia Woolf's *To the Lighthouse*, is attracted to Mrs Ramsay and her motherly behaviour and keeps trying to paint Mrs Ramsay with one of her children. However, Lily is only able to finish her portrait after Mrs Ramsay's death – in the absence of her object or even at the expense of her object – and the finished painting is a successful portrait only because Lily has found a successful relation between colours, lines, planes, masses (Woolf 1964, 167ff.).

If writing is, in exemplary fashion, freedom to synthesize the world, what is invisible to the writer is their own work, Sartre claims. The writer is least capable of synthesizing their work, relying on the reader's own freedom to synthesize it. Only then is the writer's work complete. To "make" the literary object "come into view a concrete act called reading is necessary", and the literary object "lasts only as long as this act can last. Beyond that, there are only black marks on paper" (Sartre 1993, 28). The "writer appeals to the reader's freedom to collaborate in the production of his work" (32). This is why the "writer should not seek to *overwhelm*" or to "*affect*" emotionally (34): "One does not write for slaves. The art of prose is bound up with the only régime in which prose has meaning, democracy" (47). While Sartre contrasts democracy and fascism, his view of democracy after World War II, and after the defeat of Germany and its allies, is far from complacent:

> The bad novel aims to please by flattering, whereas the good one is an exigence and an act of faith … It would be inconceivable that this unleashing of generosity provoked by the writer could be used to authorize an injustice … [T]he moment I feel myself a pure freedom I cannot bear to identify myself with a race of oppressors. Thus, I require of all freedoms that they demand the liberation of coloured people against the white race and against myself in so far as I am a part of it …
> (45–6)

Sartre is an early supporter of the postwar decolonization movements. In a Francophone context, the 1930s *négritude* movement is Sartre's contemporary artistic movement expressing a nascent anti-racist and anticolonial culture. The *négritude* movement sought to combat racism, to redefine blackness in positive terms and to reform the French Empire, stopping short of asking for independence. While the medium of the *négritude* movement is predominantly poetry, Sartre (like Bakhtin before him, see Chapter 7) strongly favours prose and the novel in *What Is Literature?* This inhibits his encounter with the *négritude* poets, such as the Martinican Aimé Césaire, whose pathbreaking, experimental *Notebook of a Return to My Native Land* was published in 1939, and the Senegalese poet Léopold Sédar Senghor. More generally, Sartre at this point has political reservations about the experimental "pure" art that Adorno considers most politically radical. However, if Sartre seems sceptical of the power of poetry in *What Is Literature?* he stresses its potential shortly afterwards in "Black Orpheus" (1948), as we will discuss.

Adorno's "Commitment" (1962) is a critique of Sartre's *What Is Literature?* published in response to the 1962 German translation. Adorno discards Sartre's optimism – his hope that freedom and political action is always possible – and, in a spirit of thoroughgoing pessimism, claims that the world "permanently puts a pistol to men's heads" (Adorno 1977b, 180). Adorno's reading of contemporary reality is that it is a "predetermined reality" of "unfreedom" – "the whole administered universe" – where "freedom becomes an empty claim" (180). Sartre is wrong to believe that "human beings are in control and decide" (182). Sartre's response to Adorno might be that he is *choosing not to choose* – choosing political apathy. Adorno himself explicitly valorizes a "dawning awareness of the approaching paralysis of politics" (as if he is diagnozing an objective global trend) and avers that this is "not a time for political art" (194). Having just declared all political resistance futile, Adorno then reasserts his familiar solution: formally experimental modernist art. He claims that, exiled from the world, "politics has migrated into autonomous art" (194). Renewing Bloch's critique of realism (Chapter 7) and anticipating the anti-representation ethos of the poststructuralist Barthes, he asserts that art "resist[s] by its form alone" (180). In their introduction to Adorno's essay, Rodney Livingstone, Perry Anderson and Francis Mulhern defend Sartre in the name of 1960s political activism. Criticizing Adorno's view of capitalism as "purged of contradiction", his "disarray" in response to the "great student demonstrations of the sixties" and his "magical" view of autonomous art, they endorse Sartre's "belief in the efficacy of individual engagement" (Livingstone *et al.* 1977b, 147, 150).

Rhiannon Goldthorpe's "Understanding the Committed Writer" is a sympathetic account of Sartre's changing and increasingly complex understanding of "commitment" (*engagement*) in literature. In *What Is Literature?* Sartre distinguishes "commitment" from "bearing witness" (*témoignage*) and "involvement" (*embrigadement*). "Involvement" is faithful allegiance to a "specific political party" (Goldthorpe 1992, 142) and set of political objectives. Poetry is the medium of "bearing witness" to historical suffering and failure (142). Lucid prose is the medium of "commitment": a writer is "committed" when he "tries to be as lucidly and as completely conscious of his involvement as possible" (Sartre quoted in Goldthorpe 1992, 142). Sartre is very aware that the writer's freedom might be heavily conditioned by an extremely bleak historical situation, but he claims that a "lucid view of the darkest situation is already, in itself, an act of optimism" in that it "implies that this situation is *thinkable*" and that we can thereby "go beyond it and resolve what to do against it, even if our decisions are desperate" (Sartre quoted in Goldthorpe 1992, 143).

However, in "Black Orpheus", his preface to an anthology of African and Caribbean poetry edited by Senghor, and in *Mallarmé, or the Poet of Nothingness* (*L'Engagement de Mallarmé*) (written from 1948 to 1952 but published in 1979), Sartre acknowledges "commitment" in pure poetry, particularly in a Mallarmean aesthetic of allusion (see Chapter 5). In his multi-volume book on Flaubert, *The Family Idiot* (1971–2), Sartre interprets Flaubert, commonly associated with pure art (*l'art pour l'art*), as committed. In "Black Orpheus", effectively, "commitment" and "bearing witness" begin to "converge" (Goldthorpe 1992, 159). Bearing witness to suffering – and emotion more generally – is no longer considered passive and defeatist or associated with overwhelming the freedom of the reader, but is viewed as a "positive project" (159): "The black man enters into history in that the intuition of suffering confers upon him a collective past and a future goal" (Sartre quoted in Goldthorpe 1992, 160). Sartre now substantially reconfigures the relation of writer and reader. The (black) writer now aims to "evoke, in deliberate shadow, the silenced object through allusive, never direct, words" (Sartre quoted in Goldthorpe 1992, 161), yoking this Mallarmean aesthetic to a "commitment to change" (158). The (white) reader extends a "sympathetic comprehension" (158). He is an "empathetic mediator" (159), open to the legitimacy of the subjective experience, values and goals of marginalized and objectified social others – "to understand is to elucidate in terms of goals" (Sartre quoted in Goldthorpe 1992, 149). Most importantly, reading is an encounter that "changes" the reader (159), an example of which is the preface we are reading and Sartre's conversion in favour of the "committed" nature of Césaire's experimentalism and *négritude* poetry more generally. Another work of importance for literary theory is Sartre's *Notebooks for an Ethics* (written from 1947 to 1948 and published posthumously), which develops further the reciprocity, mutual respect and assistance between writer and reader. Committed writing comes face to face with committed reading. In *The Problem of Method* (1960; also translated as *Search for a Method*) Sartre continues to complicate the dialectical relation between the writer's project and their situation and social conditioning. A major question is that of the "opacity" and "intelligibility" of the writer's historical experience. Sartre explores these issues in *The Family Idiot*, reading Flaubert's collapse at Pont-l'Évèque in 1844 as a hysterical episode symptomatic of his unconscious resistance to his father, his class and his historical moment.

***

In recent years contemporary feminist thinkers, from Michèle Le Doeuff to Toril Moi to Miranda Fricker, have been demonstrating Beauvoir's originality against her own intentions. Beauvoir presents *The Second Sex* (1949; Beauvoir 1953 and 2011) as a text of existentialist ethics applying Sartre's thought to a new field, patriarchy and the situation of women as an oppressed and dominated group (Le Doeuff 1991, 59). This is an example of Beauvoir's tendency to position her work as *second texts* dependent on Sartre's, in a manner ironically reminiscent or symptomatic of the workings of patriarchy as described in *The Second Sex*.

Beauvoir opens Book 2 of *The Second Sex* with the statement: "One is not born, but rather becomes, a woman" (Beauvoir 1953, 273). She argues that patriarchy determines women as a putative transhistorical and unchanging "essence", creating and imposing on them a patriarchal mythology reproduced and embellished by writers and thinkers. When real women's existential situations and choices deviate from this *essence*, instead of concluding that it misrepresents the diversity of women, it might rather be concluded that the woman in question is unfeminine and has to mend her ways. According to Beauvoir, patriarchy has created binary oppositions: subject/object, transcendence/immanence, spirit/flesh, culture/nature, life/death, day/night, etc. The valued terms in each binary opposition (subject, transcendence, spirit, culture, life, day) are reserved for man, while the undesirable terms (object, immanence, flesh, nature, death, night) are projected onto woman. Women are thereby fixed into the position of the Other or othered. However, "every existent [that is women and men] is at once immanence and transcendence" (Beauvoir 1953, 261); we are both situation and freedom, hence the "ambiguity" of our situation, according to Beauvoir. Similarly, to say that woman is flesh of course misrecognizes that "man also is flesh for woman; and woman is not merely a carnal object" (262). The same observation is true of the other binary oppositions. Beauvoir summarizes this argument in a Sartrean language reminiscent of his *Existentialism and Humanism*: "An existent *is* nothing other than what he does ... [E]ssence does not precede existence: in pure subjectivity, the human being *is not anything*" (264). However, in view of

Beauvoir's analysis, Sartre's insistence that we are distinctively human only to the extent that we transcend our situation is revealed as unwittingly translating the situation and experience of being a member of a dominant and privileged group (his own experience, one of being conditioned to be free) into the norm of authentic humanity; while unwittingly translating the situation and the experience of being a member of a dominated group into a moral flaw, an example of "bad faith" (Le Doeuff 1991, 60). Sartre's black-and-white distinction between free choice and bad faith blocks the question of the degree of unfreedom in one's situation. His understanding of situation as what is to be transcended fails to distinguish between the divergent situations of French men and women at the time: men are freer, less constrained than women. *The Second Sex*, by contrast, offers richly detailed phenomenological descriptions of varieties of French female experience in the first half of the twentieth century. In the "Conclusion" Beauvoir reprises two aspects of her analysis that effectively deviate from Sartre's work. First, she names the situation of women a form of "slavery of half of humanity" and calls for its abolition and women's "independent existence" as a precondition of mutual recognition between men and women (686). Second, Beauvoir points to an ethics of ambiguity already suggested in the "Introduction", to be practised by both men and women: "In both sexes is played out the same drama of the flesh and the spirit, of finitude and of transcendence", and both sexes should live out and "assume the ambiguity" of their situation (684). (See further her 1947 book, *The Ethics of Ambiguity*.) She also questions how the philosophy of freedom, being so agonistic, is compatible with human love relationships.

While Beauvoir is unwilling to criticize Sartre, she argues that D. H. Lawrence's texts unwittingly reproduce patriarchal mythology. Lawrence is critical of egoism, for example Gerald's egoism in *Women in Love*, and "it would at first appear that neither of the two sexes has an advantage", in that "[n]either is subject" in the existentialist sense (Beauvoir 1953, 228). However, Lawrence's monogamous heterosexual couplings are built not on "mutuality" but on male "supremacy" (228). Lawrence's *Fantasia of the Unconscious* roots "[t]hought and action. … in the phallus", making them male prerogatives and turning men's "social advantage" into a "cosmic advantage" (229). Women will not think and act for themselves – "She ought to believe in you, and in the deep purpose you stand for" (Lawrence quoted in Beauvoir 1953, 230) – and Lawrence equally frowns upon women's "independent sensuality" (230) and "sexual autonomy" (233) and has a "horror of lesbians" (231). As a result, Lawrence's provocative critique of consciousness and the Western split of spirit and body ends up, disappointingly, reproducing the sexual status quo: his advocated male "autonomous submission" to the "cosmic order" is practically indistinguishable from a "sovereign decision", while his women are made to conform to the "ideal of the 'true woman'" – the fully compliant slave who "unreservedly accepts being defined as the Other" (233).

In the introduction to *The Second Sex*, Beauvoir claims that "women do not say 'we' … The reason for this is that women lack concrete means for organizing themselves into a unit" that "can stand face to face with the correlative unit" (Beauvoir 1953, 18) or (in the new translation) "that could posit itself in opposition" (Beauvoir 2011, 8). What is lacking is a common space to support women's solidarity against patriarchy. The factory and the racially segregated community are such spaces for working-class and black struggles, respectively, but women are dispersed in private spaces. White middle-class women "feel solidarity" (Beauvoir 1953, 18) with men of their class and race, rather than with working-class and black women. *The Second Sex* calls for solidarity among women across class and race boundaries and offers itself as a virtual space supporting this difficult solidarity. Beauvoir is especially addressing white middle-class women like herself, who benefit materially from their alliance and complicity with white middle-class men, effectively asking them to abandon the benefits of idleness and luxury for the precarious and difficult pursuit of solidarity and freedom. This call to organized political action supports Le Doeuff's claim that "for twenty years, *The Second Sex* was the [women's] movement before the movement" (Le Doeuff 1991, 57).

In the chapter "The Independent Woman" Beauvoir addresses budding women writers and positions herself as an older sister advising younger ones. Like Virginia Woolf in *A Room of One's Own* (see Chapter 8), she sketches out a history of women's writing (focusing, surprisingly, on women's writing in English, with the exception of the highly praised Colette) accompanied by a double reading strategy. First, she identifies the "limitations" of women's writing and relates them to "woman's situation" (Beauvoir 1953, 671). Second, she gives encouragement and practical advice. She values "effort", boldness (664) and an "apprenticeship in abandonment and transcendence" or "liberty" (669); she authorizes women writers to feel "responsible for the universe" (670); she praises "insurgent females" (667) and rejects "reasonable modesty" (666). She argues – effectively against Sartre's *What Is Literature?* – that lucidity is not enough because "the truth itself is ambiguity" (668). Her call, "The free woman is just being born" (672), energizes new women writers to live and write freely.

Written "on the occasion of" Beauvoir's death in 1986, Luce Irigaray's "Equal or Different?" is a disturbing matricidal homage to Beauvoir (Whitford 1991a, 23). Irigaray, one of the founders of 1970s "sexual difference" feminism, had received Beauvoir's call to new women writers: "What woman has not been invigorated by it?" (Irigaray 1991b, 30). However, Irigaray argues that those who respond properly to Beauvoir's call to be free need to reject her in favour of Irigaray's own "sexual difference" feminism. "Sexual difference" feminism, first, insists on the political autonomy of women's struggles from other liberation/emancipatory movements, socialist, anticolonial, antiracist, etc.: "It is urgent for women's struggles ... to realize the importance of issues that are specific to them" (33). Second, in relation to those other movements, Irigaray posits the necessary priority of feminism because of the necessary priority of gender (or rather sexual difference) over class, race, etc.: "the primary and irreducible division" is one between "*two* [sex-specific] *genres*" (32–3). Third, she claims "sexual difference" feminism to be the only legitimate form of feminism: "The exploitation of women is based upon sexual difference and can only be resolved through sexual difference" (32). Fourth, the core task of "sexual difference" feminism is one of redefining femininity in positive terms: "defining the values of belonging to a sex-specific *genre* … giving, or restoring, cultural values to female sexuality" (32). Fifth, polarizing Beauvoir's "equality" feminism and her own "sexual difference" feminism, Irigaray accuses Beauvoir of "suppress[ing] sexual difference" – the largest-scale "genocide" in history (32)! As Whitford comments, Irigaray understands Beauvoir's calls for equality as "equivalent to the imposition of a male norm" on women and considers this to be "genocide: of women" (Whitford 1991a, 23–4). Surely, to accuse Beauvoir's equality feminism of genocide is excessive to the point of meaninglessness. The spectacle of a new generation of male thinkers who claim their originality by exaggerating their difference from their fathers and ritually killing their fathers is common enough. But Irigaray's psychodrama in this text is intriguing: Beauvoir is initially treated as a replenishing Kleinian "good breast", then quickly turned into a genocidal "bad breast" (as discussed in Chapter 6), killed by Irigaray to save women. (One of Irigaray's accusations against Beauvoir is that she didn't mother her during the traumatic reception of her first book, *Speculum of the Other Woman* [1974].) In the terms of Irigaray's influential work on the matricide underlying Western thought (see Irigaray 1991a, 34ff.), Irigaray commits a matricide of Beauvoir on the occasion of her death.

In 1994 Toril Moi compares Beauvoir to Fanon, and then assesses the respective merits of Beauvoir and French difference feminists. Moi argues that Fanon's and Beauvoir's contribution to founding contemporary postcolonial theory and feminist theory, respectively, is their demonstration of the inadequacy of both Marxist and "traditionally bourgeois" models in theorizing racism and sexism (Moi 1998, 86). However, whereas Fanon's 1952 *Black Skin, White Masks* embraces a black anti-racist racism positively redefining and politically mobilizing blackness autonomously, *The Second Sex*'s call to feminist action fails to posit the political autonomy of feminism and the value of a redefined femininity: its "deepest political flaw … consists in Beauvoir's failure to grasp the progressive potential of 'femininity' as a political discourse", and Beauvoir at the time also "vastly underestimated the potential political impact of an independent woman's movement" (86). Moi understands this divergence within the concrete political situation of the late 1940s: "While the struggle against colonialism was gaining momentum[,] … there was no sign of the future explosion of the women's movement" (87). However, in November 1971, when Beauvoir joined the Women's Liberation Movement, she was quick to affirm its autonomy: "I realised that we must fight for the situation of women, here and now, before our dreams of socialism come true … [I]t is absolutely essential for women to take their destiny in their own hands" (Beauvoir quoted in Moi 1998, 87). So if by 1971 Beauvoir had already recognized the autonomy of women's struggles, where exactly does the antagonism between Beauvoir and Irigaray (writing since the 1970s) lie? For Moi it lies between Beauvoir's purely strategic sense of the need for "independent feminist mobilization of women as women", whose ultimate aim is the disappearance of gender, and 1970s difference feminists' "focus on women's difference, often without regard for other social movements, and certainly with distinct distaste" for the ideal of equality (87–8). According to Moi, as of the 1990s this was still the most significant conflict that divided feminists. On the side of Beauvoir, there are "those who accept the [purely] strategic use of intellectual and political separatism in order to achieve a new, truly egalitarian society"; and on the side of Irigaray, "those who are convinced that women's interests are best served by the establishment of an enduring regime of sexual difference in every social and cultural field" (88). Clearly siding with Beauvoir, Moi reaffirms *The Second Sex*'s horizon of liberation: "the aim of feminism is to abolish itself" (89).

Le Doeuff's "Engaging with Simone de Beauvoir", originally delivered in 2001 as a keynote address at the Ninth International Simone de Beauvoir Conference, announces Beauvoir's resurrection after Irigaray's matricide: "Times have changed. We have changed them. It is no longer possible to claim, in the light of a certain New French Feminism, that Beauvoir is obsolete" (Le Doeuff 2006, 12). In considering directions for future work, Le Doeuff calls on readers to acknowledge the conflicts between Sartre and Beauvoir.

Miranda Fricker focuses on Beauvoir's *The Prime of Life* (*La Force de l'age*, 1960), in order to explore the emergence of Beauvoir, distinct from Sartre, as an original thinker of ambiguity. Beauvoir, Fricker argues, identifies as a writer rather than a philosopher and uses life-writing as the medium best suited to her thought and her sense that reality and the self are in excess of, and fleeing, one's attempts at synthesis. Whereas Sartre's response to the German Occupation in *Existentialism and Humanism* was that we are free to choose, Beauvoir's response was to acknowledge her complicity: "my life was not a story of my own telling, but a compromise between myself and the world at large" (Beauvoir quoted in Fricker 2003, 209). For Sartre in *What Is Literature?* the writer's task is to synthesize the world; for Beauvoir it is to acknowledge that "reality extends beyond anything that can be said about it" and to confront it as it is – "full of ambiguities, baffling, and impenetrable" – without "simplifying … ambiguities nor swaddling them in false syntheses" (Beauvoir quoted in Fricker 2003, 219). Beauvoir also strongly objects to abstract theorizing that divorces thinkers from their situation to lend their thought universal applicability – this is an "obsessional attitude" that endows "tentative patterns with universal insight and applicability" (Beauvoir quoted in Fricker 2003, 219). Fricker argues that Beauvoir identified as a writer rather than as a philosopher because "philosophy as she found it" was obsessional and "incapable of making room for ambiguity", while literature was "better able to leave ambiguity in the picture" (219). In relation to Beauvoir's understanding of the domination of women *qua* women in *The*

Second Sex, Beauvoir conveys how difficult it was at the time: "What I lacked was the idea of 'situation,' ... [b]ut there was no one, outside the framework of the class struggle, who would give me what I needed" (Beauvoir quoted in Fricker 2003, 209–10). ("Situation" could be understood in [Marxist] terms of capitalist exploitation, but the theoretical resources to understand it in terms of patriarchy were not readily available, hence the difficulty of theorizing feminist "autonomy".) Fricker therefore claims that Beauvoir's switch of focus from class to gender oppression was "a feat of political imagination" (214).

The most interesting aspect of Beauvoir's thinking, in Fricker's reading, is Beauvoir's use of narrative, particularly life-writing, to build alliance and solidarity with her past, scattered and fleeing selves. The writer is not a sovereign synthesizing consciousness understanding past selves: "self-knowledge is impossible, and the best one can hope for is self-revelation" to the reader (Beauvoir quoted in Fricker 2003, 223). Fricker argues that Beauvoir understands the self to be "broken up" (224) and fragmented because of its violent encounters with history: "History burst over me, and I dissolved into fragments ... scattered over the four quarters of the globe, linked by every nerve in me to each and every other individual" (Beauvoir quoted in Fricker 2003, 225). Fricker claims that Beauvoir primarily addresses female readers; and her alliance-building with her readers – her "feminist commitment to female solidarity" (226) – promises to bring out, through the reader, "the 'unity' to that 'scattered, broken' object that is her life" (226).

Frantz Fanon was born into the black middle class of Martinique in 1925, a French colony at the time and still a part of France today. His *Black Skin, White Masks* (1952), written in France, mixes existentialism, psychoanalysis, *négritude* poetry (Fanon was a former student of Césaire, who, like Senghor, was also a prominent politician) and phenomenological description of the experience of being a black man in France after the war, combining critique and poetic prose. In 1953 Fanon moved from France to Algeria, a French colony at the time, to work as a psychiatrist and psychoanalyst. He became involved in the Algerian liberation movement and emerged as a prominent theoretician of the exceptionally fierce Algerian liberation struggle and, more generally, of the anticolonial struggle and the process of decolonization in Africa. Fanon's major work of this period is *The Wretched of the Earth*, published in 1961 just before his early death, one year before Algerian independence in 1962. The decolonization of Africa was, by then, well underway. Libya gained independence in 1951; Sudan, Tunisia and Morocco in 1956; Ghana in 1957; Ivory Coast, Senegal, Mali and Nigeria in 1960. In the process a national middle class had emerged and was becoming powerful in these newly independent countries.

The important Chapter 5 of *Black Skin, White Masks*, "L'expérience vecue du noir" – oddly translated in the English-language edition as "The Fact of Blackness" – is about "lived experience", *expérience vecue* (not about a "fact"). In this chapter Fanon undertakes an explicit critique of Sartre's "Black Orpheus". If Goldthorpe's claim (discussed above) is that writing "Black Orpheus" and his encounter with *négritude* poetry changed Sartre, Fanon's claim is that Sartre crushed *négritude* poetry in his efforts to fit it into his pre-existing schemas and prejudices. Fanon does not so much as mention Beauvoir's *The Second Sex* – surprisingly, in view of the degree of resonance between the two texts. Equally surprisingly, his attitude towards "the woman of color" is, at best, "I know nothing of her" (Fanon 2008, 138). Like Beauvoir's reading of patriarchy, Fanon argues that racism reserves the position of subject for the white man and imposes the status of object on the black man, "seal[ing]" the black man into "crushing objecthood" (82). Using Sartre's language, Fanon claims: "I came into the world imbued with the will to find a meaning in things, … and then I found that I was an object in the midst of other objects" (82). Unlike Beauvoir, Fanon is more than willing to criticize Sartre, starting with his failure in *Being and Nothingness* to spell out that "the white man is … the master" (106). In "Black Orpheus" Sartre is using a Hegelian Marxist frame (which, incidentally, he shares with Senghor). History has a dialectical logic of thesis, antithesis, synthesis, within which *négritude* is a necessary but minor stage towards proletarian revolution and the emancipation of humanity as a whole: "negritude appears as the minor term of a dialectical progression" (Sartre quoted in Fanon 2008, 101). In Fanon's eyes Sartre attributes autonomous black acts of freedom to the workings of a disembodied historical necessity, thereby robbing them of their subjectivity. In addition Sartre denies black anti-racist and anticolonial struggles any autonomy and appropriates them as necessarily minor terms in class struggles. (The issue of "autonomy", discussed earlier in relation to Beauvoir and Irigaray, is central to Fanon as well.) In Beauvoir's terms Sartre is unable to understand a "situation" in terms other than those of class. In Fanon's terms Sartre "has destroyed black zeal" (103). Fanon describes the experience of being reobjectified by one's most powerful ally, in terms anticipating Beauvoir's language of fragmentation in *The Prime of Life*: "I burst apart" into fragments (82); "my negritude … had been broken to pieces" (106). However, Fanon is ambivalent in his attitude towards negritude.

Fanon, a Martinican, chose to identify as Algerian in solidarity with the Algerian liberation struggle; he chose identification over identity and "essence" (what/who one is). The prominent postcolonial theorist Homi K. Bhabha, in his foreword to the 1986 edition of *Black Skin, White Masks*, argued that Fanon's choice as well as his theory provide support for an anti-essentialist politics of alliance, solidarity and imaginary identification, coupled with the recognition of the "artifice" of identity (Bhabha 2008, xxxvi). Bhabha gives the example of Britain in the 1980s, when many marginalized groups chose to identify as black and to "assume the mask of the Black" (xxxvi). Bhabha also praises *Black Skin, White Masks* for highlighting "unresolved" political antagonisms (xxxvi), an important theme in his own work (see Chapter 12). His main criticism of the book is that it "ignores gender difference" (xxxvii). Ziauddin Sardar, in his foreword to the 2008 edition of *Black Skin, White Masks*, argues that Fanon is newly relevant: (neo-)colonialism "lives on" today in America's "war on terror", which "flout[s] every international law and notion of human rights", and the racism of Fortress Europe (Sardar 2008, xix).

Fanon developed his theory of colonialism and decolonization in *The Wretched of the Earth*. Its first chapter, "Concerning Violence", defended the use of violence in anticolonial struggles and was hugely controversial at the time of publication. Fanon's defence of violence is broadly existentialist: colonialism violently denied the colonized their subjectivity and freedom, turning them into objects, and violent anticolonial action, in response to the violence of colonialism, is an affirmation of human freedom. However, decolonization is a very complex process for Fanon. In the third chapter, "The Pitfalls of National Consciousness", he addresses the historical, political and cultural potential of the new African middle class and comes to wholly negative conclusions. The historical European bourgeoisie, during its early heroic period, had genuine emancipatory aspirations for the whole of humanity. Its ideology was egalitarian, and in the spirit of the Enlightenment it sought to raise up the uncivilized and less than human (in its own eyes) to "become human" – though problematically assuming that the European middle class was itself the "prototype" of humanity and civilization (Fanon 1990, 131). By contrast, the new African bourgeoisie, in Fanon's analysis, serves a "narrow nationalism" and lacks a wider "humanist content"; in this sense, it has "assimilated" the thought of the former colonial masters "in its most corrupt form" (130–31). In particular, it is self-interested, exploitative and racist, according to Fanon. After independence, its aim is to inherit the "unfair advantages which are a legacy of the colonial period", previously enjoyed by the colonizers (122); it aims to continue the colonial "exploitation of agricultural workers" (124) and is happy to serve the interests of Western big business, turning the newly independent countries into "the brothel of Europe" (123). Finally, black sub-Saharan Africa and Arab North Africa have a racist view of each other, indistinguishable from the racism "coming from the settler's lips" (130). Fanon therefore has little hope that the African national bourgeoisies can bring about genuine decolonization and harbour cultural regeneration. And yet this is exactly the core task for the newly independent states, as Fanon argues in the chapter, "On National Culture".

"On National Culture" offers a bleak view of the devastation of native cultures by colonialism, and stresses the absolute centrality of cultural regeneration in anticolonial struggles and during the lengthy process of decolonization. Under colonialism and as long as it is dominant, the native culture is a "contested culture whose destruction is sought in systematic fashion" (Fanon 1990, 131). Local traditions do not disappear, but are frozen into the empty formalism of a narrow set of automatically repeated practices (styles, stereotypes and formulae) and "a few broken-down institutions" (191). Native intellectuals either take "refuge in" clinging to existing local traditions rather than innovating and breaking new ground or they embark on a "frantic acquisition" of the colonizer's culture (190).

Fanon considers that the beginning of the "struggle for national freedom" was marked by innovative cultural production (Fanon 1990, 192). Native intellectuals turn from consumers of Western culture to cultural producers, initially producing poetry and tragedy, then "novels, short stories, and essays" (192). Poetry had been the primary genre for the *négritude* movement since the late 1930s; we discussed anticolonial and postcolonial tragedy earlier, in Chapter 2. The novel is the exemplary bourgeois literary form in origin, but its appropriation by African writers was already underway when Fanon was writing. The Igbo-Nigerian Chinua Achebe had published his tragic novel on colonization, *Things Fall Apart* – the most widely read African literary text to date – in 1958. Achebe published *No Longer at Ease*, a novel on corruption within the new black middle class, in 1960, the year that Nigeria gained independence.

Fanon's argument is that this new cultural production, in its dynamic relation to anticolonial struggles, is genuinely innovative in several respects. A major point – taken up by Sartre in his introduction to *The Wretched of the Earth* – is the change of addressee. Early on in a national liberation struggle the native writer is addressing primarily the colonizer, and the moment when the native writer begins to address "his own people" is an important break (Fanon 1990, 193). The *négritude* movement was primarily addressing European readers, trying to convince them of the need for colonial reform. Equally important, Fanon argues, is formal innovation – in both collective and individual, high and low cultural production. The frozen forms of collective oral culture now thaw: oral traditions are reanimated, and storytellers introduce "increasingly fundamental" changes (193). For example, in Algeria in 1952–3 storytellers "completely overturned" traditional methods and contents and found a newly "compact" local public (193–4), while in ceramics and pottery-making empty "[f]ormalism" was abandoned (195). New cultural production therefore combines formal and political innovation: "unusual forms of expression", "fresh" themes and "the assembling of the people" (196) towards a "fundamentally different set of relations" (196).

Fanon's analysis posits a link between formal experimentation and political radicalism, in dialogue with other theoreticians of modernism. He partly espouses a modernist aesthetic of the new, but undermines established distinctions between collective and individual, oral and written, high and low culture, which others – Horkheimer and Adorno, for example – take for granted. Fanon envisages the utopian possibility of a formally experimental and truly popular national culture that mobilizes "all classes of the people" (Fanon 1990, 198). In addition, this national culture would define a "new humanism" (198), beyond narrow nationalism and towards an "international dimension" (199). Concretely, Fanon advocates an African culture that is both national and pan-African, where the two are viewed as a "joint responsibility" (199). Fanon's hope – disappointed so far – is that a culture of nation-building can open the door of humanist communication with others and can be "accompanied" by "universalizing values" (199).

Sartre's 1961 "Preface" to *The Wretched of the Earth* highlights the important issue of Fanon's addressees. Sartre positions himself explicitly as a white Frenchman addressing white Frenchmen to force upon their attention that Fanon "speaks ... never to you"; Fanon addresses "the colonized only ... For the fathers, we alone were the speakers; the sons no longer even consider us as valid intermediaries" (Sartre 1990, 9). This, of course, is a rhetorical exaggeration. Fanon addresses the colonized primarily but not exclusively. After all, in writing the preface to Fanon's text, Sartre is being called upon to authorize Fanon in the eyes of white readers. Sartre authorizes Fanon, first, by claiming Fanon's historic significance: "the Third World finds *itself* and speaks to *itself* through his voice" (9). Second, to some degree of course Fanon was Sartre's offspring, and the anticolonial struggle is endorsed by Sartre in existentialist terms: "we only become what we are by the radical and deep-seated refusal of that which others have made of us" (15). Nevertheless, Sartre is quite emphatic that the anticolonial struggle is already free of the authority of the colonial master, forging its own destiny. Europe has been left behind with its shame. Sartre declares "our complicity" (25); every white European has benefited from colonialism. Having forced his white readers to confront their concrete situation, Sartre then condemns temporizing and suggests the only authentic choice they can possibly make: "you condemn this war but do not yet dare to declare yourselves to be on the side of the Algerian fighters" (26). In 1961 Sartre has left behind the untroubled universalism of his *Existentialism and Humanism.*

Sartre has learned from Fanon's critique in *Black Skin, White Masks.* The Algerians are recognized to be actively fighting for their freedom and the French are asked to declare their support for their struggle. Sartre also endorses aspects of Fanon's thought that implicitly critique his earlier positions. For example, he echoes Fanon's understanding of the relation between colonizer and colonized when he declares: "We were men at his expense" (Sartre 1990, 20); "with us there is nothing more consistent than a racist humanism since the European has only been able to become a man by creating slaves and monsters" (22). In this sense, he positions his own thought as the offspring of Fanon – a reversal of authority – as part of a relation of reciprocity and mutual influence.

In 1993, in *Culture and Imperialism*, Edward Said assesses the legacy of *The Wretched of the Earth.* He salutes the "preposterous reordering of things" brought about by Fanon's reversal of the relation between the West and the Third World and the pathbreaking experience of "Sartre echoing Fanon (instead of the other way around)" (Said 1993, 237). Said's reading also emphasizes Fanon's utopian humanism, neglected in Sartre's "Preface". It would be a "misreading" of *The Wretched of the Earth* to focus on "violent conflict", as this text offers "something considerably beyond" it (331). Fanon's "true prophetic genius" (328) lies in his post-nationalist politics of liberation. He is the first theorist to grasp that "orthodox nationalism followed the same track hewn out by imperialism" (330), and he therefore sought to "transfigure" national independence into a "transnational force" (325). Fanon's "incandescent power" was to envisage that nationalist identity "must be overridden" in favour of "connections among people whom imperialism separated" (330). According to Said, Fanon saw liberation not as a goal but as an ongoing "*process*" that would "somehow bind the European as well as the native together in a new non-adversarial community of awareness and anti-imperialism" (331).

Conclusion

- Heidegger critiques technology and modernity. Against the modern/technological view that turns the world into an object and exploits the earth, poetry (including Heidegger's hermeneutics) hears the call of Being, of an authentic sense of the world, and becomes its voice.
- Horkheimer and Adorno see the global postwar culture industry as the ironic triumph of fascism, engineering conformity and obedience. For Adorno the modernist dissonant composition resists this system with the recalcitrance of its form.
- The Constance School focuses on the reception of literature and the interaction between text and reader. For Jauss a text's deviation from (or opposition to) established aesthetic norms and readers' expectations is a criterion of aesthetic value. Iser argues that gaps in the text invite the reader to intertwine the text's divergent and juxtaposed perspectives.
- Sartre's early emphasis on the writer's freedom to synthesize the world and the reader's freedom to synthesize the text is increasingly coupled with attention to *situation*, in part under the influence of Beauvoir and Fanon. Beauvoir's analysis of patriarchy, anti-essentialist view of gender as socially constructed and ethics of ambiguity initiate postwar feminism and remain important in contemporary feminist criticism. Fanon develops an understanding of colonialism and postcolonial impediments to decolonization that gives culture a pivotal role in the process of decolonization and the articulation of new national and transnational perspectives.

Further reading

In relation to Adorno and Horkheimer, see Adorno 1977b, 2000a, 2001a, 2002; Bernstein 2004; Bürger 1984; Horkheimer and Adorno 1998; Kaufman 2004; Rush 2004b. For Beauvoir, see Beauvoir 1953, 2001 and 2011; Fricker 2003; Irigaray 1991b; Le Doeuff 1991 and 2006; Moi 1998. For the Constance School, see Iser 1980; Jauss 1982. For Fanon, see Fanon 1990 and 2008; Sartre 1990; Bhabha 2008. For Heidegger, see Heidegger 1975b and 1975c. For Sartre, see Sartre 1948, 1964–65 and 1993; Goldthorpe 1992.

11 From structuralism to poststructuralism
Text, power, minor literature, deconstruction

Barthes, Macherey, Foucault, Deleuze and Guattari, Derrida

Roland Barthes

Roland Barthes's (1915–80) *Mythologies* (1957) is a much-loved structuralist classic and one of the inaugural documents of cultural studies. A collection of beautifully written mini essays originally written for a literary magazine, it is a highly contingent text, self-consciously connected to the mid 1950s struggles against the French Empire.

In *Twilight of the Idols* Nietzsche attacked the idealist obsession, since Plato, with an immutable and eternal world of Being. Our world, a historical and rapidly changing world of becoming, is all there is. The world of Being and eternal essences is a world of false idols (see Chapter 5). Revising Nietzsche, Jean-Paul Sartre made his own critique of "essence" a cornerstone of his philosophy. For Sartre, there is no human nature, a universal unchanging essence of commonly shared human properties. Societies and individuals install pseudo-essences in their midst, but authentic human freedom is uncompromising negation of "essence" or "nature" (see Chapter 10). Barthes, in *Mythologies*, written from 1954 to 1956, declares himself against "postulating a human essence" (Barthes 1973, 100) and deploys anti-essentialism against the French bourgeoisie and the French Empire. The essays address contemporary myths – in the form of stories and images in magazines and newspapers, consumer goods, popular entertainments, etc. – through which the French bourgeoisie naturalizes and universalizes its values as transhistorical essences. However, while Nietzsche is a multiperspectivist and Sartre rejects what he calls the objectivist fallacy, Barthes by contrast borrows from Marxism a practice of ideological demystification: removing the veils of ideology to reveal *true* historical reality (a practice which will be the focus of his autocritique in subsequent work, to be discussed shortly). Nevertheless Barthes's Marxism is highly idiosyncratic. Sartre, it will be remembered, read anticolonial struggles as, in the final instance, class struggles. Barthes, on the other hand, is our contemporary in intuiting the irreducibility of race to class: "it will never be fair to confuse in a purely gestural identity the colonial" or the "North African workers" in Paris and "the Western worker", as this would obscure the reality of colonialism and racism (102).

To give some examples, underneath the French mythology of wine, Barthes exposes the historical reality of imposing – on the Muslim population of French colonial Algeria, "on the very land of which they have been dispossessed" – a "crop of which they have no need, while they lack even bread" (Barthes 1973, 61) (the Algerian National Liberation Front [FLN] formed in 1954). Or, in relation to the popular French tourist guide to Spain published by Hachette, under its picturesque evocation of Spain as a country suffused with the spirit of Catholic tradition, removed from daily realities and ugly truths, Barthes detects "the disease of thinking in essences" (77). He then introduces elements of historical reality: he points out that Spain's fascist dictator Franco actively supported this guide (77) and observes that in Spain Catholicism has often been a "barbaric force which has stupidly defaced the earlier achievements of Muslim civilization" (75). Barthes's commitment to anticolonial struggles and the recently launched American civil rights movement is clear. He responds to those who propagate the myth of a universal human nature – as represented by the ideology of the "family of man" – with the name of Emmett Till: "why not ask the parents of Emmett Till … what *they* think of *The Great Family of Man*?" (101). The brutal assassination of the 14-year-old Emmett Till in Mississippi in August 1955 and the speedy acquittal of his respectable white killers – reported widely in French newspapers across the political spectrum – had recently triggered the inauguration of the US civil rights movement in December 1955 (see Chapter 9).

Barthes decodes the image of another black boy: a young black soldier saluting the French flag on the cover of no. 326 of *Paris Match*, published in the summer of 1955 while anticolonial struggles were well under way in Africa. Using the language of Saussure's structuralism (see Chapter 7), Barthes treats this image as a sign uniting a signifier and a signified. The signifier in this instance is the "literal, immediate presence" of the young black soldier saluting; this is the "first-order meaning" or "denotation" (Barthes 1973, 121). The signified or the "concept" is that our black colonial subjects are good subjects loyal to France; this is the "second-order meaning" or "connotation" (122). Barthes does not mention or interpret the extreme youth of the boy soldier, who seems pre-pubescent, suggesting that the colonies are immature and unready for independence from France. He argues that bourgeois myth works by distorting a third meaning, which he aims to access. Myth's "function is to distort, not to make disappear"; the "concept" is a "*deformation*" of that deeper meaning (121–2). In relation to the smart black boy-soldier eagerly saluting the French flag, the "concept distorts" the "full" meaning of the black man's "history" (122). The myth constructs a "*pseudo-physis*", a fake nature (139; *physis* means "nature" in Greek), the eternal present of the loyal black boy, that obscures historical reality: the "contingent, historical, … *fabricated*, quality of colonialism" (143). Like Brecht's theatrical practice, the "alienation effect", before him (see Chapter 7),

Barthes's critical practice aims to denaturalize the timeless myth to reveal the historical reality that could have been otherwise and can be changed. In structuralist language, to decode the myth's signified is to expose it as a motivated, highly political interpretation of reality – as a meaning-giving production – masquerading as fact. Barthes enlists as allies formally experimental writers like (the apparently conservative) Flaubert, who questioned the mimetic nature of language and literature, moving towards an "anti-nature of language" (135); Flaubert's "great merit" was grasping that language was not to "*represent* reality, but to signify it" (136). Barthes's claim is that his own critical practice is both formalist (as Barthes understands formalism) and historical: "the more a system is specifically defined in its forms" (its characteristic myth-making signifiers) "the more amenable it is to historical criticism" (112).

Barthes distinguishes clearly between myth and its radical opposite. Myth is a weapon of oppression, myth mystifies (Barthes 1973, 9). It claims "naturalness", timeless universality and mirror-like truthfulness for its significations of reality, denying its "motivation" (126) and "contingency" (123). It assumes the "perfect intelligibility of reality" and posits itself as "pure and full" reflection of it (25) – "neutral and innocent" (123) – denying its status as "literary production" (30) and "bury[ing] the traces of this production" (154). The language of myth is the would-be "'universal' language" of the "masters" (45); theirs is a "power" that "wants to hear only the language it lends us" (46), so other languages (and their interpretations of reality) remain inaudible (44). Myth's opposite is a signifying practice in the hands of the oppressed, aiming "to transform reality" (146): it is explicitly "political" (145), self-consciously "directed towards a world to be made" (154). While the oppressor hides behind mythical facts, "[t]he oppressed *makes* the world" (149). (Barthes here anticipates Foucault's influential distinction between the old historian and the "effective historian".) Barthes leaves us in no doubt that, in Sartrean terms, the myths of oppressors are inauthentic projects, the signifying practices of the struggling oppressed authentic. Barthes makes an equally stark distinction between two kinds of readers of signifying practices: his own role as the demystifying "mythologist", exposing myths to the light of historical truth, and the deceived "myth-consumer", taking the myth's "signification for a system of facts" (131).

The great merit of Barthes's clear-cut distinctions is that they allow him to condemn the French Empire and support anticolonial struggles unequivocally. Barthes self-consciously inherits them from Marxism (Marxist demystifying science and historical truth *versus* ideological illusion) and existentialism (freedom, the authentic project and choosing to choose versus self-enslavement, inauthenticity and choosing not to choose). However, with these distinctions Barthes himself concocts a myth: a new left liberationist counter-myth, but one simplifying the opaque complexity of the historical situation. By 1961 Fanon's *The Wretched of the Earth* had outlined the post-independence problem of a self-interested African bourgeoisie occupying the vacated positions of power in an emerging neocolonial world order (see Chapter 10). By claiming to lift the veil of illusion – to reveal historical truth rather than to offer an alternative and limited interpretation of reality – the revolutionary critic seeks to occupy the position of power of the mythmakers he is criticizing. He is, very much like the mythmaking bourgoisie, denying the status of what he calls historical truth as "literary production" (30) and "bury[ing] the traces" of his "production" (154, quoted above). Barthes's later work addresses such questions and conducts an autocritique.

In *Mythologies* Barthes is already oscillating between faith in, and critique of, demystification and revolution. In questioning the "perfect intelligibility of reality" and the possibility of "full" meaning (122, quoted above), he already pulls the carpet out from under his own feet. Julia Kristeva later introduced Barthes to Bakhtin, whose heteroglossic thinking allowed Barthes to develop his theory of the "text": neither myth nor revolutionary, the text is an open-ended process interweaving many perspectives but resting with none (see Chapter 7). Barthes outlines the idea of the "text" in "The Death of the Author" (1968) and "From Work to Text" (1971), his contribution to the micro-political efflorescence (or descent into anarchy, depending on one's point of view) of the late 1960s and Paris, May 1968. In "The Death of the Author" Barthes's concept of the "text" is implicitly arguing against his earlier demystifying practice in *Mythologies*: against his tripartite distinction between a literal meaning, a distorted meaning and an undistorted hidden meaning brought to the surface by Barthes. Barthes now argues that the text hides nothing: it is all surface without depth. It is woven of many threads, some of which the critic follows, rather than searching for a hidden, originating meaning: "In the multiplicity of writing, everything is to be *disentangled*, nothing *deciphered*" (Barthes 1977b, 147). The text has no ultimate meaning and no unified and fixed meaning. In this sense, the text is "constitutively ambiguous" (148). Unlike *ambiguity* in Richards, Empson and Brooks, there is no underlying unity and reconciliation of opposites (see Chapters 8 and 9). Barthes's aphorism, "it is only language which speaks, not the author" (143) reworks Mallarmé (see Chapter 5) (though we are reminded of Heidegger too, see Chapter 10) in a direction very different from T. S. Eliot's authorial impersonality (Chapter 8). One of the many threads of "The Death of the Author" (referring back to *Mythologies*) is the Marxist claim that the author is a capitalist invention whose complement is a reader-consumer eating up the ostensive meaning of the text and moving on. Barthes radicalizes Saussure's view of language as a system of differences, seeing it as a system of arbitrary classifications embodying and embedding power inequalities. In the spirit of Bakhtin, Barthes is exploring the text, beyond the dominant *monological* language of the status quo and the dominant oppositional language of Marxism, for the inexhaustible social "heteroglossia" of minor languages.

Barthes distinguishes between "text" and "work" in favour of the former. Work, unlike text, is deciphered for a hidden meaning, etc. So is "work" what Barthes used to call "myth" and are some signifying practices – for example, some pieces of literature – more work-like while others are more text-like? Barthes asks such questions in "From Work to Text" (his answers anticipating Stanley Fish, see Chapter 9): work and text are not objects but effects of two different kinds of reading. Work is the effect of a reading that sets out to consume a book by reaching and deciphering its kernel of hidden meaning. Barthes's view is that while appearing to sacrifice himself in the search for the work's objective hidden meaning, the reader is occupying an authoritarian position that objectifies and thus seeks to dominate the work (and its other readings), even when this is done in the name of liberationist aims (Marxist, feminist, postcolonial, etc.). By contrast, Barthes outlines a kind of reading that experiences the writing and itself as interconnected ongoing productive/signifying activities: "*the Text is experienced only in an activity of production*" (Barthes 1977c, 157); "the Text ... practices the infinite deferment of the signified" (158). To capture the interconnection of reading and writing in the text Barthes discards the long-established metaphor of the "*organism*" in favour of the "*network*" (161). To clarify the non-coincidence and complementarity of the joint or twin activities of writing and reading (that reading is not simply mimetic of the writing), Barthes uses the example of playing a post-serial musical score, whose "interpreter" is "called on to be in some sort the co-author of the score" in an act of "collaboration" (163). What is at stake is not shared authority (or power-sharing) but Barthes's anarchic allegiance to the irreducibility of social heterogeneity: "the Text is that *social* space which leaves no ... subject of enunciation in position as judge, master, analyst, confessor, or decoder" (164).

In *S/Z* (1973) Barthes develops some variations on earlier themes. He rejects the distinction between denotation and connotation: there is no denotation (literal meaning), as denotation is "ultimately no more than the *last* of the connotations", the one that seems to "close the reading" (Barthes 1975, 9). He varies his earlier distinction between work and text into a new distinction between "writerly" and "readerly" texts in favour of the former (4–5). He develops the decentred multiplicity of the "network" – with "a thousand entrances" and an irreducible "plurality" that is never a "whole" – as an alternative to "structure" (5–6, 12). *S/Z* is itself a network: it is composed of theoretical fragments and fragments of practical criticism analysing Balzac's novella *Sarrasine.* There are 93 theoretical fragments in larger typeface and numbered in Latin numerals. *Sarrasine* is analysed and broken up into 561 lexias – "units of reading" (13) – in smaller typeface and numbered in Arabic numerals. The analysis mobilizes five intersecting "codes" (19) or "voices" (21): hermeneutic, semantic, proairetic (related to actions), cultural and symbolic. In spite of the intensity of close reading and critical rigour directed at *Sarrasine*, Barthes strenuously denies that it has pretensions to be a definitive or objective reading. His aim is to undermine the "naturalness" (the being-there-ness) of *Sarrasine* and of his own text, *S/Z.* Readers are invited to view *S/Z* as "*manhandling*" or "*interrupting*" *Sarrasine* (15), to build multiple connections between *S/Z* and the novella, and to connect their own improper and interruptive text to the network. Barthes's complex terminology in *S/Z* is self-consciously ad hoc and does not lay claim to being a general method of reading to be taken and uncreatively applied to other texts. In this sense, Barthes is here resisting theoretical generalities in favour of an emphasis on the freedom of interpretations.

In his "Inaugural Lecture, Collège de France", delivered on the ironic occasion of his election and admission to this exclusive institution in 1977, Barthes does allow himself some such grand theoretical generalizations:

> The object in which power is inscribed, for all of human eternity, is language ... the language we speak and write ... We do not see the power which is in speech because we forget that all language is classification, and that all classifications are oppressive ... In French (I shall take obvious examples) I am obliged to posit myself as subject before stating the action which will henceforth be no more than my attribute ... In the same way, I must always choose between masculine and feminine, for the neuter and the dual are forbidden me ... [T]o utter a discourse is not, as is too often repeated, to communicate; it is to subjugate ... [L]anguage – the performance of a language system – is neither reactionary nor progressive; it is quite simply fascist; for fascism does not prevent speech, it compels speech.
>
> (Barthes 1993c, 460–61)

However, Barthes's hyperbolic gloom aside, he does call for a specific, and in his view hopeful, politics of literature, theory and criticism. Though "there is no exit" (461), no way out, no position of exteriority in relation to language (or power), we can oppose language using language, we can oppose it from within. Barthes calls this enemy within "literature", but it is clear that what he has in mind is a writing (earlier theorized by him as "text", "network", "writerly") that includes both a certain kind of literary practice (e.g. Alain Robbe-Grillet) and his own critical practice, crossing the boundary between the literary and the critical. The tactics of "literature" is a politics of destabilizing meaning, delaying or deferring the signified, destabilizing classifications and oppositions (such as masculine and feminine). "Literature" is a utopian space or an "atopic site" (472) – *u-topia* is etymologically a non-site – within language, in the sense that it happens in-between established fields (e.g. literature and criticism) and in a process of becoming. (In the terms of *S/Z* "literature" is the *network* in-between the *structure.*) To capture, perform, enact the slipperiness of "literature" in his own writing, Barthes multiplies the signifiers and delays the meaning of "literature". "Literature" is: eccentric forces, evasion, "force of drift" (467), play, cheating, imposture, trickery, permanent revolution, displacement, theatre staging language "instead of simply using it" (463), with words "*cast* as projections, explosions, vibrations, devices, flavors" (464); "literature" is the truth of our desire, "the watcher who stands at the crossroads of all other discourses" (467); "literature" is shifting ground, anarchy, "a veritable heteronymy of things" (469), eluding, postponing, procrastinating, fragmentation, digression, excursion; "literature" is "the comings and goings of a child *playing* beside his mother, leaving her, returning to bring her a pebble, a piece of string" (476–7).

What then is Barthes doing in this inaugural lecture at the Collège de France? On the one hand, he is exposing the power of language to subjugate by imposing on us an identity based on classifications that are motivated by power relations, in the manner of *Mythologies*. However, ideological demystification (e.g. as critique of classifications) has limited value. The priority for Barthes – at the heart of his poststructuralism – is to keep on exuberantly reinventing and renewing his concepts and metaphors and reading differently. Barthes proposes *jouissance* (pleasure): a Nietzchean ethics, poetics, even erotics of the joy of becoming. The pleasure of writing and reading has been an element throughout his work, even in *Mythologies*, as the pleasure of reading these early essays (at least for this reader) attests.

Pierre Macherey

A Theory of Literary Production (1966) by Pierre Macherey (1938–) is a seminal text, dramatizing, within its own tensions, contradictions and movement, the transition from structuralism to poststructuralism, and from Marxism as the (only) truth of historical reality (as in Barthes's *Mythologies*) to an atypical Marxism interacting with other theoretical paradigms. Its impact can be felt on the work of Barthes, Derrida, Foucault and Deleuze and Guattari among others. One of Macherey's starting points is that a genuinely scientific literary criticism needs to be deductive rather than inductive: it needs to begin with general hypotheses and avoid a naïve empiricism. (This is similar to Northrop Frye's point of departure, see Chapter 9.) Macherey develops his own complex hypothesis as to the nature of literature and of literary criticism. Against structuralism, the literary text is not reducible to a stable underlying or organizing structure. It is not a closed, self-sufficient and harmonious unity or totality; it is not an interior or an inside; it doesn't have a (single hidden) meaning; it has no depth; it is not a fullness or plenitude; it is not completed; it is not self-identical; its development is not continuous; it does not describe or mirror reality; it is neither fully determined nor a completely new creation *ex nihilo*; it is neither "entirely innocent" nor "completely self-conscious" (Macherey 1978, 27). Instead, the literary text is "perhaps torn and gaping" (20), "shattered" (96), "scattered", "a thousand separate, hostile and discontinuous realities" (99). It emerges out of a "silence" (5), a "nothing" (19), an "*absence*" (85), which prior condition is to be understood in several senses.

First, Macherey understands absence as a "radical otherness" generated by the "juxtaposition and conflict of several meanings" (Macherey 1978, 84), the "difference" between "several different lines" all pursued by the text, "gaps and contradictions" in its "fabric" (99–100). Even when a text is relatively unified, Macherey is looking for its "margins": an internal or "intrinsic difference" (72, 79) that makes it "*other than it is*" (7), a "splitting" (94) or a "minute rupture" (95) in the liminal space of the text's margins, as it were, something both inside and outside, which works to undermine the binary opposition inside/outside (Derrida addressed this binary opposition in 1968 in "Plato's Pharmacy", see Chapter 1.) Second, absence points to the text's unconscious conditions of possibility. The text is "*produced* under determinate conditions" that are both "interior" to the text, in that they are shaping its conflicts, and "absent", in that the text (and the critic) is not fully aware of them (78). This historical unconscious is radically irreducible and "cannot be located" (84), i.e. the text must not be reduced to a "*single* series of conditions" (49). Macherey understands historical becoming as heterogeneous, decentred and discontinuous (anticipating Foucault). The text's conditions include not only the economic base (which is the single determining condition for orthodox Marxists), but "several levels at once" (93). These conditions cannot be fully elucidated, not even by the critic. Rejecting any form/matter model (the idea of creation or production as imposition of form on inert matter) underpinning theories of literature as creation and Marx's concept of production (Chapter 5), Macherey develops the highly resonant idea of discontinuous "modification" (50), a bricolage model of literary production. The author is a "labourer" who doesn't "manufacture" his "materials" (41); his materials are heterogeneous, borrowed already formed, and have their own disparate histories. In this sense, the composition of the text is an "*uneven development*" (originally a Marxist term for socioeconomic development); the relation of its elements is an ongoing struggle, whose direction is discontinuous in that it can be interrupted and modified at any point, by the author or the reader/critic (23).

The "absence" of literature, as developed by Macherey, is not in fact a lack but rather an excess, the text's openness to the forces of history: its *partial* determination by complex conditions of possibility, as well as its future-oriented and transformative potential. Literature produces a "rupture" and "initiates something new" (Macherey 1978, 51) exactly by holding together heterogeneous materials in open "confrontation" (59). Each one of these materials, on its own, is an already formed perspective on (and interpretation of) the world: it is a mythology or ideology that constructs an illusory full reality while claiming to mirror reality. Literature, by contrast, "distorts" or (in Barthes's terms) denaturalizes reality: it is "illusion *interrupted*" and "transformed" (61–2). "Mingling" mythologies or ideologies and staging their "contestation", literature exposes their "unreality" (59–61). Macherey thus names literature's intertextuality a "power of parody" (59).

Macherey initially adopts his teacher Louis Althusser's Marxist tripartite schema situating literature between ideology and Marxist scientific criticism. (As with Barthes's *Mythologies*, ideology is illusion, a false picture of reality, while Marxism is a science true to historical reality.) Accordingly, he describes literature as "a break from" ideology, which nevertheless falls short of the "*real break* between ideology and [Marxist] theoretical knowledge"

(Macherey 1978, 52). Ideology, literature and Marxist literary criticism – or "illusion, fiction, theory"– are three entirely separate domains, without any "bridge" connecting them (65). However, the faith that Marxism is true is in conflict, within Macherey's text, with his broader model of science – and of his own project – as developing a general hypothesis. Futhermore, the text itself undercuts its tripartite schema, undermining the schema's clear separation of literature and criticism. Macherey's critique of inside/outside undercuts the separation of three domains without a "bridge". Also, if literature does not fully "*know* itself", criticism cannot fully elucidate literature either, and both display unresolved conflicts (84). Rather than being true to historical reality, criticism, like literature, is transformative, has a "capacity to generate novelty", is "inherently provisional" and must not be "stripped of its history" (6). In dating the different sections of his book, Macherey suggests that the "uneven development" and discontinuity he discerned in literature is an element in the composition of his own critical text. The ruptures and contradictions in Macherey's text, as we have been discussing them above, further align it with literature.

Macherey's *A Theory of Literary Production* outlines a poststructuralist theory of literature – and of criticism as well – as juxtaposition and discontinuous modification of already formed materials. Macherey thus anticipates Barthes's "text" and Foucault's genealogical method. He critiques structuralism for reducing the text to a closed structure and searching for a single meaning (the text's hidden structure). He argues against interpretation, as a search for meaning, in favour of a constructivist theory of literature. Effectively he discards the question "What does it mean?" in favour of the question "How does it work?" (how is it put together and what effects does it have?), a question central to Deleuze and Guattari's *Anti-Oedipus* (1972).

Michel Foucault

"What Is an Author?" (1969) by Michel Foucault (1926–84) is a response to Barthes's "The Death of the Author". Foucault shifts attention to the discourse of criticism, since the seventeenth and especially the eighteenth century, and poses a Machereyan question: how does the figure of the author work within this discourse? The author is manufactured by criticism: it is an "author-function" (Foucault 1977b, 138) managing and directing the interpretation of a cluster of texts, grouping them together into the author's oeuvre and reading into them relations of "homogeneity, filiation, reciprocal explanation" (123). The author works as a "principle of unity" whose function it is to "neutralize the contradictions" of a book or an oeuvre (128). Foucault aims to denaturalize "familiar" categories such as the book or the oeuvre (and their assumption of a closed inside and an outside), and his concept of "discourse" (or "discursive practices") highlights the historically specific, anonymous and collective networks of local but interconnected discourses (113–14). Since the seventeenth century literary criticism has constructed the author as a "rational entity" or a "subject", though this subject is only an effect of the critics' "projections … of our way of handling texts … the traits we extract as pertinent, the continuities we assign, or the exclusions we practice" (127). First, Foucault historicizes literary criticism: before the seventeenth century texts we now call literature "were accepted, circulated, and valorized without" the attribution of an author, while scientific texts "were only considered truthful … if the name of the author was indicated" (125–6); after the seventeenth century scientific texts no longer needed the valorization of an author, while literature now began to require it. Second, Foucault connects the modern fabrication of a subject in literary criticism (the author) with its fabrication in other discourses and institutions, as part of his ongoing investigation into the diffuse and decentred but pervasive workings of modern power. For example, in relation to a new legal discourse, Foucault connects the emergence of the author-function both to the author's new property rights over his work and his becoming "subject to punishment" for a discourse considered "transgressive" (124).

Foucault has by this point moved away from his early, structuralist phase – the idea of a closed, unified and centred structure – and towards an understanding of modern power as decentralized, interconnected, discontinuous and developing unevenly. Power permeates all discursive practice and forms of knowledge and therefore cannot be overthrown centrally, but it can be contested and reversed locally. Foucault finds in Nietzsche's concept of "genealogy" and genealogical method the same understanding of power's heterogeneity and discontinuity, as well as the interimplication of power and knowledge. Foucault doesn't claim greater objectivity for his genealogical methodology and his theorization of modern power. Instead he situates himself as a political and transformative thinker whose work is intended as a form of resistance to power.

Foucault's return to Nietzsche – particularly Nietzsche's *On the Genealogy of Morals* (1887) (see Chapter 5) – is broadcast in "Nietzsche, Genealogy, History" (1971), considered a methodological manifesto for the "genealogical" work of *Discipline and Punish* (1975) and the first volume of his three-volume *History of Sexuality* (1976). Foucault distinguishes here between "history in the traditional sense" and genealogy or "effective" history (Foucault 1986c, 86–7). The traditional historian supports the "search for 'origins'" (77), "unbroken continuity" (81), foundations, unity, "constants" (87), "teleological movement" (88), "profound intentions and immutable necessities" (89) and a historiography "given to reestablishing the high points of historical development and their maintenance in a *perpetual present*" (94, my italics). (T. S. Eliot promoted the conception that great literature from Homer to his day "has a simultaneous existence and composes a simultaneous order" [Eliot 1997b, 41], see Chapter 8.) The traditional historian supports historiography as "neutral, devoid of passions, and committed solely to the truth" (95).

The genealogist or the "effective" historian, on the other hand, stresses the "singularity of events" (where an "event" is the random "reversal of the relationship of forces") (Foucault 1986c, 76, 88), "chance" (78), "dissension" and "disparity" (79), "dispersion" (81), "accidents" (80), "numberless beginnings" (81), "minute deviations ... the errors, the false appraisals, the faulty calculations" (81), "fissures", "heterogeneity" (82), the "hazardous play of dominations" (83), interpretations, "discontinuity" (88), "diverse cultures" (94). Finally the genealogist stresses that "knowledge is not made for understanding; it is made for cutting" (88): whereas the traditional historian prostrates himself before facts unaware or unwilling to acknowledge that he is anything other than impartial and objective, the genealogist or "effective" historian readily acknowledges that he is a participant in history, partial and interested.

Foucault's genealogical method has been widely influential. For example, it was a major influence on New Historicism – an important Anglo-American school of literary criticism founded by Stephen Greenblatt and others in the 1980s – as this brief summary of its major tenets will show.

- New Historicists reject the anti-historicism of American New Critics (see Chapter 9), but also reject an "earlier", "dominant", "mainstream" historicism (Greenblatt 2001, 2253). Instead they are indebted to Bakhtin (Chapter 7), Hayden White (Chapter 2) and the poststructuralists, especially Foucault, but also Said (Chapter 12).
- We cannot unproblematically rely on the historical context to elucidate a literary text because "we can have no access to a full and authentic past" (Montrose 1998, 781).
- Literature and reality interact and are mutually constitutive; literature is both "historically determined and determining" (Montrose 1998, 777).
- The literary text is an element within a cultural system – a synchronic structure of inter-related elements – that includes literary texts, but also "other genres and modes of discourse" as well as "social institutions" (Montrose 1988, 779). The meaning of a text is determined by its relations to all those other discourses rather than its relations solely within an autonomous literary history.
- New Historicists destabilize the text and its relation to reality. Stephen Greenblatt argues that the same text can function as subversive, as a kind of safety valve allowing the release of social tensions or as a hymn to social order (Greenblatt 2001).

In "What Is an Author?" Foucault outlined how modern literary criticism fabricated the author as the unitary subject or the doer hidden behind acts of literature. In *Discipline and Punish* (1975) Foucault traces the construction of "the delinquent" by modern disciplinary practices. More boldly, Foucault claims that the individual is "fabricated" by the disciplinary practices of a new, modern type of power-knowledge (Foucault 1991, 194). Modern power does not work negatively, through privation or limitation: oppressing, repressing, excluding, concealing. Instead it works positively, having "positive effects" (22): "power produces; it produces reality" (192). The individual is the "effect and object" of power-knowledge (192). At the intersection of incessant observation, theoretical elaboration and invention, discipline is the training of highly capable and productive, yet docile, bodies: the body "reduced as a 'political' force … and maximized as a useful force" (221). Since the eighteenth century and the dominance of the bourgeoisie as a class, this is the dark or "non-egalitarian" side of the Enlightenment, according to Foucault (222).

The delinquent is constructed through "processes of individualization" (22) that refer his acts back to his putative individual "nature" (99) or "soul" (295) (we are reminded of Foucault on the author). He becomes the "author of his acts" (253) through a "coercive individualization" (239) involving isolation, hierarchy and normalization; "techniques" and "sciences" converge on his body (308); his "individualization" is an "object-effect" of knowledge-power exercises in "subjection" and "objectification" (305). In this sense, the delinquent, rather than eluding the "direct hold of power" (300) or being "outside" power, is on the contrary an "institutional product" of intensified "surveillance" and "disciplinary coercion" (301). Foucault's discussion of Jeremy Bentham's Panopticon – a circular prison layout of individual cells overlooked by a central observation tower, occupied by an authority watching all the time because the watched cannot see what the watcher is doing (Foucault provides an illustration) – highlights the self-observation and self-disciplining of the delinquent, who is directed to enter into a *vertical* or hierarchical relation with the observation tower and "simultaneously plays both roles" (203) of surveyor and surveyed. The layout isolates the delinquent from other prisoners and pre-empts *horizontal* or "lateral" relations of solidarity among prisoners, who are unable to band together to attempt some resistance (200).

Foucault's example of Mettray, a French prison-farm-school for juvenile offenders, combining imprisonment with work and schooling, allows him to comment on the concerted intersection of different kinds of training – "all the coercive technologies of behaviour" (Foucault 1991, 293) – within a single institution. The disciplinary practices and power-knowledge relations pioneered within the modern prison deploy "procedures of partitioning" (isolation and individualization) and "verticality" (hierarchy) (220): a "hierarchical framework, with no lateral relation" (238), as in the Panopticon. Foucault maintains that these disciplinary practices were then disseminated in other institutions – the school, the army, the factory, the workshop, the hospital, etc. – forming a loosely connected network covering the entire social body. This is the "new era" (296) of a "carceral archipelago" or "subtle, graduated carceral net" (297) with "no outside" (301), and in this sense of the "omnipresence" of discipline (304). Education (including literary studies), and its figure of the "teacher-judge" or "educator-judge" (304), is a part of this network.

The modern diffusion of "power-knowledge relations" throughout a series of institutions or "micro-powers" means that resistance and political contestation have to be rethought accordingly (Foucault 1991, 27). On the one hand, resistance is no longer focused a priori around a central site (e.g. the king) to be overthrown in a revolution. On the other hand, the "infinitesimal distribution of power relations" (216) means that power relations are unstable and can be contested and reversed at any point and in any location in micropolitical struggles. If disciplinary power works through isolation, partitioning and verticality, resistance works horizontally or laterally: through "horizontal conjunctions", such as "spontaneous organizations" and "coalitions" (219). If disciplinary power works through the fabrication of essences – the delinquent, the pervert or indeed the student – this imposed and "non-corporeal" identity nonetheless "links" (253) groups of people together and can be the basis of solidarity and resistance.

In *The History of Sexuality. Volume 1: An Introduction* (1976) Foucault continues to focus on the modern era initiated in the seventeenth and especially the eighteenth centuries in Western Europe. His object is the diffuse proliferation of institutional discourses on sexuality, fabricating a new essence or identity: the pervert. He also continues to refine his understanding of modern power and resistance. Foucault's starting point is the hypothesis that modern power works not through the repression of sexuality, but through a "veritable discursive explosion" around sex (Foucault 1990, 17) as part of the modern "exercise of power" (18). There is a new "obligation" (20) or "imperative" (21) to talk about sex, as part of a rational public discourse aiming to manage, regulate, utilize sex into an "ordered maximization of collective and individual forces" (24–5). Once again Foucault insists on the multiplication and "dispersion of centers from which discourses emanated" and the "diversification of their forms" (34). If Freud characterized sexuality as *polymorphously perverse* (see Chapter 6), Foucault points to the "polymorphous" workings of modern power (34) – "innumerable institutional devices and discursive strategies" in medicine, psychiatry, criminal justice, etc. (30).

This burgeoning of specialist knowledges and interventions around sex now turns its attention towards the sexual acts of children, women, those attracted to their own sex, the insane and criminals in search of "the pervert" (Foucault 1990, 38–9). The aim is to fabricate "something like a nature gone awry" (39) and the "setting apart of the 'unnatural'" as a "sub-race" (39–40). For the first time, socially aberrant acts such as sodomy are attributed to a "permanent reality" (44), an individual or "personage" behind the acts, and the homosexual is born as a "singular nature" or "species"; other types of perverts are similarly classified and "entomologized" by science (43). If modern power constructs or fabricates "the pervert", its workings are concrete and its effects real (as, for example, the trial and punishment of Oscar Wilde). Incessant observation and surveillance cut into the body as "lines of indefinite penetration" (47); encroaching practices of individualization, "isolation, intensification, and consolidation of peripheral sexualities" bring about the "implantation" of perversion (48). At the same time, socially fabricated and imposed identities such as "the homosexual" (or "queer") can be appropriated and reclaimed and can become a site of resistance. (Foucault's work, and this book in particular, is one of the origins of queer theory and queer studies; see, for example, David Halperin's *Saint Foucault* [1995].)

In *The History of Sexuality. Volume 2: The Use of Pleasure* (1984) Foucault departs from modernity and turns to the management of pleasure in Greek classical antiquity, particularly the fourth century BC. Another important departure is the redirection of attention from institutional practices to the free self-fashioning of the "subject" (Foucault 1992, 6): the ethics or "aesthetics of existence" (11, 12, 89) of the elite class of citizens in the Greek democratic polis, comprised only of free male Greeks. Foucault's unacknowledged inspiration is Nietzsche's distinction between morality, as a model to be simply obeyed, and a self-fashioning ethics-aesthetics tracing a unique path in the absence of a model. The citizen of Athenian democracy, Foucault seeks to show, exercises his freedom through discretionary and voluntary mastery and control over himself or through a relation with himself: his "forms of subjectivation" and "practices of the self" (30). *Enkrateia* (temperance, moderation) is not a matter of suppressing certain desires and acts nor of passively obeying the law, but one of subtle, active and independent deliberation and judgement as to the appropriate degree, frequency, timing, conditions, etc. of his "use of pleasures" (37, 44, 53, 58). Foucault focuses on three fields requiring the exercise of the citizen's *enkrateia*: *epimeleia heautou* (care of the self, 211) in the form of an appropriate "caring for one's body" (97), diet and exercise well suited to one's body, as an "art of living" (101); management of the *oikos* (household, wife, children, slaves), including self-control in one's sexual relations with one's wife, in spite of her inferior and dependent legal status as property (151, 184); self-mastery in the male citizen's sexual relations with free young males, such that it will facilitate (and not jeopardize) the boy's adult graduation to the status of citizen. In Plato's *Symposium* the citizen's self-mastery culminates in Socrates's pursuit, no longer of pleasure, but of knowledge as to the nature of love (as part of Plato's broader project of controlling desire, see Chapter 1). Foucault endorses the Socratic dictum "Know thyself" as a "hermeneutics of the self" (6): knowing one's desires, one's character, in order to "get free of oneself" (8).

Gilles Deleuze and Félix Guattari

Gilles Deleuze (1925–95), considered a major twentieth-century philosopher, wrote extensively on literature: books on Marcel Proust (1964; 1970; 1976), Leopold von Sacher-Masoch (1967) and Franz Kafka (1975; co-written with Félix Guattari); and essays on Pierre Klossowski (1965), Michel Tournier (1967), Émile Zola (1967), Carmelo Bene (1979), Herman Melville (1989), Samuel Beckett (1992), Walt Whitman, Alfred Jarry (1993) (see Bogue 2012, 286). Deleuze's *The Logic of Sense* (1969) revolves around Lewis Carroll; and his work, including his collaborations with Félix Guattari, abounds in readings of Beckett and Melville, Antonin Artaud, Scott Fitzgerald, James Joyce,

Jack Kerouac, D. H. Lawrence, Virginia Woolf and many others. However, while Deleuze developed his film theory in the two-volume *Cinema* (1983–5), he did not produce an equivalent work devoted to literary theory. *Kafka: Toward a Minor Literature*, co-written with Guattari, is closest to such an undertaking and will be the focus of our discussion.

Deleuze's thought can be described as a broadly left-wing appropriation of Nietzsche's philosophy of becoming and critique of Plato and idealism (we discussed Deleuze's critique of Plato earlier in Chapter 1). Deleuze's engagement with Nietzsche, in *Nietzsche and Philosophy* (1962) and throughout his oeuvre, was a major influence on his friend Foucault and others. Deleuze's Nietzsche-inspired preoccupations include emphasis on becoming without a subject and without a model. The subject, whether individual or collective, though an effect of actions preceding and exceeding it, retroactively poses as the transcendent cause of these actions, in a reversal of cause and effect (we discussed Foucault's analysis of the author-function in these terms). At a collective level there is no common human essence, and in this sense Deleuze's thought is antihumanist; further, Deleuze's thought has an ecological dimension, rejecting the metaphysical privileging of humans against animals and the rest of the living world. It is anti-essentialist, in that collective subjects are constituted by actions rather than being presupposed by them as their cause. At an individual level, the self is an effect of pre-individual and collective forces. In *On the Genealogy of Morals* Nietzsche valued affirmation – bodies and instincts in an *active* state ("will to power") – against negation – bodies and instincts in a *reactive* state ("*ressentiment*"); he put forward an active or creative ethics/aesthetics tracing a path without following a model (e.g. Christian morality), i.e. without morality understood as reactive copying of a model falsely presumed to be transcendent (applicable to all, God-given, etc.). Deleuze, in ever-renewed terminology, emphasized becoming, creation, production, desire as productive rather than predicated on lack ("desiring-production" and "desiring-machines" throughout *Anti-Oedipus*, co-written with Guattari), proliferating variation without a model ("difference and repetition" or proliferating repetition-with-a-difference along divergent series in *Difference and Repetition*). Foucault's great themes, power as productive and the production of the individual, emerge in dialogue with Deleuze. Deleuze's (and Guattari's) many neologisms favour terms such as "machine" or "assemblage" to emphasize becoming without a subject.

In addition to Nietzsche, Deleuze creatively reconstructs and places himself on the line of an alternative tradition within the Western philosophical canon – a genealogy of his own philosophy of becoming including the Stoics, Hume and Spinoza. The shadow of the trinity Marx, Freud, Saussure is heavy on the entire poststructuralist generation, including Deleuze, but here Deleuze proceeds mostly through critique, aided by Guattari. Félix Guattari (1930–92), Deleuze's collaborator from 1970 until Guattari's death, was a Marxist psychoanalyst intensely critical of both Marxism and psychoanalysis. In Deleuze and Guattari's view, desire is pre-individual libidinal investment of collective social formations – sometimes politically reactive, at other times politically radical (for example, Ezra Pound desired fascism, Frantz Fanon the liberation of Algeria and the struggle against the French Empire). Desire is "impersonal and collective" and must not be "reduced to sexual relations between persons" (Colebrook 2002, 141). Deleuze and Guattari's critique of Freud in *Anti-Oedipus* is that he personalized and familialized desire. Desire is not an intra-familial drama, but plugged into the world, the driver of becoming and, as regards the political, indissociable from the immanent workings and exercise of power as well as resistance to that exercise. In relation to Marxism, Deleuze and Guattari reject the distinction between (false) ideology and (true) Marxist science, as discussed above in relation to Macherey. All we have is *simulacra* without an original, and thus neither true nor false, producing rather than representing reality, both in its most oppressive and its most liberating manifestations (from fascism to May 1968). (See the earlier discussion of Deleuze on the "simulacrum" in Chapter 1).

In relation to Saussure and structuralism, unlike Saussure, Deleuze and Guattari do not argue that language constructs or gives meaning to reality. Language is a component, a working part of reality, forming productive assemblages of discursive and non-discursive elements (or machines), in relation to which the relevant question is not "what does it mean?" but "how does it work?" (what other elements is it connected with and what effects or uses does it have?), as Deleuze and Guattari keep reiterating in *Anti-Oedipus.* For example, the call of the Greek Revolution was "Freedom or Death". In relation to literature, interpretation and hermeneutics are rejected, in favour of a new method. Deleuze's 1970 revised edition of *Proust and Signs* already shows this new orientation, bearing the traces of the start of Deleuze's collaboration with Guattari; Deleuze now focuses on the "production of signs rather than their interpretation" and approaches literature "from the vantage of function rather than meaning" (Bogue 2012, 293). In *Kafka* and in Chapter 4 of *A Thousand Plateaus* (1980), "Postulates of Linguistics", they distinguish between discursive "collective assemblages of enunciation" and non-discursive "machinic assemblages" and explore their connections. Instead of hermeneutics, they propose a pragmatics pursuing the connection of a "machinic assemblage of bodies, of actions and passions, an intermingling of bodies reacting to one another" and a "collective assemblage of enunciation, of acts and statements, of incorporeal transformations attributed to bodies" (Deleuze and Guattari 1988, 88). For example, during the Greek Revolution "Freedom or Death" was a collective assemblage of enunciation connected to non-discursive machinic assemblages, a notable machinic element being the use of fireboats.

For Deleuze and Guattari language and literature are performative: they produce or transmit "order-words" which bring about instantaneous "incorporeal transformations" (Deleuze and Guattari 1988, 88). This view of language as a realm of performative statements or speech acts is partly indebted to J. L. Austin's *How to Do Things with Words* (1962) (77). For Deleuze and

Guattari language and literature oscillate between the pole of "order-words" and the pole of "continuous variation" (Deleuze and Guattari 1988, 94) or deterritorialization. The former refers to transformations or becomings that have a point of destination (for example, in Kafka's "Metamorphosis" Gregor becomes an insect), while the latter refers to open-ended becomings (for example, Molloy's wandering in Beckett's *Molloy*). This does not mean that language, literature or literary theory are free to shape and reshape the world at will. On the contrary, Deleuze and Guattari register the shock of "extra-linguistic forces" and events (Massumi 2002, xvii). It is in this spirit that Michel Foucault read *Anti-Oedipus* as a post-1968 book registering the experience of late-1960s political activism – those "brief, impassioned, jubilant, enigmatic" years – and Deleuze and Guattari as "motivat[ing] us to go further" (Foucault 1984, xi–xii).

At least since his first book, *Empiricism and Subjectivity: An Essay on Hume's Theory of Human Nature* (1953), Deleuze had been thinking about sub-individual and collective associations, connections, external relations or transversal communications without an individual or collective subject, preceding and *constituting* subjects. In his 1989 "Preface to the English Language Edition" he captures Hume's greatness as follows:

> he constituted a multifarious world of experience based upon the principle of the exteriority of relations. We start with atomic parts, but these atomic parts have transitions, passages, "tendencies," which circulate from one to another. These tendencies give rise to *habits* … We are habits, nothing but habits – the habit of saying "I."
>
> (Deleuze 1991, x)

Deploying Deleuzian terms, Colebrook reads Woolf's *The Waves* as the power of literature to explore the process of pre-individual affects producing character; stream of consciousness and experience effecting characters rather than being "grounded in characters" (Colebrook 2002, 84). In *The Waves* affect is dislocated "from any character", perceptions are dislocated "from any object", giving way to "tendencies to become" that cannot be attributed to character or narrator – undoing any clear separation of subject, world and language (116).

The most strikingly defamiliarizing aspect of Deleuze and Guattari's thinking is that of connections without subjects, as relations of becoming between elements that precede and constitute the familiar world of subjects and objects within backgrounds. They use terms such as *assemblage* or *machine* to highlight that there is no doer behind the deed. In *Anti-Oedipus* they turn to Melanie Klein's psychoanalytic theory of schizoid part-objects (discussed earlier in Chapter 6): for the breastfeeding infant, the connection of breast and mouth precedes and constitutes persons; *mummy* and *me* are effects rather than causes of the connection of breast and mouth (Deleuze and Guattari 1984, 1, 43–5). Similarly, literary texts, literary oeuvres, literary movements, political movements, life itself can be read as assemblages without an underlying subject or territory, though subjects and territories are their very real effects. So how does one go about distinguishing between good and bad connections? In *Spinoza: Practical Philosophy* Deleuze pays tribute to Spinoza's *Ethics* for distinguishing between *good encounters* and *bad encounters*, and this ethicopolitical distinction remains a vital one throughout Deleuze's work. Good connections are *immanent* connections and bad connections are *transcendent* ones – projecting as their pseudo-cause a transcendent subject, a common essence and a common world invented by them – as I hope to elucidate in relation to Deleuze and Guattari's *Kafka*. The subject that stands back to appropriate the object has transcended experience and reality, the vital connection is lost. For Deleuze what is important is to remain amidst things, amidst the flow, your assemblage constantly active, connecting and disconnecting with other elements, in a process that seeks no end other than itself.

In *Kafka: Toward a Minor Literature* Deleuze and Guattari argue that great literature is *minor literature*, understood as a literature of immanent connections, simultaneously exposing and disassembling transcendent connections. Minor literature has a "double function: to translate everything into assemblages and to dismantle the assemblages" (Deleuze and Guattari 1986, 47). Minor literature is not the literature of an already constituted minority, representing or recognizing that minority. Minor literature is not representation but experimentation, plugged into machinic assemblages and collective assemblages of enunciation and asking "What function does it have?" (49). So, first, minor literature is not "individual" expression but "political" act (17). Second, "everything takes on a collective value" so that "what each author says individually already constitutes a common action" (17). Rather than an author, as an "enunciating subject", causing the literary text, the literary text effects a collective "subject of the statement"; it invents a virtual community or a people yet to come (18). In this sense, "[t]here isn't a subject; *there are only collective assemblages of enunciation*" (18). In "Literature and Life" Deleuze outlines the "ultimate aim of literature" as the "invention of a people who are missing" (Deleuze 1998, 4). In *Kafka*, minor literature (and Kafka's literature) is a "concern of the people", in the sense of a virtual collectivity that is "not yet constituted (for better or for worse)" but yet to come (Deleuze and Guattari 1986, 84). Minor literature is the invention of "a community whose conditions haven't yet been established" (71). (For example, Toni Morrison's *Beloved* is an open-ended call for an African-American community to come, rather than representing an existing and fully constituted African-American collectivity; see Chapter 9 for further discussion.)

Third, minor literature involves continuous linguistic variation or linguistic "deterritorialization" (Deleuze and Guattari 1986, 16). Deleuze variously describes the deterritorialization of language as a stuttering, a becoming-other and a becoming-foreign of language: "open[ing] up a kind of foreign language" within familiar language (Deleuze 1998, 6). The "deterritorialization of language" in minor literature might work through attention to the materiality of language, an "intensive" or non-signifying use of signs or lexical and syntactical invention, as in Antonin Artaud and Louis-Ferdinand Céline (Deleuze and Guattari 1986, 20, 26). Colebrook argues that for Deleuze "voice is at first noise and nonsense" (Colebrook 2000, 110). Or, rejecting referential language, minor literature might expose *order-words* as an "exercise of power" and deploy intensive language as "resistance to this exercise" (Deleuze and Guattari 1986, 23). In sum, the three characteristics of minor literature, capturing the power of *all* literature, are: "the deterritorialization of language, the connection of the individual to a social and therefore political immediacy, and the collective assemblage of enunciation" (18). Bogue points out that Deleuze and Guattari effectively connect political and formal experimentation: the "sociopolitical dimension of literature" or the concerns of Sartre's *littérature engagée* and the "practices of modernist and avant-garde formal experimentation" (Bogue 2012, 300).

We can now clarify the double function of "minor" literature for Deleuze and Guattari: "to translate everything into assemblages and to dismantle the assemblages" (Deleuze and Guattari 1986, 47, quoted above). In relation to the first function, "minor" literature is an immanent diagnosis or visionary symptomatology of the emergent forces within the institutions and discourses that make up a social world. Free indirect discourse (as discussed by Bakhtin, see Chapter 7) is understood by Deleuze and Guattari as the interaction of collective discourses effecting – rather than being caused by – seemingly transcendent narrators and characters. (See Deleuze and Guattari 1988, 77; Colebrook 2002, 109–12.) This first function is experimental rather than representational or cognitive or critical: "Criticism is completely useless. It is more important to connect to the virtual movement[s]" (58) traversing a collectivity – to prolong or accelerate "a virtuality that is already real without being actual" (48). Thus Kafka's literature connects with the "diabolical powers" of his future (Kafka quoted in Deleuze and Guattari 1986, 12): for example, in *The Trial* Josef K. investigates a bureaucratic tendency emerging within modern administered societies, beyond the actuality of the Austro-Hungarian Empire.

In relation to the second function of literature, it is a question of finding and sustaining an open-ended "line of escape" (from transcendence) – a concept borrowed from Kafka's short story "A Report to an Academy" (Deleuze and Guattari 1986, 13 and *passim*). The aim is to continue becoming: indefinite and "unlimited postponement" (Kafka quoted in Deleuze and Guattari 1986, 44), to sustain rather than to complete the line. Like a burrow, a literary text (any assemblage) has a multiplicity of points of entry and exit (3), a virtual multiplicity of lines of escape. In "Life and Literature" Deleuze, looking back on his work on literature over the years, comes to a self-suspending conclusion: "Writing" – literature, but also Deleuze's philosophy and literary criticism – is a "question of becoming, always incomplete" (Deleuze 1998, 3). Deleuze and Guattari's pluralism celebrates the pure multiplicity and diversity of *n* lines of becoming: becoming-minor, becoming-animal (in Kafka and Melville), becoming-woman (in Woolf), becoming-imperceptible are only some of the lines of becoming Deleuze and Guattari explored in relation to literature (see Chapter 10 of *A Thousand Plateaus*). Perhaps the distinctiveness of Deleuze and Guattari's literary theory, in the midst of endlessly proliferating concepts and neologisms, is the ongoing attempt to connect and keep reconnecting literature *and* the imagination (fantasy, delirium, libidinal investment) *and* formal experimentation *and* political experimentation.

Jacques Derrida

One of the best introductions to Jacques Derrida (1930–2004) for a literary-critical audience is his collection of essays, *Acts of Literature* (1992), edited by Derek Attridge. (In Chapter 1 we discussed Derrida's reading of Plato's *Phaedrus* [Derrida 1981b] and in Chapter 5 his essay on Mallarmé in *Acts of Literature* [Derrida 1992b]).

In his "Introduction: Derrida and the Questioning of Literature" Attridge outlines Derrida's understanding of literature as "potential challenge" and "resistance" to "logocentrism" or the "metaphysics of presence": the assumptions, concepts and oppositions of the Western philosophical tradition since ancient Greece and Plato (Attridge 1992, 3–4). As we discussed earlier (see Chapter 1), for Derrida this tradition sets up a system of binary oppositions, such as presence/absence, essence/appearance, true/false, good/evil, inside/outside, same/other, man/woman, etc. Within each opposition, the two terms are understood as external to each other, the former term is valued, and the latter devalued. The valued term is understood as an "inside" completely insulated from the "outside" inhabited by the devalued term. Derrida's readings (e.g. his reading of Plato's *Phaedrus*) focus on self-deconstructive moments in philosophical and literary texts, i.e. moments undoing the binary oppositions they have established, crossing the border between opposing terms and thus resisting logocentrism from within. In *The Second Sex* (1949) Simone de Beauvoir argued that patriarchy is based on the binary opposition man/woman (see Chapter 10), while in *Orientalism* (1978) Edward Said argued that the binary opposition West/Orient was fundamental to the project of imperialism (see Chapter 12). Beauvoir and Said illustrate clearly why "logocentrism" requires subversion and why there is a strong ethical dimension to Derrida's call to challenge and resist "logocentrism".

For Attridge literary studies are "dominated" by logocentrism, more than philosophy, because they lack "philosophy's long tradition" of self-critical reflection (Attridge 1992, 3). At the very least Derrida and Attridge are calling for a self-reflexive literary criticism that participates in the critique of logocentrism. It can be argued that Derrida chose to perform close readings of Mallarmé and other modernist literary texts exactly because their resistance to logocentrism is "particularly strong" (4), or that their literary practice announces, "better than elsewhere", the "subversion of logocentrism"

(Derrida quoted in Attridge 1992, 25). Or, with more finesse, it can be argued that Derrida's close readings attend to those aspects of his chosen texts that "shake the foundations" (5) of traditional literary studies and philosophy. What no one is suggesting is that all literature necessarily resists logocentrism. (Indeed Beauvoir and Said explored the degree to which particular literary texts reproduce and strengthen binary oppositions.) Derrida unsurprisingly agrees with other poststructuralists that there is "no essence of literature" (Derrida quoted in Attridge 1992, 6) and that literature is not an intrinsic and exclusive property of a specific type of text. Attridge claims that "*every* text can be read (though not necessarily without some tough and extended intellectual labor) as 'literary.' Equally, no text could be *wholly* 'literary'" (7). This undercuts the "opposition" between literature and philosophy (including literary theory and criticism), and Attridge argues that Derrida's readings of philosophical and literary texts have "patiently chipped away at" this opposition, attempting instead to think them "*together*" in their "co-implication" (13).

We "habitually" understand literary texts as "unique", singular, new, free from rules and conventions (Attridge 1992, 14) – e.g. for Jauss a text's literary value is its aesthetic distance from established aesthetic norms. Traditional philosophy, on the other hand, is understood to produce generally applicable concepts and a generalizable method. However, Derrida's readings cross the border between philosophy and literature, challenging the traditional philosophical opposition between generality and the singular. For example, his readings of literary and philosophical texts find, within those texts, and deploy terms that are *not* concepts in that they are generated in the close reading of a particular text and are not "susceptible of generalization" (9) – "*pharmakon*" (Plato), "supplement" (Rousseau), "hymen" (Mallarmé), "trace" (Nietzsche). Or they coin neologisms, such as "*différance*", which condenses two signifiers (to differ and to defer), or show that "certain familiar concepts … are not concepts at all" in that they operate in an "undecidable manner" (9). Derrida's deconstructive readings are thus "particular acts of reading" without underlying "abstractable" and exactly repeatable method and concepts (14).

For Kant, as we discussed earlier in Chapter 4, true literature (and art more broadly) is singular, in the sense that it is original and rule-breaking, free from the constraint of rules. Attridge argues that for Derrida a literary text displays and stages *not* singularity, but the "interdependence" of singularity and generality (e.g. genre conventions, concepts, binary oppositions) (Attridge 1992, 15). It is a deconstructive "act" that traverses binary oppositions between "unique and general, concrete and ideal, idiomatic and rule-governed" – "both an event and a law" (19). Derrida's term, "iterability", captures the literary text as "*at once* translatable *and* untranslatable" (Derrida quoted in Attridge 1992, 17). It generates a new meaning when read by a different critic (the same is true of a philosophical text). The literary text is a "repeatable singularity that depends on an openness to new contexts and therefore on its difference each time it is repeated" (16), crossing the borderline between the oppositions of "substance and accidents, necessity and chance" (18).

Derrida invites us to a double reading of literature both in its singularity and in its generality. Attridge argues that Derrida's ethics pays attention to a literary text in its "singularity", in the sense of its irreducible alterity: the deconstructive critic receives a "strong ethico-political summons" to attend to the "uniqueness of the other" (and of the literary text as "other") (Attridge 1992, 26). Derrida declares himself unceasingly "surprised" by critics who understand him to be arguing that "there is nothing beyond language" and summarizes his critique of logocentrism as "above all else the search for the 'other'" (Derrida quoted in Attridge 1992, 20). In its generality, literature is a Western "institution" founded in the seventeenth and eighteenth centuries in the context of modern Western democracies (23). However, it is a peculiar institution that "sheds light on institutionality" and generality, and "resists philosophical conceptuality" (24–5). (Modern thinkers have variously understood literature as outside – critical of, resistant to – rules, conventions, impoverished rationality, Western metaphysics, etc. For example, Heidegger saw poetry as visionary access to the world, considered his own philosophical work poetical and criticized modern rationality and Western metaphysics since Plato, see Chapter 10.)

In his interview with Attridge, "'This Strange Institution Called Literature'" (1989), Derrida improvises variations on these themes. Literature, as a modern Western institution, has certain rules and conventions – for example, it requires "writing … authorial property, … individual signatures" (Derrida 1992c, 40). But it is a paradoxical and "strange institution" because its law is to "defy or lift" the law (36). It is an institution that overflows its bounds, giving the "power to say everything" and to "break free of the rules" (37). For Derrida the crucial conventions or rules to defy are (as discussed above) the metaphysical oppositions and assumptions of the Western tradition since Greek antiquity – logocentrism, the metaphysics of presence, etc. Derrida is reading attentively for moments of defiance in texts that are not necessarily modern or even literary. For example, there are "moments" in the *Odyssey* as well as in *Ulysses* that "resist" a "transcendent" reading, i.e. a metaphysical reading that looks for a single meaning behind the text (45). (Derrida is close to Deleuze on "transcendence" here.) Even in Plato and other canonical philosophers, "the possibilities of rupture are always waiting to be effected" by the deconstructive reader, as Derrida tried to show in "Plato's Pharmacy" and "Khōra" (53).

Derrida uses the term "suspension" (Derrida 1992c, 50) to describe literature's equivocal defiance of metaphysical assumptions and purposes: suspension involves bracketing, displaying, exposing these assumptions (for example, assumptions of meaning and reference) but also recognition of "*dependence*" on them (48). Far from being a realm of freedom, their "recurrence" in literature is "so structural that it couldn't be a question of eliminating them", though literature's "*being-suspended* neutralizes" these assumptions (49). Derrida is not so much interested in texts thematizing or arguing against Western metaphysics and explicitly questioning the metaphysical scaffolding of traditional literary criticism (e.g. literature as an essence or object or truthful reference), but in texts "bearing and putting to work" (41) this questioning, each in a singular way, in their very practice of writing: in the "act of a literary performativity and a critical performativity (or even a performativity in crisis)" (42). Sharing with Bakhtin and poststructuralist critics the antimetaphysical sense that "[n]othing is ever homogeneous" (53), Derrida is particularly interested in "reactionary", "conservative" or "phallocentric" texts, in their intended meanings, that have paradoxical "destabilizing" and "powerful 'deconstructive' effects" in their practice of writing, texts by Joyce and Nietzsche for example (50, 59). Derrida's contentious claim is that, whatever the apparent attitude of the author, "[b]ecause of the literary dimension, what 'phallogocentric' texts display – the binary opposition of man/woman, valorization of 'man' and devaluation of 'woman' – is immediately suspended" and exposed (58). This may be the case, but we have Derrida to thank for its recognition, as phallogocentrism since the Greeks has seemed untroubled by its self-deconstructing movement.

Derrida outlines his ethics. In the absence of an "essence of literature" or an already constituted "literary object" (Derrida 1992c, 41), the literary text is both institution, sharing general rules, and singular performative questioning of the rules, a singular "signature" (66). Or rather it emerges as such in broadly deconstructive yet singular acts of reading, each repeating with a difference, each a "countersignature" in response to the text's signature. This is indeed Derrida's ethics of reading:

> My law … is *the text of the other*, its very singularity, its idiom, its appeal which precedes me. But I can only respond to it in a responsible way … if I put in play … my singularity, my signing, with another signature; for the countersignature signs by confirming the signature of the author, but also by signing in an absolutely new and inaugural way, both at once. (66–7)

Derrida links literature's repetition with a singular difference, its "iterability" (74), with a radical form of democracy, as radical openness to difference, otherness and the future, which he calls "democracy to come": "refusing to reply for one's thought or writing to constituted powers" as a form of ethical and political commitment to others (38). (Deleuze similarly connects "minor" literature with the "virtual", which is "to come".) This is envisaged as a double movement practised by author and reader (literature and literary criticism) alike, so that one can no longer distinguish between "producer and receiver" (74–5). This double movement would involve both "*singularization*" and a degree of belonging and participation in what is "*shared*", and in this sense it would take place on the "edge *between* the 'inside' and the 'outside'" (68). It can be argued that literature and responsible literary criticism embody, for Derrida, the most utopian elements of the democratic legacy of the Enlightenment.

Perhaps the weakest part of Derrida's interview is the discussion of feminist literary criticism, in spite of Attridge's insistent questioning and Derrida's declared commitment to difference and otherness. Derrida makes the useful if obvious point that great feminist writers – he only names Virginia Woolf and Hélène Cixous – cannot be assumed to be simply "non- or anti-phallogocentric" (Derrida 1992c, 59). However, Derrida seems unfamiliar with feminist criticism with the exception of Hélène Cixous, and only interested in feminism if its strategy or effects are deconstructive, i.e. as a potential part of the deconstructive project. We will be discussing Cixous and other poststructuralist feminists in the following chapter, while Lacan's and Kristeva's versions of poststructuralism were discussed in Chapter 6.

Conclusion

- Barthes's early work focuses on decoding the hidden meaning of French "myths". The critic reveals the true meaning. Under the impact of 1960s micropolitics and May 1968, Barthes crosses the boundary between literature and criticism to advocate an open-ended, provisional, experimental literary/critical practice captured by his theory of the "text": reweaving heterogeneous materials, performing an evasion of meaning, proliferating interpretations. In the absence of a position of exteriority, literature and criticism will occupy the ambiguous position of the enemy within, undercutting the distinction inside/outside, resisting settled dominant meanings.
- The Marxist Macherey also questions the distinction inside/outside. Undermining the distinction between literature and "scientific" (Marxist) criticism, he theorizes both literature and criticism as historical, provisional and transformative: particularly, as juxtaposition, confrontation and discontinuous modification of heterogeneous, already formed materials. He suggests replacing the question "What does it mean?" with the question "How does it work?"
- Foucault's genealogical method rejects objectivity in favour of the transformative and resistant figure of the "effective" historian; it assumes heterogeneity, discontinuity, singularity and the interimplication of power-knowledge. Foucault understands the author-function as a critical device of the modern Western institution of criticism, unifying and homogenizing the literary text. This fabrication of the author parallels the fabrication of a subject in other modern institutions. Modern power is productive and decentred, but this allows local resistance. Among modern micropowers, the prison fabricates the delinquent through coercive individualization involving isolation, verticality/hierarchy and normalization, while resistance takes the form of local horizontal connections – Foucault's defence of 1960s micropolitics. Discourses on

sexuality fabricate the pervert as the subject who commits aberrant acts. In search of another site of resistance Foucault turns to classical Greek self-fashioning, its ethics/aesthetics of existence and its practices of the self (*enkrateia*).

- For Deleuze and Guattari the subject is an effect of pre-individual and collective connections, "assemblages" and becomings without a subject. They distinguish between immanent and transcendent connections (attributed to a transcendent subject) in favour of the former, a life of experimental becoming, not sterile fixed identity. "Minor" literature involves immanent connections: it is not individual expression but political action; it is collective, constituting a people to come rather than representing an existing collectivity; and it "deterritorializes" language as sound, lexical or syntactical invention. It combines political and formal experimentation and invention, so literary criticism must turn from questions of meaning and interpretation to questions of production, function and pragmatics. In free indirect discourse the experimental interaction of collective discourses precedes and effects narrators and characters, and connects literature with virtual powers in a social world. Minor literature is a "collective assemblage of enunciation" (a discursive component) connecting to a "machinic assemblage" (a non-discursive social world) and looking for its "lines of escape".
- For Derrida literature is not a property of literary texts, but involves acts of reading in search of moments of defiance and subversion of *logocentrism* (metaphysical assumptions, e.g. of a single transcendent meaning, and metaphysical oppositions) in any text. Reactionary texts will have subversive moments. Literature is double: *both* institution *and* singularity, *both* rules, conventions, generality, translatability, substance, concepts *and* event, untranslatability, accidents, *signature*, *counter-signature*. Literature's doubleness is its *iterability* (repeating with a difference). Its mode is that of *suspension*: subverting *and* participating in metaphysical assumptions and thus crossing the border between outside and inside. This undermines the distinction of literature as singularity and philosophy/criticism as generality (concepts). Derrida's readings performatively cross the line, searching for non-concepts and attempting open exercises in a "democracy to come". Deconstruction is not a general method.

Further reading

For Barthes, see Barthes 1973, 1975, 1977b, 1977c, 1993c. For Derrida, see Derrida 1981b, 1992b, 1992c; Attridge 1992. For Deleuze and Guattari, see Deleuze 1998; Deleuze and Guattari 1984, 1986, 1988; Bogue 2012; Colebrook 2002. For Foucault, see Foucault 1977b, 1986c, 1990, 1991, 1992. For Macherey, see Macherey 1978.

12 Poststructuralist deviations

Mimicry, resignification, contrapuntal reading, the subaltern, Signifyin(g), hybridity

Feminist poststructuralisms (Cixous, Irigaray, Butler, Sedgwick, Spillers), postcolonial theory and race (Said, Spivak, Gates, Bhabha, Young)

Feminist poststructuralisms

The poststructuralist feminist work of Luce Irigaray (1930–) and Héléne Cixous (1937–) on *écriture féminine* (women's writing) and "sexual difference" emerged in the early 1970s in response to the post-May 1968 French women's movement and as part of that movement.

Cixous emphatically does *not* understand "women's writing" as writing by those biologically female, and her understanding of "sexual difference" is not separatist. Her most famous essay and focus of our discussion, "The Laugh of the Medusa" (1975, 1976), is a collage of allusions, most of them fleeting, to a large number of writers and thinkers in the Western tradition or, in poststructuralist terms, a text weaving together many (too many, an excessive number of) different threads. It *com-poses* a large number of irreducible ideas, all mobilized towards a multiple, excessive, open-ended over-definition of the woman to come. This is a composite utopian figure purportedly unshackled from Western metaphysics, patriarchy and capitalism, performatively evoked by Cixous's writing. With a light touch, Cixous leaves most thinkers unnamed and unquoted, but suggests we understand her writing performance as "*voler*": stealing, flying, fleeing, escaping (Cixous 1976, 887). However, Cixous's allusions are often transformative repetitions with a difference, what Derrida would call acts of "countersigning" (see Chapter 11). Cixous's strategy of ventriloquism – broadly a poststructuralist strategy of resignification – can also be compared with Irigaray's "mimicry", Butler's "resignification" and Gates's "Signifyin(g)". Cixous's own terms for women's writing – a quick series of "brief, identificatory embraces", fleetingly becoming those others through a "gift of alterability" (889) – aptly describe her own strategy here. Cixous's multiple, speedy, criss-crossing forays are at variance with Derrida's sustained close readings, and her scant quoting and referencing is provocatively unacademic, at least in an Anglo-American context.

Cixous does not name Derrida, but her project in this text – undermining the border between the metaphysical opposition of body (sexuality, emotion, sensation, reproduction) and spirit (thinking, ideas, reason, creation) – is clearly a deconstructive one. Cixous zooms in on this opposition because women, in the Western tradition, have been historically relegated to "body" and excluded from speaking and writing. Cixous aims to clear women's path to writing by deconstructing the opposition between body and spirit. She insists on the inter-implication of body and writing, and posits it as a key constituent of "women's writing". She calls such writing "sext", her neologism condensing "sex" and "text" (Cixous 1976, 885), thus following Derrida's use of undecidable neologisms with (at least) double meanings and his mobilization of the ambivalence or polyvalence of words. See also "*voler*" and her neologism, "*dé-pense*": un-think or expend excessively in a Nietzschean sense, an idea particularly developed by French thinker Georges Bataille (882).

In the *Symposium*, Socrates left sexuality and the body behind, once he was sufficiently advanced on his philosophical path. Cixous, by contrast, announces women's writing as a "return to the body" (Cixous 1976, 880): as women's reclaiming of their expropriated bodies and repressed desires – "her goods, her pleasures" (880). For *écriture féminine* questioning, research and "knowledge" are wedded to "a systematic experimentation with the bodily functions" and "erotogeneity" (a neologism condensing *eros* and *genesis*); sexual pleasure is "prolonged or accompanied by a production of forms, a veritable aesthetic activity" (876). This is a broadly psychoanalytic view. In Chapter 6 we discussed Freud, Lacan's poststructuralist reading of Freud and Kristeva's feminist-poststructuralist critical revision of Lacan in *Revolution in Poetic Language*. Freud described early pre-genital infantile sexuality as "polymorphously perverse" – sexuality as a multiplicity of erogenous zones such as the mouth and the anus, rather than focused on the genitals and reproduction – and Cixous appropriates the polymorphously perverse to describe female sexuality as a non-genital multiplicity, simultaneously alluding to Deleuze and Guattari's recently published *Anti-Oedipus* (discussed in Chapter 11) (889). Feminine sexuality, understood by Freud largely in terms of lack (the absence of a penis and penis envy), is understood by Cixous in terms of an excess of forms: it has "its thousand and one thresholds of ardor" (an allusion to Shahrazad's oral storytelling), articulating a "profusion of meanings" (885). Hysteria, particularly its bodily symptoms (such as loss of voice), Cixous conceived as a form of allusive writing with the body, and she claims Freud's patient Dora as a feminist counter-heroine and women's writing pioneer. Cixous points to a secret women's history of "admirable hysterics" and their "aphonic revolts", who found a language to speak with not by sublimating but by "furiously" inhabiting their "sumptuous" bodies (886). In an apostrophe to Dora, her muse, Cixous praises her as a "poetic body" and as "the true 'mistress' of the Signifier" (dismissing Lacan's "phallus" as the transcendental signifier), while insisting on the poverty and pain that might accompany the hysteric's revolt: resisting "social success" and "biting that tongue with her very own teeth to invent for herself a language" (886–7). Women's *writing* (*écriture*) is paradoxically predicated both on oral storytelling, voice and song as well as "pregnant" aphony and silence. Cixous's elliptical references to Lacan are antagonistic while Kristeva is not mentioned at all. However, Cixous is drawing on the former's conception of "the imaginary" and the latter's (Melanie Klein-influenced) "semiotic", in claiming for women's writing a proximity to the "drives" and a "relation to the 'mother,' in terms of intense pleasure and violence" – where the mother is a "metaphor" (one's relation to and presentation of the mother rather than the actual mother) (881–2). The Kristevan "semiotic" is brought to mind when Cixous calls on women's writing to "wreck partitions", "sweeping away syntax" (886).

Another point of departure for Cixous is Virginia Woolf's positing of "androgyny" in *A Room of One's Own* as an ideal co-existence of the masculine and the feminine within the self. Shakespeare's and Coleridge's greatness, Woolf claimed, were related to their androgynous minds (see Chapter 8). Alluding to Woolf without mentioning her, Cixous aligns women's writing with a sense of the "presence … of both sexes" in their "difference" – not their opposition – within the self (Cixous 1976, 884). As mentioned, despite Cixous's characterization of women's writing in terms of the female body, she doesn't understand "women's writing" as writing by women. On the one hand, she argues that most existing writing by women is indistinguishable from writing by men in that it "obscures women or reproduces" stereotypical representations of women as "sensitive – intuitive – dreamy, etc." (878). This writing is false, and Cixous appropriates Woolf's calls, in "Professions for Women" and *Three Guineas*, to kill the Angel in the House, "kill the lady" and even "kill the woman" (Woolf quoted in Lee 1992, xiv): "We must kill the false woman" (Cixous 1976, 880). On the other hand, Cixous argues that the rare instances of "women's writing" in the past (in her own utopian sense of "women's writing" as defined in this piece) include writing by both men and women: in French, these rare instances of a nascent women's writing include Colette, Marguerite Duras and Jean Genet. Simone de Beauvoir had praised Colette in her own sketch of women's writing in *The Second Sex* (see Chapter 10), and Cixous's odd silence on Beauvoir suggests her tacit exclusion from Cixous's vision of women's writing. In German, "women's writing" includes the poet Heinrich von Kleist. Cixous rather formulaically values poetry more than fiction and the novel. Fiction, she claims, "often grossly exaggerated all the signs of sexual opposition", and novelists were often self-circumscribed by their allegiance to "representationalism" (literature here reinforcing logocentrism in Cixous's view). By contrast, some male poets like Kleist imagined "impossible" rebellious women, "untenable in a real social framework" (879). However, she includes Joyce's *Ullyses*, particularly Molly's monologue, and considers Molly's Nietzschean affirmative yes-saying to be a constituent of women's writing (884).

Nietzsche is also strongly present, as with many of Cixous's French contemporaries. He had recently been appropriated as a left-wing poststructuralist thinker by Deleuze and Foucault (see Chapter 11). Cixous incorporates several Nietzschean themes – the origins of thought in the body, Dionysian laughter, his transvaluation of values, his ethics of affirmation and yes-saying – redescribing them as constituents of women's writing. Nietzsche's Dionysus becomes Cixous's "beautiful" and "laughing" Medusa (885). As mentioned, Cixous turns also to Georges Bataille's Nietzsche-influenced counter-economy of excess, expenditure and gift without return – counter to the capitalist economy of exchange and maximized return – to redescribe and valorize women's traditions of unpaid and undervalued work on behalf of others as "resistance" to capitalist and patriarchal society. This is a startling view and one may find it impossible or undesirable to reconceive housework as joyous expenditure of overflowing energy. For Cixous woman "gives" in an "'economy' that can no longer be put in economic terms", against "[o]pposition, hierarchizing exchange, the struggle for mastery ... governed by phallocentric values" (893). "What woman hasn't flown/stolen?" (887). Cixous endorses a textual strategy, inseparably, both of excessive giving and stealing: catachresis, improper use and abuse resist property and "propriety" (888). Repeating with a difference is a form of improper use, for example Cixous's own catachresis of Bataille.

Cixous puts together several incompatible stories in an open, additive way, including several incompatible sketches of women's history: women have interiorized sexism and self-loathing; they have suffered simultaneous sexual expropriation and silencing; they have been closer to the unconscious and less repressed; they have been creating a secret inner world not yet expressed in public; they have a history of defiance; women's resistance is just emerging or still to come; more than narrowly feminist or timidly reformist, "women's writing" is a radically utopian misappropriation of the Western tradition.

In "The Laugh of the Medusa" Cixous's "women's writing" attempts to conceive women's "sexual difference" – and the value of women speaking and listening to each other – without essentializing that difference, without eliding differences among women, without excluding men and without becoming prescriptive. The reader might also turn to "Sorties" (1975) and "Coming to Writing" (1977). Cixous has continued her genre-bending experiments, mixing theoretical/critical writing, creative writing and (auto)biography. (In Chapter 2 we discussed her rewriting of Aeshylus's *The Furies* [Cixous 2010].)

Luce Irigaray's pathbreaking *Speculum of the Other Woman* (1974) led to her being "expelled" from Lacan's *Ecole Freudienne* and her teaching position at the University of Paris VIII at Vincennes (Irigaray 2004, viii). Primarily a philosopher and psychoanalyst, Irigaray trespassed into literature by calling for a new symbolism. "This Sex Which Is Not One" (1975) attempts to clarify some of the themes of *Speculum.* I will be quoting from Porter's translation (Irigaray 1985b), but I will on occasion be adding Reeder's translation (Irigaray 1997) in square brackets. Like Cixous, Irigaray posits women's sexuality as "*plural*" – "*woman has sex organs more or less everywhere*" (1985b, 28) – and declares it a stranger to "Ownership and property [Property and propriety]"

(1985b, 31; 1997, 328). Irigaray also makes connections between women's bodies and women's writing. She shares with Cixous and Derrida a critique of "the logic that has dominated the West since the time of the Greeks" (1985b, 25).

Irigaray's particular targets are the binary opposition activity/passivity and the dominance of vision and devaluation of other senses, particularly the sense of touch, in the Western tradition. Irigaray describes the utopian figure of a woman – and simultaneously proposes and performs a women's writing – that prioritizes touch, "nearness" (Irigaray 1985b, 31), contiguity, and thus deconstructs the opposition activity/passivity. (Merleau-Ponty's work on *embodiment* is perhaps especially relevant to this project.) Irigaray describes two vaginal lips touching each other, so that it is not possible to distinguish between touching and touched, active and passive. If from the point of view of visuality there is "discrimination and individualization of form" (25) so that we can separate the two lips into two distinct and isolated forms, from the point of view of touch the two lips are not separable. Irigaray uses this symbol to reimagine women's genitals (conceived by Freud negatively as lack of a penis, see Chapter 6) and their experience of their bodies: "Thus, within herself, she [woman] is already two – but not divisible into one(s) – that caress each other" (24); women experience themselves as multiple, "at least two" (26, 28). Irigaray claims that self and other, distinct from the point of view of visuality, are not separable in this tactile model. She further claims that women's experience of their amorous encounters is tactile rather than visual, and does not distinguish between auto-eroticism and hetero-eroticism, as "the other is already within her [a part of her] and is autoerotically familiar to her" (Irigaray 1985b, 31; Irigaray 1997, 328). Nor does women's erotic experience distinguish between hetero- and homo-sexual encounters, as "all discrimination of identity" is alien to it (1985b, 31).

Irigaray pursues a connection between women's experience of their sexuality, as outlined above, and women's writing: "in what she says [her statements], too, at least when she dares, woman is constantly touching [retouches] herself" (1985b, 29; 1997, 326); "What she says is never identical with anything, moreover; rather, it is contiguous. *It touches (upon)*" (1985b, 28). Women's writing – Irigaray is primarily self-reflexively theorizing her own writing here – is a tactile amorous encounter with the other, blurring the boundary between self and other. Irigaray's strategy of "mimicry" (which we will discuss shortly) clarifies her project, but we might also briefly turn to her reading of Freud in *Speculum* (11–129). A critique usually assumes the distance between self and other, but her critique of Freud is formally innovative in that it closes the distance between Freud and herself; she critiques Freud by masquerading as Freud, through a subversive mimicry of Freud. Irigaray has been staging such encounters with male thinkers, from Plato to Nietzsche and Merleau-Ponty, though intriguingly her reading of Beauvoir in "Equal or Different?" (see Chapter 10) reintroduces distance and separation between herself and Beauvoir. Irigaray has often been accused of essentialism and of eliding the differences among women, and Margaret Whitford in *Luce*

Irigaray: Philosophy in the Feminine (1991) has done more than most to address these accusations. However, it seems clear that Irigaray is not describing the experiences of actual women but inventing and performing an ethics, including a textual ethics for women's writing.

In "The Power of Discourse and the Subordination of the Feminine" (1975) Irigaray defines *mimicry* as an indirect or oblique strategy, in contrast to the ostensibly more "direct" but, in her view, less subversive feminist strategy of demanding to be allowed to "speak as a 'masculine' subject". Historically women were reduced or relegated to mimicry (repetition without originality, reproduction without creation), and Irigaray is proposing that women "play with mimesis" in order to "try to recover the place of her exploitation by discourse, without allowing herself to be simply reduced by it". In dialogue with post-structuralist resignification or repetition with a difference, she proposes "playful repetition" as a particularly apposite feminist strategy (Irigaray 1985c, 76 throughout).

Another major poststructuralist feminist thinker is Julia Kristeva, whose work was discussed earlier (Chapters 1 and 6). In 1979 Kristeva outlined the "problems" and "dangers" of *écriture féminine*, as she saw them, in "Women's Time" (Kristeva 1986c, 195). To Kristeva its utopianism is a danger. It imagines itself outside patriarchy and capitalism, an "a-topia ... outside the law", a "counter-society" that is "harmonious, without prohibitions, free and fulfilling" (202). For Kristeva this is a problematic secular form of religious re-enchantment or "laicized transcendence" (202). Kristeva rejects its "inverted sexism" (202). Further, she claims that its "denial of the socio-symbolic contract" (203) – rejecting both participation in existing society and reformism (see, for example, Irigaray's rejection of Beauvoir, discussed in Chapter 10) – is dangerous. In psychoanalytic terms, the denial of separation and violence is "no less exposed to the risks of violence and terrorism" (208) and even leads to their return, as a return of the repressed, Kristeva argues.

Cixous and Irigaray outline a "sexual difference" version of feminism: instead of calling for equality or for the disappearance of gender, they call for the autonomy of women's struggles and argue the radical utopian potential of a revisioned sexual difference. However, queer thinkers including Judith Butler (1956–) have argued that sexual difference is conceptually dependent on heterosexuality and that a perpetuation of sexual difference, however redefined, unwittingly props up the "institution of compulsory heterosexuality".

Butler's *Gender Trouble: Feminism and the Subversion of Identity* (1990) is one of the founding texts of queer theory and the field of queer studies. The outbreak of the AIDS epidemic in the 1980s, and the ensuing demonization of gay sexuality, gave *Gender Trouble* its urgency. Butler's starting point is Simone de Beauvoir's "One is not born, rather one becomes, a woman" (Beauvoir 1953, 273). Butler argues that there is nothing natural about gender: femininity as well as masculinity have no biological basis, and express nothing interior. Femininity and masculinity are purely performative. A whole array of performances or discursive practices or signifying practices and their endless unconscious repetition bring about an effect of naturalness.

Butler argues that contemporary societies still rely on constructing "discreet and polar genders" (Butler 1990, 140), a clear division between two genders, as a support for what feminists have been calling the "institution of compulsory heterosexuality". We are therefore compelled in a variety of ways to perform and to keep on performing our gender and punished for our gender instability: "Discreet genders are part of what 'humanizes' individuals within contemporary society; indeed, we regularly punish those who fail to do their gender right" (139–40). While societies have a vested interest in concealing the performative nature of gender, drag brings this performative nature to view: "*In imitating gender, drag implicitly reveals the imitative structure of gender itself – as well as its contingency*" (137). Butler pays tribute to the drag artist Divine, who starred in John Waters's films (e.g. *Hairspray*). Divine's performances make us aware of the props, gestures and signifying practices of femininity. Seen through the performances of Divine, Marilyn Monroe is herself a female impersonator and a drag artist performing femininity.

In dialogue with Foucault (but also Barthes and Derrida, whom we discussed in Chapter 11), Butler stresses the pervasiveness of genderizing discursive practices and the unavailability of a position outside gender. Instead, as with Barthes, she hopes for destabilized and constantly resignified genders: "a fluidity of identities", "an openness to resignification" (Butler 1990, 138) and "proliferating gender configurations" (141). Butler sees identity as a normalizing, disciplinary force. Desire will always exceed any identity – in this sense she moves away from Foucault's later work on the body and pleasure in his *History of Sexuality. Volume 2: The Use of Pleasure* (see Chapter 11). The argument of queer theory is that *all* identities are performed, fabricated, unstable mixtures of "success" and "failure"; all identities are queer. We are in this sense all queer. Butler encourages her readers to engage consciously with gender stereotypes and open them to resignification. At the same time she stresses that we cannot determine in advance what performance, where, addressed to what audience is going to be subversive or, on the contrary, is going to re-enforce gender stereotypes. (For example, if a young woman were to make hyperbolic use of pink her performance might be read as an ironic comment on femininity or she might be told that she looks incredibly cute today.)

In *Gender Trouble* Butler engaged with French feminists, especially Beauvoir, Irigaray, Kristeva and Monique Wittig, also informed by 1980s feminist critiques of essentialism. In "Contingent Foundations: Feminism and the Question of 'Postmodernism'" Butler writes against those feminists "who claim that there is an ontological specificity to women … In the 1980s, the feminist 'we' rightly came under attack by women of color who claimed that the 'we' was invariably white" (Butler 1995, 49). Butler here outlines the constituents of a "radical democratic" (51) feminist politics, in response to the rampant homophobia of the times, and in dialogue with poststructuralists and anti-essentialist feminists. To summarize:

- She values contests, conflicts and antagonisms among feminists, rather than reaching consensus: "the rifts among women over the content of the term ['woman'] ought to be safeguarded and prized" (50).
- She values permanent "resignification"; the aim of a radical democratic feminist politics would be "to release the term ['woman'] into a future of multiple significations" (50).
- She calls for feminists' recognition of their unavoidable embeddedness in power relations, expressing her strong distrust of a feminist theory and politics that claims to offer a utopia "beyond the play of power" (39).

As part of this politics, Butler calls on readers to denaturalize the terms "feminism" and "woman" and to keep them multiple and open to contestation.

It seems clear that Butler is closer to Kristeva than Irigaray or Cixous, and Butler herself outlines her views on Irigaray's work in *Bodies that Matter* (1993). On the vexed question of Irigaray's essentialism, Butler argues that Irigaray is not an essentialist. Rather than *describing* an essential sexual difference, Irigaray is self-consciously deploying a textual strategy, her deliberately improper and catachrestic form of mimicry. (A strategy, we might add, which is not far removed from Butler's "resignification".) Butler, on this point, is endorsing Margaret Whitford's and Jane Gallop's readings of Irigaray. Irigaray's "two lips" and her ethics of contiguity, in keeping with Whitford, is "not itself a natural relation, but a *symbolic* articulation proper to women" (Butler 1993, 46). Or, in keeping with Gallop, Irigaray's language of essentialism is a catachrestic "rhetorical strategy" (38). Irigaray distinguishes between a (false) feminine figured within the Western binary opposition masculine/feminine and a (true) feminine "excluded in and by such a binary opposition" and appearing "only in *catachresis*" (37). This latter feminine is an "*excessive* feminine" (39) in that it "exceeds its figuration" (41). This *other* feminine performatively summoned by Irigaray comes to occupy the position of what exceeds all binary oppositions, standing for the outside of Western metaphysics. Irigaray's mimicry is intended as the "very operation of the feminine in language" (46). In sum, Butler joins those who think that Irigaray is a "strategic" essentialist, self-consciously deploying essentialism as a textual strategy. Women's genitals have been traditionally understood as a lack, wound, etc. and their reparative, positive redescription by Irigaray can be compared to the anti-racist, positive redescription of blackness by the Francophone *négritude* movement and the American Black Aesthetic Movement (see Chapters 9 and 10). Further, as for Sartre the essence of Man is to have no essence (Chapter 10), for Irigaray the essence of the true "feminine" is to have no essence, in the sense that it undermines binary oppositions and metaphysical essences and exceeds conceptuality. In this precise sense Irigaray's project is close to Heidegger's and Derrida's (Chapters 10 and 11): Irigaray's true "feminine" can be compared to Heidegger's "poetry" and Derrida's deconstruction.

Butler's critique of Irigaray is focused on the primacy of sexual difference over other forms of difference – race, class, sexual orientation, etc. – in

Irigaray's work. This is a serious problem for Butler. She argues that Irigaray's insistence on the primacy of sexual difference is an implicitly white, middle-class, heterosexual position focusing on the marginalization of women *qua* women, but inattentive to other forms of social marginalization. For Irigaray the (true) feminine is "exactly what is excluded" from binary oppositions (Butler 1993, 37). It "monopolizes the sphere of exclusion", leading to Irigaray's blindness to – and "constitutive exclusions" (42) of – other forms of difference. For Irigaray "the outside is 'always' the feminine" because Irigaray "fails to follow through the metonymic link between women and these other Others" (49) and the articulation of gender, race, class, sexual orientation. Whereas Irigaray posits sexual difference as "autonomous" and "more fundamental" than other differences, which are viewed as "*derived* from" it, Butler hopes to understand gender as "articulated through or *as* other vectors of power" (167). Butler's critique of Irigaray highlights the clash of their respective paradigms. Irigaray is looking for a language that alludes to what has been excluded from Western metaphysics, as the basis for a feminist ethics and autonomous feminist struggles. Butler is concerned with social exclusion, the complexity of "vectors" that affect women, the political shortcomings of "autonomy" as a feminist strategy and the pursuit of political alliances.

Butler acknowledges that the project of looking for the convergences and articulation of vectors of power such as gender, race, class and sexual orientation is already underway in the self-theorization of black women's writing and in the work of contemporary African-American feminists, such as Hazel Carby and Deborah McDowell, and feminists of colour such as Norma Alarcón. Alarcón theorized women of colour as "multiply interpellated" (Alarcón quoted in Butler 1993, 182), arguing that "*racializing norms*" and gender norms are "articulated through one another" (182). Indeed, in Butler's view, this is exactly the challenge of Nella Larsen's 1929 novel, *Passing*, outlining the foreclosed possibility of solidarity among black women. Butler argues that this possibility was disabled not only by white racism, but also by W. E. B. Du Bois's vision of "racial uplift" in its masculinism and adherence to bourgeois values. It is still disabled today by Irigaray's prioritizing of sexual difference, in its failure to acknowledge the articulation of sexual difference with other factors. Butler offers a close reading of *Passing* to substantiate these claims, following in the footsteps of African-American feminist literary criticism. Barbara Christian, in "The Race for Theory", suggested we read black women's writing as (self-)theorizing, and Butler sets out to "follow" her "advice" (182). McDowell's and Carby's readings of *Passing* already argue that race and sexuality are interwoven and Butler "would agree with both" (174). Butler also reads Toni Morrison's *Sula* as a revision of *Passing*, refiguring the failed "promise of connection" among black women (183) and thus supporting Butler's thesis.

Butler reads *Passing* as a critique of Du Bois and mobilizes it against Irigaray's privileging of sexual difference. The implication is that, if Irigaray had taken the time to read black women writers in addition to male white philosophers, her work would have been rather different. In relation to Du Bois and the ideology of racial uplift, Butler reads Larsen's *Passing* as exploring "the cost of uplift for black women" and the "impossibility of sexual freedom for black women" within this model (Butler 1993, 178). According to Butler, racial uplift is "construed" by Larsen as "upward class mobility" that requires the "idealization of bourgeois family life in which women retain their place in the family"; in effect it is black "masculine uplift" predicated on the perpetuation of the subordination of women, the (self-)sacrifice of black women for the sake of black men (178). As a result black women are caught in a "double-bind" between white racism and black racial uplift, against which Larsen traces the "incipient possibility of solidarity among black women" (179). (Against Butler, it can be argued that Du Bois's affirmation of spirituals, Pan-Africanism, critique of capitalism and pacifism complicate any claim that he was proposing the black assimilation of bourgeois values, see Chapter 9.)

According to Butler, Larsen's exploration of the black ideology of racial uplift grasps the inter-implication of race, class (middle-class ideals), gender (defence of white middle-class gender roles) and sexual orientation (defence of marriage and the institution of compulsory heterosexuality). Larsen thus helps Butler contest the primacy of sexual difference claimed by Irigaray and "many psychoanalytic feminists" (Butler 1993, 181). This claim has "marked" them "as white" – particularly in their "assumption" that sexual difference is "unmarked by race" (181) and that "whiteness is not a form of racial difference" (182). By contrast, Larsen makes visible historical articulations "of racialized gender, of gendered race, of the sexualization of racial ideals, or the racialization of gender norms" (182). In *Passing* Clare passes as white but her risky association with Irene and her black circle threatens to expose her as black to her white and intensely racist husband, Bellew. Butler's reading traces the convergence of race and sexuality. Clare's "risk-taking" is construed *simultaneously* as "racial crossing and sexual infidelity" that undermines middle-class norms, questioning both the "sanctity of marriage" and the "clarity of racial demarcations" (Butler 1993, 169). Conversely, sexual and racial closeting are interlinked: "the muteness of homosexuality converges in the story with the illegibility of Clare's blackness" (175). Tracing the use of the word "queering" in *Passing* Butler concludes that it is "a term for betraying what ought to remain concealed" (176), in relation to both sexuality and race.

Butler reads *Passing* as a reversal of Irigaray's claims. Irigaray, philosopher and critic, claims for her texts a literary status: performing a feminine imaginary outside the symbolic order. By contrast Butler reads *Passing*, a literary text, as self-theorizing and as an intervention in the symbolic order: Larsen "reoccupies symbolic power to expose that symbolic force in return" (Butler 1993, 185). In other words, Butler claims Larsen as an ally of her project of *resignification.*

In response to the intensification of homophobia and gay shaming after the outbreak of the AIDS epidemic in the late 1980s, gay activists pursued tactics of public visibility, and attempted to turn shaming into pride and grief into experiences of community and solidarity. (Gay Pride parades are a legacy of the period.) Outing oneself and, contentiously and divisively for the gay community, outing closeted public figures were considered highly important by some. Eve Kosofsky Sedgwick's (1950–2009) *Epistemology of the Closet* (1990) is a Foucauldian intervention in this debate. Foucault showed that, after the late eighteenth century and beginning with Romanticism, knowledge, sexuality and transgression came into "alignment with one another" and became inextricable (Sedgwick 2008, 73). In relation to the opposition homosexual/heterosexual, he traced the nineteenth-century European shift from prohibited *acts* to the discursive construction of a deviant homosexual *identity* (see Chapter 11). Sedgwick substantially revises him in order to reveal the "incoherences and contradictions" of modern and contemporary discursive constructions of homosexuality (81).

Sedgwick argues that there is an institutional assumption/presumption of heterosexuality and, in this sense, a "powerful" institutionalized ignorance of homosexuality (77). Because of this presumption gay coming-out "doesn't end anyone's relation to the closet" (81), but is neverending and incomplete – "individual revelation" has little impact on the closeting effects of "*already institutionalized* ignorance" (78). So that gay identity cannot be either *in* or *out* of the closet but has a more "imponderable and convulsive" topography (80). Sedgwick's core hypothesis in *Epistemology of the Closet* is that there are two central contradictions in the twentieth-century discursive construction of sexuality and gender.

In relation, first, to sexuality and particularly homosexual definition, there is a central contradiction between a *minoritizing* and a *universalizing* discourse. According to the minoritizing discourse there is a group of people who "'really' are gay"; the universalizing discourse, on the other hand, follows Freud and assumes the fluidity of desire and the potential bisexuality of everyone, so that the "apparently" heterosexual have "same-sex influences and desires" and vice versa (Sedgwick 2008, 85). Sedgwick claims the complete dominance – the "absolute hold" or "stranglehold" – of this double-bind, "ruling" since the beginning of the twentieth century, in every field (86). She thus substantially modifies Foucault's hypothesis in the following manner. For Foucault a discourse of homosexual *acts* was replaced by a discourse of homosexual *persons*. For Sedgwick, both incompatible paradigms co-exist (a universalizing paradigm of acts and a minoritizing paradigm of persons) and our modern predicament is to be caught in the contradiction between them.

In relation to the second central contradiction or "conceptual siege" (86) around gender, since the late nineteenth century same-sex desire has been understood through two contradictory gender "tropes": the trope of inversion and the trope of gender separatism (Sedgwick 2008, 87). According to the inversion model, a gay man is a woman's soul in a man's body, i.e. in essence a woman who desires men, so that this model preserves "an essential heterosexuality within desire itself" (87); similarly for lesbians, so that desire is always heterosexual. Within the model of gender separatism, on the contrary, desire doesn't cross gender boundaries; instead, it is "the most natural thing in the world that people of the same gender … should bond together also on the axis of sexual desire" (87). While *inversion* distinguishes sharply between identification and desire (e.g. a gay man would identify with women and desire men), *gender separatism* conflates the two (e.g. a lesbian would be woman-identified and would also desire women); *inversion* situates gay identity "at the threshold between genders" (88), for example, male homosexuality as a third sex; while *separatism* situates it within a gender. Sedgwick reminds us of the split in the nineteenth-century German homosexual rights movement between the *inversion* model of the effeminate male homosexual and the *gender separatist* model of the ultra-virile, militarist male homosexual. These models, historically, have tended towards different kinds of politics, political alliances and political exclusions. For example, the above German gender-separatist model was misogynistic, and gender separatism has tended towards alliance among lesbians and straight women. The inversion model has tended towards alliances of gay men with straight women and gay women; and alliances of lesbians with gay men (rarely with straight men). In relation to the intersection of the *two* contradictions outlined by Sedgwick – minoritizing vs. universalizing; inversion vs. gender separatism – the gender-separatist model tends towards *universalizing* homosexual potential; the "gender-*integrative*" inversion model tends towards "gay-*separatist*, minoritizing models of specifically gay identity and politics" (89). However, Sedgwick points out that these alliances and "crossings are quite contingent" (90) and their intersection cannot be generalized. For example, Freud couples a universalizing sexual definition with an "integrative, inversion" model of gender (90).

Underlying the two sets of intersecting contradictions that Sedgwick hypothesizes is the intersection of two separate forms of oppression that must not be conflated: gender oppression (sexism) and heterosexist oppression (homophobia). In spite of all the feminist and gay activism since the nineteenth century, Sedgwick feels "no optimism at all" (Sedgwick 2008, 90). Having analysed our entrapment within contradictory models of sexuality and gender, she argues – in a somewhat circular manner – that the only glimmer of hope and the "most promising project" is that of "a study of the incoherent dispensation itself" (90). Writing at the height of the AIDS crisis and infamous levels of homophobia, Sedgwick's mood is understandably bleak. But it is a testament to the success of queer studies and gay activism that *Epistemology of the Closet* now seems hyperbolic in the West. The contradictions Sedgwick describes – if indeed they are contradictions – no longer seem the "stranglehold" that she felt them to be.

While the field of queer theory arose as a (subject-less) critique of identity politics, it was critiqued for unwittingly representing privileged white Western subjects, notwithstanding Butler's work on race (discussed above). In 1997 Cathy Cohen, voicing the alienation of many queer people of colour, argued first that queer theory and politics remained "rooted in class, race, and gender privilege", having failed to grasp the multiplicity of vectors of oppression and to practise the needful articulation of sexuality, race, class and gender (Cohen

1997, 451). Second, she endorsed queer theory's commitment to the destabilization of identities, but argued that this was not a call for the liquidation of minoritarian communities and collective identifications, as these remained "paths to survival" for marginalized groups (480). In 2005 Hiram Perez, continuing the internal critique of queer theory by people of colour, seconded both of Cohen's arguments. He "speculate[d]" that queer theory still resists attempts to address the "problem of race" and – punning on Butler's *Gender Trouble* – "actively untroubles itself" over race (Perez 2005, 171). Queer theorists often implicitly assume a "transparent white subject", while addressing race is all too quickly discredited as a "retreat into identity politics" (171).

Already in 1987 Hortense Spillers's (1942–) "Mama's Baby, Papa's Maybe" had shown the extent to which the assumptions and priorities of white feminists are local and historically specific and cannot be generalized. Her starting point is the notorious Moynihan Report (1965) in the US, attributing the continuing social marginalization of African-Americans to a pathogenic black matriarchy: single-parent, female-headed households lacking the paternal authority and male leadership of the normative nuclear family. Spillers connects Monihan's social fantasy of harmful black female power to the occluded historical experience of African-American women. If the historical experience of white women was one of normative genderization within the private sphere of the patriarchal family, the historical experience of African-American women has been one of "ungendering" (Spillers 1987, 72). Slavery, as a loss of self-determination and reduction to an exchangeable commodity in the master's property, involved the symbolic gender de-differentiation of slaves. Slavery effectively outlawed the black family, as family bonds would undercut the slave's primary relation to their master and undermine property relations. Within a black family, the slave child would have belonged to its parents, questioning the slave-owner's property rights. So slavery voided motherhood symbolically and legally, while the slave child was symbolically an orphan to be bought and sold at will. Spillers argues that the white "*patriarchalized* female gender" (the only female gender there is) – an undoubted oppression for white women – nevertheless required a degree of "political, socio-cultural empowerment", while the "dispossession" of slavery led to a "*loss* of gender" and the degree of legal and moral protection that it afforded white women (77). If African-American women have been historically "*out* of the traditional symbolics of female gender", Spillers is far from calling on them to join (or remain settled in) the ranks of "gendered femaleness" within the nuclear family (80). Instead, the task is "to make a place for this different social subject" as a precondition for "gaining the *insurgent* ground as female social subject" (80).

Poststructuralism, postcolonial theory and race: Said, Spivak, Gates, Bhabha, Young

We follow Sedgwick's use of Foucault to describe the modern Western intersection of sexual orientation and gender with Said's use of Foucault to describe the modern Western function of race. Sedgwick was of course familiar with Edward Said's (1935–2003) pathbreaking *Orientalism* (1978), transposing Foucault's work to postcolonial theory and Postcolonial Studies. Said adopts Foucault's concept of "discourse" in order to describe the modern Western discourse of Orientalism:

> I have found it useful here to employ Michel Foucault's notion of a discourse ... to identify Orientalism. My contention is that without examining Orientalism as a discourse, one cannot possibly understand the enormously systematic discipline by which European culture was able to manage – and even produce – the Orient politically, sociologically, militarily, ideologically, scientifically, and imaginatively during the post-Enlightenment period.
>
> (Said 2003, 3)

Orientalism is the "nexus of knowledge and power creating 'the Oriental' [as an essence] and in a sense obliterating him as a human being" (27). As a literary critic by training, Said is especially attentive to literature, analyzing the ways in which literary works construct the Orient as the binary opposite of the West and as an eternal and immutable essence without history. While showing the participation of European literature in the project of colonialism and the discourse of Orientalism, Said is keen to claim a degree of freedom and originality for the writer and scholar:

> [U]nlike Michel Foucault, to whose work I am greatly indebted, I do believe in the determining imprint of individual writers upon the otherwise anonymous collective body of texts constituting a discursive formation like Orientalism ... Foucault believes in general that the individual text or author counts for very little ... [M]y analyses employ close textual readings whose goal is to reveal the dialectic between individual text or writer and the complex collective formation to which his work is a contribution.
>
> (23–4)

Said anticipates New Historicism here (see Chapter 11). His double readings explore texts both in their complicity and their degree of freedom. Rather than asking whether a text reproduces or resists Orientalism and imperialism, close reading would specify in what sense a text reaffirms Orientalism and in what sense it questions it.

In *Culture and Imperialism* (1993), the sequel to *Orientalism*, Said refines his method further and addresses contemporary American neoimperialism. He names and theorizes his method of reading as "contrapuntal" reading, exemplified by his reading of Conrad's *Heart of Darkness.* Said's starting point is his diagnosis of an authoritarian hardening of two intellectual camps in the 1970s and 1980s: a neoimperial or neocolonial camp (represented within literature by V. S. Naipaul, for example) blaming the Third World "for what 'they' are", as the single cause of continuing post-independence Third World malaise; and an anticolonial camp "blaming the Europeans sweepingly for the misfortunes of the present" (Said 1993, 20). This development – which Said connects with the "triumph" of the US as "the last superpower" (341) and American neoimperialism in his last chapter – is a serious international "constriction of horizons" (29). Said claims that one of its symptoms has been a "dramatic change" in Foucault and other poststructuralist "apostles of radicalism": a "disappointment in the politics of liberation" and a sense that there is "nothing to look forward to: we are stuck within a circle" (29). Against Foucault's perceived resignation, Said positions postcolonial theory and particularly his "contrapuntal" reading as an open and inclusive critical practice contributing to the urgent task of staging a dialogue between the two camps. Said is equally opposed to both – and the "loud antagonisms of the polarized debate of pro- and anti-imperialists" – because their authoritarian dogmatism and righteousness disable "interchange" (29). Said's Socratic attitude is that inside each camp "stand the blameless, the just, the faithful, led by the omnipotent, those who know the truth about themselves and others" (29).

Said's concept of "contrapuntal" reading adapts a musical term. Counterpoint is a polyphonic musical technique "involving the simultaneous sounding of two or more parts or melodies" (Collins Dictionary 2003). Said derives two simultaneous visions from Conrad's *Heart of Darkness*, made possible by Conrad's "self-consciousness as an outsider", his "exilic marginality" (Said 1993, 27) and his "dislocated subjectivity" (32). The first vision is a colonial vision. Kurtz, Marlow and Marlow's British audience on the *Nellie* have an imperial worldview – they are "creatures of their time" (33) – and Conrad cannot show us "what is *outside*" their worldview nor can he imagine an "alternative to imperialism" (28). As a result, the "oppressive force" of this vision is the sense that there is "no way out of the sovereign historical force of imperialism" (26). (Chinua Achebe, similarly, read *Heart of Darkness* as a racist text, as we discussed in Chapter 8.)

However, the self-reflexivity of Marlow's narrative makes possible a second vision. Marlow's "meticulously staged" narrative performances and the "dislocations" in his language self-reflexively "draw attention to themselves as artificial constructions" (Said 1993, 32). This "unsettles" the reader's idea of empire and of "reality itself", so that "we are in a world being made and unmade … all the time" (33). Thus, at the very least, Conrad "shows us" that Marlow's colonial vision is "contingent, acted out for a set of like-minded British hearers, and limited to that situation" (26). Further, and more importantly, Conrad thereby allows for another world beyond his own grasp. The very "provisionality" of Marlow's narrative situates it at the "juncture" of his imperial world with "another, unspecified but different" (27), so that Conrad allows a certain kind of reader to sense "a larger history … just outside" Marlow's worldview (26) and "inaccessible" to Conrad himself (32). Conrad in effect intuits that what he calls the darkness is beyond him and has an "autonomy of *its* own" (33). At the same time, Conrad's lack of "perfect synchrony or correspondence" with the project of imperialism aided him "actively to understand how the machine works" (27) and to record its "tremendous violence and waste" (28).

It is important to understand that this second vision is more than an anticolonial vision of "a non-European world *resisting* imperialism" and gaining independence (33), though it doesn't exclude the anticolonial perspective. Rather it is a simultaneous sounding of both the colonial and the anticolonial views: it "suggests the presence of a field without special historical privileges for one party" and the "disclosure of a common ground obscured by the controversy itself" (31). In other words, this second vision is not fully present in the text, but is a (Deleuzian) "virtuality" (see Chapter 11) actualized by Said's contrapuntal reading. His reading of *Heart of Darkness* is a model for the concept of the "contrapuntal", which Said only defines after this reading. A contrapuntal reading is a political reading in the broadest sense: it aims to "make concurrent those views and experiences that are ideologically and culturally closed to each other, and that attempt to distance and suppress other views and experiences"; their very juxtaposition, making them "play off each other", leads to an "exposure and dramatization of discrepancy" (37), a hopeful, politically active and enabling strategy, in Said's view. A contrapuntal reading "must take account" both of imperialism and of resistance to imperialism (79). However, literary texts and their critical readings are contrapuntal in widely varying degrees. While *Heart of Darkness* enfolds a contrapuntal virtuality, Said suggests that Kipling's *Kim* excludes it: a contrapuntal reading would have to stage, for example, *Kim*'s juxtaposition with the discourse of the movement for Indian independence emerging at the time (36). Such contrapuntal juxtapositions are reparative, in that they obey an ethical imperative to "take account" both of imperialism and of resistance to imperialism. They extend the text to "include what was once forcibly excluded" (79). In this sense, the critic is an enemy of dogmatism and authoritarianism in all its forms.

Gayatri Chakravorty Spivak's (1942–) "Can the Subaltern Speak?" (1983, 1988, 1999), initially delivered as a lecture in 1983, exists in several different published versions of widely varying length. (We will be discussing the 1999 version, in Chapter 3 of Spivak's *A Critique of Postcolonial Reason.*) This demonstrates the poststructuralist notion that the "text" is not a finished object but an open-ended process. The dispersal of Spivak's text across an open series of textual performances provides a point of access to Spivak's core assumption: that of the unpresentability of the "subaltern" (those most marginalized and excluded). In Derridean terms, the "subaltern" is traditionally (mis)represented as the devalued term in a binary opposition (see Chapter 11), and the unpresentability of the subaltern alludes to a true subaltern that exceeds its (mis)representation – any representation treating it as a full identity or claiming to fix its meaning. Similarly, Irigaray described a true feminine that exceeds its figuration (discussed above). Jean-François Lyotard thought that Holocaust victims can only be ethically presented in their unpresentability (see Chapter 9). Walter Benjamin suggested that the "tradition of the oppressed" (the history of the silenced and the defeated) is inaccessible to the traditional linear "history of the victors", but fragments of it can become visible fleetingly, from the corner of the eye, in rare moments of insight that he called the "now" (see Chapter 7).

Spivak, also discussed in Chapter 9, considers it her responsibility as a postcolonial intellectual to allude to what is outside the neocolonial and anticolonial elites from which she distances herself (following Said, as discussed above, and Ranajit Guha), as well as outside the postcolonial elite of the "liberal multiculturalist metropolitan academy" of which she is a prominent member (Spivak 1999, 309). Her critique of the "Subaltern Studies" group, Guha in particular, clarifies her particular understanding of the "subaltern". The Subaltern Studies group was influenced by the Italian Marxist thinker Antonio Gramsci (discussed in Chapter 8), using his concepts of the "subaltern", "hegemony" and the "organic intellectual" and endorsing "the intellectual's role in the subaltern's cultural and political movement into the hegemony" (269). The postcolonial project of the Subaltern Studies group was to document non-elite colonial resistance. Guha, in Spivak's reading, understands non-elite, subaltern instances of colonial resistance as "difference" from the elite (271–2), aiming to "identify" and "measure the specific" subaltern deviations from the elite (Guha quoted in Spivak 1999, 271). But he also treats subaltern groups as having "determinate vigor and full autonomy" (271–2). Spivak's broadly deconstructive critique is that Guha's project is "essentialist" and "taxonomic" (seeking to create a map of the relations of unchanging identities) (271). For Spivak Guha assumes, wrongly, that the political forces he is describing are self-conscious and already constituted identities underlying political acts of resistance. (Though Spivak doesn't clarify this, it is important to point out that Gramsci's concept of hegemony is widely considered to be anti-essentialist: political identities are constituted performatively, through political action, rather than pre-existing it.) It is obvious that many subaltern groups are highly articulate about their aims and their relations to elites and other subaltern groups, but Spivak understands the "subaltern" as singular acts of resistance outside identities.

Spivak describes the "subaltern" as "irretrievably heterogeneous" (270), a possible reference to Gilles Deleuze's decentred multiplicities (Chapter 11). Deleuze summed up poststructuralist radicalism when, in conversation with Foucault, he declared "the indignity of speaking for others" (Deleuze and Foucault 1977, 209). Deleuze credits Foucault with the insight that the theorist can no longer claim to *represent* the masses or the multiplicity of micropolitical movements (or, in Spivak's terms, the subaltern). The "theoretical fact" is that "only those directly concerned can speak in a practical way on their own behalf" (209). However, Spivak criticizes Deleuze and Foucault in terms similar to her critique of Guha, to add precision to her own vision of the unpresentability of the subaltern. Deleuze and Foucault seem to Spivak unaware of their First-World position and their privilege. They also assume, Spivak claims, that the "oppressed, if given the chance … *can speak and know their conditions*" (Spivak 1999, 269). In effect they are asking for the recognition of "subjugated" knowledges (Foucault's term) previously deemed "inadequate" and "disqualified" (267). By contrast, Spivak is intent on marking her positionality and acknowledging her privilege. She also insists that the "subaltern", as she understands it, is irretrievably silenced. Of course the oppressed have been speaking and articulating their conditions all the time, but Spivak's "subaltern" is what escapes – or is excluded from – any discourse.

Spivak is clearly in agreement with Chandra Mohanty's argument, in "Under Western Eyes" (1984), that the "Third World Woman" is an essentialist fabrication reducing the irreducible "heterogeneity" of women in the Third World (Mohanty 1984, 333). But their difference is instructive. Mohanty calls for studies of local collective struggles and localized theorizing by investigators. Spivak's heterogeneous subaltern, on the other hand, pursues the Derridean problematic of the singular or unique and its iterability. The singular or the *signature* cannot be translated fully or repeated exactly. It can only be repeated differently by a *countersignature* (see Chapter 11). The singularity in "Can the Subaltern Speak?" – Spivak's example of the "subaltern" – is the suicide of a young middle-class woman activist, Talu, Bhubaneswari Bhaduri's nickname, as retold by Spivak. Spivak interprets Talu's suicide as a highly complex political intervention that remained illegible as such even by the other women in her family, including her emancipated relatives today. That even the women closest to her saw her as "hapless" prompted Spivak's sense that "the subaltern cannot speak" (Spivak 1999, 308) and that Talu "hanged herself in vain" (311). Talu was involved in the armed struggle for Indian independence and entrusted with a political assassination. Her suicide, Spivak claims, was a complex refusal to do her mission without betraying the cause. Female suicide at the time was legible either in terms of *sati*-suicide (the self-sacrifice of a widowed wife); or in terms of the "hegemonic" anticolonial nationalist account of the fighting mother, "well remembered through the discourse of the male leaders" (307–8); or in terms of illegitimate passion and the fallen woman. Spivak claims, without any evidence, that Talu deliberately committed suicide while menstruating, in order to resist those dominant interpretations. She was neither a mother of the nation nor a fallen mother nor a *sati*-suicide, as *sati* was prohibited during menstruation. Spivak concludes that her suicide was an intricate performative act (a *speech act*). It simultaneously questioned anticolonial nationalism, "rewrote … *sati*-suicide in an interventionist way" and resisted female "imprisonment" within heterosexual passion (307). Spivak claims that Talu's "Speech Act was refused" by everyone (273) because it resisted translation into dominant discourses, but what are we to make of Spivak's attention to Talu's message? Spivak translates Talu into a postcolonial feminist deconstructive heroine mirroring Spivak's values (and our own), without producing any evidence of, for example, Talu's feminist sensibility. This jarring anachronism might be understood as an illustration of Spivak's thesis.

Spivak does not present her rendition of Talu's story as a lifting of the silence imposed on her, though she embeds in her 1999 version of "Can the Subaltern Speak?" exactly such an understanding of an earlier version. Abena Busia argued that Spivak was able to read Talu's act, and thus Talu – the subaltern – did speak and can speak. Spivak's response is double. On the one hand, she affirms that speech acts are not self-contained or self-identical but are performatively addressed to another and completed by another. In this sense, speaking involves "distanced decipherment by another, which is, at best, an interception" (Spivak 1999, 309). On the other hand, to claim that the subaltern has now spoken through Spivak's interception or intercession would be a neocolonial "missionary" claim (310). To avoid megalomaniac claims of saving the subaltern, Spivak advocates self-dramatization. Theorists must mark "their positionality as investigating subjects" (283). Spivak's retelling is the "moot decipherment by another in an academic institution"; it might be a "line of communication" between a member of subaltern groups and the "circuits of citizenship or institutionality", and it might help to insert the subaltern into the "long road to hegemony", but it must not be "identified with the 'speaking' of the subaltern" (309–10).

The story of the silencing of women of colour within anticolonial independence movements, the US civil rights movement and Western feminist movements is a familiar one. Spivak is simultaneously articulating the value of a postcolonial feminism and refusing to defend it as a salutary breakthrough. Instead she issues a call for vigilance. The task Spivak outlines for herself and her readers is that of "unlearning" our privilege (Spivak 1999, 284). The danger, as Spivak is no doubt well aware, is that the theorist's political activism exhausts itself in empty piety: self-purifying ritual performances of one's own fallen state and routine warnings of the violence of any attempt at communion with a fetishized "subaltern".

Henry Louis Gates's *The Signifying Monkey: A Theory of African-American Literary Criticism* (1988) is a foundational text in contemporary African-American Studies. Gates set out to define an African-American literary criticism whose terms would be derived from the African-American literary tradition itself. At the time, the canon of African-American literature and the new academic field of African-American Studies were in the process of being formed rather than already in place, so *The Signifying Monkey* had the double (or circular) task of simultaneously defining the tradition. What Gates discerns in the African-American literary tradition is, as it were, an African-American poststructuralism *avant la lettre* – particularly a practice and theory of critical resignification – dating more than "two centuries" (Gates 1988, 46). This is condensed in the African-American use of the word "signify" (to refer to African-American practices of critical resignification) and the folk figure of the Signifying Monkey. Going further back, Gates traces an African practice and theory of critical resignification in the Yoruba, Pan-African and black-diaspora (Caribbean and South American) figure of the trickster Esu-Elegbara (ix, 5). Against the racist view that black art is not capable of original creation, only of mimicry, the black tradition has practised and theorized itself as "Signifyin(g)". Gates proposes the written form "Signifyin(g)" for this African-American oral term. He places the "g" in parenthesis because it is silent, and capitalizes the "s" to suggest its difference from standard English. Gates does not consider African-Americans an unpresentable "subaltern" group at all, in Spivak's sense of the term. He claims to be uncovering for a Western audience what was previously hidden because of racist assumptions.

Wole Soyinka focused on the Yoruba god Ogun as a figure of the artist (see Chapter 2). Gates turns to the god Esu as a figure of the critic, condensing the African tradition's theory of "figuration and interpretation" (Gates 1988, ix). The trickster figure of Esu is the "indigenous black metaphor for the literary critic" (9), a self-reflexive, self-theorizing nodal point in the African tradition and the "primal scene of instruction for the act of interpretation" in the tradition (5). Gates argues that, unlike Western metaphysics, African resignification is essentially to do with the deferral of the signified (like Derrida's "iterability", see Chapter 11) and the deconstruction of binary oppositions. Esu "translates yesterday's words/Into novel utterances" (*Oriki Esu* quoted in Gates 1988, 3), undermining fixed meaning. He is a figure of the "transcendence of binary opposition" – of the fixed and exclusive conceptual oppositions of Western philosophy – at the "crossroads of differences", in the absence of "presence, immediacy, and transparency" (38). He is thus the potential of "unreconciled opposites living in harmony" (30). Esu embodies "indeterminacy" (8), "multiplicity", the "ambiguity of figurative language", uncertainty, "open-endedness" and "never-ending" process (21). He is "free play" that "endlessly displaces meaning, deferring it by the play of signification" (42). Gates concludes that in Yoruba and Fon hermeneutics meaning is "multiple and indeterminate" (25). Bakhtin's "double-voiced discourse" (see Chapter 7), important to the poststructuralists, is also "indigenously African" – and crucial to Gates's own method (22).

Gates speculates that Esu's partner, the monkey, survived in the African-American trickster tales, though the "degree" to which the African-American Signifying Monkey is "anthropologically related" to Esu cannot be determined (Gates 1988, 88). In the African-American vernacular tradition, tales, poems and songs about the Signifying Monkey and about Signifyin(g) self-reflexively theorize African-American figuration and interpretation. Signifyin(g) is resignification or rather a whole spectrum of resignifying strategies which Gates attempts to describe. Broadly, Signifyin(g) is a "metaphor" for "revision, or intertextuality" (xxi) – interpretation or revision that "expands on the possibilities inherent" in the text Signified upon (xi). In other words, Signifyin(g) is "repetition with a signal difference" (xxiv). If the Western tradition values alternatively originality and mimesis (in the sense of truthful representation of reality), the "originality" or distinctiveness of the African-American vernacular tradition lies in valuing "refiguration, or repetition and difference, or troping" (79). In this sense, "to Signify is to be figurative" (81), to rework linguistic or artistic figures (rather than a literal redescription).

The Signifying Monkey tales display "playful language games", attention to the materiality and the "force of the signifier" and "indirect argument" (Gates 1988, 53–4). The Signifying Monkey is, in Bakhtin's terms, double-voiced and dwells in the "space between two linguistic domains" (104), standard American English and the black vernacular. Jazz, Gates argues, continues the black vernacular Signifyin(g) tradition: jazz Signifyin(g) "*extends*" and "tropes" originals; jazz improvisation is "repetition and revision" (63), "inversion" and "devision" (104). Similarly, African-American literature includes the vernacular (oral) and the "formal" (written) tradition (xii). The written tradition "shares much" with the Western tradition, which it "repeats with a difference", but its "foundation" is the African-American vernacular tradition (xxii). The great authors of the African-American written tradition are Signifyin(g), in a complex manner, upon the Western tradition *and* upon the black vernacular tradition *and* upon each other "to a remarkable extent" (xxii). In Bakhtinian terms, they are "double-voiced" (xxiii). Gates is himself double-voiced and declares his theory of Signifyin(g) indebted on the one hand to Ralph Ellison, Zora Neale Hurston, Ishmael Reed and on the other hand to Bakhtin and poststructuralism. In turn Gates is Signifyin(g) upon both the black tradition and poststructuralism.

To give some obvious examples, Hurston's *Their Eyes Were Watching God* combines standard English and black Southern dialect. It is a novel, a Western written genre, attempting to capture the empowering artistry of the oral Signifyin(g) practices of black all-male groups. Janie, Hurston's heroine, finds her voice when she bursts into critical Signifyin(g) in response to her husband's insults (Hurston 2007, Chapter 7). In *The Color Purple*, silent Celie's act of critical Signifyin(g) on her abusive husband is Alice Walker's revision of Hurston (Walker 1983a, 170–76). In Toni Morrison's *Song of Solomon* the poor, black Northern community of Southside is Signifyin(g) on public names, in the form of ironic negations: Mains Avenue is Not Doctor Street, Mercy Hospital is No Mercy Hospital. Railroad Tommy's barbershop is a place of critical Signifyin(g) for the male community, Morrison's revision of Hurston. They respond to the radio coverage of Emmett Till's racist killing with *their* side of the story (Morrison 1989, 80ff.), but *Song of Solomon* is in turn Signifyin(g) on their patriarchal views. *Song of Solomon* also critically revises and reverses the African-American trope of migration North as journey to the Promised Land, its hero Milkman moving South to free himself.

Within the written African-American literary tradition, Gates discerns four kinds of Signifyin(g), mapped out each in relation to an important genre or author in this tradition. Black writers often claimed "no black literary antecedents whatsoever" (Gates 1988, 114), not wishing to foreground their blackness. Against this, Gates traces, first, extensive "tropological revision" within the black tradition: since the earliest written slave narratives, tropes such as the "Talking Book" (reading aloud from a book was first figured as a talking book in a 1770 slave narrative) or the ascent from South to North are shared and intensely revised (xxv). Since the Enlightenment reason and literacy had been closely equated, hence the high stakes of black literacy, but the African-American Ur-trope of the Talking Book self-reflexively thematized and explored the relation between orality and literacy, but also oral and written cultural forms (130). Second, Gates reads Hurston's *Their Eyes Were Watching God* as *formal* revision. Hurston is an important predecessor for Gates in that she explicitly theorized "Signifyin(g)" – though she did not employ the term – arguing that "originality is the modification of ideas" (Hurston quoted in Gates 1988, 118). *Their Eyes* is a formal revision of the trope of the Talking Book: it is itself a talking book or a "speakerly" text – Gates Signifyin(g) on Barthes's "writerly" text (see Chapter 11). Hurston uses free indirect discourse, so that the black vernacular and standard English, initially separated, "come together" in a "double-voiced narrative mode" (xxv).

Third, Gates maps a "hidden polemic" (Gates 1988, 110), a "critical" or "polemical" Signifyin(g) in Ellison's relation to Richard Wright and in Reed's relation to both (106–7, 111). Where they claimed originality and effectively denied the existence of a black tradition, Gates attempts to demonstrate in detail a hidden black intertextuality (120), a "concealed revision" (124), and thereby (re)constitutes or (re)invents the black canon. Fourth, Gates outlines an un-critical Signifyin(g) among black women writers, as exemplified by Alice Walker's overt homage to Hurston in *The Colour Purple* and in her criticism (see Chapter 9). In positive terms, this form of Signifyin(g) involves "loving acts of bonding rather than ritual slayings" (xxviii). It implies "unity and resemblance rather than critique and difference" and, importantly, claims descent, thereby constituting the black tradition (xxvii). It can be argued that Hurston's *Their Eyes* practises this kind of intertextuality, and that it "Signifies upon the female novel of passing" by Nella Larsen and others (xxvii).

Gates's fourth kind of Signifyin(g) can be read as his hidden polemic with Walker and her generation of black women writers. They attracted an unprecedentedly large international audience to African-American literature, but also insisted on identifying themselves as black *women* writers within a distinctive black women's tradition. Gates effectively displaces their efforts of autonomization from the black male canon (and their polemic with it), misreading them as contributing to the black autonomization from the white canon (see 258). In mapping the practice of Signifyin(g) homage among black women writers, Gates raises and simultaneously dispels the question of a distinctive black women's tradition and canon.

Gates's theory of Signifyin(g) includes all four kinds of Signifyin(g) – and others not yet mapped – as equally valid. Shared by all kinds of Signifyin(g) is an element of "*indirection*" (Gates 1988, 74), "implication" (75), "troping" (68), (re)figuration. Signifyin(g), Gates argues, is a "simultaneous, but negated, parallel discursive (ontological, political) universe" *within* the "white discursive universe" (49), in a "symbiotic" relationship with it and "grafted" onto it (50). Rather than a utopian or separatist outside and rather than a relation of exteriority, Gates claims a relation of identity as well as difference between Signifyin(g), the white literary canon and white literary theory. Like Bakhtin's "double-voiced word", the hope is that Signifyin(g) is "decoloniz[ing]" by grafting a new "orientation" onto the existing ones (50).

Homi K. Bhabha (1949–) is a postcolonial theorist committed, at least in principle, to an interstitial communication between Postcolonial Studies, African-American studies, feminism, queer theory, Marxism, etc. He puts forward the figure of the hybrid migrant, a figure with resonance in all these fields. Bhabha's "migrant" is overdetermined and polysemous, and he envisages a meeting of migrants "without an assumed or imposed hierarchy" (Bhabha 1994, 4). Toni Morrison's *Tar Baby* (1981) explores the hidden, deep-seated and intersecting hierarchies underlying a community composed entirely of migrants. Bhabha's meeting of migrants, on the other hand, might be understood as an alliance politics (discussed above in relation to Butler) or as a Derridean ethics of deconstructing binary oppositions and their hierarchies (e.g. colonizer/colonized) within the self (see Chapters 1, 11); indeed Bhabha's major influence is Derrida.

Bhabha's *The Location of Culture* (1994) casts the processes of minoritarian translation Gates calls Signifyin(g) in a global, transnational, utopian cosmopolitan perspective discernible in the work of Fanon (where it is introduced as a counterpoint to national consciousness) (see Chapter 10). Unlike Gates, who traces – in his own self-reflexive and witty terms – a "myth of origins" (Gates 1988, ix) for African-American Signifyin(g) in the African figure of Esu, Bhabha is not searching for roots. The concentration of his work is on modernity and postmodernity. Whereas Gates alludes to the African diaspora but zooms in quickly on the African-American community, Bhabha views the African diaspora (begun with the enslavement and enforced migration of Africans to the Americas) as exemplary of a larger modern history of race, class and gender oppression and resistance. Gates argues that African-Americans are double-voiced – engaging both with dominant white and minority black traditions – and bicultural. African-American double-voiced-ness – the participation in dominant language and culture as well as the African-American – is a significant condition for their resistance to dominant culture (rather than the psychic tearing asunder described by Du Bois, see Chapter 7). Bhabha couldn't agree more, celebrating the "migrant's double-vision" (Bhabha 1994, 5) and desiring to explore "narratives where double-lives are led in the postcolonial world" (213) and in the "*in-between* spaces of double-frames" (216).

In Bhabha's terms, African-American "hybridity" finds a counterpart in the cultural "hybridity" of the colonized (whose cultural transitioning *in-between* indigenous and white-colonial cultures didn't involve physical displacement), as well as the "hybridity" of postcolonial migrants in our own era of globalization (3–5, 13, 227, 236). (Bhabha's exemplary hybridity involves a powerful and a powerless term.) Bhabha locates resistance to dominant culture in a hybridity that is akin to Gates's Signifyin(g). For example, Salman Rushdie's "empowering condition of hybridity" leads to an "iteration that is ... ironic and insurgent" (227). Rushdie's postmodern intertextuality is critical and repeats with a difference (see Chapter 9). The site of political and psychic resistance is an "in-between" (1–2, 216, 219, 227). In spatial terms, it is akin to Derrida's deconstructive crossing of the border between binary oppositions or Barthes's *a-topic site*: u-topian, a non-site outside fixed hierarchical identities (such as masculine/feminine, etc.) (see Chapter 11). In temporal terms, it is outside linear history, and explicitly indebted to Walter Benjamin's "now", which captures "a moment of transition" (224), of "undecidability or unconditionality" (233) (see Chapter 7). "Border" (1), "borderline" (8), "interstices" (2), "liminality" (224), "transit" (1), "crossing" (224), "intervening" (7), "transitional" (216), etc. recur in Bhabha's writing.

Bhabha argues that the *in-between* is a site for the articulation of differences: class, gender, race. Judith Butler rejected the kind of feminism that posits the primacy of gender and explored the articulation of multiple vectors of difference (discussed above). Bhabha similarly rejects the primacy of any single form of difference in favour of the "articulation of cultural differences" (1994, 1): against "any claim to a singular or autonomous sign of difference – be it class, gender or race", he is searching for "*something else besides, in-between*" (219). Derrida valued a textual practice of border-crossings between binary oppositions: "This dislocation (is what) writes/is written" (Derrida quoted in Bhabha 1994, 108). Bhabha values a subjectivity, textual practice and politics articulating contemporary cultural differences. In relation to subjectivity, Bhabha views it as formed in-between differences and "fixed identifications" (4), so that subjectivity is "a hybridity, a difference 'within'" (13). (W. E. B. Du Bois and Virginia Woolf captured the tensions between American and black, British and woman, within the self, as discussed in Chapter 7.) The relation of differences within the hybrid self spans from the dialogic to contradictory, "ambivalent, antagonistic identifications", though even "incommensurable" differences are negotiable (2, 229). By contrast, racist subjectivity is fixed around the "fantasy of [pure] difference", without proximity or communication, as in the white European's racist stereotypes of "the simian Negro" and "the effeminate Asiatic male" as completely different from the European (108). In relation to textual practice, Derek Walcott and Toni Morrison are viewed as exemplary, in their pursuit of linguistic and cultural double-voiced-ness. Bhabha calls for an alliance politics, a "genuinely articulatory" politics of "borderline negotiations" (223), within a utopian horizon of interstitial "solidarity" among differences (3, 231). His implicit assumption is that hybrid subjectivity lends itself to alliance politics and that both are politically progressive.

Bhabha reconceptualizes community and solidarity from the "interstitial perspective" of alliance politics (Bhabha 1994, 3). His concept of community "disrupts the homogeneity of the imagined community of the nation" (230), as well as the homogeneity and naturalness of any single and fenced-in form of identity (based on the primacy of race, class or gender). In this sense, community is unhomely and uncanny, like Sethe's haunted house in *Beloved*, a site of "extra-territorial and cross-cultural initiations" (9–10). For Bhabha "minority" groups (in terms of power rather than size) are hybrid groups and, rather than focusing on any particular group, Bhabha attends to their potential political alliance, particularly the "translational time and space" in which "minority communities negotiate their collective identifications" and act "through incommensurable ... positions" (231). Solidarity by no means excludes dissension and conflicts, and includes a process of translation.

Bhabha is explicitly indebted to Walter Benjamin's concept of "translation". Far from lending itself to a facile multiculturalist mantra, Benjamin's concept highlights the "irresolution" and "liminality" of cultural translation and the "*element of resistance* in the process of transformation", as Bhabha points out (Bhabha 1994, 224). Translation involves the untranslatable: a "foreign", disjunctive, "unstable" and "indeterminate" element (227). Cultural translation – like Benjamin's "now" – is steeped in "contingency" and "indeterminacy" (234). Bhabha follows Benjamin in highlighting the "*unrepresentable*" (217) and converges with Spivak's emphasis on the unpresentability of the subaltern. Marlow in *Heart of Darkness* situates himself in the "midst of the incomprehensible" (Conrad quoted in Bhabha 1994, 213) and Bhabha recognizes "cognitive obscurity" (216) as an inevitable consequence rather than a predicament in our era of globalization. Achebe might object to Bhabha that the otherness of African people in *Heart of Darkness* is the sense of complete untranslatability rather than incomplete translation (see Chapter 8). For Bhabha, by contrast, multiculturalism requires exploration of affinity with one's cultural others, as well as acceptance of the impossibility of full and fixed knowledge of those others.

In dialogue with Bhabha, the postcolonial theorist Robert J. C. Young (1950–) develops a parallel and complementary project in *White Mythologies* and *Colonial Desire*. *White Mythologies: Writing History and the West* (1990, 2004) asks how one would go about putting together and practising a non-Eurocentric theory of history. In response to this question, Young performatively summons and maps out a new academic field of knowledge, Postcolonial Studies. In 1990 "there was no obvious discipline or place where it would fit" (Young 2004, 1). Young's role in relation to Postcolonial Studies is comparable to Gates's in relation to African-American Studies and Gilbert and Gubar's in relation to Women's Studies. *White Mythologies* inaugurates this new field by situating Said, Spivak, Bhabha and others within it, by (re)constructing its genealogy and by asking what *forms* of knowledge it might and might not pursue. The genealogy Young attributes to Postcolonial Studies is multiple. If the Ur-text of the new field is the work of Fanon, poststructuralism is also vitally important. Theory and politics – especially "tricontinental" politics, the postcolonial politics of the three continents of the South: Africa, Asia and Latin America (1) – are equally affirmed and placed in dialogue. There is a Marxist strand in the field's indebtedness to non-Western Marxisms (e.g. Fanon) or atypical versions of Western Marxism (e.g. Benjamin,

Bakhtin). There is also a programmatic willingness to listen to feminists outside the field (e.g. Kristeva, Cixous).

The question of method or mode of knowledge appropriate to Postcolonial Studies might be asked broadly like this: "How can we know *and* respect the other?" (Young 2004, 46). The questioner here is implicitly situated as white and male. While Bhabha's preferred method in the *Location of Culture* is to enter into dialogue with contemporary writers (e.g. Morrison, Walcott, Coetzee), Young opts to look back. His project is a revisionist historiography: situated (or aware of its Western "positionality", as discussed in relation to Spivak above), self-critical and reparative. Foucault and Said showed the "deep articulation of knowledge with power" (43), but Foucault singled out self-critique as the most valuable aspect of the Enlightenment (see Chapter 4). In the context of Postcolonial Studies Western knowledge and reason must pay self-critical attention to their tendency to claiming universal validity – leading to self-relativization – and bear in mind the collusion of science and knowledge in the past with Imperialism and racism. The subject/object model of knowledge – the knowing subject and the object to be known – is suspicious in itself. The result may be that the human subjects being studied are treated as less than subjects.

The work of Emmanuel Levinas, admired and promoted by Derrida, has been influential. Levinas's thought attempts to articulate respect for the other in their otherness, based on acceptance of "infinite separation" rather than cognitively "grasping" the other (Levinas quoted in Young 2004, 44). What Levinas has in mind is one person's love for another, but his ethics has influenced Spivak's sense of the unpresentability of the "subaltern" and Bhabha's insistence on cognitive obscurity in cultural translation. Levinas associates the time-honoured European ontological obsession with Unity and the One (see Chapter 3) with the violence of an incorporating self that reduces all to itself, the other to the same, and calls for a turn from ontology to ethics. Elements of ethical postcolonial knowledge will include care not to impose one's concepts and the use of dialogue, with sensitivity to imbalances of power, that allows for a "calling into question of the same by the other" – or they might involve a movement of "*the same unto the other which never returns to the same*", perhaps a becoming-other in Deleuze and Guattari's terms (Levinas quoted in Young 2004, 47, 49). For example, the *Odyssey*'s Lotos-eaters would be a more appropriate postcolonial figure than Odysseus. Derrida's response to Levinas is to question both the possibility of "absolute otherness", without any element of identity with the same, and "the ability to excise all violence in the relation to it" (47).

If Levinas and Derrida stand for Western self-critique, Young's revisionist historiography hybridizes Western thought. For example, Young understands Derrida's deconstructive critique of centre and margin as a deconstruction of the authority of the West and a contribution to the decolonization of European thought. The point is not simply that Derrida, born in colonial Algeria, might have been more preoccupied by anticolonial struggles than previously thought. The bolder move is to show the degree to which the entire poststructuralist movement was indebted to "tricontinental" political *and theoretical* movements, for example Maoism as Young sets out to demonstrate in the introduction to the revised 2004 edition. This exemplifies a reparative historiography listening for silenced voices.

In *Colonial Desire: Hybridity in Theory, Culture and Race* (1995) Young responds to Bhabha's theorization of hybridity with a genealogy of the concept of hybridity in nineteenth- and twentieth-century English scientific, cultural and literary discourses on interracial sexual encounters and mixed-race offspring. A complex picture emerges which Young formalizes into five conceptual alternatives oscillating between two poles of racial fusion and contrafusion (disjunction):

1 The "polygenist" view assumes distinct and fixed racial differences such that hybridization is not possible (any offspring of interracial sexuality are thought to be infertile or that they will become so in a generation or two).
2 "Amalgamation", in its positive version, endorses a melting-pot effect (the creation of new and viable mixed-race types).
3 The view of "decomposition" is that any amalgamation does not last either through eventual infertility or through reversion to one of the original types (so it is a variation of 1).
4 "Proximate hybridization" distinguishes between proximate and distant racial groups and only supports hybridization of the proximate.
5 Amalgamation, in its negative version, views hybridization as degeneration, i.e. the new mixed-race types are deemed inferior to the original, pure ones (Young 1995, 18 throughout).

In sum, theories of racial hybridity have oscillated between two poles: while versions of fusion envisage mixing, merging and the "evanescence of 'race'", versions of contrafusion may set racial groups "against each other" in antagonism (19).

Young discerns a similar oscillation and doubleness in Bakhtin's theorization of linguistic (and cultural) hybridity (in terms of heteroglossia, dialogism, internal dialogism, double-voiced-ness, dissonance and resonance, see Chapter 7). Using Bakhtin's terms we might say that Bakhtin's linguistic hybridity is at least double-voiced, oscillating between dissonance and resonance. (Dissonance and resonance can be mapped onto Young's double project of (self-) critique and reconstruction in *White Mythologies.*) Dialogic dissonance might include a contestatory or antagonistic dialogue between two languages/cultural perspectives, a "politicized setting of cultural differences against each other dialogically", "division and separation", a disarticulation and "subversion of authority" (Young 1995, 21–2), intervention, resistance or a "diasporizing" (in Bakhtin's terms, centrifugal) movement (25) or a movement of repulsion. Dialogic resonance might include a centripetal movement of attraction, fusion into a new language/cultural perspective, generative coalescence and coalition, a hegemony creating new spaces and new forms, a new counter-hegemonic alliance. Of course linguistic/cultural hybridity is not exclusively political, and when political not necessarily "radical", but Young concentrates on its radical political manifestations.

Young sometimes seems to suggest that only linguistic/cultural dissonance is politically radical but it is clear that both dissonance and resonance might take political forms. He maps Gates's "Signifyin(g)" and Bhabha's "hybridity" onto dissonance, Edward Brathwaite's "creolization" onto resonance (Young 1995, 21), but it seems to me that aspects of Gates's and Bhabha's work are also counter-hegemonic, articulatory, resonant. Resonant and dissonant dialogism are capacious containers of heterogeneous repertoires of dialogic linguistic/cultural practice and interaction. For example, assimilation into the majority and the articulation of a radical counter-hegemonic alliance, though hugely different, might both be forms of resonance. The most virulent form of racism and its contestation might both be forms of dissonance. These repertoires are resources for contemporary multiculturalism that Young is emphatically not setting up as a binary opposition; he values both modes, in spite of his propensity for dissonance. We might say that the relation of resonance and dissonance is one of "impossible simultaneity" (26) between the two.

For Young resonance and dissonance, fusion and contrafusion remain the ambiguous resources of twenty-first-century multiculturalism. As his work reminds us, the "interval that we assert between ourselves and the past may be much less than we assume" (Young 1995, 28). Either resource can take enabling and disabling forms, and neither is enough on its own. Is it possible to practise cultural hybridization while also celebrating our differences? These are not new problems. The premise of Young's project is that a self-critical and ethical postcolonial historiography at least clarifies the "forms" of historical "repetition" in which we are inevitably caught (28).

Conclusion

- Cixous's *écriture féminine* explores the connections of the body, sexuality and writing – the text as "sext". The erotogeneity of a multiple and excessive (rather than genital and reproductive) sexuality spills over into an excess of aesthetic forms and meanings. *Écriture féminine* is not necessarily writing by women. Its catachrestic collage-aesthetic of multiple brief "identificatory embraces" is one of *voler*: stealing/flight/excessive giving.
- Irigaray's *écriture féminine* pursues "mimicry" or playful repetition in her texts on thinkers and writers. In connecting writing to the body, she turns to tactility: touch as an alternative encounter and merging of self and other, dissolving the opposition activity/passivity. Figures such as two lips touching each other (a polysemous figure of speaking/writing, plural sexuality, solidarity) initiate her project of symbolic renewal.
- Butler outlines a strategy of gender resignification: in response to pervasive genderizing, she advocates openness to resignification, multiple,

proliferating and self-consciously contingent gender performances. Valuing conflict rather than consensus and critiquing utopianism, Butler rejects the primacy of gender and sexual difference over other differences. Turning to black women's writing (e.g. Larsen's *Passing*) and feminists of colour, she endorses their articulation of gender, race, sexuality, class.

- Sedgwick maps out contradictions in twentieth-century discourses on sexuality and gender: in relation to sexuality, the contradiction between a minoritizing and a universalizing discourse on homosexuality; in relation to gender, the contradiction between an inversion model and a gender-separatist model of homosexuality.
- Said studies Orientalism as a discourse constructing "the Oriental" as an ahistorical essence, paying particular attention to literature: the ways in which texts reproduce and participate in Orientalism *and* question and resist it. Said proposes a double, "contrapuntal" reading that avoids the neocolonial and anticolonial camps and stages a dialogue between the two. For example, Said discerns a colonial and a virtual contrapuntal vision in *Heart of Darkness*, while he extends or dialogizes *Kim* with a reparative contrapuntal reading.
- Spivak presents the unpresentability of the *subaltern*, outside neocolonial, anticolonial and postcolonial elites, including the multiculturalist liberal academy. Spivak advocates the postcolonial critic's self-reflective awareness of their positionality and privilege and their recognition of the inaccessibility of their "object".
- Gates suggests that the self-theorizing of African and African-American literary traditions anticipated poststructuralist strategies. The African trickster Esu embodies resignification, the deferral of the signified and the deconstruction of binary oppositions. African-American Signifyin(g) is double-voiced revision or repetition with a difference, both in relation to the Western written tradition and the African-American vernacular tradition. Signifyin(g) might take the form of tropological revision, formal revision, hidden polemic or homage.
- Bhabha figures the hybrid migrant's double vision. He understands "hybridity" as ironic or insurgent iteration. The "in-between" is a crossing of the border between binary opposites or the negotiation and articulation of incommensurable identities. Bhabha understands politics and "community" as an uncanny translational time/space. Cultural translation involves the untranslatable and recognition of cognitive obscurity.
- Young maps out Postcolonial Studies, reconstructing its multiple political and theoretical genealogy and exploring ethical forms of knowledge, particularly (self-)critique and reconstructive, reparative historiography. These methods or forms include self-relativization, acceptance of cognitive distance, being questioned by the other, becoming the other, critique of the limits of dialogue, deconstruction of the authority of the West, showing the non-Western origins of Western thought. Young's

genealogy of the concept of "hybridity" captures an oscillation between fusion (coalition, coalescence into new forms, reconstruction) and contrafusion (disjunction, contestation, critique). These ambiguous resources can be reclaimed towards a double postcolonial method: (self-)critique and reconstructive historiography.

Further reading

See especially Bhabha 1994; Butler 1990, 1993, 1995; Cixous 1976, 1986, 1991; Gates 1988; Irigaray 1985b, 1985c, 1991b; Kristeva 1986c; Mohanty 1984; Said 1993, 2003; Sedgwick 2008; Spivak 1999; Young 1995, 2004.

Bibliography

Achebe, Chinua. 1990. "An Image of Africa: Racism in Conrad's *Heart of Darkness*". In Achebe, *Hopes and Impediments: Selected Essays.* New York: Anchor. 1–20.

——. 2001. *Things Fall Apart.* London: Penguin.

Adorno, Theodor, Walter Benjamin, Ernst Bloch, Bertolt Brecht and George Lukács. 1977a. *Aesthetics and Politics.* London: Verso.

Adorno, Theodor. 1977b. "Commitment". Trans. Francis McDonagh. In Adorno *et al.* 1977a. 177–95.

——. 2000a. *The Adorno Reader.* Ed. Brian O'Connor. Oxford: Blackwell.

——. 2000b. "The Actuality of Philosophy". In Adorno 2000a. 24–39.

——. 2000c. "Why Philosophy?". In Adorno 2000a. 41–53.

——. 2000d. "Cultural Criticism and Society". In Adorno 2000a. 195–210.

——. 2001a. *The Culture Industry.* Ed. J. M. Bernstein. London: Routledge.

——. 2001b. "Free Time". In Adorno 2001a. 187–97.

——. 2001c. "The Schema of Mass Culture". In Adorno 2001a. 61–97.

——. 2001d. "Transparencies on Film". In Adorno 2001a. 178–86.

——. 2002. *Aesthetic Theory.* Eds Gretel Adorno, Rolf Tiedemann and Robert Hullot-Kentor. Trans. Robert Hullot-Kentor. London: Continuum.

Aeschylus. 1989. *Prometheus Bound.* Trans. James Scully and C. J. Herington. New York and Oxford: Oxford University Press.

——. 1996. *Persians.* Ed. and trans. Edith Hall. Warminster: Aris & Phillips.

——. 2002. *Oresteia.* Trans. Christopher Collard. Oxford: Oxford University Press.

Agapitos, Panagiotis, A. 2008. "Literary Criticism". In *The Oxford Handbook of Byzantine Studies.* Eds Elizabeth Jeffreys with John Haldon and Robin Cormack. New York: Oxford University Press. 77–85.

Alexander, Gavin. 2004. Editor's Introduction. In *Sidney's* The Defence of Poesy *and Selected Renaissance Literary Criticism.* London: Penguin. xviii–lxxix.

Allen, Graham. 2000. *Intertextuality.* London: Routledge.

Aquinas, Thomas. 1991. *Summa theologiae* [*The Sum of Theology*] [extract]. In Minnis *et al.* 1991. 239–43.

Arendt, Hannah. 2006. *Eichmann in Jerusalem: A Report on the Banality of Evil.* Rev. ed. London: Penguin.

Aristotle. 1986. *De anima* [*On the Soul*]. Trans. Hugh Lawson-Tancred. Harmondsworth: Penguin.

——. 1987. *Poetics.* Trans. Richard Janko. Indianapolis, IN: Hackett.

——. 1991. *Rhetoric.* Trans. George A. Kennedy. Oxford and New York: Oxford University Press.

——. 1995. *Poetics*. Ed. and trans. Stephen Halliwell. In *Aristotle: Poetics; Longinus: On the Sublime; Demetrius: On Style*. Loeb Classical Library. Cambridge, MA: Harvard University Press. 27–141.

——. 2000. *Nicomachean Ethics*. Ed. and trans. Roger Crisp. Cambridge: Cambridge University Press.

Armstrong, Isobel. 1993. *Victorian Poetry: Poetry, Poetics and Politics*. London: Routledge.

Armstrong, Tim. 2005. *Modernism: A Cultural History*. Cambridge: Polity.

Arnheim, Rudolf. 1932. *Film als Kunst* [*Film as Art*]. Berlin: Ernst Rowohlt.

Arnold, Matthew. 1993a. *Culture and Anarchy and Other Writings*. Ed. Stefan Collini. Cambridge: Cambridge University Press.

——. 1993b. *Culture and Anarchy*. In Arnold 1993a. 53–211.

——. 1993c. "The Function of Criticism at the Present Time". In Arnold 1993a. 26–51.

Asmis, Elizabeth. 1992. "Plato on Poetic Creativity". In *Cambridge Companion to Plato*. Ed. Richard Kraut. Cambridge: Cambridge University Press. 338–64.

Attridge, Derek. 1992. "Introduction: Derrida and the Questioning of Literature". In Derrida 1992a. 1–29.

Atwood, Margaret. 1986. *The Handmaid's Tale*. London: Cape.

——. 2005. *The Penelopiad*. Edinburgh: Canongate.

——. 2007. "'Everybody Is Happy Now'". *The Guardian*. 17 November. Online. www.guardian.co.uk/books/2007/nov/17/classics.margaretatwood.

Auden, W. H. 1979. "In Memory of Sigmund Freud". In *W. H. Auden. Selected Poems*. Ed. Edward Mendelson. London: Faber. 91–5.

Auerbach, Erich. 1968. *Mimesis: The Representation of Reality in Western Literature*. Trans. Willard R. Trask. Princeton, NJ: Princeton University Press.

Augustine. 1958. *On Christian Doctrine*. Trans. D. W. Robertson, Jr. Indianapolis, IN: Bobbs-Merrill.

——. 2002. *On the Trinity*. Ed. Gareth B. Matthews. Trans. Stephen McKenna. Cambridge: Cambridge University Press.

Austin, J. L. 1975. *How to Do Things with Words*. 2nd ed. Eds J. O. Urmson and Marina Sbisà. Oxford: Clarendon.

Bage, Robert. 1985. *Hermsprong*. Oxford: Oxford University Press.

Bakhtin, M. M. 1981a. *The Dialogic Imagination*. Ed. Michael Holquist. Trans. Caryl Emerson and Michael Holquist. Austin: University of Texas Press.

——. 1981b. "Discourse in the Novel". In Bakhtin 1981a. 259–422.

——. 1981c. "From the Prehistory of Novelistic Discourse". In Bakhtin 1981a. 41–83.

——. 1984. *Rabelais and His World*. Trans. Hélène Iswolsky. Bloomington, IN: Indiana University Press.

——. 1999. *Problems of Dostoevsky's Poetics*. Ed. and trans. Caryl Emerson. Manchester: Manchester University Press.

——. 2012. *Sobraniie Sochinenii v Semi Tomakh. Tom 3: Teoriia Romana*. Eds V. V. Kozhinov and I. L. Popova. Commentary S. G. Bocharov *et al*. Moscow: Iazyki slavianskikh kul'tur.

Balázs, Béla. 1924. *Der Sichtbare Mensch* [*Visible Man*]. Wien; Leipzig: Deutsch-Österreichischer Verlag.

Bally, Charles and Albert Sechehaye. 1960. "Preface to the First Edition". In Saussure 1960. xiii–xvi.

Balzac, Honoré de. 2007. *Sarrasine*. Trans. David Carter. London: Hesperus.
Baraka, Amiri [LeRoy Jones] and Lary Neal, eds. 1968. *Black Fire: An Anthology of Afro-American Writing*. New York: Wm. Morrow.
Barthes, Roland. 1973. *Mythologies*. Trans. Annette Lavers. London: Paladin.
——. 1975. *S/Z*. Trans. Richard Miller. London: Jonathan Cape.
——. 1976. *The Pleasure of the Text*. Trans. Richard Miller. London: Cape.
——. 1977a. *Image, Music, Text*. Ed. and trans. Stephen Heath. London: Fontana.
——. 1977b. "The Death of the Author". In Barthes 1977a. 142–8.
——. 1977c. "From Work to Text". In Barthes 1977a. 155–64.
——. 1993a. *A Roland Barthes Reader*. Ed. Susan Sontag. London: Vintage.
——. 1993b. *Roland Barthes by Roland Barthes* [extract]. In Barthes 1993a. 415–25.
——. 1993c. "Inaugural Lecture, Collège de France". In Barthes 1993a. 457–78.
Bates, Ernest Sutherland. ed. n.d. *The Bible Designed to be Read as Literature*. London: Heinemann.
Baudelaire, Charles. 1970. "Loss of a Halo". In Baudelaire, *Paris Spleen*. Trans. Louise Varèse. New York: New Directions. 94.
——. 1992. "The Painter of Modern Life". In *Charles Baudelaire: Selected Writings on Art and Literature*. Ed. and trans. P. E. Charvet. London: Penguin. 390–435.
——. 1993. *Les fleurs du mal*. Paris: Seuil.
Baudrillard, Jean. 1993a. *Symbolic Exchange and Death*. Trans. Iain Hamilton Grant. London: Sage.
——. 1993b. *The Transparency of Evil: Essays on Extreme Phenomena*. Trans. James Benedict. London: Verso.
——. 1994. *Simulacra and Simulation*. Trans. Sheila Faria Glaser. Ann Arbor: University of Michigan Press.
Bauman, Zygmunt. 1987. *Legislators and Interpreters*. Cambridge: Polity.
——. 2000. *Liquid Modernity*. Cambridge: Polity.
Beauvoir, Simone de. 1953. *The Second Sex*. Ed. and trans. H. M. Parshley. London: Jonathan Cape.
——. 1964. *The Ethics of Ambiguity*. 2nd ed. Trans. Bernard Frechtman. New York: Citadel.
——. 2001. *The Prime of Life*. Trans. Peter Green. London: Penguin.
——. 2011. *The Second Sex*. Trans. Constance Borde and Sheila Malovany-Chevallier. London: Vintage.
Beckett, Samuel. 1979. *The Beckett Trilogy: Molloy, Malone Dies, The Unnamable*. London: Picador.
——. 1992. *Krapp's Last Tape*. London: Faber.
——. 2006. *Waiting for Godot: A Tragicomedy in Two Acts*. London: Faber.
——. 2009. *Endgame*. London: Faber.
Beiser, Frederick. 2005. *Hegel*. New York: Routledge.
Benjamin, Walter. 1992a. *Illuminations*. Ed. Hannah Arendt. Trans. Harry Zohn. London: Fontana.
——. 1992b. "On Some Motifs in Baudelaire". In Benjamin 1992a. 152–96.
——. 1992c. "The Work of Art in the Age of Mechanical Reproduction". In Benjamin 1992a. 211–44.
——. 1992d. "Theses on the Philosophy of History". In Benjamin 1992a. 245–55.
——. 1992e. "The Storyteller". In Benjamin 1992a. 83–107.
——. 1997. *One-Way Street, and Other Writings*. Trans. Edmund Jephcott and Kingsley Shorter. London: Verso.

——. 2002. *The Arcades Project*. Eds Howard Eiland and Rolf Tiedemann. Trans. Howard Eiland and Kevin McLaughlin. Cambridge, MA: Belknap Press of Harvard University Press.

Benveniste, Émile. 1971. *Problems in General Linguistics*. Trans. Mary Elizabeth Meek. Coral Gables, FL: University of Miami Press.

Bernstein, J. M. 2004. "'The dead speaking of stones and stars': Adorno's *Aesthetic Theory*". In Rush 2004a. 139–64.

Bersani, Leo. 1978. *A Future for Astyanax: Character and Desire in Literature*. London: Marion Boyars.

Bhabha, Homi K. 1994. *The Location of Culture*. London: Routledge.

——. 2008. "Foreword to the 1986 Edition. Remembering Fanon: Self, Psyche and the Colonial Condition". In Fanon 2008. xxi–xxxvii.

Bloch, Ernst. 1977. "Discussing Expressionism". Trans. Rodney Livingstone. In Adorno *et al.* 1977a. 16–27.

Bloom, Harold. 1994. "Freud and the Sublime: A Catastrophe Theory of Creativity". In Ellmann 1994a. 173–95.

——. 1997. *The Anxiety of Influence: A Theory of Poetry*. 2nd ed. New York: Oxford University Press.

Board of Education. 1921. "The Newbolt Report on the Teaching of English in England". Online. www.educationengland.org.uk/documents/newbolt/newbolt1921.html.

Boccaccio, Giovanni. 1991. *The Genealogy of the Gentile Gods* [extract]. In Minnis *et al.* 1991. 420–38.

——. 2008. *Decameron*. Trans. J. G. Nichols. Oxford: Oneworld Classics.

Boehmer, Elleke and Steven Matthews. 2011. "Modernism and Colonialism". In Levenson 2011a. 284–300.

Bogue, Ronald. 2012. "Deleuze and Literature". *The Cambridge Companion to Deleuze*. Eds Daniel W. Smith and Henry Somers-Hall. Cambridge: Cambridge University Press. 286–306.

Booth, Wayne C. 1991. *The Rhetoric of Fiction*. 2nd ed. London: Penguin.

Borges, Jorge Luis. 1975. "On Exactitude in Science". In Borges, *A Universal History of Infamy*. Trans. Norman Thomas di Giovanni. London: Penguin.

Bouson, J. Brooks. 2000. *"Quiet as it's kept": Shame, Trauma and Race in the Novels of Toni Morrison*. Albany: SUNY Press.

Braddon, M. E. 2010. *Lady Audley's Secret*. London: Penguin.

Brantlinger, Patrick. 1988. *Rule of Darkness: British Literature and Imperialism, 1830–1914*. Ithaca, NY: Cornell University Press.

Brecht, Bertolt. 1964. "A Short Organum for the Theatre". *Brecht on Theatre*. Trans. John Willett. London: Methuen. 179–205.

——. 1977. "Against Georg Lukács". Trans. Stuart Hood. In Adorno *et al.* 1977a. 68–85.

Breton, André. 1972. *Manifestoes of Surrealism*. Trans. Richard Seaver and Helen R. Lane. Ann Arbor: Michigan University Press.

Brontë, Charlotte. 2008. *Jane Eyre*. Eds Margaret Smith and Sally Shuttleworth. Oxford: Oxford University Press.

Brontë, Emily. 2006. *Wuthering Heights*. London: Penguin.

Brooker, Peter. 2006. "Key Words in Brecht's Theory and Practice of Theatre". In *The Cambridge Companion to Brecht*. 2nd ed. Eds Peter Thomson and Glendyr Sacks. Cambridge: Cambridge University Press. 209–24.

Brooker, Peter, Andrzej Gasiorek, Deborah Longworth and Andrew Thacker, eds. 2011a. *The Oxford Handbook of Modernisms*. Oxford: Oxford University Press.

Brooker, Peter, Andrzej Gasiorek, Deborah Longworth and Andrew Thacker. 2011b. "Introduction". In Brooker *et al.* 2011a. 1–13.

Brooks, Cleanth. 1965. *Modern Poetry and the Tradition*. New York: Oxford University Press.

——. 1968. *The Well Wrought Urn: Studies in the Structure of Poetry.* London: Methuen.

——. 2001. "The Formalist Critics". In Leitch *et al.* 2001. 1366–71.

Brooks, Peter. 1992. *Reading for the Plot: Design and Intention in Narrative.* Cambridge, MA: Harvard University Press.

——. 1994. "The Idea of Psychoanalytic Criticism". In Brooks, *Psychoanalysis and Storytelling*. Oxford: Blackwell. 20–45.

Browning, Elizabeth Barrett. 1978. *Aurora Leigh and Other Poems.* Ed. Cora Kaplan. London: The Women's Press.

Bürger, Peter. 1984. *Theory of the Avant-garde.* Trans. Michael Shaw. Manchester: Manchester University Press.

Burke, Edmund. 1990. *A Philosophical Enquiry into the Origin of Our Ideas of the Sublime and the Beautiful.* Ed. Adam Phillips. Oxford: Oxford University Press.

——. 1999. *Reflections on the Revolution in France.* Oxford: Oxford University Press.

Burliuk, David, Alexander Kruchenykh, Vladmir Mayakovsky and Victor Khlebnikov. 1988. "A Slap in the Face of Public Taste". In *Russian Futurism through Its Manifestoes, 1912–1928.* Ed. Anna Lawton. Trans. Anna Lawton and Herbert Eagle. Ithaca, NY: Cornell University Press. 51–52.

Bushnell, Rebecca, ed. 2005. *A Companion to Tragedy.* Oxford: Blackwell.

Butler, Judith. 1990. *Gender Trouble: Feminism and the Subversion of Identity.* New York: Routledge.

——. 1993. *Bodies that Matter: On the Discursive Limits of "Sex".* New York: Routledge.

——. 1995. "Contingent Foundations: Feminism and the Question of 'Postmodernism'". In Seyla Benhabib, Judith Butler, Drucilla Cornell and Nancy Fraser, *Feminist Contentions.* New York: Routledge. 17–34.

——. 2002. *Antigone's Claim.* New York: Columbia University Press.

Butler, Marilyn. 2010. "Culture's Medium: The Role of the Review". In *The Cambridge Companion to British Romanticism.* 2nd ed. Ed. Stuart Curran. Cambridge: Cambridge University Press. 127–52.

Calvet, Louis-Jean. 1994. *Roland Barthes: A Biography.* Trans. Sarah Wykes. Cambridge: Polity.

Carlyle, Thomas. 1840. *Chartism.* London: J. Fraser. Online. http://archive.org/details/chartism00carlgoog.

——. 1960. *Past and Present.* London: Dent.

Carter, Angela. 1981. *The Bloody Chamber and Other Stories.* London: Penguin.

——. 1985. "Black Venus". In Carter, *Black Venus.* London: Chatto. 7–24.

——. 1987. "The Loves of Lady Purple". In Carter, *Fireworks.* Rev. ed. London: Chatto. 23–38.

Cavarero, Adriana. 2002. "On the Body of Antigone". In *Stately Bodies: Literature, Philosophy, and the Question of Gender.* Trans. Robert de Lucca and Deanna Shemek. Ann Arbor: University of Michigan Press. 13–97.

Caygill, Howard. 2004. "Walter Benjamin's Concept of Cultural History". In Ferris 2004. 73–96.

Césaire, Aimé. 1963. *La tragédie du roi Christophe.* Paris: Présence africaine.

——. 1995. *Notebook of a Return to My Native Land. Cahier d'un retour au pays natal* [Bilingual ed.]. Trans. Mireille Rosello with Annie Pritchard. Newcastle upon Tyne: Bloodaxe.

——. 2010. *A Season in the Congo*. Trans. Gayatri Chakravorty Spivak. Chicago: University of Chicago Press.

Chekhov, Anton. 2009. *The Cherry Orchard*. Trans. Tom Stoppard and Helen Rappaport. London: Faber.

Christian, Barbara. 2007. "The Race for Theory". In *New Black Feminist Criticism, 1985–2000*. Eds Gloria Bowles, M. Giulia Fabi and Arlene R. Keizer. Urbana: University of Illinois Press. 40–50.

Cixous, Hélène. 1976. "The Laugh of the Medusa". Trans. Keith Cohen and Cathy Cohen. *Signs* 1.4 (Summer): 875–93.

——. 1986. "Sorties". In Cixous and Clément 1986. 63–129.

——. 1991. "Coming to Writing". In Cixous, *"Coming to Writing" and Other Essays*. Ed. Deborah Jenson. Trans. Sarah Cornell *et al.* Cambridge, MA: Harvard University Press. 1–58.

——. 1997. "Theater, History, Ethics: An Interview with Hélène Cixous on 'The Perjured City, or the Awakening of the Furies'". With Bernadette Fort. *New Literary History* 28.3 (Summer): 425–56.

——. 2010. *La ville parjure ou le réveil des Erinyes* [*The Perjured City, or the Awakening of the Furies*]. Paris: Théâtre du Soleil.

Cixous, Hélène and Catherine Clément. 1986. *The Newly Born Woman*. Trans. Betsy Wing. Manchester: Manchester University Press.

Clinefelter, Joan L. 2005. *Artists for the Reich: Culture and Race from Weimar to Nazi Germany*. Oxford: Berg.

Coetzee, J. M. 1987. *Foe*. London: Penguin.

Cohen, Cathy J. 1997. "Punks, Bulldaggers, and Welfare Queens: The Radical Potential of Queer Politics?" *GLQ: A Journal of Lesbian and Gay Studies* 3.4 (May): 437–65.

Colebrook, Claire. 2000. "Inhuman Irony: The Event of the Postmodern". In *Deleuze and Literature*. Eds Ian Buchanan and John Marks. Edinburgh: Edinburgh University Press. 100–134.

——. 2002. *Gilles Deleuze*. London: Routledge.

Coleridge, Samuel Taylor. 1975. *Biographia Literaria*. Ed. George Watson. London: Dent.

——. 1989. *Coleridge's Criticism of Shakespeare: A Selection*. Ed. R. A. Foakes. London: Athlone.

Colish, Marcia L. 1983. *The Mirror of Knowledge: A Study in the Medieval Theory of Knowledge*. Rev. ed. Lincoln: University of Nebraska Press.

Collins Dictionary. 2003. Glasgow: HarperCollins.

Conley, Thomas M. 2005. "Byzantine Criticism and the Uses of Literature". In *The Cambridge History of Literary Criticism Volume 2: The Middle Ages*. Eds Alastair Minnis and Ian Johnson. Cambridge: Cambridge University Press. 669–92.

Conrad, Joseph. 2007. *Heart of Darkness*. Ed. Owen Knowles. London: Penguin.

Dangarembga, Tsitsi. 2001. *Nervous Conditions*. London: Women's Press.

Dante Alighieri. 1971. *The Divine Comedy of Dante Alighieri*. Trans. John D. Sinclair. London: Oxford University Press.

——. 1991a. *Il Convivio* [*The Banquet*]. In Minnis *et al.* 1991. 394–412.

——. 1991b. "Epistle to Can Grande della Scala". In Minnis *et al.* 1991. 458–69.

Darwin, Charles. 1996. *The Origin of Species*. Ed. Gillian Beer. Oxford: Oxford University Press.

Debord, Guy. 1994. *The Society of the Spectacle*. New York: Zone Books.

Defoe, Daniel. 1994. *The Fortunes and Misfortunes of the Famous Moll Flanders*. London: Penguin.

——. 2007. *Robinson Crusoe*. Eds Thomas Keymer and James Kelly. Oxford: Oxford University Press.

Deleuze, Gilles. 1983. *Nietzsche and Philosophy*. Trans. Hugh Tomlinson. London: Athlone.

——. 1986–9. *Cinema*. 2 vols. [*Cinema 1. The Movement-Image* and *Cinema 2. The Time-Image*]. Trans. Hugh Tomlinson. London: Athlone.

——. 1988. *Spinoza: Practical Philosophy*. Trans. Robert Hurley. San Francisco: City Lights.

——. 1990a. *The Logic of Sense*. Ed. Constantin Boundas. Trans. Mark Lester with Charles Stivale. London: Athlone.

——. 1990b. "Plato and the Simulacrum". In Deleuze 1990a. 253–66.

——. 1991. *Empiricism and Subjectivity: An Essay on Hume's Theory of Human Nature*. Trans. Constantin V. Boundas. New York: Columbia University Press.

——. 1998. "Literature and Life". In Deleuze, *Essays Critical and Clinical*. Trans. Daniel W. Smith and Michael A. Greco. London: Verso. 1–6.

——. 2000. *Proust and Signs: The Complete Text*. Trans. Richard Howard. London: Athlone.

——. 2004. *Difference and Repetition*. Trans. Paul Patton. London: Continuum.

Deleuze, Gilles and Michel Foucault. 1977. "Intellectuals and Power: A Conversation between Michel Foucault and Gilles Deleuze". In Foucault 1977a. 205–17.

Deleuze, Gilles and Félix Guattari. 1984. *Anti-Oedipus*. Trans. Robert Hurley, Mark Seem and Helen R. Lane. London: Athlone.

——. 1986. *Kafka: Toward a Minor Literature*. Trans. Dana Polan. Minneapolis: University of Minnesota Press.

——. 1988. *A Thousand Plateaus: Capitalism and Schizophrenia*. Trans. Brian Massumi. London: Athlone.

Derrida, Jacques. 1978. "Structure, Sign and Play in the Discourses of the Human Sciences". In Derrida, *Writing and Difference*. Trans. Alan Bass. Chicago: University of Chicago Press. 278–93.

——. 1981a. *Dissemination*. Trans. Barbara Johnson. London: Athlone.

——. 1981b. "Plato's Pharmacy". In Derrida 1981a. 61–171.

——. 1982a. *Margins of Philosophy*. Trans. Alan Bass. New York: Harvester Wheatsheaf.

——. 1982b. "Différance". In Derrida 1982a. 1–27.

——. 1982c. "The Ends of Man". In Derrida 1982a. 111–36.

——. 1992a. *Acts of Literature*. Ed. Derek Attridge. New York: Routledge.

——. 1992b. "Mallarmé". Trans. Christine Roulston. In Derrida 1992a. 110–26.

——. 1992c. "'This Strange Institution Called Literature': An Interview with Jacques Derrida". Trans. Geoffrey Bennington and Rachel Bowlby. In Derrida 1992a. 33–75.

——. 1995. "Khōra". In Derrida's *On the Name*. Ed. Thomas Dutoit. Trans. David Wood, John P. Leavey, Jr. and Ian McLeod. Stanford, CA: Stanford University Press. 89–130.

——. 1997a. *Of Grammatology*. Corrected ed. Trans. Gayatri Chakravorty Spivak. Baltimore, MD: The Johns Hopkins University Press.

——. 1997b. "… That Dangerous Supplement …" In Derrida 1997a. 141–64.

——. 1997c. "Writing before the Letter". In Derrida 1997a. 1–93.

——. 2004. "Enlightenment Past and to Come." Trans. Gulliver Cragg. *Le Monde Diplomatique*. 6 November. Online. http://mondediplo.com/2004/11/06derrida.

Dettmar, Kevin J. H. 2005. "Introduction". In *A Companion to Modernist Literature and Culture*. Eds David Bradshaw and Kevin J. H. Dettmar. Oxford: Blackwell Reference Online. www.blackwellreference.com/subscriber/tocnode.html?id=g9780631204350_chunk_g97806312043502. Accessed 23 April 2013.

Dickens, Charles. 1894. *Bleak House*. London: Chapman & Hall.

——. 1949. *Oliver Twist*. London: Macdonald.

——. 1997. *Our Mutual Friend*. Ed. Adrian Poole. London: Penguin.

——. 1998. *Hard Times*. Ed. Paul Schlicke. Oxford: Oxford University Press.

——. 1999. *David Copperfield*. Eds Nina Burgis and Andrew Sanders. Oxford: Oxford University Press.

——. 2003. *Bleak House*. Ed. Nicola Bradbury. London: Penguin.

Dickinson, Emily. 1975. "One need not be a Chamber – to be Haunted–". In *The Complete Poems of Emily Dickinson*. Ed. Thomas H. Johnson. London: Faber. 333.

Du Bois, W. E. B. 1999. *The Souls of Black Folk: Authoritative Text, Contexts, Criticism*. Eds Henry Louis Gates, Jr. and Terri Hume Oliver. New York: Norton.

——. 2007. "'Krigwa Players Little Negro Theatre': The Story of a Little Theatre Movement". In *Theatre in Theory 1900–2000: An Anthology*. Ed. David Krasner. Oxford: Blackwell. 165.

Duncan-Jones, Katherine. 2002. "Introduction". In Sidney 2002b. vii–xviii.

Duncan-Jones, Katherine and J. A. van Dorsten. 1973. "Editors' Commentary". In Sidney 1973b. 173–225.

Dutton, Richard. 1986. *Modern Tragicomedy and the British Tradition: Beckett, Pinter, Stoppard, Albee and Storey*. Norman: University of Oklahoma Press.

Eagleton, Terry. 1990. *The Ideology of the Aesthetic*. Oxford: Blackwell.

——. 1996. *Literary Theory: An Introduction*. 2nd ed. Minneapolis: University of Minnesota Press.

——. 2003. *Sweet Violence: The Idea of the Tragic*. Oxford: Blackwell.

Eco, Umberto. 1988. *The Aesthetics of Thomas Aquinas*. Trans. Hugh Bredin. London: Radius.

Eichenbaum, Boris. 1998. "Introduction to the Formal Method". In Rivkin and Ryan 1998. 8–16.

——. 2001. "The Theory of the 'Formal Method'". In Leitch *et al.* 2001. 1062–87.

Eliot, George. 1990. "The Natural History of German Life". In George Eliot, *Selected Essays, Poems and Other Writings*. Eds A. S. Byatt and Nicholas Warren. Harmondsworth: Penguin. 107–39.

——. 1994. *Romola*. Ed. Andrew Brown. Oxford: Oxford University Press.

——. 1996. *Adam Bede*. Ed. Valentine Cunningham. Oxford: Oxford University Press.

——. 2003. *The Mill on the Floss*. London: Penguin.

Eliot, T. S. 1928. *For Lancelot Andrewes: Essays on Style and Order*. London: Faber & Gwyer.

——. 1934. *After Strange Gods: A Primer of Modern Heresy. The Page-Barbour Lectures at the University of Virginia, 1933*. London: Faber.

——. 1951a. *T. S. Eliot: Selected Essays*. London: Faber.

——. 1951b. "The Metaphysical Poets". In T. S. Eliot 1951a. 281–91.

——. 1951c. "The Function of Criticism". In T. S. Eliot 1951a. 23–34.

——. 1959. *Four Quartets*. London: Faber and Faber.

——. 1962. *Notes towards the Definition of Culture.* 2nd ed. London: Faber.

——. 1964. *The Use of Poetry and the Use of Criticism: Studies in the Relation of Criticism to Poetry in England.* 2nd ed. London: Faber.

——. 1969a. *The Complete Poems and Plays of T. S. Eliot.* London: Book Club Associates.

——. 1969b. *The Waste Land.* In T. S. Eliot 1969a. 59–80.

——. 1969c. *Four Quartets.* In T. S. Eliot 1969a. 171–98.

——. 1997a. *The Sacred Wood: Essays on Poetry and Criticism.* London: Faber.

——. 1997b. "Tradition and the Individual Talent". In Eliot 1997a. 39–49.

——. 1997c. "The Perfect Critic". In Eliot 1997a. 1–13.

——. 1997d. "Hamlet and His Problems". In Eliot 1997a. 81–7.

——. 1997e. "Imperfect Critics". In Eliot 1997a. 14–38.

——. 2003. *The Waste Land.* In *The Waste Land and Other Poems.* Ed. Frank Kermode. New York: Penguin.

Ellmann, Mary. 1968. *Thinking about Women.* London: Macmillan.

Ellmann, Maud, ed. 1994a. *Psychoanalytic Literary Criticism.* London: Longman.

——. 1994b. "Introduction". In Ellman 1994a. 1–35.

Empson, William. 1950. "The Verbal Analysis". *The Kenyon Review* 12.4 (Autumn): 594–601.

——. 2004. *Seven Types of Ambiguity.* 3rd ed. London: Pimlico.

Engels, Friedrich. 1993. *The Condition of the Working Class in England.* Ed. David McLellan. Oxford: Oxford University Press.

Esslin, Martin. 1961. *The Theatre of the Absurd.* Garden City, NY: Doubleday.

Euripides. 1988a. *Euripides III: Bacchanals; Madness of Hercules; Children of Hercules; Phoenician Maidens; Suppliants.* Trans. A. S. Way. Loeb Classical Library. Cambridge, MA and London: Harvard University Press. 1–123.

——. 1988b. *Alcestis.* Ed. and trans. D. Conacher. Warminster: Aris & Phillips.

——. 2000. *Iphigenia in Tauris.* Ed. and trans. M. J. Cropp. Warminster: Aris & Phillips.

——. 2002. *Helen*; *Phoenician Women*; *Orestes.* Ed. and trans. David Kovacs. Cambridge, MA: Harvard University Press.

Fanon, Frantz. 1990. *The Wretched of the Earth.* Trans. Constance Farrington. Harmondsworth: Penguin.

——. 2008. *Black Skin, White Masks.* New ed. Trans. Charles Lam Markmann. London: Pluto.

Felman, Shoshana. 1994. "Beyond Oedipus: The Specimen Story of Psychoanalysis". In Ellmann 1994a. 76–104.

——. 1996. "Turning the Screw of Interpretation". In Vice 1996. 106–14.

Ferris, David S., ed. 2004. *The Cambridge Companion to Walter Benjamin.* Cambridge: Cambridge University Press.

Fielding, Henry. 1998. *Tom Jones.* Eds John Bender and Simon Stern. Oxford: Oxford University Press.

Fish, Stanley. 1980. *Is There a Text in This Class? The Authority of Interpretive Communities.* Cambridge, MA: Harvard University Press.

Flaubert, Gustave. 1979. *Bouvard et Pécuchet.* Ed. Claudine Gothot-Mersch. Paris: Gallimard.

——. 1986. *Madame Bovary.* Ed. Bernard Ajac. Paris: Flammarion.

——. 2005. *Bouvard and Pécuchet.* Trans. Mark Polizzotti. Champaign, IL: Dalkey Archive Press.

Foucault, Michel. 1977a. *Language, Counter-Memory, Practice: Selected Essays and Interviews*. Ed. Donald F. Bouchard. Trans. Donald F. Bouchard and Sherry Simon. Ithaca, NY: Cornell University Press.

——. 1977b. "What Is an Author?". In Foucault 1977a. 113–38.

——. 1984. "Preface". In Deleuze and Guattari 1984. xi–xiv.

——. 1986a. *The Foucault Reader*. Ed. Paul Rabinow. Harmondsworth: Penguin.

——. 1986b. "What Is Enlightenment?". Trans. Catherine Porter. In Foucault 1986a. 32–50.

——. 1986c. "Nietzsche, Genealogy, History". Trans. Donald F. Bouchard and Sherry Simon. In Foucault 1986a. 76–100.

——. 1990. *The History of Sexuality. Volume 1: An Introduction*. Trans. Robert Hurley. London: Penguin.

——. 1991. *Discipline and Punish*. Trans. Alan Sheridan. London: Penguin.

——. 1992. *The History of Sexuality. Volume 2: The Use of Pleasure*. Trans. Robert Hurley. London: Penguin.

——. 2002. *The Order of Things: An Archaeology of the Human Sciences*. London: Routledge.

Franta, Andrew. 2007. *Romanticism and the Rise of the Mass Public*. Cambridge: Cambridge University Press.

Frazer, James George. 1981. *The Golden Bough*. New York: Gramercy.

Freccero, John. 2007. "Allegory and Autobiography". In *The Cambridge Companion to Dante*. Ed. Rachel Jacoff. 2nd ed. Cambridge: Cambridge University Press. 161–80.

Freud, Sigmund. 1977. "Fragment of an Analysis of a Case of Hysteria ('Dora')". In Freud, *Volume 8: Case Histories I. "Dora" and "Little Hans"*. Ed. Angela Richards. Trans. Alix and James Strachey. Harmondsworth: Penguin. 31–164.

——. 1979. "From the History of an Infantile Neurosis (The 'Wolf Man')". In Freud, *Volume 9: Case Histories II. "Ratman", Schreber, "Wolf Man", Female Homosexuality*. Ed. Angela Richards. Trans. James Strachey. London: Penguin. 224–366.

——. 1991a. *Volume 11. On Metapsychology*. Ed. Angela Richards. Trans. James Strachey. London: Penguin.

——. 1991b. *Beyond the Pleasure Principle*. In Freud 1991a. 269–338.

——. 1991c. *The Ego and the Id*. In Freud 1991a. 339–408.

——. 1991d. "Mourning and Melancholia". In Freud 1991a. 251–68.

——. 1995. 21 September 1897 letter to Fliess. In *The Freud Reader*. Ed. Peter Gay. New York: Norton. 111–13.

——. 2001a. *The Interpretation of Dreams*. In vols 4 and 5 of *The Standard Edition of the Complete Psychological Works of Sigmund Freud*. Ed. and trans. James Strachey, with Anna Freud, Alix Strachey and Alan Tyson. London: Vintage. Vol. 4, 1–338. Vol. 5, 339–625.

——. 2001b. "Female Sexuality". In vol. 21 of *The Standard Edition of the Complete Psychological Works of Sigmund Freud*. Ed. and trans. James Strachey, with Anna Freud, Alix Strachey and Alan Tyson. London: Vintage. 225–43.

——. 2001c. "The Uncanny". Trans. Alix Strachey. In Leitch *et al.* 2001. 929–52.

Fricker, Miranda. 2003. "Life-Story in Beauvoir's Memoirs". In *The Cambridge Companion to Simone de Beauvoir*. Ed. Claudia Card. Cambridge: Cambridge University Press. 208–27.

Frye, Northrop. 1973. *Anatomy of Criticism: Four Essays*. Princeton, NJ: Princeton University Press.

——. 2001. "The Archetypes of Literature". In Leitch *et al.* 2001. 1445–57.

——. 2004. *Northrop Frye's Fearful Symmetry: A Study of William Blake.* Ed. Nicholas Halmi. Toronto: University of Toronto Press.
Gadamer, Hans-Georg. 2004. *Truth and Method.* 2nd rev. ed. Trans. Joel Weinsheimer and Donald G. Marshall. London: Continuum.
Gates, Henry Louis, Jr. 1988. *The Signifying Monkey: A Theory of African-American Literary Criticism.* Oxford: Oxford University Press.
Gay, Peter. 1996a. *The Enlightenment: An Interpretation. Vol. I: The Rise of Modern Paganism.* New York: Norton.
——. 1996b. *The Enlightenment: An Interpretation. Vol. II: The Science of Freedom.* New York: Norton.
Gayle, Addison, Jr., ed. 1971. *The Black Aesthetic.* Garden City, NY: Doubleday.
Gilbert, Sandra M. and Susan Gubar. 2000. *The Madwoman in the Attic.* 2nd ed. New Haven, CT: Yale University Press.
——. 2007. "Preface". 3rd ed. *Norton Anthology of Literature by Women: The Traditions in English.* 2 vols. New York: Norton.
Godwin, William. 1976. *Enquiry Concerning Political Justice.* Ed. Isaac Kramnick. London: Penguin.
——. 1994. *St Leon.* Ed. Pamela Clemit. Oxford: Oxford University Press.
——. 2000. *Caleb Williams.* Eds. Gary Handwerk and A. A. Markley. Peterborough, Ont.: Broadview.
Goethe, Johann Wolfgang von. 1949–59. *Faust.* 2 vols. Trans. Philip Wayne. Harmondsworth: Penguin.
——. 2011. *Wilhelm Meister.* Trans. H. M. Waidson. Richmond: Oneworld Classics.
Goldthorpe, Rhiannon. 1992. "Understanding the Committed Writer". *The Cambridge Companion to Sartre.* Ed. Christina Howells. Cambridge: Cambridge University Press. 140–77.
Goulimari, Pelagia. 2004. "Postmodernism – Minorities: A Deleuzo-Guattarian Intervention". *Postmodern Culture* 14.3 (Spring).
——, ed. 2007. *Postmodernism. What Moment?* Manchester: Manchester University Press.
Greenblatt, Stephen. 2001. "Introduction to *The Power of Forms in the English Renaissance*". In Leitch *et al.* 2001. 2250–54.
Gregory, John, ed. 1991. *The Neoplatonists.* Ed. and trans. with introduction John Gregory. London: Kyle Cathie.
Gyler, Louise. 2010. *The Gendered Unconscious: Can Gender Discourses Subvert Psychoanalysis?* London: Routledge.
Habermas, Jürgen. 1990. *The Philosophical Discourse of Modernity.* Trans. Frederick Lawrence. Cambridge: Polity.
Hall, Stuart. 2001. "Cultural Studies and Its Theoretical Legacies". In Leitch *et al.* 2001. 1898–1910.
Halliwell, Stephen. 1995. "Introduction to Aristotle's *Poetics*". In Aristotle 1995. 3–26.
Halperin, David M. 1995. *Saint Foucault: Towards a Gay Hagiography.* New York: Oxford University Press.
Hardy, Thomas. 2003. *Tess of the D'Urbervilles.* Ed. Tim Dolin. London: Penguin.
Hassan, Ihab. 1971. *The Dismemberment of Orpheus: Toward a Postmodern Literature.* New York: Oxford University Press.
Hebdige, Dick. 2003. *Subculture: The Meaning of Style.* New ed. London: Routledge.
Hegel, G. W. F. 1975. *Hegel's Aesthetics. Lectures on Fine Art.* Trans. T. M. Knox. 2 vols. Oxford: Oxford University Press.

——. 1998. "Tragedy as a Dramatic Art". In *Tragedy*. Eds John Drakakis and Naomi Conn Liebler. London: Longman. 23–52.

Heidegger, Martin. 1962. *Being and Time*. Trans. John Macquarrie and Edward Robinson. Oxford: Blackwell.

——. 1975a. *Poetry, Language, Thought*. Ed. and trans. Albert Hofstadter. New York: Perennial Library.

——. 1975b. "What Are Poets For?". In Heidegger 1975a. 89–142.

——. 1975c. "Language". In Heidegger 1975a. 187–210.

——. 1993a. *Basic Writings*. Rev. ed. Ed. David Farrell Krell. London: Routledge. 217–65.

——. 1993b. "Letter on Humanism". In Heidegger 1993a. 217–65.

——. 1993c. "The Question Concerning Technology". In Heidegger 1993a. 307–341.

——. 2000. *Introduction to Metaphysics*. Trans. Gregory Fried and Richard Polt. New Haven, CT and London: Yale University Press.

Henry, Paul. 1991. "The Place of Plotinus in the History of Thought". In Plotinus 1991. xlii–lxxxiii.

Herodotus. 2008. *The Histories*. Ed. Carolyn Dewald. Trans. Robin Waterfield. Oxford: Oxford University Press.

Hirsch, E. D., Jr. 2001. "Objective Interpretation." In Leitch *et al.* 2001. 1684–1707.

Hirschkop, Ken. 1999. *Mikhail Bakhtin: An Aesthetic for Democracy*. Oxford: Oxford University Press, 1999.

Hirst, David L. 1984. *Tragicomedy*. London: Methuen.

Hofstadter, Albert. 1975. "Introduction and References". In Heidegger 1975a. ix–xxv.

Holquist, Michael. 2002. *Dialogism*. 2nd ed. London: Routledge.

Homer. 1995. *Odyssey*. 2nd ed. rev. George E. Dimock. Trans. A. T. Murray. Cambridge, MA: Harvard University Press.

——. 1999. *Iliad*. 2nd ed. rev. William F. Wyatt. Trans. A. T. Murray. Cambridge, MA: Harvard University Press.

hooks, bell. 2001. "Postmodern Blackness". Leitch *et al.* 2001. 2478–84.

Horace. 1989. *The Art of Poetry* [*Ars Poetica*]. Trans. D. A. Russell. In *Classical Literary Criticism*. Eds D. A. Russell and M. Winterbottom. Oxford: Oxford University Press. 98–110.

Horkheimer, Max and Theodor W. Adorno. 1998. *Dialectic of Enlightenment*. Trans. John Cumming. New York: Continuum.

Hughes, Langston. 1940. *The Big Sea, an Autobiography*. New York: Knopf.

——. 2001. "The Negro Artist and the Racial Mountain". Leitch *et al.* 2001. 1313–17.

Hume, David. 1975a. *Enquiries Concerning Human Understanding and Concerning the Principles of Morals*. Ed. L. A. Selby-Bigge. 3rd ed. rev. P. H. Nidditch. Oxford: Clarendon.

——. 1975b. *An Enquiry Concerning the Principles of Morals*. In Hume 1975a. 167–323.

——. 1985. *A Treatise of Human Nature*. London: Penguin.

——. 1987a. *Essays Moral, Political and Literary*. Rev. ed. Eugene F. Miller. Indianapolis, IN: Liberty Fund.

——. 1987b. "Of the Standard of Taste". In Hume 1987a. 226–49.

——. 2008. *Principal Writings on Religion including Dialogues Concerning Natural Religion; and, The Natural History of Religion*. Ed. J. C. A. Gaskin. Oxford: Oxford University Press.

Hurston, Zora Neale. 2001a. "Characteristics of Negro Expression". In Leitch *et al.* 2001. 1146–58.

——. 2001b. "What White Publishers Won't Print". In Leitch *et al.* 2001. 1159–62.

——. 2007. *Their Eyes Were Watching God.* Introduction Zadie Smith. London: Virago.

Hutcheon, Linda. 2002. *The Politics of Postmodernism.* 2nd ed. London: Routledge.

Huxley, Aldous. 1977. *Brave New World.* London: Granada.

Huysmans, Joris-Karl. 2009. *Against Nature (À Rebours).* Ed. Nicholas White. Trans. Margaret Mauldon. Oxford: Oxford University Press.

Ibsen, Henrik. 2008a *Hedda Gabler.* Trans. Brian Friel. London: Faber.

——. 2008b. *A Doll's House.* Rev. ed. Eds Nick and Non Worrall. Trans. Michael Meyer. London: Methuen.

Irigaray, Luce. 1985a. *This Sex Which Is Not One.* Trans. Catherine Porter with Carolyn Burke. Ithaca, NY: Cornell University Press.

——. 1985b. "This Sex Which Is Not One". Trans. Catherine Porter. In Irigaray 1985a. 23–33.

——. 1985c. "The Power of Discourse and the Subordination of the Feminine". In 1985a. 68–85.

——. 1985d. *Speculum of the Other Woman.* Trans. Gillian C. Gill. Ithaca, NY: Cornell University Press.

——. 1991a. *The Irigaray Reader.* Ed. Margaret Whitford. Oxford: Blackwell.

——. 1991b. "Equal or Different?". Trans. David Macey. In Irigaray 1991a. 30–33.

——. 1997. "This Sex Which Is Not One". Trans. Claudia Reeder. In *The Second Wave: A Reader in Feminist Theory.* Ed. Linda Nicholson. New York: Routledge. 323–29.

——. 2004. "Preface". Trans. Luce Irigaray and Laine Harrington. In *Luce Irigaray: Key Writings.* London: Continuum. vii–xv.

Iser, Wolfgang. 1980. "Interaction between Text and Reader". In *The Reader in the Text: Essays on Audience and Interpretation.* Eds. Susan Suleiman and Inge Crosman. Princeton, NJ: Princeton University Press. 106–19.

Jakobson, Roman. 1987a. *Language in Literature.* Eds. Krystyna Pomorska and Stephen Rudy. Cambridge, MA: Belknap Press of Harvard University Press.

——. 1987b. "The Dominant". In Jakobson 1987a. 41–6.

——. 1987c. "Linguistics and Poetics". In Jakobson 1987a. 62–96.

James, Henry. 2011. *The Turn of the Screw.* Ed. David Bromwich. London: Penguin.

Jameson, Fredric. 1990. *Late Marxism: Adorno, or, The Persistence of the Dialectic.* London: Verso.

——. 1991. *Postmodernism, or, The Cultural Logic of Late Capitalism.* London: Verso.

Jarry, Alfred. 2003. *Ubu Roi.* Trans. Beverly Keith and G. Legman. Mineola, NY: Dover.

Jauss, Hans Robert. 1982. "Literary History as a Challenge to Literary Theory". In Jauss, *Toward an Aesthetic of Reception.* Trans. Timothy Bahti. Brighton: Harvester. 3–45.

Jeffreys, Elizabeth, ed. 1998. *Digenis Akritis: The Grottaferrata and Escorial Versions.* Trans. Elizabeth Jeffreys. Cambridge: Cambridge University Press.

Jennings, Michael. 2004. "Walter Benjamin and the European Avant-Garde". In Ferris 2004. 18–34.

Johnson, Barbara. 1996. "The Frame of Reference: Poe, Lacan, Derrida". In Vice 1996. 84–100.

Johnson, James Weldon. 2004. *Black Manhattan.* In Johnson, *Writings.* New York: Library of America.

Johnson, Samuel. 2001. "Preface to Shakespeare". In Leitch *et al.* 2001. 468–80.

Jones, Peter. 1993. "Hume's Literary and Aesthetic Theory". In Norton 1993a. 255–80.

Joyce, James. 1992. *A Portrait of the Artist as a Young Man*. Ed. Seamus Deane. London: Penguin.

——. 2008a. *Dubliners*. Ed. Jeri Johnson. Oxford: Oxford University Press.

——. 2008b. *Ulysses*. Ed. Jeri Johnson. Oxford: Oxford University Press.

Kafka, Franz. 2000. *The Trial*. Trans. Idris Parry. London: Penguin.

——. 2007. "A Report to an Academy". In *Metamorphosis and Other Stories*. Ed. and trans. Michael Hofmann. London: Penguin. 225–36.

Kane, Sarah. 1996. *Blasted & Phaedra's Love*. London: Methuen.

Kant, Immanuel. 1987. *Critique of Judgment*. Trans. Werner S. Pluhar. Indianapolis, IN: Hackett.

——. 1991a. *Kant's Political Writings*. Ed. Hans Reiss. Trans. H. B. Nisbet. 2nd ed. Cambridge: Cambridge University Press.

——. 1991b. "An Answer to the Question: 'What Is Enlightenment?'". In Kant 1991a. 54–60.

——. 2007. *Critique of Pure Reason*. Rev. 2nd ed. Ed. Norman Kemp Smith. Basingstoke: Palgrave Macmillan.

Kaufman, Robert. 2004. "Adorno's Social Lyric, and Literary Criticism Today: Poetics, Aesthetics, Modernity". In *The Cambridge Companion to Adorno*. Ed. Tom Huhn. Cambridge: Cambridge University Press. 354–75.

——. 2005. "Aura, Still". In *Walter Benjamin and Art*. Ed. Andrew E. Benjamin. London: Continuum. 121–47.

Kaufmann, Walter. 1967. "Translator's Introduction". In Nietzche 1967. 3–13.

Keats, John. 1998. *Selected Poetry*. Ed. Elizabeth Cook. Oxford World's Classics. Oxford: Oxford University Press.

——. 2008. *The Major Works: Including* Endymion, *and Selected Letters*. Ed. Elizabeth Cook. Oxford: Oxford University Press.

Kenner, Hugh. 1971. *The Pound Era*. Berkeley: University of California Press.

Kierkegaard, Søren. 2006. *Fear and Trembling*. Eds. C. Stephen Evans and Sylvia Walsh. Trans. Sylvia Walsh. Cambridge: Cambridge University Press.

King, Jeannette. 1978. *Tragedy in the Victorian Novel: Theory and Practice in the Novels of George Eliot, Thomas Hardy and Henry James*. Cambridge: Cambridge University Press.

Kipling, Rudyard. 1987. *Kim*. Ed. Edward W. Said. Harmondsworth: Penguin.

Kirwan, Christopher. 2001. "Augustine's Philosophy of Language". *Cambridge Companion to Augustine*. Eds. Eleonore Stump and Norman Kretzmann. Cambridge: Cambridge University Press. 186–204.

Komnene, Anna. 2009. *The Alexiad*. Rev. ed. Ed. Peter Frankopan. Trans. E. R. A. Sewter and Peter Frankopan. London: Penguin.

Kramer, Dale. 1975. *The Forms of Tragedy*. London and Basingstoke: Macmillan.

Kramnick, Isaac, ed. 1995. *The Portable Enlightenment Reader*. New York: Penguin.

Kristeva, Julia. 1982. *Powers of Horror: An Essay on Abjection*. Trans. Leon S. Roudiez. New York: Columbia University Press.

——. 1984. *Revolution in Poetic Language*. Trans. Margaret Waller. New York: Columbia University Press.

——. 1986a. *The Kristeva Reader*. Ed. Toril Moi. Oxford: Blackwell.

——. 1986b. "Word, Dialogue and Novel". Trans. Alice Jardine, Thomas Gora and Leon S. Roudiez. In Kristeva 1986a. 34–61.

——. 1986c. “Women’s Time”. Trans. Alice Jardine and Harry Blake. In Kristeva 1986a. 187–213.
——. 1989. *Black Sun: Depression and Melancholia*. Trans. Leon S. Roudiez. New York: Columbia University Press.
Kuhn, Thomas S. 2012. *The Structure of Scientific Revolutions*. 4th ed. Chicago: University of Chicago Press.
Lacan, Jacques. 1973. “Seminar on ‘The Purloined Letter’”. *Yale French Studies* 48: 38–72.
——. 1977a. *Écrits: A Selection*. Trans. Alan Sheridan. London: Tavistock.
——. 1977b. “The Mirror Stage as Formative of the Function of the I as Revealed in Psychoanalytic Experience”. In Lacan 1977a. 1–7.
——. 1977c. “The Agency of the Letter in the Unconscious or Reason since Freud”. In Lacan 1977a. 146–78.
——. 1979. *The Four Fundamental Concepts of Psycho-analysis*. Ed. Jacques-Alain Miller. Trans. Alan Sheridan. Harmondsworth: Penguin.
——. 1982. “Le symbolique, l’imaginaire et le réel”. *Bulletin de l’Association Freudienne* 1: 4–13.
Lang, Andrew, ed. 2010. *The Arabian Nights*. Auckland: Floating Press.
Larsen, Nella. 2007. *Passing: Authoritative Text, Backgrounds and Contexts, Criticism*. Ed. Carla Kaplan. New York: Norton.
Lawrence, D. H. 1949. *The Rainbow*. Harmondsworth: Penguin.
——. 1960. *Women in Love*. Harmondsworth: Penguin.
——. 2003. *Studies in Classic American Literature*. Eds Ezra Greenspan, Lindeth Vasey and John Wothen. Cambridge: Cambridge University Press.
——. 2004. *Psychoanalysis and the Unconscious and Fantasia of the Unconscious*. Ed. Bruce Steele. Cambridge: Cambridge University Press.
Leavis, F. R. 1933. *Mass Civilisation and Minority Culture*. In *For Continuity*. Cambridge: Gordon Fraser, The Minority Press.
——. 1964. *The Common Pursuit*. New York: New York University Press.
——. 1967. *D. H. Lawrence: Novelist*. London: Chatto & Windus.
——. 1968. “Mr. Auden’s Talent”. In *A Selection from Scrutiny*. Ed. F. R. Leavis. Vol. 1. London: Cambridge University Press. 110–14.
——. 1972a. *New Bearings in English Poetry: A Study of the Contemporary Situation*. [With “Retrospect”.] Harmondsworth: Penguin.
——. 1972b. *The Great Tradition*. Harmondsworth: Penguin.
——. 1975. *The Living Principle: English as a Discipline of Thought*. London: Chatto & Windus.
——. 1976. *Thought, Words and Creativity: Art and Thought in Lawrence*. London: Chatto & Windus.
——. 2013. *The Two Cultures? The Significance of C. P. Snow*. Cambridge: Cambridge University Press.
Le Doeuff, Michèle. 1991. *Hipparchia’s Choice: An Essay Concerning Women, Philosophy, etc*. Trans. Trista Selous. Oxford: Blackwell.
——. 2006. “Engaging with Simone de Beauvoir”. In *The Philosophy of Simone de Beauvoir*. Ed. Margaret A. Simons. Bloomington: Indiana University Press. 11–19.
Lee, Hermione. 1992. “Introduction”. In Woolf, *The Years*. Ed. Hermione Lee. Oxford: Oxford University Press. xii–xxxii.
Leitch, Vincent B. (general editor), William E. Cain, Laurie A. Finke, Barbara E. Johnson, John McGowan and Jeffrey J. Williams, eds. 2001. *The Norton Anthology of Theory and Criticism*. New York: Norton.

Levenson, Michael, ed. 2011a. *The Cambridge Companion to Modernism*. 2nd ed. Cambridge: Cambridge University Press.

——. 2011b. "Introduction". In Levenson 2011a. 1–8.

Levine, George. 1981. *The Realist Imagination: English Fiction from Frankenstein to Lady Chatterley*. Chicago: Chicago University Press.

Lévi-Strauss, Claude. 2011. *Tristes Tropiques*. Trans. John Weightman and Doreen Weightman. London: Penguin.

Lewis, Pericles. 2007. *The Cambridge Introduction to Modernism*. Cambridge: Cambridge University Press.

Linett, Maren Tova. 2010. "Modernist Women's Literature: An Introduction". In *The Cambridge Companion to Modernist Women Writers*. Ed. Maren Tova Linett. Cambridge: Cambridge University Press. 1–16.

Livingstone, Rodney, Perry Anderson and Francis Mulhern. 1977a. "Presentation I". In Adorno *et al.* 1977a. 9–15.

——. 1977b. "Presentation IV". In Adorno *et al.* 1977a. 142–50.

Locke, Alain, ed. 1997. *The New Negro*. New York: Touchstone.

Longinus. 1995. *On the Sublime*. Trans. W. H. Fyfe. Rev. Donald Russell. In *Aristotle: Poetics; Longinus: On the Sublime; Demetrius: On Style*. Loeb Classical Library. Cambridge, MA: Harvard University Press. 159–307.

Lucretius. 2001. *On the Nature of Things*. Trans. and introduction Martin Ferguson Smith. Indianapolis, IN: Hackett.

Lukács, Georg. 1977. "Realism in the Balance". Trans. Rodney Livingstone. In Adorno *et al.* 1977a. 28–59.

Lyotard, Jean-François. 1984a. *The Postmodern Condition*. Trans. Geoff Bennington and Brian Massumi. Manchester: Manchester University Press.

——. 1984b. "Answering the Question: What Is Postmodernism?" Trans. Régis Durand. In Lyotard 1984a. 71–82.

Macherey, Pierre. 1978. *A Theory of Literary Production*. Trans. Geoffrey Wall. London: Routledge & Kegan Paul.

Mallarmé, Stéphane. 1999. "Crise de vers" ["Crisis in Poetry"]. Trans. Rosemary Lloyd. In *Mallarmé: The Poet and His Circle*. Ed. Rosemary Lloyd. Ithaca, NY: Cornell University Press. 227–33.

Marcuse, Herbert. 1991. *One-Dimensional Man*. London: Routledge.

Marinetti, F. T. 2009. "The Manifesto of Futurism". Trans. Lawrence S. Rainey. In *Futurism: An Anthology*. Eds Lawrence S. Rainey, Christine Poggi, Laura Wittman. New Haven, CT: Yale University Press. 51–3.

Marx, Karl. 1977a. *Selected Writings*. Ed. David McLellan. Oxford: Oxford University Press.

——. 1977b. *Capital*. Trans. Samuel Moore and E. Aveling. In Marx 1977a. 415–507.

——. 1977c. *Economic and Philosophical Manuscripts*. Trans. David McLellan. In Marx 1977a. 75–111.

——. 2007. *Economic and Philosophic Manuscripts of 1844*. Ed. and trans. Martin Milligan. Mineola, NY: Dover.

Marx, Karl and Friedrich Engels. 1985. *The Communist Manifesto*. Trans. Samuel Moore. London: Penguin.

Maslen, R. W. 2002. "Introduction". In Sidney 2002a. 1–78.

Massumi, Brian. 2002. "Introduction: Like a Thought". In *A Shock to Thought: Expression after Deleuze and Guattari*. Ed. Brian Massumi. London: Routledge. xiii–xxxix.

Materer, Timothy. 1994. "T. S. Eliot's Critical Program". In Moody 1994. 48–59.
Meisel, Perry. 2007. *The Literary Freud*. New York: Routledge.
Metochites, Theodoros. 1969. *Epistasia kai Krisis*. In *Saggio critico su Demostene e Aristide*. Ed. Marcello Gigante. Milan: Istituto Editoriale Cisalpino. 47–83.
Miller, Arthur. 2006. *Death of a Salesman*. In *Collected Plays, 1944–1961*. Ed. Tony Kushner. New York: Library of America.
Miller, Eugene F. 1987. "Foreword". In Hume 1987a. xi–xviii.
Miller, J. Hillis. 1958. *Charles Dickens: The World of His Novels*. Cambridge, MA: Harvard University Press.
Miller, Paul J. W. 1998. "Introduction". In Pico 1998. vii–xxvii.
Millett, Kate. 2000. *Sexual Politics*. Urbana: University of Illinois Press.
Minnis, A. J. and A. B. Scott with David Wallace, eds. 1991. *Medieval Literary Theory and Criticism c.1100–c.1375: The Commentary Tradition*. Rev. ed. Oxford: Clarendon.
Minow-Pinkney, Makiko. 1996. "Mrs. Dalloway". In Vice 1996. 164–73.
Mitchell, Juliet. 2000. *Psychoanalysis and Feminism*. With a new introduction. London: Penguin.
Moers, Ellen. 1978. *Literary Women*. London: Women's Press.
Mohanty, Chandra Talpade. 1984. "Under Western Eyes: Feminist Scholarship and Colonial Discourses". *boundary 2* 12.3–13.1 (Spring/Autumn): 333–58.
Moi, Toril. 1998. "'Independent Women' and Narratives of Liberation". In *Simone de Beauvoir: A Critical Reader*. Ed. Elizabeth Fallaize. London: Routledge. 72–92.
Montrose, Louis. 1998. "Professing the Renaissance: The Poetics and Politics of Culture". In Rivkin and Ryan 1998. 777–85.
Moody, A. David, ed. 1994. *The Cambridge Companion to T. S. Eliot*. Cambridge: Cambridge University Press.
Morris, William. 1995. *News from Nowhere, or, An Epoch of Rest: Being Some Chapters from a Utopian Romance*. Ed. Krishan Kumar. Cambridge: Cambridge University Press.
Morrison, Toni. 1984. "Rootedness: The Ancestor as Foundation". In *Black Women Writers (1950–1980): A Critical Evaluation*. Ed. Mari Evans. Garden City, NY: Anchor Press/Doubleday. 339–45.
——. 1988. *Beloved*. London: Picador.
——. 1989. *Song of Solomon*. London: Picador.
——. 1991a. *Sula*. London: Picador.
——. 1991b. *Tar Baby*. London: Picador.
——. 1992. *Playing in the Dark: Whiteness and the Literary Imagination*. Cambridge, MA: Harvard University Press.
——. 1993. *Jazz*. London: Picador.
Moss, Jessica. 2007. "What Is Imitative Poetry and Why Is It Bad?". *The Cambridge Companion to Plato's* Republic. Ed. G. R. F. Ferrari. Cambridge: Cambridge University Press. 415–44.
Ngũgĩ wa Thiong'o. 1982. *Devil on the Cross*. London: Heinemann.
——. 1986. *Decolonising the Mind: The Politics of Language in African Literature*. London: James Currey; Nairobi: Heinemann.
Ngũgĩ wa Thiong'o, Taban lo Liyong and Henry Owuor-Anyumba. 2001. "On the Abolition of the English Department". In Leitch *et al.* 2001. 2092–7.
Nicholls, Peter. 1995. *Modernisms: A Literary Guide*. Basingstoke and London: Macmillan.

Nietzsche, Friedrich. 1967. *The Birth of Tragedy.* Ed. and trans. Walter Kaufmann. New York: Vintage.
——. 1968. *Twilight of the Idols and The Anti-Christ.* Trans. R. J. Hollingdale. London: Penguin.
——. 1973. *Beyond Good and Evil.* Trans. R. J. Hollingdale. London: Penguin.
——. 1974. *The Gay Science.* Trans. Walter Kaufmann. New York: Vintage.
——. 1989. *On the Genealogy of Morals.* Trans. Walter Kaufmann and R. J. Hollingdale. In *On the Genealogy of Morals; Ecce Homo.* New York: Vintage. 13–163.
——. 1992. *Ecce Homo.* Trans. R. J. Hollingdale. London: Penguin.
Norton, David Fate, ed. 1993a. *The Cambridge Companion to Hume.* Cambridge: Cambridge University Press.
——. 1993b. "An Introduction to Hume's Thought". In Norton 1993a. 1–32.
Nussbaum, Martha C. 1986. *The Fragility of Goodness: Luck and Ethics in Greek Tragedy and Philosophy.* Cambridge: Cambridge University Press.
Orr, John. 1991. *Tragicomedy and Contemporary Culture: Play and Performance from Beckett to Shepard.* London: Macmillan.
Owen, Robert. 1813–16. *A New View of Society.* Online. http://avalon.law.yale.edu/19th_century/owenpref.asp.
Paik, Nam June. 1974. "TV Garden".
Paine, Thomas. 1985. *Rights of Man.* Harmondsworth: Penguin.
Palaiologos, Andronikos. 1956. *Le Roman de Callimaque et de Chrysorrhoé.* Ed. and trans. M. Pichard. Paris: Les Belles Lettres.
Pater, Walter. 1904. "Style". In Pater, *Appreciations with an Essay on Style.* London: Macmillan. 5–38.
——. 1909. *Plato and Platonism.* London: Macmillan.
——. 1986. *The Renaissance: Studies in Art and Poetry.* Oxford: Oxford University Press.
Perez, Hiram. 2005. "You Can Have My Brown Body and Eat It, Too!". *Social Text* 23.3–4 (Fall–Winter): 171–91.
Photios. 1959–91. *Bibliotheca.* 9 vols. Ed. R. Henry. Paris: Les Belles Lettres.
Pico della Mirandola, Giovanni. 1998. *On the Dignity of Man.* Trans. Charles Glenn Wallis. Indianapolis: Hackett.
Pinter, Harold. 1991. *The Birthday Party.* 2nd rev. ed. London: Faber.
Pizan, Christine, de. 1999. *The Book of the City of Ladies.* Trans. Rosalind Brown-Grant. London: Penguin.
Plath, Sylvia. 2010a. "Stings". *Ariel.* London: Faber. 65–7.
——. 2010b. "The Arrival of the Bee Box". In Plath, *Ariel.* London: Faber. 63–4.
Plato. 1951. *The Symposium.* Trans. Walter Hamilton. Harmondsworth: Penguin.
——. 1977. *Timaeus and Critias.* Trans. Desmond Lee. Harmondsworth: Penguin.
——. 1992a. *Protagoras.* Trans. Stanley Lombardo and Karen Bell. Indianapolis, IN: Hackett.
——. 1992b. *Republic.* 2nd ed. Trans. G. M. A. Grube. Revised by C. D. C. Reeve. Indianapolis, IN: Hackett.
——. 1993. *Sophist.* Ed. and trans. Nicholas P. White. Indianapolis, IN: Hackett.
——. 1995. *Phaedrus.* Trans., with introduction and notes, Alexander Nehamas and Paul Woodruff. Indianapolis, IN: Hackett.
——. 2005. *Ion.* Trans. Trevor J. Saunders. In *Early Socratic Dialogues.* 2nd ed. Ed. Trevor J. Saunders. London: Penguin. 49–68.
——. 2010. *The Last Days of Socrates: Euthyphro, Apology, Crito, Phaedo.* New ed. and trans. Christopher Rowe. London: Penguin.

Plotinus. 1991. *The Enneads*. Trans. Stephen MacKenna. Abridged ed. Harmondsworth: Penguin.

Poe, Edgar Allan. 2003. "The Purloined Letter". In Poe, *The Fall of the House of Usher and Other Writings*. Ed. David Galloway. London: Penguin. 281–300.

Pontalis, Jean-Bertrand and Jean Laplanche. 1973. *The Language of Psycho-Analysis*. Trans. Donald Nicholson-Smith. London: Hogarth.

Porphyry. 1991. "On the Life of Plotinus and His Work." In Plotinus 1991. cii–cxxix.

Propp, Vladimir. 1968. *Morphology of the Folktale*. 2nd rev. ed. Ed. Louis A. Wagner. Trans. Laurence Scott and Louis A. Wagner. Austin: University of Texas Press.

Proust, Marcel. 1984. *La Prisonnière*. Ed. Jean Milly. Paris: Flammarion.

——. 1987. *Sodome et Gomorrhe*. Ed. Emily Eells-Ogée. Paris: Flammarion.

Psellus, Michael. 1953. *The Chronographia of Michael Psellus*. Trans. E. R. A. Sewter. New Haven, CT: Yale University Press.

Pushkin, Aleksandr. 1975. *Eugene Onegin: A Novel in Verse*. Rev. ed. Trans. and commentary Vladimir Nabokov. London: Routledge and Kegan Paul.

Quayson, Ato. 2003. "African Postcolonial Relations through the Prism of Tragedy". In Quayson, *Calibrations: Reading for the Social*. Minneapolis: University of Minnesota Press. 56–75.

Rabaté, Jean-Michel. 1994. "Tradition and T. S. Eliot". In Moody 1994. 210–22.

——. 2001. *Jacques Lacan: Psychoanalysis and the Subject of Literature*. Basingstoke: Palgrave.

Rabelais, François. 2006. *Gargantua and Pantagruel*. Ed. and trans. M. A. Screech. London: Penguin.

Racine, Jean. 1964. *Esther: Tragédie*. Ed. Gabriel Spillebout. Paris: Bordas.

Ransom, John Crowe. 2001. "Criticism, Inc.". In Leitch *et al.* 2001. 1108–18.

Reiss, Timothy J. 2005. "Using Tragedy against Its Makers: Some African and Caribbean Instances". In Bushnell 2005. 505–36.

Reynolds, Joshua. 1995. "Discourse on Art". In Kramnick 1995. 342–49.

Rhys, Jean. 1997. *Wide Sargasso Sea*. London: Penguin.

Richards, I. A. 1929. *Practical Criticism*. London: Routledge & Kegan Paul.

——. 1967. *Principles of Literary Criticism*. 2nd ed. London: Routledge & Kegan Paul.

Richardson, Samuel. 1964. *Clarissa: Preface, Hints of Prefaces, and Postscript*. Ed. R. F. Brissenden. Los Angeles: William Andrews Clark Memorial Library. Online. www.gutenberg.org/catalog/world/readfile?fk_files=1559119.

Richter, Gerhard. 1987. "Apple Trees".

Riefenstahl, Leni. 1935. *Triumph des Willens* [*Triumph of the Will*]. Written, dir. and ed. Leni Riefenstahl. Reichsparteitag-Film.

Riviere, Joan. 2008. "Womanliness as a Masquerade". In *The Routledge Critical and Cultural Theory Reader*. Eds Neil Badmington and Julia Thomas. London: Routledge. 25–33.

Rivkin, Julie and Michael Ryan, eds. 1998. *Literary Theory: An Anthology*. Rev. ed. Oxford: Blackwell.

Robertson, D. W., Jr. 1962. *A Preface to Chaucer: Studies in Medieval Perspective*. Princeton, NJ: Princeton University Press.

Roche, Mark W. 2005. "The Greatness and Limits of Hegel's Theory of Tragedy". In Bushnell 2005. 51–67.

Rose, Jacqueline. 1994. "'Daddy'". In Ellmann 1994a. 221–59.

Rosen, Michael. 2004. "Benjamin, Adorno, and the Decline of the Aura". In Rush 2004a. 40–56.

Rousseau, Jean-Jacques. 1993. *Émile*. Trans. Barbara Foxley. Everyman Library. London: Dent.

Rush, Fred, ed. 2004a. *The Cambridge Companion to Critical Theory*. Cambridge: Cambridge University Press.

——. 2004b. "Conceptual Foundations of Early Critical Theory". In Rush 2004a. 6–39.

Rushdie, Salman. 1995. *Midnight's Children*. London: Vintage.

Ruskin, John. 1985. "Unto This Last". In Ruskin, *Unto This Last and Other Writings*. Ed. Clive Wilmer. Harmondsworth: Penguin.

Said, Edward. 1993. *Culture and Imperialism*. London: Chatto & Windus.

——. 2003. *Orientalism*. London: Penguin.

Sardar, Ziauddin. 2008. "Foreword to the 2008 Edition". In Fanon 2008. vi–xx.

Sartre, Jean-Paul. 1948. *Existentialism and Humanism*. Trans. Philip Mairet. London: Methuen.

——. 1963. *The Problem of Method*. Trans. Hazel E. Barnes. London: Methuen.

——. 1964–5. "Black Orpheus". Trans. John MacCombie. *The Massachusetts Review* 6.1 (Autumn 1964–Winter 1965): 13–52. Online. www.jstor.org/stable/25087216.

——. 1981–91. *The Family Idiot: Gustave Flaubert, 1821–1857*. 5 vols. Trans. Carol Cosman. Chicago: University of Chicago Press.

——. 1988. *Mallarmé, or the Poet of Nothingness*. Trans. Ernest Sturm. University Park: Pennsylvania State University Press.

——. 1990. "Preface" [to *The Wretched of the Earth*]. In Fanon 1990. 7–26.

——. 1992. *Notebooks for an Ethics*. Trans. David Pellauer. Chicago: University of Chicago Press.

——. 1993. *What Is Literature?* Trans. Bernard Frechtman. London: Routledge.

——. 2000. *Nausea*. Trans. Robert Baldick. Harmondsworth: Penguin.

——. 2003. *Being and Nothingness: An Essay on Phenomenological Ontology*. Trans. Hazel E. Barnes. Abingdon: Routledge.

Saussure, Ferdinand de. 1960. *Course in General Linguistics*. Eds Charles Bally and Albert Sechehaye with Albert Reidlinger. Trans. Wade Baskin. London: Peter Owen.

Schoenfield, Mark. 2009. *British Periodicals and Romantic Identity*. New York: Palgrave Macmillan.

Schopenhauer, Arthur. 1969. *The World as Will and Representation*. 2 vols. Trans. E. F. J. Payne. New York: Dover.

Schuyler, George S. 1926. "The Negro-Art Hokum". *Nation* 122 (June 16): 662–3.

Sedgwick, Eve Kosofsky. 2008. *Epistemology of the Closet*. Updated ed. Berkeley: University of California Press.

Shakespeare, William. 1982. *Hamlet*. Ed. Harold Jenkins. London: Methuen.

Shelley, Percy Bysshe. 2003a. *The Major Works*. Eds Zachary Leader and Michael O'Neill. Oxford: Oxford University Press.

——. 2003b. "A Defence of Poetry". In Shelley 2003a. 674–701.

——. 2003c. *Adonais*. In Shelley 2003a. 529–45.

——. 2003d. *The Cenci*. In Shelley 2003a. 314–99.

——. 2003e. Preface to *Prometheus Unbound*. In Shelley 2003a. 229–32.

Shepard, Sam. 1984. *Fool for Love* and *The Sad Lament of Pecos Bill on the Eve of Killing His Wife*. London: Faber.

Shepherd, Geoffrey. 1973. "Editor's Introduction". In Sidney 1973a. 1–91.

Shepherd, Geoffrey and R. W. Maslen. 2002. "Editors' Notes". In Sidney 2002a. 119–256.

Shiach, Morag. 2011. "Periodizing Modernism". In Brooker 2001a. 17–30.

——, ed. 2007. *The Cambridge Companion to the Modernist Novel.* Cambridge: Cambridge University Press.

Shires, Linda M. 1999. "The Radical Aesthetic of Tess of the d'Urbervilles". In *The Cambridge Companion to Thomas Hardy.* Ed. Dale Kramer. Cambridge: Cambridge University Press. 145–63.

Shklovsky, Viktor. 1998. "Art as Technique". In Rivkin and Ryan 1998. 17–23.

Showalter, Elaine. 1982. *A Literature of Their Own: British Women Novelists from Brontë to Lessing*. New rev. ed. London: Virago.

Shusterman, Richard. 1994. "Eliot as Philosopher". In Moody 1994. 31–47.

Sidney, Philip, Sir. 1973a. *An Apology for Poetry.* Ed. Geoffrey Shepherd. Manchester: Manchester University Press.

——. 1973b. *Miscellaneous Prose of Sir Philip Sidney.* Eds Katherine Duncan-Jones and J. A. van Dorsten. Oxford: Clarendon.

——. 2002a. *An Apology for Poetry, or, The Defence of Poesy.* Eds Geoffrey Shepherd and R. W. Maslen. 3rd ed., rev. and expanded. Manchester: Manchester University Press.

——. 2002b. *Sir Philip Sidney: The Major Works.* Ed. Katherine Duncan-Jones. Oxford: Oxford University Press.

——. 2002c. *The Defence of Poesy.* In Sidney 2002b. 213–50.

Snow, C. P. 1993. *The Two Cultures.* Cambridge: Cambridge University Press.

Sophocles. 1947. *The Theban Plays: King Oedipus, Oedipus at Colonus, Antigone.* Trans. E. F. Watling. Harmondsworth: Penguin.

——. 2008. *Electra and Other Plays: Women of Trachis, Ajax, Electra, Philoctetes.* Ed. and trans. David Raeburn. New ed. London: Penguin.

Soyinka, Wole. 1973. *The Bacchae of Euripides.* In Soyinka, Vol. 1 of *Collected Plays.* London: Oxford University Press. 233–307.

——. 1988a. *Art, Dialogue, Outrage.* Ibadan: New Horn Press, 1988.

——. 1988b. "The Fourth Stage". In Soyinka 1988a. 21–34.

——. 1988c. "Between Self and System: The Artist in Search of Liberation". In Soyinka 1988a. 61–85.

——. 1998. *Death and the King's Horseman.* London: Methuen.

Spears Brooker, Jewel, ed. 2004. *T. S. Eliot: The Contemporary Reviews.* Cambridge: Cambridge University Press.

Spillers, Hortense J. 1987. "Mama's Baby, Papa's Maybe: An American Grammar Book". *Diacritics* 17.2 (Summer): 64–81.

Spinoza, Benedictus de. 2000. *Ethics.* Ed. and trans. G. H. R. Parkinson. Oxford: Oxford University Press.

Spivak, Gayatri Chakravorty. 1985. "Three Women's Texts and a Critique of Imperialism". *Critical Inquiry* 12:1 (Autumn): 243–61.

——. 1999. *A Critique of Postcolonial Reason: Toward a History of the Vanishing Present*. Cambridge, MA: Harvard University Press.

Steiner, George. 1961. *The Death of Tragedy.* London: Faber.

——. 2004. "'Tragedy', Reconsidered". *New Literary History* 35.1 (Winter): 1–15.

Sterne, Laurence. 1980. *Tristram Shandy.* Ed. Howard Anderson. New York: Norton.

Stevenson, Robert Louis. 2002. *The Strange Case of Dr Jekyll and Mr Hyde and Other Tales of Horror.* Ed. Robert Mighall. London: Penguin.

Stoker, Bram. 2011. *Dracula.* Ed. Roger Luckhurst. Oxford: Oxford University Press.

Stoppard, Tom. 2000. *Rosencrantz and Guildenstern Are Dead.* London: Faber.

Storer, Richard. 2009. *F. R. Leavis.* Abingdon: Routledge.

Stump, Eleonore. 1993. "Biblical Commentary and Philosophy". In *Cambridge Companion to Aquinas.* Eds Norman Kretzmann and Eleonore Stump. Cambridge: Cambridge University Press. 252–68.

Tennyson, Alfred. 2009. *The Major Works.* Ed. Adam Roberts. Oxford: Oxford University Press.

Thucydides. 2009. *The Pelopponesian War.* Ed. P. J. Rhodes. Trans. Martin Hammond. New York: Oxford University Press.

Tolstoy, Leo. 2002. *Anna Karenina.* Trans. Richard Pevear and Larissa Volokhonsky. New York: Penguin.

Trilling, Lionel. 1970. "Freud and Literature". In Trilling. *The Liberal Imagination: Essays on Literature and Society.* Harmondsworth: Penguin. 47–68.

Venturi, Robert and Denise Scott Brown. 2007. *Learning from Las Vegas.* New ed. Eds Kester Rattenbury and Samantha Hardingham. Abingdon: Routledge.

Vice, Sue, ed. 1996. *Psychoanalytic Criticism: A Reader.* Cambridge: Polity.

Walcott, Derek. 1990. *Omeros.* London: Faber.

——. 1996. "The Man Who Keeps the English Language Alive: An Interview with Derek Walcott" [with Rebekah Presson]. *Conversations with Derek Walcott.* Ed. William Baer. Jackson: University Press of Mississippi. 189–93.

——. 2002. *Henri Christophe.* In Walcott, *The Haitian Trilogy.* New York: Farrar, Straus and Giroux. 1–107.

Walker, Alice. 1983a. *The Color Purple.* London: Women's Press.

——. 1983b. *In Search of Our Mothers' Gardens: Womanist Prose.* San Diego: Harcourt.

Waters, John. 2002. *Hairspray.* Dir. and written by John Waters. New Line Cinema.

Watson, George. 1975. "Introduction". In Coleridge 1975. ix–xxiii.

Watt, Ian P. 1963. *The Rise of the Novel: Studies in Defoe, Richardson and Fielding.* Harmondsworth: Penguin.

White, Hayden. 2001. "The Historical Text as Literary Artifact." In Leitch *et al.* 2001. 1709–29.

Whitford, Margaret. 1991a. *Luce Irigaray: Philosophy in the Feminine.* London: Routledge.

——. 1991b. "Introduction to Section 1". In Irigaray 1991a. 23–9.

Wilde, Oscar. 1961. "The Critic as Artist: With Some Remarks upon the Importance of Doing Nothing". In Wilde, *Selected Writings.* Ed. Richard Ellmann. Oxford: Oxford University Press. 38–119.

——. 2011. *The Picture of Dorian Gray.* Ed. Nicholas Frankel. [Annotated, uncensored ed.] Cambridge, MA: Belknap Press of Harvard University Press.

Williams, Raymond. 1987. *Culture and Society, 1780–1950: Coleridge to Orwell.* [With new foreword.] London: Hogarth.

——. 1992. *Modern Tragedy.* London: Hogarth Press.

Williams, Thomas. 2001. "Biblical Interpretation". In *Cambridge Companion to Augustine.* Eds Eleonore Stump and Norman Kretzmann. Cambridge: Cambridge University Press. 59–70.

Wilson, Edmund. 1996. "The Ambiguity of Henry James". In Vice 1996. 100–106.

Wilson, Peter. 2005. "Music". In *A Companion to Greek Tragedy.* Ed. Justina Gregory. Oxford: Blackwell. 183–93.

Wollheim, Richard. 1973. *Freud.* London: Fontana.

Wollstonecraft, Mary. 1985. *Vindication of the Rights of Woman.* Harmondsworth: Penguin.

——. 2007. *Mary* and *The Wrongs of Woman.* Rev. ed. Ed. Gary Kelly. Oxford: Oxford University Press.

——. 2008a. *A Vindication of the Rights of Men; A Vindication of the Rights of Woman; An Historical and Moral View of the French Revolution*. Oxford: Oxford University Press.

——. 2008b. *A Vindication of the Rights of Men*. In Wollstonecraft 2008a. 1–62.

Woolf, Virginia. 1929. *A Room of One's Own*. London: Hogarth.

——. 1964. *To the Lighthouse*. Harmondsworth: Penguin.

——. 1991. *Three Guineas*. London: Hogarth.

——. 1992. *Orlando: A Biography*. London: Hogarth.

——. 1996. *Mrs Dalloway*. London: Penguin.

——. 2003. "George Eliot". In Woolf, *The Common Reader. Volume 1*. Ed. Andrew McNeillie. London: Vintage. 162–72.

——. 2004. *A Room of One's Own*. London: Penguin.

——. 2007. *Jacob's Room: Authoritative Text, Virginia Woolf and the Novel, Criticism*. New York: Norton.

——. 2008. "Professions for Women". In Woolf, *Selected Essays*. Ed. David Bradshaw. Oxford: Oxford University Press. 140–45.

Wordsworth, William. 1998. "Lines Written a Few Miles above Tintern Abbey". In *William Wordsworth: Selected Poetry*. Eds Stephen Gill and Duncan Wu. Oxford: Oxford University Press. 57–61.

——. 2007. *The Excursion*. Eds Sally Bushell, James A. Butler and Michael C. Jaye with David García. Ithaca, NY: Cornell University Press.

——. 2012. "Preface to *Lyrical Ballads*". In *Romanticism: An Anthology*. 4th ed. Ed. Duncan Wu. Oxford: Wiley-Blackwell. 506–17.

Wyatt, Jean. 2008. "*Love*'s Time and the Reader: Ethical Effects of *Nachträglichkeit* in Toni Morrison's *Love*". *Narrative* 16.2 (May): 193–221.

Yeats, W. B. 2000. "The Second Coming". In *Selected Poems*. Rev. ed. Ed. Timothy Webb. London: Penguin. 124.

——. 2001. *The Major Works: Including Poems, Plays and Critical Prose*. New ed. Ed. Edward Larrissy. Oxford: Oxford University Press.

Young, Robert J. C. 1995. *Colonial Desire: Hybridity in Theory, Culture, and Race*. London: Routledge.

——. 2004. *White Mythologies: Writing History and the West*. 2nd ed. London: Routledge.

Zambrano, María. 2012. *La tumba de Antígona* [*Antigone's tomb*]. Ed. Virginia Trueba Mira. Madrid: Cátedra.

Žižek, Slavoj. 1991. *Looking Awry: An Introduction to Jacques Lacan through Popular Culture*. Cambridge, MA: MIT Press.

Index

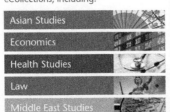